MW01203908

Walter Rauschenbusch

Published Works and Selected Writings

in Three Volumes

General Editor: William H. Brackney

Editors and Contributors

Ralf Dziewas
Priscilla Eppinger
Erich Geldbach
David Gushee
Andrea Strübind
Philip Thompson

Mercer University Press
In conjunction with
Acadia Centre for Baptist and Anabaptist Studies
American Baptist Historical Society

Walter Rauschenbusch, the last photo, 1918.

Walter Rauschenbusch

Published Works and Selected Writings

in Three Volumes

General Editor: William H. Brackney

Volume III

A Theology for the Social Gospel and Other Writings

With a Theological Introduction by William H. Brackney

MERCER UNIVERSITY PRESS
In conjunction with
Acadia Centre for Baptist and Anabaptist Studies
American Baptist Historical Society
2018

Endowed by
TOM WATSON BROWN
and
THE WATSON-BROWN FOUNDATION, INC.

MUP/ H962

Published by Mercer University Press
1501 Mercer University Drive
Macon, Georgia 31207

9 8 7 6 5 4 3 2 1

Books published by Mercer University Press are printed on acid-free paper that meets the requirements of the American National Standard for Information Sciences—Permanence of Paper for Printed Library Materials.

Grateful acknowledgment is to the Samuel B. Colgate Memorial Library of the American Baptist Historical Society in Atlanta, Georgia, for granting permission for the use of images and texts in this volume.

The initials on the cover are a transposition of Walter Rauschenbusch's actual initials designed by Kathryn E. Brackney, who has granted all rights for its use.

The dust jacket is designed by Burt&Burt.

ISBN 978-0-88146-678-2
Cataloging-in-Publication Data is available from the Library of Congress

Contents Volume III

Acknowledgments

This volume is the third in a three-volume set that fulfills four objectives: to establish a textual authority for Walter Rauschenbusch's major published works; to provide analyses of Rauschenbusch's life and works from historical, ethical, and theological perspectives; to gather the most extensive Rauschenbusch bibliography available; and to provide a sampling of Rauschenbusch shorter writings, correspondence, and select photographic artifacts.

Mercer University Press and its director, Dr. Marc Jolley, are to be commended for taking on larger projects of interest to the religious scholarly community and this one in particular. It is the centenary year of the recognition of Professor Rauschenbusch's death and the Press has done us all a great service by preserving this material. Dr. Jolley has been a patient editor and promoter of this project throughout.

The publication of the set coincides with the conference held at the Cecil B. Day Campus of Mercer University in Atlanta, Georgia, "The Legacy of Walter Rauschenbusch," April 9-11, 2018. A wide variety of scholars presented analyses of Rauschenbusch's life and thought, convened jointly by the Acadia Centre for Baptist and Anabaptist Studies of Acadia University, the American Baptist Historical Society, and Mercer University.

For this volume, we are particularly indebted to many archivists, technical volunteers, and specialist readers. They include, in Germany, Andrea Strübind, Dominik Gautier, Ines Pieper, Ralf Dziewas, Theresa Pieper, and Erich Geldbach; in Canada, Evan Colford, Scott Butler, Susan DeMont, Roger Prentice, and Kathryn Brackney; in the U.S., Phillip Thompson, Priscilla Eppinger, Janet Winfield, Jill Sweetapple, Marge Nead, Jackie Howell, Paul Minus, Paul B. Rauschenbusch, and Robert D. Cunningham.

We gratefully acknowledge permission to reproduce texts and photographs in the collections of the American Baptist Historical Society, the Archives of Colgate Rochester Crozer Divinity School, and the Orchard Community Church (formerly Latta Road Baptist Church), Greece, New York.

The Editorial Committee

Second German Baptist Church, New York City, ca.1880s.
(artist's sketch)

First German Baptist, Rochester, New York.
(Rauschenbusch Family Church)

Strong Hall, Rochester Theological Seminary, ca. 1908.

Rockefeller Hall, Rochester Theological Seminary, ca. 1885.

Faculty of Rochester Theological Seminary, ca. 1900. Walter Rauschenbusch is front row, left, with President A. H. Strong, third from left.

Tommy Douglas,
Social Gospel and Political Leader in Canada.

Rauschenbusch Window, Samuel Colgate Memorial Chapel,
Colgate Rochester Crozer Divinity School.

A THEOLOGICAL INTRODUCTION TO WALTER RAUSCHENBUSCH

What follows is methodologically an exercise in historical theology. In appreciating issues of context, biography, and historiography, historical theologians can create an image of a character that may be in contrast with the actual literary remains of the figure under consideration. That is the goal of the ongoing task of interpretation. Here, we will explore the interaction of Walter Rauschenbusch with other theologians in and beyond the Social Gospel movement and their influence upon him. The "Historical Introduction" to Volume I of this work should be read in tandem with this theological analysis.

In Walter Rauschenbusch, one sees the culmination of a new direction in American Christian theology. Rauschenbusch was perhaps not as original as some biographers thought him to be,[1] but he gathered the bits and pieces of a theoretical and practical social gospel like no one else.[2] His final major work, *A Theology for the Social Gospel* (1917), was a bold attempt to work like a systematic theologian and it summarized a career of theological development.

In assessing Walter Rauschenbusch's theology, one must begin with his own self-understanding. He thought modestly of his capacities as a theologian: "I am not a doctrinal theologian either by professional training or by personal habits of mind. Professional duty and intellectual liking have made me a teacher of Church History, and the events of my life, interpreted by my religious experiences, have laid the social problems on my mind." His theology was praxis-oriented: "We have a social gospel. We need a systematic theology large enough to match it and vital enough to back it."[3] He defended his contribution by asserting, "theology has often received its most fruitful impulses when secular life and movements have set it new problems."[4]

---

[1] For instance, Dores R. Sharpe and Max Stackhouse. See Max L. Stackhouse, "The Formation of a Prophet: Reflections on the Early Sermons of Walter Rauschenbusch." *Andover Newton Quarterly* 9 (1969): 137-159.

[2] Compare Washington Gladden, Josiah Strong, George Herron, and the British thinkers, Frederick Robertson, Frederick Maurice, Charles Kingsley, and Richard Heath.

[3] Walter Rauschenbusch, *A Theology for the Social Gospel* (New York: Macmillan Co., 1917), 1.

[4] Rauschenbusch, *A Theology for the Social Gospel*, "Foreword."

German Theological Genes[5]

Our analysis commences with genetic influences. American interest in German scholarship and educational methods reached a peak from 1830 to 1890, with a large number of American students and professors on sabbatical leave visiting and studying at German universities. The most popular destinations were Halle and Göttingen, then Berlin, that attracted the largest number of American students in the nineteenth century.[6] Among the prominent German theologians of the era, the following are of major import to the making of the worldview of August Rauschenbusch, and later to his son, Walter: Johann Neander, Albrecht Ritschl, Albert Schäffle, Adolf Stoecker, Julius Kaftan, Adolf von Harnack, Karl Kautsky, Isaac Dorner and Rudolf Hermann Lotze. Details of each follow.[7]

An important link with August Rauschenbusch was Johann Wilhelm August Neander (1789-1850).[8] Neander converted from Judaism to Christianity in 1806 and, in 1813, he was appointed as Professor for Church History and History of Dogma in the University of Berlin. He considered church history to be the history of steady growth, reaching towards increasingly greater unity in the human race. He was influenced by the German *Erweckung* (Awakening) movement and by Romanticism, and wanted to determine the effect of the divine spirit in history—with reference to both the wider context, and also on the basis of individual personalities. He was critical of the then-progressive modern age because of its focus on humans—not the Spirit of God—placing humans at the centre of history. In matters of church politics, however, he turned his back on the censorship of David Friedrich Strauss's historical-critical work *Das Leben Jesu* [*The Life of Jesus*], published in 1835. He also distanced himself from denominational Neo-Lutheranism, a movement that stressed 17th-century orthodoxy and opposed contemporary biblical scholarship. To this end, he co-founded the *Deutsche Zeitschrift für Christliche*

---

[5] We are indebted to Dominik Gautier of Carl von Ossietsky University in Oldenburg for material in this section.

[6] Other universities were Heidelberg, Leipzig, München, Strasbourg, Freiburg, Jena, and Bonn. Jurgen Herbst, *The German Historical School in American Scholarship: A Study in the Transfer of Culture* (Ithaca, NY: Cornell University Press, 1965), 14-22, contains a useful description of German schools, leading scholars and the learning culture.

[7] Links with these German thinkers are found in Walter's reading lists and in the lectures he attended while traveling in Europe.

[8] Neander was born David Mendel, on 17 January 1789 in Göttingen and died 14 July 1850 in Berlin.

Wissenschaft und Christliches Leben [*"German Magazine for Christian Science and Christian Life"*]. His major work was the *Allegemeine Geschichte der christlichen Religion und Kirche* [*"General History of the Christian Religion and Church"*] (1825–1852), which was published in six volumes.[9]

The towering German influence upon Walter Rauschenbusch was Albrecht Ritschl (1822-1889). Ritschl was a Professor of Dogmatic Theology and Ethics at the University of Göttingen from 1864 to 1889. His enduring theological contribution is considered to be a New Testament understanding of reconciliation, which he considered, in continuity with the Old Testament, is not God's reconciliation, but could be better described as reconciliation between humans. Against this background, Ritschl understood Christianity to be a practical way of life: according to Ritschl, revelation relates to the continuous growth of God's kingdom in history.[10] Therefore, Christian action and a Christian way of life should also reflect God's kingdom. Ritschl's major work was *Die christliche Lehre von der Rechtfertigung und Versöhnung* [*The Christian Teachings of Justification and Reconciliation*] (1870–1874), published in three volumes.[11] Ritschl, who had a strong following in the United States, had constant interaction with both August and Walter Rauschenbusch.[12]

Albert Eberhard Friedrich Schäffle (1831-1903) was a widely-read economist who propounded the "Organismal Theory" in the Social Sciences. According to this theory, society can be understood as a unified social body, whose biological impetus and motivating forces could be discovered, and highlighted for the development of society and social life. The Prussian government periodically banned Schäffle's works because his analysis of social

---

[9] Alf Christophersen, "Johann Wilhelm August Neander" in *Religion in Geschichte und Gegenwart* (*RGG*), Vol. 6, (Tübingen: Mohr Siebeck, 2005), 164–165. Karl Theodor Schneider, *August Neander. Beiträge zu seinem Leben und Wirken,* (Schleswig: J. Schneider, 1894).

[10] As early as 1892 Rauschenbusch recognized Ritschl's contribution to "basileic" theology in bringing it forward into his own thinking.

[11] Eilert Herms, "Albrecht Ritschl", in *RGG*, Vol. 7, 536–538; Helga Kuhlmann, *Die theologische Ethik Albrecht Ritschls* (München: C. Kaiser Verlag, 1992); also Matthias Neugebauer, "Albrecht Ritschl. Unterricht in der christlichen Religion" in: Rebekka A. Klein/Christian Polke/Martin Wendte editors, *Hauptwerke der Systematischen Theologie. Ein Studienbuch,* (Tübingen: UTB, 2009), 209–226.

[12] William Newton Clarke, *Outline of Christian Theology* (1898); William Adams Brown, *Christian Theology in Outline* (1906); Gerald Birney Smith, *Social Idealism and the Changing Theology: A Study of the Ethical Aspects of Christian Doctrine* (1913); Henry Churchill King, *Reconstruction in Theology* (1901). Rauschenbusch heard Ritschl lecture at the Universities of Bonn and Göttingen.

impetus was linked with socialist concepts. Against the background of Chancellor Otto von Bismarck's social legislation, Schäffle attempted to gain a senior management post, but his efforts failed, despite the fact that he was assisted by Bismarck in the process. His major work was *Das gesellschaftliche System der menschlichen Wirtschaft* ("*The Social System of the Human Economy*") (1867).[13] Rauschenbusch observed the results of Schäffle's frustrated theories in Bismarkean Germany and quoted him with appreciation: "History still turns on the axis of religion."[14]

Adolf Stoecker (1835-1909) came to Berlin in 1897 as a court chaplain to Kaiser Wilhelm II. He supported the idea of the Protestant [Lutheran] Church being independent of the state, with "strong roots" in the people, so that it would establish itself as a force for conservative order. In this way, he believed that social issues should come into focus, which would potentially be solved not only by the Inner Mission, also known as Home Mission, but also by means of political action.

To this end, Stoecker founded the Christian-Social Workers' Party [*Christlich-Soziale Arbeiterpartei* (CSAP)] in 1878. In an attempt to disengage the workers from their commitment to social democracy, he reflected prevailing anti-Semitic attitudes and accused liberal Judaism of being the cause of the impoverishment of the middle classes and lower bourgeoisie. In this way, combatting Judaism came to be at the core of Christian social practice for Stoecker. He mobilised the masses with this message, and broadcast his ideas through the German church's conservative communities. From 1880 to 1893, he was a member of the imperial German government, the Reichstag. He openly supported Wilhelm I and Wilhelm II's social ideas, and was co-founder of the Evangelical-Social Congress (ESK). Although he left the Conservative Party and the ESK in 1896, his influence on the socially committed Protestant community continued after this time. A collection of his essays and speeches can be found in the publication *Christlich-Sozial* [*Christian-Social*] (1885).[15]

---

[13] Dirk Kaesler, "Albert Eberhard Friedrich Schäffle" *Neue Deutsche Biographie* (*NDB*), 22, Berlin 2005, 521–522; Arnold Ith, *Die menschliche Gesellschaft als sozialer Organismus. Die Grundlinien der Gesellschaftslehre Albert Schäffles*, (Zürich: Speidel & Wurzel, 1927).

[14] Walter Rauschenbusch, *The City Vigilant* 1/5 (May 1894).

[15] Martin Greschat "Adolf Stoecker", in *RGG*, 7, 1744–1745; Günter Brakelmann/Martin Greschat/Werner Jochmann, "Adolf Stoeckers" in *Protestantismus und Politik. Werk und Wirkung* (Hamburg: Christians, 1982).

Another key influence on Rauschenbusch was Julius Wilhelm Martin Kaftan (1848-1926). He drafted a form of Christian dogmatics in the tradition of Albrecht Ritschl, and he taught in the University of Berlin from 1883 in the chair once occupied by Friedrich Schleiermacher. According to Kaftan, religion was to be understood as a tangible-practical value system that was founded in God and experienced in faith, as compared to purely theoretical constructs. Consequently, his involvement in the social committee of the German Evangelical Church, his contribution to the foundation of the Evangelical-Social Congress (ESK) and his membership of the *Freunden der Christlichen Welt* (Friends of the Christian World) should be seen in the context of this understanding of religion. His major works include *Das Wesen der christlichen Religion* ("The Nature of the Christian Religion") (1888) and *Dogmatik* ("Dogmatic Theology") (1897).[16]

In the development of Albrecht Ritschl's way of thinking, Adolf von Harnack (1851-1930) was a key figure. He broke away from Lutheran Confessionalism—as evidenced, among other things, by his involvement in the foundation of the *Theologischen Literaturzeitung* ("Theological Journal for Literature") (1876) and the magazine *Die Christliche Welt* ("The Christian World") (1886). His 1880 appointment as Professor for Church History at the University of Berlin was very controversial, as far as the State Church was concerned, following a dispute over his liberal textbook on the history of Christian dogma. On the basis of his reading of Albrecht Ritschl's theology, he understood Jesus' Gospel of the Kingdom of God as being aligned with practical godliness, in terms of which the dogmatic and ethical consolidation also needed to be criticised. In this way, he became an exponent of Culture-Protestantism, a movement in which the human culture in Christianity is stressed, and through which it should be promoted in the 19th century context.

Far beyond just the field of Theology, von Harnack was involved in many scientific and research organisations in the German Empire, and with his international renown, he also highlighted the significance and relative importance of Berlin on the world stage. Politically, he worked as an advisor in the fields of education and social policy. From 1890, he was actively involved in the Evangelical-Social Congress (ESK). He was a supporter of the First World War, but he advocated for moderate goals or targets for the war. He was initially hesitant in his support of the Weimar Republic, but increasingly

---

[16] Markus Schröder, "Julius Wilhelm Martin Kaftan" in *RGG*, Vol. 4, 733; Christina Costanza, *Einübung in die Ewigkeit. Julius Kaftans eschatologische Theologie und Ethik* (Göttingen: Vandenhoeck & Ruprecht, 2009).

he came to encourage and back the concept of the Republic. As a result, he assumed a critical distance towards National Protestantism, and he criticised growing anti-Semitism in Germany. His major works include three volumes of the *Lehrbuch der Dogmengeschichte* ("Textbook of History of Dogma") (1886–1890), as well as *Das Wesen des Christentums* ("The Nature of Christianity") (1900).[17]

The journalist Karl Kautsky (1854-1938), another subject in Rauschenbusch's reading, was strongly influenced by Friedrich Engels. In 1875, Kautsky became a member of the Social Democratic Party of Austria (SPÖ), and from 1883 to 1917, he was the editor-in-chief of the *Neuen Zeit* (*New Times*), the primary means of communication for the Social Democratic Party of Germany (SPD) and the international workers' movement. He was very influential in the dissemination of Karl Marx's ideas and concepts and in the programmatic development of the SPD, as well as having a strong influence on the Second International, the original Socialist International. He can be counted among the opponents of the First World War, and while employed in a short-term role as state secretary in the Foreign Office, Kautsky worked on documentation regarding Germany's joint guilt for the First World War.[18]

While not as direct an influence upon Rauschenbusch as other German theologians, Isaak August Dorner (1809-1884) was certainly a large figure in the context of new theological trends, particularly in the doctrine of Christology. Dorner taught at Tübingen where he was appointed professor extraordinarius of theology and five years later he moved to the University of Kiel as professor ordinarius. Thereafter he taught at Königsberg, Bonn and Göttingen, finally settling at the University of Berlin in 1862. His work stood in contrast to that of David Strauss who propounded a mytho-poetic hermeneutic for the four Gospels. Dorner set forth an exhaustive study of the doctrine of Christ, establishing Christology as the leading Christian doctrine going forward.[19] He produced magisterial works, including *Entwicklungsgeschicte der*

---

[17] Wolf-Dieter Hauschild, "Adolf von Harnack," in: *RGG*, Vol. 3, 1457–1459; Christian Nottmeier, *Adolf von Harnack und die deutsche Politik 1890–1930. Eine biographische Studie zum Verhältnis von Protestantismus, Wissenschaft und Politik* (Tübingen: Mohr Siebeck, 2004); Gunther Wenz, *Der Kulturprotestant. Adolf von Harnack als Christentumstheoretiker und Kontroverstheologe* (München: Herbert Utz Verlag, 2001).

[18] Günter Brakelmann, "Karl Kautsky" in *RGG*, Vol. 4, 913; Ingrid Gilcher-Holtey, *Das Mandat des Intellektuellen. Karl Kautsky und die Sozialdemokratie* (Berlin: Siedler Verlag, 1986).

[19] Paul T. Phillips, *A Kingdom on Earth: Anglo-American Social Christianity, 1880-1940.* University Park, PA: Pennsylvania State University Press, 1996), 20.

Lehre von der Person Christi ("The Historical Development of the Doctrine of Christ": 1835), *Das Princip unserer Kirche nach dem inner Verhaltniss seiner zwei Seiten betrachtet* ("The Principles of Our Church Concerning the Interrelationships of the Two Views": 1841), and *Geschicte der protestantischen Theologie* 1867: ("History of Protestant Theology").

Following Dorner's new Christological directions, was Rudolf Hermann Lotze (1817-1881) a colleague of Albrecht Ritschl who taught philosophy at Göttingen. In response to the rationalism of contemporary philosophy and the demands for scientifically verifiable evidence, Lotze emphasized the importance of personality and ethical relationships with others, through which the knowledge of God is evident. As William R. Hutchinson has pointed out, Lotze's 'teleological idealism' portrayed God and humanity as constitutive elements in one great and necessary ethical reality. Lotze's approach was to provide a foundation for theological liberalism well into the twentieth century.[20] His major influential work was *Microcosmus: An Essay Concerning Man and His Relation to the World* (2 vols, 1885).

Recently, the influence of Julius Wellhausen[21] on Walter Rauschenbusch has come to light. Wellhausen was already well-published in German as Rauschenbusch earned his theological degrees and began to study prominent German scholars. It is now known that Rauschenbusch read Wellhausen's *Israelitische und jüdische Geschichte* ("History of Israel and Judaism") published in 1894 and drew upon it extensively for his early manuscript, "Christianity Revolutionary" and later *Christianity and the Social Crisis*. Rauschenbusch was enamored of a scientific, historical study of ancient Israel and particularly the evolution of a prophetic tradition that he saw as fulfilled in Jesus. Steven Cassedy has extensively compared the texts of Wellhausen and Rauschenbusch and demonstrates significant verbal dependence of Rauschenbusch upon Wellhausen, notably in prophetic vocabulary and phrases pertaining to

---

[20] William R. Hutchinson, *The Modernist Impulse in American Protestantism* (Cambridge, MA: Harvard University Press, 1976), 124-125.

[21] Julius Wellhausen (1844-1918) was one of the most prominent biblical scholars and Orientalists of his era. He held academic positions at Griefswald, Halle, Marburg, and Göttingen, ultimately holding the position of *professor ordinarius* at Marburg and Göttingen. His work on the Five Books of Moses was definitive (*Prolegomena zur Geschichte Israels: Prolegomena to the History of Ancient Israel,* Berlin: 1892), asserting the 'documentary hypothesis' for a multiple authorship in stages of the Torah.

the Kingdom.[22] Both theologians believed that Jesus was recovering a lost prophetic tradition and in modern terms for Rauschenbusch, laying a foundation for a radical reshaping of the historical churches and the restoration of the Kingdom as Jesus taught it.[23]

Taken as a whole, the number of German thinkers who had an impact on Rauschenbusch's developing theology reflected the range of universities and traditions in the German context. Jurgen Herbst has made two important points in this regard. First, the German-trained scholars who sought to connect academic methods with the democratic idea of equality fared best when they joined their efforts with organized religion, notably in the Social Gospel movement. Secondly, in one way or another, the American scholars who were trained to one degree or another in German universities were all educational reformers. These included Richard T. Ely, Francis Peabody, and Shailer Mathews. The Social Gospel movement in the United States helped them to focus on real social and economic issues.[24]

Walter Rauschenbusch also had a personal experience in the German educational context. The theological tradition of the Gymnasium in Gütersloh was also important to the shaping of Rauschenbusch's theological perspective. Established in 1851 by devotees of the *Erweckung*, the secondary school created a theologically orthodox curriculum that blended loyalty to a pious monarch, Frederick Wilhelm IV, with pre-critical bible teaching: "love for God, love for king and fatherland, and love for science and art."[25]

Rauschenbusch immersed himself in Latin, Greek, French, and Hebrew, as gateways to both the original Scriptures and literary classics. His classes included languages, mathematics, history, geography, and religion. He wrote

---

[22] Steven Cassedy, "Walter Rauschenbusch, the Social Gospel Movement, and How Julius Wellhausen Unwittingly Helped Create American Progressivism in the Twentieth Century" in *Sacred History, Sacred Literature: Essays on Ancient Israel, the Bible, and Religion in Honor of R. E. Friedman on His Sixtieth Birthday*, ed. Richard Elliott Friedman and Shawna Dolansky (Winona Lake, IN: Eisenbrauns, 2008), 318-319, argues that Rauschenbusch follows a Hegelian analysis of Jewish history set forth by Wellhausen and borrows precise phrases from Wellhausen, often without any attribution.

[23] As Cassedy puts it, p. 323, Wellhausen the historian, supplied Rauschenbusch the political activist, with the notion of restoration, and as an admirer of Otto von Bismarck, would have been surprised to see his methods and conclusions having an impact in the politics of another country.

[24] Herbst, *The German Historical School*, 174; 182; 186.

[25] Quoted in Minus, *American Reformer*, 20. On the precise nature of the curriculum, see the "Introduction" to Vol. I, above, xvi-xvii.

essays on Homer, Cicero, Goethe, and Lessing. But the most profound influence was Theodor Braun, the chaplain and teacher of religious subjects at Gütersloh. Braun was a thoroughgoing Pietist who emphasized individual religious experience, using a conversionist model of ministry. Walter was much swayed by Braun's sermons. In class Braun stressed the biblical and historical foundations of Christianity that involved memorization of Luther's writings, thirty-two hymns, and dozens of bible verses. Rauschenbusch especially loved the bible classes and church history. He concluded that the four gospels were "the best of the entire bible," a canon within the canon. Importantly, it was Theodor Braun who lectured on the Kingdom of God in the two testaments, a theme that would dominate Rauschenbusch's teaching a decade later.[26]

Rauschenbusch's biographers have identified an important theological influence that surfaced during his studies at Gütersloh. As a Baptist in an orthodox Lutheran setting, Rauschenbusch was disallowed the opportunity to participate in the sacrament of Holy Communion. This created in him an attitude of anti-sacramentalism. Later during a visit in 1891 when visiting a consecration service for Anglican bishops at Westminster Abbey, he chafed at the "bowing, kneeling, marching and wheeling of the prelates."[27] Christopher Evans has summed up the essence of Rauschenbusch's disinclination toward sacramentalism as involving: impeding the ministry of the laity, Pietist influences, foreign rituals (Latin language), undemocratic hierarchy, and the decision of a close friend to become a Roman Catholic priest.[28]

Transatlantic Theological Antecedents

English theological interest in social Christianity actually preceded Rauschenbusch's work and greatly influenced him. In contrast to earlier thinkers like Wilhelm Visser't Hooft, Charles Hopkins, and George Hammar, (who held that the social gospel was essentially an American phenome-

[26] Quoted in Minus, *American Reformer*, 26-27.

[27] Walter Rauschenbusch, *The Righteousness of the Kingdom*, 234.

[28] Christopher Evans, *The Kingdom is Always but Coming: A Life of Walter Rauschenbusch* (Grand Rapids, MI: Eerdmans, 2004), 29. The close friend was Edward (Ed) Joseph Hanna of Rochester (1860-1944) who became Archbishop of San Francisco, 1915-1935.

non), Robert T. Handy contended that the social gospel movement was a diversified one, paralleling movements in other lands and itself influenced directly by them.[29]

The English foray into Social Christianity was determinant in Rauschenbusch's theological perspective. Throughout the second half of the nineteenth century, English Protestant theology was in transition. A crystallized form of Evangelicalism was interacting continuously with biblical higher criticism, Social Darwinism, Romanticism, and latitudinarianism. Often, the Church of England was the forum for theological ferment.[30] Gradually in the late 1840s, influenced by the Chartist Movement, a coterie of Anglican clergy and writers coalesced around a social interpretation of Christianity.[31] English Social Christianity writers actively promoted principles of social justice in addressing the acute issues of economic and social distress.[32] Among those who advanced the cause were J. M. Ludlow, Charles Kingsley, Frederick Robertson, and the leading thinker, F. D. Maurice.[33] To this list must be also added John Ruskin and Joseph Mazzini.

---

[29] See Robert T. Handy, "The Influence of Mazzini on the American Social Gospel," *Journal of Religion* 29/2 (April 1949): 115. Handy was following the earlier theses of Conrad H. Moehlmann, "Walter Rauschenbusch and His Interpreters" *Crozer Quarterly* 23(1946): 47, and Maurice Latta, "The Background for the Social Gospel in American Protestantism" *Church History* 5 (1936): 256. Latta's exact words were "worldwide in scope, which have everywhere brought about similar reactions in the field of religion... and the vigorous enunciation of a social ethic." In 1928 the Dutch theologian, Willem A. Visser't Hooft, characterized American Social Gospellers as "pantheistic utopians": *The Background of the Social Gospel in America* (St. Louis, MO: Bethany Press, 1963; [1928]), 151; 178.

[30] The best overall analyses of Christian Socialism include Owen Chadwick, *The Victorian Church, 2 Parts* (London: Adam and Charles Black, 1970), 346-353, John R. H. Moorman, *A History of the Church in England* (London: Adam and Charles Black, 1953), 355-56; 380-381; David Hempton, "Religious Life in Industrial Britain" in *A History of Religion in Britain: Practice and Belief from the Pre-Roman Times to the Present*, ed. by Sheridan Gilley and W. J. Shiels (Oxford: Basil Blackwell, 1994), 306-322. David Bebbington, *Evangelicalism in Modern Britain: A History from the 1730s to the 1980s* (London: Routledge, 1989), 211-217, offers an evangelical perspective on the social gospel.

[31] Prominent Anglican biblical scholars were involved in the movement, notably Fenton J. A. Hort, Brooke Foss Westcott, and Richard C. Trench.

[32] Phillips, *A Kingdom on Earth*, xviii; Robert T. Handy, *The Social Gospel in America, 1870-1920* (New York: 1966), 5.

[33] Included in regular gatherings at Lincoln's Inn or Queen Street to hear bible studies led by Maurice, were Cuthbert Ellison, Archie Campbell, Charles Walsh, Daniel and Alexander Macmillan, Tom Hughes, Georgiana Hare (Maurice's future wife), Walter Cooper, and Lloyd Jones. They were described as "a sprinkling of law students, doctors, an

John Malcolm Forbes Ludlow (1821-1911) was not theologically trained, but contributed organizationally to the English Christian Socialist movement. A lawyer by training, he helped to found the Christian Working-Men's College in Great Ormond Street, London, in 1854, and from 1875-90 he was editor of the influential *Christian Socialist* newspaper.[34] Ludlow was influenced in his appreciation of Socialism by French Protestants and he believed that Christianity was the fulfillment of whatever was good in Socialism.[35] He was a confidante of F. D. Maurice and especially Charles Kingsley, offering editorial critique for their ideas.[36]

Of singular importance in theological transition was Frederick Denison Maurice (1805-1872). Raised a Unitarian, some authors think he long exhibited nonconformist tendencies with a greater sense of an established church.[37] He described his task as "theological grubbing," but his contribution was that of a seminal thinker.[38] His expressed concept of God was as a Father, and he could not understand how a God whose primary characteristics were goodness and mercy could allow for eternal punishment.[39] Maurice's father continually stressed the unity of God and the universality of God's love.[40] God is immanent and seeks a relationship with humankind.

---

architect, an engineer, and a chemist, all professing Christians… some Tories, cautious Reformers, and not a few ardent Radicals." Florence Higham, *Frederick Denison Maurice* (London: SCM Press, 1947), 62-67.

[34] The best biographies of Ludlow are N. C. Masterman, *J. M. Ludlow, Builder of Christian Socialism* (Cambridge: Cambridge University Press, 1963), and E. R. Norman, "Ludlow, John Malcolm Forbes (1821-1911)" rev. H. C. G. Matthew *ODNB* http://www.oxforddnb.com/index/101037696/John-Ludlow, accessed 1 October 2016.

[35] Chadwick, *The Victorian Church*, 348.

[36] Further on Ludlow, see P. R. Allen, "F. D. Maurice and J. M. Ludlow," *Victorian Studies* 11/4 (1968): 461-482.

[37] Compare David Young, *F. D. Maurice and Unitarianism* (Oxford: Oxford University Press, 1992), 92, with Philips, *Kingdom on Earth*, 2. Young argues that Maurice's views of the Fatherhood of God, divine unity, rejection of the penal substitutionary atonement theory, rejection of original sin and everlasting punishment, and a social concern were all derived from his father, Michael Maurice.

[38] Alec R. Vidler, *The Theology of F. D. Maurice* (London: SCM Press, 1948), 22. David Bebbington has affirmed the importance of Maurice as "stirring some to contemplate the divine pattern for the nation: *Evangelicalism in Modern Britain*, 212.

[39] Maurice wrote, "we have a Father in Heaven who does not forget us, who never becomes indifferent to us, who never ceases to desire our good." F. D. Maurice, *Sermons Preached in the Country* (London: Macmillan, 1873), 316.

[40] Young, *Maurice and Unitarianism*, 96, 133-135. Notable was Michael's admiration for the Baptist minister, Robert Hall, Jr., of Bristol.

Driven like many of his English contemporaries by "reasonableness," he rejected traditional supernaturalism and wanted to accommodate historical criticism of the bible and contemporary scientific theories. He rejected the Calvinistic idea of human depravity.[41] He employed a philosophic vocabulary to open new possibilities that stressed a broader view of the world, a new Christology, a new view of humanity, and a revised understanding of the church.[42] One critic wrote of his tendency toward the limits of sound doctrine that he believed that time and eternity co-existed in humans. For the critic, Maurice apparently had a difficult time recognizing the idea of an eternal state as distinct from temporal conditions. Ordinary people may recognize eternal life as a great and present reality, Maurice believed.[43] This kind of theological reflecting led to his dismissal from King's College for unorthodox views.[44] Yet, his *Essays and Reviews* (1860) was considered one of the two most influential books in Anglican history.[45]

Maurice unfolded a new Christology. For him, the death of Christ was

> far more than peace-making...it is actually and literally the death of you and me...we *are* dead, actually absolutely dead; and let us believe further that we *are* risen , and that we have each a life, our only life—a life not of you nor me, but a universal life—in Him. He will live in us, and

---

[41] Instead, Maurice believed that man never ceased to be a child of God, having an innate character that is truer and more real than sin: F. D. Maurice, *The Church as a Family: Twelve Sermons on the Occasional Services of the Prayer-Book. Preached in the Chapel of Lincoln's Inn* (London: John W. Parker, 1850), 35.

[42] Maurice was much influenced by Romanticism, where he moved away from a mechanistic view of the world to one where human feelings were given priority and personal experience could provide the basis for a reasonable faith. His pilgrimage was like that of former Unitarian Samuel Taylor Coleridge, Charles Lamb, and William Wordsworth. See Young, *Maurice and Unitarianism*, 115-123.

[43] Frederick Maurice, *Theological Essays* (London: Macmillan, 1853), 366; Jones, *Christian Socialist Revival*, 13. Maurice thought of eternal life as a certain quality, not life unending. He found the idea of everlasting torment barbaric. The *Essays* were Maurice's 17 "Articles of Religion," a confessional statement "intended to turn the mindset of British Christianity in a new direction," so states Olive J. Brose, *Frederick Denison Maurice: Rebellious Conformist* (Athens, OH: Ohio University Press, 1971), [214]; 202-229, in the best analysis available.

[44] Una Pope-Hennessy, *Canon Charles Kingsley: A Biography* (London: Chatto and Windus, 1948), 119.

[45] Peter d'A. Jones, *The Christian Socialist Revival 1877-1914: Religion, Class, and Social Conscience in Late-Victorian England* (Princeton, NJ: Princeton University Press, 1968), 7-12.

quicken us with all life and all love...experience the reality of loving God, and loving our brethren.[46]

Maurice revealed an enlarged view of the church in his book, *The Kingdom of Christ* (1838; 1842). The work was a sketch of a worldview in broad outline. At its center was the author's idea of how heaven and earth had been joined in Jesus Christ. Christ was the archetypal man, the full declaration of man and God.[47] A biographer rightly observed that the incarnation was the master-note of all Maurice's teaching:

> He saw clearly that the doctrine of the Incarnation means, in the first place, that God has a plan for the world; it means that order and progress in human civilization is real... it means in the development of that plan each age of the world has its own special work to do: it means that progress through order is not only a vital fact of human existence, but that it is its vital law: it means that there *is* a Christian ideal for society, for no human relationship can really be outside the Divine kingdom...[48]

Man, Maurice wrote, now had communion with God in the ascended Christ. With the Incarnation, Christ ushered in his rule, that Maurice called the "Kingdom of Christ."[49] He wrote, "There rose up before me the idea of a *CHURCH UNIVERSAL*, not built upon human inventions or human faith, but upon the very nature of God himself, and upon the union which He has formed with His creatures."[50] His view of the universal church ran along completely new lines:

> The world contains the elements of which the Church is composed. In the Church, these elements are penetrated by a uniting, reconciling power. The Church is therefore, human society in its normal state; the

[46] J. F. Maurice, *The Life of Frederick Denison Maurice* (London: Charles Scribner's Sons, 1884), Vol. I: 106-107.

[47] Regarding the Holy Spirit, Maurice spoke of the Spirit as a "uniting Spirit" uniting the Father and the Son, and humankind as well: F. D. Maurice, *The Prayer–Book and the Lord's Prayer* (London: John W. Parker, 1902), 185.

[48] Charles William Stubbs, D.D., *Charles Kingsley and the Christian Social Movement* (London: Blackie & Son, 1899), 21-22. Bishop Edward R. Wickham, *Church and People in an Industrial City* (London: Lutterworth, 1957), 193, thought Maurice "earthed the Gospel."

[49] Brose, *Rebellious Conformist* (Athens, OH: Ohio University Press, 1971), 155.

[50] Frederick Maurice, *The Kingdom of Christ* (London: Darton and Clark, 1838), Vol. I: 14. The book began as a response to Quaker thought and went through several printings to 1983.

> World, that same society irregular and abnormal. The world is the Church without God; the Church is the world restored to its relation with God, taken back by Him into the state for which He created it.[51]

The Church, for Maurice, as a new covenant, the new Israel, baptized in Christ's name, became all men.[52] As all humanity is an organic unity, so in Christ the Church is an organic unity. He chose the devices and rites of the Church of England and found its universality in its baptism and doctrine:

> A universal Church is found existing, acknowledging the Trinity, acknowledging the Atonement as the foundations of its being. These great truths are expressed in Sacraments; their relation to the constitution of the Church and of society gradually unveiled in the written word; their meaning interpreted to the people, by a ministry connecting one generation with another; their meaning expressed in various acts of allegiance, and offices of thanksgiving, intercession, communion.[53]

Maurice's theology made the church universal and its mandate as the kingdom of Christ, obligatory upon all people. Maurice may well have been the first writer among Social Christians to employ the metaphor "kingdom" for the vision of a contemporary society based upon Christian compassion rather than materialism.[54] The outward signs of the kingdom were the sacraments (especially the Lord's Supper), the written Word (including the creeds), the episcopal ministry, outward worship, and being in constant warfare against disorder among men.[55] He was repulsed by singleness, competition, and sectarianism.[56] Unlike his contemporary Evangelicals, Maurice's idea of the Church was inclusive, thanks to the love of God. For that reason, Maurice was critical of American ideas of the separation of church and state, because by God's law they were necessarily united.[57]

---

[51] Maurice, *Theological Essays*, 403.

[52] Vidler, *The Theology of F. D. Maurice,* 77-78.

[53] Maurice, *Kingdom of Christ*, Vol. I: 58.

[54] Phillips, *A Kingdom on Earth,* 1.

[55] Frank Mauldin McClain, *Maurice: Man and Moralist* (London: S.P.C.K., 1972), 139.

[56] Maurice, *Theological Essays*, 25.

[57] McClain, *Man and Moralist,* 143. He thought the task of the American Episcopal Church was to serve as a model in the midst of an unstable evolving democratic social structure.

From his theological understanding of the church, Maurice worked out a theology of social activism that was based on his idea of the atonement.[58] Young has summarized his thinking on the church:

> God through his act of creation has given human life a structure and order, which man is to recognize and with which he is to cooperate. God has already established his kingdom, a fellowship embracing all mankind...The Christian Socialist Movement was therefore a spiritual enterprise seeking to assert God's order.[59]

Maurice was never a radical social reformer, but one who practiced an educational approach for the working classes. Social Christianity was, for F. D. Maurice, an essentially religious movement, based upon certain theological precepts, the object of which was the creation of social harmony in place of social discord.[60] His influence in the United States was profound and widespread.[61] Walter Rauschenbusch pursued the same educative strategy creating harmony in place of discord.[62]

Frederick W. Robertson (1816-1853) was another Anglican priest of great interest to Rauschenbusch. He served in working class Brighton in the south of England.[63] His theological contribution was to move theology away

---

[58] Maurice wrote that "the proper constitution of man is his constitution in Christ...When he offered Himself to God, He took away the sin of the world. We have no right to count ourselves sinners, seeing we are united in him." F. D. Maurice, *The Epistles of St. John* (London: Macmillan, 1867), 110. Young, *Maurice and Unitarianism*, 216-224, observes three components to Maurice's theology of the atonement: union, sacrifice, and battle.

[59] Young, *Maurice and Unitarianism*, 182, ref. Maurice, *Politics for the People*, I (1848) and Maurice, *Life of Maurice*, Vol. II: 44.

[60] Phillips, *Kingdom on Earth*, xvi.

[61] See C. G. Brown, "Frederick Denison Maurice in the United States, 1860-1920" *Journal of Religious History* 10/1 (1978): 50-69.

[62] *Proceedings of the Baptist Congress*, 1889, 40; Minus, *American Reformer*, 69, 74, 187. Minus also contends that Rauschenbusch differed from Maurice's Anglican sacramental theology. Further to the dependence of Rauschenbusch on Maurice, Evans (*The Kingdom is Always, But Coming*, 91), suggests that Rauschenbusch did not attempt to contact any Christian Socialist leaders during his trip in 1879-83 through Britain to Germany, while Winthrop Hudson has pointed out (Rauschenbusch, *Selected Writings*, 16-27) that Leighton Williams, close confidante of Rauschenbusch, visited Maurice in 1859, was drawn to his developing doctrine of Christian Socialism and high churchmanship, and continued his admiration for the English brand of Christian Socialism in the Brotherhood of the Kingdom.

[63] Phillips, *A Kingdom on Earth*, xiv, n.3.

from the doctrine of the atonement of Christ to the Incarnation, much as Maurice had done. He emphasized the humanity of Christ over His divine nature, a major departure from contemporaneous Evangelicalism. Robertson was read widely in the United States, particularly alongside the works of Horace Bushnell.

In a context where English formal theology was divided by blurred positions between High Church men and Evangelicals, the new front of the 1840s that was advanced by men like F. D. Maurice provided a middle ground.[64] Robertson was much enamored of Maurice:

> I sympathize deeply with Mr. Maurice. I do not agree with him entirely, either theologically or economically…he loves to see the soul of good, as Shakespeare says, in things evil. I desire to see the same; therefore I love him, and so far I am at one with him…he is every inch a man, and a right noble one.[65]

What Robertson was struggling with in 1851 was his situation among a working-class parish and their needs and the program of emerging Christian Socialism to improve the conditions of the workingmen.[66]

Robertson was much influenced theologically by historical literary figures like William Shakespeare, John Bunyan, and John Milton, and contemporaries like Lord Byron, Percy Shelley, Thomas Macaulay, John Keats, and especially William Wordsworth.[67] The theological gateway for Robertson came with a dramatic shift in his Christology in his pastoral ministry. He

---

[64] The categories at mid-century were "High Church," roughly the equivalent of "Anglo-Catholic" who stressed formal liturgy and a positive outlook on Roman Catholics and Greek Orthodox; "Evangelicals" who included Pietists and pro-revival types of churches, many of who lived by a traditional confession of faith; "Old Dissent" that included Methodists Congregationalists, and Presbyterians; and "Sacramental Socialists" that included men like Maurice, Ludlow, and Robertson. See Kenneth Hylson-Smith, *High Churchmanship in the Church of England, from the Sixteenth Century to the Late Twentieth Century* (Edinburgh: T. & T. Clark, 1993), Bebbington, *Evangelicalism in Modern Britain,* Timothy Larsen, *Contested Christianity: The Political and Social Contexts of Victorian Theology* (Waco, TX: Baylor University Press, 2004), 59-77.

[65] Frederick Robertson to Mrs. Hutton, 26 November 1851 in *Life and Letters of Frederick W. Robertson, M.A.* edited by Stopford A. Brooke, M.A. (Boston, MA: Fields, Osgood, & Co., 1870), Vol. II: 8.

[66] Robertson was involved in the Workingman's Institute, an association of 1,100 men in Brighton. He advocated a library and reading rooms, with lectures to inform workingmen of an improved life. *Life and Letters of Robertson*, II: 140-141.

[67] He also read with appreciation John Keble and William E. Channing.

gradually reoriented all of his doctrine from an Evangelical stress on the deity of Christ to the Incarnation that he called "the blossoming of humanity."[68] He believed the doctrine of the Divinity of Christ was waning and those who held it (Evangelicals) had petrified it into a theological dogma without life or warmth. Instead, he advised, "Begin as the Bible begins, with Christ the Son of Man. Begin with him as God's character revealed under the limitations of humanity." Robertson's pathway moved him between Evangelicals who gave Christ only a lukewarm intellectual homage and Unitarians like Channing who only admired Christ.[69]

Having built the case for understanding the true humanity of Christ, Robertson next moved to bridge God to the needs of humanity. While at first he disclaimed Socialist tendencies, and being called a Radical, he finally acknowledged the label: "No doubt I am called a Radical, but my radicalism is not political, but religious—a principle, and not a scheme, a conviction of the rights of others...I had tried to *feel* the meaning of Christ's words and to make my heart beat with His and so I became what they call a Radical."[70] Robertson became obsessed with his chosen motto for life: "None but Christ...to feel as He felt; to judge the world, and to estimate the world's maxims, as He judged and estimated. That is the one thing worth living for. To realize that, is to feel 'none but Christ.'"[71] As Paul Minus has shown, it was the 'spirit of the Cross' that was the key to Robertson's Christology. The cross was the ultimate example of Christ's humanity and self-sacrifice: here God spoke to the needs of humanity.[72] A young pastor in New York City, Walter Rauschenbusch, would read such words and be lifted to a new plane of thinking.[73]

Charles Kingsley (1819-1875), yet another priest in the Church of England, was a university historian, novelist, and later Canon of Westminster. He was of a similar bent to Maurice, embracing his Socialism, Darwinian thought, and thinking of Maurice as the 'elder prophet' and himself as the young priest. Although ordained an Anglican, Kingsley disliked dogmatic

---

[68] *Life and Letters of Robertson*, II: 167.

[69] *Life and Letters of Robertson*, II: 169.

[70] Frederick Robertson to Mr. Moncrief, 1849, in *Life and Letters of Robertson*, I: 149-150.

[71] *Life and Letters of Robertson*, I: 150.

[72] Minus, *American Reformer*, 44-45.

[73] In his journal, Rauschenbusch made ten entries quoting Robertson, the most telling of which was, "To the question, 'Who is my neighbor?' I reply as my Master did by the example that He gave: 'the alien and the heretic.'" Minus, *American Reformer*, 45.

theology and was deeply troubled by the condemnatory lines of the Athanasian Creed.[74] In Maurice, however, Kingsley found a coherent view of the Scriptures and the very foundations of the Church of England.[75] His wife, Francis, gave him a copy of Maurice's *Kingdom of Christ*, which was dedicated to Kingsley's old headmaster, Derwent Coleridge.

The young priest threw himself into the evolving Chartist Movement at a Chartist Mass Meeting in April 1848. From this experience Kingsley learned of the power of organized associations.[76] By the early 1850s Kingsley had moved beyond Chartism and was a convinced Christian Socialist who advocated cooperative labor associations and wrote regularly for periodicals like *Politics for the People*[77] and *The Christian Socialist.*[78] Dabbling in moral tales, poetry and essays, one of his outstanding accomplishments was the popular children's book, *Waterbabies: A Fairy Tale for a Land Baby* (1862-63), that revealed the exploitation of a chimney sweep in Victorian Britain and, through satire, a progressive view of human origins. Walter Rauschenbusch read that book and commented on Kingsley's contributions to Christian Socialism.

The key to Kingsley's theological underpinning to Christian Socialism was that human selfishness lies at the foundation of social evils. It was a matter of God's declarations through the prophets and martyrs. Kingsley saw himself as a 'Muscular Christian' who preached the divine likeness of the whole of

---

[74] Pope-Hennessy, *Canon Charles Kingsley*, 101.

[75] Kingsley's first book, *The Saint's Tragedy* (1848), was published under Maurice's patronage, and Kingsley's *nom de plume*, "Parson Lot," was suggested at a gathering at Maurice's house where Kingsley jokingly said he felt like the patriarch Lot in the cities of the Plain in Genesis 14: Stubbs, *Charles Kingsley*, 115.

[76] The Chartists advanced a revolutionary platform (The People's Charter, published 8 May 1838) for political and social change in Britain, beginning in 1838 and extending to 1858. The Charter contained six points: universal suffrage, a secret ballot, no property qualifications for MPs, remuneration of MPs, equal constituencies of MPs, and annual elections of MPs. At first Kingsley was not part of the movement, but eventually he was drawn to it. See Malcolm Chase, *Chartism: A New History* (Manchester: Manchester University Press, 2007).

[77] *Politics for the People* ran 17 issues, May-July 1848.

[78] Charles Kingsley, "Tracts on Christian Socialism" in *Parson Lot, Cheap Clothes and Nasty* (London: W. Pickering, 1850). Maurice, Kingsley, and Ludlow held Chartism to be secular and believed that Christian Socialism blended the right antidote to Chartism: Pope-Hennessy, *Canon Charles Kingsley*, 73. The *Christian Socialist* was published November 1850-June 1851, then continued till 1891 under other auspices. Chadwick, *The Victorian Church*, 356, called it the first coherent attempt to state the Christian view of a socialist society.

mankind. Using the Bible he advocated vociferously for universal suffrage, an economic blend of free trade and communism, organized labor, and elevation of the poor.[79]

Of Kingsley's six points of Christian Socialism, the beginning was "politics according to the Kingdom of God," or what he called "Bible politics." He was compelled to respond to the popular criticism that the Bible supported priest-craft, superstition, and tyranny. He urged workingmen to realize there will be "no true freedom without virtue, no true science without religion, no true industry without the fear of God, and love of your fellow citizens."[80]

Some of Kingsley's best thinking was revealed in his poetry:

> Weep, weep, weep and weep
> For pauper, dolt and slave!
> Hark! From wasted moor and fen,
> Feverous alley, stifling den,
> Swells the wail of Saxon men—
> Work! or the grave!
> Down, down, down and down
> With idler, knave and tyrant!
> Why for sluggards cark and moil?
> He that will not live by toil
> Has no right on English soil!
> God's word's our warrant![81]

He was not above using biblical apocalyptic hyperbole:

> Gather you, Gather you, hounds of Hell—
> Famine, and Plague and War; Idleness, Bigotry, Cant, and Misrule,
> Gather and fall in the snare!
> Hireling and Mammonite, Bigot and Knave, Crawl to the battle field, sneak to your grave,
> In the Day of the Lord at Hand.[82]

---

[79] Kingsley joined a group that F. D. Maurice gathered at Lincoln's Inn to circulate among the parishes to conduct social and religious work. See Guy Kendall, *Charles Kingsley and His Ideas* (London: Hutchinson & Co., 1947), 44-51.

[80] Pope-Hennessy, *Canon Charles Kingsley*, 102-103.

[81] Quoted in Stubbs, *Charles Kingsley*, 12-13.

[82] Quoted in Kendall, *Charles Kingsley and His Ideas*, 70.

Charles Kingsley's influence cast a long shadow. In 1877 Stewart Headlam led a company of High Church Anglican Clergy directly inspired by Kingsley's teaching, in organizing the Guild of St. Matthew, in part to promote the study of social and political questions in light of the Incarnation. Working in large towns, its members felt the "absolute need of preaching in season and out of season 'Gospel of the Kingdom,' the fact that the Church is a real living society on this earth, working for the greatest good of the greatest number, and embodying in her sacraments and creeds the strongest assertions of true 'liberty, equality and fraternity ever given to the world..."[83] A decade later in the United States, Walter Rauschenbusch and his friends organized the Brotherhood of the Kingdom, with much the same vision.

Distantly related to Anglican social Christianity was John Ruskin. Ruskin (1819-1900) was a literary and art critic, a philanthropist, and ultimately the Slade Professor of Fine Art at the University of Oxford. A man of the established Church who reflected much on biblical themes to reach conservative moral values,[84] he welded together aesthetic romanticism and Christian morality.[85] Ruskin had a commitment to improving the life quality of industrial workers and he offered his services as an instructor at Working Men's College, Toynbee Hall, and Oxford House at Bethnel Green, ostensibly to bring culture and beauty to the working classes. Demonstrating his penchant for the Romanticist metaphor, Ruskin wrote upon I Timothy 2:10,

> You are yourselves the Church, and see that you be finely adorned, as women professing godliness, with the precious stones of good works, which may be quite briefly defined for the present, as decorating the entire Tabernacle; and clothing your poor sister, with yourselves. Put roses in *their* hair, put precious stones also on *their* breasts; see that they are clothed in your purple and scarlet, with other delights; and that they also learn to read the gilded heraldry of the sky; and upon the earth, be taught, not only the labors of it, but the loveliness.[86]

---

[83] Quoted in Stubbs, *Charles Kingsley*, 151-152. Other manifestations of Christian Socialist advocacy include the Christian Social Union (1889-1919), the Industrial Christian Fellowship, founded in 1920, the Christian Socialist League 1894-98), and the Christian Socialist Society (1886-1892).

[84] A compendium of his biblical comments is found in John Ruskin, *The Bible References of John Ruskin,* edited by Mary and Ellen Gibbs (New York: Henry Frowde, 1898; repr.: Folcroft, PA: Folcroft Library Editions, 1977).

[85] Evans, *The Kingdom Is Always but Coming*, 74.

[86] Quoted in Gibbs, *Bible References of John Ruskin,* 229.

In the 1880s, Rauschenbusch 'absorbed' volumes of Ruskin, whom he declared in a 1910 sermon, "the most Christ-like thinker in all literature." According to one biographer, Rauschenbusch was indebted to Ruskin not only for his superb literary style and high descriptions of art, but also "for the social message of this revolutionary spirit—for this cultured , artistic, literary stylist who wrote about cathedrals and paintings," but also being the prophet of a new age.[87]

Another thinker, actually of Italian origins, Giuseppe (Joseph) Mazzini (1802-1875), was pointedly influential on Walter Rauschenbusch. Mazzini had joined the *Carbonari* in Italy who nurtured a vision for a united Italy and he also agitated republicanism as a member of the secret society of "Young Italy." He was imprisoned and upon release, lived in exile in Switzerland, Paris, and then London.

Mazzini's thinking was plainly theological in character. One writer has characterized him as a Jansenist Catholic who developed a moralistic view of God, mixing God, natural law, and human law.[88] A leading spokesman of liberal nationalism and republicanism, he was also a student of literary criticism. Numerous English and American socialist thinkers regarded his work highly,[89] including Hugh Price Hughes, William S. Rainsford, W. D. P. Bliss, John R. Commons, and George D. Herron.[90] Richard Heath's book, The Captive City of God, or the Churches Seen in Light of the Democratic Ideal, drew heavily upon Mazzini's 1844/1858 essays.[91]

According to Rauschenbusch biographer, Dores R. Sharpe, Rauschenbusch was a student of Mazzini all of his life.[92] He exclaimed of Mazzini, "Have you ever met Mazzini?... He is a prophet to whom God has given lessons of the past...He measures the great men of our time by the attitude they

---

[87] Evans, *The Kingdom Is Always, but Coming*, 74; Sharpe, *Walter Rauschenbusch*, 197, 426.

[88] Donovan Smucker, *The Origins of Walter Rauschenbusch's Social Ethics* (Montreal, QC: McGill-Queens University Press, 1994), 114.

[89] His works filled six volumes and were published in an English translation in 1870 and in the US in the 1880s. See Charles William Stubbs, *God and the People: The Religious Creed of a Democrat, Being Selections from the Writings of Joseph Mazzini* (London: T. Fischer Unwin, 1896).

[90] As did Woodrow Wilson, David Lloyd George, Gandhi, and Sun Yat-sen.

[91] See also Walter Rauschenbusch, "Christianity Revolutionary," 378.

[92] Sharpe, *Walter Rauschenbusch*, 197, 426.

take to its movement. It is a book of religion. To some it may even be a book of devotion."[93]

Deeply concerned about the effects of industrialization and ruthless individualism, Mazzini had a solid religious foundation to his convictions. Robert Handy has pointed out key theological elements in Mazzini, including his first principle of God rooted in divine idealism and the immanence of God. Mazzini believed that "the Divine Law was evident in Life…the proper role of the individual in this Divine economy was to make a contribution to the progress of humanity while on earth."[94] Another writer spoke of Mazzini's watchwords as "duty, not rights; self-service, not self-seeking; association and not competition; God and not the opinions of mankind."[95] Always an activist, Mazzini wrote, "Workingmen, we live in an epoch similar to Christ. We live in the midst of a society as corrupt as the Roman Empire, feeling in our innermost soul, the need of reanimating it and transforming it."[96] Quite likely, Mazzini also contributed to Rauschenbusch's kingdom theology. For example, he wrote, "We seek the kingdom of God on earth, as it is in heaven, or rather that we can become a preparation for heaven…"[97] His populist idea of a Holy Church was that it would be led by a Spirit of Truth to direct its actions.

Beyond the Anglican examples of Christian Socialist writing were Nonconformist engagements of social concerns.[98] Among the leading Nonconformists were the Baptist John Clifford and the Methodist, Hugh Price

---

[93] *Colloquium* I (November 1889): 28. A classmate of Rauschenbusch, F.W.C. Meyer, contended in 1929 that Walter drew heavily upon Mazzini, Karl Marx, and Leo Tolstoy, as well as American thinkers Henry George, Edward Bellamy, Josiah Strong, and Washington Gladden. See Evans, *The Kingdom Is Always but Coming*, 49, n.2, and Sharpe, *Walter Rauschenbusch*, 65, 84, 138, 197, 426, who thought Mazzini was a primary influence.

[94] Handy, "The Influence of Mazzini on the Social Gospel," 120.

[95] Quoted in "Mazzini" *The New Encyclopedia of Social Reform*, ed. by W. D. P. Bliss and Rudolph M. Binder (New York; London: Funk and Wagnalls, 1908), 760.

[96] Giuseppi Mazzini, *An Essay on the Duties of Man: Addressed to Workingmen* (London, Toronto: J. M. Dent, 1844), 103. This was actually written in 1844 and reissued in 1858 and 1892.

[97] Mazzini, *Essay on the Duties of Man*, 21.

[98] Peter d'A. Jones, *The Christian Socialist Revival*, 330, has observed that while Anglicans tended to be incarnational, generally Nonconformists were immanentists, lacking any ideological or dogmatic dependence upon beliefs from British sociologists in general. See also Edward Norman, *Church and Society in England 1770-1970* (Oxford: Oxford University Press, 1976), 4.

Hughes, close friends in the cause.[99] Clifford (1836-1923) had personal connections with the working classes as a lad of eleven who worked 12-hour work days in a lace factory and had "cruel impressions of the men and their work."[100] His theological roots were among the General Baptists, an Arminian side of the denominational family.[101] In the 1880s, he caught the trend of the times, writing that everywhere everything social was astir. Recalling the antislavery crusade of William Wilberforce a half century earlier, Clifford was familiar with Maurice, Kingsley, Westcott, and Ruskin, as well as American writers like Richard Ely and William Bliss. He became directly acquainted with the plight of workers during the London Dock Strike of 1889 and about the same time read Ralph Waldo Emerson's *Essays* that stressed self-reliance, and John Ruskin's work that described man as "capable of an infinite height of marvelous developments."[102] All social problems were spiritual at heart, Clifford concluded.

In the 1890s Clifford was president of The Ministers' Union, a socially active association, and the next year he was president of the Christian Socialist League.[103] His theological position was revealed in almost one hundred arti-

---

[99] Paul T. Phillips' recent analysis also includes the contributions to English Christian Socialism of R. W. Dale, A. M. Fairbairn, and R. J. Campbell (Congregationalists), and Philip Wicksteed (Unitarian). These Nonconformist thinkers followed a stream of Christological Incarnationism or immanentism, the New Theology (including the moral influence theory of the atonement and biblical higher criticism), plus an interest in economics and the social sciences: *A Kingdom on Earth*, 12-18. In contrast, David W. Bebbington continues the evangelical argument that the social gospel in Britain was grounded in Evangelicalism: *Evangelicalism in Modern Britain*, 211-212, replicating the American Evangelical 'school' of Timothy Smith and Donald Dayton.

[100] Quoted in David Thompson, "John Clifford's Social Gospel" *Baptist Quarterly* 21/5 (May, 1986): 201. Christologically, Clifford was an incarnational thinker. He was able to broaden the doctrine of Christ from an individual to realizing himself as all humanity. For a favorable biography of Clifford by a close colleague, consult James H. Rushbrooke, "Clifford, John," *DNB Supplement 1922-30*, 189-190. In contrast, Bebbington alleged that Clifford lifted a phrase from the 1848 *Communist Manifesto* of Marx and Engels in a speech to the Baptist Union: *Evangelicalism in Modern Britain*, 212.

[101] One of the cardinal tenets of the English General Baptists was religious liberty, that Clifford understood to be the freedom to interpret the will of Christ in the light of growing knowledge and change.

[102] Thompson, "John Clifford's Social Gospel," 204.

[103] The League believed that the principles of Jesus Christ are directly applicable to all social and economic questions...demanding reconstruction of society upon a basis of

cles and books across a half century. Beginning in 1872 he wrote as an increasingly committed Christian Socialist in articles like "Jesus Christ and Modern Social Life" (1872), "Socialism and the Teaching of Christ" (1884; 1897), "Christianity the True Socialism" (1885), "The Christian Conception of Society" (1891), and "The Housing of the Poor" (1902).[104] In 1900 at the autumn meetings of the Baptist Union in Leicester, Clifford persuaded his colleagues to pass resolutions demanding land reform, housing and education legislation, care of the aged poor, and licensing reform.[105] Clifford again used his position as president of the newly formed Baptist World Alliance in 1905 to urge an international brotherhood to deal with contemporary social concerns. His most extensive theological presentation was in his Angus Lectures of 1906, published as *The Ultimate Problems of Christianity*, in which he focused on God as Father of everyone, Jesus as redeemer and king,[106] and every man as a child of God redeemed by Christ with ultimate calling and potential. For Clifford, socialism was not a class movement, but divine. As early as 1888 he wrote in his diary,

> This day has deeply impressed me…with the need for more attention to the social problems of the day. Churches should have social missionaries attached to them, should also become organizations for the promotion of the social welfare of the people. Workers should be trained who should not be *theological*. The church has made too much of theology. 'Ethical Culture' is a reaction against extravagances and follies of the theological party…[107]

---

association and fraternity: John H. Y. Briggs, *The English Baptists of the 19th Century* (Didcot: Baptist Historical Society, 1994), 327.

[104] Two of these tracts (1897, 1908) were labeled "Fabian," by which Clifford meant the collective ownership of the means of production.

[105] Jones, *Christian Socialist Revival*, 394.

[106] According to A. C. Underwood, *A History of the English Baptists* (London: Kingsgate Press, 1947), 225-229 [228], Clifford attributed his Christological emphasis to his mother who told him to "find out the teaching of Jesus; make sure of that, and then stick to it, no matter what may happen." "Christ," he said, "has been to me the centre of intelligent repose, as well as the guide and inspiration of my life, my Savior and Master, Leader and Companion, Brother and Lord."

[107] Entry for 16 September 1888, quoted in Sir James Marchant, *Dr. John Clifford, CH: Life Letters and Reminiscences* (London: Cassell and Co., 1924), 81. The "party" Clifford was referring to was the Evangelical Alliance, in the Baptist family headed up by Charles Haddon Spurgeon.

Clifford's programme included better organization of charity, moralizing relations between masters and men in the commercial and industrial worlds, higher wages, better education, preaching of the gospel, and fellowship with Christ.[108]

Through the Baptist Congress (1880-1913) and the Baptist World Alliance (Philadelphia, 1911), Rauschenbusch heard Clifford say, "we must advocate and work for the social gospel ... charity must not be accepted as a substitute for justice."[109]

Hugh Price Hughes (1847-1902), the founder of the Methodist Forward Movement, held that the principles of Christianity must be applied as much to society as to the individual, with a Christology that called for social reconstruction on a Christian basis. Influenced by T. H. Green at Balliol College, Oxford, Joseph Mazzini, and F. D. Maurice, Hughes sought to revive the social vision of John Wesley with a Pentecostal urgency: "Wesley," he wrote, "extended the Gospel to the lives of all men, and to the whole life of every person."[110] Hughes believed that with a new social vision, social harmony among the classes would result, and the poor would be uplifted by the humanitarian example of Christian service. Concerned that Nonconformist evangelicals had become overly individualistic, he wrote, "My wish is to apply Christianity to every aspect of life."[111]

From this survey of key figures invested in social Christianity in the English context, several common theological principles are evident. They include a doctrine of an immanent God, the importance of God identifying with humanity in the Incarnation, the unity of humanity, often expressed as the brotherhood of all mankind. Overarching, there is the interpretation of the Gospel on a social or collective basis. These themes are drawn from a well of changing theological patterns in English universities from the 1840s. The lead voice was Frederick Maurice and the watershed reached Church of England and Nonconformist spheres of influence.

American Theological Foundations of Social Christianity

We gain further understanding of Walter Rauschenbusch's contribution to the social gospel in the work of Josiah Strong, Washington Gladden,

---

108 Thompson, "John Clifford's Social Gospel," 208.

109 Quoted in Thompson, "John Clifford's Social Gospel," 215.

110 Quoted in William McGuire King, "Hugh Price Hughes and the British Social Gospel," *Journal of Religious History* 13/1 (1984): 73.

111 Hugh Price Hughes, *Social Christianity* (New York: 1890), 21.

Shailer Mathews, and Richard Ely all of whom both predated and paralleled the work of Walter Rauschenbusch.[112]

A contemporary of Rauschenbusch with a national reputation for his work on American social reform, was Josiah Strong. Strong (1847-1916), a Congregationalist minister in Cheyenne, Wyoming, and Sandusky and Cincinnati, Ohio, was later an administrator and organizer in ecumenical organizations.[113] More of a popularizer than an academic theologian, his impact on the development of the social gospel was nevertheless profound.

Strong's outstanding contribution to American thought was *Our Country: Its Possible Future and Its Present Crisis* (1885). Thinking in the context of the settlement of the western frontier and its potential religious character, Strong laid out nine "threats" to the future of America, and beyond, to the world. These included immigration, Romanism, secularist public education, Mormonism, intemperance, socialism, wealth, exhaustion of public lands, and the weak moral influence in the cities. His thesis was that America was facing a crisis of identity and the answer to the crisis lay with the Anglo-Saxon race, pre-eminent in the United States. "We are living in extraordinary times. Few suppose that these years of peaceful prosperity, in which we are quietly developing a continent, are the pivot on which is turning the nation's future," he wrote.[114]

One analyst has identified four basic themes in Josiah Strong's theology: the immanence of God, an optimistic view of human nature, the realization of the Kingdom of God on earth, and a crisis facing the church, commonly known as a "cataclysmic" interpretation.[115] Like other social gospel advocates of the 1890s, Strong had a commitment to scientific progress, particularly the

---

[112] Smucker, *Social Ethics of Walter Rauschenbusch*, 93-94, identifies Gladden and Strong as American Ritschelians.

[113] Strong was raised in an ancestral Puritan family, educated at Western Reserve College and Lane Theological Seminary. He was active in the Congregationalist American Home Missionary Society and in 1886 was elected American General Secretary of the Evangelical Alliance until being forced from his position by conservative leaders. He became the leader of a new organization, the League for Social Service (1898-1916) and was a founder of the Federal Council of the Churches of Christ in the USA. He was editor of the League's magazine, *The Gospel of the Kingdom.* He authored twelve books.

[114] Josiah Strong, *Our Country: Its Possible Future and Its Present Crisis* (New York: Baker and Taylor for the American Home Missionary Society, 1885), 15.

[115] Dorothea R. Muller, "The Social Philosophy of Josiah Strong: Social Christianity and American Progressivism," *Church History* 28/2 (June 1959): 187-188.

theory of evolution, and a unified or organic theory of society.[116] According to the laws of nature, Strong believed that "God was purposing, guiding, overruling, accomplishing," and that the Kingdom of God was a world-wide society in which "all human life, physical, intellectual, moral, spiritual, social, industrial, and political would be brought into harmony with the will of God."[117] From his biblical studies, he thought the central teaching of Jesus was his revelation of the Kingdom.

Strong's view was that the sinfulness and imperfection of human society was not inevitable, necessary, or permanent. Once selfishness was overcome, man had the capacity with the aid of science and collective action, to usher in a new social spirit, a spirit of brotherhood and of love. Change had to occur both for individuals and the environment.[118]

Walter Rauschenbusch paid a high tribute to Strong as one of those men who had matured their thought when he was yet a young man, producing a spirit in him that kindled and compelled him.[119]

Washington Gladden (1836-1918) was an early voice in the United States for social concerns implied in the Gospel, and a contemporary of Walter Rauschenbusch. In the history of American thought, Washington Gladden is usually cast in the proximity of Lyman Abbott, Graham Taylor, George A. Gordon, and Walter Rauschenbusch. Rauschenbusch and Gladden actually first met in Columbus, Ohio, in 1916.

From his pastoral base at First Congregational Church in Columbus, Ohio, Gladden became one of the key personalities of the New Theology and the development of the Social Gospel.[120] He was the first notable minister to

---

[116] Through the League, Strong inspired American Social Christians to use social science methods and to collect statistical data. See Phillips, *A Kingdom on Earth*, 92.

[117] Josiah Strong, *The Next Great Awakening* (New York: 1902), 102, 104; "What the Kingdom Is," *The Gospel of the Kingdom* 2/1 (January 1910): 1-2.

[118] Strong, "The Next Great Awakening," 115; "Religious Movements for Social Betterment"; Muller, "Social Philosophy," 201.

[119] Walter Rauschenbusch, *Christianizing the Social Order* (New York: Macmillan Co., 1912), 9.

[120] Gladden was a distinguished graduate of Williams College who was raised in the Burned Over District of Western New York. He served Congregational churches in Brooklyn and Morrisania, New York, and North Adams and Springfield, Massachusetts, before a thirty-six year tenure as pastor of First Congregational Church, Columbus, Ohio. He was also an editor of secular and religious periodicals. His important works were *Working People and Their Employers* (1876) and *The Christian Way: Whither It Leads and How to*

advocate unions, a leader of progressive social thought in the later nineteenth century.

Gladden's biographers have classified him as an evangelical liberal theologian. Jacob Dorn has observed that Gladden was not theologically trained and his work was the product of his own spiritual pilgrimage.[121] Reacting against the orthodox Calvinism of his youth, Gladden moved close to Horace Bushnell's ideas of the atonement, and he accommodated himself to contemporary evolutionary thought and biblical criticism. His was a rational faith and one that was rooted in social experience. He attempted to bridge the "come-outers" and "stay-inners" by affirming historic confessions (he thought the Westminster Confession was a useful historical symbol) and defending liberal Congregationalists. He followed the lead of Baptist theologian, William Newton Clarke, that the bible was a progressive revelation that was filtered through human experience. It was a unique revelation but the bible was not of uniform value. Gladden employed a popularization approach to Bible study in classes and lectures that gave him wide currency in American religious life.[122] As Kenneth Cauthen has noted, Gladden was an evangelical liberal, returning to orthodox positions of the uniqueness of Christ, the depravity of humanity, and cautioning against an overreach of criticizing orthodoxy.[123]

Pastoral settings and experience created priorities in Gladden's theology. His idea of the social gospel was rooted in his concern for the working classes. Industrialization and urbanization drove him to embrace reform. In the 1870s he witnessed firsthand the effects of a depression. Around him were victims of unemployment, ruined families, exploitation of laborers, the plight of the Black population, the failure of Reconstruction, and the persistence of an impoverished class in the city slums. He noted Ida Tarbell's accusations of tainted money in the Standard Oil tycoon John D. Rockefeller's gifts to religious and charitable works.

Go On (1877), among thirty-five titles. He supported the American Institute of Social Service and was a member of its successor, the National Committee for Studies in Social Christianity.

[121] Dorn, *Prophet of the Social Gospel*, 142; see also Evans, *The Kingdom Is Always but Coming*, 52-55.

[122] Two of his books illustrated this interest: *Who Wrote the Bible?* (1891) and *Seven Puzzling Bible Books* (1897).

[123] Kenneth Cauthen, *The Impact of American Religious Liberalism* (New York: Harper and Row, 1962), 87.

Well-informed, Gladden read Thomas Carlisle and John Ruskin and applied their ideas of social reform. In several recorded sermons, he gave biographical sketches of Frederick Maurice, Charles Kingsley, and Hugh Price Hughes.[124] Gladden's own theology began with a larger view of God's Fatherhood than his Calvinistic upbringing allowed for. For him, God was the Father of all men, as he asserted in *Being a Christian: What It Means and How to Begin* (1876) and *The Christian Way: Whither It Leads and How to Go On* (1877). As a corollary, this meant that there was a "most glorious and perfect goodness…natural to man." Evil could be eradicated by the restoration of clear thinking, improved family relations and the creation of a universal brotherhood. [125]

At the heart of Gladden's thinking was a universal law of love for God and man. He believed that any religion that did not emphasize social questions was not authentically Christian. Here was the kingdom of God, as Gladden understood it: "the whole social organism so far as it is affected by divine influences."[126] From his past he conceived of the Kingdom as future, but in his mature thinking, the Kingdom was also to be a present reality. His Christmas message in 1893 indicated that the ideas of the Second Coming of Christ and a subsequent golden age had been displaced in his thinking by "a continuous kingdom of law and love, with no breaks, nor interregnums, nor cataclysms."[127]

Like most progressives in this era, Gladden was optimistic about the full realization of the Kingdom. He saw progress in economics, political reform, and social improvement. This was for him the greatest evidence that the Kingdom was in fact present. Thus, the Kingdom was not to be equated with the Church. In his book, *The Church and the Kingdom* (1894), the church was the institution that modeled the values of the kingdom and declared it. The kingdom was of divine origin and enablement and could not be realized through any forces other than truth and love.[128] Unlike more radical social reformers

---

[124] Dorn, *Prophet of the Social Gospel*, 184, asserts that there was no linear connection between the two movements, but this has been largely rebutted by contemporary studies.

[125] Washington Gladden, "The Supreme Friendship," Sermon, 1910, cited in Dorn, *Prophet of the Social Gospel*, 189.

[126] *The Church and the Kingdom* (New York: Fleming H. Revell Co., 1894), 6.

[127] Washington Gladden, "Christmas Sermon," 1893, cited in Dorn, *Prophet of the Social Gospel*, 194.

[128] Washington Gladden, *The Church and the Kingdom* (New York: Fleming H. Revell, 1894), 9-13.

like George D. Herron, Gladden remained loyal to the church with the Kingdom.

A recent writer has argued that it was Shailer Mathews who made the most important contributions to Modernism in the service of the Social Gospel.[129] Modernism was "a determination to use scientific, historical, social methods in understanding and applying evangelical Christianity to the needs of living persons."[130] Within his "modernist framework," It was Mathews who laid the intellectual groundwork for the emerging social gospel movement.[131] Trained for the contemporary Baptist ministry, his specialized work was in the fields of historical and comparative theology.[132] In his 1897 book, *The Social Teaching of Jesus: An Essay in Christian Sociology,* he introduced his thinking.[133] Following the Scottish theologian, Robert S. Candlish's earlier work, Mathews underscored the prominent place of the Kingdom of God. In itself, it suggests a social relationship. "The kingdom," he wrote, "is the goal of effort, the reward of persecution, and the abode of blessedness."[134] Mathews set aside the theory of a descending Kingdom of God in favor of Jesus' words, "Thy Kingdom Come," as a present reality. It was intended to be an ideal social order in which the relation of men to God is that of sons, and therefore

---

[129] Paul T. Phillips, *A Kingdom on Earth: Anglo-American Social Christianity, 1880-1940* (University Park, PA: The Pennsylvania State University Press, 1996), 32.

[130] Shailer Mathews, *The Faith of Modernism* (New York: Macmillan Co., 1924), 46. See also William R. Hutchinson, *The Modernist Impulse in American Protestantism* (Durham, NC: Duke University Press, 1992), 275-282.

[131] Dorrien, *Soul and Society*, 30.

[132] Mathews had a B.A. from Colby College in Maine and the three-year certificate from Newton Theological Institution. He did further study for two years at the University of Berlin under Hans Delbruck and Ignaz Jastrow in history and Adolf Wagner in political economics. He was also mentored by Albion W. Small at Colby and Ernest D. Burton at Newton, both of whom he later joined at the University of Chicago. Early in his career, Mathews taught New Testament and was drawn to the scientific study of religion. On Mathews and his contribution, see Kenneth Cauthen, "The Life and Thought of Shailer Mathews: Introduction" in *Jesus on Social Institutions* (Philadelphia, PA: Fortress Press, [1928] repr. 1971), xlvi-liii, and Shailer Mathews, *New Faith for Old: An Autobiography* (New York: Macmillan, 1936).

[133] Dorrien, *Soul and Society*, 31, called it the most influential text produced in the social gospel movement. The book was in print for three decades, replaced ultimately by a revised edition, published as *Jesus on Social Institutions* (New York: Macmillan, 1928).

[134] Here Mathews makes no distinction between the terms "Kingdom of God" and "Kingdom of Heaven." *Social Teachings of Jesus*, 42, following Hans Hinrich Wendt, *The Teaching of Jesus*, trans. John Wilson 2 vols. (New York: Charles Scribner's Sons, 1892), I: 370.

to each other, that of brothers.[135] Thus, Mathews thought the Kingdom is an actual anticipated social order. There is to be a universal reign of love---the fatherhood of God and the brotherhood of men,[136] which Mathews called a new social order. [137] For Mathews, an ideal society is not beyond human attainment, but it is the natural possibility for man's social capacities and powers.

From Mathews' point of view, how is an ideal society realized? It is evolutionary, organic, and transformational. Persons who will usher in the kingdom must be transformed in a moral sense into groups of men and women each possessed of the same spirit taught by Jesus. The Kingdom, he thought, was a concrete reality rather than an idea, and it was to be progressively realized. Mathews believed the Church's evangelizing effort on the part of the church was not to be urged on the ground of the benefit to individuals, but the profound significance and helpfulness in all matters of social advance.[138]

A decade later, having interacted with a growing number of leaders speaking the language of the social gospel, Mathews published two additional books advancing his understanding of social Christianity: *The Church and the Changing Order* (1907) and *The Social Gospel* (1910). In his 1907 book that paralleled (from the same publisher) Rauschenbusch's *Christianity and the Social Crisis,* Mathews saw an impending crisis where the masses were being alienated from the churches. A class distinction had emerged with leading Protestant churches identified with employers, salaried persons and farmers, and those disenfranchised "others" who were associated with providing the personal services to the prevailing class, he believed.[139] Identifying serious social problems like materialism, family relations, employment of women and children, he called upon the church to be courageous and develop a role as a social leader: "The greatest service which the church can render society just at present would be to contribute the spirit of Jesus to the ideals which are provocative of discontent."[140]

What Mathews called the "gospel of brotherhood," equated with the kingdom of God, was an assertion that "a man cannot be a Christian in the

[135] Mathews, *Social Teachings of Jesus*, 54.

[136] Mathews, *Social Teachings of Jesus*, 62.

[137] Mathews, *Social Teachings of Jesus,* 77.

[138] Mathews, *Social Teachings of Jesus,* 207, 217, 224.

[139] Shailer Mathews, *The Church and the Changing Order* (New York: Macmillan Co., 1907), 120.

[140] Mathews, *Church and the Changing Order*, 126.

truest sense of the word, except he be interested in bringing in a social life in which honesty and kindliness shall not be a hindrance to any legitimate success in business and politics."[141] Only the church that sets before itself this social service is working in the spirit of its Master; it alone really appreciates its responsibility in converting society into the kingdom of God. It alone is really preaching "the old Gospel."[142]

In *The Social Gospel,* Matthews again took up the message of the Kingdom of God, noting that no selfish man can be saved until he quits his selfishness. He listed principles of the gospel: love, fraternity, a better social order, and a message of hope. The emerging sociologist spoke to how the Kingdom must affect marriage, divorce, children, government, war and peace, social classes, and wealth. He observed the conflict that had ensued between the poor and rich, and the forces that must be engaged in legislation, missions, education, and the church.[143]

Following the emerging principles of social psychology, Mathews believed that the causes of poverty were many and there was no single remedy. The very structure of social life and its innumerable forces make for selfishness and cruelty, thriftlessness, vices of all sorts, but particularly drunkenness. Poverty, he wrote, itself breeds poverty.[144] Here, Mathews was building a social scientific foundation for the social gospel that reflected his associations at the University of Chicago and for some observers, the American social gospel as a whole.[145]

Like Rauschenbusch, Matthews urged that the Church should be brought in to union with other forces that are making a new social order.[146] More than any other theologian of his time, "Mathews elaborated the liberal

---

[141] Mathews, *Church and the Changing Order*, 147.

[142] Mathews, *Church and the Changing Order,* 115. In the table of contents, Mathews listed "the necessity of a social gospel" as a topic of chapter V (vii).

[143] Shailer Mathews, *The Social Gospel* (Philadelphia, PA: The Griffith and Rowland Press, 1910), 24-28.

[144] Mathews, *Social Gospel,* 92.

[145] Compare the observation of Visser 't Hooft, *Background of the Social Gospel*, 149-151, with Kenneth L. Smith and Leonard I. Sweet, "Shailer Mathews: A Chapter in the Social Gospel Movement, Part II" *Foundations: A Baptist Journal of History and Theology* 19/1(1976): 220.

[146] Shailer Mathews, *The Church and Changing Order* (New York: The Macmillan Co, 1907), 6; 9.

modernist understanding of Christianity as a particular kind of social movement."[147] Walter Rauschenbusch regarded Mathews' book, *The Social Teachings of Jesus*, as "incisive."

An important theological influence upon Rauschenbusch from a lay perspective was that of Richard Ely.[148] Rauschenbusch discovered Ely early in his ministry in New York City and the friendship continued through Rauschenbusch's life. Ely was an engaged Episcopalian who commented broadly on the Christian's response to social concerns from his academic expertise in political economy.

Ely was well read in the English social Christian literature, notably the writings of Frederick Maurice.[149] Ely developed a theological understanding to undergird his response to a list of social problems, including the implications of the stock exchange on the control of wealth, child labor in factories, taxation and public utilities, city housing for the poor, and the plight of colored (sic) people. As he saw it, the gospel is divided into two parts: the first is theology and the second is sociology, the science of society. He built upon the words of the Lord's Prayer, "Thy kingdom come," in writing that Christian principles should be applied to potential solutions of social problems. "Every opportunity," he wrote, "to bring to pass righteousness in this world is one that a Christian cannot neglect...the working-classes need intellectual and moral enlightenment."[150]

Ely followed the Christological lead of English theologians Maurice and Robertson. In the gospels, he saw where Jesus turned his disciples away from themselves to the "plenteous harvest," thus assuming a collectivism in the mission of Jesus.[151] An incarnational thinker, Ely observed that modern Christians had forgotten the cross of Christ. The cross meant for Ely that Christians should lead a life of renunciation, as Jesus did: "Hence we must take up our cross." The enunciation of Christ's two commandments, to love God and to love one's neighbor, was the ethical basis of Ely's activism. Here he thought the American Church had fallen short by contenting itself with repeating plat-

---

[147] Dorrien, *Soul in Society*, 35.

[148] For a brief biographical sketch of Ely, see the "Historical Introduction" to Vol. I, above.

[149] Minus, *American Reformer*, 63.

[150] Richard T. Ely, *Social Aspects of Christianity and Other Essays* (New York: Thomas Y. Crowell, 1889), 21; 31.

[151] Ely, *Social Aspects*, 19.

itudes. His ecclesiology was more provocative: "There is in the Church a conscience which can be pricked...there is a power back of the Church in her divine Master which makes for righteousness and which urges her on to a higher life. What is needed is to go back to Christ and learn of him."[152]

According to Dores R. Sharpe, Rauschenbusch read Ely's address on "Natural Monopolies and Local Taxation" in 1886.[153] Apparently, Rauschenbusch first personally encountered Richard Ely when the lecture that became "Social Aspects of Christianity" was presented to a gathering of Baptist ministers in 1888.[154] Christopher Evans points out that Rauschenbusch "devoured" Ely's books and shared his suspicion of socialism.[155] In his second great book, *Christianizing the Social Order* (1912), Rauschenbusch cited Ely on the importance of the cross of Christ, the labor movement, and Ely's opposition to socialism.[156] At this point, Rauschenbusch was himself not inclined to be associated with Socialism.

Finally, among American influences upon Rauschenbusch, was Francis Greenwood Peabody.[157] Peabody, a Congregationalist and then a Unitarian minister, was a correspondent with Rauschenbusch and a published thinker on ethical issues. In placing a priority for theology over sociology, Peabody was a leading interpreter and student of German theology in the United States, helping to create at Harvard a substantial German theological repository.

---

[152] Ely, *Social Aspects*, 49.

[153] Sharpe, *Walter Rauschenbusch*, 64.

[154] Minus, *American Reformer*, 63.

[155] Evans, *The Kingdom Is Always, but Coming*, 65.

[156] Rauschenbusch, *Christianizing the Social Order*, 290, 401, 438.

[157] Peabody (1847-1936) was lecturer in ethics and Plummer Professor of Christian Morals at Harvard Divinity School from 1880-1912. He was minister in Cambridge, Massachusetts and dean of the Divinity School, helping to move it from a denominational orientation to a non-sectarian institution. He introduced the teaching of Christian Social Ethics at Harvard (the College and the Divinity School) and was among the foremost interpreters of German theology in the United States. See Jurgen Herbst, "Francis Greenwood Peabody: Harvard's Theologian of the Social Gospel," *Harvard Theological Review* 54/1 (January 1961): 45-69. His published works include *Jesus Christ and the Social Question* (1900), *The Christian Life in the Modern World* (1914), and *The Religious Education of an American Citizen* (1917). For a perspective on his Christology, see Prescott Browning Wintersteen, *Christology in American Unitarianism: An Anthology of Outstanding Nineteenth and Twentieth Century Unitarian Theologians, with Commentary and Historical Background* (Boston, MA: The Unitarian Universalist Christian Fellowship, 1977), 87-93.

Seven years before Rauschenbusch's "big book," Peabody had published *Jesus Christ and the Social Question* (1900),[158] among the first titles of a long list on the topic to come from the Macmillan Company in the next two decades.[159] Peabody reflected both German influences and the English writers among the Social Christian community, noting especially Maurice, Kingsley, and Ruskin.[160] An eloquent speaker and writer, he often paraphrased biblical content, e.g.: "By this shall all men know that ye are wise men of business, if ye have love one to another."[161]

A good deal of Peabody's attention was directed at the industrial order and the ethical implications involved. He rejected the idea of a class struggle and sought an "industrial peace" and an "industrial justice."[162] While he thought the issues raised in an industrial economy were beyond specific instructions given by Jesus, likewise any sense of Christian economics, sociology or a science of modern society defined by Jesus, the teachings of Jesus did have a bearing upon modern industrial life. He drew richly upon the gospels of Matthew and Luke, particularly the parables of householders, laborers, and fishermen.[163] Basically he saw Jesus teaching the principle of industrial fidelity, or the scrupulous behavior of one's daily business commanding the commendation of God. Christian ideals, he believed carried the details of everyday life to a higher plane on a new horizon.[164] He raised the principle he saw in Jesus' teaching that seemed to subordinate profit to personality as a test of any industrial scheme. He found in Great Britain in the cooperative projects, such as at Rochdale, an example of a moral movement that illustrated the teaching

---

[158] Francis Greenwood Peabody, *Jesus Christ and the Social Question: An Examination of the Teaching of Jesus in Its Relation to Some of the Problems of Modern Social Life* (New York: The Macmillan Co., 1905), 274, indicates that Peabody was inspired at least in part by Heinrich J. Holtzmann, *Die ersten Christen und die soziale Frage* ("The First Christians and the Social Question"), (Frankfurt am Main: n.p., 1880; 1882). Holtzmann (1832-1910) was a professor of New Testament at the University of Strasbourg. Holtzmann's work was in the tradition of Ritschl and may well be the progenitor of titles linking the teachings of Jesus with social questions.

[159] Peabody's book went through eight printings between November 1900 and June 1905.

[160] Peabody, *Jesus Christ and the Social Question*, 32-38.

[161] Peabody, *Jesus Christ and the Social Question*, 316.

[162] Peabody, *Jesus Christ and the Social Question*, 273.

[163] Peabody, *Jesus Christ and the Social Question*, 278.

[164] Peabody, *Jesus Christ and the Social Question*, 280.

of Jesus and inculcated the virtues of patience, thrift, and loyalty, which in turn make personal character.[165]

For Peabody, the doctrine of social horizon and of social origin meet in the social ideal of Jesus Christ. The world constitutes the location of the kingdom of God and individuals are inspired to become instruments of that kingdom.[166] Here he sharpened his focus on a key idea: "The kingdom of God, according to Jesus, is to be found in the gradually realized, and finally perfected, brotherhood of man.[167]

Like others who were revising the theology of the kingdom, Peabody allowed that the kingdom might not come about peaceably because men of violence may take it by force. While the rich will have difficulty entering the kingdom, the poor, the blind, the maimed, and the lame will be welcomed. Peabody was certain that a new system of labor would prevail where workers would be paid according to their needs. His focus on the coming kingdom saw its realization in collectivism that was coming about in his lifetime. Quoting the German biblical theologian, Oskar Holtzmann, he believed the fundamental ideals of socialism are to be referred back to Jesus.[168]

Rauschenbusch's Evolving Theology: Eclecticism

Beyond Systematics

Walter Rauschenbusch was aware of the great German and Dutch dogmatic theologians of the eighteenth and early nineteenth centuries whom his father had admired and imitated, men like Amesius (William Ames), Gottfried Leibnitz, Johann Hamann, and F. D. E. Schleiermacher. In another important sense, Rauschenbusch was introduced to American English-speaking

[165] Peabody, *Jesus Christ and the Social Question*, 282. The Rochdale mill town in greater Manchester, England, produced a co-operative project where membership co-operative economics were practiced.

[166] Peabody, *Jesus Christ and the Social Question*, 285.

[167] Peabody, *Jesus Christ and the Social Question,* 286.

[168] Peabody, *Jesus Christ and the Social Question*, 287. Oskar Holtzmann (1859-1934) was a well-known New Testament theologian at the University of Giessen, the author of *Jesus Christus und das Gemeinschaftsleben der Menschen* ("Jesus Christ and the Life of the Community") (Freiburg: J. C. B. Mohr, 1893). An eloquent writer, Peabody often paraphrased the words of Jesus: "By this shall all men know that ye are wise men of business, if ye have love one to another." (p. 316)

systematic theology as a student at Rochester Theological Seminary of Augustus Hopkins Strong. Strong succeeded Ezekiel G. Robinson[169] as theologian and took the school in some important new directions. During Rauschenbusch's sojourn at Rochester Theological Seminary as a student, Strong was slowly undergoing a transition in several areas of his thinking.

Strong's theology went through distinct phases: 1876; 1886; 1892; 1896; and 1907.[170] In the earliest edition of his published classroom notes, Strong exhibited a traditional, evangelical, orthodox theology characterized by a high view of the scriptures as revelation, a forensic understanding of justification, and a propitiatory view of the atonement in a modified Calvinistic context. Having studied under the progressive theologian, Ezekiel G. Robinson, at first, Strong bore no marks of interaction with the methods of the New Theology or the emerging emphasis on divine immanence. In the second edition of his published notes in 1886, Strong moved into idealism to develop a philosophic basis for the biblical awareness of deity. By the 1892 edition, according to Carl F. H. Henry's analysis,[171] Strong had a more positive regard for immanence, and he developed his own terminology, "ethical monism," to express his interest in science and the Boston University school of Personalism.[172] By 1907, the once conservative, evangelical A. H. Strong changed to a

[169] Robinson (1815-1894) was one of the most celebrated Baptist educators of the nineteenth century. He was founding president and professor of theology at Rochester Theological Seminary and later Brown University. Theologically, Robinson was a Kantian eclectic, or a developing theologian, influenced by Barnas Sears, Theodore Parker, and Horatio B. Hackett; among German and Dutch theologians, August Tholuck, Martin Kahler, George Calixtus, A. T. Lydecker and Coccejus; and finally the British Romanticists, Samuel T. Coleridge and P. T. Forsyth. His systematic work was published at the conclusion of his career: *Christian Theology* (Rochester, NY: E.B. Andrews, 1894). On his contribution, see Brackney, *Genetic History of Baptist Thought*, 270-271; 319-324.

[170] Carl F. H. Henry has exhaustively covered the scores of articles and lectures between editions of his lectures that demonstrate Strong's pilgrimage toward new positions: *Personal Idealism and Strong's Theology* (Wheaton, IL: The Kampen Press, 1951), 65-94.

[171] Henry's doctoral dissertation at Boston University focused on the changes in Strong's theology from a conservative, evangelical orientation to a set of positions much reflective of E. G. Robinson, Hermann Lotze, and Borden P. Bowne. Critics of Strong's final positions found him hesitant, attempting to hold onto old doctrines but with a vocabulary that signaled a new theory of religious knowledge. Henry, *Personal Idealism and Strong's Theology*, 228-229.

[172] Personalism was a school of thought advanced in 1898 by Borden Parker Bowne and later by Edgar J. Brightman both associated with Boston University School of Theology. Influenced by Herman Lotze in Germany and Henry Churchill King at Oberlin Col-

Personalistic idealism, an affirmation of the relationship of science and religion, a new naturalistic understanding of miracles, theistic evolution, a truncated view of original sin, and a modified kenotic Christology, and a postmillennial eschatology of an enlarging kingdom of Christ.[173]

Strong's influence was abidingly relevant, throughout Walter Rauschenbusch's active career.[174] Firstly, Strong was Rauschenbusch's teacher and a close family friend. As a student at Rochester Seminary, Rauschenbusch could well be characterized as a conservative evangelical. Indeed, President Strong was troubled by several views that Rauschenbusch exhibited, but in 1897 he hired Rauschenbusch to teach in the German Department and in 1902 to take up a major faculty chair in the main English program.[175] When Rauschenbusch published his first book, *Christianity and the Social Crisis* (1907), Strong was lavish in his praise: he believed the book would be "as epoch-making as

---

lege, it was an attempt to mediate Hegelian modes and scientific positivism. Stressing ethical relationships between God and humanity, Personalist thinkers offered strong support to the Social Gospel: Hutchinson, *The Modernist Impulse*, 126. The major treatise of the movement was Borden P. Bowne, *Personalism* (Boston, MA: Houghton Mifflin and Co., 1908).

[173] Augustus Hopkins Strong, *Systematic Theology: A Compendium Designed for the Use of Theological Students* (Philadelphia, PA: American Baptist Publication Society, 1907): the pertinent passages are: Preface (vii-xii; 26-29; 105-110); miracles, (117-133); inspiration, (212-222); personality of God, (252-254); emanation, (383-86); personality of humanity, (515-16); theory of Dorner, (686-688); ethical theory of the atonement, (750-771).

[174] Note especially Rauschenbusch's dedicatory inscription in *A Theology for the Social Gospel* (1917): "This book is inscribed with reverence and gratitude to Augustus Hopkins Strong for forty years president of Rochester Theological Seminary, My teacher, colleague, friend, humanist and lover of poetry, a theologian whose best beloved doctrine has been the mystic union with Christ."

[175] President Strong was not without his concerns for Rauschenbusch's theology, particularly Rauschenbusch's view of the atonement: "When you say that you do not point inquirers to the cross as making it possible for God to forgive, do you mean that it is your judgment [that] God can forgive without atonement? In teaching history would you be indifferent as between Augustine and Pelagius, or would you make the study of deepening the student's conception of sin? While we wait for more definite news from Prof. [Benjamin] True, please answer these questions in confidence. Faithfully yours, Augustus H. Strong." A. H. Strong to Walter Rauschenbusch 25 April 1888 (Rauschenbusch Collection RG 1003, Correspondence Files, American Baptist Historical Society, Atlanta, Georgia).

Henry George's *Progress and Poverty* and it's going to do much to show Christians their duty."[176] A decade later Strong criticized Rauschenbusch's omission of the idea of union with Christ (the foundation of Strong's *Systematic Theology*) in *A Theology for the Social Gospel*.[177]

That supportive comment from his president notwithstanding, the mature Rauschenbusch was increasingly impatient with the methods of systematic theologians. In an article in the prestigious *American Journal of Theology* in 1907, Rauschenbusch opined,

> Systematic theology embodies the net results of all theological studies. It is the capitalized hoard of all their earnings, and just as economic capital hates to see its securities depreciate, so theology dislikes to discover that some golden candlestick, which it has long lighted in honor of its Lord, is only plated and that the brass is wearing through. It is pathetic to watch the scholastic theologians of the sixteenth century, when their venerated authorities were flouted by the men of the new learning, and the textbooks which they had laboriously learned to expound were dumped into the gulf of oblivion with a splash.[178]

Even more strongly, in 1917, he virtually dismissed systematic theology:

> Theology is the esoteric thought of the Church. Some of its problems are unknown and unintelligible except where the Church keeps an interest in them alive. Even the terminology of theology is difficult for anyone to understand unless he has lived under church influence for years...Theology became an affair of experts.[179]

In his own theological pilgrimage, Strong exhibited the same transitions that Rauschenbusch did in developing a full-blown articulation of the social gospel. President Strong and Professor Rauschenbusch remained close personal friends until Walter's death.[180]

---

[176] A. H. Strong to Walter Rauschenbusch, 27 June 1907 (Rauschenbusch Family Collections, RG 1003, American Baptist Historical Society, Atlanta, Georgia).

[177] Smucker, *Rauschenbusch's Social Ethics,* 44. Walter disagreed, responding that all life was to be transformed by faith and knowledge of Christ.

[178] Walter Rauschenbusch, "The Influence of Historical Studies on Theology," *American Journal of Theology* 11/1 (January 1907): 118.

[179] Walter Rauschenbusch, *A Theology for the Social Gospel* (New York: Macmillan, 1917), 15-16.

[180] Strong was involved in an experimental blood transfusion procedure to save Walter's life.

Here an important observation is useful: Rauschenbusch was essentially a historical theologian. He wrote in 1906, "In the history of doctrine, we see the doctrines in the making."[181] He was certainly educated in systematic thought and read great systematic theologians, but in the end he collected biblical exegesis, the life of Christ, the history of the apostolic age, practical theology, missions, and ethics all under the history of doctrine that he understood as the dominant and modern branch of theology. He believed that continuity—understanding human development as a linear progression—is a necessary equipment for the theologian. "The scientific study of history is the best method for training the scientific temper and the critical faculty in theologians; and the critical faculty is absolutely necessary."[182] The German influence on Walter Rauschenbusch was profound in treating theology as a science or *wissenschaft,* "the unity of teaching and research or discovery… suggesting that education is a process of growing and becoming."[183]

The implications of historical method for Rauschenbusch's theology included an emphasis upon the life of Christ (particularly the incarnation), the emergence in history and beyond, of the Kingdom of God, and the real possibility of social reform.[184] He reflected in a letter to Cornelius Woelfkin,

---

[181] Walter Rauschenbusch, "Address to the Theological Conference," *Post-Express* (May 9, 1906).

[182] Rauschenbusch, "The influence of Historical Studies," 119.

[183] https://en.wikipedia.org/wiki/Wissenschaft, accessed 4 November 2016.

[184] Kenneth Cauthen observed in his analysis of Rauschenbusch that he made no attempt to deal with many of the questions in which a systematic thinker would be interested. Cauthen believed some of his convictions lacked clarity (*Impact of American Religious Liberalism*, 93). A systematic analysis of Rauschenbusch's theological position produces the following doctrinal observations: (1) he had a democratic view of God in which Jesus democratized the idea of God; (2) God is both immanent and transcendent, coming close to a form of pantheism; (3) inspiration, more experiential and dynamic, is more important than revelation; (4) a high view of man and his capacities flows through Rauschenbusch' writings: "I believe in the miraculous power of the human personality"; (5) sin is equated with tragedy, frustration, suffering, and destruction; (6) Rauschenbusch lays more stress on social sin than biological evil; (7) there is an equal concern for both social and individual salvation: the atonement has covered all mankind in changing their status before God; redemption amounts to restoration of God-consciousness through Jesus Christ; (8) he refers to the church as the social factor in salvation: the church continues the work of Jesus but is not the equivalent of the Kingdom of God; and (9) there is a split frame in eschatological terms with an emphasis upon the coming eternal reign of God and the present developing Kingdom in history.

> The American ideals of Democracy have dominated my intellectual life. My literary and professional work for years has been characterized by the consistent effort to work out democratic interpretations of history, religion, and social life...I am, therefore, not merely an American in sentiment, but have taken our democratic principles very seriously, and used my life to inculcate and spread them here and abroad.[185]

Baptist Pietism

A second set of defining theological characteristics of Walter Rauschenbusch's theology relate to his Pietistic Baptist orientation.[186] Donovan Smucker has defined Pietism in general to mean,

> the Protestant reaction against orthodox intellectualism and formalism in favour of a personal, devotional, subjective, individualist, conversionist evangelicalism that stresses vital religious experience. The pietist movement as understood here stems from the seventeenth century.[187]

The Pietist tradition signaled that a radical return to the authority of scripture was at the foundation of Rauschenbusch's experience. As F. Ernest Stoeffler has pointed out, Pietist doctrine, preaching and ethics were based squarely on the New Testament. Pietist biblical interpretation could often seem legalistic, but Pietists were committed to biblical norms and suspicious of any kind of rationalism.[188]

Closely related to biblical authority, Pietists were people of deep, vivid religious experience.[189] Pietists historically were also engaged with their environment and culture. They were activists upon what they held to be scriptural

---

[185] Walter Rauschenbusch to Cornelius Woelfkin, 1918, (Rauschenbusch Family Collections, RG 1003, Box 91, American Baptist Historical Society, Atlanta, Georgia).

[186] Among the uses of the term "pietist," "pietism," "piety," among Baptist thinkers, see Edwin S. Gaustad, *Baptist Piety: The Last Will and Testimony of Obadiah Holmes* (New York: Arno Press, 1980), 70-72; William G. McLoughlin, *New England Dissent, 1630-1833: The Baptists and the Separation of Church and State*, 2 vols. (Cambridge, MA: Harvard University Press, 1971), I: 30-32; II: 707-708; and Adolf Olson, *A Centenary History, As Related to the Baptist General Conference of America* (Chicago, IL: Baptist General Conference Press, 1952), 12-13.

[187] Smucker, *The Origins of Walter Rauschenbusch's Social Ethics*, 9.

[188] Stoeffler, *Rise of Evangelical Pietism*, 20-21.

[189] Stoeffler, *Rise of Evangelical Pietism,* 13-14. In the use of this term, one must be careful not to transform Pietism from its historical context into a generic term. See, for instance, McLoughlin, *New England Dissent*, I: 6, 28, 30, where the writer refers to a "pietistic movement."

ultimatums. Baptists of varying types engaged Pietist practices in Britain through the Puritan-Separatist tradition, in Europe through a Separatist offshoot of the Reformed and Lutheran Churches, in the Netherlands through the Precicianist movement, and in America through the revivalist movements of the 18th and 19th centuries.[190] From his conversion in 1836, August Rauschenbusch was a thoroughgoing German Pietist, whose spiritual pilgrimage was further enhanced in May 1850 when he was baptized a believer in the Baptist tradition.[191] From childhood, Walter felt the overpowering Pietist, Baptist influence of his father, August.

In Walter Rauschenbusch's reading of Baptist and Anabaptist history, there were sufficient instances in the late sixteenth and early seventeenth centuries to connect Baptists legitimately with Dutch Mennonites and English Separatists.[192] Here he joined a popular school of Baptist teachers who connected the two streams seamlessly.[193] In the eighteenth century, Baptists in the American colonies joined the Great Awakening and emphasized the richness of the public ordinance of believer's baptism by immersion. In the Revolutionary Era, as he understood the religious history, Rauschenbusch was aware of "evangelists" of the New England and Middle Colonies who travelled south on tours to preach and plant churches. In his own immediate context his father was part of the Second Great Awakenings that much benefitted the Baptist movement: we recall August was converted to Baptist principles in 1850, part of the Baptist domestic missionary experience. This shift in basic Christian identity became iconic in the Rauschenbusch family.

In later years as he reflected on Baptist experiential theology, Rauschenbusch found other elements he could affirm. He had sufficient opportunity to

---

[190] Konrad Anton Fleischmann, founder of the German Baptist movement in the US, was formerly a Swiss Separatist.

[191] Minus, *American Reformer*, 2-3. The vast majority of details about August's early years are taken from *Leben und Wirken von August Rauschenbusch, Professor am theologishen Seminar zu Rochester in Nordamerika angefangen von ihn selbst, vollendet und herausgegeben von seinem Sohn Walter Rauschenbusch* (Cassel: Kommissionsverlag von J. G. Oncken, Nachfolger, Gmbh; and Cleveland, OH: Peter Ritter, 1901).

[192] On this approach, see the later work of Glen H. Stassen, "Anabaptist Influence in the Origin of Particular Baptists" *Mennonite Quarterly Review* 36 (October 1962): 322-48, and "Opening Menno Simon's Foundation Book" *Baptist History and Heritage* 32/2 (1998): 34-44.

[193] See contemporaries like Thomas Armitage, Albert H. Newman, Henry C. Vedder, and W. J. McGlothlin. Hudson argued this was ultimately attributable to Thomas Crosby's 1738-40 history.

observe and consider sacramental theology and High-Church ecclesiology among the Catholics, Lutherans, and Anglicans, respectively, and he rejected all. Sacramental theology belonged to the past and the prelacy of the Church of England was pompous. Some churches, he observed, made much of ritual and sacrament, while others made much of a formulated creed. He wrote sardonically,

> Imagine Jesus, with the dust of Galilee on his sandals, coming into the Church of St. Sophia in Constantinople in the fifth century, listening to dizzy doctrinal definitions...watching the priests performing the gorgeous acts of worship, reciting long and set prayers, and offering his own mystical body as a renewed sacrifice to their God![194]

Further to Rauschenbusch's Pietism, one study has demonstrated that in his first two years as pastor at Second German Baptist in New York City, he reflected the Pietism of his upbringing, emphasizing the holiness of God, human sinfulness, and the importance of a personal conversion.[195] In 1917 at the end of his life, he reminisced,

> I felt the call of God, and after a long struggle extending through several years, I submitted my will to his law. Henceforth God was consciously present in my life, and this gave it a sense of solemnity and worth. This gave a decisive reinforcement to my will, and turned my life in the direction of service and, when necessary, self-sacrifice; so salvation came to me.[196]

Himself a Pietist, Donovan Smucker felt that the most enduring influences of Pietism upon Walter Rauschenbusch were a quest for religious reality and a warm compassion for people.[197]

In Baptist ecclesiology Rauschenbusch affirmed the democratic congregationalism and emphasis upon preaching and personal experience with Christ. "The Christian faith as Baptists hold it, sets spiritual experience boldly to the front as the one great thing in religion. We are an evangelistic body.

---

[194] Walter Rauschenbusch, *Christianity and the Social Crisis* (New York: Macmillan Co., 1907), 94; "Why I am a Baptist, My First Reason," 2.

[195] Heinz D. Rossol, "More than a Prophet" *American Baptist Quarterly* 29/2 (June 2000): 129-153; also cited in Evans, *The Kingdom Is Always but Coming,* 59.

[196] Walter Rauschenbusch to Lemuel Call Barnes 10 May 1918 (Rauschenbusch Family Collection, RG 1003, Box 39, American Baptist Historical Society, Atlanta, Georgia); also re-printed in *Walter Rauschenbusch: Selected Writings,* edited by Winthrop S. Hudson (New York: Paulist Press, 1984), 44-45.

[197] Smucker, *Rauschenbusch's Social Ethics,* 29.

We summon all men to conscious repentance from sin, to conscious prayer for forgiveness."[198]

From Rauschenbusch's reading of Continental Anabaptist history and American and English Baptist development, Baptists and their Anabaptist kin better exhibited the qualities of prophetic Christianity than other denominations. Historically, he found Baptist principles imbedded in the sixteenth century Anabaptist wing of the Reformation. Here the English writer and historian, Richard Heath,[199] was very influential. Rauschenbusch was indebted to Heath's book, *Anabaptism, from Its Rise at Zwickau to its Fall at Münster 1521-1536* (1895) for the continuity of certain ideals to his own generation.[200] Heath had written,

> Anabaptism is not dead; it slumbers in the heart of the Poor Man, and will assuredly rise again. For the voice that proclaimed liberty of conscience in Christendom, to which, therefore, we owe all that results therefrom—liberty of thought, liberty of worship, free speech, and a free press—the voice that proclaimed the Common Life to be of far higher importance than the individual life, the true Community to be the divine unit rather than the individual, the family or the nation—that voice cannot be hushed in any tomb or kept silent under the heavy stone of conventional religion. For that voice is not in one man only, but in all.[201]

---

[198] Rauschenbusch, "Why I am a Baptist. My First Reason," 1.

[199] See the biographical detail on Heath in the "Introduction" to Vol. I, xxxvi-xxxvii.

[200] Heath and Rauschenbusch were frequent correspondents. Sixteen letters from Richard Heath 1901-1908 covered contemporary topics as well as their joint interest in Anabaptist origins of the Baptists. For instance, Heath wrote, "...Have you made progress with your studies in Anabaptism? I hope the American public will listen to you and begin to do justice to that grand period in Baptist history. If the Baptists could only be immersed in the Anabaptist spirit, they might at the present time lead the Christian world. The river of the Anabaptist cause goes a long way to explain the littleness of English history since the Commonwealth and the still more miserable character of German history.

This said, there is to be a Baptist Congress held at Berlin in August and I have taken the liberty to suggest that the Secretary of the Baptist Union that they should suggest that the English delegates should read my book on Anabaptist history as a key to the present dangerous condition of affairs in Germany and in fact throughout Christendom. I hope your stay in Germany has improved your health and that will be as I expect it will be, of the utmost benefit to your children. I remain yours sincerely, Rich Heath." Richard Heath to Walter Rauschenbusch, 12 May 1908 (Rauschenbusch Family Collection, RG 1003, Correspondence Files, American Baptist Historical Society, Atlanta, Georgia).

[201] Richard Heath, *Anabaptism, from Its Rise at Zwickau to Its Fall at Münster 1521-1536* (London: Alexander and Shepheard 1895), 193-194. In Heath's interpretation of

Because Christianity was becoming less clerical, less ceremonial, less dogmatic, and more democratic, more spiritual, and more ethical, Rauschenbusch believed Baptists had an enormous responsibility and opportunity to become the vanguard of modern Christianity by recovering and championing the fundamentals deep in their heritage.[202]

Finally, Rauschenbusch's ecclesiology underscored the American doctrines of separation of church and state and religious liberty. Here his theology was drawn from his cultural experience and education in the United States. As a "culture-Protestant," to employ Dr. Cauthen's category,[203] Rauschenbusch was emphatic on the separation of church and state:

> Our Baptist churches decline all alliances with the State. They accept no dictation from the State in their spiritual affairs. They ask no favors from the State, except that they accept such exemption from taxation as the State grants to all institutions which labor for the common good and are not for private profit. Baptists insisted on separation between church and State at a time when the principle was novel and revolutionary...Baptists have the far nobler and prouder position ...of being pioneers in that principle toward which the civilized nations are slowly drifting.[204]

Little wonder that he would reflect on a situation in his childhood where he exclaimed his role model was John the Baptist![205]

A "New Theologian"

Christopher Evans has painted a portrait of Walter Rauschenbusch and the rise of the social gospel as inseparable with theological liberalism.[206] In

---

Anabaptism, the community overshadowed the individual, creating for Rauschenbusch a contradicting image with his Pietist individualist spirituality. I am indebted to Dr. Priscilla Eppinger for pointing out this contradiction.

[202] Walter Rauschenbusch, "Baptists in History," *The Baptist Observer*, October 1906.

[203] Cauthen, *Impact of American Liberalism*, 93.

[204] Rauschenbusch, "Why I am a Baptist, My Second Reason," 4.

[205] Walter Rauschenbusch, "Reminisces of My Life" (Mss. dated December, 1900 in Rauschenbusch Family Collection, ABHS, Box 139).

[206] Evans, *The Kingdom Is Always but Coming*, 49. This is a major thesis of the book, which has a subplot of presenting a history of American liberal theology with Colgate Rochester Divinity School and Rochester, New York, playing a major role in the narrative. According to W. Kenneth Cauthen (formerly of Crozer Theological Seminary), *American Religious Liberalism*, 87, the origins of this narrative are found in George Hammar, *Christian Realism in Contemporary American Theology* (Uppsala: A. B. Lundequistska Bokhandeln, 1940), 146-150.

doing so, he follows the lead of Gary Dorrien who had previously argued that after Rauschenbusch left seminary, he embraced liberal German theological tradition that his father had raised him to dread.[207] In the present analysis, however, the terminology, "New Theology," is preferred. In short, the "New Theology" was a response to new questions and new methods in the theological disciplines. As William Hutchison has suggested, the principal antecedents to Rauschenbusch include German theologians, English Broad Churchmen, and Americans like Newman Smyth, Horace Bushnell, Charles A. Briggs, Henry Ward Beecher, H. C. King, Gerald B. Smith, and importantly, Theodore Munger, who defined the term, "New Theology."[208]

Munger's key contribution was his 1883 book, *The Freedom of Faith,* that set forth the manifesto of the New Theology.[209] Among the categories of doctrine he revised were the doctrine of God, Christ, morality, immortality, atonement, and eschatology. For him, the New Theology was a definite movement that attempts to link the truth of the past with the truth of the present in the interest of the Christian faith. In his description, he was indebted to Maurice, Robertson, and Bushnell, among others.

Specifically, Munger described seven key features of the "New Theology": (1) a broader use of reason in theology: revelation rests upon reason, revelation is reasonable; (2) Scripture should be interpreted in a more natural way: he observed a trend toward a more historical, contextual understanding of the Bible, not just fitting texts together to form a doctrine; (3) a recognition of a new relation of theology to natural science: the external world is a revelation of God; (4) the theory of physical evolution is the probable method of physical creation; (5) Theology is not just the science of God, but the science

---

[207]Dorrien, *Soul in Society*, 23. Noteworthy was the assessment of Dores R. Sharpe, *Walter Rauschenbusch*, 12, who as a Liberal thinker himself, characterized Rauschenbusch as "generating a liberal social movement calling for a fresh study of social and religious conditions and institutions, a new interpretation of the principles of Jesus…a new evangelism, the reconstruction of the social order, and the education of Christian people in support of a liberal social view of Christianity."

[208] "New Theology" is preferred here because it is the most generic term actually used in the historical context. It is the least prejudicial term allowing liberals and modernists to continue to be seen as "evangelicals," and it is the *objet de critiques* of many scholarly reviews such as from the Hodges at Princeton. See Hutchinson's comment, "The New Theology had to pay the price of its success in spreading and institutionalizing liberal ideas." Hutchison, *Modernist Impulse*, 110.

[209] An excellent summary of the development of the New Theology, Munger, *et.al.* is in Hutchison, *Modernist Impulse*, 76-110.

of the relations between God and man; (6) there is no line of distinction between the sacred and the secular: "the kingdoms of this world are becoming the kingdom of the Lord Jesus Christ"; (7) Eschatology must be restated: he equated the "eternal" with moral and spiritual meaning. Man is under probation, Munger believed, because he is a moral being undergoing a formative process.[210] Munger concluded his description of the New Theology by saying, "it is reception to the breathing of the Spirit, passive, yet quick to respond to the heavenly visions that do not cease to break upon the darkened eyes of humanity."[211]

University of Chicago Professor Gerald B. Smith added a decade later his conviction that,

> the historical method of studying religion must be pushed to its logical conclusion. We must insist that the outcome of critical scholarship shall be judged by its actual moral quality, not by the superficial test of mere conformity to a system.[212]

Smith, much indebted to Albrecht Ritschl, then went on to deconstruct ecclesiastical ethics in favor of a new ethical basis for transforming theology. He noted the decline of the importance of miracles and the sacramental, a new understanding of the Bible that focuses upon its capacity to quicken one's religious and moral ideals rather than focusing on its origins, a new emphasis upon divine immanence, the influence of psychology on ideas like regeneration, a new ethical understanding of the work of Christ, and the ethical needs of training ministers.[213]

Smith was fully committed to the fruits of scientific investigation and developments of technology, like the steam engine and telephone communication. So theology ought to be open to new ideas. He concluded his Yale Lectures with a contrast between the old aristocratic understanding of Christianity and the ethical values of modern democratic strivings. Smith thought he was responding via the New Thought or New Theology to a summons to a work of theological reconstruction, which would enable Christianity actually

---

[210] Theodore T. Munger, *The Freedom of Faith* (Boston, MA: Houghton Mifflin, 1883), Munger, 11, 13, 16, 25, 27, 32, 27.

[211] Munger, *Freedom of Faith*, 44.

[212] Gerald Birney Smith, *Social Idealism and the Changing Theology* (New York: The Macmillan Co., 1913), xxii.

[213] Smith, *Social Idealism*, 205-219. In his "new understanding" of the atonement and Christian nurture, he affirmed the views of Horace Bushnell (219).

to make its contribution to the development of modern civilization, a kind of "environing God," as he termed it.[214]

In his final major work, *A Theology for the Social Gospel*, Walter Rauschenbusch subtly employed the terminology "New Theology" in the context of the Apostle Paul, and underscored in a footnote his appreciation for two key essays, King's *Reconstruction in Theology*, and Smith's *Social Idealism and the Changing Theology*.[215]

A Christological Foundation

In all aspects and periods of his thought, Walter Rauschenbusch was Christologically grounded. Of the different identifiable types of "New Theologians" at the turn of the nineteenth century, Walter Rauschenbusch was an evangelical liberal. This meant basically that he strove for a biblical foundation for his social gospel, to cite George Hammar's categories.[216]

As Rauschenbusch used critical historical Jesus scholarship to plumb the gospels, he was concerned with a proper Christology:

> He [Jesus] was neither a theologian, nor an ecclesiastic, nor a socialist. But if we were forced to classify him either with the great theologians who elaborated the fine distinctions of scholasticism; or with the mighty popes and princes of the Church who built up their power in his name; or with the men who are giving their heart and life to the propaganda of a new social system, where would we place him?[217]

Following the lead of Frederick Maurice, Charles Kingsley and Frederick Robertson, Rauschenbusch was an incarnational theologian: he valued the life of Christ, His teachings, and their implications as the core of his theology. In the main, Rauschenbusch wrote in his last book,

> the theological significance of the life of Christ has been comprised in the incarnation, the atonement, and the resurrection.... The social gospel

---

[214] Smith, *Social Idealism*, 226; 243.

[215] Henry Churchill King, *Reconstruction in Theology* (New York: Macmillan, 1901); Rauschenbusch, *Theology for the Social Gospel*, 3, 4, 5, 7, 9, 13n, 14, 20, 21.

[216] Hammar, *Christian Realism in Contemporary American Theology*, 158. See also Cauthen, *American Religious Liberalism*, 89.

[217] Rauschenbusch, *Christianity and the Social Crisis*, 92. Ironically, as Rauschenbusch published his first great book in 1907, he seemed not to be aware of Albert Schweitzer's work on the historical Jesus, published the previous year. Schweitzer upended the Harnack thesis that undergirded Rauschenbusch's perspective on Jesus and the early church. See Dorrien, *Restructuring the Common Good*, 29.

would interpret all the events of his life, including his death, by the dominant purpose, which he consistently followed, the establishment of the Kingdom of God.[218]

Rauschenbusch seemed to dismiss the two-nature debates of the fourth and fifth centuries as excessively metaphysical and pursuing a 'false tail.' Trying to define the divinity of Christ, Rauschenbusch thought of divinity as a pre-existent endowment that he brought to the womb of Mary. It was not a physical matter of his conception, but manifested in "spiritual processes" of desire, choice, affirmation, and self-surrender within his will.[219] Character, not nature, was for him the locus of Christ's divinity.

Of great insight to Rauschenbusch's Christology was the Ritschelian understanding of personhood that was put forth in the United States by Borden Parker Bowne at Boston University. Ritschl had written that theology takes as its fundamental truth the full conception of God as a "Person Who establishes the Kingdom of God as the final end of the world, and in it assures to every one who trusts in Him supremacy over the world." Further, Ritschl reasoned, "Personality, is likewise a predicate of man, but only in a derivative fashion." Ritschl followed Martin Luther's teaching that God is Love, that humans also exhibit Love, and that human love springs from the revelation of God in Christ.[220] The world of persons thus created an ethical web of relationships that was attested to by actual human experience.[221] Bowne further postulated "a world of persons with a Supreme Person at the head as the conception to which we come as the result of our critical reflections." It is the experience of God as a person that validates one's theology, because as Bowne pointed out, "experience is first and basal in all living and thinking, and all theorizing must go out from experience as its basis, and must return to it for verification."[222]

---

[218] Rauschenbusch, *A Theology for the Social Gospel*, 149-150.

[219] Rauschenbusch, *A Theology for the Social Gospel*, 150.

[220] Albrecht Ritschl, *The Christian Doctrine of Justification and Reconciliation: The Positive Development of the Doctrine, English Translation*, edited by H. R. Macintosh and A. B. Macaulay (Edinburgh: T & T Clark, 1902), 228; 238; James Orr, *The Ritschelian Theology and the Evangelical Faith* (London: Hodder and Stoughton, 1905), 112-113, provides a contemporary affirmation of Ritschl.

[221] Ritschl wrote, "The task of Jesus Christ in His vocation, or the final aim of His life, viz., the Kingdom of God, is directly the final aim of God in the world, and is known by Him (Jesus) to be such." Quoted in Orr, *The Ritschelian Theology*, 128.

[222] Borden Parker Bowne, *Personalism* (Boston, MA and New York: Houghton Mifflin and Co., The Riverside Press, Cambridge, 1908), 277-278; 303.

Rauschenbusch wrote that it was by virtue of Jesus' personality that he became the initiator of the Kingdom of God. Jesus' personality was a new type among humanity. Jesus experienced God in a new way, he was spiritually intimate with the Father, and he communed directly with God. Being a unique form of humanity, Jesus was able to overcome human temptations: mysticism, pessimism, asceticism, and superficial religion. The personality of Jesus, thus understood, was a call to emancipation and transformation to others down through the ages. "What was personal with him became social within the group of the disciples. His life became a collective and assimilating force and a current of historic tradition."[223]

In his final summation of his Christology, Rauschenbusch says,

> Jesus experienced God in a new way. The ethical monotheism, which he inherited from the prophets, was transformed within his spirit and through his experiences into something far lovelier and kinder. Jehovah, the keeper of covenants and judge of his people, was changed into the Father in heaven who forgives sins freely, welcomes the prodigal, makes his sun to shine on the just and unjust, and asks for nothing but love, trust, and cooperative obedience. This intuition of God was born in a life that neither hated nor feared, and so far as it is adopted in any single life or in the life of humanity, it banishes hate and fear. An overpowering consciousness of God is needed in order to offset and overcome the tyranny of the sensuous life and its temptations. This consciousness of God, which we derive from Jesus, is able to establish centres of spiritual strength and peace, which help to break the free sweep of evil in social life. Jesus set love into the centre of the spiritual universe, and all life is illuminated from that centre. This is the highest idealistic faith ever conceived, and the greatest addition ever made to the spiritual possessions of mankind....So we have in Jesus a perfect religious personality, a spiritual life completely filled by the realization of a God who is love. All his mind was set on God and one with him.[224]

'Basileic' (Kingdom/Reign of God) Theology: The Kingdom Theology of the Social Gospel

Walter Rauschenbusch's theology of the Kingdom (*basileia tou theou*) was in contrast with earlier interpretations, including Origen's spiritualization of the kingdom, Augustine's equating of the kingdom with the Church, the

---

[223] Rauschenbusch, *A Theology for the Social Gospel*, 155-[164].

[224] Rauschenbusch, *A Theology for the Social Gospel,* 154-155.

common Reformation idea that the kingdom and the invisible church were the same, and the eschatological manifestation of the kingdom in Johannes Weiss, Albert Schweitzer, and various groups of dispensationalists.

In the nineteenth century background of a renewed interest in kingdom theology lay yet another contribution of Albrecht Ritschl. A major new direction in Ritschl's articulation of the doctrine of God was his understanding and the import he gave to the Kingdom of God. In his thinking, God as Love is revealed in His Son and a community that is subject to His will.[225] This association of mankind thus subject to the will of God extensively and intensively, is the most comprehensive possible concept that exhibits reciprocal moral action of its members.[226] Based upon Romans 14: 16-18, Ritschl wrote, "the kingdom of God is the divinely ordained end of the preaching of Christ, including the demand for change of heart and for faith,...and forming the principal subject of prayer to God."[227] Ecclesiologically, Ritschl delineated between the church as a worshipping community, identified as followers of Christ, and those who act reciprocally from love and call into existence that fellowship of moral disposition and moral blessings which extends, through all possible gradations, to the limits of the human race. Churches, he observed, require constitutions and sacraments; the kingdom does not depend in the least on these for its continued existence.[228] God's personal end, and the ultimate end of the world, become the same through the Kingdom of God.[229] Significantly for the coming social Christianity and social gospel movements, Ritschl also believed that the interrelations between the love of God and the

---

[225] Ritschl, *Justification and Reconciliation*, 282.

[226] Ritschl, *Justification and Reconciliation*, 284.

[227] Albrecht Ritschl, *Instruction in the Christian Religion*, trans. Alice Mead Swing, in Albert Temple Swing, *The Theology of Albrecht Ritschl* (New York: Longmans, Green, and Co., 1901), 174. Further, "The kingdom of God is the divinely vouchsafed for highest good of the community founded through his revelation in Christ, but it is the highest good only in the sense that it forms at the same time the ethical ideal, for whose attainment the members of the community bind themselves together through their definite reciprocal action."

[228] Ritschl, *Justification and Reconciliation*, 285.

[229] Ritschl, *Justification and Reconciliation*, 291.

kingdom of God results in a moral order that prepares the way for the Kingdom of God among human beings.[230] So, in fact Ritschl paved the way for basileic theology that points to the Kingdom of God as realized in the present.

Rauschenbusch conceived the relationship of politics and religion in Kingdom theology in his early years and maintained through his life, according to Klaus Jürgen Jaehn. But that historian also concedes that one generation earlier, Frederick Maurice in England had conceived the idea of combining Christian Socialism with the concept of the Kingdom of God.[231] So one can legitimately connect Rauschenbusch's basileic theology with earlier Anglican Broad Churchmen. Further, as we have seen, Rauschenbusch followed Ritschl's emphasis on the definition, role, history, scope, and location, ecclesiology and eschatology of the Kingdom of God.[232] In fact in his reading notes, Rauschenbusch wrote, "The entire Gospel was a *logos tēs basileias* (a "word of the kingdom"), coining the phrase "basileic," and in his manuscript, "Christianity Revolutionary," Jesus' thoughts about the Kingdom circle like a host of planets 'round a central sun."[233]

In precise theological terms, what did Walter Rauschenbusch mean by the Kingdom coming into human history?[234] History, he thought, was a gradual revelation of God's will. At its heart in his generation, for Rauschenbusch, the kingdom was an experiential matter: "The powers of the kingdom of God well up in the individual soul; that is where they are born and that is where the starting point must be."[235] In 1907 he wrote that the Kingdom was connected with Jesus, who fulfilled the Kingdom, declared that it was close at

---

[230] Ritschl, *Justification and Reconciliation,* 317; Ritschl, *Instruction in the Christian Religion*, 239-240, where Ritschl declared "the ethical task of the kingdom of God is performed as the universal task of the Christian community only when all the duties of the narrower circles of life conditioned by nature…are done according to the special principles of each, under the inspiration of love to one's neighbour as their final motive."

[231] Jaehn, *Rauschenbusch: The Formative Years*, 46-47.

[232] Smucker, *Origins of Rauschenbusch's Social Ethics*, 87-94. On the eschatological dimensions of Ritschl's development of the kingdom, See Orr, *The Ritschlian Theology*, 160, where he notes Ritschl's idea of the Kingdom as the *Selbstzweck* ("work of sacrifice") and the *Endszweck* ("concluding work") of God in the creation of the world.

[233] Quoted in Minus, *American Reformer,* 81; "Christianity Revolutionary" (Unpublished manuscript in Rauschenbusch Papers, ABHS, Atlanta, Georgia, Box 101), 79.

[234] Rauschenbusch was plainly Ritschelian, consciously building upon Immanuel Kant, Friederich Schleiermacher, and Ritschl in underscoring the ethical importance of the Kingdom. See *A Theology for the Social Gospel*, 138-139, note 1.

[235] Walter Rauschenbusch, "The Kingdom of God," *Cleveland's Young Men* (January 9, 1913) quoted in Gary Dorrien, *Soul in Society*, 27.

hand, and that it was the center of all Jesus' teaching: parables, moral instructions, and prophetic predictions. God was the creator of the kingdom, he said, and Jesus patiently fostered its growth, cell by cell. He was clear that Jesus believed that God was the real creator of the Kingdom; it was not set up by man-made evolution.[236] Translating the kingdom into his era, Rauschenbusch understood it to be a social hope or a collective conception, involving the whole social life of man.[237] It was not, he believed, a matter of getting individuals to heaven, but of transforming the life on earth into the harmony of heaven.[238] The kingdom of God stood at counterpoint with a 'kingdom of evil' that Rauschenbusch equated with rampant capitalism, exploitation of various groups, and even the darkness of the medieval church. "Jesus desired to found a society resting on love, service, and equality...God is a father, men are neighbors and brothers; let them act accordingly....The kingdom of God is the true human society..."[239]

In his second large book, *Christianizing the Social Order* (1912), Rauschenbusch indelibly imprinted Christianization of the social order with the theological meaning of the Kingdom of God. "No man is intellectually prepared to understand Jesus Christ, Rauschenbusch wrote, "until he has understood

---

[236] Rauschenbusch, *Christianity and the Social Crisis*, 63. Among the various Rauschenbusch descriptive statements of his understanding of the kingdom were: "the sum of all divine and righteous forces on earth..."all pure aspirations God-ward"... "individual men and women who freely do the will of God because they love it"..."a growing perfection in the collective life of humanity..." (*BOKL*, 1893); "a collective conception, involving the whole social life of man" (*CSC*, 65); "an approximation to a perfect social order"; "The Kingdom of God is always but coming" (*CSC*, 421); "the progressive transformation of all human affairs by the thought and spirit of Christ" (*CSO*, 458); "the energy of God realizing itself in human life" (*TSG*, 141); "that God's will shall be done on earth even as it is now in heaven" in "The Kingdom of God" *Cleveland's Young Men* 27 (January 9, 1913); the reign of God among men on earth (*CSO*, 82); "the kingship of God that always means the emancipation and democracy of people" (*CSO*, 91); "a life of humanity organized on the basis of solidarity and love" (*DWBC*, 59); "the reign of God" (*SPJ*, 49); "the highest and broadest idea in sociology and ethics" (*SPJ*, 59); the kingdom of God means justice, freedom, fraternity, labor, joy" (*SPJ*, 75); "a religious social life on earth" (*SPJ*, 75); "a dynamic expression of accepted sociological principles" (*SPJ*, 78).

[237] Here he followed the earlier basileic theology of Francis Peabody, who saw the kingdom in two worlds, heavenly and earthly, its present potentiality and its future realization. Peabody, *Jesus Christ and the Social Question*, 100.

[238] As he put it in *Christianity and the Social Crisis*, 65, "it is not a matter of saving human atoms, but of saving the social organism." Here he was addressing the old evangelical position by offering a new soteriological model.

[239] Rauschenbusch, *Christianity and the Social Crisis*, 54, 60, 63, 65, 71.

the meaning of the Kingdom of God." The point of his thesis in that sequel was to show that the faith of the Kingdom of God is "fundamentally adapted to inspire and guide us in christianizing the social order."[240] In this, his first major theological publication, Rauschenbusch was careful to define his idea of the church:

> The Church, the organized expression of the religious life of the past, is one of the most potent institutions and forces in western civilization. All parties woo its favor and moral influence. It cannot help throwing its immense weight on one side or the other. If it tries not to act, it thereby acts; and in any case its choice will be decisive for its own future.[241]

And to underscore an important distinction, Rauschenbusch wrote, "We are the church as we worship together; we are the Kingdom as we live justly and lovingly with one another."[242]

The Christological foundations of the Kingdom in Rauschenbusch's thought must not be missed: "All his teachings center about it. His life was given to it. His death was suffered for it. When a man has once seen that in the gospels, he can never unsee it again."[243]

Rauschenbusch also contended that as the Reformers had rediscovered Paul's doctrine of justification by faith, his generation was called to rediscover the Christ of the synoptic gospels.[244]

A decade after the 'great book,' Rauschenbusch's basileic theology was even more fully developed. In the following excerpts, he made eight major points:

> (1) The kingdom of God is divine in its origin, progress and consummation. It was initiated by Jesus Christ…it is sustained by the Holy Spirit and it will be brought to its fulfillment by the power of God in his own time….It has a rightful place in theology; (2) The Kingdom of God contains the teleology of the Christian religion; (3) The Kingdom of God is both present and future. Like God it is all tenses, eternal in the midst of

[240] Walter Rauschenbusch, *Christianizing the Social Order* (New York: Macmillan Co., 1912), 49.

[241] Rauschenbusch, *Christianity and the Social Crisis*, xxii.

[242] Walter Rauschenbusch, *The City Vigilant* 1/5 (May 1894).

[243] Quoted in C. Howard Hopkins, *A Gospel for the Social Awakening: Selections from the Writings of Walter Rauschenbusch*, edited by Benjamin E. Mays (New York: Association Press, 1950), 13.

[244] Walter Rauschenbusch, "A Conquering Idea," *The Examiner* 31 July 1892; also in Hudson, *Walter Rauschenbusch: Writings*, 73.

> time; (4) Even before Christ, men of God saw the Kingdom of God as the great end to which all divine leadings were pointing; (5) The Kingdom of God is humanity organized according to the will of God. [It] is a progressive reign of love in human affairs; (6) Since the Kingdom is the supreme end of God, it must be the purpose for which the Church exists; (7) Since the Kingdom is the supreme end, all problems of personal salvation must be reconsidered from the point of view of the Kingdom; (8) The Kingdom of God is not confined within the limits of the Church and its activities. It embraces the whole of life.[245]

The Kingdom responded to all the old and all the new elements of Rauschenbusch's own religious life, and was eminently practical. It was the "saving of the lost, the teaching of the young, the pastoral care of the poor and frail, the quickening of starved intellects, the study of the Bible, church union, political reform, the reorganization of the industrial system, international peace…the idea is as big as humanity, for it means the divine transformation of all human life."[246] That transformation came about through the thought and spirit of Christ.[247]

For Rauschenbusch, the Kingdom was never to be reduced to its constituent parts, because "the reign of God was the sum of all divine and righteous forces on earth."[248] He saw the Kingdom as "the first and most essential dogma of the Christian faith."[249]

Democratic, Nationalistic Theology

Rauschenbusch was imbued with a double spirit of nationalism. Firstly, he held a lifelong, familial appreciation for German culture in an age of German nationalism. We have seen his appreciation for German Anabaptism from his father. Especially in his four-year sojourn in Gütersloh, Walter experienced Germany as the home of his ancestors, a centre of university education among the best in the world, an environment in which to speak and read the German language, home to a number of his relatives, and a place of

[245] Rauschenbusch, *A Theology for the Social Gospel*, 139-145, *passim.*
[246] Rauschenbusch, *Christianizing the Social Order*, 93-94.
[247] Rauschenbusch, *Christianizing the Social Order*, 458.
[248] Rauschenbusch, "Kingdom of God," 79.
[249] Rauschenbusch, *Christianizing the Social Order*, 49.

great tourist attraction to the young seeker.[250] Moreover, he witnessed Bismarck's Germany at the height of its political unification, buttressed by a *kultur Protestantism*.[251]

Secondly, he held deep convictions about his family's adopted country's ideals and the theological implications. In his much-quoted series, "Why I am a Baptist," he asserted,

> We are Americans because we were born so. But it is our duty and our right clearly and increasingly to understand what our country stands for and to adopt as our personal principles those ideals of democracy and equality on which our national life is founded. We are Americans by birth, but we must become Baptists by conviction.[252]

Here he was likening the adoption of theological convictions to patriotic principles. The author of a textbook in German on American democracy, *Die Politische Verfassung unseres Landes: Ein Handbuch zum Unterrichte fur die deutsche-amerikanische Jugend* (1902),[253] Rauschenbusch thought of the United States as an apex in the development of democratic ideals, the model for western nation-states. Here he reflected the thinking of Josiah Strong, among others. Strong had concluded in 1895,

> I believe it is fully in the hands of the Christians of the United States during the next ten or fifteen years, to hasten or retard the coming of Christ's kingdom in the world by hundreds, and perhaps thousands, of years. We of this generation and nation occupy the Gibraltar of the ages which commands the world's future.[254]

---

[250] Minus, *American Reformer*, 32-33;71-82: Minus titled his chapter on Rauschenbusch in Europe, "The Seeker;" Evans, *The Kingdom is Always, but Coming*, 27.

[251] On this issue, see Gunther Wenz, *Der Kulturprotestant. Adolf von Harnack als Christentumstheoretiker und Kontroverstheologe* (München: Herbert Utz Verlag, 2001) and Herbst, *The German Historical School*, 164. This was a blend of Protestant religion and the ideals of the Bismarkian state in the 1870s and 1880s. It involved large numbers of professors who freely gave their services to the state in exchange for *Lehrfreiheit* ("academic freedom"). Professors Gneist, von Humboldt, and Wagner all held high positions in the Prussian Council of State or the Imperial Diet.

[252] Walter Rauschenbusch, "Why I am a Baptist," *The Rochester Baptist Monthly*, (November1905): Prelude.

[253] "The Political Constitution of our Country: A Guide to Teaching for German-American Youth."

[254] Strong, *Our Country*, 227.

In addition to Walter Rauschenbusch's affection for the United States and liberal democracy, his geographical and social context was a subtle influence as well. As former Rochester city historian Blake McKelvey has argued, Rochester was an unusual city in which to mature and work. Prosperous during Walter's entire lifetime, Rochester was a deeply philanthropic city. Industries and the wealthy supported educational and health care institutions.

Beyond these assets, Rochester earned a reputation as a religiously and politically liberal environment. In the decade of the 1870s the Rev. Newton Mann defended the theory of evolution, Byron Adams, minister at the Plymouth Ave. Church, was ejected in 1880 from the Rochester Presbytery for holding unorthodox views, and Algernon Crapsey at St. Andrews Episcopal Church, who became a national figure accused of heresy in the Protestant Episcopal Church, was removed from his pulpit in 1906. Responsive to the working people of Rochester, Paul Moore Strayer's Third Presbyterian Church in 1908 started a series of lectures, the People's Sunday Evenings, that focused on social concerns. The Labor Lyceum was an important forum to Rauschenbusch, as was a strong YMCA. The various churches in the city formed a federation of churches that eventually dropped evangelical terminology from its bylaws in order to allow the Unitarians to participate. On the evangelical side of the ledger, the great evangelist, Wilbur Chapman, in 1907 held a regional series of revival meetings where two hundred thousand people were involved in 200 meetings. Baptist-affiliated Rochester Seminary was open to multiple denominations, as of course was the Baptist-related University of Rochester.[255]

Rauschenbusch ended his final book, *A Theology for the Social Gospel*, by presciently observing the connection between theology and the political sphere: "The era of prophetic and democratic Christianity has just begun. This concerns the social gospel, for the social gospel is the voice of prophecy in modern life."[256]

---

[255] Smucker, *Origins of Walter Rauschenbusch's Social Ethics*, 81. Historian Philip Thompson found an instance in the 1920s of the liberal tradition of the City Club in Rochester where police threatened to arrest one of the invited speakers who was reputed to be a Bolshevik. One of Rauschenbusch's faculty successors, Conrad Moehlman, was president of the Club. Note from Philip Thompson to the editor, 16 January 2017.

[256] Rauschenbusch, *A Theology for the Social Gospel*, 279.

Summary

To attempt to depict fully the theology of Walter Rauschenbusch is to recover the pieces of a mosaic across time. Consequently, Walter Rauschenbusch's theology across four decades can best be described functionally as eclectic. His doctrine of God emphasized human discovery over divine self-disclosure. God has predestined a democratic process as a personal moral will; he is also a kindly Christ-like Father who desires the full redemption of all. Some analysts stress Rauschenbusch's commitment to the immanence of God.[257] Likewise, his understanding of Christology was ethical rather than metaphysical or doctrinal. Jesus is at once in continuity with other humans, and constitutes the moral perfection of the human race. The doctrine of Christ for Rauschenbusch was tied up in the realization of the Kingdom of God as an emerging divine community under the will of God. As to the atonement of Christ, Rauschenbusch traced the traditional biblical narrative, adding that it was a kingdom of evil that killed Christ, that Jesus tasted death like every human, Jesus' suffering identified God with the human race, and that the death of Christ transformed the spiritual status of humans before God to a community of the redeemed.

Rauschenbusch had a high view of the capacity of humanity: this clearly placed him within the socially liberal frame of reference. On an individual basis, Rauschenbusch parted company with traditional Calvinist ideas of total depravity, affirming the power and transformation of education and morality.[258] He recognized the nature of sin as mostly social and the result of human passions and ignorance. The human will can be corrected and the ignorance of humanity can be educated. With respect to the inheritance of sin, Rauschenbusch was inclined toward inherited social sin (through institutions) rather than biologically transmitted sin. He mostly emphasized the social nature of salvation, the increasing social transformation toward a perfect society, but he stopped short of any form of utopian society actually achieved on earth. This echoed contemporary liberal thinking. Yet, he also reinforced his own individual experience of regeneration. Here he could be fitted among liberal evangelicals.

Rauschenbusch modified the doctrine of last things considerably. His background was rooted in cataclysmic eschatology, but he gradually shifted toward a modified postmillennialism. History and the Kingdom of God are

[257] Cauthen, *Impact of American Religious Liberalism*, 94-95.

[258] See Dorrien, *Reconstructing the Common Good,* 39.

relentless in the march toward redemption. The distinction between the saved and the damned is replaced by God's ultimate redemption of all creation. Rauschenbusch did not give up his belief that beyond the present life, there will be an ultimate divine consummation of all things. His eschatology best reveals his theological eclecticism.

Rauschenbusch read widely, interacting with scores of writers and ideas as revealed in his journals. His was not a straight-line pilgrimage. He was indebted to his German scholastic background, the Pietism of his own family experience, a Baptist understanding of the church, an incarnational Christology, all leading to a focus on the Kingdom of God. His affection for the United States encapsulated his overall theological agglomerate into a *kultur Protestantismus*.[259]

As he summed up his own theology, consumed by his social vision, he observed its comprehensiveness:

> The body of ideas which we call the social gospel is not the product of a fad or temporary interest; it is not an alien importation or a novel invention; it is the revival of the most ancient and authentic gospel, and the scientific unfolding of essential elements of Christian doctrine which have remained undeveloped all too long; the rise of the social gospel is not a matter of choice but of destiny; the digestion of its ideas will exert a quickening and reconstructive influence on every part of theology.[260]

---

[259] This idea of a cultural Protestantism had roots in the German national experience. Robert Handy has commented on the American experience: "Most Protestants in the America of 1890 saw themselves as belonging both to a denominational tradition and to the national religion, a religion of civilization—and they experienced little or no tension between them. More than they knew, evangelicals were convinced that theirs was a Christian civilization on the way to victory and perfection" Robert T. Handy, *A Christian America: Protestant Hopes and Historical Realities, Second Edition* (New York: Oxford University Press, 1984), 99.

[260] Rauschenbusch, *A Theology for the Social Gospel*, 26.

A Theology for the Social Gospel

Editorial Introduction

A Theology for the Social Gospel was Rauschenbusch's final major work. Friends and colleagues had long pressed him to create a theological basis for his overall program. The opportunity for the book came in the 1917 invitation to deliver the Nathaniel W. Taylor Lectures at Yale University. In writing the book, he frankly admitted that he was not a systematic theologian, and in fact held the discipline in questionable value. His approach was based upon the published theologies of William Adams Brown, William Newton Clarke, and Augustus H. Strong in an historical context. After initial chapters focusing upon the importance of the social gospel in re-orienting the task of theology, he covered doctrinal categories of sin (six chapters), the fall, and evil; salvation; the atonement; the church and the ordinances; and eschatology. It is in this book that Rauschenbusch redefined several classic theological ideas, like focusing on social and corporate over individual sin; the relevance of the church in combatting social ills; stressing a pragmatic kingdom of evil; the priority of a present kingdom of God; and the real possibility of human achievement. Some sympathetic critics found the last book lacking in imagination, repeating former assertions, but with less spirit.

This book is inscribed
with reverence and gratitude
to
Augustus Hopkins Strong
for Forty Years
President of Rochester Theological Seminary,
My Teacher, Colleague, Friend,
Humanist and Lover of Poetry,
A Theologian whose best beloved doctrine
has been
the Mystic Union with Christ

Foreword

In April, 1917, I had the honour of delivering four lectures on the Nathaniel W. Taylor Foundation before the Annual Convocation of the Yale School of Religion. These lectures are herewith presented in elaborated form.

The Taylor Lectures are expected to deal with some theme in Doctrinal Theology, but the Faculty in their invitation indicated that a discussion of some phase of the social problem would be welcome. I have tried to obey this suggestion and still to remain well within the original purpose of the Foundation by taking as my subject, "A Theology for the Social Gospel."

Of my qualifications for this subject I have reason to think modestly, for I am not a doctrinal theologian either by professional training or by personal habits of mind. Professional duty and intellectual liking have made me a teacher of Church History, and the events of my life, interpreted by my religious experiences, have laid the social problems on my mind. On the other hand, it may be that the necessity of approaching systematic theology from the outside may be of real advantage. Theology has often received its most fruitful impulses when secular life and movements have set it new problems.

Of the subject itself I have no cause to speak modestly. Its consideration is of the highest importance for the future of theology and religion. It bristles with intellectual problems. This book had to be written some time, and as far as I know, nobody has yet written it. I offer my attempt until some other man comes along who can plough deeper and straighter.

I wish to assure the reader who hesitates in the vestibule, that the purpose of this book is wholly positive and constructive. It is just as orthodox as the Gospel would allow. I have dedicated it to an eminent representative of the older theology in order to express my deep gratitude for what I have received from it, and to clasp hands through him with all whose thought has been formed by Jesus Christ.

My fraternal thanks are due to my friends, Professor James Bishop Thomas, Ph.D., of the University of the South, and Professor F. W. C. Meyer of Rochester Theological Seminary, who have given a critical reading to my manuscript and have made valuable suggestions.

Contents

CHAPTER I

THE CHALLENGE OF THE SOCIAL GOSPEL TO THEOLOGY

We have a social gospel. We need a systematic theology large enough to match it and vital enough to back it.

This is the main proposition of this book. The first three chapters are to show that a readjustment and expansion of theology, so that it will furnish an adequate intellectual basis for the social gospel, is necessary, feasible, desirable, and legitimate. The remainder of the book offers concrete suggestions how some of the most important sections of doctrinal theology may be expanded and readjusted to make room for the religious convictions summed up in " the social gospel."

Some of my readers, who know the age, the tenacity, and the monumental character of theology well, will smile at the audacity of this proposal. Others, who know theology still better, will treat this venture very seriously. If theology stops growing or is unable to adjust itself to its modern environment and to meet its present tasks, it will die. Many now regard it as dead. The social gospel needs a theology to make it effective; but theology needs the social gospel to vitalize it. The work attempted in this book is doomed to futility if it has only the personal ideas of the author behind it. It is worthy of consideration only if the needs of a new epoch are seeking expression in it, and in that case its personal defects are of slight importance.

The argument of this book is built on the conviction that the social gospel is a permanent addition to our spiritual outlook and that its arrival constitutes a stage in the development of the Christian religion.

We need not waste words to prove that the social gospel is being preached. It is no longer a prophetic and occasional note. It is a novelty only in backward social or religious communities. The social gospel has become orthodox.

It is not only preached. It has set new problems for local church work, and has turned the pastoral and organizing work of the ministry into new and constructive directions. It has imparted a wider vision and a more statesmanlike grasp to the foreign mission enterprise. In home missions its advent was signalized by the publication, in 1885, of "Our Country" by Josiah Strong. (*Venerabile nomen!*) That book lifted the entire home mission problem to a higher level. The religious literature uttering the social gospel is notable both for its volume and its vitality and conviction. The emotional fervour of the new convictions has created prayers and hymns of social aspiration, for which the newer hymn books are making room. Conservative denominations have formally committed themselves to the fundamental ideas of the social gospel and their practical application. The plans of great interdenominational organizations are inspired by it. It has become a constructive force in American politics.

This new orientation, which is observable in all parts of our religious life, is not simply a prudent adjustment of church methods to changed conditions. There is religious compulsion behind it. Those who are in touch with the student population know what the impulse to social service means to college men and women. It is the most religious element in the life of many of them. Among ministerial students there is an almost impatient demand for a proper social outlet. Some hesitate to enter the regular ministry at all because they doubt whether it will offer them sufficient opportunity and freedom to utter and apply their social convictions. For many ministers who have come under the influence of the social gospel in mature years, it has signified a religious crisis, and where it has been met successfully, it has brought fresh joy and power, and a distinct enlargement of mind. It has taken the place of conventional religion in the lives of many outside the Church. It constitutes the moral power in the propaganda of Socialism.

All those social groups which distinctly face toward the future, clearly show their need and craving for a social interpretation and application of Christianity. Whoever wants to hold audiences of working people must establish some connection between religion and their social feelings and experiences. The religious organizations dealing with college men and women know that any appeal which leaves out the social note is likely to meet a listless audience. The most effective evangelists for these two groups are men who have thoroughly embodied the social gospel in their religious life and thought. When the great evangelistic effort of the "Men and Religion Forward Movement" was first planned, its organizers made room for "Social Service" very hesitatingly. But as soon as the movement was tried out before the public, it became clear that only the meetings which offered the people the social application of religion were striking fire and drawing crowds.

The Great War has dwarfed and submerged all other issues, including our social problems. But in fact the war is the most acute and tremendous social problem of all. All whose Christianity has not been ditched by the catastrophe are demanding a christianizing of international relations. The demand for disarmament and permanent peace, for the rights of the small nations against the imperialistic and colonizing powers, for freedom of the seas and of trade routes, for orderly settlement of grievances, these are demands for social righteousness and fraternity on the largest scale. Before the War the social gospel dealt with social classes; to-day it is being translated into international terms. The ultimate cause of the war was the same lust for easy and unearned gain which has created the internal social evils under which every nation has suffered. The social problem and the war problem are fundamentally one problem, and the social gospel faces both. After the War the social gospel will "come back" with pent-up energy and clearer knowledge.

The social movement is the most important ethical and spiritual movement in the modern world, and the social gospel is the response of the Christian consciousness to it. Therefore it had to be. The social gospel registers the fact that for the first time in history the spirit of Christianity has had a chance to form a working partnership with real social and psychological science. It is the religious reaction on the historic advent of democracy. It seeks to put the democratic spirit, which the Church inherited from Jesus and the prophets, once more in control of the institutions and teachings of the Church.[1]

The social gospel is the old message of salvation, but enlarged and intensified. The individualistic gospel has taught us to see the sinfulness of every human heart and has inspired us with faith in the willingness and power of God to save every soul that comes to him. But it has not given us an adequate understanding of the sinfulness of the social order and its share in the sins of all individuals within it. It has not evoked faith in the will and power of God to redeem the permanent institutions of human society from

[1] In his "Social Idealism and the Changing Theology," embodying the Taylor Lectures for 1912, Professor Gerald B. Smith has shown clearly the discrepancy created by the aristocratic attitude of authority in theology and the spread of democracy in modern ethical life, and has insisted that a readjustment is necessary in theology at this point to conform it to our ethical ideals. Professor Smith expresses the fear that our critical methods by themselves will lead only to a barren intellectualism. That feeling has been one motive in the writing of the present book.

their inherited guilt of oppression and extortion. Both our sense of sin and our faith in salvation have fallen short of the realities under its teaching. The social gospel seeks to bring men under repentance for their collective sins and to create a more sensitive and more modern conscience. It calls on us for the faith of the old prophets who believed in the salvation of nations.

Now, if this insight and religious outlook become common to large and vigorous sections of the Christian Church, the solutions of life contained in the old theological system will seem puny and inadequate. Our faith will be larger than the intellectual system which subtends it. Can theology expand to meet the growth of faith? The biblical studies have responded to the spiritual hunger aroused by the social gospel. The historical interpretation of the Bible has put the religious personalities, their spiritual struggles, their growth, and their utterances, into social connection with the community life of which they were part. This method of interpretation has given back the Bible to men of modernized intelligence and has made it the feeder of faith in the social gospel. The studies of "practical theology" are all in a process of rejuvenation and expansion in order to create competent leadership for the Church, and most of these changes are due to the rise of new ideals created by the social gospel. What, then, will doctrinal theology do to meet the new situation? Can it ground and anchor the social gospel in the eternal truths of our religion and build its main ideas into the systematic structure of Christian doctrine?

Theology is not superior to the gospel. It exists to aid the preaching of salvation. Its business is to make the essential facts and principles of Christianity so simple and dear, so adequate and mighty, that all who preach or teach the gospel, both ministers and laymen, can draw on its stores and deliver a complete and unclouded Christian message. When the progress of humanity creates new tasks, such as world-wide missions, or new problems, such as the social problem, theology must connect these with the old fundamentals of our faith and make them Christian tasks and problems.

The adjustment of the Christian message to the regeneration of the social order is plainly one of the most difficult tasks ever laid on the intellect of religious leaders. The pioneers of the social gospel have had a hard time trying to consolidate their old faith and their new aim. Some have lost their faith; others have come out of the struggle with crippled formulations of truth. Does not our traditional theology deserve some of the blame for this spiritual wastage because it left these men without spiritual support and allowed them to become the vicarious victims of our theological inefficiency?

If our theology is silent on social salvation, we compel college men and women, workingmen, and theological students, to choose between an unsocial system of theology and an irreligious system of social salvation. It is not hard to predict the outcome. If we seek to keep Christian doctrine unchanged, we shall ensure its abandonment.

Instead of being an aid in the development of the social gospel, systematic theology has often been a real clog. When a minister speaks to his people about child labour or the exploitation of the lowly by the strong; when he insists on adequate food, education, recreation, and a really human opportunity for all, there is response. People are moved by plain human feeling and by the instinctive convictions which they have learned from Jesus Christ. But at once there are doubting and dissenting voices. We are told that environment has no saving power; regeneration is what men need; we cannot have a regenerate society without regenerate individuals; we do not live for this world but for the life to come; it is not the function of the church to deal with economic questions; any effort to change the social order before the coming of the Lord is foredoomed to failure. These objections all issue from the theological consciousness created by traditional church teaching. These half-truths are the proper product of a half-way system of theology in which there is no room for social redemption. Thus the Church is halting between two voices that call it. On the one side is the voice of the living Christ amid living men to-day; on the other side is the voice of past ages embodied in theology. Who will say that the authority of this voice has never confused our Christian judgment and paralysed our determination to establish God's kingdom on earth?

Those who have gone through the struggle for a clear faith in the social gospel would probably agree that the doctrinal theology in which they were brought up, was one of the most baffling hindrances in their spiritual crisis, and that all their mental energies were taxed to overcome the weight of its traditions. They were fortunate if they promptly discovered some recent theological book which showed them at least the possibility of conceiving Christian doctrine in social terms, and made them conscious of a fellowship of faith in their climb toward the light. The situation would be much worse if Christian thought were nourished on doctrine only. Fortunately our hymns and prayers have a richer consciousness of solidarity than individualistic theology. But even to-day many ministers have a kind of dumb-bell system of thought, with the social gospel at one end and individual salvation at the other end, and an attenuated connection between them. The strength of our faith is in its unity. Religion wants wholeness of life. We need a rounded system of doctrine large enough to take in all our spiritual interests.

In short, we need a theology large enough to contain the social gospel, and alive and productive enough not to hamper it.

CHAPTER II

THE DIFFICULTIES OF THEOLOGICAL READJUSTMENT

Any demand for changes in Christian doctrine is sure to cause a quiver of apprehension and distress. Religious truth is the truth our souls live by and it is too dear to be scrapped and made over. Even to grant the possibility of the need of change means a loss of assurance and certitude, and that hurts. The passionate interest of many in the beliefs which have been the food of their spiritual life for years creates a social resistance to change in religious thought. Every generation tries to put its doctrine on a high shelf where the children cannot reach it. For instance, the Methodist Church will not be charged with sitting on the clock, but its creed has been put beyond the reach even of the highest body of the Church. Its "Articles of Religion" were an adaptation of the Thirty-Nine Articles of the Church of England by John Wesley; to-day they seem to have the better of the starry universe, for they can never change: "The General Conference shall not revoke, alter, nor change our Articles of Religion, nor establish any new standards or rules of doctrine contrary to our present existing and established standards of doctrine."

I have entire sympathy with the conservative instinct which shrinks from giving up any of the dear possessions which have made life holy for us. We have none too much of them left. It is a comfort to me to know that the changes required to make room for the social gospel are not destructive but constructive. They involve addition and not subtraction. The social gospel calls for an expansion in the scope of salvation and for more religious dynamic to do the work of God. It requires more faith and not less. It offers a more thorough and durable salvation. It is able to create a more searching sense of sin and to preach repentance to the respectable and mighty who have ridden humanity to the mouth of hell.

The attacks on our inherited theology have usually come from the intellectuals who are galled by the yoke of uncritical and unhistorical beliefs brought down from pre-scientific centuries. They are entirely within their right in insisting that what is scientifically impossible shall not be laid as an obligatory belief on the neck of modern men in the name of religion. But the rational subtractions of liberalism do not necessarily make religion more religious. We have to snuff the candle to remove the burnt-out wick, but we may snuff out the flame, and all the matches may prove to be damp. Critical clarifying is decidedly necessary, but power in religion comes only through the consciousness of a great elementary need which compels men to lay hold of God anew. The social gospel speaks to such a need, and where a real harmony has been established it has put new fire and power into the old faith.

The power of conservatism is not all due to religious tenderness and loyalty. Some of it results from less worthy causes. Doctrinal theology is in less direct contact with facts than other theological studies. Exegesis and church history deal with historical material and their business is to discover the facts. New facts and the pressure of secular scientific work compel them to revise their results and keep close to realities. Doctrinal theology deals with less substantial and ascertainable things. It perpetuates an esoteric stream of tradition. What every church demands of its systematic theologians is to formulate clearly and persuasively what that church has always held and taught. If they go beyond that they are performing a work of supererogation for which they do not always receive thanks.

Theoretically the Church is the great organization of unselfish service. Actually the Church has always been profoundly concerned for its own power and authority. But its authority rests in large part on the stability of its doctrine. The Roman Catholic Church has always been in the nature of a defensive organization to maintain uniformity of teaching. The physical suppression of heresy was merely the last and crudest means employed by it to resist change. The more subtle and spiritual forms of pressure have doubtless been felt by every person who ever differed with his own church, whatever it was. This selfish ecclesiastical conservatism is not for the Kingdom of God but against it.

Theology needs periodical rejuvenation. Its greatest danger is not mutilation but senility. It is strong and vital when it expresses in large reasonings what youthful religion feels and thinks. When people have to be indoctrinated laboriously in order to understand theology at all, it becomes a dead burden. The dogmas and theological ideas of the early Church were those ideas which at that time were needed to hold the Church together, to rally its forces, and to give it victorious energy against antagonistic powers. To-day many of those ideas are without present significance. Our reverence for them is a kind of ancestor worship. To hold laboriously to a religious belief which does not hold us, is an attenuated form of asceticism; we chastise and starve our intellect to sanctify it by holy beliefs. The social gospel does not need the aid of church authority to get hold of our hearts. It gets hold in spite of such authority when necessary. It will do for us what the Nicene theology did in the fourth century, and the Reformation theology in the sixteenth. Without it theology will inevitably become more and more a reminiscence.[1]

The great religious thinkers who created theology were always leaders who were shaping ideas to meet actual situations. The new theology of Paul was a product of fresh religious experience and of practical necessities. His idea that the Jewish law had been abrogated by Christ's death was worked out in order to set his mission to the Gentiles free from the crippling grip of the past and to make an international religion of Christianity. Luther worked out the doctrine of "justification by faith" because he had found by experience that it gave him a surer and happier way to God than the effort to win merit by his own works. But that doctrine became the foundation of a new theology for whole nations because it proved to be the battle-cry of a great social and religious upheaval and the effective means of breaking down the semi-political power of the clergy, of shutting up monasteries, of secularizing church property, and of increasing the economic and political power of city councils and princes. There is nothing else in sight to-day which has power to rejuvenate theology except the consciousness of vast sins and sufferings, and the longing for righteousness and a new life, which are expressed in the social gospel.

Every forward step in the historical evolution of religion has been marked by a closer union of religion and ethics and by the elimination of non-ethical religious performances. This union of religion and ethics reached its highest perfection in the life and mind of Jesus. After him Christianity quickly dropped back to the pre-christian stage. Ceremonial actions and orthodox beliefs became indispensable to salvation; they had a value of their own, quite apart from their bearing on conduct. Theology had the task of defending and inculcating these non-ethical ingredients of religion, and that pulled theology down. It is clear that our Christianity is most Christian when religion and ethics are viewed as inseparable elements of the same sin-

---

[1] President H. C. King's "Reconstruction in Theology" gives an admirable summary of the causes for dissatisfaction with the old doctrinal statements, and of the fundamental moral and spiritual convictions which demand embodiment in theology. See also Prof. Gerald B. Smith's lucid analysis in his "Social Idealism and the Changing Theology. "

gle-minded and wholehearted life, in which the consciousness of God and the consciousness of humanity blend completely. Any new movement in theology which emphatically asserts the union of religion and ethics is likely to be a wholesome and christianizing force in Christian thought.

The social gospel is of that nature. It plainly concentrates religious interest on the great ethical problems of social life. It scorns the tithing of mint, anise and cummin, at which the Pharisees are still busy, and insists on getting down to the weightier matters of God's law, to justice and mercy. It ties up religion not only with duty, but with big duty that stirs the soul with religious feeling and throws it back on God for help. The non-ethical practices and beliefs in historical Christianity nearly all centre on the winning of heaven and immortality. On the other hand, the Kingdom of God can be established by nothing except righteous life and action. There is nothing in social Christianity which is likely to breed or reinforce superstition. The more the social gospel engages and inspires theological thought, the more will religion be concentrated on ethical righteousness. The social gospel is bound to be a reformatory and christianizing force inside of theology.

Theology is the esoteric thought of the Church. Some of its problems are unknown and unintelligible except where the Church keeps an interest in them alive. Even the terminology of theology is difficult for anyone to understand unless he has lived under church influence for years. Jesus and his followers were laymen. The people felt that his teaching was different from the arguments of their theologians, less ponderous and more moving. When Christianity worked its way from the lower to the higher classes, its social sympathies became less democratic and fraternal, its language less simple, and its ideas more speculative, elaborate and remote. Origen felt he had to apologize for the homely Greek and the simple arguments o Jesus. Theology became an affair of experts. The first duty of the laymen was to believe with all their hearts what they could not possibly understand with all their heads.

The practical result has been that laymen have always assented as they were told, but have made an unconscious private selection of the truths that seemed to contain marrow for them. The working creed of the common man is usually very brief. A man may tote a large load of theology and live on a small part of it. If ministers periodically examined their church members as professors examine their classes, they would find that a man can be in the rain a long time and not become wetter under the skin. Even in the Middle Ages, when all philosophy was theology and when religious doubt was rare, the laity seem to have had their own system of faith. In the memoirs of statesmen and artists and merchants, in the songs of the common people, and in the secret symbolism of the masons and other gilds, we find a simple faith which guided their life. They believed in God and his law, in immortality and retribution, in Christ and his mercy, in the abiding difference between righteousness and evil, and by this faith they tried to do their duty where God had given them their job in life.

The social gospel approximates lay religion. It deals with the ethical problems of the present life with which the common man is familiar and which press upon his conscience. Yet it appeals to God, his will, his kingdom; to Christ, his spirit, his law. Audiences who are estranged from the Church and who would listen to theological terminology with frank scorn, will listen with absorbed interest to religious thought when it is linked with their own social problems.

Theology ought not to pare down its thought to the rudimentary ideas of untrained people. But every influence which compels it to simplify its terms and to deal with actual life is a blessing to theology. Theological professors used to lecture and write in Latin. There is perhaps no other language in which one can utter platitudes so sonorously and euphoniously. It must have been a sanitary sweating off of adipose tissue when theology began to talk in the vernacular. It will be a similar increase of health when theology takes in hand the problems of social redemption and considers how its doctrines connect with the Kingdom of God in actual realization.

The renovating effect of the social gospel would aid theology to meet the really modern religious needs. Heart religion is always a cry of need. Men pray because a burden is on their life; sickness threatens them; a child is in danger; some morbid passion has gained a footing in their mind or body and can not be shaken off; some evil has been done which can not be undone. The need is beyond their own strength. So they cry to a higher Power to help, to forgive, to cleanse, to save.

Now, many of the fears and burdens which drove men to the altars of their gods in the past are being eased in modern life. People are learning to trace diseases to natural causes instead of the evil eye, or the devil, or the anger of God. Even the streptococcus has a friendlier look than the omnipresent devils that haunt a Burmese hill tribe. Men used to feel acute guilt if they had committed some ritual oversight, such as touching a taboo thing, eating meat on Friday, or working on the Sabbath. The better teachings of modern Christianity and general religious indifference have combined to reduce that sort of fear and guilt.

On the other hand we are becoming much more sensitive about collective sins in which we are involved. I have a neighbour who owns stock in a New England cotton mill. Recently the company opened a factory in North Carolina and began to employ child labour. This man's young daughter faded away when she was emerging from childhood, and so he thinks of the other girls, who are breathing cotton fluff for him. A correspondent wrote me whose husband, a man of national reputation, had bought stock in a great steel company. She is a Jewess and a pacifist. When the plant began to devote itself to the manufacture of shrapnel and bombs in 1915, she felt involved. But what was her husband to do with the stock? Would it make things better if he passed the war-stained property to another man? I know a woman whose father, back in the nineties, took a fortune out of a certain dirty mill town. She is now living on his fortune; but the children of the mill-hands are living on their misfortune. No effort of hers can undo more than a fraction of the evil which was set in motion while that fortune was being accumulated.

If these burdens of conscience were foolish or morbid, increased insight and a purer Christian teaching would lift them. But it is increased insight and Christian feeling which created them. An unawakened person does not inquire on whose life juices his big dividends are fattening. Upper-class minds have been able to live parasitic lives without any fellow-feeling for the peasants or tenants whom they were draining to pay for their leisure. Modern democracy brings these lower fellow-men up to our field of vision. Then if a man has drawn any real religious feeling from Christ, his participation in the systematized oppression of civilization will, at least at times, seem an intolerable burden and guilt. Is this morbid? Or is it morbid to live on without such realization? Those who to-day are still without a consciousness of collective wrong must be classified as men of darkened mind.

These are distinctly modern burdens. They will continue to multiply and increase. Does the old theology meet them? Was it competent to meet the religious problems raised by the war? Can personal forgiveness settle such accounts as some men run up with their fellow-men? Does Calvinism deal adequately with a man who appears before the judgment seat of Christ with $50,000,000 and its human corollaries to his credit, and then pleads a free pardon through faith in the atoning sacrifice?

Religious experience, as William James has shown us, has many varieties, and some are distinctly higher than others. The form most common among us has come through an intense concentration on a man's own sins, his needs, his destiny. In the Old Testament we have a number of accounts describing how men of the highest type of God-consciousness made their fundamental experience of God and received their prophetic mission. In none of these cases did the prophet struggle for his personal salvation as later Christian saints have done. His woe did not come through fear of personal damnation, but through his sense of solidarity with his people and through social feeling; his hope and comfort was not for himself alone but for his nation. This form of religious experience is more distinctively Christian than any form which is caused by fear and which thinks only of self. It contains larger possibilities of personal growth and religious power.

The social gospel creates a type of religious experience corresponding closely to the prophetic type. It fuses the Christian spirit and the social consciousness in a new outreaching toward God and in remarkable experiences of his comfort and inspiring power. This is the most youthful, modern, and effective form of present-day religion.

Religious experience reacts on theology. Consider the men who have turned theological thought into new channels — Paul, Augustine, Luther, Fox, Wesley, Schleiermacher. These were all men who had experienced God at first hand and while tinder the pressure of new problems. Then they generalized on the basis of their experience. Paul, for instance, had borne the weight of the Law; he had found his own efforts futile; he had found Christ gracious, free, and a power of life. On this experience he built his theology. A like experience under Catholic legalism enabled Luther to understand Paul; he revitalized the Pauline theology, built a theology of emancipation on that, and threw out of religious practice and thought what was not in agreement with his experience and its formula.

The rank and file of us have no genius and can not erect our personal experience into a common standard. But our early experiences act as a kind of guide by which we test what seems to have truth and reality. We select those theoretical ideas which agree with our experience, and are cold to those which have never entered into our life. When such a selective process is exercised by many active minds, who all act on the same lines, the total effect on theological thought is considerable. This is a kind of theological referendum, a democratic change in theology on the basis of religious experience.

Connect these two propositions: that an experience of religion through the medium of solidaristic social feeling is an experience of unusually high ethical quality, akin to that of the prophets of the Bible; and second, that a fresh and clearly marked religious experience reacts on theology. Can we not justly expect that the increasing influence of the social gospel and all that it stands for, will have a salutary influence on theology? The social gospel has already restored the doctrine of the Kingdom of God, which held first place with Jesus but which individualistic theology carefully wrapped in several napkins and forgot. Theology always needs rejuvenation. Most of all in a great epoch of change like ours. Yet change always hurts. If change must come, the influence of the social gospel is the most constructive and wholesome channel by which it could possibly come. Surely theology will not become less Christian by widening the scope of salvation, by taking more seriously the burden of social evil, and by learning to believe in the Kingdom of God. The proclamation of the social gospel would evoke the prophetic spirit in the exponents of doctrinal theology. Then they would have to seek boldness and authority from the living spirit of God. Theology has a right to the forward look and to the fire of religious vision.

Chapter III

Neither Alien Nor Novel

In these introductory chapters my aim is to win the benevolent and serious attention of conservative readers for the discussions that are to follow. I have thus far tried to show that the spread of the social gospel will inevitably react on theology, and that this influence is likely to be constructive and salutary. Let us add the important fact that the social gospel imports into theology nothing that is new or alien.

Frequent attempts have been made in the history of our religion to blend alien elements with it. The early Gnostics and the mediaeval Albigenses, for instance, tried to combine historical Christianity with dualistic conceptions of the universe and strict asceticism. Modern Mormonism, Theosophy, and Christian Science represent syncretistic formations, minglings of genuine Christianity with new and alien elements.

The belief in the universal reign of law, the doctrine of evolution, the control of nature by-man, and the value of education and liberty as independent goods, — these are among the most influential convictions of modern life and have deeply modified our religious thought. But they are novel elements in theology. They are not alien, but certainly they held no such controlling position in the theology of the past as they do with us. We may discover prophetic forecasts of them in the Bible, but we have to look for them.

On the other hand the idea of the redemption of the social organism is nothing alien. It is simply a proper part of the Christian faith in redemption from sin and evil. As soon as the desire for salvation becomes strong and intelligent enough to look beyond the personal sins of the individual, and to discern how our personality in its intake and output is connected with the social groups to which we belong, the problem of social redemption is before us and we can never again forget it. It lies like a larger concentric circle around a smaller one. It is related to our intimate personal salvation like astronomy to physics. Only spiritual and intellectual immaturity have kept us from seeing it clearly before. The social gospel is not an alien element in theology.

Neither is it novel. The social gospel is, in fact, the oldest gospel of all. It is "built on the foundation of the apostles and prophets." Its substance is the Hebrew faith which Jesus himself held. If the prophets ever talked about the "plan of redemption," they meant the social redemption of the nation. So long as John the Baptist and Jesus were proclaiming the gospel, the Kingdom of God was its central word, and the ethical teaching of both, which was their practical commentary and definition of the Kingdom idea, looked toward a higher social order in which new ethical standards would become practicable. To the first generation of disciples the hope of the Lord's return meant the hope of a Christian social order on earth under the personal rule of Jesus Christ, and they would have been amazed if they had learned that this hope was to be motioned out of theology and other ideas substituted.

The social gospel is nothing alien or novel. When it comes to a question of pedigree and birth-right, it may well turn on the dogmas on which the Catholic and Protestant theologies are based and inquire for their birth certificate. They are neither dominant in the New Testament nor clearly defined in it. The more our historical investigations are laying bare the roots of Catholic dogma, the more do we see them running back into alien Greek thought, and not into the substance of Christ's message nor into the Hebrew faith. We shall not get away again from the central proposition of Harnack's History of Dogma, that the development of Catholic dogma was the process of the Hellenization of Christianity; in other words, that alien influences streamed into the religion of Jesus Christ and created a theology which he never taught nor intended. What would Jesus have said to the symbol of Chalcedon or the Athanasian Creed if they had been read to him?

The doctrine of the Kingdom of God was left undeveloped by individualistic theology and finally mislaid by it almost completely, because it did not support nor fit in with that scheme of doctrine. In the older handbooks of theology it is scarcely mentioned, except in the chapters on eschatology; in none of them does it dominate the table of contents. What a spectacle, that the original teaching of our Lord has become an incongruous element in so-called evangelical theology, like a stranger with whom the other doctrines would not associate, and who was finally ejected because he had no wedding garment! In the same way the distinctive ethics of Jesus, which is part and parcel of his Kingdom doctrine, was long the hidden treasure of suppressed democratic sects. Now, as soon as the social gospel began once more to be preached in our own time, the doctrine of the Kingdom was immediately loved and proclaimed afresh, and the ethical principles of Jesus are once more taught without reservation as the only alternative for the greedy ethics of capitalism and militarism. These antipathies and affinities are a strong proof that the social gospel is neither alien nor novel, but is a revival of the earliest doctrines of Christianity, of its radical ethical spirit, and of its revolutionary consciousness.

The body of ideas which we call the social gospel is not the product of a fad or temporary interest; it is not an alien importation or a novel invention; it is the revival of the most ancient and authentic gospel, and the scientific unfolding of essential elements of Christian doctrine which have remained undeveloped all too long; the rise of the social gospel is not a matter of choice but of destiny; the digestion of its ideas will exert a quickening and reconstructive influence on every part of theology.

The verification of these propositions lies in the future. But I believe that a survey of the history of theology during the last hundred years would already corroborate the inevitableness and the fruitfulness of the essential ideas of the social gospel. The trend of theology has been this way, and wherever the social nature of Christianity has been clearly understood, a new understanding for other theological problems has followed. The limits of this book do not permit such a survey, and I have not the accurate and technical knowledge of the literature of doctrinal theology to do justice to the subject. It would be an attractive subject for a specialist to trace the genesis and progress of the social gospel in systematic theology. The following paragraphs are simply by way of suggestion.

So far as my observation of doctrinal handbooks goes, it seems that those writers whose minds were formed before the eighties rarely show any clear comprehension of social points of view. We move in a different world of thought when we read their books. It would pay the reader to test this for himself by reading the table of contents and scanning crucial sections of any standard American theologian of the first half of the nineteenth century. The terms, the methods, the problems, and the guiding interests lie far away. If any social ideas do occur, they are most often the dutiful explanation of ideas derived from Hebrew religion. Those individuals of that era who did strike out into social conceptions of Christianity deserve the name and honour of prophets.

Among the earlier German theologians Friedrich Schleiermacher, Richard Rothe, and Albrecht Ritschl seem to me to deserve that title. The constructive genius of Schleiermacher worked out solidaristic conceptions of Christianity which were far ahead of his time, Ritschl built his essential ideas of the kingdom of evil and the Kingdom of God on Schleiermacher's work, and stressed the teaching of Luther that our service to God consists, not in religious performances, but in the faithful work we do in our secular calling. The practical importance of these elements of Ritschl's theology is proved by the strong social spirit pervading the younger Ritschlian school. The moderate liberals grouped in the " Evangelisch-soziale Kongress " and organized as "Freunde der Christlichen Welt" and "Freunde evangelischer Freiheit" all have social orientation. Professor Herrmann and Professor Troeltsch have definitely faced the relation between systematic theology and the social task of Christianity. The monumental work of Troeltsch, "die Soziallehren der christlichen Kirchen und Gruppen," is the first and chief attempt to apply the methods of the history of doctrine to the social convictions and hopes of the Churches. Conservative theology is naturally less responsive to the newer influences. But the wonderful work of the " Innere Mission " since Wichern, and the social reconstruction of Germany, in which the conservative parts of the nation have taken a full share, have not left their conception of the mission of Christianity untouched.

Switzerland democratizes whatever it handles. The "Religiös-sozialen" in German Switzerland have more political radicalism and more religious enthusiasm for the doctrine of the Kingdom of God than the corresponding German groups. They have done thorough and inspiring work on the combination of social and theological ideas, especially Ragaz, Kutter, Matthieu, Benz, and Reinhardt.

Social and democratic idealism is one of the most active ingredients in Catholic Modernism. The French Protestants, though they number only about 700,000, have produced a social and socialist literature of a richness and maturity which puts our greater numbers to shame, and witnesses to the intellectual fertility of French life. Auguste Sabatier, Charles Secrétan, Tomy Fallot, Wilfred Monod, Elie Gounelle, and Paul Passy occur to me among those who have given doctrinal formulation to the social gospel.

Great Britain has been the foremost capitalistic nation for a century and a half. Its religion and theology have necessarily matched its individualistic political economy and political philosophy. When the early Christian Socialists, Frederick Denison Maurice and Charles Kingsley, first asserted solidaristic ideas on theology and social questions, they justly felt that they were preaching a new and prophetic gospel in the midst of a Babylon of competitive selfishness. The trend of things is strikingly brought out by the contrast between their lonely position in the revolutionary year of 1848 and the Anglican Congress of 1908, where Christian Socialism was in possession of the platform and only Lord Cecil made a stand against it. It is significant that, so far as the social gospel is concerned, the High Church section has become Broad, and some of its intellectual leaders are weaving solidaristic ideas into their most sacramental and ecclesiastical doctrines. At the same time the Free Church leaders have worked their way out of individualistic Evangelicalism, and are freely applying their heritage of democratic faith to the social problems.

Of course I am not now discussing the popular propaganda of social Christianity, nor the growth of organizations for its practical application, but simply the reaction of the social gospel on doctrinal theology.[1] In our country, many of the younger men in the North who have written on theology have shown that the problems of society are a vital concern with them, and their fresh theological work consists largely in understanding the relation between social life and religion. I am thinking of William A. Brown, John W. Buckham, William H. P. Faunce, Thomas B. Hall, William DeWitt Hyde, Rufus Jones, Henry C. King, Shailer Mathews, Francis G. Peabody, Gerald B. Smith, George B. Stevens, and James B. Thomas, but I am sure this enumeration is very incomplete. Some of the best work is done in the class rooms, and has not yet come out in print.

When we contrast the neglect of the social contents of Christianity in former generations, and the fertile intellectual work now being given to this part of theology, a strong probability is established that the social gospel is not a passing interest, but that it is bound to become one of the permanent and commanding ingredients of theology.

---

[1] I sketched the Social Awakening in the Churches in the first part of "Christianizing the Social Order." But that was written in 1912.

Chapter IV

The Consciousness of Sin

It remains now to pass in review the doctrines which would be affected by the social gospel and which ought to give more adequate expression to it. On some of the more speculative doctrines the social gospel has no contribution to make. Its interests lie on earth, within the social relations of the life that now is. It is concerned with the eradication of sin and the fulfilment of the mission of redemption. The sections of theology which ought to express it effectively, therefore, are the doctrines of sin and redemption.

The Christian consciousness of sin is the basis of all doctrines about sin. A serious and humble sense of sinfulness is part of a religious view of life. Our consciousness of sin deepens as our moral insight matures and becomes religious. When we think on the level of law or public opinion, we speak of crime, vice, bad habits, or defective character. When our mind is in the attitude of religion, we pray: "Create in me a clean heart, O God, and renew a right spirit within me." When a man is within the presence and consciousness of God, he sees himself and his past actions and present conditions in the most searching light and in eternal connections. To lack the consciousness of sin is a symptom of moral immaturity or of an effort to keep the shutters down and the light out. The most highly developed individuals, who have the power of interpreting life for others, and who have the clearest realization of possible perfection and the keenest hunger for righteousness, also commonly have the most poignant sense of their own shortcomings.

By our very nature we are involved in tragedy. In childhood and youth we have imperious instincts and desires to drive us, and little knowledge to guide and control us. We commit acts of sensuality, cruelty, or dishonour, which nothing can wipe from our memory. A child is drawn into harmful habits which lay the foundation for later failings, and which may trip the man again when his powers begin to fail in later life. How many men and women have rushed with the starry eyes of hope into relations which brought them defilement of soul and the perversion of their most intimate life, but from which they could never again extricate themselves by any wrench. "Forgive us our trespasses. Lead us not into temptation." The weakness or the stubbornness of our will and the tempting situations of life combine to weave the tragic web of sin and failure of which we all make experience before we are through with our years.

Any religious tendency or school of theology must be tested by the question whether it does justice to the religious consciousness of sin. Now, one cause of distrust against the social gospel is that its exponents often fail to show an adequate appreciation of the power and guilt of sin. Its teachings seem to put the blame for wrong-doing on the environment, and instead of stiffening and awakening the sense of responsibility in the individual, it teaches him to unload it on society.

There is doubtless truth in this accusation. The emphasis on environment and on the contributory guilt of the community, does offer a chance to unload responsibility, and human nature is quick to seize the chance. But the old theology has had its equivalents for environment. Men unloaded on original sin, on the devil, and on the decrees of God. Adam began soon after the fall to shift the blame. This shiftiness seems to be one of the clearest and most universal effects of original sin.

Moreover, there is an unavoidable element of moral unsettlement whenever the religious valuation of sin is being reconsidered. Paul frequently and anxiously defended his gospel against the charge that his principle of liberty invited lawlessness, and that under it a man might even sin the more in order to give grace the greater chance. We know what the Hebrew prophets thought of the sacrificial cult and moral righteousness, but we are not informed about the unsettling effect which their teaching may have had. If we could raise up some devout priest of the age of Amos or Isaiah to give us his judgment on the theology of the prophets, he would probably assure us that these men doubtless meant well, but that they had no adequate sense of sin; they belittled the sacrifices instituted by Moses; but sacrificing, as all men knew, was the true expression and gauge of repentance.

In the early years of the Reformation, Catholic observers noted a distressing looseness in the treatment of sin. Men no longer searched their consciences in the confessional; they performed no works of penance to render satisfaction to God and to prove their contrition; they no longer used the ascetic means of holiness to subdue their flesh and to gain victory over the powers of darkness. Luther had taught them that God required nothing but faith, and that all accounts could be squared by agreeing to call them square. By any standard of measurement known to Catholics, the profounder consciousness of sin was with the old theology and its practical applications. In point of fact, the Reformation did upset the old means of moral control and did create widespread demoralization. But in time, Geneva, Holland, or Scotland showed a deeper consciousness of sin than Rome or Paris. The sense of sin found new outlets.

The delinquencies of a new movement are keenly observed because they are new; the shortcomings of an old system are part of the accepted scheme of life. If the exponents of the old theology have taught humanity an adequate consciousness of sin, how is it that they themselves have been blind and dumb on the master iniquities of human history? During all the ages while they were the theological keepers of the conscience of Christendom, the peasants in the country and the working class in the cities were being sucked dry by the parasitic classes of society, and war was damning poor humanity. Yet what traces are there in traditional theology that the minds of old-line theologians were awake to these magnificent manifestations of the wickedness of the human heart? How is it that only in the modern era, since the moral insight of mankind has to some extent escaped from the tuition of the old theology, has a world-wide social movement arisen to put a stop to the exploitation of the poor, and that only in the last three years has war been realized as the supreme moral evil? One of the culminating accusations of Jesus against the theological teachers of his time was that they strained out gnats and swallowed camels, judiciously laying the emphasis on the minor sins and keeping silence on the profitable major wrongs. It is possible to hold the orthodox doctrine on the devil and not recognize him when we meet him in a real estate office or at the stock exchange.

A health officer of Toronto told me a story which illustrates the consciousness of sin created by the old religious teaching. If milk is found too dirty, the cans are emptied and marked with large red labels. This hits the farmer where he lives. He may not care about the health of Toronto, but he does care for the good opinion of his own neighbourhood, and when he drives to the station and finds his friends chuckling over the red labels on his cans, it acts as a moral irritant. One day a Mennonite farmer found his cans labeled and he swore a worldly oath. The Mennonites are a devout people who take the teachings of Christ seriously and refuse to swear, even in law-courts. This man was brought before his church and excluded. But, mark well, not for introducing cow-dung into the intestines of babies, but for expressing his belief in the damnation of the wicked in a non-theological way. When his church will hereafter have fully digested the social gospel, it may treat the case this way: "Our brother was angry and used the name of God profanely in his anger; we urge him to settle this alone with God. But he has also defiled the milk supply by unclean methods. Having the life and health of young children in his keeping, he has failed in his trust. Voted, that he be excluded until he has proved his lasting repentance." The result would be the same, but the sense of sin would do its work more intelligently.

In his " Appeal to the Christian Nobility," Luther said that in consequence of the many fast days and the insistence of the priests on their observance, the people had come to a point where they regarded it as a greater sin to eat butter on a fast day than to lie, swear, or commit fornication. An eminent minister in New York enumerated as the chief marks of a Christian that he attends church, reads the Bible, and contributes to the support of public worship. A less eminent minister in the same place mentioned as the four sins from which a Christian must abstain, drinking, dancing, card playing, and going to the movies. And this in New York where the capitalistic system of the nation comes to a head!

It may well be that with some individuals there is a loss of seriousness in the sense of sin as a result of the social gospel. But on the whole the result consists chiefly in shifting the emphasis and assigning a new valuation to different classes of sins. Attention is concentrated on questions of public morality, on wrongs done by whole classes or professions of men, on sins which enervate and submerge entire mill towns or agricultural states. These sins have been side-stepped by the old theology. We now have to make up for a fatal failure in past teaching.

We feel a deep consciousness of sin when we realize that we have wasted our years, dissipated our energies, left our opportunities unused, frustrated the grace of God, and dwarfed and shamed the personality which God intended when he called us into life. It is a similar and even deeper misery to realize that our past life has hurt and blocked the Kingdom of God, the sum of all good, the essential aim of God himself. Our duty to the Kingdom of God is on a higher level than all other duties. To aid it is the supreme joy. To have failed it by our weakness, to have hampered it by our ignorance, to have resisted its prophets, to have contradicted its truths, to have denied it in time of danger, to have betrayed it for thirty pieces of silver, this is the most poignant consciousness of sin. The social gospel opens our eyes to the ways in which religious men do all these things. It plunges us in a new baptism of repentance.

CHAPTER V

THE FALL OF MAN

We are familiar with the teachings of traditional theology on the first entrance of sin into the life of the race: the state of innocence of our first parents; the part played by Satan in tempting them; the motives and experiences of the fall; the apostasy of the entire race through the disobedience of its head; the transmission of depravity and death to all; the imputation of Adam's guilt to all his descendants; the ruin of the divine plan for humanity by the perversity of sin.

The motives of theology in elaborating so fully an event so remote were partly philosophical and partly religious.

The philosophical motive was the desire for a coherent explanation of our universe and its present baffling mixture of good and evil. The story of the fall, as interpreted by theology, furnished an outline for a philosophical history of the race. It was the first act in a great racial tragedy which was to end with the final judgment. The fact that a mind like Milton's took the fall as the theme for a great epic, and that his poem was accepted as a poetic treatment of the highest realities, shows how the doctrine of the fall dominated common thought.

The religious motive in elaborating the doctrine of the fall was the desire to bring all men under conviction of sin and condemnation in order that all might realize their need of grace and salvation. There was no need to prove the guilt of any one individual when all were in a state of corruption. It was not a question of this act or that, but of the state of apostasy from which all acts proceeded and by which even our virtues are contaminated. The terribleness of sin became clear only by scanning the height from which man had fallen. He once had a pure consciousness of God; he now has a mind darkened by sin and unable to know God. He had a will set on holiness; he now has a will set on evil and rebellion. He had love of goodness, harmony of the higher and lower powers, freedom from suffering, power over nature, and the grace of God. He lost it all. Consequently he is unable to save himself. Only the grace of God can save him. We can see this religious motive at work in the great theologians of sin and grace, Paul, Augustine, Luther, and Calvin. They abased man to glorify God's mercy. They took away all "boasting." They shut all doors on the prisoner of sin except the door of grace in order to compel him to emerge through that.

It is important to realize that the story of the fall is incomparably more fundamental in later theology than it was in biblical thought. The conspicuous place given to Genesis in the arrangement of the Hebrew canon, itself concentrated the attention of later times on it. The story now embodied in Genesis 3 was part of the Jahvist narrative, a document of Ephraimitic origin dating back to the ninth century B.C. The original purpose of the story was not to explain the origin of sin, but the origin of death and evil. There are scarcely any allusions to the story in the Old Testament. The prophets were deeply conscious of the sins of men, but they did not base their teachings on the doctrine of the fall. Not till we reach post-biblical Jewish theology is there any general interest in the story of Adam's fall. Even then the story of the fall of the angels in Genesis 6 attracted more interest.

In the synoptic sayings of Jesus there is not even a reference to the fall of Adam. In the fourth gospel there is one allusion, (John 8:44). Jesus, of course, had the clearest consciousness of the chasm between the will of God and the actual condition of mankind. The universality of sin was a matter of course with him; it was presupposed in all his teaching. But he was concerned only with those sources of sin which he saw in active work about him: first, the evil heart of man from which all evil words and actions proceed; second, the social stumbling blocks of temptation which make the weak to fall; and third, the power of the Kingdom of Evil. On the other hand the first origin of evil seems to have been so distant in his mind that it did not readily slip into any discussions of sin which are preserved to us. His interest was practical and not speculative, religious and ethical and not philosophical.

Not until we come to Paul do we find any full and serious use of the story of the fall in the Bible. He twice (Romans 5 and 1 Corinthians 15) set over against each other the carnal humanity descended from Adam and characterized by sin and mortality, and the spiritual humanity descended from Christ and characterized by holiness and eternal life. These passages belong to the theological portions of Paul's writings and were eagerly seized by the patristic writers as congenial raw material for their work.

When once theology concentrated on the story it was expanded by exegetical inferences, by allegorical embellishments, and by typology, until it conveyed far more than it actually contained. It comes as a shock to realize, for instance, that the story in Genesis itself does not indicate that the writer understood the serpent to be Satan, or Satan to be speaking through the serpent. Moreover, we find so few traces of any belief in Satan in Hebrew thought before the Exile that it seems doubtful if contemporary readers would have understood him to be meant unless further indications made the reference clear.

Here, then, we have two different methods of treating the story of the fall. Theology has given it basic importance. It has built its entire scheme of thought on the doctrine of the fall. Jesus and the prophets paid little or no attention to it. They were able to see sin clearly and to fight it with the highest energy without depending on the doctrine of the fall for a footing. Only with Paul is the story clearly of religious importance, and even with him it is not as central as for instance the antagonism between spirit and flesh. It offered him a wide spiritual perspective and a means of glorifying Christ.

Two things seem to follow. First, that the traditional doctrine of the fall is the product of speculative interest mainly, and that the most energetic consciousness of sin can exist without drawing strength from this doctrine. Second, that if the substance of Scriptural thought, the constant and integral trend of biblical convictions, is the authoritative element in the Bible, the doctrine of the fall does not seem to have as great an authority as it has long exercised.

How does this affect the special gospel? What doctrinal teaching on this point is able to give it the most effective backing?

The social gospel is above all things practical. It needs religious ideas which will release energy for heroic opposition against organized evil and for the building of a righteous social life. It would find entire satisfaction in the attitude of Jesus and the prophets who dealt with sin as a present force and did not find it necessary to indoctrinate men on its first origin. It would have no motive to be interested in a doctrine which diverts attention from the active factors of sin which can be influenced, and concentrates attention on a past event which no effort of ours can influence.

Theology has made the catastrophe of the fall so complete that any later addition to the inheritance of sin seems slight and negligible. What can be worse than a state of total depravity and active enmity against God and his will?[1] Consequently theology has had little to say about the contributions which our more recent forefathers have made to the sin and misery of mankind. The social gospel would rather reserve some blame for them, for their vices have

[1] The Helvetic Confession, II, Chapter 8: "We understand original sin to be the native corruption of man which has passed from our first parents to us; through which, being sunk in depraved desires, averse to good, inclined to every evil, full of every wickedness, of contempt and hatred of God, we are unable to do or even to think any good whatever."

afflicted us with syphilis, their graft and their wars have loaded us with public debts, and their piety has perpetuated despotic churches and unbelievable creeds. One of the greatest tasks in religious education reserved for the social gospel is to spread in society a sense of the solidarity of successive generations and a sense of responsibility for those who are to come after us and whom we are now outfitting with the fundamental conditions of existence. This is one of the sincerest and most durable means of spiritual restraint. It is hard to see how the thought of Adam and Eve can very directly influence young men and women who are to be the ancestors of new generations. In so far as the doctrine of the fall has made all later actions of negligible importance by contrast, it blocks the way for an important advance in the consciousness of sin.

The traditional doctrine of the fall has taught us to regard evil as a kind of unvarying racial endowment, which is active in every new life and which can be overcome only by the grace offered in the Gospel and ministered by the Church. It would strengthen the appeal of the social gospel if evil could be regarded instead as a variable factor in the life of humanity, which it is our duty to diminish for every young life and for every new generation.

These, it seems to me, are the points at which the social gospel impinges on the doctrine of the fall of man.

Of course evolutionary thought has radically changed the conceptions about the origin of the race for those whose thinking is done under the influence of evolutionary science. Such will take little interest in the discussion of this chapter. But there are many conservative minds who can not recast their thought in wholly new moulds; the story of the fall is a serious religious and intellectual burden to some of them. The more theology bases all its reasoning on the doctrine of the fall, the greater is the collapse and mental distress when a man comes to realize that the biblical story of the fall will not bear the tremendous weight which the theological system of the past has put upon it. For such the attitude suggested in this chapter seems to offer a way which is satisfying to both the religious and the scientific conscience. They can not be going far wrong if they take the attitude taken by the Hebrew prophets and by Jesus himself, concentrating their energies on the present and active sources of evil and leaving the question of the first origin of evil to God. On that basis it is possible to preach both an individualistic and a social gospel with full effectiveness.

CHAPTER VI

THE NATURE OF SIN

It is not easy to define sin, for sin is as elastic and complicated as life itself. Its quality, degree, and culpability vary according to the moral intelligence and maturity of the individual, according to his social freedom, and his power over others. Theologians have erred, it seems to me, by fitting their definitions to the most highly developed forms of sin and then spreading them over germinal and semi-sinful actions and conditions.

We are equipped with powerful appetites. We are often placed in difficult situations, which constitute overwhelming temptations. We are all relatively ignorant, and while we experiment with life, we go astray. Some of our instincts may become rampant and overgrown, and then trample on our inward freedom. We are gifted with high ideals, with a wonderful range of possibilities, with aspiration and longing, and also weighted with inertia and moral incapacity to achieve. We are keenly alive to the call of the senses and the pleasures of the moment, and only dimly and occasionally conscious of our own higher destiny, of the mystic value of personality in others, and of God.

This sensual equipment, this ignorance and inertia, out of which our moral delinquencies sprout, are part of our human nature. We did not order it so. Instead of increasing our guilt, our make-up seems to entitle us to the forbearing judgment of every onlooker, especially God. Yet no doubt we are involved in objective wrong and evil; we frustrate our possibilities; we injure others; we disturb the divine harmonies. We are unfree, unhappy, conscious of a burden which we are unable to lift or escape.

Sin becomes guilt in the full sense in the degree in which intelligence and will enter. We have the impulse to live our life, to exercise our freedom, to express and satisfy the limitless cravings in us, and we are impatient of restraint We know that our idleness or sensuality will cripple our higher self, yet we want what we want. We set our desires against the rights of others, and disregard the claims of mercy, of gratitude, or of parental love. Our self-love is wrought up to hot ill-will, hate, lying, slander, and malevolence. Men press their covetousness to the injury of society. They are willing to frustrate the cause of liberty and social justice in whole nations in order to hold their selfish social and economic privileges. Men who were powerful enough to do so, have left broad trails of destruction and enslavement through history in order to satisfy their selfish caprice, avarice, and thirst for glory.

Two things strike us as we thus consider the development of sin from its cotyledon leaves to its blossom and fruit. First, that the element of selfishness emerges as the character of sin matures. Second, that in the higher forms of sin it assumes the aspect of a conflict between the selfish Ego and the common good of humanity; or, expressing it in religious terms, it becomes a conflict between self and God.

The three forms of sin,—sensuousness, selfishness, and godlessness—are ascending and expanding stages, in which we sin against our higher self, against the good of men, and against the universal good.

Theology with remarkable unanimity has discerned that sin is essentially selfishness. This is an ethical and social definition, and is proof of the unquenchable social spirit of Christianity. It is more essentially Christian than the dualistic conception of the Greek Fathers, who thought of sin as fundamentally sensuousness and materiality, and saw the chief consequence of the fall in the present reign of death rather than in the reign of selfishness.

The definition of sin as selfishness furnishes an excellent theological basis for a social conception of sin and salvation. But the social gospel can contribute a good deal to socialize and vitalize it.

Theology pictures the self-affirmation of the sinner as a sort of solitary duel of the will between him and God. We get a mental image of God sitting on his throne in glory, holy and benevolent, and the sinner down below, sullenly shaking his fist at God while he repudiates the divine will and chooses his own. Now, in actual life such titanic rebellion against the Almighty is rare. Perhaps our Puritan forefathers knew more cases than we because their theological God was accustomed to issue arbitrary decrees which invited rebellion. We do not rebel; we dodge and evade. We kneel in lowly submission and kick our duty under the bed while God is not looking.

The theological definitions of sin have too much the flavour of the monarchical institutions under the spiritual influence of which they were first formed. In an absolute monarchy the first duty is to bow to the royal will. A man may spear peasants or outrage their wives, but crossing the king is another matter. When theological definitions speak of rebellion against God as the common characteristic of all sin, it reminds one of the readiness of despotic governments to treat every offence as treason.

Sin is not a private transaction between the sinner and God. Humanity always crowds the audience-room when God holds court. We must democratize the conception of God; then the definition of sin will become more realistic.

We love and serve God when we love and serve our fellows, whom he loves and in whom he lives. We rebel against God and repudiate his will when we set our profit and ambition above the welfare of our fellows and above the Kingdom of God which binds them together.

We rarely sin against God alone. The decalogue gives a simple illustration of this. Theology used to distinguish between the first and second table of the decalogue; the first enumerated the sins against God and the second the sins against men. Jesus took the Sabbath commandment off the first table and added it to the second; he said the Sabbath is not a taboo day of God, but an institution for the good of man. The command to honour our parents is also ethical. There remain the first three commandments, against polytheism, image worship, and the misuse of the holy name. The worship of various gods and the use of idols is no longer one of our dangers. The misuse of the holy name has lost much of its religious significance since sorcery and magic have moved to the back-streets. On the other hand, the commandments of the second table grow more important all the time. Science supplies the means of killing, finance the methods of stealing, the newspapers have learned how to bear false witness artistically to a globeful of people daily, and covetousness is the moral basis of our civilization.

God is not only the spiritual representative of humanity; he is identified with it. In him we live and move and have our being. In us he lives and moves, though his being transcends ours. He is the life and light in every man and the mystic bond that unites us all. He is the spiritual power behind and beneath all our aspirations and achievements. He works through humanity to realize his purposes, and our sins block and destroy the Reign of God in which he might fully reveal and realize himself. Therefore our sins against the least of our fellow-men in the last resort concern God. Therefore when we retard the progress of mankind, we retard the revelation of the glory of God, Our universe is not a despotic monarchy, with God above the starry canopy and ourselves down here; it is a spiritual commonwealth with God in the midst of us.

We are on Christian ground when we insist on putting humanity into the picture. Jesus always deliberately and energetically bound man and God together. He would not let us deal with man apart from God, nor with God apart from man. We can not have forgiveness from God while we refuse forgiveness to any man. "What ye have done to these, ye have done to me; what ye have not done to these, ye have not done to me." This identification of the interests of God and man is characteristic of the religion of Jesus. Wherever God is isolated, we drop back to a pre Christian stage of religion.

Sin is essentially selfishness. That definition is more in harmony with the social gospel than with any individualistic type of religion. The sinful mind, then, is the unsocial and anti-social mind. To find the climax of sin we must not linger over a man who swears, or sneers at religion, or denies the mystery of the trinity, but put our hands on social groups who have turned the patrimony of a nation into the private property of a small class, or have left the peasant labourers cowed, degraded, demoralized, and without rights in the land.[1] When we find such in history, or in present-day life, we shall know we have struck real rebellion against God on the higher levels of sin.

We have defined sin. But we need more than definition. We need realization of its nature in order to secure the right religious attitude toward it.

Sin is always revealed by contrast to righteousness. We get an adequate intellectual measure of it and feel the proper hate and repugnance for it only when we see it as the terrible defeat and frustration of a great good which we love and desire.

Theology has tried to give us such a realization of sin by elaborating the contrast between the sinless condition of Adam before the fall and his sinful condition after it. But there are objections to this. In the first place of course we do not know whether Adam was as perfect as he is portrayed. Theology has ante-dated conceptions of human perfection which we have derived from Jesus Christ and has converted Adam into a perfect Christian. Paul does nothing of the kind. In the second place, any interpretation of the nature of sin taken from Adam will be imperfect, because Adam's situation gave very limited opportunities for selfishness, which is the essence of sin. He had no scope to exhibit either the virtues or the sinful vices which come out in the pursuits of commerce or politics. The only persons with whom he could associate were God, Eve, and Satan. Consequently theology lacked all social details in describing his condition before and after the fall. It could

[1] I have just been reading "The Secret of Rural Depopulation," an account of the condition of the agricultural laborers in England, by Lieut-Col. D. C Pedder, 1904. Fabian Tract No. 118. The Fabian Society, 3 Clement's Inn, Strand, W. C., London.

only ascribe to him the virtues of knowing and loving God and of having no carnal concupiscence, and, by contrast, after the fall he lost the love and knowledge of God and acquired carnal desires. Thus a fatal turn toward an individualistic conception of sin was given to theology through the solitariness of Adam.

A better and more Christian method of getting a religious realization of sin is to bring before our minds the positive ideals of social righteousness contained in the person of Christ and in the Kingdom of God, and see sin as the treasonable force which frustrates and wrecks these ideals and despoils the earth of their enjoyment It is Christ who convicts the world of sin and not Adam. The spiritual perfection of Jesus consists in the fact that he was so simply and completely filled with the love of God and man that he gave himself to the task of the Kingdom of God without any reservation or backsliding. This is the true standard of holiness. The fact that a man is too respectable to get drunk or to swear is no proof of his righteousness. His moral and religious quality must be measured by the intelligence and singleheartedness with which he merges his will and life in the divine purpose of the Kingdom of God. By contrast, a man's sinfulness stands out in its true proportion, not when he is tripped up by ill-temper or side-steps into shame, but when he seeks to establish a private kingdom of self-service and is ready to thwart and defeat the progress of mankind toward peace, toward justice, or toward a fraternal organization of economic life, because that would diminish his political privileges, his unearned income, and his power over the working classes.

It follows that a clear realization of the nature of sin depends on a clear vision of the Kingdom of God. We can not properly feel and know the reign of organized wrong now prevailing unless we constantly see it over against the reign of organized righteousness. Where the religious conception of the Kingdom of God is wanting, men will be untrained and unfit to see or to estimate the social manifestations of sin,

This proposition gives a solemn and terrible importance to the fact that doctrinal theology has failed to cherish and conserve for humanity the doctrine of the Kingdom of God. Christ died for it. Theology has allowed it to lead a decrepit, bed-ridden and senile existence in that museum of antiquities which we call eschatology. Having lost its vision of organized righteousness, theology necessarily lost its comprehension of organized sin, and therewith its right and power to act as the teacher of mankind on that subject. It saw private sin, and it set men to wrestling with their private doubts or sexual emotions by ascetic methods. But if sin is selfishness, how did that meet the case?

It would be unfair to blame theology for the fact that our race is still submerged under despotic government, under war and militarism, under landlordism, and under predatory industry and finance. But we can justly blame it for the fact that the Christian Church even now has hardly any realization that these things are large-scale sins. We can blame it in part for the fact that when a Christian minister in our country speaks of these sins he is charged with forgetting the simple gospel of sin and salvation, and is in danger of losing his position. This comes of shelving the doctrine of the Kingdom of God, or juggling feeble substitutes into its place. Theology has not been a faithful steward of the truth entrusted to it. The social gospel is its accusing conscience.

This is the chief significance of the social gospel for the doctrine of sin: it revives the vision of the Kingdom of God. When men see the actual world over against the religious ideal, they become conscious of its constitutional defects and wrongs. Those who do their thinking in the light of the Kingdom of God make less of heresy and private sins. They reserve their shudders for men who keep the liquor and vice trade alive against public intelligence and law; for interests that organize powerful lobbies to defeat tenement or factory legislation, or turn factory inspection into sham; for nations that are willing to set the world at war in order to win or protect colonial areas of trade or usurious profit from loans to weaker peoples; and for private interests which are willing to push a peaceful nation into war because the stock exchange has a panic at the rumour of peace. These seem the unforgivable sins, the great demonstrations of rebellious selfishness, wherever the social gospel has revived the faith of the Kingdom of God.

Two aspects of the Kingdom of God demand special consideration in this connection: the Kingdom is the realm of love, and it is the commonwealth of labour.

Jesus Christ superimposed his own personality on the previous conception of God and made love the distinctive characteristic of God and the supreme law of human conduct Consequently the reign of God would be the reign of love. It is not enough to think of the Kingdom as a prevalence of good will. The institutions of life must be fundamentally fraternal and cooperative if they are to train men to love their fellowmen as coworkers. Sin, being selfish, is covetous and grasping. It favours institutions and laws which permit unrestricted exploitation and accumulation. This in turn sets up antagonistic interests, increases law suits, class hostility, and wars, and so mis-educates mankind that love and cooperation seem unworkable, and men are taught to put their trust in coercive control by the strong and in the sting of hunger and compulsion for the poor.

Being the realm of love, the Kingdom of God must also be the commonwealth of co-operative labour, for how can we actively love others without serving their needs by our abilities? If the Kingdom of God is a community of highly developed personalities, it must also be an organization for labour, for none can realize himself fully without labour. A divinely ordered community, therefore, would offer to all the opportunities of education and enjoyment, and expect from all their contribution of labour.

Here again we realize the nature of sin over against the religious ideal of society. Sin selfishly takes from others their opportunities for self-realization in order to increase its own opportunities abnormally; and it shirks its own labour and thereby abnormally increases the labour of others. Idleness is active selfishness; it is not only unethical, but a sin against the Kingdom of God. To lay a heavy burden of support on our fellows, usually on the weakest classes, and to do no productive labour in return, is so crude a manifestation of sinful selfishness that one would suppose only an occasional instance of such delinquency could be found, and only under medical treatment. But in fact throughout history the policy of most States has been shaped in order to make such a sinful condition easy and perpetual. Men who have been under the teachings of Christianity all their lives do not even see that parasitism is a sin. So deeply has our insight into sin been darkened by the lack of a religious ideal of social life. Henry Drummond, who was one of the early prophets of the Kingdom idea, long ago pointed out that parasites are on the way to perdition, physically, intellectually, and morally. We shall not be doing our thinking in a Christian way until we agree that productive labour according to the ability of each is one of "the conditions of salvation."

The accepted definition of sin as selfishness is therefore wholly in line with the social gospel, and the latter can back tip the old theology with impressive examples of high-power selfishness which seem to have been overlooked. They can hardly fail to create a more searching consciousness of sin in every Christian mind. Indeed, many a Christian man, surveying the chief ambitions and results of his life in the light of the Kingdom of God, will have to begin his repentance over again and cry, *Mea culpa.*

There is evangelistic force in this social comprehension of the nature of sin. It offers searching and unsettling arguments and appeals to evangelistic preachers. If popular evangelists have not used them it can hardly be for lack of effectiveness. Is it because they are too effective?

If theology absorbs this understanding of the nature of sin, it will become a strong intellectual support of the social gospel, and come into fuller harmony with the spirit of the prophets and of the teaching of Jesus, The social gospel is part of the "return to Christ."

CHAPTER VII

THE TRANSMISSION OF SIN

How is sin transmitted from generation to generation? How is it made enduring and universal throughout the race?

This is by no means an academic question. Theology ought to be the science of redemption and offer scientific methods for the eradication of sin. In dealing with any epidemic disease, the first thing is to isolate the bacillus, and the second to see how it propagates and spreads. We must inquire for the lines of communication and contagion by which sin runs vertically down through history, and horizontally through the strata of contemporary society.

Theology has dealt with this problem in the doctrine of original sin. Many modern theologians are ready to abandon this doctrine, and among laymen it seems to carry so little sense of reality that audiences often smile at its mention. I take pleasure, therefore, in defending it. It is one of the few attempts of individualistic theology to get a solidaristic view of its field of work. This doctrine views the race as a great unity, descended from a single head, and knit together through all ages by unity of origin and blood. This natural unity is the basis and carrier for the transmission and universality of sin. Depravity of will and corruption of nature are transmitted wherever life itself is transmitted.

Science, to some extent, corroborates the doctrine of original sin. Evil does flow down the generations through the channels of biological coherence. Idiocy and feeble-mindedness, neurotic disturbances, weakness of inhibition, perverse desires, stubbornness and anti-social impulses in children must have had their adequate biological causes somewhere back on the line, even if we lack the records.

Even in normal individuals the animal instincts preponderate over the spiritual motives and restraints. All who have to train the young find themselves marshalling motives and forces to strengthen the higher desires against the drag of unwillingness. "The spirit is willing, but the flesh is weak," is a formula of Jesus. Paul's description of the struggle of flesh and spirit in his life is a classical expression of the tragedies enacted in the intimate life of every one who has tried to make his recalcitrant Ego climb the steep path of perfection: "The good which I would I do not; but the evil which I would not, that I practise."

According to orthodox theology man's nature passed through a fatal debasement at the beginning of history. According to evolutionary science the impulses connected with our alimentary and reproductive organs run far back in the evolution of the race and are well established and imperious, whereas the social, altruistic, and spiritual impulses are of recent development and relatively weak. We can take our choice of the explanations. In either case a faulty equipment has come down to us through the reproductive life of the race.

There is, then, a substance of truth in this unpopular doctrine of original sin. But the old theology over-worked it. It tried to involve us in the guilt of Adam as well as in his debasement of nature and his punishment of death. It fixed on us all a uniform corruption, and made it so complete that all evil resulting from personal sins seems trivial and irrelevant. If our will is so completely depraved, where do we get the freedom on which alone responsibility can be based? If a child is by nature set on evil, hostile to God, and a child of the devil, what is the use of education? For education presupposes an appetite for good which only needs awakening, direction, and spiritual support.

The texts usually cited in support of the doctrine can not justly be made to bear such universal significance.[1] The proof-text method, in trying to prove our original sin, has proved its own. The basic passage in Romans 5:12-21, is so difficult that even the exact methods of modern exegesis have not made Paul's meaning sure. Augustine based his influential argument on the Vulgate translation of verse 12, which is certainly faulty.

Theology was right in emphasizing the biological transmission of evil on the basis of race solidarity, but it strained the back of the doctrine by overloading it. On the other hand, it slighted or overlooked the fact that sin is transmitted along the lines of social tradition. This channel is at least as important as the other and far more susceptible of religious influence and control. Original sin deals with dumb forces of nature; social tradition is ethical and may be affected by conscious social action. Only the lack of social information and orientation in the past can explain the fact that theology has made so little of this.

---

[1] Gen. 6:5; 8:21; Psalms 14:1-3; 51:5; 58:3; Isaiah 48:8; John 3:5-6; Romans 5:12-14; Eph. 2:3.

The evil habits of boyhood,—lying, stealing, cigarette smoking, profane and obscene talk, self-pollution,—are usually set up in boys by the example and social suasion of boys just one stage older than they, young enough to be trusted companions, and old enough to exercise authority. One generation corrupts the next.

The permanent vices and crimes of adults are not transmitted by heredity, but by being socialized; for instance, alcoholism and all drug evils; cruel sports, such as bull-fights and pugilism; various forms of sex perversity; voluntary deformities, such as foot-binding, corseting, piercing of ears and nose; blood-feuds in Corsica; lynching in America. Just as syphilitic corruption is forced on the helpless fœtus in its mother's womb, so these hereditary social evils are forced on the individual embedded in the womb of society and drawing his ideas, moral standards, and spiritual ideals from the general life of the social body.

That sin is lodged in social customs and institutions and is absorbed by the individual from his social group is so plain that any person with common sense can observe it, but I have found only a few, even among the modern hand-books of theology, which show a clear recognition of the theological importance of this fact.[2] The social gospel has from the first emphasized it, and our entire religious method of dealing with children, adolescents, students, industrial and professional groups, and neighbourhoods, is being put on a different basis in consequence of this new insight. Systematic theology is not running even with practical theology at this point. A theology for the social gospel would have to say that original sin is partly social. It runs down the generations not only by biological propagation but also by social assimilation.

Theologians sometimes dispatch this matter easily as "the force of evil example." There is much more in it. We deal here not only with the instinct of imitation, but with the spiritual authority of society over its members.

---

[2] O. Kirn, "Grundriss der evangelischen Dogmatik," p, 82: "Heredity is not the only channel through which sin is spread and increased. Defective education, evil example, and the direct incitement to sin by unjust treatment or seduction, are of at least equal importance. The sin that we inherit is only a fragment of the totality of sin existing in the race. We ought especially to replace the theological conception of hereditary guilt by the realization of the fact that guilt attaches not only to the individual, but that there is a common guilt of social groups in widening circles, till we reach the guilt of the whole race for the moral conditions pervading all humanity." See also Clarke, "Outline of Christian Theology," pp. 218-221; Brown, "Christian Theology in Outline," p. 278; Pfleiderer, "Grundriss der christlichen Glaubens-und Sitten-lehre," p. 122.

In the main the individual takes over his moral judgments and valuations from his social class, profession, neighbourhood, and nation, making only slight personal modifications in the group standards. Only earnest or irresponsible persons are likely to enter into any serious opposition or contradiction, and then often on a single matter only, which exhausts their power of opposition. The deep marks which such a struggle with our group, especially in youth, leaves on our memory shows how hard it was at the time.

A group may be better or worse than a given member in it. It may require more neatness, fortitude, efficiency, and hard work than he is accustomed to. In that case the boy entering a good shop or a fine college fraternity is very promptly educated upward. On the other hand, if a group practises evil, it will excuse or idealize it, and resent any private judgment which condemns it. Evil then becomes part of the standards of morality sanctioned by the authority of society. This confuses the moral judgment of the Individual. The faculty of inhibition goes wrong. The magnetic pole itself shifts and the compass-needle of conscience swings to S.E.

Theology has always been deeply interested in the problem of authority in religion. The problem of authority in sin is of equal importance. Religious faith in the individual would be weak and intermittent unless it could lean on permanent social authorities. Sin in the individual is shame-faced and cowardly except where society backs and protects it This makes a decisive difference in the practical task of overcoming a given evil.

The case of alcoholic intoxication may serve as an example. Intoxication, like profanity and tattooing, is one of the universal marks of barbarism. In civilization it is a survival, and its phenomena become increasingly intolerable and disgusting to the scientific and to the moral mind. Nevertheless alcoholic drinking customs have prevailed and still prevail throughout civilization. What has given the practice of injecting a seductive drug into the human organism so enduring a hold? Other drug habits, such as the opium, cocaine, or heroin habits, are secretive and ashamed. Why does the alcohol habit flourish in the open? Aside from the question of the economic forces behind it, of which I shall speak later, the difference is due to social authority.

In the wine-drinking countries wine is praised in poetry and song. The most charming social usages are connected with its use. It is the chief reliance for entertainment and pleasure. Laughter is supposed to die without it No disgrace is attached to mild intoxication provided a gentleman carries his drink well and continues to behave politely. Families take more pride in their wine-cellars than in the tombs of their ancestors. Young men are proud of the amount of wine and beer they can imbibe and of the learning which they refuse to imbibe. Until very recent years a total abstainer in middle class European society was regarded with disquietude of mind and social impatiençe, like a person advocating force revolution or political assassination. He was a heretic, and his freedom of conscience had to be won by very real sufferings.

This justification and idealization of alcoholism by public opinion made it incomparably harder to save the victims, to prevent the formation of the drinking habits in new cases, and to secure legislation. Governments were, of course, anxious to suppress the disgusting drunkenness of the labouring classes, which interfered with their working efficiency, but the taming of the liquor trade was hard to secure as long as men high up in Parliament, the established Church, and Society considered investments in breweries, distilleries, and public houses a perfectly honourable source of income.

The rapid progress in the expulsion of the liquor trade in America would have been impossible if the idealization of the drinking customs had not previously disappeared from public opinion. The chief plea of the brewers now is that beer displaces distilled liquor and promotes temperance. In "the People's Sunday Evening," a popular theatre meeting in Rochester, N. Y., we have for seven years publicly invited and challenged the Brewers' Exchange and all the liquor trade organizations to discuss the social and moral utility of moderate drinking on our platform. They accepted the first time, but had to go to Buffalo for a lawyer to make the speech. After that we were never able to secure a response. The use of liquor is still common in America, but its social authority has been overcome. So far as I can see, this was done by the churches before either business or science lent much aid, and the decisive fact which set the voice of some of the denominations free was their refusal to tolerate in their membership persons financially interested in the liquor business, or to receive contributions from them.

In the case of alcoholism we can watch a gradual breaking down of the social authority of a great evil In the case of militarism we are watching the reverse process. Before the War the military institutions of our nation were weak and public opinion condemned war. Enthusiasm for peace was one of the clearest social convictions of the Church. This state of mind was one of the causes for our mental reactions at the outbreak of the war. In the course of three years we have swung around. At first preparedness was advocated as a dire necessity under the actual circumstances. But soon other voices began to mingle with this. We were soft and flabby, without training in order and obedience. It would do our boys and young men a world of good to be under military discipline and drill for years. It would improve the American character. Prophets of war asserted that war is essentially noble, the supreme test of manhood and of the worth of a nation. The corresponding swing in the attitude of the churches was made slowly and with deep reluctance and searching of heart by many ministers. But it was made. Those who remained faithful to the religious peace convictions which had been orthodox a short time ago, were now extremists, and the position of a public spokesman of religion became exceedingly difficult for one who believed that war is inherently evil and in contradiction to Christianity. The problem of Jesus took on new forms and dealt with his pacifism and non-resistance. The ejection of the traders from the temple with a scourge of small cords, and the advice to the disciples to sell their cloaks and buy swords, took rank as important parts of the gospel.

In these ways religion, being part of the national life, had to adjust its convictions and teachings in order to permit the idealization of war. If the nations emerge into a long peace with disarmament, this war will be recorded as a holy and redemptive war. If preparedness and universal service become permanent institutions of American life, profound changes in the popular philosophy of life and in religious thought will follow. Social institutions always generate the theories adapted to them.

The idealization of evil is an indispensable means for its perpetuation and transmission. But the most potent motive for its protection is its profitableness. Ordinarily sin is an act of weakness and side-stepping, followed by shame the next day. But when it is the source of prolific income, it is no longer a shame-faced vagabond slinking through the dark, but an army with banners, entrenched and defiant. The bigger the dividends, the stiffer the resistance against anything that would cut them down. When fed with money, sin grows wings and claws.

The other outlets for sinful selfishness, such as over-eating and sexual excess, soon reach their natural limit and end in nausea and disgust, or they eliminate the sinner. Polygamy gave full scope to the lust of great men, but Solomon's thousand concubines seem to be the limit in history and story. We have never heard of a man becoming a millionaire in the line of wives.

Property, too, used to be limited. Too much land or cattle or clothing became unmanageable. The main satisfaction of the rich was to have many guests and dependents, and to spend bountifully. The rise of the money system enlarged the limits of acquisition. Money could be bred from money. To-day a man can store millions in paper evidences of wealth in a safe deposit box, and collect the income from it with a stenographer, a lawyer, and a pair of shears. He can acquire tens of millions, hundreds of millions. Imagine the digestive organs expanding to the size of a Zeppelin.

If "the love of money is the root of all evil" and if selfishness is the essence of sin, such an expansion of the range and storage capacity of selfishness must necessarily mark a new era in the history of sin, just as the invention of the steam-engine marked a new era in the production of wealth. Drink, over-eating, sexualism, vanity, and idleness are still reliable standardized sins. But the exponent of gigantic evil on the upper ranges of sin, is the love of money and the love of power over men which property connotes. This is the most difficult field of practical redemption and the most necessitous chance of evangelism.

The theological doctrine of original sin is an important effort to see sin in its totality and to explain its unbroken transmission and perpetuation. But this explanation of the facts is very fragmentary, and theology has done considerable harm in concentrating the attention of religious minds on the biological transmission of evil. It has diverted our minds from the power of social transmission, from the authority of the social group in justifying, urging, and idealizing wrong, and from the decisive influence of economic profit in the defense and propagation of evil. These are ethical facts, but they have the greatest religious importance, and they have just as much right to being discussed in theology as the physical propagation of the species, or creationism and traducianism. There is the more inducement to teach clearly on the social transmission and perpetuation of sin because the ethical and religious forces can really do something to check and prevent the transmission of sin along social channels, whereas the biological transmission of original sin, except for the possible influence of eugenics, seems to be beyond our influence.

CHAPTER VIII

THE SUPER-PERSONAL FORCES OF EVIL

Individualistic theology has not trained the spiritual intelligence of Christian men and women to recognize and observe spiritual entities beyond the individual. Our religious interest has been so focused on the soul of the individual and its struggles that we have remained uneducated as to the more complex units of spiritual life.

The chief exception to this statement is our religious insight into the history of Israel and Judah, into the nature of the family, and the qualities of the Church. The first of these we owe to the solidaristic vision of the Old Testament prophets who saw their nation as a gigantic personality which sinned, suffered, and repented. The second we owe to the deep interest which the Church from the beginning has taken in the purity of family life and the Christian nurture of the young. The third we owe to the high valuation the Church has always put on itself. It has claimed a continuous and enduring life of its own which enfolds all its members and distinguishes it from every other organization and from the totality of the worldly life outside of it. It is hard to deny this. Not only the Church as a whole, but distinctive groups and organizations within the Church, such as the Friends or the Jesuit Order, have maintained their own character and principles tenaciously against all influences. This is the noblest view that we can take of the Church, that the spirit of her Lord has always been an informing principle of life within her, and that, though faltering, sinning, and defiled, she has kept her own collective personality intact. Paul's discussion of the Church as the body of Christ (1 Cor. 12) is the first and classical discussion in Christian thought of the nature and functioning of a composite spiritual organism.

The Church is not the only organism of that kind, though pre-eminent among them all. Others are less permanent, less distinctive, less attractive, and less self-assertive, but the spiritual self-consciousness of the Church is built up on the social self-consciousness which it shares with other social organisms.

Josiah Royce, one of the ablest philosophical thinkers our nation has produced, has given us, in his "Problem of Christianity" his mature reflections on the subject of the Christian religion. The book is a great fragment, poorly balanced, confined in the main to a modern discussion of three great Pauline conceptions, sin, atonement, and the Church. The discussion of the Church is the ablest part of it; I shall return to that later. Following the lead of Wundt's Völkerpsychologie, Professor Royce was deeply impressed with the reality of super-personal forces in human life. He regards the comprehension of that fact as one of the most important advances in knowledge yet made.

"There are in the human world two profoundly different grades, or levels, of mental beings, — namely, the beings that we usually call human individuals, and the beings that we call communities. Any highly organized community is as truly a human being as you and I are individually human. Only a community is not what we usually call an individual human being because it has no one separate and internally well-knit physical organism of its own; and because its mind, if you attribute to it any one mind, is therefore not manifested through the expressive movements of such a single separate human organism. Yet there are reasons for attributing to a community a mind of its own.— The communities are vastly more complex, and, in many ways, are also immeasurably more potent and enduring than are the individuals. Their mental life possesses, as Wundt has pointed out, a psychology of its own, which can be systematically studied. Their mental existence is no mere creation of abstract thinking or of metaphor; and is no more a topic for mystical insight, or for phantastic speculation, than is the mental existence of an individual man."[1]

This conception is of great importance for the doctrine of sin. I have spoken in the last chapter about the authority of the group over the individual within it, and its power to impose its own moral standard on its members, by virtue of which it educates them upward, if its standard is high, and debases them, if it is low. We need only mention some of the groups in our own national social life to realize how they vary in moral quality and how potent they are by virtue of their collective life: high school fraternities; any college community; a trade union; the I. W. W.; the Socialist party; Tammany Hall; any military organization; an officers' corps; the police force; the inside group of a local political party; the Free Masons; the Grange; the legal profession; a conspiracy like the Black Hand.

---

[1] "Problem of Christianity" I, pp. 164-167.

These super-personal forces count in the moral world not only through their authority over their members, but through their influence in the general social life. They front the world outside of them. Their real object usually lies outside. The assimilative power they exert over their members is only their form of discipline by which they bring their collective body into smooth and efficient working order. They are the most powerful ethical forces in our communities.

Evil collective forces have usually fallen from a better estate. Organizations are rarely formed for avowedly evil ends. They drift into evil under sinister leadership, or under the pressure of need or temptation. For instance, a small corrupt group in a city council, in order to secure control, tempts the weak, conciliates and serves good men, and turns the council itself into a force of evil in the city; an inside ring in the police force grafts on the vice trade, and draws a part of the force into protecting crime and brow-beating decent citizens; a trade union fights for the right to organize a shop, but resorts to violence and terrorizing; a trust, desiring to steady prices and to get away from antiquated competition, undersells the independents and evades or purchases legislation. This tendency to deterioration shows the soundness of the social instincts, but also the ease with which they go astray, and the need of righteous social institutions to prevent temptation.

In the previous chapter it was pointed out that the love of gain is one of the most unlimited desires and the most inviting outlet for sinful selfishness. The power of combination lends itself to extortion. Predatory profit or graft, when once its sources are opened up and developed, constitutes an almost overwhelming temptation to combinations of men. Its pursuit gives them cohesion and unity of mind, capacity to resist common dangers, and an outfit of moral and political principles which will justify their anti-social activities. The aggressive and defensive doings of such combinations are written all over history. History should be re-written to explain the nature of human parasitism. It would be a revelation. The Roman *publicani*, who collected the taxes from conquered provinces on a contract basis; the upper class in all slave-holding communities; the landlord class in all ages and countries, such as East Prussia, Ireland, Italy, and Russia; the great trading companies in the early history of commerce; — these are instances of social groups consolidated by extortionate gain. Such groups necessarily resist efforts to gain political liberty or social justice, for liberty and justice do away with unearned incomes. Their malign influence on the development of humanity has been beyond telling.

The higher the institution, the worse it is when it goes wrong. The most disastrous backsliding in history was the deterioration of the Church. Long before the Reformation the condition of the Church had become the most serious social question of the age. It weighed on all good men. The Church, which was founded on democracy and brotherhood, had, in its higher levels, become an organization controlled by the upper classes for parasitic ends, a religious duplicate of the coercive State, and a chief check on the advance of democracy and brotherhood. Its duty was to bring love, unity and freedom to mankind; instead it created division, fomented hatred, and stifled intellectual and social liberty. It is proof of the high valuation men put on the Church that its corruption seems to have weighed more heavily on the conscience of Christendom than the corresponding corruption of the State. At least the religious Revolution antedated the political Revolution by several centuries. To-day the Church is practically free from graft and exploitation; its sins are mainly sins of omission; yet the contrast between the idea of the Church and its reality, between the force for good which it might exert and the force which it does exert in public life, produces profounder feelings than the shortcomings of the State.

While these pages are being written, our nation is arming itself to invade another continent for the purpose of overthrowing the German government, on the ground that the existence of autocratic governments is a menace to the peace of the world and the freedom of its peoples. This momentous declaration of President Wilson recognizes the fact that the Governments of Great States too may be super-personal powers of sin; that they may in reality be only groups of men using their fellow-men as pawns and tools; that such governments have in the past waged war for dynastic and class interests without consulting the people; and that in their diplomacy they have cunningly contrived plans of deception and aggression, working them out through generations behind the guarded confidences of a narrow and privileged class.[2]

There is no doubt that these charges justly characterize the German government There is no doubt that they characterize all governments of past history with few exceptions, and that even the democratic governments of to-day are not able to show clean hands on these points. The governments even of free States like the Dutch Republic, the city republics of Italy, and the British Empire have been based on a relatively narrow group who deter-

---

[2] These ideas and phrases are drawn from the President's Address to Congress on April 2nd, 1917.

mined the real policies and decisions of the nation. How often have we been told that in our own country we have one government on paper and another in fact? Genuine political democracy will evidence its existence by the social, economic, and educational condition of the people. Generally speaking, city slums, a spiritless and drunken peasantry, and a large emigration are corollaries of class government If the people were free, they would stop exploitation. If they can not stop exploitation, the parasitic interests are presumably in control of legislation, the courts, and the powers of coercion. Parasitic government is sin on a high scale. If this war leads to the downfall or regeneration of all governments which support the exploitation of the masses by powerful groups, it will be worth its cost.

The social gospel realizes the importance and power of the superpersonal forces in the community. It has succeeded in awakening the social conscience of the nation to the danger of allowing such forces to become parasitic and oppressive. A realization of the spiritual power and value of these composite personalities must get into theology, otherwise theology will not deal adequately with the problem of sin and of redemption, and will be unrelated to some of the most important work of salvation which the coming generations will have to do.

CHAPTER IX

THE KINGDOM OF EVIL

This chapter will be the last step in our discussion of the doctrine of sin. We have sought to show that in the following points a modification or expansion is needed in order to give the social gospel an intellectual basis and a full medium of expression in theology.

1.Theological teaching on the first origin of sin ought not to obscure the active sources of sin in later generations and in present-day life, by which sin is quickened and increased. An approximation to the reticence of Jesus and the prophets about the fall of man, and to their strong emphasis on the realistic facts of contemporary sin, would increase the practical efficiency of theology.

2. Since an active sense of failure and sin is produced by contrast with the corresponding ideal of righteousness, theology, by obscuring and forgetting the Kingdom of God has kept the Christian world out of a full realization of the social sins which frustrate the Kingdom. The social gospel needs above all a restoration of religious faith in the Reign of God in order to create an adequate sense of guilt for public sins, and it must look to theology to furnish the doctrinal basis of it.

3. The doctrine of original sin has directed attention to the biological channels for the transmission of general sinfulness from generation to generation, but has neglected and diverted attention from the transmission and perpetuation of specific evils through the channels of social tradition.

4. Theology has not given adequate attention to the social idealizations of evil, which falsify the ethical standards for the individual by the authority of his group or community, deaden the voice of the Holy Spirit to the conscience of individuals and communities, and perpetuate antiquated wrongs in society. These social idealizations are the real heretical doctrines from the point of view of the Kingdom of God.

5. New spiritual factors of the highest significance are disclosed by the realization of the super-personal forces, or composite personalities, in society. When these backslide and become combinations for evil, they add enormously to the power of sin. Theology has utilized the terminology and re-

sults of psychology to interpret the sin and regeneration of individuals. Would it stray from its field if it utilized sociological terms and results in order to interpret the sin and redemption of these super-personal entities in human life?

The solidaristic spiritual conceptions which have been discussed must all be kept in mind and seen together, in order to realize the power and scope of the doctrine to which they converge: the Kingdom of Evil.

In some of our swampy forests the growth of ages has produced impenetrable thickets of trees and undergrowth, woven together by creepers, and inhabited by things that creep or fly. Every season sends forth new growth tinder the urge of life, but always developing from the old growth and its seeds, and still perpetuating the same rank mass of life.

The life of humanity is infinitely interwoven, always renewing itself, yet always perpetuating what has been. The evils of one generation are caused by the wrongs of the generations that preceded, and will in turn condition the sufferings and temptations of those who come after. Our Italian immigrants are what they are because the Church and the land system of Italy have made them so. The Mexican peon is ridden by the Spanish past Capitalistic Europe has fastened its yoke on the neck of Africa. When negroes are hunted from a Northern city like beasts, or when a Southern city degrades the whole nation by turning the savage inhumanity of a mob into a public festivity, we are continuing to sin because our fathers created the conditions of sin by the African slave trade and by the unearned wealth they gathered from slave labour for generations.

Stupid dynasties go on reigning by right of the long time they have reigned. The laws of the ancient Roman despotism were foisted by ambitious lawyers on mediaeval communities, to which they were in no wise fitted, and once more strangled liberty, and dragged free farmers into serfdom. When once the common land of a nation, and its mines and waters, have become the private property of a privileged band, nothing short of a social earthquake can pry them from their right of collecting private taxes. Superstitions which originated in the third century are still faithfully cultivated by great churches, compressing the minds of the young with fear and cherished by the old as their most precious faith. Ideas struck out by a wrestling mind in the heat of an argument are erected by later times into proof-texts more decisive than masses of living facts. One nation arms because it fears another; the other arms more because this armament alarms it; each subsidizes a third and a fourth to aid it. Two fight; all fight; none knows how to stop; a planet is stained red in a solidarity of hate and horror.

The entomologist Fabre investigated the army cater-pillar, which marches in dense thousands, apparently under some leadership which all obey. But Fabre found there is no leadership. Each simply keeps in touch with the caterpillar just ahead of it and follows, follows on. The one article of faith is to follow the leaders, though none of the leaders knows whither they are going. The experimenter led the column to march in a circle by getting the front rank in touch with the rear, and now they milled around helplessly like lost souls in Dante's Hell.

If this were the condition of humanity, we should be in a state of relative innocency and bliss. The front-rank caterpillars are at least not trying to make something out of the rest, and are not leading them to their destruction by assuring them that they are doing it for their good and for the highest spiritual possessions of the caterpillar race. Human society has leaders who know what they want, but many of them have manipulated the fate of thousands for their selfish ends. The sheep-tick hides in the wool of the sheep and taps the blood where it flows warm and rich. But the tick has no power to alter the arterial system of the sheep and to bring the aorta close to the skin where it can get at it. Human ticks have been able to do this. They have gained control of legislation, courts, police, military, royalty, church, property, religion, and have altered the constitution of nations in order to make things easy for the tick class. The laws, institutions, doctrines, literature, art, and manners which these ruling classes have secreted have been social means of infection which have bred new evils for generations.

Any reader who doubts these sad statements can find the facts in the books, though mostly in foot-notes in fine print. It is also going on in real life. We can watch it if we look at any nation except our own.

This is what the modern social gospel would call the Kingdom of Evil. Our theological conception of sin is but fragmentary unless we see all men in their natural groups bound together in a solidarity of all times and all places, bearing the yoke of evil and suffering. This is the explanation of the amazing regularity of social statistics. A nation registers so and so many suicides, criminal assaults, bankruptcies, and divorces per 100,000 of the population. If the proportion changes seriously, we search for the disturbing social causes, just as we search for the physical causes if the rhythm of our pulse-beat runs away from the normal. The statistics of social morality are the pulse-beat of the social organism. The apparently free and unrelated acts of individuals are also the acts of the social group. When the social group is evil, evil is over all.

The conception of a Kingdom of Evil is not a new idea. It is as old as the Christian Church and older. But while our modern conception is naturally historical and social, the ancient and mediaeval Church believed in a Kingdom of evil spirits, with Satan at their head, which is the governing power in the present world and the source of all temptation.

The belief in evil spirits is so common in ethnic religions that the relative absence of that belief in the Old Testament is proper cause for wonder. There are only a few passages referring to evil spirits, and a few referring to a spiritual being called Satan. It is altogether likely that the belief in dangerous and malicious spirits held a much larger place in the popular religious life of the Jewish people than we would gather from their literature. If the higher religious minds, who wrote the biblical books, purposely kept the popular beliefs down and out of sight, that gives remarkable support to those who regard the belief in personal evil spirits as a seamy and dangerous element of religion.

After the Exile the religion of the Jews was filled with angels and devils, each side built up in a great hierarchy, rank above rank. Evidently this systematized and theological belief in a satanic kingdom was absorbed from the Eastern religions with which the Jews came into close contact during the Exile. The monotheism of the Hebrew faith held its own against the dualism of the East, but the belief in Satan is a modified dualism compatible with the reign of Jehovah. The apocalyptic system is a theology built up on this semi-dualistic conception, describing the conflict of the Kingdom of Satan against God and his angels and his holy nation, and the final triumph of God.

The belief in the Satanic Kingdom and the apocalyptic theology were transferred from Judaism to Christianity as part of the initial inheritance of the new religion from the old, and any one familiar with patristic literature and with popular mediaeval religion needs no reminder that this was one of the most active and effective parts of the religious consciousness. The original belief was reinforced by the fact that all the gods and the daimonia of the Græco-Roman world were dyed black and classified as devils and evil spirits by the aggressive hostility of the Church. This process was repeated when the mediaeval Church was exorcising the pagan gods from the minds and customs of the Teutonic nations. All these gods remained realities, but black realities.

Popular superstition, systematized and reinforced by theology, and inculcated by all the teaching authority of the mediaeval Church, built up an overwhelming impression of the power of evil. The Christian spirit was thrown into an attitude of defence only. The best that could be done was to hold the powers of darkness at bay by the sign of the cross, by holy water, by sacred amulets, by prayer, by naming holy names. The church buildings and church yards were places of refuge from which the evil spirits were banned. The gargoyles of Gothic architecture are the evil spirits escaping from the church buildings because the spiritual power within is unbearable to them. I recently witnessed a corner-stone laying at a new Catholic church. The bishop and the clergy thrice moved in procession around the foundation walls, chanting; an acolyte carried a pailful of holy water, and the bishop liberally applied it to the walls. So the rectangle of masonry became an exempt and disinfected area of safety. Under the sunshine of an American afternoon, and with a crowd of modern folks around, it was an interesting survival.

The belief in a demonic Kingdom was in no wise attacked in the Reformation. Luther's sturdy belief in devils is well known. Indeed, the belief which had been built up for centuries by the Church, came to its terrible climax during the age of the Reformation in the witch trials. From A. D. 1400 to 1700, hundreds of thousands of women and girls were imprisoned, tortured, and burned. These witch trials were grounded on the belief in the satanic kingdom. Thomas Aquinas furnished the theological basis; the Inquisition reduced it to practice; Innocent VIII in 1484 in the bull *Summis desiderantes* lent it the highest authority of the Church; the *Malleus Maleficarum* (1487 or 1488) codified it; lawyers, judges, informers, and executioners exploited it for gain; information given by malice, fear, or the shrieks of the tortured made the contagion self-perpetuating and ever spreading. It prevailed in Protestant countries equally with Catholic. To believe in the machinations of evil spirits and their compact with witches was part of orthodoxy, part of profounder piety. If the devil and his spirits are not real but a figment of social imagination, yet at that time the devil was real, just as real as any flesh and blood being and far more efficient. Theology had made him real. The Reformation theology did not end this craze of horror. Aside from the humane religious spirit of a few who wrote against it, it was the blessed scepticism of the age of Enlightenment and the dawn of modern science which saved humanity from the furies of a theology which had gone wrong.

The passive and defensive attitude toward the satanic Kingdom of Evil still continues wherever the belief in evil spirits and in the apocalyptic theology is active. Bunyan's "Pilgrim's Progress" presents a dramatic record of the Calvinistic religious consciousness in its prime. In all the wonderful adventures and redoubtable combats of Christian and his companions and heavenly aids, they are on the defensive. The only exception that I can remember occurs in the second part, when Christian's wife and children, personally conducted by Great-Heart, pass by Doubting Castle where Christian and Hopeful were imprisoned by Giant Despair.

"So they sat down and consulted what was best to be done: to wit, now they were so strong, and had got such a man as Mr. Great-Heart for their conductor, whether they had not best to make an attempt upon the giant, demolish his castle, and if there were any pilgrims in it, to set them at liberty, before they went any further. So one said one thing, and another said the contrary. One questioned if it was lawful to go upon unconsecrated ground; another said they might, provided their end was good; but Mr. Great-Heart said, "Though that assertion offered last cannot be universally true, yet I have a commandment to resist sin, to overcome evil, to fight the good fight of faith; and pray, with whom should I fight this good fight, if not with Giant Despair? I will therefore attempt the taking away of his life and the demolishing of Doubting Castle."

So they passed from the defensive to the offensive attitude and demolished the castle. The serious deliberations of the party show that Bunyan realized that this was a new departure. He was, in fact at that moment parting company with the traditional attitude of theology and religion, and putting one foot hesitatingly into the social gospel and the preventive methods of modern science. Note that it was Mr. Great-Heart who made the move.

To-day the belief in a satanic kingdom exists only where religious and theological tradition keeps it alive. It is not spontaneous, and it would not originate anew. Its lack of vitality is proved by the fact that even those who accept the existence of a personal Satan without question, are not influenced in their daily life by the practical belief in evil spirits. The demons have faded away into poetical unreality. Satan alone remains, but he has become a literary and theological devil, and most often a figure of speech. He is a theological necessity rather than a religious reality. He is needed to explain the fall and the temptation, and he re-appears in eschatology. But our most orthodox theology on this point would have seemed cold and sceptical to any of the great theologians of the past.

No positive proof can be furnished that our universe contains no such spiritual beings as Satan and his angels. Impressive arguments have been made for their existence. The problem of evil is simplified if all is reduced to this source. But the fact confronts us, and I think it can not be denied, that Satan and his angels are a fading religious entity, and that a vital belief in demon powers is not forthcoming in modern life.

In that case we can no longer realize the Kingdom of Evil as a demonic kingdom. The live realization of this belief will be confined to narrow circles, mostly of pre-millennialists; the Church would have to use up its precious moral authority in persuading its members to hold fast a belief which all modern life bids them drop. Yet we ought to get a solidaristic and organic conception of the power and reality of evil in the world. If we miss that, we shall see only disjointed facts. The social gospel is the only influence which can renew the idea of the Kingdom of Evil in modern minds, because it alone has an adequate sense of solidarity and a sufficient grasp of the historical and social realities of sin. In this modern form the conception would offer religious values similar to those of the old idea, but would not make such drafts on our credulity, and would not invite such unchristian superstitions and phantasms of fear.

The ancient demonic conception and the modern social conviction may seem at first sight to be quite alien to each other. In fact, however, they are blood-kin.

The belief in a Satanic kingdom, in so far as it was not merely theology but vital religious faith, has always drawn its vitality from political and social realities. The conception of an empire of evil fastened on Jewish thought after the Jews had an opportunity during the Exile to observe imperialism at close range and to be helpless under its power. The splendor of an Oriental court and its court language deeply influenced the Jewish conception of God. He was surrounded with a heavenly retinue, and despotic ideas and phraseology were applied. The same social experiences also enlarged the conception of the reign of evil. The little evil spirits had been enough to explain the evil of local Jewish communities. But a great malign power was needed as the religious backing of the oppressive international forces in whose talons the Jewish race was writhing. Satan first got his vitality as an international political concept.

The political significance of the belief in the Satanic kingdom becomes quite clear in the relation of the early Church to the Roman Empire. The Apocalypse of John is most enlightening on this fact. The Empire is plainly described as the creature and agent of the Satanic powers. The Beast with the seven heads had received its dominion from the great Dragon. The great city, which is described as the commercial and financial centre of the world, falls with a crash when Satan and his host are overthrown by the Messiah. Evidently the political system of Rome and the demonic powers are seen as the physical and spiritual side of the same evil power.

Early Christianity is usually described as opposed to paganism, and we think of the pagan religion as a rival religious system. But it was also a great social force penetrating all community life, the symbol of social coherence and loyalty. Its social usages let no one alone. It became coercive and threatening where religious actions had political significance, especially in the worship of the emperor. Christians believed the pagan gods to be in reality demon powers, who had blinded and enticed men to worship them. Whoever did worship them came under their defiling power. Idolatry was an unforgivable sin. All the life of the Church aimed to nerve Christians to suffer anything rather than come under the control of the dark powers again from which baptism had saved them. When the choice confronted them and they were pinned to the wall, the hand that gripped them was the hand of the Roman Empire, but the face that leered at them was the face of the adversary of God. So the belief in a Satanic kingdom of evil drew its concrete meaning and vitality from social and political realities. It was their religious interpretation.

In the Middle Ages, when the Roman Empire had become a great memory, the Papacy was the great international power, rich, haughty, luxurious, domineering, commanding the police powers of States for its coercive purposes, and claiming the heritage of the emperors. The democratic movements which sprang up during the eleventh and twelfth centuries and headed toward a freer religion and a more fraternal social life, found the papacy against them. Then the Apocalypse took on new life. The city on the seven hills, drunk with the blood of the saints, and clad in scarlet, was still there. The followers of Jesus who suffered in the grip of the international hierarchy did not see this power as a Christian Church using oppressive measures, but as an anti-christian power, the tool of Satan and the adversary of God. This belief was inherited by Protestantism and was one of its fighting weapons. Once more it was a political and social reality which put heat and vitality into the belief in the reign of Satan.

To-day there is no such world-wide power of oppression as the Roman Empire or the mediaeval papacy. The popular superstitious beliefs in demonic agencies have largely been drained off by education. The conception of Satan has paled. He has become a theological devil, and that is an attenuated and precarious mode of existence. At the same time belief in original sin is also waning. These two doctrines combined, the hereditary racial unity of sin, and the supernatural power of evil behind all sinful human action, created a solidaristic consciousness of sin and evil, which I think is necessary for the religious mind. Take away these two doctrines, and both our sense of sin and our sense of the need of redemption will become much more superficial and will be mainly concerned with the transient acts and vices of individuals.

A social conception of the Kingdom of Evil, such as I have tried to sketch, makes a powerful appeal to our growing sense of racial unity. It is modern and grows spontaneously out of our livest interests and ideas. Instead of appealing to conservatives, who are fond of sitting on antique furniture, it would appeal to the radicals. It would contain the political and social protest against oppression and illusion for which the belief in a Satanic kingdom stood in the times of its greatest vitality. The practical insight into the solidarity of all nations in their sin would emphasize the obligation to share with them all every element of salvation we possess, and thus strengthen the appeal for missionary and educational efforts.

The doctrine of original sin was meant to bring us all under the sense of guilt. Theology in the past has labored to show that we are in some sense partakers of Adam's guilt. But the conscience of mankind has never been convinced. Partakers in his wretchedness we might well be by our family coherence, but guilt belongs only to personality, and requires will and freedom. On the other hand an enlightened conscience can not help feeling a growing sense of responsibility and guilt for the common sins under which humanity is bound and to which we all contribute. Who of us can say that he has never by word or look contributed to the atmospheric pressure of lubricious sex stimulation which bears down on young and old, and the effect of which after the war no man can predict without sickening? Whose hand has never been stained with income for which no equivalent had been given in service? How many business men have promoted the advance of democracy in their own industrial kingdom when autocracy seemed safer and more efficient? What nation has never been drunk with a sense of its glory and importance, and which has never seized colonial possessions or developed its little imperialism when the temptation came its way? The sin of all is in each of us, and every one of us has scattered seeds of evil, the final multiplied harvest of which no man knows.

At the close of his great invective against the religious leaders of his nation (Matt. 23), Jesus has a solidaristic vision of the spiritual unity of the generations. He warns his contemporaries that by doing over again the acts of their forefathers, they will bring upon them not only the blood they shed themselves, but the righteous blood shed long before. By solidarity of action and spirit we enter into solidarity of guilt. This applies to our spiritual unity with our contemporaries. If in the most restricted sphere of life we act on the same sinful principles of greed and tyranny on which the great exploiters and despots act, we share their guilt. If we consent to the working principles of the Kingdom of Evil, and do not counteract it with all our strength, but perhaps even fail to see its ruinous evil, then we are part of it and the salvation of Christ has not yet set us free.

I should like to quote, in closing this discussion, a remarkable passage from Schleiermacher's systematic theology, which describes the Kingdom of Evil without calling it by that name. I need not say that Schleiermacher was one of the really creative minds in the history of Protestant theology, a man who set new problems and made old problems profounder, thus fertilizing the thoughts even of those who know nothing of him. Speaking of the universal racial sin of humanity he said:

> "If, now, this sinfulness which precedes all acts of sin, is produced in every individual through the sinful acts and condition of others; and if on the other hand every man by his own free actions propagates and strengthens it in others; then it is something wholly common to us (gemeinschaftlich). Whether we view this sinfulness as guilt and as conscious action, or as a principle and condition of life, in either aspect it is something wholly common, not pertaining to every individual separately or referring to him alone, but *in each the work of all, and in all the work of each.* In fact we can understand it justly and completely only in this solidarity. For that reason the doctrines dealing with it are never to be taken as expressions of individual self-consciousness, but they are expressions of the common consciousness. This solidarity is a unity of all places and all times. The peculiar form which this racial sinfulness takes in any individual, is simply an integral part of the form it takes in the social group to which he belongs, so that his sin is incomprehensible if taken alone and must always be taken in connection with the rest. This principle runs through all the concentric circles of solidaristic consciousness, through families, clans, tribes, nations, and races; the form

which sinfulness takes in any of these can be understood only in connection with the rest. Therefore the total force exerted by the flesh against the spirit in all human actions incompatible with the consciousness of God, can be truly realized only when we see the totality of all contemporary life, never in any part alone. The same holds true of the succession of generations. The congenital sinfulness of one generation is conditioned by the sinfulness of those who preceded, and in turn conditions the sin of those who follow."[1]

Ritschl, another incisive and original theological thinker, adopted this solidaristic conception of sin, and its correlated ideas in the doctrine of salvation, as the basis of his theological system. He thinks that this, and not the theory of subjective religion which is commonly quoted in connection with his name, is Schleiermacher's epoch-making contribution to theology.[2] Certainly the passage I have quoted shows what a capacity of religious vision is evoked by a religious comprehension of the solidarity of human life. "The consciousness of solidarity is one of the fundamental conditions of religion, without which it can neither be rightly understood nor rightly lived."[3]

---

[1] Schleiermacher, "Der Christliche Glaube," §71, 2. 3rd edition. The translation and italics are mine. A few unessential phrases are omitted to shorten the quotation.

[2] Ritschl, "Rechtfertigung und Versöhnung," I, p. 555.

[3] Ritschl, I, p. 496.

CHAPTER X

THE SOCIAL GOSPEL AND PERSONAL SALVATION

We take up now the doctrine of salvation. All that has been said about sin will have to be kept in mind in discussing salvation, for the conceptions of sin and salvation are always closely correlated in every theological or religious system.

The new thing in the social gospel is the clearness and insistence with which it sets forth the necessity and the possibility of redeeming the historical life of humanity from the social wrongs which now pervade it and which act as temptations and incitements to evil and as forces of resistance to the powers of redemption. Its chief interest is concentrated on those manifestations of sin and redemption which lie beyond the individual soul. If our exposition of the superpersonal agents of sin and of the Kingdom of Evil is true, then evidently a salvation confined to the soul and its personal interests is an imperfect and only partly effective salvation.

Yet the salvation of the individual is, of course, an essential part of salvation. Every new being is a new problem of salvation. It is always a great and wonderful thing when a young spirit enters into voluntary obedience to God and feels the higher freedom with which Christ makes us free. It is one of the miracles of life. The burden of the individual is as heavy now as ever. The consciousness of wrong-doing, of imperfection, of a wasted life lies on many and they need forgiveness and strength for a new beginning. Modern pessimism drains the finer minds of their confidence in the world and the value of life itself. At present we gasp for air in a crushing and monstrous world. Any return of faith is an experience of salvation.

Therefore our discussion can not pass personal salvation by. We might possibly begin where the old gospel leaves off, and ask our readers to take all the familiar experiences and truths of personal evangelism and religious nurture for granted in what follows. But our understanding of personal salvation itself is deeply affected by the new solidaristic comprehension furnished by the social gospel.

The social gospel furnishes new tests for religious experience. We are not disposed to accept the converted souls whom the individualistic evangelism supplies, without looking them over. Some who have been saved and perhaps reconsecrated a number of times are worth no more to the Kingdom of God than they were before. Some become worse through their revival experiences, more self-righteous, more opinionated, more steeped in unrealities and stupid over against the most important things, more devoted to emotions and unresponsive to real duties. We have the highest authority for the fact that men may grow worse by getting religion. Jesus says the Pharisees compassed sea and land to make a proselyte, and after they had him, he was twofold more a child of hell than his converters. To one whose memories run back twenty or thirty years, to Moody's time, the methods now used by some evangelists seem calculated to produce skin-deep changes. Things have simmered down to signing a card, shaking hands, or being introduced to the evangelist. We used to pass through some deep-soil ploughing by comparison. It is time to overhaul our understanding of the kind of change we hope to produce by personal conversion and regeneration. The social gospel furnishes some tests and standards.

When we undertook to define the nature of sin, we accepted the old definition, that sin is selfishness and rebellion against God, but we insisted on putting humanity into the picture. The definition of sin as selfishness gets its reality and nipping force only when we see humanity as a great solidarity and God indwelling in it In the same way the terms and definitions of salvation get more realistic significance and ethical reach when we see the internal crises of the individual in connection with the social forces that play upon him or go out from him. The form which the process of redemption takes in a given personality will be determined by the historical and social spiritual environment of the man. At any rate any religious experience in which our fellow-men have no part or thought, does not seem to be a distinctively Christian experience.

If sin is selfishness, salvation must be a change which turns a man from self to God and humanity. His sinfulness consisted in a selfish attitude, in which he was at the centre of the universe, and God and all his fellow-men were means to serve his pleasures, increase his wealth, and set off his egotisms. Complete salvation, therefore, would consist in an attitude of love in which he would freely co-ordinate his life with the life of his fellows in obedience to the loving impulses of the spirit of God, thus taking his part in a divine organism of mutual service. When a man is in a state of sin, he may be willing to harm the life and lower the self-respect of a woman for the sake of his desires; he may be willing to take some of the mental and spiritual values out of the life of a thousand families, and lower the human level of a whole mill-town in order to increase his own dividends or maintain his autocratic sense of power. If this man came under the influence of the mind of Christ, he would see men and women as children of God with divine worth and beauty, and this realization would cool his lust or covetousness. Living now in the consciousness of the pervading spiritual life of God, he would realize that all his gifts and resources are a loan of God for higher ends, and would do his work with greater simplicity of mind and brotherliness.

Of course in actual life there is no case of complete Christian transformation. It takes an awakened and regenerated mind a long time to find itself intellectually and discover what life henceforth is to mean to him, and his capacity for putting into practice what he knows he wants to do, will be something like the capacity of an untrained hand to express artistic imaginations. But in some germinal and rudimentary form salvation must turn us from a life centred on ourselves toward a life going out toward God and men. God is the all-embracing source and exponent of the common life and good of mankind. When we submit to God, we submit to the supremacy of the common good. Salvation is the voluntary socializing of the soul.

Conversion has usually been conceived as a break with our own sinful past. But in many cases it is also a break with the sinful past of a social group. Suppose a boy has been joining in cruel or lustful actions because his gang regards such things as fine and manly. If later he breaks with such actions, he will not only have to wrestle with his own habits, but with the social attractiveness and influence of his little humanity. If a working man becomes an abstainer, he will find out that intolerance is not confined to the good. In primitive Christianity baptism stood for a conscious break with pagan society. This gave it a powerful spiritual reaction. Conversion is most valuable if it throws a revealing light not only across our own past, but across the social life of which we are part, and makes our repentance a vicarious sorrow for all. The prophets felt so about the sins of their nation. Jesus felt so about Jerusalem, and Paul about unbelieving Israel.

We call our religious crisis "conversion" when we think of our own active break with old habits and associations and our turning to a new life. Paul introduced the forensic term "justification" into our religious vocabulary to express a changed legal status before God; his term "adoption" expresses the same change in terms derived from family life. We call the change "regeneration" when we think of it as an act of God within us, creating a new life.

The classical passage on regeneration (John 3) connects it with the Kingdom of God. Only an inward new birth will enable us to "see the Kingdom of God" and to "enter the Kingdom of God." The larger vision and the larger contact both require a new development of our spirit. In our unregenerate condition the consciousness of God is weak, occasional, and suppressed. The more Jesus Christ becomes dominant in us, the more does the light and life of God shine steadily in us, and create a religious personality which we did not have. Life is lived under a new synthesis.

It is strange and interesting that regeneration is thus connected with the Kingdom of God in John 3. The term has otherwise completely dropped out of the terminology of the fourth gospel. If we have here a verbatim memory of a saying of Jesus, the survival would indicate how closely the idea of personal regeneration was originally bound up with the Kingdom hope. When John the Baptist first called men to conversion and a change of mind, all his motives and appeals were taken from the outlook toward the Kingdom. Evidently the entire meaning of "conversion" and "regeneration" was subtly changed when the conception of the Kingdom disappeared from Christian thought. The change in ourselves was now no longer connected with a great divine change in humanity, for which we must prepare and get fit. If we are converted, what are we converted to? If we are regenerated, does the scope of so divine a transformation end in our "going to heaven?" The nexus between our religious experience and humanity seems gone when the Kingdom of God is not present in the idea of regeneration.

Through the experience and influence of Paul the word "faith" has gained a central place in the terminology of salvation. Its meaning fluctuates according to the dominant conception of religion. With Paul it was a comprehensive mystical symbol covering his whole inner experience of salvation and emancipation, which flooded his soul with joy and power. On the other hand wherever doctrine becomes rigid and is the pre-eminent thing in religion, "faith" means submission of the mind to the affirmations of dogma and theology, and, in particular, acceptance of the plan of salvation and trust in the vicarious atonement of Christ. Where the idea of the Church dominates religion, "faith" means mainly submission to the teaching and guidance of the Church. In popular religion it may shrivel up to something so small as putting a finger on a Scripture text and "claiming the promise."

In primitive Christianity the forward look of expectancy was characteristic of religion. The glory of the coming dawn was on the Eastern clouds. This influenced the conception of "faith." It was akin to hope, the forward gaze of the pioneers. The historical illustrations of faith in Hebrews 11 show faith launching life toward the unseen future.

This is the aspect of faith which is emphasized by the social gospel. It is not so much the endorsement of ideas formulated in the past, as expectancy and confidence in the coming salvation of God. In this respect the forward look of primitive Christianity is resumed. Faith once more means prophetic vision. It is faith to assume that this is a good world and that life is worth living. It is faith to assert the feasibility of a fairly righteous and fraternal social order. In the midst of a despotic and predatory industrial life it is faith to stake our business future on the proposition that fairness, kindness, and fraternity will work. When war inflames a nation, it is faith to believe that a peaceable disposition is a workable international policy. Amidst the disunion of Christendom it is faith to look for unity and to express unity in action. It is faith to see God at work in the world and to claim a share in his job. Faith is an energetic act of the will, affirming our fellowship with God and man, declaring our solidarity with the Kingdom of God, and repudiating selfish isolation.

"Sanctification," according to almost any definition, is the continuation of that process of spiritual education and transformation, by which a human personality becomes a willing organ of the spirit of Christ. Those who believe in the social gospel can share in any methods for the cultivation of the spiritual life, if only they have an ethical outcome. The social gospel takes up the message of the Hebrew prophets, that ritual and emotional religion is harmful unless it results in righteousness. Sanctification is through increased fellowship with God and man. But fellowship is impossible without an exchange of service. Here we come back to our previous proposition that the Kingdom of God is the commonwealth of co-operative service and that the most common form of sinful selfishness is the effort to escape from labor. Sanctification, therefore, can not be attained in an unproductive life, unless it is unproductive through necessity. In the long run the only true way to gain moral insight, self-discipline, humility, love, and a consciousness of coherence and dependence, is to take our place among those who serve one another by useful labor. Parasitism blinds; work reveals.

The fact that the social gospel is a distinct type of religious experience is proved by comparing it with mysticism. In most other types of Christianity the mystic experience is rated as the highest form of sanctification. In Catholicism the monastic life is the way of perfection, and mystic rapture is the highest attainment and reward of monastic contemplation and service. In

Protestantism, which has no monastic leisure for mystic exercises, mysticism is of a homelier type, but in almost every group of believers there are some individuals who profess to have attained a higher stage of sanctification through "a second blessing," "the higher life," "complete sanctification," "perfect love," Christian Science, or Theosophy. The literature and organizations ministering to this mystical life, go on the assumption that it far transcends the ordinary way in spiritual blessings and sanctifying power.

Mysticism is a steep short-cut to communion with God. There is no doubt that under favorable conditions it has produced beautiful results of unselfishness, humility, and undauntable courage. Its danger is that it isolates. In energetic mysticism the soul concentrates on God, shuts out the world, and is conscious only of God and itself. In its highest form, even the consciousness of self is swallowed up in the all-filling possession of God. No wonder it is absorbing and wonderful. But we have to turn our back on the world to attain this experience, and when we have attained it, it makes us indifferent to the world. What does Time matter when we can live in Eternity? What gift can this world offer us after we have entered into the luminous presence of God?

> The mystic way to holiness is not through humanity but above it. We can not set aside the fundamental law of God that way. He made us for one another, and our highest perfection comes not by isolation but by love. The way of holiness through human fellowship and service is slower and lowlier, but its results are more essentially Christian. Paul dealt with the mystic phenomena of religion when he dealt with the charismata of primitive Christianity, especially with glossolalia (1 Cor. 12-14). It is a striking fact that he ranks the spiritual gifts not according to their mystic rapture, but according to their rational control and their power of serving others. His great chapter on love dominates the whole discussion and is offered as a counter-poise and antidote to the dangers of mysticism.[1]

Mysticism is not the maturest form of sanctification. As Professor Royce well says: "It is the always young, it is the childlike, it is the essentially immature aspect of the deeper religious life. Its ardor, its pathos, its illusions,

[1] I have set this forth fully in my little book, "Dare We Be Christians?" (Pilgrim Press, Boston.) In my "Prayers of the Social Awakening" (Pilgrim Press), I have tried to connect the social consciousness with the devotional life by prayers envisioning social groups and movements. Professor Herrmann's "The Communion of the Christian with God " deals with the difference of the mystic way and the way of service.

and its genuine illuminations have all the characters of youth about them, characters beautiful, but capricious."[2] There is even question whether mysticism proper, with rapture and absorption, is Christian in its antecedents, or Platonic.

I believe in prayer and meditation in the presence of God; in the conscious purging of the soul from fear, love of gain, and selfish ambition, through realizing God; in bringing the intellect into alignment with the mind of Christ; and in re-affirming the allegiance of the will to the Kingdom of God. When a man goes up against hard work, conflict, loneliness, and the cross, it is his right to lean back on the Eternal and to draw from the silent reservoirs. But what we get thus is for use. Personal sanctification must serve the Kingdom of God. Any mystic experience which makes our fellowmen less real and our daily labour less noble, is dangerous religion. A religious experience is not Christian unless it binds us closer to men and commits us more deeply to the Kingdom of God.

Thus the fundamental theological terms about the experiences of salvation get a new orientation, correction, and enrichment through the religious point of view contained in the social gospel. These changes would effect an approximation to the spirit and outlook of primitive Christianity, going back of Catholicism and Protestantism alike.

The definitions we have attempted are not merely academic and hypothetical exercises. Religion is actually being experienced in such ways.

In the Bible we have several accounts of religious experiences which were fundamental in the life of its greatest characters. A few are told in their own striking phrases. Others are described by later writers, and in that case indicate what popular opinion expected such men to experience. Now, none of these experiences, so far as I see, are of that solitary type in which a soul struggles for its own salvation in order to escape the penalties of sin or to attain perfection and peace for itself. All were experienced with a conscious outlook toward humanity. When Moses saw the glory of God in the flaming bush and learned the ineffable name of the Eternal, it was not the salvation of Moses which was in question but the salvation of his people from the bondage of Egypt. When young Samuel first heard the call of the Voice in the darkness, it spoke to him of priestly extortion and the troubled future of his people. When Isaiah saw the glory of the Lord above the Cherubim, he realized by contrast that he was a man of unclean lips, but also that he dwelt

[2] Royce, "Problem of Christianity," I, p. 400.

among a people of unclean lips. His cleansing and the dedication which followed were his preparation for taking hold of the social situation of his nation. In Jeremiah we are supposed to have the attainment of the religion of the individual, but even his intimate experiences were all in full view of the fate of his nation. Paul's experience at Damascus was the culmination of his personal struggle and his emergence into spiritual freedom. But his crisis got its intensity from its social background. He was deciding, so far as he was concerned, between the old narrow nationalistic religion of conservative Judaism and a wider destiny for his people, between the validity of the Law and spiritual liberty, between the exclusive claims of Israel on the Messianic hope and a world-wide participation in the historical prerogatives of the first-born people. The issues for which his later life stood were condensed in the days at Damascus, as we can see from his own recital in Galatians 1, and these religious issues were the fundamental social questions for his nation at that time.

We cannot afford to rate this group of religious experiences at a low value. As with us all, the theology of the prophets was based on their personal experiences. Out of them grew their ethical monotheism and their God-consciousness. This was the highest element in the spiritual heritage of his people which came to Jesus. He re-interpreted and perfected it in his personality, and in that form it has remained the highest factor among the various historical strains combined in our religion.

These prophetic experiences were not superficial. There was soul-shaking emotion, a deep sense of sin, faith in God, longing for him, self-surrender, enduement with spiritual power. Yet they were not ascetic, not individualistic, not directed toward a future life. They were social, political, solidaristic.

The religious experiences evoked by the social gospel belong to the same type, though deeply modified, of course, by the profound differences between their age and ours. What the wars and oppressions of Israel and Judah meant to them, the wars and exploitations of modern civilization mean to us. In these things God speaks to our souls. When we face these questions we meet God. An increasing number of young men and women,—and some of the best of them—are getting their call to repentance, to a new way of life, and to the conquest of self in this way, and a good many older men are superimposing a new experience on that of their youth.

Other things being equal, a solidaristic religious experience is more distinctively Christian than an individualistic religious experience. To be afraid of hell or purgatory and desirous of a life without pain or trouble in heaven was not in itself Christian. It was self-interest on a higher level. It is not strange that men were wholly intent on saving themselves as long as such dangers as Dante describes were real to their minds. A man might be pardoned for forgetting his entire social consciousness if he found himself dangling over a blazing pit. But even in more spiritual forms of conversion, as long as men are wholly intent on their own destiny, they do not necessarily emerge from selfishness. It only changes its form. A Christian regeneration must have an outlook toward humanity and result in a higher social consciousness.

The saint of the future will need not only a theocentric mysticism which enables him to realize God, but an anthropocentric mysticism which enables him to realize his fellow-men in God. The more we approach pure Christianity, the more will the Christian signify a man who loves mankind with a religious passion and excludes none. The feeling which Jesus had when he said, "I am the hungry, the naked, the lonely," will be in the emotional consciousness of all holy men in the coming days. The sense of solidarity is one of the distinctive marks of the true followers of Jesus.

CHAPTER XI

THE SALVATION OF THE SUPER-PERSONAL FORCES

In discussing the doctrine of sin we faced the fact that redemption will have to deal not only with the weakness of flesh and blood, but with the strength of principalities and powers.[1] Beyond the feeble and short-lived individual towers the social group as a super-personal entity, dominating the individual, assimilating him to its moral standards, and enforcing them by the social sanctions of approval or disapproval.

When these super-personal forces are based on an evil principle, or directed toward an evil purpose, or corrupted by some controlling group interest which is hostile to the common good, they are sinners of sublimer mould, and they block the way of redemption. They are to us what demonic personalities were to earlier Christian minds. Men of religious vision have always seen social communities in that way. The prophets dealt with Israel and Judah, with Moab and Assyria, as with personalities having a continuous life and spirit and destiny. Jesus saw Jerusalem as a man might see a beloved woman who is driven by haughtiness and self-will into tragic ruin.

In our age these super-personal social forces present more difficult problems than ever before. The scope and diversity of combination is becoming constantly greater. The strategy of the Kingdom of God is short-sighted indeed if it does not devote thought to their salvation and conversion.

The salvation of the composite personalities, like that of individuals, consists in coming under the law of Christ. A few illustrations will explain how this applies.

Two principles are contending with each other for future control in the field of industrial and commercial organization, the capitalistic and the co-operative. The effectiveness of the capitalistic method in the production of wealth is not questioned; modern civilization is evidence of it. But we are also familiar with capitalistic methods in the production of human wreckage. Its one-sided control of economic power tempts to exploitation and oppres-

---

[1] Chapter VIII.

sion; it directs the productive process of society primarily toward the creation of private profit rather than the service of human needs; it demands autocratic management and strengthens the autocratic principle in all social affairs; it has impressed a materialistic spirit on our whole civilization.

On the other hand organizations formed on the co-operative principle are not primarily for profit but for the satisfaction of human wants, and the aim is to distribute ownership, control, and economic benefits to a large number of co-operators.

The difference between a capitalistic organization and a co-operative comes out clearly in the distribution of voting power. Capitalistic joint stock companies work on the plan of "one share, one vote." Therewith power is located in money. One crafty person who has a hundred shares can outvote ninety-nine righteous men who have a share apiece, and a small minority can outvote all the rest if it holds a majority of stock. Money is stronger than life, character, and personality.

Co-operatives work on the plan of "one man, one vote." A man who holds one share has as much voting power as a man with ten shares; his personality counts. If a man wants to lead and direct, he can not do it by money power; he must do it by character, sobriety, and good judgment. The small stockholders are not passive; they take part; they must be persuaded and taught. The superior ability of the capable can not outvote the rest, but has to train them. Consequently the co-operatives develop men and educate a community in helpful loyalty and comradeship. This is the advent of true democracy in economic life. Of course the co-operative principle is not a sovereign specific; the practical success of a given association depends on good judgment and the loyalty of its constituents. But the co-operatives, managed by plain men, often with little experience, have not only held their own in Europe against the picked survivors of the capitalistic competitive battle, but have forged steadily ahead into enormous financial totals, have survived and increased even during the war, and by their helpful moral influence have gone a long way to restore a country like Ireland which had long been drained and ruined by capitalism.

Here, I think, we have the difference between saved and unsaved organizations. The one class is under the law of Christ, the other under the law of mammon. The one is democratic and the other autocratic. Whenever capitalism has invaded a new country or industry, there has been a speeding up in labor and in the production of wealth, but always with a trail of human misery, discontent, bitterness, and demoralization. When co-operation has invaded a country there has been increased thrift, education, and neighborly feeling, and there has been no trail of concomitant evil and no cries of protest. The men in capitalistic business may be the best of men, far superior in ability to the average committee member of a co-operative, but the latter type of organization is the higher, and when co-operation has had as long a time to try out its methods as capitalism, the latter will rank with feudalism as an evil memory of mankind.

Super-personal forces are saved when they come under the law of Christ. A State which uses its terrible power of coercion to smite and crush offenders as a protection to the rest, is still under brutal law. A State which deals with those who have erred in the way of teaching, discipline, and restoration, has come under the law of Christ and is to that extent a saved community. "By their fruits ye shall know them." States are known by their courts and prisons and contract labor systems, or by their juvenile courts and parole systems. A change in penology may be an evidence of salvation.

A State which uses its superior power to overrun a weaker neighbor by force, or to wrest a valuable right of way from it by instigating a *coup d'état*, or uses intimidation to secure mining or railway concessions or to force a loan at usurious rates on a half-civilized State, is in mortal sin. A State which asks only for an open door and keeps its own door open in return, and which speaks as courteously to a backward State as to one with a big fleet, is to that extent a Christian community.[2]

With composite personalities as with individuals "the love of money is the root of all evil." Communities and nations fall into wild fits of anger and cruelty; they are vain and contemptuous of others; they lie and love lies; they sin against their critical conscience; they fall in love with virile and magnetic men just as women do. These are the temptations and dangers which every democracy will meet and from which it will recover with loss and some shame. But, as has been said before, evils become bold and permanent when there is money in them. It was the need of protecting wealth against poverty which made the courts and the criminal law so cruel in the past. It was theological superstition which started the epidemic of witch trials in Europe, but it was the large fees that fell to the lawyers and informers which made that craze so enduring. Nearly all modern wars have had their origin in the covetousness of trade and finance.[3]

---

[2] This matter of saving the community life has been discussed more fully in my book, "Christianizing the Social Order," the Macmillan Company, 1912.

[3] See historical instances in F. C. Howe, "Why War?"

If unearned gain is the chief corrupter of professions, institutions, and combinations of men, these super-personal beings will be put on the road to salvation when their graft is in some way cut off and they are compelled to subsist on the reward of honest service.

The history of the Church furnishes a striking example. For generations before the Reformation the condition of the Church and of the ministry was the sorest social question of the time, weighing heavily on the conscience of all good men. The ministrations of the Church, the sacrament of the altar, the merit gained by the sacrifice of the mass, the penitential system, the practice of indulgences, had been turned into means of great income to the Church and those who were in control of it. The rank and file of the priests and monks were from the common people, and their incomes were poor. But the higher positions of the Church and the wealthier monasteries were in possession of the upper classes, who filled the lucrative places with their younger sons or unmarried daughters. Where rich sinecures existed and an immense patronage was in the gift of the higher churchmen, the rake-off was naturally practised and perfected. Everyone who had paid for getting his position, recouped his investment. The highest institution of service had become the most glaring example of graft. Since the Church always resisted the interference of the laity, and since the oligarchy which surrounded the papacy was itself the chief beneficiary of the ecclesiastical graft, reform was successfully blocked out, or quickly lapsed when it was attempted.

It was this profit system in the Church which produced the religious unrest and finally the revolutionary upheaval of the Reformation in some nations. Men were not dissatisfied with the doctrines of the Church. There were surprisingly few theological heretics. Wycliffe and his followers are the only ones that gained popular influence, and his chief interest, too, was in the social utilization of the wealth of the Church. Men like Savonarola were not doctrinal reformers, but were trying to cleanse the Church of its graft and the resulting idleness and vice. The ideal of "the poverty of the Church" which was common to men so unlike as Saint Bernard, Arnold of Brescia, Saint Francis, and all the democratic sects, must be understood over against the vested wealth, the graft, and the semi-governmental power of the Church. They wanted the Church voluntarily to give up its wealth, and to put its ministers on the basis of service and the daily bread.

The Church refused to take this heroic path of repentance of its own free will. So it was compelled to take it. In all the countries which officially adopted the Reformation, the possessions and vested incomes of the Church were secularized. The sinecures mostly disappeared. The bishops lost their governmental functions. Everywhere the reform movements converged on this impoverishment of the Church with a kind of collective instinct Luther's theses on indulgences got their popularity not by their new and daring theology, for they were a hesitating and wavering statement of a groping mind,— but by the fact that they touched one of the chief sources of papal income. Several of the great doctrines of the Reformation got their vitality by their internal connection with the question of church property.

The process of reformation which stripped the Church of its landed wealth and privileges was nothing beautiful. It was high-class looting. Only a small portion of the wealth was used to endow education and charity. Most of it was seized by kings, princes, and nobles. This gave a new lease of life to autocracy, and in England set up some of the splendid aristocratic families, who still consume what was once given to God. But this unholy procedure did cleanse the Church and its ministry of graft. When there were few large incomes, the rake-off perforce ceased. A body of ministers developed who were on the whole educated, clean, and willing to serve to the best of their understanding on a meagre salary. A great profession had been saved. Its salvation did not come from theology, as theology would have us believe. Where the Roman Catholic clergy is on the basis of hard work and plain income, it has shown similar improvement. The remedy which purified the ministry and the Church "so as by fire" was that "poverty of the Church" which the medieval reformers had demanded. The average minister will not be in doubt that he has married the Lady Poverty, and that this keeps him from wantonness.

The salvation of the super-personal beings is by coming under the law of Christ. The fundamental step of repentance and conversion for professions and organizations is to give up monopoly power and the incomes derived from legalized extortion, and to come under the law of service, content with a fair income for honest work. The corresponding step in the case of governments and political oligarchies, both in monarchies and in capitalistic semi-democracies, is to submit to real democracy. Therewith they step out of the Kingdom of Evil into the Kingdom of God.

CHAPTER XII

THE CHURCH AS THE SOCIAL FACTOR OF SALVATION

What is the function of the Church in the process of salvation? What is it worth to a man to have the support and guidance of the Church in saving his soul?

If we listen to the Church's own estimate of itself it is worth as much as oxygen is to animal life. It is indispensable. "Outside of the Church there is no salvation." Very early in its history the Church began to take a deep interest in itself and to assert high things about itself. Every community is inclined to develop an expanded self-consciousness if the opportunity is at all favorable, and the Christian Church has certainly not let its opportunity go begging. Some historian has said, it is a wonder that the Church has not been made a person in the Godhead.

It is important to remember that when its high claims were first developed; they were really largely true. Christianity was in sharp opposition not only to the State but to the whole social life surrounding it. It created a Christian duplicate of the social order for its members, as far as it could. Christian influences were not yet diffused in society and literature. The Christian spirit and tradition could really be found nowhere except in the organized Christian groups. If the individual was to be impregnated with the saving power of Christianity, the Church had to do it. There was actually no salvation outside of the Church. But the statements in which men of the first generations expressed their genuine experience of what the Church meant to them, were turned into a theological formula and repeated in later times when the situation had changed, and when, for a time, the Church was not the supreme help but a great hindrance. The claims for the indispensability of the Church and its sacraments and officers became more specific as the hierarchic Church developed. First no man could be saved outside of the Church; next he could not be saved unless he was in right relation to his bishop; and finally he could not be saved unless he submitted to the Roman pontiff.

What are the functions of the Church in salvation, and how indispensable is it? And what has the social gospel to say to the theological valuation of the Church?

The Church is the social factor in salvation. It brings social forces to bear on evil. It offers Christ not only many human bodies and minds to serve as ministers of his salvation, but its own composite personality, with a collective memory stored with great hymns and Bible stories and deeds of heroism, with trained aesthetic and moral feelings, and with a collective will set on righteousness. A super-personal being organized around an evil principle and set on predatory aims is the most potent breeder of sin in individuals and in other communities. What, then, might a super-personal being do which would be organized around Jesus Christ as its impelling power, and would have for its sole or chief object to embody his spirit in its life and to carry him into human thought and the conduct of affairs?

If there had never been such an organization as the Christian Church, every great religious mind would dream of the possibility of creating something like it. He would imagine the happy life within it where men shared the impulses of love and the convictions about life which Jesus imparted to humanity. If he understood psychology and social science, he would see the possibilities of such a social group in arousing and guiding the unformed spiritual aspirations of the young and reinforcing wayward consciences by the approval or disapproval of the best persons, and its power of reaching by free loyalty springs of action and character lying too deep for civil law and even for education to stir. He might well imagine too how the presence of such a social group would quicken and balance the civil and political community.

How far the actualities of church life fall short of such an ideal forecast, most of us know but too well. But even so, the importance of the social factor in salvation is clear from whatever angle we look at it What chance would a disembodied spirit of Christianity have, whispering occasionally at the key-hole of the human heart? Nothing lasts unless it is organized, and if it is organized of human life, we must put up with the qualities of human life in it.

Within the field it has chosen to cultivate, the local church under good leadership is really a power of salvation. During the formative years of our national growth the churches gathered up the available resources of education, history, philosophy, eloquence, art, and music, and established social centres controlled by the highest possessions known to people whose other resources were the family, money, gossip, the daily paper, and the inevitable vices. The great ideas of the spiritual life God, the soul, duty, sin, holiness, eternity would today be wholly absent in many minds, and in most others would be but flickering lights, if the local churches did not cherish and affirm them, and make them glorious and persuasive by the most effective combination of social influences ever accumulated by any organization during a history lasting for centuries and spread through many nations.

We are so accustomed to the churches that we hardly realize what a social force they exert over the minds they do influence. If we could observe a native Christian church in a pagan people, after the Christian organization is once in operation as a social organism, and is weaning families and village communities from pagan customs and assimilating them to the new ideas, we should realize better the power of conservation exerted in our own communities.[1] The new religion of Christian Science provides another chance for such a realization. It expounds a new religious book alongside of the Bible, and a new prophet alongside of Christ, and thus creates a novel religious consciousness among its own people. It has taken many nervous, unhappy, and burdened persons, and has given health to their bodies and calmness and self-control to their minds by attacking and subduing their souls with a dogmatic faith, till they learn to contradict the rheumatic facts of life and to ignore even the presence of death by looking the other way. If we could see the old churches as clearly as we see this new church, we should realize their power.

The men who stand for the social gospel have been among the most active critics of the churches because they have realized most clearly both the great needs of our social life and the potential capacities of the Church to meet them. Their criticism has been a form of compliment to the Church. I think they may yet turn out to be the apologists whom the Church most needs at present. They are best fitted to see that while the Church influences society, society has always influenced the Church, and that the Church, when it has dropped to the level of its environment, has simply yielded to the law of social gravitation. This is true of the delinquencies of the Church in past ages, which lie heavily on our minds when we want to describe the Church as the great organism of salvation. Those whose expectations are created by the claims of the Church about itself may well be profoundly dis-

[1] "Social Christianity in the Orient," by Emma Rauschenbusch Clough, Ph.D. (Macmillan Company) is a striking narrative of the revolutionary effect of the introduction of Christianity in an Indian pariah tribe.

appointed when they go through some of the bad chapters of Church History. If they have to judge it by its own absolute religious criteria as the body of Christ and the exponent of his spirit, the gap between the ideal and the reality is painful. The fact is that the Church has watered its own stock and can not pay dividends on all the paper it has issued. It has made claims for itself to which no organization composed of humans can live up. If we see it simply as an attempt to give social expression to the life derived from Christ, we shall not feel too deeply disappointed when we see it fail. True social insight knows that its sins were always the sins of the age. If the Church was autocratic and oppressive, so were all governments. There was graft in the Church, but the feudal aristocracy was founded on graft, and it never fought it as the Church fought simony.

A fresh understanding for the indispensableness of the Church is gaining ground today in Protestant theology in spite of the increased knowledge of the past and present failures of the Church. This is an attempt to overcome the exaggerated individualism into which Protestantism was thrust by the violent reactions of the Reformation. When men were in the throes of a revolution against a Church which claimed everything, they naturally denied every claim by which the enemy could brace its authority. They denied the authority of the tradition and decrees of the Church and made the Bible the sole source of truth. They denied the doctrine of the eucharist because the mass was the chief monopoly right from which the Church drew material income and spiritual reverence. They emphasized and elaborated the doctrine of election because it effectively eliminated the middle-man in salvation; for it put man into direct contact with the source of salvation, and made the decree of salvation wholly independent of any human act or church mediation. But the result of this great polemical reaction against the Church was a system of religious individualism in which the social forces of salvation were slighted, and God and the individual were almost the only realities in sight.

Of course in actual practice the Protestant churches exercised very stout control over their members. Calvin, in a celebrated passage of the Institutes comes close to a social appreciation of the functions of the Church:

> "But, as it is now our purpose to discourse of the visible Church, let us learn, from her single title of Mother, how useful, nay, how necessary the knowledge of her is, since there is no other means of entering into life unless she conceive us in the womb and give us birth, unless she nourish us at her breasts, and, in short, keep us under her charge and

> government, until, divested of mortal flesh, we become like the angels.— Moreover, beyond the pale of the Church no forgiveness of sins, no salvation, can be hoped for, as Isaiah and Joel testify.— The paternal favour of God and the special evidence of spiritual life are confined to his peculiar people, and hence the abandonment of the Church is always fatal."[2]

But all of us who have had to acquire our social and historical comprehension laboriously will appreciate how little the old Protestant system stimulated and developed the understanding of the social factor in redemption.

The individualism of Reformation theology is being overcome by a new insistence on the importance of the Church. This trend of thought is not due, as in Anglican theology, to a renascence of Catholicism, but to a combination of purified Protestantism and modern social insight. I have been struck by the eminence of some of the prophets of this new solidaristic strain in theology.

Schleiermacher in his earlier "Reden über die Religion" still interpreted the religious sense of dependence as an individual experience. Maturer reflection showed him that all personal life is determined by the spirit of the community with which it is organically connected. This is true of the religious life too. Our sin is due to the feebleness with which we realize God. Jesus lived in complete and unbroken consciousness of God. Contact with him can so strengthen the God-consciousness in us that we are able to overcome the power of sin and rise to newness of life. But the memory of his life and the consciousness of salvation in him are transmitted to us only by the Church. We share his consciousness by sharing the common faith and experience of the Church. The new life of the individual is mediated by the social organism which is already in possession of that life.

"The Protestant theology of our age rests on the foundation laid by Schleiermacher; all theologians some directly, some more indirectly are seeking to establish the connections between the religious personality of the individual and the common consciousness of the Church."[3]

Ritschl, the most vigorous and influential theological intellect in Germany since Schleiermacher, is evidence of this. He abandoned the doctrine of original sin but substituted the solidaristic conception of the Kingdom of Evil. He held that salvation is embodied in a community which has experienced salvation; the faith of the individual is part of the faith of the Church.

---

[2] Calvin, "Institutes of the Christian Religion" Book IV, i, 4.

[3] Pfleiderer, Glaubens-und Sittenlehre. §55.

The Church and not the individual is the object of justification; the assurance of forgiveness for the individual is based on his union with the Church.

In American thought the most striking utterance on the indispensable importance of the Church in salvation has come from an eminent outsider, a philosopher and not a theologian, Professor Royce. He had worked out "the philosophy of loyalty" in other fields, and then applied it to religion in "the Problem of Christianity" (1913). This book is the mature product of his life, and its argument is evidently uplifted by the conviction that he had discovered some highly important facts.

Professor Royce, as has been said before, held that there are in the human world two profoundly different grades or levels of mental beings, namely individuals and communities, and he calls it the most significant of all moral and religious truths "that a community, when unified by an active, indwelling purpose, is an entity more concrete and less mysterious than any individual man, and can love and be loved as a husband and wife love." What is love between man and man, becomes loyalty when it goes out from a man to his community.

Professor Royce felt profoundly on the sin of the individual. "The individual human being is by nature subject to some overwhelming moral burden, from which, if unaided, he cannot escape. Both because of what has been technically called original sin, and because of the sins that he himself has committed, the individual is doomed to a spiritual ruin from which only a divine intervention can save him." (Lecture III,) He "cannot unaided win the true goal of life. Help must come to him from some source above his own level."

The individual is saved, if at all, by membership in a community which has salvation. When a man becomes loyal to a community, he identifies himself with its life; he appropriates its past history and memories, its experiences and hopes, and absorbs its spirit and faith. This is the power which can lift him above his own level.

The Christian religion possesses such a community. It first comes into full view in the Pauline epistles. How it originated is a mystery like the origin of life, for loyalty is always evoked by the loyalty of those who already have it. Paul did not create it; he only formulated its ideas.

Professor Royce thinks the creation of the Church was the most important event in the history of Christianity. Not Christ but the Church is the central idea of Christianity. He rates Jesus largely as an indispensable basis on which the Church could form and stand. He thinks we know little about him, and that Jesus defined the Christian ideas inadequately. But his name was the great symbol of loyalty for the Church. The doctrines about him were developed because they were necessary for the consolidation of the Church.

This slighting of Jesus is one of the most unsatisfactory elements in Royce's thought. If the awakening of loyalty is "a spiritual triumph beyond the wit of man;" if "you are first made loyal through the power of someone else who is loyal;" if "no social will can make the community lovable unless loyalty is previously effective;" then the origin of "the beloved community" is the great problem in the history of Christianity, and everything points to Jesus as the only solution. He performed the miracle of the origin of life. A proper evaluation of Jesus as the initiator would have been the natural and necessary consummation of this entire doctrine of salvation by loyalty.

A tacit condition is attached to all the high claims made by Professor Royce and others on behalf of the Church: If the Church is to have saving power, it must embody Christ. He is the revolutionary force within it. The saving qualities of the Church depend on the question whether it has translated the personal life of Jesus Christ into the social life of its group and thus brings it to bear on the individual. If Christ is not in the Church, how does it differ from "the world?" It will still assimilate its members, but it will not make them persons bearing the family likeness of the first-born son of God.

Wherever the Church has lost the saving influence of Christ, it has lost its saltness and is a tasteless historical survival. Therewith all theological doctrines about it become untrue. Antiquity and continuity are no substitute for the vitality of the Christ-spirit. Age, instead of being a presumption in favor of a religious body, is a question-mark set over against its name. The world is full of stale religion. It is historically self-evident that church bodies do lose the saving power. In fact, they may become social agencies to keep their people stupid, stationary, superstitious, bigoted, and ready to choke their first-born ideals and instincts as a sacrifice to the God of stationariness whom their religious guides have imposed on them. Wherever an aged and proud Church sets up high claims as an indispensable institution of salvation, let it be tested by the cleanliness, education, and moral elasticity of the agricultural labourers whom it has long controlled, or of the slum dwellers who have long ago slipped out of its control.

This conditional form of predicating the saving power and spiritual authority of the Church is only one more way of asserting that in anything which claims to be Christian, religion must have an immediate ethical nexus and effect. This marks an essential difference between the claims made for the Church in Catholic theology, and the emphasis on the functions of the Church made in the social gospel. The Catholic doctrine of the Church made its holiness, its power to forgive sin, and the efficacy of its sacraments independent of the moral character of its priests and people; the social conception makes everything conditional on the spiritual virtues of the church group. The Catholic conception stakes the claims of the Church and its clergy on the due legal succession and canonical ordination of its chief officers. This imports legal conceptions derived from the imperial Roman bureaucracy into the organism of the Christian Church, which has nothing to do with any bureaucracy. It gives an unquestioned status to some corrupt, venal, or ignorant bishop in Southern Italy; makes the ecclesiastical validity of the entire Anglican clergy dubious; and denies all standing to Chalmers, Spurgeon, or Asbury. The social gospel, on the other hand, tests the claims and powers of any Church by the continuity of the apostolic faith within it and by its possession of the law and spirit of Jesus.

The saving power of the Church does not rest on its institutional character, on its continuity, its ordination, its ministry, or its doctrine. It rests on the presence of the Kingdom of God within her. The Church grows old; the Kingdom is ever young. The Church is a perpetuation of the past; the Kingdom is the power of the coming age. Unless the Church is vitalized by the ever nascent forces of the Kingdom within her, she deadens instead of begetting.

CHAPTER XIII

THE KINGDOM OF GOD

If theology is to offer an adequate doctrinal basis for the social gospel, it must not only make room for the doctrine of the Kingdom of God, but give it a central place and revise all other doctrines so that they will articulate organically with it

This doctrine is itself the social gospel. Without it, the idea of redeeming the social order will be but an annex to the orthodox conception of the scheme of salvation. It will live like a negro servant family in a detached cabin back of the white man's house in the South. If this doctrine gets the place which has always been its legitimate right, the practical proclamation and application of social morality will have a firm footing.

To those whose minds live in the social gospel, the Kingdom of God is a dear truth, the marrow of the gospel, just as the incarnation was to Athanasius, justification by faith alone to Luther, and the sovereignty of God to Jonathan Edwards. It was just as dear to Jesus. He too lived in it, and from it looked out on the world and the work he had to do.

Jesus always spoke of the Kingdom of God. Only two of his reported sayings contain the word "Church" and both passages are of questionable authenticity. It is safe to say that he never thought of founding the kind of institution which afterward claimed to be acting for him.

Yet immediately after his death, groups of disciples joined and consolidated by inward necessity. Each local group knew that it was part of a divinely founded fellowship mysteriously spreading through humanity, and awaiting the return of the Lord and the establishing of his Kingdom. This universal Church was loved with the same religious faith and reverence with which Jesus had loved the Kingdom of God. It was the partial and earthly realization of the divine Society, and at the Parousia the Church and the Kingdom would merge.

But the Kingdom was merely a hope, the Church a present reality. The chief interest and affection flowed toward the Church. Soon, through a combination of causes, the name and idea of "the Kingdom" began to be displaced by the name and idea of "the Church" in the preaching, literature, and theological thought of the Church. Augustine completed this process in his *De Civitate Dei.* The Kingdom of God which has, throughout human history, opposed the Kingdom of Sin, is to-day embodied in the Church. The millennium began when the Church was founded. This practically substituted the actual, not the ideal Church for the Kingdom of God. The beloved ideal of Jesus became a vague phrase which kept intruding from the New Testament. Like Cinderella in the kitchen, it saw the other great dogmas furbished up for the ball, but no prince of theology restored it to its rightful place. The Reformation, too, brought no renascence of the doctrine of the Kingdom; it had only eschatological value, or was defined in blurred phrases borrowed from the Church. The present revival of the Kingdom idea is due to the combined influence of the historical study of the Bible and of the social gospel.

When the doctrine of the Kingdom of God shriveled to an undeveloped and pathetic remnant in Christian thought, this loss was bound to have far-reaching consequences. We are told that the loss of a single tooth from the arch of the mouth in childhood may spoil the symmetrical development of the skull and produce malformations affecting the mind and character. The atrophy of that idea which had occupied the chief place in the mind of Jesus, necessarily affected the conception of Christianity, the life of the Church, the progress of humanity, and the structure of theology. I shall briefly enumerate some of the consequences affecting theology. This list, however, is by no means complete.

1. Theology lost its contact with the synoptic thought of Jesus. Its problems were not at all the same which had occupied his mind. It lost his point of view and became to some extent incapable of understanding him. His ideas had to be rediscovered in our time. Traditional theology and the mind of Jesus Christ became incommensurable quantities. It claimed to regard his revelation and the substance of his thought as divine, and yet did not learn to think like him. The loss of the Kingdom idea is one key to this situation.

2. The distinctive ethical principles of Jesus were the direct outgrowth of his conception of the Kingdom of God. When the latter disappeared from theology, the former disappeared from ethics. Only persons having the substance of the Kingdom ideal in their minds, seem to be able to get relish out of the ethics of Jesus. Only those church bodies which have been in opposition to organized society and have looked for a better city with its foundations in heaven, have taken the Sermon on the Mount seriously.

3. The Church is primarily a fellowship for worship; the Kingdom is a fellowship of righteousness. When the latter was neglected in theology, the ethical force of Christianity was weakened; when the former was emphasized in theology, the importance of worship was exaggerated. The prophets and Jesus had cried down sacrifices and ceremonial performances, and cried up righteousness, mercy, solidarity. Theology now reversed this, and by its theoretical discussions did its best to stimulate sacramental actions and priestly importance. Thus the religious energy and enthusiasm which might have saved mankind from its great sins, were used up in hearing and endowing masses, or in maintaining competitive church organizations, while mankind is still stuck in the mud. There are nations in which the ethical condition of the masses is the reverse of the frequency of the masses in the churches.

4. When the Kingdom ceased to be the dominating religious reality, the Church moved up into the position of the supreme good. To promote the power of the Church and its control over all rival political forces was equivalent to promoting the supreme ends of Christianity. This increased the arrogance of churchmen and took the moral check off their policies. For the Kingdom of God can never be promoted by lies, craft, crime or war, but the wealth and power of the Church have often been promoted by these means. The medieval ideal of the supremacy of the Church over the State was the logical consequence of making the Church the highest good with no superior ethical standard by which to test it. The medieval doctrines concerning the Church and the Papacy were the direct theological outcome of the struggles for Church supremacy, and were meant to be weapons in that struggle.

5. The Kingdom ideal is the test and corrective of the influence of the Church. When the Kingdom ideal disappeared, the conscience of the Church was muffled. It became possible for the missionary expansion of Christianity to halt for centuries without creating any sense of shortcoming. It became possible for the most unjust social conditions to fasten themselves on Christian nations without awakening any consciousness that the purpose of Christ was being defied and beaten back. The practical undertakings of the Church remained within narrow lines, and the theological thought of the Church was necessarily confined in a similar way. The claims of the Church were allowed to stand in theology with no conditions and obligations to test and balance them. If the Kingdom had stood as the purpose for which the Church exists, the Church could not have fallen into such corrup-

tion and sloth. Theology bears part of the guilt for the pride, the greed, and the ambition of the Church.

6. The Kingdom ideal contains the revolutionary force of Christianity. When this ideal faded out of the systematic thought of the Church, it became a conservative social influence and increased the weight of the other stationary forces in society. If the Kingdom of God had remained part of the theological and Christian consciousness, the Church could not, down to our times, have been salaried by autocratic class governments to keep the democratic and economic impulses of the people under check.

7. Reversely, the movements for democracy and social justice were left without a religious backing for lack of the Kingdom idea. The Kingdom of God as the fellowship of righteousness, would be advanced by the abolition of industrial slavery and the disappearance of the slums of civilization; the Church would only indirectly gain through such social changes. Even today many Christians can not see any religious importance in social justice and fraternity because it does not increase the number of conversions nor fill the churches. Thus the practical conception of salvation, which is the effective theology of the common man and minister, has been cut back and crippled for lack of the Kingdom ideal.

8. Secular life is belittled as compared with church life. Services rendered to the Church get a higher religious rating than services rendered to the community.[1] Thus the religious value is taken out of the activities of the common man and the prophetic services to society. Wherever the Kingdom of God is a living reality in Christian thought, any advance of social righteousness is seen as a part of redemption and arouses inward joy and the triumphant sense of salvation. When the Church absorbs interest, a subtle asceticism creeps back into our theology and the world looks different.

9. When the doctrine of the Kingdom of God is lacking in theology, the salvation of the individual is seen in its relation to the Church and to the future life, but not in its relation to the task of saving the social order. Theology has left this important point in a condition so hazy and muddled that it has taken us almost a generation to see that the salvation of the individual and the redemption of the social order are closely related, and how.

10. Finally, theology has been deprived of the inspiration of great ideas contained in the idea of the Kingdom and in labor for it. The Kingdom of

[1] After the death of Susan B. Anthony a minister commented on her life, regretting that she was not orthodox in her beliefs. In the same address he spoke glowingly about a new linoleum laid in the church kitchen.

God breeds prophets; the Church breeds priests and theologians. The Church runs to tradition and dogma; the Kingdom of God rejoices in forecasts and boundless horizons. The men who have contributed the most fruitful impulses to Christian thought have been men of prophetic vision, and their theology has proved most effective for future times where it has been most concerned with past history, with present social problems, and with the future of human society. The Kingdom of God is to theology what outdoor colour and light are to art. It is impossible to estimate what inspirational impulses have been lost to theology and to the Church, because it did not develop the doctrine of the Kingdom of God and see the world and its redemption from that point of view.

These are some of the historical effects which the loss of the doctrine of the Kingdom of God has inflicted on systematic theology. The chief contribution which the social gospel has made and will make to theology is to give new vitality and importance to that doctrine. In doing so it will be a reformatory force of the highest importance in the field of doctrinal theology, for any systematic conception of Christianity must be not only defective but incorrect if the idea of the Kingdom of God does not govern it.

The restoration of the doctrine of the Kingdom has already made progress. Some of the ablest and most voluminous works of the old theology in their thousands of pages gave the Kingdom of God but a scanty mention, usually in connection with eschatology, and saw no connection between it and the Calvinistic doctrines of personal redemption. The newer manuals not only make constant reference to it in connection with various doctrines, but they arrange their entire subject matter so that the Kingdom of God becomes the governing idea.[2]

---

[2] William Adams Brown, "Christian Theology in Outline," p. 192: "We are witnessing to-day a reaction against this exaggerated individualism (of Reformation theology). It has become an axiom of modern thought that the government of God has social as well as individual significance, and the conception of the Kingdom of God obscured in the earlier Protestantism is coming again into the forefront of theological thought." See the discussion on "The View of the Kingdom in Modern Thought" which follows. Albrecht Ritschl, in his great monograph on Justification and Reconciliation, begins the discussion of his own views in Volume III (§2) by insisting that personal salvation must be organically connected with the Kingdom of God. He says ("Rechtfertigung und Versöhnung," III, p. 111): "Theology has taken a very un-equal interest in the two chief characteristics of Christianity. Everything pertaining to its character as the redemption of men has been made the subject of the most minute consideration; consequently redemption by Christ has been taken as the centre of all Christian knowledge and life, whereas the ethical conception of Christianity contained in the idea of the Kingdom of God has

In the following brief propositions I should like to offer a few suggestions, on behalf of the social gospel, for the theological formulation of the doctrine of the Kingdom. Something like this is needed to give us " a theology for the social gospel."

1. The Kingdom of God is divine in its origin, progress and consummation. It was initiated by Jesus Christ, in whom the prophetic spirit came to its consummation, it is sustained by the Holy Spirit, and it will be brought to its fulfilment by the power of God in his own time. The passive and active resistance of the Kingdom of Evil at every stage of its advance is so great, and the human resources of the Kingdom of God so slender, that no explanation can satisfy a religious mind which does not see the power of God in its movements. The Kingdom of God, therefore, is miraculous all the way, and is the continuous revelation of the power, the righteousness, and the love of God. The establishment of a community of righteousness in mankind is just as much a saving act of God as the salvation of an individual from his natural selfishness and moral inability. The Kingdom of God, therefore, is not merely ethical, but has a rightful place in theology. This doctrine is absolutely necessary to establish that organic union between religion and morality, between theology and ethics, which is one of the characteristics of the Christian religion. When our moral actions are consciously related to the Kingdom of God they gain religious quality. Without this doctrine we shall have expositions of schemes of redemption and we shall have systems of ethics, but we shall not have a true exposition of Christianity. The first step to the reform of the Churches is the restoration of the doctrine of the Kingdom of God.

2. The Kingdom of God contains the teleology of the Christian religion. It translates theology from the static to the dynamic. It sees, not doctrines or rites to be conserved and perpetuated, but resistance to be overcome and great ends to be achieved. Since the Kingdom of God is the supreme purpose of God, we shall understand the Kingdom so far as we understand

---

been slighted. ... It has been fatal for Protestantism that the Reformers did not cleanse the idea of the ethical Kingdom of God or Christ from its hierarchical corruption (i.e. the idea that the visible Church is identical with the Kingdom), but worked out the idea only in an academic and unpractical form." Kant first recognized the importance of the Kingdom of God for ethics. Schleiermacher first applied the teleological quality of Christianity to the definition of its nature, but he still treated now of personal redemption and now of the Kingdom of God, without adequately working out their connection. Ritschl has done more than any one else to put the idea to the front in German theology, but he does not get beyond a few great general ideas. He was born too early to get sociological ideas.

God, and we shall understand God so far as we understand his Kingdom. As long as organized sin is in the world, the Kingdom of God is characterized by conflict with evil. But if there were no evil, or after evil has been overcome, the Kingdom of God will still be the end to which God is lifting the race. It is realized not only by redemption, but also by the education of mankind and the revelation of his life within it.

3. Since God is in it, the Kingdom of God is always both present and future. Like God it is in all tenses, eternal in the midst of time. It is the energy of God realizing itself in human life. Its future lies among the mysteries of God. It invites and justifies prophecy, but all prophecy is fallible; it is valuable in so far as it grows out of action for the Kingdom and impels action. No theories about the future of the Kingdom of God are likely to be valuable or true which paralyze or postpone redemptive action on our part. To those who postpone, it is a theory and not a reality. It is for us to see the Kingdom of God as always coming, always pressing in on the present, always big with possibility, and always inviting immediate action. We walk by faith. Every human life is so placed that it can share with God in the creation of the Kingdom, or can resist and retard its progress. The Kingdom is for each of us the supreme task and the supreme gift of God. By accepting it as a task, we experience it as a gift. By labouring for it we enter into the joy and peace of the Kingdom as our divine fatherland and habitation.

4. Even before Christ, men of God saw the Kingdom of God as the great end to which all divine leadings were pointing. Every idealistic interpretation of the world, religious or philosophical, needs some such conception. Within the Christian religion the idea of the Kingdom gets its distinctive interpretation from Christ, (a) Jesus emancipated the idea of the Kingdom from previous nationalistic limitations and from the debasement of lower religious tendencies, and made it world-wide and spiritual. (b) He made the purpose of salvation essential in it. (c) He imposed his own mind, his personality, his love and holy will on the idea of the Kingdom, (d) He not only foretold it but initiated it by his life and work. As humanity more and more develops a racial consciousness in modern life, idealistic interpretations of the destiny of humanity will become more influential and important. Unless theology has a solidaristic vision higher and fuller than any other, it can not maintain the spiritual leadership of mankind, but will be outdistanced. Its business is to infuse the distinctive qualities of Jesus Christ into its teachings about the Kingdom, and this will be a fresh competitive test of his continued headship of humanity.

5. The Kingdom of God is humanity organized according to the will of God. Interpreting it through the consciousness of Jesus we may affirm these convictions about the ethical relations within the Kingdom: (a) Since Christ revealed the divine worth of life and personality, and since his salvation seeks the restoration and fulfilment of even the least, it follows that the Kingdom of God, at every stage of human development, tends toward a social order which will best guarantee to all personalities their freest and highest development This involves the redemption of social life from the cramping influence of religious bigotry, from the repression of self-assertion in the relation of upper and lower classes, and from all forms of slavery in which human beings are treated as mere means to serve the ends of others, (b) Since love is the supreme law of Christ, the Kingdom of God implies a progressive reign of love in human affairs. We can see its advance wherever the free will of love supersedes the use of force and legal coercion as a regulative of the social order. This involves the redemption of society from political autocracies and economic oligarchies; the substitution of redemptive for vindictive penology; the abolition of constraint through hunger as part of the industrial system; and the abolition of war as the supreme expression of hate and the completest cessation of freedom, (c) The highest expression of love is the free surrender of what is truly our own, life, property, and rights. A much lower but perhaps more decisive expression of love is the surrender of any opportunity to exploit men. No social group or organization can claim to be clearly within the Kingdom of God which drains others for its own ease, and resists the effort to abate this fundamental evil. This involves the redemption of society from private property in the natural resources of the earth, and from any condition in industry which makes monopoly profits possible. (d) The reign of love tends toward the progressive unity of mankind, but with the maintenance of individual liberty and the opportunity of nations to work out their own national peculiarities and ideals.

6. Since the Kingdom is the supreme end of God, it must be the purpose for which the Church exists. The measure in which it fulfils this purpose is also the measure of its spiritual authority and honour. The institutions of the Church, its activities, its worship, and its theology must in the long run be tested by its effectiveness in creating the Kingdom of God. For the Church to see itself apart from the Kingdom, and to find its aims in itself, is the same sin of selfish detachment as when an individual selfishly separates himself from the common good. The Church has the power to save in so far as the Kingdom of God is present in it. If the Church is not

living for the Kingdom, its institutions are part of the " world." In that case it is not the power of redemption but its object It may even become an anti-Christian power. If any form of church organization which formerly aided the Kingdom now impedes it, the reason for its existence is gone.

7. Since the Kingdom is the supreme end, all problems of personal salvation must be reconsidered from the point of view of the Kingdom. It is not sufficient to set the two aims of Christianity side by side. There must be a synthesis, and theology must explain how the two react on each other. (See Chapter X of this book.) The entire redemptive work of Christ must also be reconsidered under this orientation. Early Greek theology saw salvation chiefly as the redemption from ignorance by the revelation of God and from earthliness by the impartation of immortality. It interpreted the work of Christ accordingly, and laid stress on his incarnation and resurrection. Western theology saw salvation mainly as forgiveness of guilt and freedom from punishment. It interpreted the work of Christ accordingly, and laid stress on the death and atonement. If the Kingdom of God was the guiding idea and chief end of Jesus — as we now know it was — we may be sure that every step in His life, including His death, was related to that aim and its realization, and when the idea of the Kingdom of God takes its due place in theology, the work of Christ will have to be interpreted afresh.

8. The Kingdom of God is not confined within the limits of the Church and its activities. It embraces the whole of human life. It is the Christian transfiguration of the social order. The Church is one social institution alongside of the family, the industrial organization of society, and the State. The Kingdom of God is in all these, and realizes itself through them all. During the Middle Ages all society was ruled and guided by the Church. Few of us would want modern life to return to such a condition. Functions which the Church used to perform, have now far outgrown its capacities. The Church is indispensable to the religious education of humanity and to the conservation of religion, but the greatest future awaits religion in the public life of humanity.

Chapter XIV

The Initiator of the Kingdom of God

The social gospel has an inherent interest in history. Individualistic theology sees everywhere countless sinful individuals who must all go through the same process of repentance, faith, justification, and regeneration, and who in due time die and go to heaven or hell. The historical age in which a person lived, or the social class or race to which he belonged, matters little. This religious point of view is above time and history. On the other hand the social gospel tries to see the progress of the Kingdom of God in the flow of history; not only in the doings of the Church, but in the clash of economic forces and social classes, in the rise and fall of despotisms and forms of enslavement, in the rise of new value-judgments and fresh canons of moral taste and sentiment, or the elevation or decline of moral standards. Its chief interest is the Kingdom of God; and the Kingdom of God is history seen in a religious and teleological way. Therefore the social gospel is always historically minded. Its spread goes hand in hand with the spread of the historical spirit and method.

This dominant interest in the creation and progress of social redemption influences the approach to the theological problems of the person and work of Christ. We want to see the Christ who initiated the Kingdom of God. Theologians have always tried to make their christology match with their conception of salvation. If they believed salvation to consist chiefly in the knowledge of God, they emphasized the personality and the doctrine of Christ as the complete revelation of God. If they made salvation to consist chiefly in the mystic impartation of divine life and immortality, their christology laid chief stress on the union of the divine and human in the incarnation and in the sacraments. If salvation consists above all in the expiation of guilt, the forgiveness of sins, the justification of the sinner, and the remission of his penalties, then we need a Christ who made atonement for our sins, rendered satisfaction to God for our delinquencies, and offset our guilty defects by his infinite merit and divine virtue. Each conception of salvation made a pragmatic selection and construction of the facts. Each was fragmentary, but without necessarily excluding other series of ideas. So now the social gospel, without excluding other theological convictions, demands to understand that Christ who set in motion the historical forces of redemption which are to overthrow the Kingdom of Evil.

This is surely not an illegitimate interest. It is a return to the earliest messianic theology; whereas some of the other christological interests and ideas are alien importations, part of that wave of "Hellenization" which nearly swamped the original gospel.

Being historically minded and realistic in its interests, the social gospel is less concerned in the metaphysical problems involved in the trinitarian and christological doctrines. The speculative problem of christological dogma was how the divine and human natures united in the one person of Christ; the problem of the social gospel is how the divine life of Christ can get control of human society. The social gospel is concerned about a progressive social incarnation of God.

The social gospel is believed by trinitarians and unitarians alike, by Catholic Modernists and Kansas Presbyterians of the most cerulean colour. It arouses a fresh and warm loyalty to Christ wherever it goes, though not always a loyalty to the Church. All who believe in it are at one in desiring the spiritual sovereignty of Christ in humanity. Their attitude to the problems of the creeds will usually be determined by other influences.

Yet there are certain qualities in the social gospel which may create a feeling of apathy toward the speculative questions. It is modern and is out for realities. It is ethical and wants ethical results from theology. It is solidaristic and feels homesick in the atomistic desert of individualism.

The social gospel joins with all modern thought in the feeling that the old theology does not give us a Christ who is truly personal. Just as the human race, when it appears in theology, is an amorphous metaphysical conception which could be more briefly designated by an algebraic symbol, in the same way the personality of Jesus is not allowed to be real under theological influence. If it does stand out vital and resolute, it is in spite of theology and not because of it. Some of the greatest theologians, men who wrote epoch-making treatises about Christ, such as Athanasius, give no indication that the personality of Jesus was live and real to them. When those who have been trained under the old religious beliefs come under the influence of historical teaching, the realization that Jesus was actually a person, and not merely part of a "scheme of redemption," often comes as a great and beneficent shock. He has been made part of a scheme of salvation, the second premise in a great syllogism. The social gospel wants to see a personality able to win hearts, dominate situations, able to bind men in loyalty and make them think like himself, and to set revolutionary social forces in motion.

Every event and saying in the life of Christ has, of course, been scanned intensely and used over and over for edification or theological proof. But in the main the theological significance of the life of Christ has been comprised in the incarnation, the atonement, and the resurrection. The life in general served mainly to connect and lead up to these great events, and to found the Church.[1] The things in which Jesus himself was passionately interested and which he strove to accomplish, do not seem to count for much. The impartation of divine life and immortality to the race was accomplished when he was a babe. The atonement might actually have been frustrated if the life effort of Jesus had been successful, for if the Jews had accepted his spiritual leadership, they would not have killed him.

The social gospel would interpret all the events of his life, including his death, by the dominant purpose which he consistently followed, the establishment of the Kingdom of God. This is the only interpretation which would have appealed to himself. His life was what counted; his death was part of it. The historic current of salvation which went out from him is the prolongation of that life into which he put his conscious energy.

Theology has made the divinity of Christ a question of nature rather than character. His divinity was an inheritance or endowment which he brought with him and which was fixed for him in his pre-existent state. He was divine on account of what took place at one moment in the womb of one Jewish woman rather than on account of all that took place in the inner depths of his spirit when he communed with his Father and fought through the issues of his life. Theology has been on a false trail in seeking the key to his life in the difficult doctrine of the two natures. That doctrine has never been settled. The formula of Chalcedon was a compromise. Any attempt to think precisely about the question results in a caricature; safety lies in vagueness. We shall come closer to the secret of Jesus if we think less of the physical process of conception and more of the spiritual processes of desire, choice, affirmation, and self-surrender within his own will and personality. The mysteries of the spiritual world take place within the will.

[1] The treatment of his "work" under the three heads of prophet, priest, and king, which is an hereditary scheme in theology, seems antique and far-fetched. Moreover, his kingly office mainly begins with his resurrection. His kingly work in historical life has been treated with neglect.

To repeat: The social gospel is not primarily interested in metaphysical questions; its christological interest is all for a real personality who could set a great historical process in motion; it wants his work interpreted by the purposes which ruled and directed his active life; it would have more interest in basing the divine quality of his personality on free and ethical acts of his will than in dwelling on the passive inheritance of a divine essence.

The fundamental first step in the salvation of mankind was the achievement of the personality of Jesus. Within him the Kingdom of God got its first foothold in humanity. It was by virtue of his personality that he became the initiator of the Kingdom.

His personality was an achievement, not an effortless inheritance. His temptations and struggles were not stage-combats. At every point of his life he had to see his way through the tangle of moral questions which invited to errors and misjudgments; his clarity of judgment was an achievement. Not only in the desert but all the way he had to re-affirm his unity with the will of God and make all aims subservient to the Kingdom of God. The inclination early set in to eliminate the element of temptation, of effort, of vigorous action and reaction, and to show him calm, majestic, omniscient, the effortless master of all forces. This was supposed to be the proper demonstration of divinity in human form; in fact it was a demonstration of feeble imagination and of Gnostic tendencies in his interpreters. Possibly God might be revealed in a life wholly placid and complete; certainly the Kingdom of God could not be initiated by such a life, for the Kingdom of God means battle. In all other cases we judge the ethical worth of a man by the character he achieves by will and effort. If he has any unusual outfit of nature we deduct it in our estimate. How can we claim high ethical value for the personality and character of Jesus if no effort of will was necessary to achieve it?

Jesus lived out his own life. Like every other Ego he existed for himself as well as for others. He was asserting and defending his right to be himself when he stood up for others. The problems of human life were not simply official problems to him, but personal problems. But unlike others, he did not fall into the sin of selfishness, because he succeeded in uniting the service of the common good with the affirmation of his selfhood.

The personality which he achieved was a new type in humanity. Having the power to master and assimilate others, it became the primal cell of a new social organism. Even if there had been no sin from which mankind had to be redeemed, the life of Jesus would have dated an epoch in the evolution of the race by the introduction of a new type and consequently new social standards. He is the real revelation of God. Other conceptions have to be outlived; his has to be attained.

In the words of one of the most personal and original idealistic philosophers:

> "The consciousness of the absolute unity of the human and the divine life is the profoundest insight possible to man. Before Jesus it did not exist. Since his time, we might say to this day, it has been almost lost again, at least in secular philosophy. Jesus evidently had this insight. How did he get it? There is nothing very wonderful in rediscovering the truth after another man has found the way; but how the first, separated by ages before and after by the sole possession of this insight, obtained it, this is matter for profound wonder. Therefore it is really true that Jesus of Nazareth, in a unique way, true of no other, is the only begotten and first born Son of God, and that all ages, if they are capable of understanding him at all, must recognize him as such. It is true enough that now any man can rediscover this doctrine in the writings of the apostles and appropriate it in his own convictions. It is also true, and we assert it, that the philosopher,—as far as he knows,—discovers the same truths independently of Christianity, and sees them with a clearness and breadth of vision which traditional Christianity can not match. Yet it remains for ever true that we, our entire age, and all our philosophical investigations are based on Christianity, and our thinking proceeds from it; that this Christian faith has entered in the most manifold ways into our entire culture; and that we all would not be what we are, unless this powerful principle had preceded us historically. It remains incontestably true that all those who since Jesus have arrived at union with God, have attained it only through him and by his mediation. Thus in every way it is confirmed that to the end of time all wise men will bow before this Jesus of Nazareth, and the more of life they have themselves, the more humbly will they acknowledge the exceeding glory of this great personality."[2]

Jesus experienced God in a new way. The ethical monotheism which he inherited from the prophets was transformed within his spirit and through his experiences into something far lovelier and kinder. Jehovah, the keeper of covenants and judge of his people, was changed into the Father in heaven who forgives sins freely, welcomes the prodigal, makes his sun to shine on

---

[2] Johann Gottlieb Fichte, "Die Anweisung zum seligen Leben," Lecture VI. 1806. The translation is mine.

the just and unjust, and asks for nothing but love, trust, and co-operative obedience. This intuition of God was born in a life that neither hated nor feared, and so far as it is adopted in any single life or in the life of humanity, it banishes hate and fear. An overpowering consciousness of God is needed in order to offset and overcome the tyranny of the sensuous life and its temptations. This consciousness of God which we derive from Jesus is able to establish centres of spiritual strength and peace which help to break the free sweep of evil in social life. Jesus set love into the centre of the spiritual universe, and all life is illuminated from that centre. This is the highest idealistic faith ever conceived, and the greatest addition ever made to the spiritual possessions of mankind.

With such a Father spiritual intimacy is possible. With a despotic God prayer is a series of court obeisances and a secret fencing for personal independence. But given such a God as Jesus knew, and the consciousness of him would steal in everywhere and envelop all life in peace. It made righteousness a joy and sin repulsive. Any one who has ever been under a clear and happy realization of God will remember how spontaneous goodness becomes.

So we have in Jesus a perfect religious personality, a spiritual life completely filled by the realization of a God who is love. All his mind was set on God and one with him. Consequently it was also absorbed in the fundamental purpose of God, the Kingdom of God. Like the idea of God, the conception of the Kingdom was both an inheritance and a creation of Jesus; he received it and transformed it in accordance with his consciousness of God. Within his mind the punitive and imperialistic elements were steeped out of it, and the elements of love and solidarity were dyed into it. The Reign of God came to mean the organized fellowship of humanity acting under the impulse of love.

By virtue of this consciousness of God Jesus rose above three temptations which have beset other religious spirits.

The first temptation is mysticism. Those who have been initiated into the secret inner way of God, and have experienced the sweetness of losing self in the all-comprehending and holy Life, are tempted to turn in high disdain from the small and material contacts and duties which bind the soul on the wheel that ever revolves and never gets anywhere, and to seek the tranquility and forgetfulness of mystic absorption. This is one of the temptations of the noblest souls.

Jesus was not a mystic in the narrower sense of the escape from the world. He is our great example of prayer and of intimate communion with God. But the Kingdom of God engaged his will and set his task in the midst of men. He drew his strength from God, but he put it forth in the world. The Kingdom of God put divine significance into all his minor duties and saved life from religious disdain. We all know the common statue of Buddha, with his hands relaxed and inactive in his lap, his eyes unseeing and visionary, his lips in the smile of mystic contentment. We can not see Jesus so.

The second temptation is pessimism. Religion creates a profound sense of the evil in life. Those whose ears are attuned to hear the deepest organ note of the universe, hear a groan of travail from the under deep. Consequently pessimism has been the sombre habitation of many noble religious minds from Buddha to Schopenhauer. The dualism of the first century, both philosophical and religious, was an expression of pessimism. Christianity was sucked thigh-deep into this quicksand. Its earliest speculative theologians, the Gnostics, were so pessimistic that to them the creation of the world was a blunder or a crime, and the Creator-God of Judaism got no reverence from them for perpetrating this world.

Jesus was not a pessimist. Since God was love, this world was to him fundamentally good. He realized not only evil but the Kingdom of Evil; but he launched the Kingdom of God against it, and staked his life on its triumph. His faith in God and in the Kingdom of God constituted him a religious optimist. Even when his life was overshadowed by opposition, seeming failure, and death, his prevailing temper was not melancholy, but youthful and triumphant He had no use for the studied melancholy of periodical fasting. Why should his friends fast? They were having a wedding time. Why pour the new wine of gladness into the old sad bottles, and why sew a new patch on a garment that was dropping to pieces?

The third temptation of religious spirits is asceticism and otherworldliness. Both are related to pessimism. The monk repudiates the social life which tempts him, scours the stains of worldliness from his soul by spiritual exercises, wears the earthly integument thin by hunger and castigation, and enjoys the other world by anticipation whenever angels visit him or he has a vision of divine glory. All Christians who yearn to escape from this vale of tears and whose life is really set on another world, are to that extent pessimistic. The asceticism and other-worldliness of ancient and mediaeval Christianity were results of its "Hellenization" as Harnack calls it. It took a thousand years of history, great social and intellectual changes, and an unparalleled religious revolution to set Christianity even partly free from these influences of its early Greek and Oriental environment.

Jesus was neither ascetic nor other-worldly. He formulated the distinctive difference between himself and John the Baptist in the saying that John ate not and drank not, while he himself ate and drank, and quoted the critics who called him a glutton and wine-bibber. He believed in a life after death, but it was not the dominant element in his teaching, nor the constraining force in his religious life. There are sayings in the gospels which are ascetic, and more that are apocalyptic; but Jesus, I believe, was neither. In so far as these sayings were really his own, their ideas were part of the equipment furnished him by his age and religion; they were not the essential products of his life. His mind was not at all of the same family type as those who wrote and re-wrote the apocalyptic literature. He fasted when he was absorbed in thought; so did Socrates; so do others. He went without food, sleep, and home-life because he was set on a big thing. This is the revolutionary asceticism of the Kingdom of God, but that is wholly different from the individualistic and other-worldly asceticism of the Nitrian desert.

My own conviction is that the professional theologians of Europe, who all belong by kinship and sympathy to the bourgeois classes and are constitutionally incapacitated for understanding any revolutionary ideas, past or present, have overemphasized the ascetic and eschatological elements in the teachings of Jesus. They have classed as ascetic or apocalyptic the radical sayings about property and non-resistance which seem to them unpractical or visionary. If the present chastisement of God purges our intellects of capitalistic and upper-class iniquities, we shall no longer damn these sayings by calling them eschatological, but shall exhibit them as anticipations of the fraternal ethics of democracy and prophecies of social common sense.

Jesus communed with God; he realized the evil in the world; and he held his life with a light grasp. Yet he escaped the noble temptations of religion contained in mysticism, pessimism, asceticism, and other-worldliness. Out of the same ingredients, communion with God, realization of evil, and religious intensity and self-control, he built a higher synthesis. His attitude to life was the direct product of his twofold belief, in the Father who is love and the Kingdom of God which is righteousness. Mediaeval Christianity, which was mystic, ascetic, and other-worldly, was not built on his synthesis. On the other hand the social gospel can be. His affirmation of life is the ideal basis for the social gospel. No religion involving the negation of life is really compatible with it. It remains to be seen whether anything like the social gospel can make headway in Buddhistic countries; and if it does, whether it will not transform the old Buddhism.

His communion with God and his devotion to the Kingdom of God set Jesus free and also bound him. They freed him from the conservatism of inherited religion and from the coercion of the social order; they bound him to a life of obedience and to the utter service of men. The harmony of these antinomies is one of the distinctive qualities of his personality.

He was a loyal son of his nation, a believer in its traditions and its worth, and we know how deeply he was moved by his foresight of its disaster. His religious life was inseparable from that of his nation. There were no novel or alien elements in it, as with Paul or Philo, which might have laid the basis for departures. He never cut loose from the religion of his fathers, and never told his followers to leave the synagogue and found the Church. He was no come-outer.

But he had a higher law and allegiance within him. In so far as the religious customs of Judaism conflicted with his consciousness of God or with the reign of love, he broke with them. He contravened the Sabbath regulations when they inflicted suffering or interfered with acts of mercy. He set aside the entire principle of clean and unclean food because it had no ethical truth in it. The Sermon on the Mount was a deliberate declaration that the old moral law was insufficient and that new ethical standards were needed for the new era. His invective against the scribes and Pharisees repudiated, not only the clerical "system" which was exploiting religion, but the models, definitions, and casuistry of current theology. Aside from his action of cleansing "the house of prayer" from the chatter of the market, he scarcely mentioned the temple and its sacrifices, except to rank them below love and reconciliation. Ceremonial acts were not the proper expression of his consciousness of God. He realized religion in acts expressing love and fellowship, or in breaking with the Kingdom of Evil. Under his teaching the burden of time, expense and routine through which religious men sought to appease God's anger or court his favour, dropped away. If God was love, why these doings? "The Gentiles think they shall be heard for their many-worded prayers; be not like them; your Father knows."

Such a change of attitude toward the ritual institutions of religion, when it has become common, has availed to purge the religion of whole nations of its non-ethical inheritances; it has reinforced the progressive elements of society by turning the energies of religion from the maintenance of conservative institutions to the support of movements for political emancipation and social justice. Such a change in religion inaugurates new eras in history.

Now, such changes, when they have happened, have been due in part to a renaissance of this attitude of Jesus. In the case of the Protestant Reformation it was mainly due to a revival of Paul's attitude of freedom over against the Law. But Paul's freedom was one of the treasures which he derived from Christ.

With Jesus this spiritual attitude toward the religious customs of his people was the consistent outworking of his consciousness of God and of his conception of the reign of God. In making his stand on each of the points which brought him into conflict, he was achieving his own personality.

The God whom Jesus bore within him was not the God of one nation. The reign of God which he meant to establish was not a new imperialism with the chosen people on the top of the pile. The gospels show us Jesus in the act of crossing the racial boundary lines and outgrowing nationalistic religion. He recognized the religious qualities in a pagan; he foresaw that the Kingdom of God would cut across the old lines of division; he held up the hyphenated and heretical Samaritan as a model of humane kindness. Every time a wider contact was offered him, he seized it with a sense of exultation, like the discoverer of a new continent. That world-wide consciousness of humanity, which is coming to some in protest against the hideous disruption and hatred of the War, was won by Jesus at less cost under the tuition of God and the Kingdom ideal.

Jesus lived in a world of high thought and set his face toward the greatest of all aims. But he talked peacefully with simple people, and was impatient when his friends did not want him annoyed by children. He was valorous, fearless, an outdoor man, and an invincible fighter. But he was so tender to the sick and so comradely with the poor that "Christ-like" has remained one of the aristocratic adjectives in our language, and men like Saint Francis, who followed him and grew like him, have stood out as the beloved souls, the rare flowers of esoteric humanity.

He was a proud spirit who lived out his own life and asserted himself against all the weight of authority, against his king, against the supreme court of his nation, against Moses, against professional theology and the lawyer caste, against the power of custom, against his home community, against his own mother. But he had a thirst for friendship, an unfailing insight into the subtler motives and longings of men and women, a thrilling responsiveness to the emotions of masses of men, and an unexampled sense of the sacredness of personality.

He bowed to law and order. He paid his taxes, and advised others to do it. He sent a leper to the proper officer to get his sanitary certificate. But he had no spiritual awe for the exponents of the present social order. He challenged its moral basis. He dropped into the silence of a passive resister when he faced a typical court, and he was felt then and ever since as a force against despotism.

The personality of Jesus is a call to the emancipation of our own personalities. He has multiplied free souls. Every such soul counts in the progress of mankind. They are rare. They are most effective in the redemption of society when they are free from the acrid qualities of rebellion. Those who have derived their spiritual freedom and their social spirit from Jesus are most likely to have the combination of freedom with love and gentleness. This ought to be the distinctive mark of Christ within the social movement. Is it true that Jesus has been experienced as a Liberator more frequently apart from theology than within it? If so, why?

To think out any one of these convictions, or to achieve any one of these harmonies, so that all life can become simple, whole-hearted, and divinely intelligible through its truth, is a great achievement for a life-time. Luther was one of the most dynamic personalities in history, one of the epoch-making religious minds. Yet it took him years of morbid struggle to emerge from the gloom of religious fear into Christian assurance, and to cut across the labyrinth of church methods by the shortcut of simple faith. And after achieving this discovery, he imposed his emancipating faith on others as a sovereign formula, and would not let others advance beyond the point he had reached. With Jesus these great inward convictions were not academic theory, but life and action. They were the reality on which he staked all. They were so much his own that he acted on them as a matter of course, with a self-possession which did not have to weigh and consider, but struck ahead, and struck right.

In the case of biological mutations the question is not only whether the new type is valuable, but also whether it will breed true and succeed in perpetuating itself against the competition of other types. Jesus not only achieved the kind of religious personality which we have tried to bring before our memory and imagination, but he succeeded in perpetuating his spirit. What was personal with him became social within the group of the disciples. His life became a collective and assimilating force and a current of historic tradition.

His disciples were human stuff, and all of them doubtless were thin conductors for the powerful current they had to convey. His Jewish friends were full of older ideas, and most of them seem to have sagged back toward conservative Judaism. Luke's narrative about Peter and Stephen, and Paul's profound trouble of mind about the Judaizing brethren are evidence. As soon as the Church moved out into the Greek world, a process of assimilation began which left little of the real Jesus in sight. The historical research of the last forty years has written a new chapter about the sufferings of Jesus. Imagine him coming into a Gnostic conventicle in A. D. 150, or into the Church of Cyprian in A. D. 250, or into high mass at the Church of the Lateran in A. D. 1250, and trying to discover what it was all about.

And yet he survived. He has come through to this day with his thought and his personality still vital, *sui generis*, and far ahead of our day. Whenever his spirit has been embodied again in a striking degree in some individual, people have gathered around that man, hungry for salvation. Any man in whom the Jesus-strain reappears clearly is felt to be a kind of superman. If Tolstoi, for instance, had never begun to follow Christ in his life, he would be simply one of a group of brilliant Russian novelists. Since he received something of the mind of Jesus into his mind, he became one of the prophetic figures of our age and no one can tell how much he contributed, through others, to enable Russia, newly free, to make the one sincere and penetrating utterance made on behalf of democracy and peace in the Spring and Summer of 1917. In the same way those religious movements in which the distinctive ideas and spirit of Jesus have broken forth again, have been the fruitful and prophetic movements in religion. Their power of attack can best be measured by the ferocity with which the Kingdom of Evil has trampled on them.

The Kingdom of God is not a concept nor an ideal merely, but an historical force. It is a vital and organizing energy now at work in humanity. Its capacity to save the social order depends on its pervasive presence within the social organism. Every institutional foothold gained gives a purchase for attacking the next vantage-point. Where a really Christian type of religious life is created, the intellect and its education are set free, and this in turn aids religion to emancipate itself from superstition and dogmatism. Where religion and intellect combine, the foundation is laid for political democracy. Where the people have the outfit and the spirit of democracy, they can curb economic exploitation. Where predatory gain and the resultant inequality are lessened, fraternal feeling and understanding become easier and the sense of solidarity grows. Where men live in the consciousness of solidarity and in the actual practice of love with their fellow-men, they are not far from the Kingdom of God. The great thing in the salvation of humanity is that salvation is present. Life begets life.

Yet it is a matter of unspeakable difficulty for the Kingdom of God to make headway against the inherent weakness of human nature and the social entrenchments of the Kingdom of Evil. "The risks of temporary disaster which great ideals run, appear to be directly proportioned to the value of the ideals. Great truths bear long sorrows."[3] The more we do justice to this fact, the more we shall realize that the initiation and perpetuation of the historical movement of redemption was the essential thing. Jesus was the initiator. To show this more and more clearly is the service the social gospel asks of doctrinal and historical theology. By this avenue of approach we shall appreciate the human dimensions of Jesus. The individualistic theology was the creation of men with little historical training and historical consciousness, and to that extent the problems they set were the product of uneducated minds. The full greatness of the problem of Jesus strikes us when we see him in his connection with human history. Our own consciousness of God's love and forgiveness, our inward freedom, our social feeling, the set of our will toward the achievement of the Kingdom of God, our fellowship with the "two or three" in which we have a realization of the higher presence, we owe to our connection with the historical force which Jesus initiated. Where did he himself get what he had? At what fountain did he drink?

[3] Royce, " Problem of Christianity" I, 54.

Chapter XV

The Social Gospel and the Conception of God

My main purpose in this book has been to show that the social gospel is a vital part of the Christian conception of sin and salvation, and that any teaching on the sinful condition of the race and on its redemption from evil which fails to do justice to the social factors and processes in sin and redemption, must be incomplete, unreal, and misleading. Also, since the social gospel henceforth is to be an important part of our Christian message, its chief convictions must be embodied in these doctrines in some organic form.

Now, the doctrines of sin and salvation are the starting-point and goal of Christian theology. Every essential change or enlargement in them is bound to affect related doctrines also. It will be the object of the remaining chapters of the book to indicate how the social gospel would re-act on the doctrine of God, of the Holy Spirit and inspiration, of the sacraments, of eschatology, and of the atonement.

The conception of God held by a social group is a social product. Even if it originated in the mind of a solitary thinker or prophet, as soon as it becomes the property of a social group, it takes on the qualities of that group. If, for instance, a high and spiritual idea of God is brought to a people ignorant and accustomed to superstitious methods of winning the favour or help of higher beings, it will soon be coarsened and materialized. The changes in the Hebrew conception of God were the result of the historical experiences of the nation and its leaders. The Christian idea of God has also had its ups and downs in the long and varied history of Christian civilization.

A fine and high conception of God is a social achievement and a social endowment. It becomes part of the spiritual inheritance common to all individuals in that religious group. If every individual had to work out his idea of God on the basis of his own experiences and intuitions only, it would be a groping quest, and most of us would see only the occasional flitting of a distant light. By the end of our life we might have arrived at the stage of voodooism or necromancy. Entering into a high conception of God, such as the Christian faith offers us, is like entering a public park or a public gallery of art and sharing the common wealth. When we learn from the gospels, for instance, that God is on the side of the poor, and that he proposes to view anything done or not done to them as having been done or not done to him, such a revelation of solidarity and humanity comes with a regenerating shock to our selfish minds. Any one studying life as it is on the basis of real estate and bank clearings, would come to the conclusion that God is on the side of the rich. It takes a revelation to see it the other way.

Wherever we encounter such a strain of social feeling in our conceptions of God, it is almost sure to run straight back either to Jesus or the prophets. The Hebrew prophets were able to realize God in that way because they were part of a nation which had preserved the traditions of primitive fraternal democracy. The prophets emphasized God's interest in righteousness and solidarity because they were making a fight to save their people from the landlordism and oppression under which other peoples have wilted and degenerated. When, therefore, we to-day feel the moral thrill of Hebrew theism, we are the heirs and beneficiaries of one untamed nation of mountain-dwellers. When such a conception of God is transmitted to other nations or to later times, it is the exportation of the most precious commodity a nation can produce.

On the other hand, if a conception of God originates among the exploiting classes in an age of despotism, it is almost certain to contain germs of positive sinfulness which will infect all to whom it is transmitted.

Christianity is an old religion. Its youth was lived in the midst of a matured and dying imperial despotism. At first it was an illegal organization, suppressed by the Empire, and in turn the Empire was described in our Apocalypse as "the Beast." This hostility was a saving element which made the Church somewhat immune to the despotic influences, as long as it lasted. But in time the Church came under the control and spiritual influence of the upper classes, and finally of the Roman State. We know that the effects of this social environment were wrought into the constitutional structure of the Church. The Roman Catholic Church is still the religious replica of the Roman imperial organization. Harnack thinks this is the characterization which comes closest to its real nature. Did this environment also influence the theological and religious conceptions about God?

Later the Western Church passed through the age of feudalism. Feudalism was a social order in which the military, judicial, and executive powers were under the control of the same class which controlled the one great source of wealth at that time, the agricultural land. What such a combination of private property power and governmental powers of coercion comes to was brought home to us by the revelations about the rubber trade in the Belgian Congo a few years ago. Of this feudal social order the Church was an integral and active part. The temper and attitude of the dominant part of the clergy was deeply affected by this social environment. Did it also shape the conception of God? Did it create habits of mind which came out in the religious appeals, the illustrations and arguments used, and the tacit presuppositions of all argument?

Our imagination has only a short reach. In conceiving a higher world we have to take the familiar properties and figures of our material world, and enlarge and refine them as best we can. As long as kings and governors were the greatest human beings in the public eye, it was inevitable that their image should be superimposed on the idea of God. Court language and obeisances were used in worship and when men reasoned about God, they took their illustrations and analogies from those who were a close second to God.

Athanasius, for instance, in order to explain how the incarnation could save the human race from death and give immortal life, says that when a great king takes residence in one house in a city, the whole city enjoys great honour and is not in danger from any enemy or bandit invasion. In the same way the physical presence of the incarnate Logos dispelled the evil of death. This is one of the principal arguments in his mind. But in fact it is no argument at all except on monarchical assumptions.

In his epoch-making book, "Cur Deus Homo" Anselm bases his discussion on the proposition that God's "honour" has been violated by human sin. Man is wholly subject to God, and bound to fulfil all his demands. If he falls short, God is under no obligation to show him favour, and must exact satisfaction for the violation of his honour. He cannot simply forgive sin. It is not enough if the sinner henceforth performs his whole duty. "Satisfaction" must be rendered by some adequate work of merit over and above the legal requirements of God. This equivalent man is unable to render. Christ is able. On this basis Anselm builds his theory of the atonement. It has often been pointed out that Anselm derived his idea of "satisfaction" from the Teutonic practice of commuting physical punishment into a financial payment.[1] I think Anselm, an Italian and a churchman, was also influenced by the "satisfactions" in the penitential practice of the Church. But beyond all

[1] This was first established by my friend Professor Hermann Cremer in his monograph, "Die Wurzeln des anselmischen Satisfactionsbegriffes." Studien und Kritiken, 1880.

these contemporary influences of law and custom was the pervasive impression of autocratic power and monarchical self-assertion, which rates an offence against the members of the royal family or against the governing class far more highly than other crimes, and makes the king's "honour" a concern for which nations must go to war.

God's right of arbitrary decision, which has been asserted in many connections, runs back to the same autocratic sources. Duns Scotus and his followers even held that the death of Christ was necessary only because God declared it necessary. If he had been willing to accept the obedience of some good angel, that too would have sufficed. We are most familiar with the arbitrary power of God in the doctrine of election. The right of God to select some individuals for eternal life and leave others to eternal punishment, entirely apart from any question of personal merit or demerit, was always based on the ground of the "sovereignty" of God, that is, the divine autocracy. If a city rebelled, all lives were forfeited; if the King had only 50 councillors hung, or every tenth citizen sold into slavery, it was an act of royal clemency worthy of praise. By the fall all men were in a state of damnation; if God elected some to salvation and left the others as they were, it was divine grace; nor was he under obligation to explain his reasons in picking the favoured.

Scholastic arguments reach few people; imaginative pictures of spiritual ideas are subtle and pervasive, God was imagined far above, in an upper part of the universe, remote from humanity but looking down on us, fully aware of all we do, interfering when necessary, but very distinct. In Greek theology this distinctness was due to philosophical influences. In popular theology the remoteness of great men perhaps had more to do with shaping this idea than philosophy.

The sense of fear which has pervaded religion has doubtless been, at least in part, a psychological result of the despotic attitude of parents, of school-masters, of priests, and of officials all the way from the town beadle to the king. To uncounted people God has not been the great Comforter but the great Terror. The main concern in religion was to escape from his hands. Luther longed that he "might at last have a gracious God"—*einen gnädigen Gott*; the word is the same which was applied to princes and nobles when they were good-natured. Luther sweated with fear when he walked alongside of the body of the Lord in a Corpus Christi procession. To what extent was this due to the fact that he was constantly beaten by his parents and by his school-masters, and taught to be afraid of everything? Men enriched the Church enormously with gifts of land as insurance premiums that God would not do anything horrible to them. When farmers are afraid enough to part with land, it must be a deep fear.

The mediaeval methods of earning religious merit and of securing intercession were the product of fear and a close duplicate of the conditions existing under economic and political despotism. God was a feudal lord, holding his tenants in a grip from which there was no escape, exacting what was due to him, and putting the delinquent in a hot prison which was even worse than the terrible holes underneath the duke's castle. By special self-denial the religious peon could win "merit" to offset his delinquencies. The saints and the blessed Virgin had much merit. The Church had power to assign some of this to those who stood in with the Church. The intercession of the saints counted; every one knew that it was a great thing for a poor man if a nobleman spoke for him to the judge; it would be so in heaven too. Things go by favour; the more aristocracy, the more pull.

Thus the social relations in which men lived, affected their conceptions about God and his relations to men. Under tyrannous conditions the idea of God was necessarily tainted with the cruel hardness of society. This spiritual influence of despotism made even the face of Christ seem hard and stern. The outlook into the future life was like a glimpse into a chamber of torture.

The conflict of the religion of Jesus with autocratic conceptions of God is therefore part of the struggle of humanity with autocratic economic and political conditions. This carries the social movement into theology. Theologians therewith have their share in redeeming humanity from the reign of tyranny and fear, and if we do not do our share emphatically and with a will, where do we belong, to the Kingdom of God or the Kingdom of Evil? The worst form of leaving the naked unclothed, the hungry unfed, and the prisoners uncomforted, is to leave men under a despotic conception of God and the universe; and what will the Son of Man do to us theologians when we gather at the Day of Doom?

Here we see one of the highest redemptive services of Jesus to the human race. When he took God by the hand and called him "our Father," he democratized the conception of God. He disconnected the idea from the coercive and predatory State, and transferred it to the realm of family life, the chief social embodiment of solidarity and love. He not only saved humanity; he saved God. He gave God his first chance of being loved and of escaping from the worst misunderstandings conceivable. The value of Christ's idea of the Fatherhood of God is realized only by contrast to the despotic ideas which it opposed and was meant to displace. We have classified theology as Greek and Latin, as Catholic and Protestant. It is time to classify it as despotic and democratic. From a Christian point of view that is a more decisive distinction.

Paul has preserved for us the deep impression of liberation and relief which the Christian idea of God made on him and his contemporaries: "For (when you became Christians) you did not receive the spirit of slavery to fill you with fear once more, but you received the spirit of sonship which leads us to cry, 'Our Father.'" The Gnostics, some of whom were exceedingly able minds, attracted to Christianity by its spiritual contents, believed that Christ had for the first time in cosmic history brought to mankind a revelation of the real God. All the other God-ideas had been counterfeits and caricatures imposed on humanity by lower and evil spiritual beings to enslave them. This is a striking expression of the feeling that the God mirrored in the teaching and person of Christ was in a wholly different class from all others.

Of course the Christian conception of God was not kept pure. The pall of darkness rising from despotic society constantly obscured and eclipsed it. The imagery of coercion and tyranny always suggested itself anew. The triumph of the Christian idea of God will never be complete as long as economic and political despotism prevail.

The value of the Reformation should be re-assessed from this point of view. Luther tore the idea of "merit" out of theology. Christ alone had merit. By his blood he had paid the whole debt once for all. Man need not earn merit. He cannot earn merit. It would be a sin for him to try. That ended the contract labour system in religion. God was reconciled. He had been angry but he was now kind and ready to forgive. The sinner need only believe and accept the great transaction made on his behalf. That ended the reign of fear for those who understood. The saints and their intercession were dismissed; they never had any merit either; the sinner could deal with God and Christ direct. Purgatory was gone; only hell proper remained. It was a religious Seisachtheia, like that in Athens under Solon's laws, a great unloading, a revolution in the field of the spiritual life, and the condition for the coming of political and economic liberty.

But the restoration of the Christian conception of God was by no means complete. Despotic government was still in full swing when the Reformation theology was written. Luther and Calvin were not personally in sympathy with democracy. The age of absolutism and of Louis XIV was just ahead. The long era of witch-trials had just begun. The spell of fear was broken only for a few. The fundamental assumptions about God remained.

The inherited forensic terminology of theology suggested the old lines of thought. As long as religion borrows its terms from the procedure of law-courts, the spirit of coercion and terror leaks in. Legal ideas are not congruous with the Christian consciousness of salvation. The idea of "justification" did not come to us from Jesus and it does not blend well with his way of thinking. For Paul and Luther "justification by faith" was an emancipating idea; it stood for an immense simplification and sweetening of the process of salvation. They used the terminology of legalism to deny its spirit. To us, who are not under the consciousness of Jewish or Roman Catholic legality, "justification" does not convey the same sense of liberation, but the phrase is now a vehicle by which legal and often despotic ideas come back to plague us.

The social gospel is God's predestined agent to continue what the Reformation began. It arouses intelligent hatred of oppression and the reign of fear, and teaches us to prize liberty and to love love. Therefore those whose religious life has been influenced by the social gospel are instinctively out of sympathy with autocratic conceptions of God. They sense the spiritual taint which goes out from such ideas. They know that these religious conceptions are used to make autocratic social conditions look tolerable, necessary, and desirable. Like Paul, the social gospel has not "received the spirit of bondage again unto fear." It is wholly in sympathy with the conception of the Father which Jesus revealed to us by his words, by his personality, and by his own relations to the Father.

This reformatory and democratizing influence of the social gospel is not against religion but for it. The worst thing that could happen to God would be to remain an autocrat while the world is moving toward democracy. He would be dethroned with the rest. For one man who has forsaken religion through scientific doubt, ten have forsaken it in our time because it seemed the spiritual opponent of liberty and the working people. This feeling will deepen as democracy takes hold and becomes more than a theory of government. We have heard only the political overture of democracy, played by fifes; the economic numbers of the program are yet to come, and they will be performed with trumpets and trombones.

The Kingdom of God is the necessary background for the Christian idea of God. The social movement is one of the chief ways in which God is revealing that he lives and rules as a God that loves righteousness and hates iniquity. A theological God who has no interest in the conquest of justice and fraternity is not a Christian. It is not enough for theology to eliminate this or that autocratic trait. Its God must join the social movement. The real God has been in it long ago. The development of a Christian social order would be the highest proof of God's saving power. The failure of the social movement would impugn his existence.

The old conception that God dwells on high and is distinct from our human life was the natural basis for autocratic and arbitrary ideas about him. On the other hand the religious belief that he is immanent in humanity is the natural basis for democratic ideas about him. When he was far above, he needed vice-regents to rule for him, popes by divine institution and kings by divine right. If he lives and moves in the life of mankind, he can act directly on the masses of men. A God who strives within our striving, who kindles his flame in our intellect, sends the impact of his energy to make our will restless for righteousness, floods our sub-conscious mind with dreams and longings, and always urges the race on toward a higher combination of freedom and solidarity, — that would be a God with whom democratic and religious men could hold converse as their chief fellow-worker, the source of their energies, the ground of their hopes.

Platonic philosophy in the first century made God so transcendent that it had to devise the Logos-idea to bridge the abyss between the silent depths of God and this world, and to enable God to create and to reveal himself. Theology shrank from imputing suffering to God. Patripassianism seemed a self-evident heresy. To-day men want to think of God as close to them, and spiritually kin to them, the Father of all spirits. Eminent theologians insist that God has always suffered with and for mankind and that the cross is a permanent law of God's nature: "The lamb has been slain from the beginning of the world." Through the conception of evolution and through the social movement we have come to see human life in its totality, and our consciousness of God is the spiritual counterpart of our social consciousness. Some, apparently, would be willing to think of God as less than omnipotent and omniscient if only he were working hard with us for that Kingdom which is the only true Democracy.

Two points still demand discussion. The first is the problem of suffering.

The existence of innocent suffering impugns the justice and benevolence of God, both of which are essential in a Christian conception of God.

The simplest solution is to deny the existence of unjust suffering; to trust that good and ill are allotted according to desert; and if the righteous Job suffers great disaster, to search for his secret sin. This explanation broke down before the facts. How about the man born blind? What personal sin had merited his calamity?

Dualism took the other extreme. It acknowledged that the good suffer, and stressed the fact. But it exculpated the good God by making the evil God the author of this world, or at least its present lord.

Christianity has combined several explanations of suffering. It grounds it in general on the prevalence of sin since the fall. It has ascribed a malignant power of afflicting the righteous to Satan and his servants. It has taken satisfaction when justice was vindicated in some striking case of goodness or wickedness. It has held out a hope of a public vindication of the righteous in the great judgment, and of an equalization of their lot by their bliss in heaven and the suffering of the wicked. (This element, however, was weakened in Protestantism by the disappearance of purgatory and the tacit assumption that all who are saved at all will enjoy an equal bliss. Purgatory was a great balancer and equalizer.) Finally, Christianity has taught that God allots suffering with wise and loving intent, tempering it according to our strength, relieving it in response to our prayer, and using it to chasten our pride, to win us from earthliness to himself, and to prepare us for heaven. This interpretation does not assert the justice of every suffering, taken by itself, but does maintain its loving intention.

All these are powerful and comforting considerations. But they are shaken by the bulk of the unjust suffering in sight of the modern mind. These Christian ideas are largely true as long as we look at a normal village community and its individuals and families. But they are jarred by mass disasters. The optimism of the age of rationalism was shaken by the Lisbon earthquake in 1755, when 30,000 people were killed together, just and unjust. The War has deeply affected the religious assurance of our own time, and will lessen it still more when the excitement is over and the aftermath of innocent suffering becomes clear. But that impression of undeserved mass misery which the war has brought home to the thoughtless, has long been weighing on all who understood the social conditions of our civilization. The sufferings of a single righteous man could deeply move the psalmists or the poet of Job. To-day entire social classes sit in the ashes and challenge the justice of the God who has afflicted them by fathering the present social system. The moral and religious problem of suffering has entered on a new stage with the awakening of the social consciousness and the spread of social knowledge.

If God stands for the present social order, how can we defend him? We can stand the pain of travail, of physical dissolution, of earthquakes and accidents. These are the price we pay for the use of a fine planet with lovely appurtenances and for a wonderful body. We can also accept with reasonable resignation the mental anguish of unrequited love, of foiled ambition, or of the emptiness of life. These are the risks we run as possessors of a highly organized personality amid a world of men. But we can not stand for poor and laborious people being deprived of physical stature, youth, education, human equality, and justice, in order to enable others to live luxurious lives. It revolts us to see these conditions perpetuated by law and organized force, and palliated or justified by the makers of public opinion. None of the keys offered by individualistic Christianity fit this padlock.

The social gospel supplies an explanation of this class of human suffering, Society is so integral that when one man sins, other men suffer, and when one social class sins, the other classes are involved in the suffering which follows on that sin. The more powerful an individual is, the more will he involve others; the more powerful a class is, the more will it be able to unload its own just suffering on the weaker classes. These sufferings are not "vicarious;" they are solidaristic.

Our solidarity is a beneficent part of human life. It is the basis for our greatest good. If our community life is righteous and fraternal, we are enriched and enlarged by being bound up with it. But, by the same law, if our community is organized in a way that permits, encourages, or defends predatory practices, then the larger part of its members are through solidarity caged to be eaten by the rest, and to suffer what is both unjust and useless.

It follows that ethically it is of the highest importance to prevent our beneficent solidarity from being twisted into a means of torture.

Physical pain serves a beneficent purpose by warning us of the existence of abnormal conditions. It fulfils its purpose when it compels the individual to search out the cause of pain and to keep his body in health. If he takes "dope" to quiet the consciousness of pain without healing the causes, the beneficent purpose of pain is frustrated.

Social suffering serves social healing. If the sense of common humanity is strong enough to set the entire social body in motion on behalf of those who suffer without just cause, then their troubles are eased and the whole body is preserved just and fraternal. If the predatory forces are strong enough to suppress the reactions against injustice and inhumanity, the suffering goes on and the whole community is kept in suicidal evil. To interpret the sufferings imposed by social injustice in individualistic terms as the divine chastening and sanctification of all the individuals concerned, is not only false but profoundly mischievous. It is the equivalent of "dope" for it silences the warning which the suffering of an innocent group ought to convey to all society without abolishing the causes. It frustrates the only chance of redemptive usefulness which the sufferers had.

All this applies to our conception of God. The idea of solidarity, when once understood, acts as a theodicy. None of us would want a world without organic community of life, any more than we would want a world without gravitation. The fact that a careless boy falls down stairs does not condemn gravitation, nor does the existence of evil community life condemn God who constituted us social beings. The innocent suffering of great groups through social solidarity simply brings home to us that the tolerance of social injustice is an intolerable evil. The great sin of men is to resist the reformation of predatory society. We do not want God to be charged with that attitude. A conception of God which describes him as sanctioning the present social order and utilizing it in order to sanctify its victims through their suffering, without striving for its overthrow, is repugnant to our moral sense. Both the Old Testament and the New Testament characterizations of God's righteousness assure us that he hates with steadfast hatred just such practices as modern communities tolerate and promote. If we can trust the Bible, God is against capitalism, its methods, spirit, and results. The bourgeois theologians have misrepresented our revolutionary God. God is for the Kingdom of God, and his Kingdom does not mean injustice and the perpetuation of innocent suffering. The best theodicy for modern needs is to make this very clear.

Finally, the social gospel emphasizes the fact that God is the bond of racial unity.

Speaking historically, it is one of the most universal and important characteristics of religion that it constitutes the spiritual bond of social groups. A national god was always the exponent of national solidarity. A common religion created common sympathies. Full moral obligation stopped at the religious boundary line. The unusual thing about the Good Samaritan was that he disregarded the religious cleavage and followed the call of humanity pure and simple.

The mingling of populations and religions in modern life makes the influence of religion less noticeable, but it still works as a bond of sympathy. It is easiest to trace it where the religious cleavage coincides with the racial or political cleavages. The French Catholics in Quebec and the English Protestants in Ontario; the Irish and the Ulstermen; the Catholic Belgians and the Protestant Dutch; the Latin nations of America and the United States; the mention of the names brings up the problem. The Balkans are a nest of antagonisms partly because of religious differences. It has been fortunate for the American negro that the antagonism of race and social standing has not been intensified in his case by any difference of religion.[2]

The spread of a monotheistic faith and the recognition of a single God of all mankind is a condition of an ethical union of mankind in the future. This is one of the long-range social effects of Christian missions. The effects of Christianity will go far beyond its immediate converts. Every competing religion will be compelled to emphasize its monotheistic elements and to allow its polytheistic ingredients to drop to a secondary stage.

But it is essential to our spiritual honesty that no imperialism shall masquerade under the cover of our religion. Those who adopt the white man's religion come under the white man's influence. Christianity is the religion of the dominant race. The native religions are a spiritual bulwark of defence, independence, and loyalty. If we invite men to come under the same spiritual roof of monotheism with us and to abandon their ancient shelters, let us make sure that this will not be exploited as a trick of subjugation by the Empires. As long as there are great colonizing imperialisms in the world, the propaganda of Christianity has a political significance.

God is the common basis of all our life. Our human personalities may seem distinct, but their roots run down into the eternal life of God. In a large way both philosophy and science are tending toward a recognition of the truth which religion has felt and practised. The all-pervading life of God is the ground of the spiritual oneness of the race and of our hope for its closer fellowship in the future.

The consciousness of solidarity, therefore, is of the essence of religion. But the circumference and spaciousness of the fellowship within it differ widely. Every discovery of a larger fellowship by the individual brings a glow of religious satisfaction. The origin of the Christian religion was bound up

---

[2] I have seen Southern pamphlets undertaking to prove that the negroes are not descended from Adam, but have evolved from African jungle beasts. The very orthodox authors were willing to accept the heretical philosophy of evolution for the black people, though of course they claimed biblical creation for the white. The purpose of this religious manoeuvre is to cut the bond of human obligation and solidarity established by religion, and put the negroes outside the protection of the moral law.

with a great transition from a nationalistic to an international religious consciousness. Paul was the hero of that conquest. The Christian God has been a breaker of barriers from the first. All who have a distinctively Christian experience of God are committed to the expansion of human fellowship and to the overthrow of barriers. To emphasize this and bring it home to the Christian consciousness is part of the mission of the social gospel, and it looks to theology for the intellectual formulation of what it needs.

We have discussed three points in this chapter: how the conception of God can be cleansed from the historic accretions of despotism and be democratized; how it can be saved from the indictment contained in the unjust suffering of great social groups; and how we can realize God as the ground of social unity. Freedom, justice, solidarity are among the aims of the social gospel. It needs a theology which will clearly express these in its conception of God.

CHAPTER XVI

THE HOLY SPIRIT, REVELATION, INSPIRATION, PROPHECY

The doctrine of the Holy Spirit is one of the most religious of all Christian doctrines. It is not primarily a product of reflection, but of the great religious emotions and experiences. Perhaps for that very reason it has been relatively a neglected section of doctrinal theology. It deals with the most intimate and mystic experiences of the soul, and does not seem to belong to the field especially cultivated by the social gospel.

But in fact the social nature of religion is clearly demonstrated in the work of the Holy Spirit. The prophets of the Old Testament were not lonely torches set aflame by the spirit of God; they were more like a string of electric lights along a road-side, which, though far apart, are all connected and caused by the same current. They transmitted not only their ideas but their spiritual receptivity and inspiration to one another. The great men of whom we think as solitary miracles of religious power were surrounded and upborne in their day by religious groups which have now melted back into oblivion. Their prophetic consciousness was awakened and challenged by historic events affecting the social group to which they belonged. "The burden of the Lord" was not for themselves but for their community. They knew that their revelation was to be a message. Their religious experiences were moments of intense social consciousness.

The Christian Church began its history as a community of inspiration. The new thing in the story of Pentecost is not only the number of those who received the tongue of fire but the fact that the Holy Spirit had become the common property of a group. What had seemed to some extent the privilege of aristocratic souls was now democratized. The spirit was poured on all flesh; the young saw visions, the old dreamed dreams; even on the slave class the spirit was poured. The charismatic life of the primitive Church was highly important for its coherence and loyalty in the crucial days of its beginning. It was a chief feeder of its strong affections, its power of testimony, and its sacrificial spirit. Religion has been defined as "the life of God in the soul of man." In Christianity it became also the life of God in the fellowship of man. The mystic experience was socialized.

The doctrine of the inspiration of the Bible, as we all know, has passed through profound changes in recent years. The change has all been away from religious individualism and toward a social comprehension of the religious facts.

The process of inspiration was formerly conceived as a transaction between God and the individual. The higher the doctrine of inspiration, the more solitary was the inspired individual. It would have defeated the purpose of the doctrine to admit the presence of outside influences. Even the intellect and personality of the recipient were sometimes represented as passive and quiescent. Philo, whose ideas the early Church followed, said: "A prophet gives forth nothing at all of his own, but acts as interpreter at the prompting of another in all his utterances, and as long as he is under inspiration he is in ignorance, his reason departing from its place, and yielding up the citadel of the soul, when the divine Spirit enters into it and strikes at the mechanism of the voice." In extreme orthodoxy it was a liberal concession to grant that the divine power utilized and respected the literary style and individual outlook of the writer.

The modern conception of inspiration not only recognizes the free operation and the contributions of the distinctive psychical equipment of the inspired person, but seeks in every way to get beyond the individual to the social group which produced him, to the spiritual predecessors who inspired him, and to the audience which moved him because he hoped to move it. We might characterize the progress of the historical study of religion in the last fifty years as a progressive effort to interpret religious individuals by their social contacts. The great work of biblical criticism has been to place every biblical book in its exact historical environment as a preliminary to understanding its religious message. The "*religionsgeschichtliche Methode*" takes up the work where the critical method drops it, and reaches out still further, beyond the ideas and purposes of the literary person to the religious drifts and desires and beliefs of his age, to which he more or less consciously reacted.

Every one who has shared in the results of this work will appreciate how helpful and fruitful this process at its best has been. It has opened up the inspiration of the past and released social values which had been completely locked away under the individualistic method of interpretation. The historical method has already done what the social gospel might wish it to do. Here we have a completed laboratory experiment proving the value and efficiency of a social understanding of religion. The only question is whether we can win just as strong a sense of the presence of God from this complicated social process of inspiration, as when God was believed to have dictated the books by a psychological miracle. It can be done, but the interpreter needs personal acquaintance with inspiration to do it.

In another direction, however, we have not yet overcome the narrowing influence of the old, mechanical views of inspiration.

Those who have had first-hand experience of inspiration either in their own souls or in the life of others, have always combined reverence for the authority of the word of the Lord and a realization of the human frailty and liability to error in the prophet. Paul and his churches had a rich experience of inspiration. Writing to the Thessalonians he asserts the right of prophesying, but takes the duty of critical scrutiny by the hearers as a matter of course: "Quench not the spirit" (in yourselves); despise not prophesying (in others); scrutinize all utterances; appropriate what is good" Inspiration did not involve infallibility when men knew it by experience.

When the inspirationalism of the primitive Church died out, the understanding of its nature grew artificial, just as the understanding of Old Testament inspiration had become centuries earlier. It was not to the interest of church leaders to emphasize that the laity had once possessed the gift of inspiration and the right of utterance. Consequently the realization of the charismatic life of the primitive Church was allowed to fade from the memory of Christians. The apostles alone stood out in the historical perspective as the possessors of inspiration. Their human frailties and fallibilities were forgotten or suppressed; they were conventionalized and fitted with haloes. Their utterances were infallible. Inspiration and infallibility were almost convertible terms. Being so high a gift, inspiration was strictly circumscribed, and was supposed to have ceased when the canon of the New Testament was completed. This, on the whole, has remained the popular orthodox view down to recent times. Now, so high a conception of inspiration discourages the stirring of the prophetic spirit in living men. A man might well claim that God had spoken to his soul and laid a message upon him. But who would want to claim that he is infallible? Psychical experiences are evoked by expectancy. If men do not expect to be regenerated, few will have the experience. If they do not expect to be inspired, few will make their way single-handed to such an experience. The Church has reversed all the maxims of Paul except the last. It has quenched the spirit; it has discountenanced prophesying; it has forbidden intellectual scrutiny of inspiration so far as the biblical books were concerned. The only thing it encouraged was to cleave to that which is good.

The old view of inspiration is supposed to be more deeply religious than the new. It did involve a more reverent and passive attitude of mind. But it robbed us of part of our consciousness of God. A religious man knows that he has no merit of his own, and that all his righteousness was wrought in him by God. To suppose that he can set his own will on God and work out his own salvation is sub-christian. We ought to have the same consciousness of God's influence on our intellectual comprehension of Christian truth. To suppose that we can work out a living knowledge of the truth from a sacred book without the enlightening energy of the spirit of God is sub-christian and rationalistic. On the other hand, to be conscious of the divine light, to listen to the inner voice, to read the inspired words of the Bible with an answering glow of fire, is part of the consciousness of God to which we are entitled. There are many degrees of clarity and power in this living inspiration, and heavy admixtures of human error, passion, and false sentiment, but the same is true of the experiences of regeneration and sanctification. It is the business of the Church to encourage, temper, and purify the intellectual, as well as the emotional and volitional experiences of its members.

At this point the social gospel coincides with the most energetic religious consciousness. Traditional theology has felt the need of inspired prophets and apostles chiefly in order to furnish the system of doctrine with a firm footing of inerrancy and infallibility. The doctrine of inspiration is not treated as part of the glorious results of redemption, and as the Christian salvation of the human intellect, but as part of the prolegomena of theology. The social gospel, on the other hand, feels the need of present inspiration and of living prophetic spirits in order to lead humanity toward the Kingdom of God. Wherever the Church is set in the centre and her aim is to keep the body of doctrine intact as delivered to it, inspiration will be located at the beginning of the line of tradition, and at most the power of infallible interpretation will be claimed for popes and church councils. Wherever the Kingdom of God is set to the front, inspiration will spontaneously spring into life at the points where the conflict is hot and active in the present. A theology adapted to the social gospel, therefore, will recognize inspiration as an indispensable force of our religion and an essential equipment of redemption. The social order can not be saved without regenerate men; neither can it be saved without inspired men.

The value of the regenerate individual for the advancement of the Kingdom of God consists largely in his prophetic quality. If the Holy Spirit works on his soul so that he has a vision of the Kingdom of God and its higher laws, then to some extent he will be living ahead of his age. In the qualities of his personality and in his judgments of men and events he will be a witness to the divine order of society, and will challenge the right of the world as it now is. If this prophetic insight is not dulled by ignorance and made erratic by eccentricities of character, but is guided by education and balance of character, its social force is very great.

Individualistic religion has bred saints, missionaries, pastors, and scholars, but few prophets. Some of its so-called prophets have been expounders of the prophecy of others. Religions of authority have no real use for prophets except to furnish a supernatural basis for doctrine. Hence prophecy used to be put on a level with miracles as "evidences of the Christian religion." Where the main interest is to keep doctrine undisturbed, living prophecy seems a dangerous and unsettling force.

Genuine prophecy springs up where fervent religious experience combines with a democratic spirit, strong social feeling, and free utterance. Some sense of antagonism between the will of God and the present order of things is necessary to ignite the spirit of the prophet.

This was the combination which produced the Hebrew prophets. We have the same combination in those manifold radical bodies which preceded and accompanied the Reformation. They all tended toward the same type, the type of primitive Christianity. Strong fraternal feeling, simplicity and democracy of organization, more or less communistic ideas about property, an attitude of passive obedience or conscientious objection toward the coercive and militaristic governments of the time, opposition to the selfish and oppressive Church, a genuine faith in the practicability of the ethics of Jesus, and, as the secret power in it all, belief in an inner experience of regeneration and an inner light which interprets the outer word of God. These radical bodies did not produce as many great individuals as we might have expected because their intellectuals and leaders were always killed off or silenced. But their communities were prophetic. They have been the forerunners of the modern world. They stood against war, against capital punishment, against slavery, and against coercion in matters of religion before others thought of it. It was largely due to their influence that the Puritan Revolution had its prophetic elements of leadership. The Free Churches throughout the world, consciously or unconsciously, clearly or dimly, have passed beyond the official types of orthodox Protestantism and have taken on some of the characteristics of the early radicals. Great church bodies now stand as a matter of course on those principles of freedom and toleration which only the boldest once dared to assert. The power of leadership is with those organizations and movements which have some prophetic qualities and trust to the inner light.

To-day it is the social gospel which has the democratic outlook and the sense of solidarity. If it also has spiritual fervor, it will have prophetic power.

The social gospel is not a doctrine turned backward to the sources of authority, but a faith turned forward to its task. It sees before it the Kingdom of Evil to be overcome, and the Kingdom of God to be established, and it cries aloud for an inspired word of God to give faith and power and guidance. If theology is to answer to the needs of the social gospel, it ought to assign to prophecy a definite place among the permanent forces of redemption. In recognizing the need of inspiration and prophecy the social gospel is more religious than the orthodox type, and more positive than that liberal type of theology which is chiefly interested in historical criticism.[1]

---

[1] I shall return to this subject once more at the end of the last chapter.

CHAPTER XVII

BAPTISM AND THE LORD'S SUPPER

The sacraments have occupied a large place in the worship and life of the Church, and a correspondingly wide room in theology. The Catholic Church is the institution of sacramental salvation. The Reformation was in large part a movement for cleansing the sacramental practices and doctrines. The disastrous split between the Lutheran and Zwinglian churches was due to differences about the significance of one of the sacraments. Large historical denominational bodies have formed about the effort to restore the genuine practice and doctrine of baptism. Evidently the conception of the sacraments has long been an active volcanic region in theology. The old controversial zeal has been followed by relative apathy. Except under "High Church" influences the importance of the sacraments in practical church life seems to be lessening and the issues are being forgotten.

Can the religious spirit of the social gospel give any fresh spiritual meaning to the ancient ordinances, or add anything to the theological interpretation of them? I confess I doubt it. The two fields of interest lie far apart at present. But as a challenge to thought perhaps the following considerations may have some use.

When the act of baptism was initiated by John the Baptist and continued for a time by Jesus, it was not a ritual act of individual salvation, but an act of dedication to a religious and social movement. Baptism at the Jordan was not received to save the individual by himself, or in a future life; it was received in view of the impending Messianic salvation and as an act of allegiance to a new order of things. The baptism of John can not be separated from his preaching; the former received its meaning and content from the latter. His preaching called men to repent of their old way of living, to quit grafting, and to begin to live in fraternal helpfulness. Baptism was the dramatic expression of an inward consent and allegiance to the higher standards of life which were to prevail in the Messianic community. It was the symbol of a revolutionary movement.

There is no indication that Jesus or his disciples practised baptism during the Galilean period of his work. When the practice was resumed by the primitive Church, it was once more an act of obedience and faith in view of the impending Messianic Kingdom at the return of the Lord. The ritual act now got its ethical interpretation from the remembered sayings of the Master and from the fraternal life of the Christian group.

Baptism was profoundly affected by the great change which came over Christianity when it left its Jewish environment and was assimilated by Greek religious and social life. It was gradually filled with new meanings. It was an act cancelling the guilt of all past sins; an act of regeneration; an act of exorcization, cleansing from the defilement of pagan worship and life. But it was less and less a dedication to the coming Kingdom of God. It still had a great social significance, for it was the act by which the individual stepped out of pagan society and into the fellowship of the Christian group, with its love, its dangers, and its limitations.

This change in the meaning and content of baptism was confirmed by the spread of infant baptism since the middle of the second century. The immediate cause for the baptism of young children was the belief that baptism is necessary for salvation, combined with the ever urgent facts of infant mortality. Origen, and still more Augustine, tied up the church practice with the doctrine of original sin. Baptism had been the symbol of a revolutionary hope, an ethical act which determined the will and life of the person receiving it. It was now a ceremony performed on a babe to save it from the guilt and power of original sin and to assure its salvation in heaven in case of its death.

Here again new social elements sprang up. The practical necessities of the case created a social backing for the young candidate. Since his own responses were still inarticulate, grown-up sponsors recited the creed and other formulas for him, and this service established a social relationship which often lasted for life. Since the faith of the child was still undeveloped, theology taught that the sponsors and the Church were to supply it.

In modern time much finer ideas have been attached to infant baptism. The act is based on the organic unity of the family; the parents thereby dedicate the child to God and pledge themselves to give it Christian nurture; the child is by baptism incorporated into the organism of the Church and made to share in its saving power; the act expresses the consciousness of the Church that the child is a child of God and has a right to claim the divine paternity. These are much more Christian ideas than those which first called infant baptism into existence.

Scarcely any Christian institution has experienced such changes and deteriorations as baptism, but of them all the loss of outlook toward the Kingdom of God was one of the most regrettable. Could the social gospel—at least in some instances—fill baptism with its original meaning? We could imagine a minister and a group of candidates who unite in feeling the evil of the present world-order and the promise and claims of the impending Christian world-order, together using baptism to express their solemn dedication to the tasks of the Kingdom of God, and accepting their rights as children of God within that Kingdom. In those churches in which baptism is administered in infancy, confirmation would offer the next best opportunity to impress and express such convictions. In the catechumenate the ancient Church put the candidate through long processes of exorcization to expel the demon powers which had infected him in his pagan life. Those churches which practise confirmation have shifted the instruction of the catechumenate to precede confirmation; those churches which practise adult baptism are much in need of a period of systematic instruction before baptism. It would be a really rational and Christian form of exorcization to break the infection of the sinful and illusive world-order and to explain the nature of a distinctively Christian order of life.

Such a restoration of its earliest meaning might save baptism from the religious and theological emptiness which now threatens its very existence. Its older doctrinal meanings have leaked away or evaporated. In the ancient Church it was closely connected with the prevalent belief in demonism. Patristic and scholastic theology bound it up with original sin. But we do not live in a realizing sense of demon powers, and original sin and baptismal regeneration seem to be marked for extinction. To say that Christ commanded it and that we must obey his ordinance, is equivalent to confessing that the act has lost its enthusiasm and its religious conviction. It is simply an order, which must be obeyed. Why not connect baptism with the Kingdom of God? It has always been an exit and an entrance; why not the exit from the Kingdom of Evil and the entrance into the Kingdom of God? That would, under right teaching and with the right people, give it solemn impressiveness. It would make it a truly Christian act. Baptism has always been dogged by superstitions, and thrust down into paganism. The individualistic interpretation of it as an escape from damnation tainted it with selfishness. Contact with the Kingdom of God would restore baptism to its original ethical and spiritual purity.

The Lord's Supper, like Baptism, has had a tragic history.

The meal in the upper room at Jerusalem was the last of many meals in which Jesus had broken the bread with his friends in the close intimacy of their wandering life. The spirit of all the previous meals was in this last meal. It was pervaded by the same strong and holy feelings of friendship which make the disappointment of Jesus in the garden so pathetic. It is a question whether Jesus' thought ran beyond the group of his friends when he asked for a repetition of the meal; it seems at least very unlikely that he purposed a cult act such as actually developed. His purpose was to create an act of loyalty which would serve to keep memory and fidelity alive until he should return and eat and drink with them again in the Kingdom of God. Jesus had created a wonderful social group. He wanted it to hold together. The Lord's Supper came into existence through strong religious and social feeling and its purpose was the maintenance of the highest loyalty.

In the primitive Church the memorial act was part of a fraternal meal in which the Christian group met in religious privacy to express its peculiar unity and coherence. Such communistic meals, to which every member contributed his portion of food, were quite common among the religious and fraternal societies of the time. Communistic meals produce solidaristic feelings even today. Paul was not a marked exponent of democratic emotions, but he was deeply shocked when he learned that the social character of the common meal at Corinth had been debased by the intrusion of the class divisions of the outside world. The well to do gathered in coteries to eat their plentiful supplies, while the poor sat neglected and ashamed. His feeling testifies to the social beauty and power which the Lord's Supper then possessed. (1 Cor. 11:17-34.)

There can be no doubt that the Lord's Supper has always had a powerful influence in consolidating the fraternal organization of the Church. It has always been an inner privilege, for which preparation had to be made, and from which a man might be excluded; consequently it was prized. In the European State Churches, people who have become wholly indifferent to church life, still attend communion once a year and would regard it as a loss to be shut out from it. In the early Church, discipline consisted largely in barring offenders from communion. The humiliation and sacrifices assumed by penitents in order to get back into the full solidarity of the Church shows that strong social feelings were at work here. Reconciliation among the members preceded communion. None could share in the Lord's Supper who were in a state of enmity with other Christians. Thus people were compelled to face Christ's law of love and forgiveness, and pluck the bitter root of pride and ill-will from their hearts. This, too, was a social value of the ceremony. The rubric of the Book of Common Prayer still empowers the minister to warn notorious offenders to stay away, and to do the same "with those, betwixt whom he perceiveth malice and hatred to reign, not suffering them to be partakers of the Lord's Table, until he know them to be reconciled." This is expressed also in the beautiful invitation:

"Ye who do truly and earnestly repent you of your sins, and are in love and charity with your neighbours, and intend to lead a new life, following the commandments of God, and walking from henceforth in his holy ways: Draw near with faith, and take this holy sacrament to your comfort, and make your humble confession to Almighty God, devoutly kneeling."

In the first generation, and perhaps later, the Lord's Supper still had an outlook toward the coming of the Lord. We find this still in a significant phrase in Paul, who otherwise emphasized other lines of thought: "For as often as ye eat this bread and drink this cup, ye proclaim the Lord's death *till he come*" Now, to the larger part of the primitive Church the coming of the Lord signified the coming of the millennial reign of peace and righteousness on earth. The Lord's Supper was, therefore, connected with the realization of the social ideals and hopes of the Church. The prevalence of prophecy in the charismatic life of primitive Christianity points in the same direction. It acted as an interpretation of the Lord's Supper.

The outlook toward the coming of the Lord became dim as time went on. The eucharistic act was cut loose from the fraternal meal, and that was a great lessening of its social value. The meal was still held occasionally in the evening, but turned into a charitable performance where the rich fed the poor, and it finally ceased. The eucharistic act was connected with the church worship on Sunday morning. It developed sacramental qualities in two directions; it was mystic food, in which the Lord was present and through which his grace and power and immortal life nourished the soul; and it was a sacrifice offered to God. The fact that it was the central mystery of the esoteric ritual of the church made it very important as a bond of unity, but the fraternal feeling of the early days was lessened. It intensified the consciousness of God rather than the consciousness of man. The fraternal meal of Jesus became a chief means of creating the priesthood of the Catholic Church, and the main door through which superstitious beliefs came in. In time it became the mass, in which the priest partook of the bread and wine while the people watched him doing it. He might even go through the whole performance alone, for the benefit of a deceased person, according to the terms of an endowment. Thus the Lord's Supper lost its meaning because it was in the hands of a body which had neither social outlook nor democratic emotions.

The Protestant Reformation concentrated on the reform of the Lord's Supper. The laity shared more fully in it. The private mass was abolished. Some of the social feeling was restored. But not the social outlook. The act turned backward and not forward. It is an act of remembrance; in it we appropriate the atoning death of our Saviour. Where it is experienced most deeply, it is a mystic act of fellowship between the unseen Lord and the silent soul of the worshipper.

For a time the great act of fraternal love became the object of bitter controversial feelings between Catholic and Protestant, and between Lutheran and Calvinist, and exercised a very unsocial and divisive influence.

While the great churches were bitterly contending over the question whether their Lord was physically or spiritually present, and if physically, whether by transubstantiation or consubstantiation, the persecuted Anabaptists, who had neither the right to meet nor to exist, had the spirit of the original institution among them. As in the primitive Church, their service was preceded by searching of heart and reconciliation, so that all might be one in Christ. As in the upper room at Jerusalem, they acted in full view of death, and their main thought was to gain strength for imprisonment and torture by once more touching the garment-hem of their Lord. They often dwelt on the fact that many grains of wheat had been crushed and had felt the heat of the oven to make this bread, and many berries of the vine had been pressed in the wine-press to make this wine; in the same way the followers of Jesus must pass through affliction and persecution in order to form the body of the Lord. Thus these poor proletarians, hunted by the tyrannical combinations of Church and State, Catholic and Protestant alike, returned to the original spirit of the Lord's Meal and realized that Real Presence about which others wrangled.

Can the social gospel contribute to make the Lord's Supper more fully an act of fraternity and to connect it again with the social hope of the Kingdom of God?

In the Lord's Supper we re-affirm our supreme allegiance to our Lord who taught us to know God as our common father and to realize that all men are our brethren. In the midst of a world full of divisive selfishness we thereby accept brotherhood as the ruling principle of our life and undertake to put it into practice in our private and public activities. We abjure the selfish use of power and wealth for the exploitation of our fellows. We dedicate our lives to establishing the Kingdom of God and to winning mankind to its laws. In contemplation of the death of our Lord we accept the possibility of risk and loss as our share of service. We link ourselves to his death and accept the obligation of the cross.

It is open to any minister to emphasize thoughts such as these, connecting the Lord's Supper with the Kingdom of God. All who have the new social consciousness would feel their appeal. Any person encountering antagonism or loss for the sake of the Kingdom would find comfort and strength in connecting his troubles with the cross of Christ. The Lord's Supper was instituted by Jesus in full view of his death. We can fully share his spirit only when we too confront the possibility of suffering in the same cause.

The emphasis on such thoughts would be the reaction of the social gospel on the religious and theological content of the Lord's Supper. They would be a challenge to the Church to realize its mission as the social embodiment of the Christ-spirit in humanity. They would constitute a spiritual preparation for the actual experience of the Real Presence that Presence which requires a social group of two or three because love and the sense of solidarity are necessary to enable him to be in the midst of us.

CHAPTER XVIII

ESCHATOLOGY

Eschatology raises two questions of profound interest to the human mind. First, What is the future of the individual after his brief span of years on earth is over? Second, What is to be the ultimate destiny of the human race?

These questions are important to every thoughtful mind, and they are inseparable from religion. Religion is always eschatological. Its characteristic is faith. It lives in and for the future. In all other parts of our life we deal with imperfect things, fluctuating, conditioned, relative, and never complete. In religion we seek for the final realities, the absolute values, the things as God sees them, complete, in organic union.

All religions of higher development have some mythology about the future. The Christian religion needs a Christian eschatology. To be satisfying to the Christian consciousness any teaching concerning the future life of the individual must express that high valuation of the eternal worth of the soul which we have learned from Christ, and must not contradict or sully the revelation of the justice, love, and forgiving mercy of our heavenly Father contained in his words, his life, and his personality. Any doctrine about the future of the race which is to guide our thought and action, must view it from distinctively Christian, ethical points of view, and must not contradict what is historically and scientifically certain.

In fact, however, our traditional eschatology never was a purely Christian product, growing organically from Christian soil and expressing distinctively Christian convictions. It is more in the nature of an historical mosaic combining fragments of non-christian and pre-christian systems with genuine Christian ideas. It took shape under special historical conditions, and was broken up and shaped afresh to express other conditions, but in no case was it shaped to suit our modern needs. Like all eschatologies it expresses ideas about the universe, but these cosmic conceptions are pre-scientific. The world portrayed in them is the world of the Ptolemaic system, a world three stories high, with heaven above and hell beneath. During the formative centuries the Oriental and Greek religious life, which deeply influenced Christianity, was dualistic, and whatever influences have come from that source are not only historically but essentially unchristian. A Christian mind can get most satisfaction by contemplating how the genius of the Christian religion took this heterogeneous and often alien material and made something approximately Christian of it after all.

As a consequence eschatology is usually loved in inverse proportion to the square of the mental diameter of those who do the loving. Calvin was the greatest exegete of his day and he wrote commentaries on nearly all the books of the Old and New Testaments, but he gave the Apocalypse a wide berth. No interpretation of this main biblical source ever won general consent as long as it was interpreted doctrinally. The wise threw up their hands; those who devoted their minds to it, often suffered from mild obsession. Our generation is the first in eighteen hundred years to understand this book as its author, or authors, meant it to be understood, and now it is one of the most enlightening and interesting books of them all. In primitive Christianity eschatology was in the centre of religious interest and thought. Today it is on the circumference, and with some Christians it lies outside the circumference. Theologians of liberal views are brief or apologetic when they reach eschatology. This situation is deeply regrettable. Perhaps no other section of theology is so much in need of a thorough rejuvenation.

Those who believe in the social gospel are especially concerned in this element of weakness in theology. The social gospel seeks to develop the vision of the Church toward the future and to co-operate with the will of God which is shaping the destinies of humanity. It would be aided and reinforced by a modern and truly Christian conception about the future of mankind. At present no other theological influence so hampers and obstructs the social gospel as that of eschatology. All considerations taken from the life of the twentieth century cry out for something like the social gospel; but the ideas of the first century contained in eschatology are used to veto it. Those who have trained their religious thinking on the Hebrew prophets and the genuine teachings of Jesus are for the social gospel; those who have trained it on apocalyptic ideas are against it. This is all the more pathetic because the premillennial scheme is really an outline of the social salvation of the race. Those who hold it exhibit real interest in social and political events. But they are best pleased when they see humanity defeated and collapsing, for then salvation is nigh. Active work for the salvation of the social order before the coming of Christ is not only vain but against the will of God. Thus eschatology defeats the Christian imperative of righteousness and salvation.

Historical science and the social gospel together may be able to affect eschatology for good. Historical criticism by itself makes it look imbecile and has no creative power. The social gospel has that moral earnestness and religious faith which exerts constructive influence on doctrine.

In the first place, the social gospel can at least give us a sympathetic understanding and right valuation of some of the elements contained in the inherited body of ideas. A merely theological comprehension of it is a false understanding. It must be understood historically in connection with the social situations which created its parts, like the buildings on an old college campus, or like the Constitution and its amendments.

Those parts of Christian eschatology which deal with the future of the race are on the whole derived from Judaism, and we owe their ethical qualities to the valiant democratic spirit of the prophets. Their "Day of Yahveh" became our "Great Judgment;" the time of peace and righteousness which was to follow it became the Christian millennium. The whole was originally the religious equivalent of a wholesome revolution in which the oppressing class is eliminated and the righteous, poor get relief. This central section of Christian eschatology was the product of the brave fight which Jehovah and his people made together for the ancestral freedom of the common people. The idea of a resurrection of the dead did not come into eschatology through growing individualism, but out of the feeling that the righteous who had died before the inauguration of the new order were entitled to a share in the common happiness. Demonology and satanology, which pervaded Jewish eschatology after the exile, were, as we have pointed out, in part a religious expression of social and political hatred and despair.

Those parts of eschatology which deal with the future of the individual were in the main derived from contemporary Greek life. Greek religion was characterized by a profound desire for immortality and an equally deep sense of the sin and sadness of this earthly life. The "mysteries" ministered to this desire; Christianity did it more effectively. In turn these religious desires brought out and strengthened those eschatological facts and ideas in Christianity which could serve them. Here we have one chief cause for the increasing other-worldliness of Christianity. Now, this attitude of weariness and resignation, which led to the immense popularity of ascetic ideals of life, was in part a product of the Roman Empire. It had clamped down its bureaucracy and its tax-gathering apparatus on all Mediterranean civilization; the method was political subjugation; the aim was economic exploitation. The self-government of the Greek states by which the citizens might have been protected, had been put under safe control. Revolt was useless. If we imagine a single empire today permanently holding the seas and continents in its grip, and enriching its aristocracy from the industry of others, with every way of escape barred, we shall understand the apathy of men under the Roman Empire. The escape into immortality was the only way to freedom left to all. This social condition left deep traces in Christian eschatology.

Thus social causes contributed to the origin of eschatological ideas. Other social causes led to their disappearance. Amid the doctrinal changes of the Protestant Reformation eschatology remained unchanged except that purgatory was cut out. It had no support in the canonical Scriptures. That was one motive. But, also, the belief in purgatory had become a prolific source of income for the Church. Hell was unalterable; no gifts or indulgences could unlock its gates. The penalties to be absolved in purgatory could be lightened by indulgence, and shortened by the prayers and pious works of friends. The indulgence system was built on this belief, and innumerable endowments were provided for masses to be read for the repose of the souls in purgatory. Now, the income bearing property of the Church and the clergy living on it constituted the greatest social and economic problem of the age before the Reformation. Wherever the Reformation received the support of government, church property was "secularized" or confiscated. When Protestant theology denied the existence of purgatory, it denied that the Church could render any quid pro quo for its vested incomes, and this weakened the legal and moral hold of the Church on its endowments, and cut under some of the most offensive practices of the Church. Unless these practical considerations had made purgatory a social issue, it may be questioned whether the lack of biblical support for the doctrine would have sufficed to suppress it. The resulting contest of Protestant theology against the doctrine of purgatory induced it, by its necessary reactions, to assert that the fate of the soul is fixed at death and the saved enter into glory.

Perhaps the modern hesitancy about the doctrine of hell also has social causes. Despotic governments formerly accustomed men to frequent, public, and very horrible executions, and to long and hopeless imprisonments. Since the spread of democracy has somewhat weakened the cruel grip of the governing classes, the criminal law has become more humane. Capital punishments have become less frequent, less public, and less cruel. The outfit of prisons has improved. There is an increasing feeling that punishment should not be merely vindictive and terrifying, but remedial and disciplinary, aiming at the salvation and social restoration of the offender. Our prisons are our human hells, where men are cut off from all that exercises a saving influence on our lives the love of wife and child and home, work and play, contact with nature, hope, ambition, only fear and coercion are in full force. If democracy should further weaken the hold of the governing classes on the penal system of the country; and if Christianity should impress us with the divine worth of "the least of these" in prison and our obligation to offer them salvation; and if the prison system becomes redemptive; can theology then continue to get the moral approval of mankind for a divine prison which is not educational and redemptive, but wholly without change or end?

Thus eschatology has all along been influenced by social causes, while keeping on its own conservative path of tradition. The Jewish people under social and political oppression, and the primitive Church under persecution wept and prayed our eschatology into existence. Our Apocalypse is wet with human tears and must be read that way. Ever since, some sections of eschatology have been vivified, others modified, and some consigned to oblivion through the pressure of social causes. Has not the social consciousness of our age, speaking through the social gospel, also a right to be heard in the shaping of eschatology?

Any reformatory force taking hold of eschatology can not expect a fresh start, but must reckon with its traditional contents and its biblical and theological sources. It may clear our path to lay down several propositions about this material coming from the past.

1. In everything contributed by the Old Testament we should seek to distinguish what is due to the divine inspiration of the prophets. We are under no obligation to accept the mythical ideas and cosmic speculations of the Hebrew people, their limited geography, their primitive astronomy, the historical outlook of the book of Daniel, or the Babylonian and Persian ideas which flowed into their religious thought. What has authority for us is the ethical and religious light of men who had an immediate consciousness of the living God, and saw him now and hereafter acting for righteousness, for the vindication of the oppressed classes, and for the purging of the social life of the nation. These elements of the Old Testament carry authority because they are in spiritual consensus with the revelation of God in Christ.

2. We should learn to distinguish clearly between prophecy and apocalypticism. There is as much difference between them as between Paul and Pope Gregory I. From apocalypticism we get the little diagrams which map out the history of the human race on deterministic methods, as if God consulted the clock. From the same source the active belief in demonology, the

reliance on miraculous catastrophes, and the blue light of unreality have always come into eschatology. Those who fill their minds with it, thereby tie themselves to all backward things. Apocalyptic believers necessarily insist on the verbal inerrancy of Scripture and oppose historical methods, for their work consists in piecing mosaics of texts. Historically we can appreciate the religious value of apocalypticism in later Judaism, just as we can appreciate the religious value of the belief in transubstantiation or of scholastic theology. But as a present-day influence in religion it is dangerous. It has probably done more to discredit eschatology than any other single influence.

3. In the New Testament it is our business to sift out what is distinctively Christian in origin and spirit. It stands to reason that the leaven of the Christian spirit was not able at once to transform the inherited ideas of Jews and Gentiles of the first generation. For instance, Christianity had to struggle hard with the stubborn nationalistic pride of Judaism which claimed either a monopoly of messianic salvation or at least special privileges within it. Even Paul, the chief exponent of international religion, could not get away from his pro-Jewish feelings, and thought God was saving the Gentiles in order to stir up the Jews and get them saved. Jesus did not make the judgment depend on nationality but on the sense of human solidarity, and repeatedly foreshadowed that the Jews would be supplanted. In the Apocalypse we are carried back into Jewish feeling and points of view. The mind of Jesus Christ is our criterion for an ethical scrutiny of these ingredients.

4. The effort to systematize the eschatological statements of biblical writers has always been muddled by the supposition that they all thought alike. There was, as yet, no orthodoxy. All were deeply interested in these questions, and men of strong conviction made their own formulations. The Apocalypse, Paul, and the fourth gospel are strikingly unlike.

The Apocalypse expounds the old social hope of Israel. The great woes and the overthrow of the mystic Babylon have political significance. There are a thousand years of messianic peace on this earth. Even after the last eruption of Satan and the great judgment the new earth is still on the old earth; the new Jerusalem comes down here, and there are trees, and a river, and happy people.

Paul, on the other hand, has no room for a millennium of flesh and blood men on a material earth. The coming of Christ would usher in a cosmic change; the material world would end and the groaning of dying creation would cease; the living and the dead would receive spiritual bodies; therewith the last enemy, Death, would be overcome, and God would be all in all. In Paul the Jewish and the Greek streams of thought join. Probably in this, as in other things, Paul stood for a new theology; the Apocalypse comes nearer to being the prevalent view of the first generation.

In the fourth gospel and the epistles of John we see the future translated into the present tense. The chief points of primitive eschatology, the antichrist, the parousia, the judgment, the resurrection, are still acknowledged; but there are many antichrists now present; the coming of the Comforter takes the place of the parousia; the judgment takes place when men accept or reject the light; the spiritual transformation into eternal life takes place now. Eschatology is dissolved into Christology; the Kingdom of God gives way to the Church. It is far more instructive spiritually to see these different views side by side than to see them mangled and forced into conformity.

5. The most troublesome problem at present is to determine what Jesus himself thought about the future. A group of able scholars has put such emphasis on the eschatological sayings of Jesus that he himself has been turned into an apocalyptic enthusiast and the authority of his ethical teaching has been impaired by being yoked with apocalyptic expectations. This school of thought has done valuable work, but the future will probably show that it has overworked its working hypothesis.

Ordinary critical analysis eliminates a good deal of eschatological material as later accretions. The earliest of the documentary sources of the gospels, "Q," contains least.[1]

All human analogies make it certain that his followers coloured his ideas with their own previous conceptions. They could not help it. Language is rich on the lower, and thin on the higher, spiritual levels. Men of high religious power have often become poetical makers of language because they had to wrestle with their medium of expression and coin new figures and terms. They must use the lower terminology to express the inexpressible. Their followers, the loyal lower souls, invariably coarsen and materialize their teachings, taking the figures for realities and the accidental for the substance. The more original and spiritual a teacher is, the larger will be the inevitable ratio of misunderstanding. We must remember that the sayings of Jesus were repeated and transmitted orally for years before our earliest documents were written.

[1] Harnack, " Sayings of Jesus" p. 250. "The tendency to exaggerate the apocalyptic and eschatological elements in our Lord's message and to subordinate to this the merely religious and ethical elements, will ever find its refutation in Q."

We see the whole situation incorrectly when we tacitly assume that the ideas of Jesus were uniform throughout his teaching ministry. If we take the doctrine of his real humanity seriously, he was a growing personality, and his ideas were in the making. A man's ideas are developed by reacting on the ideas of his fellow men by assent or dissent. It is vital to this problem to know in what direction Jesus was working, into apocalypticism or out of it. We can see that he began with a Jewish horizon and broke his way into a world-wide and human world. How about his eschatology? His earliest parables are a decisive answer. He chose that form of teaching because he wanted to veil and yet reveal his polemical departure from current messianic ideas. He took his illustrations from organic life to express the idea of the gradual growth of the Kingdom. He was shaking off catastrophic ideas and substituting developmental ideas. John had put the judgment at the beginning of the Messiah's work; Jesus pushed it over to the end. He had no taste for that part of the Messianic program. In short, apocalypticism was part of the environment in which he began his thinking; it was not his personal product; he was emancipating himself from it. This is essential.

The intellect of Jesus was religious and prophetic; it was not constructed for apocalypticism. It had too many windows. Paul's ethical teaching got its orientation from his eschatology. The ethics of Jesus would have remained the same if the range of time had lengthened before him. His mind did push impetuously forward, but not toward a scheme of distant events, but toward the immediate saving acts of God. To him the Kingdom of God was both future and present. Whoever can harbour that antimony has risen above apocalypticism.

6. The eschatological schemes of primitive Christianity were all based on the supposition that the end would come soon. If Paul expected a longer interval in his later life, it was a matter of years, not of centuries. The actual duration of the present world for nineteen hundred years has disrupted the whole outline. The judgment and the general resurrection of the dead were necessary parts of the Jewish eschatology because the judgment was needed to decide who was to share in the Messianic happiness, and the resurrection enabled the dead to have their part in it. But what is the use of the judgment if the fate of every man is decided at his death and he goes directly to heaven or hell? And why should a Christian of the first century receive his body again at the general resurrection when he has lived in heaven without it for eighteen hundred years?

History is a revelation of God's will. God thinks in action, and speaks in events. His historical realities are a surer word of God than any prophecy. The least of us today knows things which would have revolutionized the eschatology of the apostles. Are we obedient to the revelation of God if we think more of the sprouting grain than of the full ear, and artificially put ourselves back where we do not belong?

7. The early Catholic Church dealt reverently with the primitive eschatology, and yet changed it profoundly. The earthly millennium was very dear to the common people, but the intellectuals and college graduates who had studied Greek philosophy, had no use for it. The Gnostics hated it, and the semi-Gnostic Alexandrian theology undermined it. What sort of religious ideal was this which pictured fertile fields and vineyards, lots of babies romping, and old men holding on to life for a hundred years? How did that chime with a holy desire for heaven and the "angelic life" of asceticism? Moreover how did the theocratic and fraternal social order pictured in the millennial ideal square with the Roman Empire, the present distribution of property, the eminence of the upper classes, the permanence of church institutions, and the power of the bishops? (Church historians usually dwell on the theological objections to the "carnal" millennial ideas, but fail to see how distasteful the social elements of the millennial ideal must have been to those who controlled the teaching of the Church.) So the millennium was dropped out, while the safer and more distant parts of the Jewish eschatology were retained. Personal immortality, of course, had long ago crowded the racial eschatology aside in point of real interest.

But the most decisive fact in transforming the substance of primitive eschatology was the Church itself. Its future was now the future of Christianity. In Jewish eschatology there was no Church in the picture; only the people. In primitive Christian thought the Church was real, but it was like a temporary house put up to shelter the believers till the Lord came and the real salvation began. But the Parousia did not come, and the temporary shelter grew and grew, and became the main thing. Even if the doctrines of eschatology had been kept unchanged, they would no longer have been the same after the Catholic Church had come on the scene.

The considerations discussed above are necessary, it seems to me, for a proper understanding and valuation of the biblical material in traditional eschatology. A few constructive propositions can now be made about the future of the race.

1. The future development of the race should have a larger place in practical Christian teaching. The great ethical issues of the future lie in this field, and the mind of Christian men and women should be active there. If we can not be guided by moral and spiritual thought, we shall be guided by bitter experience. The Great War is in truth a grim discussion of the future of the race on this planet, but a discussion with both reason and religion left out. We have the amplest warrant for directing the prophetic thought of religious men toward the social and political future of humanity, for all eschatology derived from Hebrew sources dealt with these interests. A stronger emphasis on the future of the race will simply restore the genuinely Christian emphasis. But if Christian teachers are to teach truth about history, they must have truth to teach. If all ministers and Bible School teachers should now suddenly begin to talk on these subjects, the angels above would probably be astonished to see a still thicker vapour of partisan fury and nationalistic egotism rising from all countries.

2. All Christian discussions of the past and the future must be religious, and filled with the consciousness of God in human affairs. God is in history. He has the initiative. Where others see blind forces working dumb agony, we must see moral will working toward redemption and education. A religious view of history involves a profound sense of the importance of moral issues in social life. Sin ruins; righteousness establishes, and love consolidates. In the last resort the issues of future history lie in the moral qualities and religious faith of nations. This is the substance of all Hebrew and Christian eschatology.

3. We need a restoration of the millennial hope, which the Catholic Church dropped out of eschatology. It was crude in its form but wholly right in its substance. The duration of a thousand years is a guess and immaterial. All efforts to fix "times and seasons" are futile. But the ideal of a social life in which the law of Christ shall prevail, and in which its prevalence shall result in peace, justice and a glorious blossoming of human life, is a Christian ideal. An outlook toward the future in which the "spiritual life" is saved and the economic life is left unsaved is both unchristian and stupid. If men in the past have given a "carnal" colouring of richness to the millennial hope, let us renounce that part, and leave the ideals of luxury and excess to men of the present capitalistic order. Our chief interest in any millennium is the desire for a social order in which the worth and freedom of every least human being will be honoured and protected; in which the brotherhood of man will be expressed in the common possession of the economic resources of society;

and in which the spiritual good of humanity will be set high above the private profit interests of all materialistic groups. We hope for such an order for humanity as we hope for heaven for ourselves.

4. As to the way in which the Christian ideal of society is to come, — we must shift from catastrophe to development. Since the first century the divine Logos has taught us the universality of Law, and we must apply it to the development of the Kingdom of God. It is the untaught and pagan mind which sees God's presence only in miraculous and thundering action; the more Christian our intellect becomes, the more we see God in growth. By insisting on organic development we shall follow the lead of Jesus when, in his parables of the sower and of the seed growing secretly, he tried to educate his disciples away from catastrophes to an understanding of organic growth. We shall also be following the lead of the fourth gospel, which translated the terms of eschatology into the operation of present spiritual forces. We shall be following the lead of the Church in bringing the future hope down from the clouds and identifying it with the Church; except that we do not confine it to the single institution of the Church, but see the coming of the Kingdom of God in all ethical and spiritual progress of mankind. To convert the catastrophic terminology of the old eschatology into developmental terms is another way of expressing faith in the immanence of God and in the presence of Christ. It is more religious to believe in a present than in an absent and future Christ. Jesus saw the Kingdom as present and future. This change from catastrophe to development is the most essential step to enable modern men to appreciate the Christian hope.[2]

5. This process will have to utilize all constructive and educational forces in humanity. In our conception of personal regeneration, likewise, we have been compelled to think less of emotional crises and more of religious nurture and education. The coming of the Kingdom of God will be the regeneration of the super-personal life of the race, and will work out a social expression of what was contained in the personality of Christ.

---

[2]Pfleiderer, "Grundriss der christlichen Glaubenslehre" §177, has this fine summary: "The primitive Christian faith in the return of Christ and the establishment of his Kingdom on earth embodied the ideal of an earthly realization of the Kingdom of God. It set up the extensive and intensive penetration of humanity by the Christian spirit as the aim and task of history. The victorious coming and kingly rule of Christ on earth is achieved by the organization of all mankind in a fellowship of children of God, and by the continuous ethical transformation of all society through the power of the Christian spirit. But since this takes place within the historic life of nations, the process is bound to human conditions and limits."

6. The coming of the Kingdom of God will not be by peaceful development only, but by conflict with the Kingdom of Evil. We should estimate the power of sin too lightly if we forecast a smooth road. Nor does the insistence on continuous development eliminate the possibility and value of catastrophes. Political and social revolutions may shake down the fortifications of the Kingdom of Evil in a day. The Great War is a catastrophic stage in the coming of the Kingdom of God. Its direct effects will operate for generations. Our descendants will have a better perspective than we to see how all the sins of modern civilization have brought forth death after their own kind, and how the social repentance of nations may lay the foundation for a new beginning.

7. An eschatology which is expressed in terms of historic development has no final consummation. Its consummations are always the basis for further development. The Kingdom of God is always coming, but we can never say "Lo here." Theologians often assert that this would be unsatisfactory. "A kingdom of social righteousness can never be perfect; man remains flesh; new generations would have to be trained anew; only by a world-catastrophe can the Kingdom of glory be realized." Apparently we have to postulate a static condition in order to give our minds a rest; an endless perspective of development is too taxing. Fortunately God is not tired as easily as we. If he called humanity to a halt in a "kingdom of glory" he would have on his hands some millions of eager spirits whom he has himself trained to ceaseless aspiration and achievement, and they would be dying of ennui. Besides, what is the use of a perfect ideal which never happens? A progressive Kingdom of righteousness happens all the time in installments, like our own sanctification. Our race will come to an end in due time; the astronomical clock is already ticking which will ring in the end. Meanwhile we are on the march toward the Kingdom of God, and getting our reward by every fractional realization of it which makes us hungry for more. A stationary humanity would be a dead humanity. The life of the race is in its growth.

Since at death we emigrate from the social life of mankind, the future life of the individual might seem to lie outside of the scope of our discussion. But in truth our conceptions of the life hereafter are deeply affected by the fundamental convictions of the social gospel.

There is no inherent contradiction whatever between the hope of the progressive development of mankind toward the Kingdom of God and the hope of the consummation of our personal life in an existence after death. The religious belief in the future life is often bitterly attacked by social radicals because in actual practice the deep interest in it which is cultivated by the Church, weakens interest in social justice and acts as a narcotic to numb the sense of wrong. The more the social gospel does its work within the Church, the more will this moral suspicion against the doctrine of the future life lessen.

Belief in a future life is not essential to religious faith. The religious minds who speak to us from the pages of the Old Testament, though they probably believed in future existence, apparently gained neither comfort nor incentive from that belief. There is doubtless an increasing number of religious men and women today who find their satisfaction in serving God now, but expect their personal existence to end at death.

The hope that we shall survive death is not a self-evident proposition. When it is intelligent, it is an act of faith, — a tremendous assertion of faith. It may get support from science, from philosophy, or from psychical research, but its main supports are the resurrection of Christ, his teachings, and the common faith of the Christian Church, which all embolden the individual. Further, the sense of personality, which is intensified and ennobled by the Christian life, and rises to the sense of imperishable worth in the assurance that we are children of God.

The hope of a higher life for the race does not solve he problem of the individual. It is a matter of profound satisfaction to those whose life has really matured and been effective to think that they have made a contribution to the richness and the redemption of the race. But none of us lives out his life fully. There are endowments in us which have never been put to use for others, and tastes and cravings which have been starved md suppressed. Moreover only a small percentage of men and women under present conditions are able to develop their powers beyond the feeblest beginnings. A large percentage die in childhood; uncounted others lave been used up by labour, — shrunken and intimidated souls. Where do they come in? Is it enough for them to think that they have been laid like sills in the mud that future generations may live in the mansion erected on their dead bodies and souls? Besides, the best society on earth can not last for ever. This planet may end at any time and it is sure to die by collision or old age some time. What then will be the net product of all our labours? Plainly a man has a larger and completer hope if he looks forward to eternal life for himself as well as to a better destiny for the race.

4. It is our business, however, to christianize both expectations. It is possible to fear hell and desire heaven in a pagan spirit, with a narrow-

minded selfishness that cares nothing for others, and is simply an extension to the future life of the grabbing spirit fostered by the Kingdom of Evil. The desire for heaven gets Christian dignity and quality only when it arises on the basis of that solidaristic state of mind which is cultivated by the social gospel.

Two theories, quite unlike, are held as private opinions by many Christian individuals, though not sanctioned by traditional theology. The theory of conditional immortality is largely based on evolutionary ideas. It holds that only those will survive who have attained to a spiritual life capable of surviving. The theory of re-incarnation, which has been held by a few eminent minds in theology and by many outside of it, comes to us mostly through theosophical channels from the East. It teaches that we live in a succession of lives, each of them adapted to the spiritual attainments of the individual and disciplinary in its effect; through them we can gradually exhaust the possibilities of human life and rise to spiritual levels above man.

5.The social gospel could utilize the latter idea if it were commonly held. It would be an attractive idea to those who have fought for humanity, to come back to this earth and help on the Cause once more, beginning afresh on the basis of the experiences and character attained in the present life. The reward of a fine life, then, would be more life of the same kind. On the other hand there would be remarkable chances of retribution and purgation. A man who has prostituted women, might be re-incarnated as a prostitute and see how he likes it. A woman who has lived softly on the proceeds of child labour might be re-born as a little Georgia girl working in a cotton mill. A man who has helped to lynch a negro, might be born in a black skin and be lynched by his own grandsons.

Both theories, however, are somewhat aristocratic in their effect. When we consider the terrible inequality of opportunity for spiritual development in our present world, it does not convey a sense of Christian solidarity to think of a minority climbing into eternal life while the majority wilt away like unfertilized blossoms.

The theory of re-incarnation seems to offer a fair chance for all, provided each soul is really started in the exact environment which it has earned by its past life and in which it can best develop for the future. Theosophists have devised a spiritual bureaucracy of "Masters" or higher spiritual beings who manage this very essential matter. In actual practice it is interesting to observe that those who profess to have a recollection of past existences, all seem to have been stately and famous personages. They do sometimes become savages or courtesans for one life-time to expiate dark deeds of vengeance, or as interesting slumming expeditions. The plain people who just raise hogs or sell cheese in one existence, seem to forget it in the next, which is very human.

It is a more serious question whether this doctrine is not incompatible with social unrest and indignation. If the poor are in their present condition because they have deserved it in a previous life, why should we worry about them? The present child-labourers may be former stock-holders who have come back to get the other side, and we should be interfering with justice by trying to uplift them. If people living in bad tenements are in the conditions best adapted to their future spiritual development in later incarnations, we may be tampering with things too high for us in condemning the tenements. This doctrine explains the present inequalities too well. It seems to cut the nerve of the social movement much more effectively than the hope of heaven ever did.

Of course the Christian realm of grace would disappear, and a reign of Karma and exact retribution would supplant it.

6. The most unattractive element in the orthodox outlook on the future life is the immediate fixity of the two states. When we die, our destiny is immediately and irrevocably settled for us. As the Westminster Larger Catechism (Question 86) has it:

> The communion in glory with Christ, which the members of the invisible church enjoy immediately after death, is in that their souls are then made perfect in holiness and received into the highest heavens, where they behold the face of God in light and glory; waiting for the full redemption of their bodies, which even in death continue united to Christ, and rest in their graves as in beds, till at the last day they be again united to their souls. Whereas the souls of the wicked are at their death cast into hell, where they remain in torments and titter darkness; and their bodies kept in their graves, as in their prisons, until the resurrection and judgment of the great day.

This belief was novel at the time of the Reformation, and the precision and emphasis of this statement are directed against the idea of purgatory. The idea of a fixed condition is so unlike any life we know and so contradictory of our aspirations that our imagination stands still before a tedious sameness of bliss. The rich diversification in Dante shows the possibility of the other view.[3] We want the possibility of growth. We can not conceive of finite existence or of human happiness except in terms of growth. It would be more satisfactory for modern minds and for Christian minds to think of an unlimited scale of ascent toward God, reaching from the lowest to the highest, within which every spirit would hold the place for which it was fitted, and each could advance as it grew. This would satisfy our sense of justice. Believers in the social gospel will probably agree that some people have deserved hell and ought to get theirs. But no man, in any human sense of justice, has deserved an eternity of hell. On the other hand, it jars our sense of justice to see some individuals go to heaven totally exempt. They have given hell to others and ought to have a taste of it somewhere, even if they are regenerate and saved men.

7. This idea would also satisfy our Christian faith in the redeeming mercy of God. In this ascending scale of beings none would be so high that he could not be drawn still closer to God, and none so low that he would be beyond the love of God. God would still be teaching and saving all. If we learned in heaven that a minority were in hell, we should look at God to see what he was going to do about it; and if he did nothing, we should look at Jesus to see how this harmonized with what he taught us about his Father; and if he did nothing, something would die out of heaven. Jonathan Edwards demanded that we should rejoice in the damnation of those whom the sovereign election of God abandoned to everlasting torment Very justly, for we ought to be able to rejoice in what God does. But we can not rejoice in hell. It can't be done. At least by Christians. The more Christian Christ has made a soul, the more it would mourn for the lost brothers. The conception of a permanent hell was tolerable only while God was conceived as an autocratic sovereign dealing with his subjects; it becomes intolerable when the Father deals with his children.

To-day many Protestants are allowing the physical fires of hell to go out, and make the pain of hell to consist in the separation from God. They base the continuance of hell, not on the sovereign decree of God but on the progressive power of sin which gradually extinguishes all love of good and therewith all capacity for salvation. But this remains to be proven. Who has ever met a man that had no soft spot of tenderness, no homesick yearning after uprightness left in him? If God has not locked the door of hell from the

---

[3] Prof. William Adams Brown, in the closing pages of his "Christian Theology in Outline" points out the need for progress, and explains the hold which the doctrine of purgatory has on Catholics.

outside, but men remain in it because they prefer the darkness, then there is bound to be a Christian invasion of hell. All the most Christian souls in heaven would get down there and share the life of the wicked, in the high hope that after all some scintilla of heavenly fire was still smouldering and could be fanned into life. And they would be headed by Him who could not stand it to think of ninety-nine saved and one caught among the thorns.

The idea of two fixed groups does not satisfy any real requirement. Men justly feared the earlier Universalist doctrine that all men enter salvation at death. That took sin lightly and offended the sense of justice. The idea of a scale of life in which each would be as far from God and in as much darkness and narrowness as he deserved, would constitute a grave admonition to every soul. Indeed it would contain more summons to self-discipline than the present idea that as long as a man is saved at all, he is saved completely and escapes all consequences. To-day the belief in hell has weakened in great numbers of people, and in that case there is no element of fear at all to aid men in self-control. The Christian idea would have to combine the just effects of sin for all and the operation of saving mercy on all.

8. Our personal eschatology is characterized by an unsocial individualism. In the present life we are bound up with wife and children, with friends and work-mates, in a warm organism of complex life. When we die, we join—what? A throng of souls, an unorganized crowd of saints, who each carry a harp and have not even organized an orchestra. The question is even debated whether we shall know each other in heaven, and whether we shall remember and have a sense of our identity. What satisfaction would there be in talking to Isaiah or Paul if they could not remember what books they wrote and at last set our minds at rest on those questions of criticism? Anyone trained in the mind of Christ by the social gospel wants organic relations of duty and friendship. How can we become more Christ-like on earth or in heaven except by love and service? The chief effort of the Holy Spirit in our earthly life was to develop our capacity for love and our sense of solidarity and responsibility. Is this training to go for nothing in heaven, or is this present life the real preparation for the kind of life we are to live there, and the basis for promotion and growth? If the future life is to be the consummation of all that is good and divine here, it must offer fellowship with God and man. This is the point to be insisted on in our popular teaching, and not the painlessness and the eternal rest.

9. And how about labour and service? Is not our heaven too much a heaven of idleness? It looks as if it had been conceived by oppressed and ex-

ploited people who regarded labour as a curse and wanted a rest more than anything else. The social gospel wants to see all men on earth at productive work, but none doing too much of it. It carries that expectation into the idea of heaven. Dr. William N. Clarke, who was a most loving heart and had no child of his own, makes the point in his "Outline of Christian Theology" (pp. 419-20) that a third part of humanity dies in childhood, with undeveloped personality. "This significant fact has never yet been admitted to the popular thought of the future life, or exerted its due influence in theology." If these youthful spirits are to grow and develop, they must live a life of free and responsible action. If the children in heaven need education and care, " opportunities of usefulness and help must open in inexhaustible abundance to those who are farther advanced in holy experience, and the heavenly life must be intensely active and interesting." Dr. Clarke thought this was " a vast enrichment of our ideas of the other world."

This is a thought worthy of a man who followed a Master that gathered the children to his heart The social gospel would add the kindred fact that a further large proportion of individuals are left so underdeveloped by our earthly social system that they deserve a heavenly post-graduate course to make it up to them. It would be a great joy in heaven to find men trooping in from mines and shops, and women from restaurant kitchens and steaming laundries, and getting their long delayed college education.

This suggests another form of service. We are all conscious of having failed in some of our human relations, giving indifference instead of sympathy, idleness instead of service, laying our burdens on others without lending a hand with theirs. Some have done little in the sum total of their life except to add to the weight on others, and monopolizing the opportunities which ought to have been shared by many. The future life offers a chance for reparation, not by way of kindness but of justice. Suppose that a stockholder has taken large dividends out of a mill-town, leaving only the bare minimum to the workers, and stripping their lives of what could humanize them. He followed the custom of his day, and the point of view of his social class hid the injustice from his conscience. But in the other world he sees things differently and becomes a belated convert to the social gospel. About him are the men and women whose souls he has starved. Would not justice demand that he remain on the lower levels of life with them until he was able to take upward with him all whom he had retarded? Suppose that a man sent a child into life without accepting the duties of fatherhood, breaking the spirit of a girl and her family, and leaving his child to be submerged in poverty and vice. Would it not be just and Christian to require that he serve the soul of his child until it is what it might have been? Such labour and expiation might well keep us busy for some part of eternity, and in doing it, relationships of love and service would be formed which would make us fit to live closer to the Source of Love.

Of course some of the ideas I have ventured to put down are simply the play of personal fancy about a fascinating subject. There are only a few things which we can claim with any assurance, and these are not based on a single prediction, or on some passage, the origin or meaning of which may be disputed, but on the substance of the gospel of Christ. These are: that the love of God will go out forever to his children, and especially to the neediest, drawing them to him and, where necessary, saving them; that personality energized by God is ever growing; that the law of love and solidarity will be even more effective in heaven than on earth; and that salvation, growth, and solidarity are conditioned on interchange of service.

The worth of personality, freedom, growth, love, solidarity, service, these are marks of the Kingdom of God. In Christ's thought the Kingdom of God was to come from heaven to earth, so that God's will would be done on earth as it is in heaven. So then it exists in heaven; it is to be created on earth. All true joys on earth come from partial realizations of the Kingdom of God; the joy that awaits us will consist in living within the full realization of the Kingdom. Our labour for the Kingdom here will be our preparation for our participation hereafter. The degree in which we have absorbed the laws of the Kingdom into our character will determine our qualification for the life of heaven. If in any respect we have not been saved from the Kingdom of Evil, we shall be aliens and beginners in the Kingdom of God. Thus heaven and earth are to be parts of the same realm. Spiritual influences come to us; spiritual personalities go out from us. When our life is in God it has continuity.

CHAPTER XIX

THE SOCIAL GOSPEL AND THE ATONEMENT

To countless Christian minds the doctrine of the atonement has been the marrow of theology. We have reserved it for the close of our discussion. Does the social gospel contain anything which would verify, interpret, quicken, or expand that doctrine? And what form of the doctrine would best express and support the social gospel?

The theological interpretation of the death of Christ has a long and varied history. It will aid us in estimating our modern needs if we pass it briefly in review.

To the first disciples the death of their Lord was an astonishing catastrophe, an unexpected, terrible, and apparently impossible outcome of the work of the Messiah. For that very reason they craved an explanation of the event which would interpret it as a fundamental part of God's plan. Their method was to prove that it had been foretold throughout the Scripture and foreshadowed by typology. Paul was the first to give the death of our Lord a really central position in a theological system.

But the early Church never appropriated or utilized more than a few leading ideas of Paul. The most popular and elaborate theological explanation was the theory that Christ's death was a ransom paid to Satan. By the fall the human race became subject to Satan, and he had a rightful claim on it as its sovereign. God in mercy desired to emancipate humanity from the thraldom of Satan, but would not use his superior power to wrest from him what was his by legal right. So he offered Christ to Satan as a ransom in exchange, and Satan gladly accepted. But in killing the sinless Christ, Satan overstepped his legal claims and thereby forfeited all his rights. Or, according to other Fathers, Satan was attracted by the human beauty of Christ, but did not realize that this was the incarnate Logos; the marriage of Mary to Joseph had concealed from him the mystery of the incarnation. God knew beforehand that even if Satan took possession of the ransom, he could never hold Christ. So God offered Satan a bait and tricked him. When Satan tried to imprison Christ in Hades, he burst the gates and came forth with a throng of souls. This legal negotiation between two sovereigns reminds one of modern diplomacy. A few Fathers objected to the element of trickery, but on the whole this was the orthodox theology till Anselm of Canterbury substituted something better for it in A. D. 1098.

Anselm's doctrine was a real advance in ethical and religious insight. Its main points are these: Our sin has robbed God of the honour due him; an equivalent must be offered him before he can forgive sin; we ourselves can not render the "satisfaction" due to him; God alone can; therefore God had to become man; being divine and sinless, his death furnished an offset and equivalent for the boundless sins of mankind.

This theory has furnished the ground-work for orthodox theology ever since Anselm. Yet it raises unanswerable questions and in some respects offends our Christian convictions. How can it satisfy justice to have an innocent one die in place of the guilty? How can God pay an equivalent to himself? If the debt due to God has been paid by the death of Christ, why is it any longer an act of grace on the part of God to remit sin? The debt we owe to God is not a financial but a moral debt; another man may discharge a debt of $100 for me, but no man can discharge my obligations as a son or as a father for me; how then can the debt we owe to God be paid by another? If Christ fulfilled the law for us, why are we still obliged to fulfil it? These questions shock our Christian feeling. This is where we get when we try to formulate the relations between God and us on the basis of law and in forensic terms. It ends in wiping out the love and mercy of God, our most essential Christian conviction.

The Reformation made no essential change in this doctrine. Lutherans and Calvinists on the whole taught the same outline of atonement. God, in mercy toward fallen humanity, sent his Son, who shared both the divine and human nature, in order to redeem and reconcile. The justice of God demands the condemnation of all. God can exercise mercy only if vicarious satisfaction is rendered. The infinite worth of the divine nature in Christ makes his suffering an equivalent for the infinite sins of mankind. Christ experienced the wrath of God in his suffering, and that wrath is now satisfied, so that God can forgive.

These traditional theological explanations of the death of Christ have less biblical authority than we are accustomed to suppose. The fundamental terms and ideas—"satisfaction," substitution," "imputation," "merit"—are post-biblical ideas, and are alien from the spirit of the gospel.

It is important to note that every theory of the atonement necessarily used terms and analogies taken from the social life of that age, and that the spirit and problems of contemporary life are always silent factors in the construction of theory. The early Church set the model of formulating the doctrine in the terminology of sacrifice. To us sacrificing is a matter of antiquarian knowledge, kept alive mainly by the Bible. To Christians of the first three centuries it was a social institution which they saw in operation all about them. Paul saw in the death of Christ the solution of the great social problem of his life, the abolition of the Jewish Law and the emancipation of Gentile missions. The theory that the death of Christ was a ransom to Satan was the outgrowth of the semi-dualistic religion of the Empire and the prevalent belief in the rule of demons. Anselm's theory seems to me clearly the product of the penitential practices of the medieval Church, within which Anselm lived and moved and which was his social order. Every priest in the confessional was constantly assessing the delinquencies of men in terms of penalty and merit, and assigning so much inconvenience or suffering as a "satisfaction" for so much sin. Perhaps the commercial and governmental theories of later Protestantism were the natural social product of the age of capitalistic merchants and of limited monarchies.

These social realities which lay back of the theories gave them their influence and convincing power at the time they originated and for a long time thereafter, but when these social realities disappear, the theories of the atonement based on them become artificial and unconvincing, and sometimes repulsive. Analogies and illustrations taken from the priestly slaughtering of animals or the ritual functions of the Jewish high-priest are remote from our imagination, and instead of clarifying the facts, they themselves need elaborate explanation. Forensic methods and the dealings of autocratic rulers arouse our moral antagonism and have brought the teachings about the atonement under suspicion.

Our dominant ideas are personality and social solidarity. The problems which burden us are the social problems. Has the death of Christ any relation to these? Have we not just as much right to connect this supreme religious event with our problems as Paul and Anselm and Calvin, and to use the terminology and methods of our day? In so far as the historical and social sciences have taught our generation to comprehend solidaristic facts, we are in a better situation to understand the atonement than any previous generation.

As Christian men we believe that the death of our Lord concerns us all. Our sins caused it. He bore the sin of the world. In turn his death was somehow for our good. Our spiritual situation is fundamentally changed in consequence of it. But how? How did he bear our sins? How did his death affect God? How did it affect us? These three questions we shall discuss.

How did Jesus bear sins which he did not commit?

The old theology replied, by imputation. But guilt and merit are personal. They can not be transferred from one person to another. We tamper with moral truth when we shuffle them about. Imputation is a legal device to enable the law to hold one man responsible for the crime committed by another. Imputation sees mankind as a mass of individuals, and the debts of every individual are transferred to Christ. The solution does not lie in that way.

Neither is it enough to say that Jesus bore our sins by sympathy. His contact with sin was a matter of experience as well as sympathy, and experience cuts deeper. Child-birth and travail reveal the realities of life to a woman more than sympathetic observation.

How did Jesus bear our sins? The bar to a true understanding of the atonement has been our individualism. The solution of the problem lies in the recognition of solidarity.

By his human life Jesus was bound up backward and forward and sideward with the life of humanity. He received the influences of the historical life of the Jewish people through the channels of social tradition, and he transmitted the effects of his own life and personality to the future through the same channels. Palestine was only a little corner of the Roman Empire, but the full life of humanity was there, just as a man's little finger is filled with the flow of life which nourishes his whole body. Even the feeblest mind has some consciousness of the tide of life playing about him. The stronger and more universal a human personality is, the more will he consciously absorb the general life and identify himself with it. To a genius, or to one whose social feeling is made vivid and sensitive by love, even small experiences unlock life, and from a small circle one may prolong great sectors into the wider concentric circles. Jesus had an unparalleled sense of solidarity. Thereby he had the capacity to generalize his personal experiences and make them significant of the common life.

Now, this race life of ours is pervaded by sin; not only by sporadic acts of folly, waywardness, vice or crime which spring spontaneously from human life, but by organized forces and institutions of evil which have stabilized the power of sin and made it effective. Our analysis of race sin culminated in the recognition of a Kingdom of Evil (Chapter IX). Jesus lived in the midst of that Kingdom, and it was this which killed him.

Every personal act of sin, however isolated it may seem, is connected with racial sin. Evil social customs and ideas stimulate or facilitate it; in turn it strengthens the social suggestion to evil for others.

But personal transgression does not develop moral force and resentment enough to slay the prophets of God. It takes public and organized evil to do that. When a travelling pedlar cheats a farmer's wife, he is part and parcel of an ancient system of business which overreaches the customer if it can. But if the pedlar learns that a socialist editor is advocating a system of production which would abolish him and his cunning, he does not waylay and kill the editor to stop his pen. On the other hand if trade and finance have developed a lucrative system of evil income, such as the American slave trade, or the English opium trade, or the universal liquor traffic, or Five Power Loans to China, or a monopoly of colonial trade, then it will resist interference. The gigantic collective pedlar will blast reputations by the press he controls, break men financially by the bank credit he controls, or ruin men politically by the party machinery or official power he controls. When Evil is organized, the prophets suffer. There is probably not a single State of our Union which has not seen the reputation and financial or political standing of good men killed in cold blood because they sincerely opposed high class graft.

These public evils so pervade the social life of humanity in all times and all places that no one can share the common life of our race without coming under the effect of these collective sins. He will either sin by consenting in them, or he will suffer by resisting them. Jesus did not in any real sense bear the sin of some ancient Briton who beat up his wife in B. C. 56, or of some mountaineer in Tennessee who got drunk in A. D. 1917. But he did in a very real sense bear the weight of the public sins of organized society, and they in turn are causally connected with all private sins.

As one looks across human history with a mind enlightened by the thought of the Kingdom of God, he sees a few great permanent evils which have blighted the life of the race and of every individual in it They always change their form and yet remain the same in substance. Seize and fight the power of evil at any point, as you will, and soon one of these ruling evils will lift its head and strike back at you. The stronger and more influential a man's life is, and the broader his moral interests, the deeper will be his experience of these chief evils. I have been impressed with the fact that so many of them plainly converged on Jesus and had a part in doing him to death.

These evils were not as gigantic and fully developed in Palestine as they have been in the great Empires, including our own. But the fact that even in this remote corner of the ancient world they were present and virulent, proves their universal power in the life of the race. There are few communities, a cross-section of which would not reveal their presence. Jesus experienced his full collision with them when he came to the capital of his nation in the last week. There is a reason why prophets are most likely to die at Jerusalem.

To make this clear I shall enumerate six sins, all of a public nature, which combined to kill Jesus. He bore their crushing attack in his body and soul. He bore them, not by sympathy, but by direct experience. In so far as the personal sins of men have contributed to the existence of these public sins, he came into collision with the totality of evil in mankind. It requires no legal fiction of imputation to explain that "he was wounded for our transgressions, he was bruised for our iniquities." Solidarity explains it.

The most persistent force which pushed Jesus toward death, the earliest on the field and the latest on the watch, was religious bigotry. At that time it was embodied in the intellectual expounders and the devotees of Judaism rather than in the priests. Jesus acknowledged the earnestness and outward rectitude of his opponents. The traditional zeal of Judaism, the solemn injunctions of their most sacred books, and the punishments the nation had incurred by slackness and tolerance in the past, seemed ample justification of the vigor with which they set themselves against a man who seemed to flout the Sabbath, to disregard the laws of fasting, to eat with profane and unwashed hands, to overthrow the entire doctrine of clean and unclean food, and to confuse all moral distinctions between good and bad by associating with irreligious men. He was suspected of far-reaching designs against the religion of Jehovah; he had offered to substitute a temple not made with hands for their ancestral sanctuary.

So they counteracted him by innuendo and direct charges, and tried to entrap him. The great invective of Jesus shows that he regarded their influence as the chief cause for the frustration of his work. They were the active agents in the legal steps which led to his death and exerted the pressure to which Pilate had to yield. Secular governors are but poor persecutors compared with men of religion. The persecutions of the Roman Empire against Christians were feeble and occasional as compared with the zeal of the Inquisition. It takes religion to put a steel edge on social intolerance. Just because it is so high and its command of social loyalty so great, it is pitiless when it goes wrong.

Religious bigotry has been one of the permanent evils of mankind, the cause of untold social division, bitterness, persecution, and religious wars. It is always a social sin. Estimate the harm which the exponents of religion have done simply by suppressing the prophetic minds who had received from God fresh thought on spiritual and intellectual problems, and by cowing those who might have followed the prophets.

Jesus was killed by ecclesiastical religion. He might have appeared in almost any highly developed nation and suffered the same fate. Certainly after religion bore his name, there were a thousand situations in which he would have been put to death by those who offered salvation in his name. Innumerable individuals contribute their little quota to make up this collective evil, and when once the common mind is charged with it, it gets innumerable outlets. This sin, then, was borne by Jesus, not by imputation, nor by sympathy, but by direct experience.

A second social evil which contributed to kill him was the combination of graft and political power. Those who are in control of the machinery of organized society are able to use it for selfish and predatory ends, turning into private profit what ought to serve the common good. In the Oberammergau Passion Play the whole plot turns on the cleansing of the temple. This interpretation has found scholarly support. The market was originally outside the temple gates. A location inside would be a trading privilege. Did the pious hierarchy take no offence at the chaffering and dickering inside of the sacred enclosure? Or was somebody making something out of it? Knowing what we do of human nature and the versatility of graft, it does not seem likely that the concessionaires got their inside stands for love. If this conjecture is true, the feeling that the Galilæan prophet was on the side of right would explain the ready yielding to his command; and the active concern of the traders and the hierarchy in their common business would explain the energy with which the hostile action henceforward moved against him.

We are on sure ground when we realize that the prophetic leadership of Jesus endangered the power of the ruling class. There is always an oligarchy, wherever you look; monarchial and republican forms of government are both protective devices for the-group-that-controls-things. This group is the universal government. For every oligarchy political power is convertible into financial income and social influence, thus satisfying the powerful double instinct for money and for power.

In the case of the Jewish people, the Romans held the chief power and collected the main taxes through the concessionaires called the publicani or publicans. But considerable powers were left to the native oligarchy, especially the control of the institutions of religion, and from the loyalty of the Jews to their ancestral and centralized faith a modest income in cash and considerable social prestige could be harvested. Even distant colonies in the pagan cities remitted the annual temple tax, and a poor widow dropped her two farthings. Also it was pleasant to be called Rabbi, and to get the best seats in the synagogue. Their sincere concern for their religion was reinforced by concern for their special privileges as the custodians of the religious institutions and jurisdictions.

Jesus was a prophet of religion; they were exploiters of religion. This added durable fuel to their bigotry. They assumed that Jesus planned to stir up the revolutionary elements, and they feared that a messianic revolt would lose them the remnants of their power. "Whatever is to be done?" the fourth gospel reports them as saying; "if we let him alone like this, everybody will believe in him, and then the Romans will come and suppress our holy Place and our nation." Caiaphas formulated the situation with Machiavellian frankness:" You know nothing about it. You do not understand it is in your interest that one man should die for the People instead of the whole nation being destroyed."[1]

A third historic evil is the corruption of justice. We remember how often the Hebrew prophets denounced the judges who took bribes against the poor. Bearing false witness was so constant an evil that it got a place in the decalogue. Jesus took an illustration of the power of prayer from the case of a widow and a hard judge; though the judge cared neither for religion nor public opinion, she got the better of him by sheer feminine persistence. But it was hard for widows who had no pull.

Injustice between man and man is inevitable and bad enough. But it is far worse when the social institution set up in the name of justice gives its support to injustice. What nation can claim to be free from this? We have thought of the political prisons of autocratic Russia as a remnant of the dark ages, but the War has shown that even in free countries the judicial process can swiftly break conscientious convictions and the most cherished rights, of democracy. In our own country the delays and appeals permitted by our legal procedure set up a terrible inequality between the rich and poor. Years of

[1] John 11:47-50.

public agitation have produced no adequate change. Even if the judge is wholly free from bias, the law itself in all countries, presumably, is on the side of property. The British Parliament, "the mother of free institutions" has always been an assembly of propertied men; only in recent years has it contained an efficient minority of representatives of the working class. Our own legislatures rarely contain any spokesman of the class which needs a voice most of all.

As soon as Jesus was arrested, he became a victim of the courts. In the ecclesiastical court, we are told, distorted and bribed testimony was used. His followers were not present and we have no report of eye-witnesses. It may be that he never made the claim that he would come as the apocalyptic Messiah, and that it was concocted in order to have a political charge to present in the Roman court. The priestly court condemned him on a priestly charge; he was a heretic and blasphemer.

In the Roman court the pull of the upper classes and the pressure of mob clamour were allowed to influence judicial procedure. It was Pilate's high privilege to protect a man whom he felt to be innocent; he had the military power of Rome to back his verdict. He yielded to pressure because his own career, as we know from secular history, was corrupt; the Jews threatened to "get him," and he knew they could. So he took some water and demonstratively washed his hands of what he yet consented to do. Pilate's wash-bowl deserves to be a mystic symbol, the counter-part of the Holy Grail.

So Jesus made experience of one of the permanent sins of organized society, bearing in his own body and soul what so many thousands of the poor and weak have borne before and after, the corruption of justice.

A fourth permanent social sin which participated in the death of Jesus was the mob spirit and mob action. The mob spirit is the social spirit gone mad. The social group then escapes from the control of its wiser and fairer habits, and is lashed into action by primitive passions. The social spirit reacts so powerfully on individuals, that when once the restraints of self-criticism and self-control are shot back, the crowd gets drunk on the mere effluvia of its own emotions. We know only too well that a city of respectable and religious people will do fiendish acts of cruelty and obscenity.

There are radical mobs and conservative mobs. Well-dressed mobs are more dangerous than ragged mobs because they are far more efficient Entire nations may come under the mob spirit, and abdicate their judgment.

Rarely are mobs wholly spontaneous; usually there is leadership to fanaticize the masses. At this point this sin connects with the sins of selfish leadership which we have analysed before. Sometimes the crowd turns against the oligarchy; usually the oligarchy manipulates the crowd.

So it was in the case of Jesus. The mob shouted for the physical force man and against the man who embodied the better spirit of the Jewish nation. There was "patriotism" in this choice. Pilate realized that, and tried to play on it by calling Jesus the king of the Jews, but the native politicians outplayed him. The choice was prophetic. It was the Barabbas type which led the nation to its doom in the Jewish War and the later risings of the Jewish patriots.

So this pervasive sin of community life, the intoxication of the social spirit, before which so many prophets and semi-prophets have had to quail, contributed to the death of Jesus. He bore it, not by sympathy or imputation, but by experience.

The fifth universal sin of organized society which co-operated in the death of Christ was militarism. So far as we know, Jesus never passed through an actual war. He probably never saw his home burned, his father killed, his sisters ravished, nor was he ever forced to bear arms. But that he had convictions on war is plain from his sayings. "He that taketh the sword shall perish by the sword," shows clear comprehension of the fact that in war neither side gains, and that the reactions of war are as dangerous as the direct effects; of which fact ample demonstrations are before us.

If the words spoken in his lament over Jerusalem are authentic, he not only foresaw that the present drift would carry his nation to war and destruction, but he regarded the acceptance of his leadership as the one means by which his people might have escaped their doom:" If thou hadst known in this day the things that make for peace! But now they are hidden from thine eyes." To his mind, then, the Kingdom of God must have had a conscious and definite relation to war and force revolution.

With his arrest Jesus fell into the hands of the war system. When the soldiers stripped him, beat his back with the leaded whip, pressed the wreath of thorns into his scalp, draped a purple mantle around him and saluted this amusing king of the Jews, and when they blindfolded and struck him, asking him to prophesy who it was and spitting in his face, — this was the humour of the bar-rack room. This was fun as the professional soldiers of the Roman Empire saw it. The men who drove the spikes through his hands and feet were the equivalent of a firing-squad told off for duty at an execution, and when they gambled for his clothes, they were taking their soldiers' perquisites.

The last of this group of racial sins is class contempt. Class pride and its obverse passion, class contempt, are the necessary spiritual product of class divisions. They are the direct negation of solidarity and love. They substitute a semi-human, semi-ethical relation for full human fraternity. The class system, therefore, is a sinful denial of the Kingdom of God, and one of the characteristic marks and forces of the Kingdom of Evil.

It is almost universal. Our capitalistic semi-democracy has alleviated it but not overcome it. Indeed, while some other nations are slowly breaking up the class systems erected in the past, the present economic tendencies in our country, if allowed to go on, will inevitably build up a durable class system. Economic facts mock at political theory. Sixty-five per cent of the national property before the war was held by two per cent of the population. The war has contributed enormously to the aggregation of great fortunes.[2] Parasitic incomes produce class differences; class differences create class pride and class contempt.

This sin has always rested heavily on the great mass of mankind. It expresses itself in social customs and in the laws of a nation. Where an aristocracy exists, either its members are formally exempt from the degrading forms of punishment, as in Russia, or they are ostensibly liable to them but practically exempt by the inability to put them in prison or keep them there.

In Roman law crucifixion was a punishment reserved for offenders of the lowest classes. No Roman citizen could be crucified. Cicero flung it at Verres as a culminating accusation in the counts of his misrule that he had crucified a Roman. When Jesus was nailed to the tree, therefore, he bore not only the lightning shoots of physical pain imposed by the cruelties of criminal law, but also that contempt for the lower classes which has always dehumanized the upper classes, numbed and crippled the spiritual self-respect of the lower classes, and set up insuperable barriers to the spirit of the Kingdom of God.

Religious bigotry, the combination of graft and political power, the corruption of justice, the mob spirit, militarism, and class contempt,—every

---

[2] The Minority Report of the Senate Committee on Finance, August 13, 1917, contains tables of 95 industrial corporations and 50 railways in which the average income of 1911-13 is deducted from the net income of 1916, leaving special war profits of 100%, 400%, 1400%, 4500% in some cases. Thus the Bethlehem Steel Corporation made over 1300% or $40,518,860, and the Du Pont Powder Co. over 1400% or $76,581,729.

student of history will recognize that these sum up constitutional forces in the Kingdom of Evil. Jesus bore these sins in no legal or artificial sense, but in their impact on his own body and soul. He had not contributed to them, as we have, and yet they were laid on him. They were not only the sins of Caiaphas, Pilate, or Judas, but the social sin of all mankind, to which all who ever lived have contributed, and under which all who ever lived have suffered.[3]

The spiritual insight of Jesus himself has added a further step to this solidaristic interpretation of his death. In the parable of the Vineyard he described the religious history of his nation as a continuous straggle, with God and his prophets on one side, and the selfish exploiters of religion on the other, and set his own impending death at the end of the prophetic succession as its culmination. This was an historical, social, and solidaristic interpretation of his death.

At the close of the invective against the religious leaders (Mathew 23) he again outlined this historical process, in which the ruling classes of the past had always silenced the living voices of God, but managed to utilize them posthumously among the decorative elements and authorities of religion. He warned his own generation that they were on the point of repeating this sin by persecuting the new prophets whom he would send. Thereby they would prove that they were "the sons of them that slew the prophets;" they would "fill up the measure of their fathers;" and would bring upon themselves "all the righteous blood shed on the earth."

His thought is that by repeating the sins of the past we are involved in the guilt of the past. We are linked in a solidarity of evil and guilt with all who have done the same before us, and all who will do the same after us. In so far then as we, by our conscious actions or our passive consent, have repeated the sins which killed Jesus, we have made ourselves guilty of his death. If those who actually killed him stood before us, we could not wholly condemn them, but would have to range ourselves with them as men of their own kind.

[3] I have not seen this analysis attempted before. My attention has been called to a sermon by President William DeWitt Hyde, on "The Sins which Crucified Jesus," in the collection of "Modern Sermons by World Scholars," Vol. IV, in which he follows a similar line of inquiry. He specifies the envy of the hierarchy, the money-love of Judas, slander, and the servility of Pilate. But, except in the first part, dealing with the hierarchy, he does not place the discussion under the category of solidarity, and that is the decisive point of my argument See also Henry Sloane Coffin, "Social Aspects of the Cross."

This is Christ's own theology. It is not a legal theory of imputation, but a conception of spiritual solidarity, by which our own free and personal acts constitute us partakers of the guilt of others.

Along two lines we have replied to the question how the sins of the world were borne by Jesus: First, the realistic forces which killed Jesus were not accidental and personal causes of his death, but were the reaction of the totality of racial sin against him; and second, the guilt of those who did it spreads to all who re-affirm the acts which killed him. The key to the problem is contained in the realization of solidarity.

We have understood only one side of the atonement when we comprehend how the sins of humanity converged in the death of Jesus and were borne by him. The next question is, in what sense this can be said to affect God and to change the relation of humanity to him.

The first step toward a true view of the atonement is to see the death of Christ as an integral part of his life. Theology has made a fundamental mistake in treating the atonement as something distinct, and making the life of Jesus a mere staging for his death, a matter almost negligible in the work of salvation.

It is not given to all to die a significant death. Usually, as we age or sicken, the work of our life and the things we have loved and lived for, begin to drop from our hands. Instead of dying fighting, we die what our pagan forefathers called a "straw-death." Sometimes a brave life ends in a dishonorable death. The death of Jesus was wholly of one piece with his life. He gathered all the radiance of his character and purpose in a focus-point of blazing light, and there he died.

In living his life and dying his death as he did, Jesus lived out, confirmed, and achieved his own personality. He did it for himself, as well as for God and humanity. There was no "merit" in the medieval sense in it; nothing superfluous which he could hand over and credit to others to make up their defects. Just as we owe God the complete best that is in us, so Jesus too owed life and death to God. He was under the law he had proclaimed, that "from him to whom much is given, much shall be required."

His death was not simply an infliction from without. He acccpted his suffering not as a fate to be warded off, but with inward assent and acceptance. He knew it was coming. "I must go on my way to-day and to-morrow and the day following; for it can not be that a prophet perish out of Jerusalem." When the time came he "set his face steadfastly to go to Jerusalem." The struggle in the garden was only the last act. Every step was a conflict and a temptation, but whenever the time came for the next step, Jesus was ready. The spiritual and redemptive value of his death was not in the quantity of his mental or physical suffering; (that is a caricature of the atonement;) it was in the willingness with which he took on himself this highest and hardest part of his lifework.

The life of Jesus was a life of love and service. At every moment his life was going out toward God and men. His death, then, had the same significance. It was the culmination of his life, its most luminous point, the most dramatic expression of his personality, the consistent assertion of the purpose and law which had ruled him and formed him.

The law under which he lived was the mind and will of God; the purpose for which he lived was the Kingdom of God. Jesus had to learn that law and try out that purpose. He had it within him, but the great experiences of his life brought the will of God and the needs of the Kingdom to his consciousness. The events leading up to his death were of the highest educational importance to his spirit. Here he learned fully the divine attitude toward malignant sin. He entered into that attitude, made it his own, and thus revealed God at the point where the sin of the world and the mind of God were in sharpest antagonism.

He was evidently deeply helped by contemplating the life of the prophets before him. The historical precedents furnished by them took on the significance of a spiritual law to him. He constantly connected his own work with theirs. His mental contact was not with high-priests and kings, but with the men who bore the living God in their hearts and braved the craft of priests or the yell of the mob to speak his word. He taught his disciples to see themselves in the same succession. They were to take opposition as part of their day's work and not mind it The consciousness of standing with the prophets was so uplifting to him that he made this the culmination of the beatitudes, bidding his followers to rejoice and be exceeding glad if they tasted the same scorn and hate. What the death of Jesus now does for us, the death of the prophets did for him. None of the later theories of the atonement are taught, or even touched, in the sayings of Jesus, except perhaps at the Lord's Supper. The only clear interpretation of his death from his own mind is this, that he ranged his sufferings in line with those of the prophets. This lifts the experiences and functions of the prophets to a very high level in the redemption of mankind.

We said that through his sufferings Jesus came into full understanding of God's attitude toward malignant sin, and adopted it. God's attitude is combined of opposition and love. God has always borne the brunt of human sin while loving us. He too has been gagged and cast out by men. He has borne our sins with a resistance which never yields and yet is always patient. Within human limits Jesus acted as God acts. The non-resistance of Jesus, so far from being a strange or erratic part of his teaching, is an essential part of his conception of life and of his God-consciousness. When we explain it away or belittle it, we prove that our spirit and his do not coalesce.

In the Sanhedrim, in the court of Pilate, amid the jests of the soldiers, Jesus had to live out the Father's mind and spirit. He did it in the combination of steadfastness and patience. The most striking thing in his bearing is his silence. He never yielded an inch, but neither did he strike back, or allow others to do it for him. "If my kingdom were on a level with yours," he said to Pilate, "my followers would fight to protect me." He did not answer force by force, nor anger by anger. If he had, the world at that point would have subdued him and he would have fallen away from God. If he had headed the Galilæans to storm Pilate's castle, he would have been a God-forsaken Christ.

But his attitude was not soft. He resisted. He fought. Even on the cross he fought. He never fought so hard as then. But not with fist or stick on a physical level of brute force, but by the quietness which both maddens and disarms. If he had blustered, he would have been conquered. Christian art has misreported him when it makes him suffer with head down. His head was up and he was in command of the situation.

We have cleared the way for the question, how this obedience unto death affected God. Of course, any attempt to answer this question on the part of any human mind, inspired or uninspired, is an attempt to express more than it can conceive. "God is in heaven, and thou art on earth; therefore let thy words be few." All theories on the atonement prove how unlovely the image of man is when he enlarges it and projects it to the skies. For a Christian man the only sure guide in speaking of God is the mind of Christ. That is our logic and metaphysic.

If we think of God in a human way, it seems as if the death of Jesus must have been a great experience for God. Pantheistic philosophy represents God as coming to consciousness in the spiritual life of men and rising as our race rises. If we believe that he is immanent in the life of humanity and in a fellowship of love with us as our Father, it does not seem too daring to think that our little sorrows and sins might be great sorrows to him, and that our spiritual triumphs might be great joys. What, then, would it mean to God to be in the personality of Jesus and to go through his suffering and death with him? If the principle of forgiving love had not been in the heart of God before, this experience would fix it there. If he had ever thought and felt like the Jewish Jehovah, he would henceforth think and feel as the Father of Jesus Christ If Christ was the divine Logos—God himself expressing himself—then the experience of the cross reacted directly on the mind of God.

We may conceive the effect of Christ's life and death on God in another way.

As long as humanity lives within the Kingdom of Evil, it is out of spiritual unity and fellowship with God, and God is forced into an attitude of opposition where he desires to be in an attitude of love and help. Christ was the first to live fully within the consciousness of God and to share his holy and loving will. He drew others into his realization of God so that they too freely loved God and appropriated his will as their own. Thus he set in motion a new beginning of spiritual life within the organized total of the race, and this henceforth pervaded the common life. This was the embryonic beginning of the Kingdom of God within the race. Therewith humanity began to be lifted to a new level of spiritual existence. To God, who sees the end enfolded in the beginning, this initiation of a new humanity was the guarantee of its potential perfection.

This would alter the relation between God and humanity from antagonism to co-operative unity of will; not by a legal transaction, but by the presence of a new and decisive factor embodied in the racial life which affected its spiritual value and potency. When men would learn to understand and love God; and when God could by anticipation see his own life appropriated by men, God and men would enter into spiritual solidarity, and this would be the only effective reconciliation.[4]

In this change of relations Christ would be the initiator. His obedience would be the germinal cell from which the new organism would grow. His place within it would be unique. But his aim and effort would be to make himself not unique, but to become "the first-born among many brethren."

But what place does his death hold in this process of reconciliation? No place apart from his life, his life-purpose, and the development and expression of his personality; a very great place as the effective completion of his life. Men were coming into fellowship with the Father before his death hap-

[4] This line of thought in substance follows Schleiermacher.

pened, and before they knew that it was to happen. Jesus labored to unite men with God without referring to his death. If he had lived for thirty years longer, he would have formed a great society of those who shared his conception and religious realization of God, and this would have been that nucleus of a new humanity which would change the relation of God to humanity. Indeed, we can conceive that in thirty years of additional life Jesus could have put the imprint of his mind much more clearly on the movement of Christianity, and protected it from the profound distortions to which it was subjected. There would have been an ample element of prophetic suffering without physical death. Death came by the wickedness of men.

But taken in connection with his life, as the inevitable climax of his prophetic career, his death had an essential place in his work of establishing solidarity and reconciliation between God and man. It was his supreme act of opposition to sin; not even the fear or the pangs of death could make him yield anything of what God had given him to hold. It was the supreme act, also, of obedience to God, to which he was moved by love to God and loyalty to his Kingdom. Moreover, as we shall see, his power to assimilate others to his God-consciousness and to gather a new humanity, was influenced by his death, and the creation of such an effective nucleus is essential to any real reconciliation.

This conception is free from the artificial and immoral elements inherent in all forensic and governmental interpretations of the atonement. It begins with the solidarity between God and Christ, and proceeds to the solidarity between God and mankind. It deals with social and religious realities. It connects the idea of reconciliation and the idea of the Kingdom of God. It does not dispense with the moral effort of men and the moral renewal of social life but absolutely demands both. It furnishes a mystic basis for the social revolution. It would be a theological conception which the social gospel could utilize and enforce.

Finally we must inquire how the atonement affected men. What did the death of Christ add to his life in the way of reconciling, and redemptive power? The answer to this can not be narrowed down to a single influence. An event like the death of Jesus influences human thought and feeling in many ways. I shall mention three.

First: It was the conclusive demonstration of the power of sin in humanity. I can not contemplate the force and malignancy of the six social and racial sins which converged on Jesus without a deep sense of the enormous power of evil in the world and of the bitter task before those who make up the cutting edge of the Kingdom of God. In various ways this realization comes to all who think of the cross of Christ. But the solidaristic interpretation of the killing power of sin is by far the most impressive. The cross forever puts a question-mark alongside of any easy treatment of sin.

Now, the surest way to make sin pall on us is to watch it go its full length. The first beginnings of drink, vice, or war are of exciting interest, but the fourth and fifth act make us very sick. If realistic art would only be faithful and tell the whole story to the end, preachers might suspend business. An evening out; a broken girl; a shamed family; a syphilitic baby; scrophulous bodies for several generations. Show us the last results at the beginning and we should sober up.

Moreover, the moral cure worked by sin is most effective in some way when we see our sin working in another life. A man may be willing to gamble with his own life and take the risk of his sport, but he may shrink from making another life pay for it by agony or death, — provided he realizes the connection. Therefore it is the business of all who profit by sin to make the exploited sinner forget the social effects of his sin. The more innocent and lovable the victim, the more poignant the remorse when we realize what we have done.

When discussing the problem of suffering, (Chapter XV), we made the point that pain in the physical organism has a beneficent preventive use and purpose, and that social suffering serves the same purpose for society, provided it can be effectively brought home, and provided there is enough sense of sympathy and solidarity to care.

From all these points of view the suffering of Christ is an incomparable demonstration of sin. Here we see human sin in its mature and social form; the victim has not contributed to it, so that the guilt can not be divided, palliated, or shifted; the one who suffered was loving and lovable beyond all others; yet great social forces combined with the utmost energy to kill him.

As soon as the passion of the moment subsided and the "interests" were safe again, men were impressed with the innocence of Jesus. The more they realized the holiness of his life, the strength of his love, the divine value of his person, the more would they feel the sinfulness of the sin committed there. Besides, the blame was not confined to those who did the act; all the interpretations of the Church emphasized the universality of the guilt. Every Christian has had his eye fixed on the cross as a place of engrossing interest. Whatever the theories of the atonement might be, was the death of Jesus not bound to produce a deeper moral earnestness of life, a wider sense of sin, and more self-restraint and thoughtfulness?

Suffering is Nature's publicity method to secure attention to something that is wrong. All history demonstrates that men are stupid and callous to suffering, even to their own suffering, and that only the most effective means will arouse them to put a preventive stop to what is destroying them. In all reverence I would say that the cross of Christ was the most tremendous publicity success in the history of mankind. No event in history has received such earnest and constant attention. None has spread so much seriousness, and made men realize the sin of humanity from so many angles. None has so impressed them with their own complicity in it and the solidarity of humanity in sin.

In so far as a genuine consciousness of sin is the first step toward redemption from sin, the cross was an essential part of the redemptive process. The life of Christ never spread such a realization of sin as his death has done.

Second : the death of Christ was the supreme revelation of love.

Love is the social instinct of the race. In all its many forms it binds man to man. Every real improvement of society gives love a freer chance. Every genuine progress must be preceded by a new capitalization of love.[5]

Jesus put love to the front in his teaching. He was ready to accept love for God and man as a valid equivalent for the customary religious and ethical duties. His own character and action are redolent of virile and energetic love.

If Jesus had died a natural death, posterity would still treasure his teaching, coupled with the commentary of his life, as the most beautiful exposition of love. But its effectiveness was greatly increased by his death. Death has a strange power over the human imagination and memory. A pathetic or heroic death wins a place for a weak and cowardly man. If a significant death is added to a brave and self-sacrificing life, the effect is great. A righteous man might well pray for this as the last great blessing of his life, that his death might interpret the higher meaning of his life and weld all his labors into one by the flame of suffering. This crowning grace was given to Jesus. His death underscored all he said on love. It put the red seal of sincerity on his words. "Greater love hath no man than that he give his life for his friends." Unless he gives it for his enemies too.

---

[5] The social importance of the Christian doctrine of love is treated somewhat fully in my little book, "Dare We Be Christians? " (Pilgrim Press.)

The human value of his love was translated into higher terms by the belief that Christ revealed and expressed the heart and mind of God. If Christ stood for saving pity and tender mercy and love that seeks the lost, then God must be that kind of a God. It is a question if the teaching of Jesus alone could have made that the common faith of millions. His death effectively made God a God of love to the simplest soul, and that has transformed the meaning of the universe and the whole outlook of the race. Surely the character of the God a man worships reacts on the man. Suppose that our life has mocked our creed of love a thousand times; how many times would our life have mocked at love if love were not in our creed? Suppose the dualism of the first century had written pessimism and ascetic resignation into our creed. Suppose that instead of the Father of Jesus Christ we had a God who embodied the doctrine of the survival of the fit, the rule of the strong, and the suppression of the weak, how would that have affected the spiritual character of Western civilization? How much chance would there have been for democracy? Instead of that, love has been written into the character of God and into the ethical duty of man; not only common love, but self-sacrificing love. And it was the death of Christ which furnished the chief guarantee for the love of God and the chief incentive to self-sacrificing love in men.

It is true that the self-sacrifice generated by Christianity has been misdirected and used up for nothing in ascetic Christianity. But no one can well deny that the sum total of self-sacrifice evoked by Christianity has been and is enormous, and that its influence on the development of Christian civilization has been very great. Some of the legal conceptions of the atonement have obscured the love of God in the death of Christ. But the fact that the Christian consciousness has reacted against any despotic elements in the character of God, is proof of the fact that the essentially Christian idea had done its work in us and overcome the sinful alloy with which it was mixed.

Since we live in the fellowship of a God of love, we are living in a realm of grace as friends and sons of God. We do not have to earn all we get by producing merit. We live on grace and what we do is slight compared with what is done for us.

This conviction, too, is based on the death of Christ. Belief in the atonement has enabled religious souls first to break away from self-made righteousness and to realize salvation as a gift. With their eye on the cross of Christ they denied the merit system, first of Judaism, later of the Catholic Church. The great religious characters are those who escaped from themselves and learned to depend on God, — Paul, Augustine, Saint Francis, Tauler on whom Luther fed, Luther himself.

Self-earned righteousness and pride in self are the marks of religious individualism. Humility is the capacity to realize that we count for little in ourselves and must take our place in a larger fellowship of life. Therefore humility and dependence on grace are social virtues.

The cross is the monumental fact telling of grace and inviting repentance and humility.

Thus the death of Christ was the conclusive and effective expression of the love of Jesus Christ for God and man, and his complete devotion to the Kingdom of God. The more his personality was understood to be the full and complete expression of the character of God, the more did his death become the assurance and guarantee that God loves us, forgives us, and is willing to do all things to save us.

It is the business of theologians and preachers to make the atonement effective in producing the characteristic of love in Christian men and women. If it does not assimilate them to the mind of Christ it has missed its purpose. We can either be saved by non-ethical sacramental methods, or by absorbing the moral character of Jesus into our own character. Let every man judge which is the salvation he wants.

The social gospel is based on the belief that love is the only true working principle of human society. It teaches that the Kingdom of Evil has thrust love aside and employed force, because love will support only a fraternal distribution of property and power, while force will support exploitation and oppression. If love is the fundamental quality in God, it must be part of the constitution of humanity. Then it can not be impossible to found society on love. The atonement is the symbol and basis of a new social order.

Third: the death of Christ has reinforced prophetic religion.[6]

Historical criticism has performed an inestimable service to true religion by clearing up the historical antagonism between priest and prophet in the Old Testament, and labeling the literary documents of Jewish religion according to the religious interest which produced or re-edited them. This antagonism is a permanent element in the Christian religion, and part of the conflict between the Kingdom of God and the Kingdom of Evil. A comprehension of the difference between prophet and priest is essential to a clear understanding of Jesus and to intelligent discipleship.

---

[6] The importance of prophecy within the Christian religion has been discussed in part in Chapter XVI.

The priest is the religious professional. He performs religious functions which others are not allowed to perform. It is therefore to his interest to deny the right of free access to God, and to interpose himself and his ceremonial between the common man and God. He has an interest in representing God as remote, liable to anger, jealous of his rights, and quick to punish, because this gives importance to the ritual methods of placating God which the priest alone can handle. It is essential to the priestly interest to establish a monopoly of rights and functions for his group. He is all for authority, and in some form or other he is always a spokesman of that authority and shares its influence. Doctrine and history as he teaches it, establish a *jure divino* institution of his order, which is transmitted either by physical descent, as in the Aaronic priesthood, or by spiritual descent through some form of exclusive ordination, as in the Catholic priesthood. As history invariably contradicts his claims, he frequently tampers with history by Deuteronomic codes or Pseudo-Isidorian Decretals, in order to secure precedents and the weight of antiquity. He is opposed to free historical investigation because this tears open the protective web of idealized history and doctrine which he has woven about him. He is the middle man of religion, and like other middle-men he is sincerely convinced that he is necessary for the good of humanity and that religion would perish without him. But underneath all is the selfish interest of his class, which exploits religion.

The prophet becomes a prophet by some personal experience of God, which henceforth is the dominant reality of his life. It creates inward convictions which become his message to men. Usually after great inward conflicts and the bursting of priest-made barriers he has discovered the way of access to God, and has found him wonderful, — just, merciful, free. As a result of his own experience he usually becomes the constitutional enemy of priestly religion, the scorner of sacrificial and ritual doings, a voice of doubt about the doctrines and the literature which shelter the priest. He too is a middleman, but he wants no monopoly. His highest desire is to have all men share what he has experienced. If his own caste or people claim special privileges as a divinely descended caste or a chosen people, he is always for some expansion of religious rights, for a crossing of boundaries and a larger unity. His interest is in freedom, reality, immediateness, —the reverse of the priestly interest. His religious experience often gives a profound quickening to his social consciousness, an unusual sense of the value of life and a strong compassion with the suffering and weak, and therefore a keen feeling for human rights and indignation against injustice. He has a religious conviction that God is against oppression and on the side of the weak.[7]

The religion of the priest and the religion of the prophet grow side by side, on the same national soil and from the same historic convictions, but they are two distinct and antagonistic religions. The usual distinctions which separate religions and denominations are trivial compared with this. This difference cuts across most other lines of cleavage. Since the Reformation, however, the personal qualities which marked the prophet have become to some extent the mark and foundation of continuous religious bodies. Over against Catholicism, Protestantism has, in its noblest periods, had prophetic quality; over against the Established Churches the Free Churches have a prophetic mission. But the flame of prophetic religion is always dying down for lack of oxygen. It burns only when there is something worth burning for. It kindles wherever the Kingdom of God is clashing with the Kingdom of Evil. You can tell where the conflict is on today when you hear the voice of prophetic religion. In every religious body, even in those that have repudiated priestliness, you have the undeveloped and unconscious priest and prophet side by side; mixed types, like Ezekiel and Savonarola; embryonic prophets; spent prophets; prophets who have given up; prophets whose bodies and minds have been hurt and thrown out of equilibrium. God knows his own.

The prophet is always the predestined advance agent of the Kingdom of God. His religion flings him as a fighter and protester against the Kingdom of Evil. His sense of justice, compassion, and solidarity sends him into tasks which would be too perilous for others. It connects him with oppressed social classes as their leader. He bears their risk and contempt. As he tries to rally the moral and religious forces of society, he encounters derelict and frozen religion, and the selfish and conservative interest of the classes which exploit religion. He tries to arouse institutional religion from the inside, or he pounds it from the outside. This puts him in the position of a heretic, a free thinker, an enemy of religion, an atheist. Probably no prophet escaped without bearing some such name. His opposition to social injustice arouses the same kind of antagonism from those who profit by it. How far these interests will go in their methods of suppressing the prophets depends on their power and their needs. I have been impressed with the fact that though

[7] I wish to call attention in advance to a book which is still in preparation, "Religion, its Prophets and its Exploiters," by Professor James Bishop Thomas, Ph.D., of the University of the South. It presents with impressive clearness the historic antagonism between priest and prophet.

Christianity began in a renascence of prophetism, scarcely any personality who bears the marks of the prophet can be found in Church History between A. D. 100 and A. D. 1200. Two main explanations suggest themselves: that their own capacity for self-sacrifice led the potential prophets into the monasteries and put them under monastic obedience; and that the Catholic Church, which embodies the priestly principles, suffocated the nascent prophets by its spiritual authority and the physical force it could command.

In this way the death of Jesus has taken personal hold on countless religious souls. It has set them free from the fear of pain and the fear of men, and given them a certain finishing quality of strength. It has inspired courage and defiance of evil, and sent men on lost hopes. The cross of Christ put God's approval on the sacrificial impulse in the hearts of the brave, and dignified it by connecting it with one of the central dogmas of our faith. The cross has become the motive and the method of noble personalities.

It has compelled reflection on the value of the prophets for the progress of humanity. What might have been a sporadic and unaccountable religious instinct, has been lifted to the level of a law of history and religion.

> By the light of burning heretics Christ's bleeding feet I track,
> Toiling up new Calvaries ever with the cross that turns not back.
> And these mounts of anguish number how each generation learned
> One new word of that grand Credo which in prophet-hearts hath burned
> Since the first man stood God-conquered with his face to heaven
> upturned.[8]

The death of Jesus was the clearest and most conspicuous case of prophetic suffering. It shed its own clarity across all other, less perfect cases, and interpreted their moral dignity and religious significance. His death comforted and supported all who bore prophetic suffering by the consciousness that they were "bearing the marks of the Lord Jesus" and were carrying on what he had borne. The prophet is always more or less cast out by society and profoundly lonely and homeless; consequently he reaches out for companionship, for a tribal solidarity of his own, and a chieftainship of the spirit

---

[8] From James Russell Lowell's "Present Crisis." This poem is the finest expression I know of the historic function of prophet-hood within the solidarity of mankind and its spiritual progress.

to which he can give his loyalty and from which he can gather strength. Then it is his rightful comfort to remember that Jesus has suffered before him.

Thus the cross of Christ contributes to strengthen the power of prophetic religion, and therewith the redemptive forces of the Kingdom of God. Before the Reformation the prophet had only a precarious foothold within the Church and no right to live outside of it. The rise of free religion and political democracy has given him a field and a task. The era of prophetic and democratic Christianity has just begun. This concerns the social gospel, for the social gospel is the voice of prophecy in modern life.

Source: Walter Rauschenbusch, *A Theology for the Social Gospel.* New York: The Macmillan Co., 1917. First edition, November 1917; copy from Vaughan Memorial Library, Acadia University.

"Christianity Revolutionary"/ The Righteousness of the Kingdom

Editorial Introduction

In 1891 or 1892[1] while on a study leave in Germany, it is known that Rauschenbusch began a large study of the church's failure to understand Christianity rightly. At that time, he began to reflect on the priority of the Kingdom of God. This produced a full-scale manuscript that he entitled, "Christianity Revolutionary." What has seemed like an odd title may have reflected an idiomatic German equivalency.[2] He sent the 450-page onion skin manuscript to his close colleagues, Leighton Williams and Nathaniel Schmidt. Williams's comments were gentle (he thought it was dull) toward the pastoral side, while Schmidt in his 90-page response was quite critical of what he thought were Rauschenbusch's superficial biblical interpretations. The original pages include the handwriting of both readers. Apparently, Rauschenbusch was put off by the magnitude of critique from his friends, because he set aside the comprehensive revision process for about 16 years.

Rauschenbusch revisited his manuscript in 1895 and in 1905-07 when he used portions of it in his new book project, *Christianity and the Social Crisis* (See Vol. I). He also mined the manuscript for several articles he published in the early 1900s. Ideas from the manuscript were evident in his book, *The Social Principles of Jesus* (1916: see Vol. II).[3] According to Max Stackhouse, then a Harvard student preparing a doctoral dissertation on Rauschenbusch in the mid-1960s, the onion skin pages were found scattered in unorganized material that Dores R. Sharpe had accumulated in the 1930s in anticipation of his biography on Rauschenbusch. Stackhouse queried extensively Glenn B. Ewell, the librarian at Colgate-Rochester, and Edward C. Starr the curator at the American Baptist Historical Society, also at Rochester, and reported that there were two theories about the provenance of "Christianity Revolutionary." One was that Sharpe had come by the material himself, the other was that the manuscripts were temporarily lost in the basement of a Rochester home and sent to the seminary library where they were filed separately under several titles.[4] According to Stackhouse, it

---

[1] Paul Minus favored 1891, Max Stackhouse, 1892.

[2] Some analysts have reversed the words and used the title "Revolutionary Christianity." Rauschenbusch did not. See Minus, *American Reformer,* 79.

[3] Christopher Evans traces some of the history of "Christianity Revolutionary" in his book, *The Kingdom Is Always but Coming*, 93-98; 103; 122; 175; 177; 278-79.

[4] This is a plausible theory because Rauschenbusch's library and some of his personal effects were dispersed in the local German Baptist community.

was he who recognized Schmidt's and Williams's handwriting and he reassembled the unified corpus.

Thus, after over seven decades, in 1968 Walter Rauschenbusch's earliest book-length project re-emerged under the creative editorial hand of Max Stackhouse who re-titled the work, *The Righteousness of the Kingdom*, published by Methodist-related Abingdon Press in Nashville. Stackhouse prepared a 59-page ethical/theological introduction paying little attention to the critical literary and archival issues. He attributed the work to Rauschenbusch, and scores of students and scholars have since followed that pathway.[5]

It is likely that Rauschenbusch had no clear intent of trying to publish this work as such, especially after 1907. Doubtless he was continually aware of its existence, because he drew phrases etc. from it. Noteworthy also was his desire that none of his work be published after his death and his request that his papers be destroyed upon his death.

The original manuscript is produced here for two reasons: as an example of the first literary project of Walter Rauschenbusch, and secondly to delineate Rauschenbusch's own work from that of Max Stackhouse. We have restored the original title, "Christianity Revolutionary" and note that Rauschenbusch later added the title to a typescript addendum, "The Righteousness of the Kingdom" at some point in the first decade of the twentieth century.

NOTE: **Boldfaced,** bracketed numbers have been inserted in the text that indicate pagination of the original manuscript.

---

[5] Stackhouse was more interested in the contemporary ecclesial context of his find than its provenance. In a footnote to his introduction, he said, "The document as found was not in final form. Several short sections listed in an outline are found in the manuscript only as a list of topics, and others stand in only partially revised form. Still others are revisions of chapters in Rauschenbusch's private variety of shorthand and speed writing, seemingly revised in response to Schmidt's criticisms. In reconstructing the manuscript, I have attempted to use the latest and most complete statements. I have revised or reorganized only in those instances where it seemed necessary by virtue of grammar, where a phrase might lead to misunderstanding today, where the organization required transitions, where Rauschenbusch's notes indicate that he intended it, where the joining of a partially revised chapter to the rest of an unrevised version demanded word or sentence changes. In two places three points were made in the text, and only two were used in a summary paragraph. I supplied the missing point in his language. I struck out one full paragraph that was badly written and unrelated to the flow of argument." [Walter Rauschenbusch, *The Righteousness of the Kingdom*, edited and Introduced by Max L. Stackhouse (Nashville, TN: Abingdon Press, 1968), 20, n.12)].

[beginning of typewritten introduction, added circa 1911-1916]
[1]

"The Righteousness of the Kingdom"

The purpose of this essay is to set forth in a straightforward and practical way what Jesus taught concerning right and wrong in human conduct.

It would be a mistake to represent Jesus merely as an ethical teacher. His purpose above all things was to make God known and loved among men. To leave the Father out of Christ's teaching is to blot the sun out of the day. But on the other hand he was not merely a guide in mystical religion. He came to found a new society on earth and he laid down the principles of conduct which were to govern men in this new society. Nor did he regard this as a matter of secondary importance. The bulk of his teachings as recorded in the first three Gospels is on questions of conduct. Questions of ceremonial were slighted by him; he took them up only when they were thrust upon him by others, and then it was only to unwrap and rescue some question of justice or mercy which was tangled up in the ceremony and in danger of suffocation. In doctrinal discussions also he frequently showed that the ethical aspect was the one that mainly interested him; that in fact he refused to consider theological questions when divorced from their ethical outcome. "Will the number of the saved be smaller?" "See that you are saved yourself" (Luke 13, 23).

We cannot conceal from ourselves the fact that the Christian Church has not, on the whole, apportioned its interest in the same way. It has split on questions of ceremonial, like the use of leavened or unleavened bread in communion, but not on the question of violent resistance to wrong. [2] It has been shaken for centuries on doctrinal questions, like the relation of the persons of the Trinity, but not so much on the relation of rich and poor. There is a clean-limbed vigor in the discussion of doctrine, which seems to change to the halting step of the half-blind in the treatment of human relations as affected by Christian discipleship. We know of many tracts setting forth the scheme of salvation, but we do not recall a single popular and full statement of the kind of conduct imposed by Christ upon his followers.
Yet the need of a bold and legible presentation of the Master conception of righteousness has perhaps never been greater than to-day. It is needed for the church; for the modern Jews and Greeks are not asking for signs and

wisdom as the credentials of the church, so much as for the fruits of a new life, for a conduct palpably different from any they are used to. It is needed for the world; for the great task of our epoch is the re-casting of social institutions, and it will depend largely on us how much of Christ's conceptions of social relations will be infused into the metal which is now glowing in the furnace of modern thought. [3] The teaching of Jesus was always fragmentary. He spoke as the needs of his hearers prompted. There is none of the rounded symmetry of an elaborate system, going back to the beginnings and working everything out to the details. On some matters he spoke frequently and at great length; others he never touched; not because he was indifferent to them, but because he could take the knowledge of them for granted with his hearers. He never dwelt on the wickedness of murder or the sinfulness of stealing. The ethical training of the Jewish people in the past had taken care of that part of his task. He accepted as his own the moral heritage of Israel, wrought out by Moses and the prophets. It was not his task to raze those gigantic foundation walls to the ground, but rather to build upon them the shining pillars which were to support the temple of a perfect humanity. He had not come to destroy but to fulfill. He set in where the Law stopped. The Law said: "Thou shalt not murder"; he said: "yea, nor shalt thou be angry with thy brother." The Law said: "Thou shalt not commit adultery"; he said: "thou shalt not even lust." The Law said: "thou shalt not send away thy wife without a legal document defining her status and permitting her to marry another"; he said: "thou shalt not send away thy wife at all save for the cause of fornication." The Law said: "thou shalt keep the word thou hast sworn to"; he said: "thou shalt keep thy word without swearing to it." The Law said: "if a man smites out thine eye, thou shalt not smite out his two eyes, but only one"; he said: "thou shalt smite out none at all." The Law drew a white circle of love around all men of Jewish faith and nationality and said: "thou shalt hate none within this circle; [4] what is beyond thou mayest hate"; he blotted out the circle and drew it again around all humanity and said: "thou shalt hate none and love all." Thus he fulfilled the law, as one fills a vase that has been but half full.

In systematizing the ethical principles of Jesus, we must not forget then that he presupposes the plain moral convictions of humanity, and that he will not allow his followers to drop back of the lines of righteousness drawn by the past experience of the race. On the other hand we must not forget that he refuses to stop with them. The moral maxims of the past are buoys to mark the channel as far as explored; they are not invitations to anchor, but to sail on.

There is a noble union of the conservative and the progressive element in this position, which constitutes a permanent principle of action for the builders of the Kingdom of God. They must not destroy; they must accept and reverently disentangle the convictions of right and wrong which the past thought of humanity has matured. But they must not stop there; they must fulfill and always keep on fulfilling. The Christian conceptions of righteousness are gradually saturating public opinion in the civilized nations. The regard for human life and the sympathy for suffering which were formerly distinctively Christian virtues have become matters of simple humanity. The righteousness of the scribes and Pharisees is moving forward. If the righteousness of the disciples of the Master is still to keep its pre-eminence, they must break camp and move forward into the untried regions of the future though there be but a few blood-stained foot-prints to show the way. [5] Questions of right and wrong enter into our relations to our fellow-men, to ourselves and to God. We shall take up the teachings of Jesus in that order.

In discussing our relations to our fellow-men, we shall speak first of our treatment of their life, their reputation and their property, for these are common to all; then of the special relations existing between men and women; and finally of the relations of the individual to the State.

The Decalogue summed up the duties toward the life of others in the commandment: "Thou shalt do no murder." Jesus did not repeat this commandment, except to say that he regarded obedience to it as a matter of course with his followers. He did not even broaden it by forbidding any impairment of the life of another. To damage the life of another was so evidently a wrong that Jesus did not stop to label it as such. Of course he knew that cases of injury consciously inflicted on others would occur even among the disciples. Some steward entrusted with the care of others, some men singled out by virtue of native ability or inherited position to be a leader and provider among men, would forget his obedience to the absent Master and his obligation to the souls entrusted to him, and instead of serving their wants would compel them to minister to his luxuries. For such a one the Master foretells weeping and gnashing of teeth and a portion among the hypocrites; and we cannot help asking ourselves whether there are not in modern society an appalling number who own the Master's name, but who [6] are rioting with their Master's property and inflicting injury on their fellow-servants.

It might happen too that a disciple inflicts an injury on another so slight perhaps that it would hardly be called an injury by others, such as calling a man Raca or fool. Perhaps the disciple has himself forgotten it. But as he comes to offer his gift upon the alter the nearness of God brings up the memory of his sin, as fire brings out the faded blackness of sympathetic ink. In that case he must let no fancied duty towards God or sacredness of ritual stand in his way, but he must drop everything and make amends to his brother.

To injure another is wrong, of course. Even to hate another, without injurious action, is intolerable. But mere abstinence from injury and hate does not satisfy the Lord. Indifference is not the attitude of the disciples towards the life of others. Nothing short of positive love will do. We must love him as well as we love the being we love best—ourselves. If we do that we shall not injure him. We have a very intimate and vivid sense of what is sweet or bitter to ourselves; if we would but be just as sensitive on behalf of our brother, identifying our feelings with his by love, and do to him what we would have others do to us if we were in the same position, we shall do well by his life.

The manifestation of love on which Jesus dwelt most, is love to the suffering and restoration of life that is in any way injured. It is that portion of love's duty which imposes the severest strain and to which human nature needs most encouragement; hence the special [7] emphasis on it. The most earnest things that were said by Jesus on the duty of restoring injured life were said without words. The ineffable tenderness with which he met all cases of suffering, the impetuous touch he gave to the crouching leper, the patient fidelity with which he received all who needed him at eventide in Capernaum, even when he was weighed down by the exertion and drained by output of sympathy—all this was teaching that burned the obligation of loving the suffering back to life into the imagination and memory of mankind. It has not been in vain. If we consider the strength of natural selfishness and the callousness produced by our own struggle for existence, there is cause for deep gratitude in the many agencies of restoration in the Christian world and for the universal conviction of human duty in that direction which the civilized world owes so largely to Jesus. And if we have not yet learned from Christ to seek out the perishing life and save it, we have very generally learned our duty to save it at least when it seeks us.

When Jesus came to Nazareth and the roes in the synagogue where he had so often sat, and saw before him the familiar faces of the friends of his youth, he selected a passage from Isaiah as best expressing to them the new consciousness which was animating him and the purpose to which he had consecrated his life. It was a passage embodying the divinely given desire to go out with a glad message to the poor, to release the captives, to restore sight to the blind and freedom to the crushed. If that embodied the life-work of Christ, it embodies the life-work of Christianity, and the fidelity of Christ's followers will have to be measured by this standard.

When John the Baptist in the prison of Machaerus heard no **[8]** message of judgement and the sweeping hosts of the Lord, he sent to inquire frankly of Jesus if he really was the Messiah.

[end of typewritten introduction]

[beginning of typewritten version of chapter i: provenance uncertain, but after 1900]

CHAPTER I.

Christianity Revolutionary [1] Christianity is in its nature revolutionary. This fact is apparent from the spiritual ancestry to which it traces its lineage. Jesus was the successor of the Old Testament prophets. The people discerned this kinship and whispered that he must be Elijah or Jeremiah, or some one of the prophets (Matth. 16, 4). Jesus himself asserted it. Like the prophets he was rejected in his own country (Matth. 13, 57); like them he would to suffer at the hands of the wicked husbandmen, and like them perish at Jerusalem (Luke. 20, 9-18; 13, 33). He calls his forerunner a prophet predicts for his followers the persecution and death which is the lot of the prophets (Matth. 9, 11-13; 23, 29-36).

And who were these prophets, to whose spirit and purposes Jesus felt so close a kinship, and whose lot he expected to share?

The prophets were the revolutionists of their age. They were dreamers of Utopias. They pictured an ideal state of society, in which the poor should be judged with equity and the cry of the oppressed would be heard no more; a time in which men would beat their idle swords into plowshares and their spears into pruning-hooks, because then the nations would learn war no more (Is. 2, 4).

Nor did not expect such a change to glide in without a struggle. A day of vengeance would have to precede it, which would be like a refiner's fire and like fullers' soap. The Lord would have a reckoning with those that oppressed the hireling in his wages, [2] the widow and the fatherless, and those who took advantage of the stranger's weakness (Mal. 3, 2, 5). He would come upon the high ones and the kings of the earth, and gather them like prisoners in the dungeon; for they had eaten up the vineyard; the spoil of the poor was in their houses; they had crushed the people and ground the faces of the poor (Is. 24, 21-22; 3, 13-15).

And the prophets were not impractical dreamers and declaimers. They were men of action. They overthrew dynasties. They were popular agitators, tribunes of the people. They rebuked to their faces kings who had taken the plain man's wife or tricked him out of his ancestral holding.

Such were the men whose successor Jesus professed to be. That does not imply that he sanctioned all their actions or proposed to copy all their methods. It does imply that of all the forces in the past of his nation the prophets were the most worthy of his approval and most akin to his spirit.

But the prophets were the revolutionary element in Israel.

The revolutionary character of Christ's work appears also from the elements in contemporary life to which he allied himself.

He found the people on fire with the Messianic hope. That drew them to the Jordan to hear John. That riveted their eyes on Jesus when he spoke of the acceptable year of the Lord and [3] declared that it was now at hand. They longed to count him on their side. They were on the alert to take the signal of revolt from his lips and to follow him as their king (John 6, 14-15).

It is true, Jesus steadfastly refused to fulfill their expectations. We shall discuss the reason for that later. Yet he did appeal to the Messianic hope. He found his followers among those in whom that hope was liveliest. He came so near to fulfilling the people's idea of the Messiah that they were always on the verge of expectation. Even at the very end, the assumption of little public state on his part was sufficient to revive their hopes, and they hailed him as the Messiah coming to claim the kingdom of his father David. The Sadducean enemies of the Messianic movement likewise identified him with it, and regarded it as only a question of time when he would raise his standard and plunge the nation into war with Rome (John 11, 47-50).

The contents of the Messianic hope of course varied. With some it was dyed in blood; with others it was irradiated by heaven. But this element was common to all who entertained it: they were weary of present conditions; they were longing for a radically different state of affairs; and they were sure that it would come and eager to help it on. In other words, the Messianic hope was a revolutionary hope.

Even the hopes of the most spiritually minded were tinged by this element. Mary praises the Lord for showing strength with [4] his arm in scattering the proud; for putting down princes and exalting them of low degree; for filling the hungry with good things and sending the rich away empty (Luke 1, 51-53). These were the thoughts of her whose blood ran in the veins of Jesus, and who had the fashioning of his early years. In the song of Zacharias the Messianic hope is summed up in a mighty uprising of Jehovah, a casting down of the powerful and wicked, and then spiritual peace and temporal prosperity for the poor and righteous (Luke 2, 34-35).

When we turn to the man whom Jesus himself has called the choicest fruit of his nation's past, we find the same language:

"Make ye ready the way of the Lord!
Make his paths straight!
Every valley shall be filled
And every mountain and hill shall be brought low;
And the crooked shall become straight,
And the rough way smooth."

Here is a general straightening out and leveling as a preparation for the coming of the Messiah. His practical advice to the people explains what he meant by straightening out the crooked ways and razing the high places: "He that hath two coats let him impart to him that hath none; and he that hath food let him do likewise." According to John, the abolition of social inequality is the first step in the Messianic renewal. His conception of the Messiah's [5] work is expressed in flaming images of destruction and overthrowing: a dusty threshing-floor, a sifting of wheat and chaff, a consuming fire, a crashing down of rotten trees. John's baptism, in which his preaching found its drastic expression, was a revolutionary symbol. It signified a turning away from old ways and a consecration to the new. It was the rite of initiation into "the remnant," which would be prepared for the coming of the Messiah and fit for the new order of things to be ushered in by the Messianic judgment.

Jesus expressly asserted the revolutionary character of his work. He declared that he had come to cast fire upon the earth and he only longed to see it kindled. He was hiding a leaven in the world's trough of meal, and the mass would be in a ferment until the leaven had done its work.

If there was a new spirit, there would have to be new forms. The old cracked skins could not contain the young, bubbling wine. It would be a foolish conservatism merely to patch bits of new cloth over the most shameless rents in the tattered garments wherewith society was seeking to cover its nakedness. A new spirit plus new forms and customs and institutions; what is that but revolution?

Jesus declared that the change he was inaugurating was so radical, that after its consummation it would be found that the first had become last, and the last first. Ideas now dominant would then be smiled over, and ideas now ridiculed would be triumphant. [6] Men now on top in society and state and church, would go to the bottom, and many now despised would then be honored and would reign over the tribes of Israel. Such a reversal of values presupposes sweeping changes in the general conceptions and judgements prevalent in human society, and necessarily also in the social and political institutions in which these conceptions find their embodiment.

Jesus knew the difficulties of his undertaking. He knew that those who have seats at the banquet of life where the old wine is served, have little taste for the new, and that power and privilege are not resigned without a struggle. He foresaw a division of humanity into hostile camps. Two in a household would be ranged against the other three. The strongest ties in the world would snap under the pressure of this new force. He foresaw this. If ever a heart was tender, surely it was his. Yet he did not shrink from precipitating such a conflict. His attitude became even more revolutionary as he went on; his language grew sterner, his opposition to the powers that were, grew more unyielding, until it became plain that the most moral community of that age, and perhaps the most religious community of any age, was engaged in irreconcilable conflict with Jesus Christ.

This interpretation of Christ's work is borne out by the attitude of his contemporaries toward him. Those who had anything to gain by a change, followed him. Those who had anything to lose by it, feared and hated him. Self-interest is short-sighted, but [7] its sight is marvelously keen for all that comes within the range of its vision. The politicians of that age were no duller than those of to-day. When the chief priests and scribes and elders, the dignitaries of society as it then existed, combined to put the Galilean down at all hazard, they were not stabbing at a shadow. They were right in holding him to be their foe. It was either his life or their privileges, and they knew it.

Indeed Christ's work could not but be revolutionary. He was sent by God, with his Father's thoughts and his Father's will in his heart, in order to make those thoughts known on earth and to secure obedience to that will.

Now, if the world were lovingly doing God's will to the extent of its knowledge, Christ's work would have been educational, and not revolutionary. With words of love he might have led his willing flock to the richer pastures. But that is not the state of the world. Men do not hasten to the light. The individual stifles his conscience and the community stones its prophets. Men keep a very firm grip on their own particular lusts and the wrongs by which they gain. And the evil of centuries has found its proper expression and manufactured its fitting tools in the laws, the customs, the opinions and traditions prevailing in human society. It is all one mass that hangs together. As John says: “The whole world lies embedded in wickedness.” [8] Given such a world, and given a great Christ who comes to see God’s will done on earth, and what can be the result, but a collision, an upheaval, a revolutionary movement, which must last and be revolutionary, until either the world is brought into submission, or Christ is conquered and gives up his attempt?

We find, then, that the historical antecedents of Christianity, the contemporary forces with which it was allied, the express statements of Jesus, the attitude of his contemporaries, and the very idea of his work and mission, unite in proving that it was really a revolutionary movement. It is not within the scope of this chapter to watch the impact of this force upon the world in subsequent history. But a glance at the history of Christianity as we find it in the apostolic writings of the New Testament, will serve to show that its revolutionary mission was not immediately lost sight of.

The bulk of Paul’s writings and the power of his mind have somewhat overshadowed in our estimate of the apostolic age that section of the early church, which looked to Peter and James rather than to Paul for its doctrine and standard of life. And yet the Jewish Christian churches were a most important part of early Christianity, and in some directions perhaps preserved the original character of the movement more intact than the Gentile churches.

The Apocalypse sprang from this soil. In gleaming imagery [9] it portrays the overthrow of the brutal world-powers and the inauguration of the kingdom of Christ. In veiled words the wickedness of Rome, its luxury, its rottenness, its oppression, are pictured. The Christians of that age knew what was meant by “the great city that reigns over the kings of the earth,” and that is “drunk with the blood of the saints.” Many hearts doubtless were longing for the sounding of hallelujahs over her fall.

The letter of James is another expression of the thoughts prevailing among the Jewish Christians. There is something of the sternness of the Old Testament prophets in his denunciation of the incipient corruption of the church by property distinctions. “The faith of our Lord Jesus Christ” and “the respect of persons” still seem incompatible to him. He reminds his brethren who were so eager to make things pleasant for the rich visitors of the church, that the oppression of the church had come from that class, while the poor had been chosen as heirs of the kingdom. There is no complacent justification of existing conditions in such words as these: “Go to now, ye rich, weep and howl for your miseries that are coming upon you.

Your gold and your silver are rusted and their rust shall be for a testimony against you and shall eat your flesh as fire. Behold the hire of the laborers who mowed your fields, which is of you kept back by fraud, crieth out, and the cries of them that reaped have entered into the ears of the Lord of Sabaoth." Such thoughts were probably far more general in the early church than we now sup-**[10]** pose.

With Paul the revolutionary element is not so dominant. His mind worked in other directions. But the evil of the present state of things, the certainty of an approaching Messianic judgment, and the establishment of a new world-era were among his fundamental teachings. And in fact he did do revolutionary work. However truthfully he protested that he was establishing the law, he was really making it unnecessary. The Jews were not altogether wrong, when they called him "the man that teacheth all men everywhere against the people, and the law; and this place," and when they repeated before Felix the charge they had raised against Christ before Pilate: "we have found this man a pestilent fellow and a mover of insurrections among all the Jews throughout the world." Paul was overthrowing the intertwined mass of the religion and politics of Judaism. And in heathen civilization he dropped a living seed, which in the course of its growth was to burst asunder the masonry of its edifice. Very early men felt that he was attacking the principle of unity which held the Roman world together. It was not merely a misunderstanding when men accused him of turning the world upside down, and of proclaiming another sovereign in the place of Caesar (Acts 17, 7). We pass lightly over the passages in which he speaks of Christ as superior to "all government and authority and power and lordship and every name that is named," and calls him "the blessed and only Potentate, the King of kings and Lord of lords." But in those days of abject **[11]** servility to human power, when the statue of the emperor stood in every market-place and divine honors were paid to the lord of the earth, we incline to think the Christians felt those words to be something more than pious phrases. At any rate the emperors soon came to feel the subversive power of these religious thoughts.

[end of typewritten version of chapter 1]

[start of handwritten version of manuscript, circa 1891-92] **[1]**

CHAPTER I.

CHRISTIANITY IS IN ITS NATURE REVOLUTIONARY.

1.) Its revolutionary character is apparent from the spiritual ancestry to which it traces its lineage. Jesus was the successor of the Old Testament prophets. The common people of his day discerned this kinship and whispered that he must be Elijah or Jeremiah or some other of the prophets (Mt. 16, 4). He himself repeatedly drew the parallel between the work and lot of the prophets and his own. Like the prophets he was rejected in his own country (Mt. 13, 57). Like the prophets he was to suffer at the hands of the wicked husbandmen (Lk. 20, 4-18). Like all the prophets he must perish at Jerusalem (Lk. 13, 34-35). His forerunner he calls a prophet, a second Elijah (Mk. 9, 11-13; Lk. 7, 26); and to his followers he predicts that like the prophets they will be slandered and persecuted (Mt. 5, 10-12), and at last like the prophets meet their death (Mt. 23, 29-36).

Now what were these prophets, to whose spirit and purpose Jesus felt so close a kinship, and whose lot he expected to share?

The prophets were the revolutionists of their age. They were dreamers of Utopias. They pictured an ideal state of society in which the poor should be judged with equity and the cry of the oppressed should no longer be heard; a time in which men would beat their idle swords into ploughshares and their spears into pruning hooks, for then the nations would learn war no more (Is. 2, 4). No slight amelioration contented them; nothing but a change so radical that they dared to represent it as **[2]** a repealing of the ancient and hallowed covenant and the construction of a new one. A proposal to abolish the Constitution of the United States would not seem so revolutionary to us as this proposal must have seemed to the contemporaries of the prophets.

They did not expect such a change to glide in without a struggle. A day of vengeance would have to precede it. It would be like a refiner's fire and like fullers' sope (Mal. 3, 2). The Lord would have a reckoning with those that oppressed the hireling in his wages, the widow, and the fatherless, and those that turned aside the stranger from his right (Mal. 3, 5). He would come upon the high ones and the kings of the earth, and gather them as prisoners are gathered in the dungeon, and shut them up in prison (Is. 24, 21-22.). For they had eaten up the vineyard; the spoil of the poor was in their houses; they had beaten God's people to pieces; they had ground the faces of the poor (Is. 3, 13-15).

Nor were the prophets mere impractical dreamers and declaimers. They were men of action. They overthrew dynasties. They were popular agitators, tribunes of the people. They rebuked to their faces kings who had taken the plain man of his wife or tricked him out of his ancestral holding.

These were the men whose successor Christ professed to be. This does not imply that he sanctioned all their actions or proposed to copy all their methods. But it does imply that of all the forces in the national history of Israel the prophets were the most worthy of his approval and most akin to his spirit.

But the prophets were the revolutionary element in Israel. [3] 2.) The revolutionary character of Christ's work appears also from the elements in contemporary life to which he allied himself.

The Messianic hope, kindled and fanned by the prophets, was still glowing in the hearts of the people. When John the Baptist lifted up his voice by the Jordan, men were on the alert immediately, querying "whether haply he were the Messiah." (Lk. 3, 15). The atmosphere of Palestine was surcharged with this electricity. When, in the synagogue at Nazareth, Jesus chose for his text that passage of Isaiah which tells of glad tidings to the poor, of release to the captives, of liberty to the bruised, and of the acceptable year of the Lord, "the eyes of all in the synagogue were fastened upon him." The passage was universally understood to refer to the Messianic era. They were breathlessly eager to hear what attitude he would assume. And what was his attitude? He told them the time had now come: "To-day hath this scripture been fulfilled in your ears." (Lk. 4, 16-21).

It is plain that the people counted him as their own. They were waiting to see him raise the standard of revolt and were ready to follow him as their king (Jo. 6, 14-15). And in spite of all apparent disappointments to which he subjected them, they had their eye on him still. When at the very end he entered Jerusalem with something of public state, all their hopes revived and they hailed him as the Messiah coming to claim the Kingdom of his father David.

It is true that Christ steadfastly refused to fulfill their expectations. We shall discuss [4] later on his reasons for doing so. Yet the fact remains that he did appeal to the Messianic hope. He found his followers among those in whom that hope was liveliest. He came so near to fulfilling the people's idea of the Messiah that they were always on the verge of expectation. To the Sadducean enemies of the Messianic movement he seemed, even at the end of his ministry, so closely connected with the movement that they regarded it as only a question of time when he would lead the revolt and plunge the nation into war with Rome (John 11, 47-50).

The contents of the Messianic hope of course varied. With some it was dyed in blood, with others it was irradiated by heaven. But this element was common to all who entertained it: they were weary of present conditions; they were longing for a radically different state of affairs; and they were sure that it would come and were ready to help it on. In other words, the Messianic hope was a revolutionary hope.

That this revolutionary element existed even among the most spiritually minded men and women is discernible from the recorded words of those choice souls among whom Jesus, by God's own appointment, spent his early years and by whom his thoughts were moulded. The hymns in the first two chapters of Luke, judged by internal evidence, express the Messianic hope before it had been modified by the teachings and the life of Jesus. Note the revolutionary tone:

> [5] "He hath shewed strength with his arm;
> He hath scattered the proud in the imagination of their heart. He hath put down princes from their thrones
> And hath exalted them of low degree.
> The hungry he hath filled with good things;
> And the rich he hath sent empty away." (Lk. 1, 51-53).
> Those were the thoughts of her whose blood ran in the veins of Jesus and who had the fashioning of his early years.
> Zacharias blesses Jehovah for having raised up a horn of salvation,
> "Salvation from our enemies, and from the hand of all that hate us;
> ... That he would grant unto us,
> That we, being delivered out of the hands of our enemies
> Should serve him without fear
> In holiness and righteousness before him all our days." (Lk. 1, 71, 74, 75).

In these two songs the thought of the Messianic victory predominates, and Simeon thinks more of the conflict which shall precede it and which will bring about the prostration of some and the elevation of others: "Behold this child is set for the falling and the rising of many in Israel; and for a sign which is spoken against; yea and a sword shall pierce through thine own soul; that thoughts out of many hearts may be revealed." (Lk. 2, 34-35). But in them all is the prophetic hope: a mighty uprising of Jehovah, a casting down of the powerful and wicked, and then peace and prosperity for the poor and righteous. [6] And when finally we turn to the man whom Jesus himself has called the choicest fruit of the all past, we find the same revolutionary language.

"Make ye ready the way of the Lord!
Make his paths straight!
Every valley shall be
And every mountain and hill shall be brought low;
And the crooked shall become straight,
And the rough way smooth."

Here is a general straightening out and leveling as a preparation for the coming of the Messiah. His advice to the people explains what he meant by straightening out the crooked ways and razing the high places: "He that hath two coats let him impart to him that hath none; and he that hath food let him do likewise." The abolition of social inequality, according to John, was the first step in the Messianic renewal. His conception of the Messiah's work is likewise expressed in flaming images of destruction and overthrowing: a dusty threshing-floor, a sifting of wheat and chaff, a consuming fire, a crashing down of rotten trees. The baptism of John, in which his preaching found its dramatic expression, was a revolutionary symbol. It was the baptism of repentance; a turning away from old ways and a consecration to the new; it was the rite of initiation into "the remnant," which would be prepared for the coming of the Messiah and fit for the new order of things to be ushered in by the Messianic judgment. [7] 3.) The revolutionary character of his work is expressly asserted by Christ.

He came to cast fire upon the earth, and he longed to see it kindled. He had come to hide a leaven in the world's trough of meal, and it would be in a ferment until the leaven had done its work.

He brought a new spirit and the new spirit would demand new forms of life. Men then as now had small discernment for the new spirit, but they raised a decided protest against the abolition of old forms and the evolution of new ones. He might bring new wine, if he wished, but let him put it in the old vessels. But Jesus told them that they must not think that his young, bubbling wine could be bottled up in the old cracked wine-skins, or that it would not suffice him reverently to patch bits of new cloth on the most shameless rents of the tattered garment wherewith society was seeking to cover its nakedness. A new spirit plus new forms and customs and institutions; that means revolution.

The change he was inaugurating was so radical, that after its consummation it would be found that the first had become last and the last first. Ideas now dominant would then be smiled over. Institutions now regarded as existing, *jure divino*, would then be recognized as having existed *jure diabolico*. Men now on top in society and state and church, would go to the bottom, and many now despised and neglected would then be honored and would reign over the tribes of Israel. Such [8] a reversal of values presupposes sweeping changes in the general conceptions and judgments prevalent in human society, and necessarily also in the social and political institutions in which these conceptions and judgments find their embodiment.

Jesus knew very well the difficulties of the work he had undertaken. He knew that those who have seats at the banquet where the old wine is served have little taste for the new. He knew that those who hold the places of power and privilege will seldom resign them without a struggle. He foresaw a terrible conflict, a division of humanity into hostile camps. A man would be set at variance with his father, and a daughter with her mother. Two in a household would be ranged against the other three. The strongest ties in the world would snap ~~if~~ when they encountered this new force.

Jesus foresaw all this. If ever a heart was tender, surely it was his. Yet he did not shrink from precipitating the world into such a conflict. His was the revolutionary spirit, loving and inflexible.

Moreover his attitude became more revolutionary as he went on; his language grew sterner, his opposition to the powers that were, more unyielding, until it grew plain that the most moral community of that age, and perhaps the most religious society of any age, was engaged in irreconcilable conflict with Jesus Christ; a conflict which could end only with the overthrow of one of the conflicting forces. We know that it did end with the apparent overthrow of the one and the actual overthrow of the other. [9] 4.) This interpretation of the tendency of Christ's work is borne out by the attitude of his contemporaries. Those who had anything to gain by a change, followed him and heard him gladly. Those who had anything to lose by a change, feared him. They feared him enough to hate him. They hated him enough to kill him. Self-interest is short-sighted, but its sight is marvelously keen for all that comes within the range of its vision. When the chief priests and scribes and elders, the dignitaries of society as it then existed, combined to put him down at all hazard, they were not stabbing at shadows. They were closing with a deadly foe and they knew it. It was either his life or their privileges. They had no mind to be placed at the bottom in any overturning process of his.

5.) In fact, if we consider what Christ's work really consisted in, we shall perceive that it could not but be revolutionary. He was sent by God, with his Father's thoughts and this Father's will in his heart, to make those thoughts known on earth and to secure obedience to that will.

Now if the world were lovingly doing God's will to the extent of its knowledge, and anxiously seeking more knowledge in order better to obey God, then Christ's work would have been educational and not revolutionary. With words of love he would **[10]** have led his willing flock to the richer pastures and purer water prepared for them. But that is not the state of the world. The crucifixion of Jesus gives the lie to that theory of life, and he that has eyes to see, can see along the track of history a long line of Calvaries, where successive generations have sought to choke the word of God calling them to righteousness. It has ever been easy for man to obey his lusts and hard to resist them. And the evil of centuries has found its proper expression and manufactured its fitting tools in the laws, the customs, the opinions and traditions prevailing in human society, so that an old man who had seen much of life, and yet loved mankind, sadly summed up his thoughts in the judgment: "The whole world is embedded in wickedness."

Now, given such a world, and given a great Christ who comes to see God's will done on earth, and in the nature of the case, there must be a collision, an upheaval, a revolutionary movement which must last and be revolutionary until either the world is brought into submission or Christ is conquered and gives up his attempt.

6.) It is not within the purpose of this chapter to trace the course of the revolutionary movement initiated by Jesus, but simply to point out that the historical antecedents of Christianity, the contemporary forces with which it was allied, the **[11]** express statements of Christ himself, the attitude of his contemporaries to him, and the very nature of his work, mite to prove that it was really a revolutionary movement. Still, a glance at the history of Christianity, as we find it in the apostolic writings of the New Testament, may serve still further to establish this point.

One of the earliest books of the New Testament in point of time is the Apocalypse. In gleaming imagery it portrays the overthrow of the brutal world powers and the inauguration of the Kingdom of Christ. In veiled words the wickedness of Rome, its luxury, its rottenness, its oppression are pictured. The Christians of that age knew what was meant by "the great city that reigns over the kings of the earth" and that "is drunk with the blood of the saints," and doubtless many hearts longed for the sounding of hallelujahs over her fall.

Another early expression of Christian thought as it prevailed among the Jewish Christians, is found in the Letter of James. There is something of the sternness of the Old Testament prophets and of John the Baptist in his rebuke of the incipient corruption of the church by property distinctions. "The faith of our Lord Jesus Christ" and the "respect of persons" seem incompatible to him. He reminds those who incline to bestow church distinctions on the man [12] with the gold ring and the fire working, that the rich are the oppressors of the church and the blasphemers of Christ's work; while the poor are the ones whom God has chosen to be heirs of the Kingdom. Read this and see whether it sounds like complacent justification of existing conditions: "Go to now, ye rich, weep and howl for your miseries that are coming upon you. Your riches are corrupted, and your garments are moth-eaten. Your gold and your silver are rusted and their rust shall be for a testimony against you and shall eat your flesh as fire. Ye have laid up your treasure in the last days. Behold the hire of the laborers who mowed your fields, which is of you kept back by fraud, crieth out; and the cries of them that reaped have entered into the ears of the Lord of Sabaoth." [James 5, 1-4] Such thoughts were probably far more general in the early church than we now suppose. The force and the bulk of Paul's teaching have in our minds overshadowed everything else in the / apostolic church.

With Paul the revolutionary element is not so dominant. His mind worked in other directions and elaborated the thoughts of his Master on another side. But the evil of the present state of things, the certainty of an approaching Messianic judgment, and the establishment of a new world era were among his fundamental teachings. In fact he did do revolutionary work. However much and truthfully he protested that he was establishing the law, he was really making it unnecessary; he was leveling the distinctive prerogatives of the Jews and subverting everything in which they put their trust and pride. They were not altogether wrong when they called him "the man that teacheth all men everywhere against the people, and the law, and this place," and when they repeated before Felix the charge they had raised against Christ before Pilate: "we have found this man a pestilent fellow and a mover of insurrections among all the Jews throughout the world." There was truth in it. So far as Judaism was concerned, the whole intertwined mass of its religion, its politics and its society, Paul's work was revolutionary. And in heathen civilization he dropped a living seed which in the course of its growth was to burst asunder the masonry of its edifice and make it totter and fail. Very early men felt that he was attacking the principle of unity which held the Roman world together. It was not a mere misunderstanding when men accused him of turning the world upside down and of opposing Caesar by proclaiming Jesus as king (Acts 17, 7). We pass lightly over the passages in which he speaks of Christ as superior to "all government and authority and power and lordship and every name that is named," and calls him "the blessed and only Potentate; the King of kings and Lord of lords." But in those days of abject servility to human power, when the statue of the emperor stood in every market-place and divine honor was paid to the lord of the earth, we incline to think the Christians feel those words to be more than pious phrases. At any rate the emperors soon came to feel the subversive power of these religious thoughts.

[beginning of typewritten beginning of chapter II: provenance c.1911-1916] **[12]**

CHAPTER II.

THE KINGDOM OF GOD

What, now is the aim of this revolutionary movement inaugurated by Jesus? What word is inscribed on the banner he raised?

"The kingdom of God"! That is the phrase forever recurring in his teaching. About that his thoughts circle like a host of planets round a central sun.

And what is the "Kingdom of God"? Jesus discusses many aspects of it, its value, its laws of growth, its blessings, its obstacles; but for a definition of what he meant by the words we look in vain. Why? Because his hearers were familiar with the words and with the idea contained in them. Jesus did not create the conception. It was there; the heritage of his nation's past, and the most living hope of its present. Therefore to understand Jesus we must put ourselves in the position of his contemporaries and realize in our own mind the ideas with which the past had stocked the common mind of the Jewish people.

The conceptions which ruled the religious life of Israel were the idea of the covenant and the theocracy. Jehovah had chosen Israel as peculiarly his own. He fought its battles through the Judges. He reigned through the kings. He gave the laws. He spoke through the prophets. He heard the prayers of his people and interfered against their oppressors. If the people walked in his law, his bless- **[13]** in was promised to be upon them; they would till the ground in peace; the harvests would not fail; sickness would not come nigh them; their children would multiply like the young lambs of the flock. That is the Jewish ideal of life: a righteous community, ordered by divine laws, governed by God's ministers, having intercourse with the Most High, and blessed by him with the good things of life.

But the realization lagged wearily behind the ideal. The people were recreant to their obligations. The kings were more often creatures of the harem than vice-gerents of God. We hear the passionate protests of the prophets against the venality of judges and the covetousness of the nobles, and in the Psalms the poor and meek sob for redress of wrongs. The national independence was lost. The rivers of Babylon saw the mute grief of Jewish exiles. After the return Jerusalem was ground under the heels of successive oppressors.

But the faith of this wonderful nation rose triumphant above this contradiction between their faith in a sublime vocation and their actual wretchedness. Its spirit was not crushed. Its faith was not relinquished. It must have fulfilment, somewhere, some time. The perfect reign of God in Israel would yet be. Fair above the failures of the present rose the image of a glorious future. It took its outlines from periods of prosperity in the past, and its colors were pressed from the woes of the present. Every prophet saw it darkly and prophesied in part, but every one added some touch [14] and its lineaments grew ever clearer, till all the nation fixed its eyes on that hope.

It is not possible to trace here the long development of the Messianic hope, and the various forms it assumed in the two parts of Isaiah, in Ezekiel, in Daniel, and in the abundant apocalyptic literature after the exile. Its historic continuity was never broken, and in the days of Jesus the nation was full of eager anticipation of the Messiah's coming who was to initiate the new era by a mighty display of power in the judgement of the wicked and the liberation of the people of God.

The Messianic hope, then, was the hope for the perfection of the theocracy. Its contents varied with the character of those who entertained it. The majority perhaps looked for national revenge and temporal enjoyment. Some hoped for spiritual quickening. But this was common to them all, including John the Baptist; this belongs to the essence of the Messianic hope: that the theocratic idea was at last to have its perfect realization in a kingdom of God on earth, with the Messiah as its head, Israel as its dwelling-place and organ, and all the world as the sphere of its manifestation.

Now what attitude did Jesus assume toward the Messianic hope of his day? Did he oppose it as wrong, foolish and perilous? Was he indifferent to it, as to something remote from his own work? Or did he accept it, elevate it, and strive to realize it?

Evidently the latter. He used the vocabulary of the Messianic [1] movement. He selected his followers from the circle most imbued with Messianic ideas. His attitude and preaching could not have been, and indeed were not, understood by his hearers as referring to anything but the fulfilment of the common hope of the nation.

The assertion that Jesus identified himself with the Messianic hope, does not imply that he proposed to fulfil every hope of everyone of his contemporaries, nor even that he agreed with the conceptions entertained by a majority of them. That hope was a growth of centuries and its end was not identical with its inception. It was a popular idea that shaded off into innumerable tints, and not a rigid formula or scheme that had to be accepted entire or rejected entire. In agreeing with some Jesus could not help disagreeing with others. But the essence of the hope he must have accepted, else his words would have been misleading, and he would not have been Israel's Messiah, the fulfiller of its national religious life. If he protested that not one iota of the law should perish till it had come to its full fruition, he could not cast aside as false or useless the central idea of the Old Testament, the idea of the theocracy, the hope of God's perfect reign in humanity.

Two things are essential to the programme formulated in Christ's revolutionary parole: First, the idea of a kingdom necessarily implies a social ideal; it speaks of a perfect community. Secondly the fulfillment of that ideal is expected on this earth and on the hither side of death. "Thy Kingdom come; thy will be done on earth."

[end of typewritten beginning of chapter 2] [Continuation of original manuscript version of Chapter II, c.1891-1892]

[13]

CHAPTER II.

THE REVOLUTIONARY PROGRAM

What, now is the aim of this revolutionary movement inaugurated by Jesus? What word is inscribed on the banner he raised?

"The Kingdom of God!" That is the phrase forever recurring in his teaching. About that his thoughts circle like a host of planets 'round a central sun. Observe the radiance of that central thought, and the whole constellation is darkened.

What is the "Kingdom of God"? Jesus discusses many aspects: he speaks of its value, its laws of growth, its blessings, its obstacles; but for a definition of it we look in vain. Why is that? Because the idea of the Kingdom of God was a conception with which his hearers were familiar. Jesus did not create the conception, but only to correct it. The body of it was there, the heritage of past centuries and the most living hope of that age. Hence if we would understand Jesus as his contemporaries understood him, we must put ourselves in their position. We must trace the origin and growth of the idea of the Kingdom of God and find what the phrase stood for with the men to whom Jesus spoke.

The foundation on which the religious and national life of Israel rested was the conviction that Jehovah had chosen this one nation from among all the people of the earth to be particularly his own. He had made an eternal covenant with them; if they obeyed him, he would protect them against their enemies, prosper them in all their ways, reveal his glory among them and be their God. He would be their King. He would give them laws. He would also, like other Oriental monarchs, be the supreme judge; but unlike them, he would judge without regard of persons, **[14]** especially over the widow, the fatherless, and the stranger (Deut. 10, 14-18).

The leadership of Moses or the Judges was not a contradiction of the Kingship of Jehovah. For it was he that raised them up and gave them wisdom and victory. They were merely the great King's commissioner, holding their power from him and not in their own right. The demand for the institution of a human Kingship was a defection from the theocratic idea, but even the self-exaltation of Oriental autocrats and adulation of courtiers were not able to eradicate that idea from the heart of the nation. It found most unpleasant utterance now and then through the prophets.

The idea of Jehovah's covenant with Israel and his Kingship over it became the very soul of the nation. It was its comfort in adversity, its pride in prosperity, its admonition in sin, it unifying hope even in despair. That idea has made Israel's history unique. It commenced a structure of national life so enduring, that though an omnipotent hand has overthrown the edifice, yet eighteen centuries have not availed to rumble and disintegrate the ruins.

But the realization often lagged wearily behind the idea. The people were recreant to their covenant obligations. The nation was split in two. It was given into the hands of the Gentiles. The land withheld its fruit. Righteousness and peace were fled. We hear the passionate protests of the prophets against the venality of judges and the covetousness of the nobles. In the Psalms we hear the sobs of the poor and meek begging for redress of wrong. The Kings were but seldom vice-regents of Jehovah. More often they were creatures of the harem, aping their royal neighbours, seeking even to undermine the nation's faith in its God. **[15]** In this contradiction between their faith in a sublime vocation on the one hand and their experience of actual servitude and wretchedness on the other, the nation began to work out the Messianic hope. Their faith must have fulfillment, somewhere, sometime. The perfect reign of God in Israel would yet be. Fair above the failures of the present rose the image of a glorious future. It took its outlines from periods of prosperity in the past and its colors were pressed from the woes of the present. Every prophet saw it darkly and prophesied in part, but every one added some touch, and its lineaments grew ever clearer, till all the nation fixed its eyes on that hope.

From the root of Jesse, the bulk of which was fallen and dead, a fresh sprout would shoot up. A king would arise who would have the spirit of Jehovah, the spirit of wisdom and understanding, the spirit of counsel and might, the spirit of knowledge and of the fear of Jehovah. He would judge the poor with righteousness and reprove with equity on behalf of the meek (Is. 11,1-5). He would be worthy of divine names: "Wonderful counsellor, mighty God, father of eternity, prince of peace (Is. 9, 6). The nation would flock around him as to an ensign lifted up. He would lead them to victory against the Gentiles. Under his sway the earth would blossom. Universal peace would reign. Even the beasts would destroy no more. And the nations, seeing the glory of Israel, would gather to Jehovah's mountain to learn his ways and walk in his paths. Sin would be blotted out. The spirit of God would be poured out on all, the earth would be full of the knowledge of the Lord as the waters cover the sea. [16] The Babylonian exile had not crushed the Messianic hope. The weary centuries following the exile did not starve it. Its record is preserved in the apocalyptic literature of that period. Since the revolution under the Maccabees, it seemed almost on the point of fulfillment. But again, the fortunes of the nation declined and the hope was projected into the remoter future. At the time of Jesus, the Herodian and Roman rule were heavy on the people. There was a restless waiting for the promised salvation. It was so intense that even the heathen world began to be in anticipation of some great event in Judea. From the time of Tiberius to Hadrian's prophets and Messiahs arose in rapid succession, calling the Jews to arise against the Rome. The New Testament gives the most vivid picture of the eagerness with which the people were ready to hail either John the Baptist or Jesus as the Messiah, if they would but claim the title.

The Messianic hope, then, was the hope for the perfection of the theocracy. Begotten by the spirit of God and nourished by the prophets, it had survived to the days of Jesus. It was the most powerful and the most divine fact in the national and religious life of his people. Its contents varied with the character of those who entertained it. The majority perhaps looked for national revenge and temporal enjoyment. Some hoped for spiritual quickening. But this was common to them all, including John the Baptist; this belongs to the essence of the Messianic hope: that the theocratic idea was at last to have its perfect realization in a Kingdom of God, with the Messiah as its head, Israel as its dwelling-place and organ, and all the world as the sphere of its manifestation. [17] We are now ready for the question: What attitude did Jesus assume toward the Messianic hope of his day? Did he oppose it as wrong, foolish and perilous? Was he indifferent to it, as to something remote from his own work? Or did he accept it, elevate it, and strive to realize it?

Evidently the latter. He formulated no new ideal, but proclaimed that the existing ideal was now on the verge of fulfilment. "The Kingdom of God is at hand." He used the vocabulary of the Messianic movement. He selected his followers from the circle most imbued with Messianic ideas. His attitude and preaching could not have been, and indeed were not, understood by his hearers as referring to anything but the establishment of the perfect theocracy.

And how could it have been otherwise? Jesus was not the successor of Greek philosophers teaching a system of self-culture. He was the successor and heir of the great thoughts of Israel. These, he said, he had come to fulfill. And if he protested that not an iota of the law should perish until it had come to its full fruition, would he cast aside as useless that greatest of all the Old Testament ideas, the idea of the theocracy? Here, if anywhere, his mission must be to fulfill and not to destroy. And to fulfill **[18]** surely does not mean to supplant, to substitute something in its place which to all intents is not the same thing nor a fuller development of the same thing. If Jesus had brushed aside the idea of the reign of God on earth, he would have brushed aside the entire Old Testament and the entire past of Israel. And if any of the professed followers of Christ teach a Christianity in which that same idea is not the core and center, then they may protest their belief in the Old Testament, in its inspiration, its inviolability by criticism, and its divine contents, but they belie their own words. In theory they call it holy and wise, in practice they call it foolish and impracticable.

The assertion that Jesus identified himself with the Messianic hope, does not imply that he proposed to fulfill every hope of everyone of his contemporaries, nor even that he agreed with the conceptions entertained by a majority of them. The Messianic hope was a growth of centuries and its end was not identical with its inception. It was a popular idea that shaded off in innumerable tints, and not a rigid formula or scheme that had to be accepted entire or rejected entire. So in agreeing with some Jesus could not help disagreeing with others.

Surveying the development of the Messianic idea, we find that there is a **[19]** steady movement in certain directions; not a movement in a straight line, but a progress like the flow of a river, turned aside at one point by the peculiarities of one powerful personality, doubling on itself for a while under a temporary reactionary movement, and yet on the whole moving forward. And comparison shows that, in contradicting some popular conceptions and developing others, Jesus was working in the same direction in which the spirit of God had been slowly leading the prophets.

1.) The Messianic idea developed in the direction of universality.

Prophecy was like a man climbing the winding stairs of a tower and gaining a wider and more glorious outlook with every window reached. The prophets of the first period, Joel, Amos, Hosea, speak only of a national salvation. Isaiah and Micha (Is. 2, 2-4; Micah 4, 1-4) tell of Gentiles coming to inquire of the God of Jacob, and of Assyria and Egypt forming with Israel a holy triad of nations (Is. 19, 18-25). The more Israel came in contact with the great empires, the larger grew the Messianic hope. The isles of the heathen and men beyond the rivers of Ethiopia would become suppliants to Jehovah (Zeph. 2, 11; 3, 10). They would bless themselves with his name, and recognize all their religion as [20] lies and emptiness (Jer. 4, 2; 16, 19). Then Jehovah alone would be king on earth (Zach. 14, 9) and the knowledge of his glory would fill the earth as the waters cover the sea (Hab. 2, 14). Finally universality became so prominent a feature of its Messianic hope, that a few at least rose to the idea that it was for just this purpose of being a light to the Gentiles that Israel had been chosen (Is. 40-66).

This conviction had, in the time of Christ, issued in a wide-spread Jewish missionary activity. As Jesus puts it, they were compassing sea and land to make one proselyte. They numbered their adherents in the highest circles, especially among the women at Rome, and some years later Paul finds "devout proselytes" in all the Jewish congregations of Asia Minor. But this tendency to universality was hampered by the extreme nationalism of Judaism. All might share in the Messianic blessings, but only by becoming Jews and taking upon them the yoke of the law. That the Gentiles as Gentiles were to have a share in the Messianic salvation was unthinkable. We know how hard it was even for the apostles to strip off this narrowness, and how Paul waged a life-long battle against its effort to re-enslave the church.

The position of Jesus appears to have developed gradually on this point as on all others. He began his work, as was natural, among his own people. He concentrated his efforts on winning them to own him and obey him (Mt. 23, 34). He commanded his disciples on their missionary journeys not to [21] go into the way of the Gentiles, nor into the Samaritan cities, but to go to the lost sheep of the house of Israel (Mt. 10, 5-6). Yet wherever he comes in contact with heathen, the wall of partition crumbles at his touch. He talks freely to the Samaritan woman and stays several days in her village. He is won by the faith of the Syro-Phoenician woman to do that which he had refused. The fact that the centurion at Capernaum was a heathen did not conceal from him that in this man dwelt a faith surpassing any that he had found in Israel, and he was led to prophesy that many like this man would come from the East and the West to share in the Kingdom, while sons of the Kingdom would be cast forth into the darkness without. In this disregard for names and regard for facts; in this unfailing hold on inward realities lay the guarantee that Christ would limit his work not by the bounds of nationality, but by the bounds of humanity. Faith and not Judaism qualified for the Kingdom. Unbelief and not uncircumcision disqualified for it. Therefore when his efforts for Israel as a whole had been unavailing, he told them that "the Kingdom of God would be taken from them and given to a nation bringing forth the fruits thereof." And so at the end he sent out his disciples to proclaim the glad tidings to all the nations. [22] We find, then, that the Kingdom of God as Christ saw it, was not outwardly limited by the boundaries of any one nation. We have already touched on the fact that this outward universality was the necessary consequence of its inward universality. But we must expand that thought.

2.) The conception of the Messianic salvation developed in the direction of spirituality. The circle within which it would be manifested was widened; but at the same time the nature of its blessings and consequently the character of those capable of receiving them, were differently conceived.

The early prophets spoke mainly of national independence and supremacy, and of temporal prosperity. Every Israelite would have a share in the blessing by virtue of being a member of the chosen nation.

But in time national experience taught the prophets that no outward reconstruction and no enforced obedience to the law would suffice. Jeremiah had seen the people slip back as soon as the strong arm of Josiah which had forced them up, was withdrawn. A spiritual renewal was necessary [23] as the basis for the bestowal of outward blessings. But if that was true, then not all of Israel would share in it, for it was but too evident that there were hearts too hard to yield. They would have to be weeded out. A great judgment would have to precede the Messianic salvation, and only "the remnant" would be saved.

In the nature of the case this conception could not be shared by all. Only those who were spiritual could discern that the profoundest chasm is not between nation and nation, nor even between those who perform outward rites and those who do not, but between those who have the love and fear of God in their hearts and those who have not. The children of this world stick to outward lines of demarcation. Accordingly, in spite of the growing plainness of prophetic preaching on this point, we find the people in the days of Christ still convinced that every child of Abraham who was in outward conformity with the law, was entitled to a share in the Messiah's blessings as his birthright. There were some who saw it differently. Simeon had watched ecclesiastical life in Jerusalem long enough to foresee that there would be a rising for some in Israel, but a falling for others. John the Baptist foretold a terrible sweeping out of the chaff and a hewing down of evil trees.

He [24] bade those who were comforting themselves with their descent from Abraham, to look to their hearts; repentance alone would qualify them for the Kingdom; as for children of Abraham, God could turn the Jordan pebbles into as many of them as he wanted.

Jesus took up the same message. In the synagogue at Nazareth he proclaimed that the Messianic visitation was at hand. Then he spoke of the conditions of participating in it. He pointed out that in the days of Elijah it was a Sidonian widow to whom alone the prophet was sent. And in the days of Elisha it was only a Syrian leper who was cleansed, while Israel remained unblessed. The inference was that in the day of the Messiah also it would be spiritual fitness and not nationality that would ensure the blessing. It was that which angered the people: that they were to be placed on the same insecure and conditional footing with the rest of mankind. In praising the faith of the heathen centurion and in denouncing Chorazin and Bethsaida as worthy of greater punishment than the accursed cities of Phoenicia, he likewise overthrows the prerogative of nationality and establishes spirituality as the qualification for citizenship in the Kingdom. "Except ye turn and become as little children, ye shall in no wise enter into the Kingdom." "Except a man be born anew, he cannot see the Kingdom of God." [25] The tendency of prophetic development, then, was toward the recognition of the spiritual nature of the Kingdom of God. And this tendency finds its consummation in Christ's own conception. He proposed to found his Kingdom on spirit and not on matter. He gathered as the material for its upbuilding the poor in spirit, the meek, the merciful, and not the men who possessed temporal power and wealth, and the ability of wielding the forces of this world. By his entire life he showed that he regarded the spiritual nature of man, the religious and moral element, as the core of the individual life and the real formative force in the life of society.

History assents to his position. Ideas and convictions are the enduring revolutionary forces. Changed institutions without changed convictions to uphold them from beneath are likely to slump together. In nations where religion has decayed or stands as a propped-up skeleton in churchly robes; where the sobriety and morality of the common people are sapped and poisoned; where the body politic has gristle in-[26]stead of bone, the flabby mass may indulge in contortions, but it cannot march to greatness. Righteous and God-fearing men and women are the material with which the progress of human society can be made enduring. The infusion of a new principle, a new conviction into the thought-life of humanity is the condition of every onward step in the organization of society. The perfect humanity must be a growth, building itself up by vital forces from within, like the chambered nautilus secreting its own shell.

But while Jesus began his work on the inward and spiritual side of human life, he did not propose to let it end there. That is the falsity of the conception of the Kingdom current among Christians today. They have learned so thoroughly the lesson that the Kingdom of God is righteousness and peace and joy in the Holy Ghost, that they are ready to close the book there. Social reformers shrug their shoulders at religion and labor away at environment as the source of social regeneration. "Nay," says the church, "not from without, but from within," and the church is right, as social reformers have found out and will find out yet more. But when the church silently adds "only within," it brings down on itself the severest invective of its professed Master. There was nothing that Jesus resented so much as an attempt to divorce the inward [27] from the outward; to be saying "Lord, Lord!" and then not to obey him; to parade as a good tree and yet bring no fruit or bitter fruit. There was a man who had two sons. And he said to the elder, "Go work to-day in my vineyard." And he answered: "Certainly, Father, my will is consecrated to thee," but he did not go but sat on the fence and rejoiced in the assurance of his sonship within. The father made the same request of the younger. He was surly and muttered as he sat still: "In the place I am not at all sure that he is my father; in the second place I think I only imagined that he spoke to me; and in the third place I am not going anyway." But after a while he climbed over the fence into the vineyard and began hoeing away, assuring himself that he did not do it on his father's account, but because he liked it. And the father wished that he had a third son who would both say yes and do yes.

Prosperity unsustained by righteousness ends in rottenness. Therefore Jesus did not begin his work by creating prosperity. Righteousness, if it has its full course, produces all prosperity. Therefore Jesus did begin with making men know and do righteousness, knowing well that if [28] they did that, all things would be added to them. But woe to him that seeks to shut up the spirit of God in his own heart or in the hearts of others, and forbids it from going out into the world to do its creative work there; that speaks of a spiritual kingdom and means a kingdom of feelings and words and air and intangible moonshine; that looks for a kingdom of earth in heaven, but neither hopes nor desires a kingdom of heaven on earth; that asks for a "pure gospel" and means a disembodied spirit that haunts churches, but never ventures out into the market and the stock exchange and the real estate office.

Christ initiated his Kingdom on earth by establishing a community of spiritual men, in inward communion with God and in outward obedience to him. This was the living germ of the Kingdom. But it was not the purpose of this community merely to dismiss one after the other of its members into heaven and to leave the world as it was, nor was the increase of its membership the only method of extending its power. By the power of the spirit dwelling in it, it was to overcome the spirit dominant in the world, and thus penetrate and transform the world. In place of cruel customs it was to establish merciful customs. It was [29] to push up steadily the average standard of right making it approximate to the absolute standard of God. It was to break the enslaving power of lies by the enfranchising power of truth. Every such step forward, every increase in mercy, every obedience to justice, every added brightness of truth would be an extension of the reign of God in humanity, an incoming of the Kingdom of God. The more men became saturated with the thoughts of Christ; the more they came to judge all actions from his point of view; the more they conformed the outward life of society to the advancing inward standard; the more would Christ be the dominant force in the world, and all humanity become the true theocracy.

That this development would not be a peaceful one, he foretold and demonstrated in his life. But that the spirit of God can overthrow the resisting spirit of this world and oust it from one position after another he also asserted and demonstrated. He also promised that at all the important junctures of this process and especially at its consummation God would interfere with awful judgments and demonstrations of his power from on high, cooperating with the spiritual work of the church in securing the triumph of Christ. [30] 3.) There was a progress in prophetic thought in the value ascribed to spiritual means as against external means in the establishment of the Messianic Kingdom. At first force was the means which the Messiah was to use and which those had to use who would anticipate his work. The reforming kings of Israel and Judah, instigated and upheld by the prophets, used force in suppressing the enemies of God and in bringing his people into obedience to the law. The Messiah was to be a warrior king, crushing the heads of enemies, breaking their forces like potsherds, and distributing their booty to his followers.

But with the growing strength of the prophetic order and the influence of their teaching on the life of the nation, the tremendous force contained in the weapons of the spirit was increasingly recognized. During the exile the national government was non-existent. If the life and unity of the nation had depended on that, it would have dropped asunder like a barrel when the hoops are cut. But the national unity was maintained. The sense of oneness was increased. Patriotism and ardor for the law had never burned with so steady and persistent a fire. Evidently it was not by might nor by power, but by the spirit of Jehovah that great things were to be done. The suffering steadfastness of the godly had proved to be a power with men and prevailing with God. The Messianic salvation would be achieved by the same means. (The proph. expectations of a powering out of the spirit) **[31]** These thoughts were dimly perceived by the prophets and treasured in some hearts. Spiritual men discerned with more or less clearness that as the qualifications for the Messianic Kingdom and its blessings were spiritual, so the means for its establishment must be spiritual also. But the majority of men put their trust in outward means. They expected that the Messiah would drive out the Romans by force. They showed their trust in arms by their readiness to seize them. They were impatient with Jesus for delaying so long his summons to arms. Even John the Baptist, spiritual as his conceptions were, seems to have expected a mighty display of power, and when in his prison cell he listened in vain for the alarms of a rising nation and heard only of preaching and healing, he began to question whether this were indeed he for whom Israel was waiting.

Christ's choice of means was made at the outset of his work and consistently adhered to till the end. In the lonely days following his baptism he faced the temptations that pressed upon him in his official capacity and settled on his course. He decided first that he would not use his official power for self-gratification, not even to save himself from pain; in the second place that he would not seek to attract men **[32]** by miraculous display; and finally that he would not ally himself with that Messianic faction of his people, which had hate for its motive and force for its means, even if by that means he might gain the kingdoms of the world and the glory thereof. The latter two refer to the means to be chosen for his work.

In declining to gain adherents by the display of power he put aside the influence which would most readily have gained him the leadership of his nation. They were all on the alert for high-colored marvels. Paul mentions it as the distinguishing characteristic of Jewish religious life that they were ever asking for signs. "Master, we would see a sign from thee" (Mt. 12, 38). "What then doest thou for a sign, that we may see and believe thee? What workest thou? Our fathers ate the manna in the wilderness" (Jo. 6, 30-31). Even to the cross that temptation followed him: "Let him now come down from the Cross, and we will believe on him" (Mt. 27, 42).

Jesus refused their request over and over again, to the distress of his disciples and the pleasure of his opponents. He called those who were clamoring for a sign, "an evil and adulterous generation." When he did perform works of power he shunned publicity as much as possible. He restrained those who had been healed from hawking the news about. He did [33] regard his restoration of the wretched and stricken and his victorious conflict with the sinister forms of insanity, as demonstrations that a power stronger than the Prince of this world, the power of the Kingdom of God, was present in the world (Mt. 11, 2-5; 12, 22-29). If men could not perceive that fact in any other way, let these ocular demonstrations at least make them hesitate and think; let the signs be signs, beacon-lights to show the way to him. He was willing to have his works serve this purpose after they had been wrought, but he did not work them in order to serve this purpose. He worked them in order to relieve definite cases of pain and sorrow then before him. But display he discarded. One of the evangelists in speaking of his unostentatious method of work was reminded of the passage in Isaiah 42 concerning the servant of Jehovah:

"He shall not quarrel nor be loud voiced,
Neither shall anyone hear his voice in the streets."

And why did he refuse a means so ready, so effective for impressing the people? If it had been his aim to build up a strong organization, to attract money and influence, to gain great numbers, and to make them blindly obedient to his word, he could have chosen no better way [34] than to do what they asked for, to let manna fall from heaven, or do some other dazzling and awe-inspiring miracle. But if he wanted to make men know God and love one another, why should he work miracles? Would the sight of a miracle give a Sadducee the child-like spirit? Would it make a Pharisee love a publican as his brother? Would it not simply frighten people into that outward conformity to the commands of God which his soul loathed? No, display would not serve his purpose. To use the power of God for such ends as would be accomplished by leaping from the pinnacles of the temple would be tempting God and prostituting his power.

The second means which it would have been natural to use, was force. Its use was expected by the disciples. It was almost forced on him by the people. It was feared by the Sadducean conservatives. Jesus refused to use it.

He forbade his disciples from using it even in defense of what was the holiest on earth to them (Mt. 26, 51-52). Before Pilate he disavowed the use of force for his whole movement as something incompatible with its very nature (Jo. 18, 36). It would have been an endeavor to set up the Kingdom of God by a compact of obedience to the Prince of this world. Imagine Christ raising an army. [35] National bigotry and jealousy would have been enflamed. The cave of passions would have been unlocked and the world demonized. Fancy Jesus inspiring his troops before battle by a sermon on brotherly love, on love to their enemies, and on forgiving seventy times seven times.

Both the display of power and the use of force are essentially of this world. The children of this world are expert in their use. The kings of the earth have used them from time immemorial. They are effective on their own plane. But in the nature of the case they cannot achieve any results that are higher than their own plane. Display can inspire terror or admiration, but not love. Force can extort assent or compel submission; it cannot awaken faith or persuade to willing obedience. External means can work external and mechanical changes; they cannot change the spirit or purify the spring of life. The Kingdom of God was to be based on the spiritual life, therefore carnal means could not establish it.

The spiritual means adopted by Jesus was the preaching of the truth. The truth, and not the sword, makes free. It has a germinating, productive life, so that if it [36] is sown into the hearts of men it will take root there and do its work. Not that all hearts will receive it alike or be equally fruitful, anymore than all soil will bring an equal harvest. Yet those who are the truth, will perceive it and respond to it and follow him. On that response and adherence he founds his Kingdom (Jo. 18, 36-37). He that has found with him the words of eternal life, will not go away in spite of perplexities and disappointments (Jo. 6, 66-68). [37] The power indwelling in truth itself was in his case multiplied by its exemplification in his life, by its attestation in his suffering, by the power of his personality, by the community of believers testifying to it, and by the influence of the spirit of God on the minds of his hearers. But of these forces we shall speak in a subsequent chapter. We deal here with the means he proposed to use and did use. His means were simply the truth. With that he shook the self-confidence of the religious, aroused men and women hardened in open sin, and induced wealthy men to forsake their wealth. With that he re-animated a nation, frightened princes, attacked a system hoary with age, drove its defenders to bay, and single-handedly did battle with the learning, the wealth and the influence of his times.

There are few of the principles of Jesus are so often insisted on to-day, as this of the spiritual means of establishing the Kingdom. Whenever the church is [38] invited to influence legislation for the abolition of wrong, it replies with a shrug of the shoulders, that it is not its province to use legislation supported by force, because its weapons are spiritual. The words are true enough, but the spirit of them is frequently false. They are too often but a convenient excuse for inaction, for skulking from the arena of actual life and confining attention to "the soul" and its soarings and droopings.

It is true that, like Christ, we wield no sword but the truth. But mark well, that sword was a sword in his hands and not a yard-stick. It cut into the very marrow of his generation. It was mighty to the casting down of strongholds. So it has proved itself wherever it has been used in dead earnest. Their lies reveal their true nature, as when Satan was touched by the spear of Ithuriel. Then injustice quails on its throne, chafe, sneer, abuse, hurl its spear, tenders its gold, and finally offer to serve as truth's vassal. But the truth that can do such things is not an old woman, wrapped in the spangled robes of earthly authority, bedizened with golden ornaments, the marks of honor given by injustice in [39] turn for services rendered, and muttering dead formulas of the past. The truth that can serve God as the mightiest of his archangels is robed only in love, her weighty limbs unfettered by needless weight, calm-browed, her eyes terrible with beholding God.

Verily, if the people of God loved not tradition, not accepted words but truth; if they had the discernment of God's will and thoughts, the clear eye for the real relation of things, the terrible precision of judgement which continued intercourse with truth and obedience to it are bound to give; if they had Christ's utter fearlessness in speaking the truth, in calling wrong wrong whoever did it, and right right wherever it was found; if wealth and honor and the favor of men, which are all in the gift of the Prince of this world and his ministers were but as the froth of wine when weighed against the love of truth; then the church could exultingly strip off all other weapons and go forth in its naked strength with a sling and a few shining pebbles.

Jesus deliberately rejected force and chose truth. The Catholic Church did not follow his example when it [40] used the rack, and not the truth, on Jew and heretic. The Reformers did not follow Christ's example when they leaned on princes and consented to have whole countries change their faith as monarchy directed. The ruling church in any country does not follow his example when it secures or even consents to laws that in any way hamper or put on an unequal footing other religious bodies. The established churches of all countries do not follow his example when they derive their support from tithes or taxes, if but one solitary man is thus compelled to pay an unwilling penny. Truth asks no odds. She will not ask that her antagonist's feet be put in shackles before she will cross swords with him. Christ's Kingdom needs not the spears of Roman legionaries to prop it, nor even the clubs of Galilean peasants. Whenever Christianity shows an inclination to use constraint in its own defense or support, it thereby furnishes presumptive evidence that it has become a thing of this world, for it finds the means of this world adapted to its ends. [41] Christ deliberately rejected display as a means and chose truth. Defenders of Christianity have done it an ill service when they made of Christ's miracles one of the great proofs of the truth of his words and the reality of his mission. They endeavor to give to the world the signs, which Christ refused it. They have turned into a demonstration of the truth that which Christ at most pointed out as an indication of the source of truth, and they have been sent to the Caesar to whom they appealed. They have conceded that the Kingdom of God came with outward demonstration, that it could be seen with the eye, felt with the hand and its presence or absence ascertained by the trained intellect; and so the keen eye, the sensitive hand and the trained intellect have undertaken to sit as a tribunal on the Kingdom of God.

But the most serious departure from Christ's method is the general adoption of display as a means of attracting followers to Christ. Dazzling miracles, it is true, the Protestant churches at least do not undertake to work. It neither leaps from the pinnacles of the temple to astonish the gaping crowd, nor does it cause manna to fall from heaven. But it gets as near as it can in many [42] cases. We do not speak of the Catholic missionary whose retinue and mitred magnificence convinced the heathen Prussians that his must be the true church. Papal splendor, jewelled Crucifixes, glittering processions, robes, incense,—what is all that but the means which all the emperors of the world have used to fire the imagination, prostrate the judgment and subdue the will? The Catholic Church has sought to use display, that potent instrument of the world, to build up the Kingdom of God. It has failed. It has built up an organization, a hierarchy, but it has failed to make the people among whom it exists spiritual, pure, just, independent, tenacious of purpose, children of light. The Catholic Church has done most good where it has been most devoid of splendor, in simple country parishes.

Wherever its display is most perfected, it breeds superstitution and blind obedience with some, and unbelief and hypocrisy with others.

But Protestants while condemning Rome, have too often tried to steal a feather from Rome's gay plumage. They erect stately churches on the finest avenues; they fit them with costly woods and soft cushions; mellow light fills them; organ tones [43] surge through them and trained voices warble in them. Why is all this? Partly from the luxury of the men and women who worship their Nazarene Christ there and are too accustomed to ease to miss it for an hour. But partly also from the feeling that this is necessary to draw men in. Are the pews empty? Do the masses pass by the church indifferent? God to, let us build a new front and fresco the interior; then men will behold and say, "Verily, this church has influence and wealth; we will go there with our wives and daughters." As for the preacher, he must prophesy unto us smooth things.

Display in buildings, display in furnishings, display in music and liturgy, display in rhetoric, display if possible in the numbers attending – who that is familiar with modern church work will say that this is not a large part of its working capital, whereby we hope to attract and retain the multitude? And who on the other hand will point out anything parallel to it in the methods of Jesus? If some men to-day had the power to work miracles would they not use them as a means of attraction? Is not something of that sort actually [44] advertised as part of the program in some public meetings?

When constraint is to be used on behalf of religion, or when men put trust in the attractive power of display for the upbuilding of the Kingdom, then it is that Christian men should insist on the spiritual weapons of Christianity, and not when they are asked to express themselves in regard to injustice or sin. Such an expression is a declaration of the truth, the wielding of the one spiritual weapon entrusted to the church.

4.) Finally, with the development of prophetic thought came an increased recognition of the value of the individual personality.

The covenant of God with Israel was a covenant with the nation. The individual shared in it as a member of the nation, not because of individual qualifications. The blessings were national blessings. The sins were dealt with as national sins, and the punishments were visited on the nation. The religious desires of the godly man had to seek God through the medium of the whole people. For his assurance of acceptance with God, he had to fall back on Jehovah's mighty deeds for his nation. In the temple he approached God through [45] the priests, the representatives of all.

And yet there was that in the soul of the godly man which sought direct access to the heart of God. There was a sense of spiritual relationship to God which was nearer and surer than anything mediated by blood descent. There was a refusal to be classed merely as a unit of a mass in which there were many of a spirit totally alien. The personality demanded recognition as a separate ethical entity. The righteous man longed for forgiveness of sins for himself, and assurance of it to himself.

The growth of this personal element in Israel's religious life is traceable in the prophets. It received no full satisfaction. The national disasters culminating in the exile fell upon the just also who had not deserved them. Indeed they felt the blow most severely of all. But in the Messianic age that would be changed. A great deed of salvation would be wrought assuring them of forgiveness. That personal intercourse with God which had found its fullest demonstration in the prophets would become common to all. The spirit of God would be poured out on [46] all. They would all be prophets, knowing the Lord and bearing his will in their hearts. The constraint of the old forms of worship would widen out. The glory of the Lord would dwell among all his people.

In Christ the demands of the human personality found full recognition.

He taught that every man was personally responsible for his acceptance of the Messianic salvation. It would not come to all alike. Every man must personally strive to enter the narrow gate. The men of violence only would not succeed. If a man loved property or family too well, he could have no share. There would be a great division, as when the shepherd parts the sheep and the goats. One would be taken, the other would be left. The wise virgins would enter into the joy of the marriage feast, the foolish would be left in the outer darkness. There was no salvation to the entire nation or to entire classes. He that turned, became as a child, and was born from above, would enter the Kingdom, though it were a publican or that one a harlot. He that refused, would not enter, though he [47] be a teacher in Israel, or that one a ruler endowed with all the virtues.

Christ taught the forgiveness of sins for the individual soul. He assured the palsied man, the great sinner, and the crucified malefactor of forgiveness and acceptance. He insisted that it was not sufficient to have men saved in the bulk, but that even the stray sheep must be brought in and the lost coin found, because it was not the will of the Father that even one of the insignificant ones perish. All sins could now be forgiven, even blasphemy; the only thing that could put a man outside the pale of forgiveness was that condition of heart which called white black and black white, and could not distinguish between the working of the spirit of God and the working of Beelzebub. This assurance of the forgiving love of God found its ultimate expression in the death of Christ. If God so loved the world that he gave his only begotten son, then we have surety that God desires not our death but our life.

Furthermore the Messianic salvation of Christ offers complete satisfaction for all the spiritual desires of the individual. They that mourn shall be comforted. They that hunger and thirst [48] after righteousness shall be filled. They that labor and are heavy laden shall find rest. In him we shall have the light of life to guide us in darkness; the bread of life that we may hunger no more; the water of life that becomes a spring within us and makes us sources from which rivers of living water flow out. Peace in the midst of tribulation; joy made full; the sight of God and converse with the spiritual world; all these are promised to him that fulfills the conditions of the Kingdom of God.

Christ recognizes the separate value of the human personality. He makes it individually responsible. He assures it of personal forgiveness and offers it satisfaction for all its desires. He offers the perfection of personal life to those that receive him. In the old covenant the entire nation was called the Son of Jehovah; even when the name was applied to the king, it was in his official capacity. Now the humblest member of the Kingdom is to be a child of God and a brother of Christ. And these names are given because there is an underlying fact to which they correspond. These are no longer of this world. Their life is not entirely derived from it; their character is not explainable [49] on earthly grounds; their aims are not limited by the life of time. They share the life of Christ as the branches share the life of the vine. They feed on his life, and hence shall live because of him, as he lives because of the Father (Jo. 6, 57). Because they believe on him who is the resurrection and the life, they shall live even though they die. They shall be with Christ in the place prepared for them and shall see his glory, and be honored by the Father.

Summing up now the results of the foregoing discussion, we find that Jesus adopted the theocratic idea and professed himself to be the Messiah who was to bring it to its fulfillment. This adoption necessarily implied assent to the essential core of the theocratic idea: the idea of an ideal human society, constituted according to divine laws and governed by God.

We find, however, that Jesus differed from his contemporaries on various points and that in the divergence he was advancing along the lines already traced by the development of Old Testament prophecy. 1) He extended the limits of the Kingdom. For the idea of God's nation he substituted the idea of God's humanity. In place of a small Kingdom organized [50] on rigid laws and by its smallness and homogeneity capable of uniformity, the theocracy was now to be a Kingship of God in all nations binding their diversity together by unity of spirit and oneness of sovereignty. 2) He changed the basis of citizenship in the Kingdom. He substituted spiritual descent and relationship for natural descent and outward coherence. 3) He repudiated external means, force and display, and relied upon truth and love and the powers of the spirit to overcome opposing forces and establish the Kingdom. 4) He recognized the human personality as a responsible unit, which stands or falls according to its personal deserts, and offered to it the full satisfaction of its highest desires and the ultimate perfection of its personal life.

We anticipate objections from various quarters.

It will be objected by some that God's designs have changed since Christ. The theocracy of Israel has failed and a new theocracy is not a part of God's plans. All that he desires now is the salvation of many souls. Therefore we must bend our energies to see many individuals awakened, justified, regenerated, sanctified and finally saved in heaven.

This is practically the position of the great mass of evangelical Christians to-day. The indexes of Calvinistic systematic [51] theologies show at a glance, that, so far from having the contents arranged with the Kingdom of God as the starting point and centre, there are only isolated references to it. The hymnology of the Christian Church shows the same striking fact; the burthen of the hymns relating to man is the salvation of the individual and not the salvation of the world. And so far as our observation goes, the idea of the Kingdom of God on earth is a forgotten idea among the mass of Christian people, except among certain bodies where it is very much alive in a peculiar form.

We object to this conception that it is unscriptural. It is untrue by defect. It is right in preaching the redemption and perfection of the individual life. It is wrong in not preaching the perfection of the collective life of humanity. How far traditional theology has departed from the teaching of Christ can be seen by comparing the table of contents of a "systematic theology" with that of a "biblical theology." It is the province of biblical theology simply to group and systematize the actual teachings of Christ, and as a result the books attempting that task all make the idea of the Kingdom the vertebral idea around which the other thoughts are grouped in a coherent organism. [52] In our own discussion we have endeavored to follow the same method and have arrived at the same result. Christ does teach the perfection of the personal life, but he makes the salvation of the individual the subsidiary idea. A man is saved according as he enters or does not enter the Kingdom. Even in the passage where personal regeneration is taught in the most exact and emphatic language, it is spoken of as the condition of seeing the Kingdom of God and entering into it (Jo. 3, 3).

It would be difficult and hazardous to say what has been the cause of this gradual swinging away from the teaching of Christ. Even in the writings of Paul less space is devoted to the Kingdom than to the church and the upbuilding of the individual. But Paul by no means lost sight of the Kingdom. It lay in the nature of the case that he was compelled to think out and discuss especially the practical questions of the new life as it was seeking to take shape in the personal life and in the life of the churches.

The same causes continued to operate later and under the powerful influence of Paul's writings the thought of the church continued to run in the grooves carved out by him. But while with him the perfection of the Kingdom was a near and living hope which easily [53] subjugated all other thoughts and aims, that faith died out in the church later. The hope of the immediate coming of Christ faded out. The manly faith which started out to overcome the world shrank into a lean old age, rubbing itself to keep up its own vitality and content to save itself. In place of a church invading the world and wrestling with it, spirit against spirit, we see a church fleeing out of the world and in solitude, with fastings, prayers and flagellations, guarding the flickering rush-light of personal godliness from the mocking breath of the world.

It seems to us due to the same lack of faith when the church of the present day takes the defensive attitude against the world instead of the offensive. Or is it not a defensive attitude when the saving of one's soul in heaven is the sum of Christian hope to so many? In place of the parable of the mustard seed and the leaven we shall have to invent a new one: The Kingdom of God is like unto a burning ship, from which a few escape in a boat and rest on their oars at a distance in helpless contemplation.

The assertion that the theocratic idea has been abandoned by God is a misconstruction of the facts. Did Jehovah miscalculate when he attempted the up- [54] building of a reign of God, and has he now corrected his plans? Or did he grow weary of one way and is now attempting another? God never fails nor grows weary. His human instruments may fail Him and be cast aside for new ones, but His plans are not abandoned. He does not destroy but he fulfills. The smaller is lost sight of because it is merged in the greater. The outline of His plans changes constantly, but it is a change like the change in the contours of a beach when the tide is rising.

When the personal element was magnified in the New Testament, the collective element, with which the Old Testament dealt, was not abandoned. How could it be? If there was that in the nature of the Jewish nation which justified God in treating it as a composite personality that could be held responsible for moral actions and conditions and rewarded or punished as a personality, then the same personality and responsibility must still inhere in the nature of communities, nations and races. And if God once regarded the collective life as a force to be dealt with in the erection of his Kingship on earth, has the increased importance attached to the individual life caused God to lose his interest in the forces he once valued so highly? [55] A second objection comes from those who acknowledge the permanence of the theocratic idea and the purpose of Christianity to bring about a perfect humanity on earth, but who hold that the only way to act on humanity is to act on individuals. Let the units of society be changed, they say, and society itself will be changed. The only way in which the Kingdom of God can be extended is to seek the conversion of as many persons as possible.

There is certainly much truth in this. Jesus began the establishment of the Kingdom by gathering a few men who had the spirit of the Kingdom in them. Every man of that sort is a new light set in the darkness, a grain of salt in the corruption of the world. The hope of changing the world by a mere change of system was not shared by Christ. He wanted changed men; men who obeyed the spirit and not the flesh; men in whom the potent spell of the visible and temporal was broken and who beheld the power and felt the value of the invisible and eternal; men in whom the world's rules and judgments were no longer dominant, but God's will and thoughts reigned supreme; men in whom profit [56] and pleasure had been dethroned, and right and love enthroned. Without such men no Kingdom of God will be established on earth. Every such man is an advanced fulcrum on which God can rest his lever in overturning the world.

And yet we hold that the multiplication of such men is not the only service that we can render the Kingdom, nor is the extension of the Kingdom necessarily co-extensive with the multiplication of such. The principles and aims of an organization may be better or worse than the men constituting the organization. If the organization is better than the men, it is likely to be changed for the worse very quickly. If it is worse, a change for the better will be made only if it is taken in hand with all seriousness. For instance, it would be hard to prove that the people of the South had a higher moral or religious average in 1870 than in 1850; yet in 1850 men owned their fellow-men, and in 1870 they did not. The constitution of the community had become more righteous, though the number of righteous persons in it may not have increased greatly or at all. Again, there were only a few years intervening between the reign of Oliver Cromwell and the Restoration of the Stuarts; the number of godly men cannot have diminished so much [57] during that interval. And yet what a difference between the England of the Commonwealth and the England of Charles the Second! Or once more, who will say that the business men of America are cruel and heartless men? Yet our business life is very nearly as cruel as the grind-stones of a grist-mill.

Evidently the collective life of a body of men is not quite equivalent to the sum of all its units when taken separately. By contact with others certain propensities, good or evil, as the case may be, are checked and sunk out of sight, while others are called forth and given a potency that they would never have in the man by himself. A railway director rises in prayer-meeting and speaks of his desire to be a true follower of Christ and to have the same mind that was in him. Next day in the board of directors he advocates the smashing of a small rival line. "He is a hypocrite," says the world. Perhaps so; perhaps not. Human nature is subtle and capacious enough to contain both actions within itself. Perhaps the best aspirations that were in that man were brought out by the spirit of the community in the one case and [58] he was lifted above his usual self. In the other case by the traditions and customs and codes of railway management he did worse things than he would do in a private capacity and perhaps never thought that they were bad. Indeed as our business life goes, it would not be inconceivable that all his fellow-directors were in the prayer-meeting as active participants.

It is not enough to christianize individuals; we must christianize societies, organizations, nations, for they too have a life of their own which may be made better or worse. Christ addressed Capernaum and Bethsaida as responsible personalities. He lamented over Jerusalem as a whole. He told his disciples to leave communities refusing them to their fate. We find Paul acting on that principle repeatedly. Throughout the Old Testament God dealt with Israel as a whole, which could rise or fall. In the book of Revelation the spirit addressed whole Churches with praise or blame, and the forces of evil are represented as corporate beings, the beast, the harlot, the false prophet.

And on the other hand the church is constantly present to the mind of Paul, not as a sand heap of many grains, but as a great body with many members, [59] all framed and knit together, growing up into unity and fullness of life, developing not into full-grown men, but into a full-grown Man.

There is a corporate life developed in a body of men. Even a chance mass meeting will begin to be a unity after it has responded to the same thought for half an hour, and that unity will be good or bad according to the thoughts that have united it. Humor or passion will sweep over the multitudinous souls like the breath of bellows over the iron in the furnace, and they begin to fuse. The individual loses himself in the whole. He finds himself applauding as the rest applaud, laughing at things he else holds sacred, enthusiastic about that which was indifferent to him and may be so again when he is out of this crowd. The subsequent speakers, if they have the oratorical sensitiveness, will find themselves led by or wrestling with a kind of huge personality, a good or evil spirit, whose unity in consent or dissent they can feel.

If that is true of a random gathering, it is much more true of a stable organization, of a church, a club, a party, a nation. Every common sorrow, every joy that has thrilled all, unites them, as the many pieces of a violin vibrate into unity in constant use. There comes to be a Common feeling, a common judgement, which can be [60] forecast and wrought upon, and which yet at times surprizes its most expert manipulators by the elemental spontaneity of its uprising. Before our civil war there was a jangle of voices in the North, a big ant-hill of apparently confused and separate interests. But the jangling voices became the roar of a cataract. Before the eyes of a wondering world a huddle of states arose a nation. Indeed, what was that war of the Union but the nation's assertion of its oneness, the refusal of a living being to be drawn and quartered? What were the struggles of Germany, Italy, Greece, Poland, Ireland, but the struggles of personalities for a personal life, the efforts of nations to be nations and not aggregations of individuals?

And if the life of a body is so powerful and independent a factor in the life of humanity, shall it not find its independent recognition from those who would revolutionize the world? Shall only the children of this world become the children of God, and not the kingdoms of the world become the Kingdom of God and of his Christ?

There is a continuity of life in an organization. The men who unite in it create its laws and institutions according to their own nature and according to the aims they have in mind. But those laws and institutions, once established, confirm, strengthen **[61]** and perpetuate the nature from which they arose, and give the organization the power of assimilating new elements to itself. Witness the marvelous continuity of life, and uniformity of thought and feeling and purpose in the Jesuit Order. Its members have come and gone, like the particles constituting a human body, but like a human body the Jesuit Order has remained the same. Their antagonists, the Port-Royalists, have during a much shorter term of life demonstrated the assimilative power of an organization in which a vigorous spirit lives. Schools and colleges have their peculiar genius, and stamp their graduates with their various seals and superscriptions.

In short, the efforts for the extension of the Kingdom of God are insufficient, if they address themselves to the individual alone. A world of regenerated individuals is not necessarily a regenerated world. The laws of nations, the customs of society, the institutions of corporate life, though indirectly affected by every personal change, may perpetuate wrong and warp the individuals, and a conscious effort must be made to reconstruct them, until they cease to be based on selfishness and force and begin to be based on love and justice. Every step toward such reconstruction, as well as every individual conversion, is an extension of the **[62]** reign of God, for God reigns where his will is done.

The individual and collective life of humanity act and react on each other. Every changed individual life makes a changed society possible. Every change for the better in the construction of society makes a higher perfection of the individual possible. Each is an originating centre of power. Each, therefore, is a citadel to be captured in the name of God.

A third objection will come from those who believe in the speedy second coming of Christ. With them the Kingdom of God is really a living hope which inspires and sustains them. They do believe in a glorified humanity with Christ as King, and the rapid spread of their ideas in our own day proves anew the virility of that faith in whatever form it may appear. And wherever their life proves that they actually regard the present world-era as short, too short to amass property or to lay the foundations of an enduring family life (I Cor. 7, 29-31), their faith seems to me far more worthy of respect and more apostolic than the attitude of the average Christian who tries to be prosperous before he **[63]** dies and hopes to be prosperous after he dies, but lets this world wag on its even way to that final collision, which he has been told will come sometime, but which is too far off to disturb his digestion or influence his testamentary arrangements.

Now, though these believe in the Kingdom of God, many of them will not agree to what has been said. They hold that the Kingdom will come when Christ returns. Then the government of the world will fall to him and to his saints, and justice and peace will reign. But until then, the Kingdom exists only in the church; its only increase is in the increase of the church; its only province is to snatch individuals from the mass of the world that they may be ready for the coming of the Lord. As for the world, it cannot be saved till Christ comes. The life of the world may be modified by the existence of the church in it, but radical changes are not to be expected. An endeavor on the part of the church to work radical changes would be a vain waste of energy; some think it would be a wicked and adulterous compact with Satan and his kingdom. The apostles made **[64]** no effort to influence the social or political life of the world. They watched for the coming of Christ and expected it to be done then.

It is true that Christ promised the completion of the Kingdom at his coming again. Now the tares are still growing in the wheat field (Mt. 13, 24-30), and the useless sea-creatures mingle with the fish in the drag-net (Mt. 13, 47-50). Then the separation will be made; the sheep will be parted from the goats (Mt. 25, 31-46); the wise virgins will be admitted to the joy of the marriage-feast, and the foolish left in the darkness (Mt. 25, 1-13); all false disciples will then be rejected (Mt. 7, 21-27; 22, 11-14); and the true followers will be gathered from all parts of the earth (Mt. 8, 11) to claim their inheritance in the Kingdom and share in its joy.

It is true also that the apostles expected the speedy return of Christ. James admonished the brethren to be patient of injuries until the coming of the Lord, who was already standing before the door (James 5, 7-9). Peter regarded the end of all things as at hand (I Peter 4, 7) and the salvation of Christ ready to be revealed (1, 5). Paul till near the end of his life, hoped to be alive at the coming of the Lord (I Thess. 4, 15-17). The day of the Lord was very near at hand (Rom. 13, 11-14). **[65]** This hope was so much alive in some of the churches that they felt seriously troubled about the few Christians who had already died and so seemed unable to have their share in the Kingdom (I Thess. 4, 13-18). With this expectation pressing upon them, it was natural that they attempted no change in existing conditions, even if they had had any means of influencing them. They were like travelers in an inn, sitting booted and cloaked, listening for the knock that calls them to horse, and hence caring little if in their room of the inn the windows are draughty and the fire nearly out. And for those who really share their expectation that attitude of mind is still the natural one. But if they claim the right to disregard the state of this world, because its construction is so soon to pass away, we demand of them the proof of their sincerity. If they think the time is short, let them "have wives as though they had none; let them weep, as though they wept not; let them rejoice as though they rejoiced not; let them buy as though they possessed not." But if any man surfeits himself with the pleasure and wealth of this world, and beats his fellow-servants that are in his power, **[66]** and enlarges his barns and increases his investments and looks well to the securities thereof, then that man may protest a thousand times that he is looking for the coming of the Lord and he may be ever so diligent in figuring over the times and half times of Daniel, yet his words are idle words, and his faith is a nut without a kernel.

But do Christians really hold that belief to-day? They say they do; but do they? Can they? Eighteen centuries have passed away and the end has not yet come. There have been honest men at many periods in the history of the church who fervently believed in the immediate appearance of Christ; the Montanists believed it; about the year 1000 there was a very wide-spread belief that the end would come with that year; great numbers were in expectation at the time of the Reformation; the Fifth Monarchy men were a force in politics during the English Commonwealth. During this century men have had enough faith to set the day over and over again. The hope of them all has come to naught; it has lost itself in the sand. They are worthy of honor. But did God want them to believe what was not true? **[67]** We shall be told that Christ commands his servants to watch at all hours, because they never know when the Son of man will come. It is true; but in what does the watching consist? In expectation or in obedience? What steward is prepared for the coming of his master, the one that is peering out of the gable window all the day to spy the first dust-cloud that signals his return, or the one that keeps the house in the order his master loves to see? If expectation were a preparation for Christ's return, surely the people of day would have been prepared for his first coming; they were full of expectation; yet when he came they crucified him.

Christ appeared the first time when "the fullness of the time" had come (Gal. 4, 4). He will appear the second time when the fullness of the time shall have come. When that will be, depends largely on us. In all the dealings of God with men the human factor is the variable quantity. God has so conditioned himself that within certain limits he allows us free action, and [68] the fulfillment of His counsel is hastened or retarded according to our obedience or disobedience. Paul saw in his day that the day of the Lord would not come till certain hindrances which he met in his work, were removed, and until the missionary work of the world as he knew it, was completed (II Thess. 2, 1-12). We, if we have eyes to see, can also see certain forces that are antagonistic to Christ and that must go down if he is to reign; and we can see work still to be done in the world to make it a fit habitation for our Lord. Is not then our duty plain?

Or shall we wail at the slightness of our forces and weapons, and say that we can accomplish nothing till he comes with re-enforcements and artillery of heavier calibre? Have we not the flashing sword of truth which has grown keener with the using? Have we not the persevering faith that can cart a mountain away in wheel-barrow loads? What weapons shall Christ bring that we have not now? He can come in power and glory, the sword in his hand and his avenging angels with him. But [69] then it will be to sift and scatter and punish, and not to convert and win and upbuild. Or shall he at the end convince the world by force and display, the means he always discarded?

We have power if we will but use it; power to win stubborn hearts; power to uncover social lies; power to make injustice blush and skulk away; power to break the chains of Christ's enslaved brothers; power to shame immodesty into hiding places. Will it be no service to Christ to use such power? Will he be indifferent to it? Or does he care only for the conversion of men? Frederick William I of Prussia was always enlisting recruits for his giant battalion, but he never led it into battle. Recruits have been enlisted for Christ these sixty generations. Every one had but a short term in which he was on the battle-field, and then he passed away to another world. Is the only service a soldier can render that he enlists others, who in turn will die without having seen battle? [70] This world is a battle-ground, not a gymnasium in which we punch inflated balls to increase our own muscle. Our work tells, if we make it tell. We can change the world. None of us knows how much. None can tell what a place this earth would be if all the force that has been spent on spiritual gymnastics, had been put into fighting wrong and seeing God's will done on earth; and we surmise that heaven would have been filled, if not with more, yet with stronger, braver souls.

The fact is that the experience of all these centuries has been a long commentary on one of the prominent doctrines of Jesus: the gradualness of the coming of the Kingdom. The prophets expected it suddenly. The coming of the Messiah, the judgement, the destruction of the wicked, the erection of the perfect reign of God, all this they saw as one event. John the Baptist expected it that way too. Christ emphasized the gradualness of it. It was a growth like the growth of a mustard-plant. It was an organic process like the fermen- [71] tation of yeast. "So is the Kingdom of God, as if a man should cast seed upon the earth; and should sleep and rise, night and day, and the seed should spring up and grow, he knoweth not how. The earth beareth fruit of herself; first the blade, then the ear, then the full corn in the ear. But when the fruit is ripe, straightway he putteth forth the sickle, because the harvest is come." This gradualness follows from the nature of the case. If he had used compulsion, he could have achieved great results quickly. Because he wanted an organic growth, he had to bide his time. There is no saying how much the process might have been quickened and may yet be quickened by the energetic fidelity of his followers. But hitherto the process has been slow.

And yet we are to be on the alert for his coming. Though all experience tells us that it will not come immediately, yet we are to [72] act as if it were coming immediately. How is that possible? How can we keep ourselves always in a state of tension? We can do it only by understanding the law of evolution in the Kingdom. It is always at hand. When Jesus taught, he said the Kingdom had come; signs of its actual presence were visible (Mt. 11, 3-5; 12, 28); some men were near it (Mt. 12, 34), some entering it (Mt. 21, 31), some in it (Mt. 11, 11). Yet on the other hand he bids his disciples seek it and pray for its coming (Mt. 6, 10, 33). It has come; it is coming. As God is in all three tenses, the God that was and is and shall be, so is the Kingdom behind which is the force of the living God. It is forever coming. Hence it is forever pressing. The time is always short. One era after the other passes away. The need is always desperate. The opportunities never return, and where we have failed to answer the call of God and to throw in our strength, history will always show a hiatus which is but slowly closed. Our missing effect in this era becomes [73] a missing cause in the next era. In the days of Jesus was the time for the Jewish nation. If it had known in that day the things that made for peace, who will say what the splendor of that people might have been and what the effect on the world? As a nation Israel failed and the whirlwind of judgement swept the chaff from the threshing-floor. The prophetic discourse of Jesus can hardly be understood in any other way than that the destruction of the Jewish nation was a coming of Christ. And if that was a coming of Christ, was it the only one? Have there been no other judgements of God on cities and nations that failed in the hour of their trial? Has not our own generation seen "the glory of the coming of the Lord," seen Him "treading out the wine-press where the grapes of wrath were stored"? The religious man believes that God did terrible things in the far Past, and that he will do great things in the far Future. The spiritual [74] man sees God doing terrible things now. He sees the great Avenger standing ever within the shadow of history. He feels the spirit of the living Christ working in the hearts of men that think they know him not. He feels his breath coming across the frozen fields of the earth, and new life blossoms. In the moanings of the nations, in their feverish stirring, in the shrill laugh of skepticism, in the gropings of fanatics, he sees the working of him who, like his Father, is ever working without haste and without rest, and with beating heart he whispers to himself: "The Kingdom of God is at hand; arise!"

This then is the program of the Christian revolution: the Kingdom of God on earth. It includes a twofold aim: the regeneration of every individual to divine sonship and eternal life; and the victory of the spirit of Christ over the spirit of this world in every form of human society and a corresponding alteration in [75] all the institutions formed by human society. These two are simultaneous aims. Every success in the one is a means for a new success in the other.

That the aim is vast, we know, and we rejoice in it. In this all-embracing aim is found that unity of life for the want of which modern Christian life is crippled. What earnest man has not felt this division of his life? All the week he gives to his business, and on Sunday he serves God. How? By prayer and praise, by testifying, by an expression of his inward experience, by teaching children religious truths. This is all good, but is this all? Speak to him about doing something for God, and he will think you mean giving his money for religious purposes, speaking in prayer-meeting, teaching Sunday school, or taking part in a mission. He will not think of his daily work to which he yet devotes nine tenths of his time and strength. If he is a shoe-maker, he will not refer your question about serving God to making better shoes. [76] If he is a plumber, he will not refer it to the sanitary washing of joints. That part of his life has nothing to do with serving God, except that he keeps from doing wrong in it. The serving of Christ, according to the average conception, lies in doing "religious" work, in working on people's souls. If you hear a young lawyer say that he means to give himself entirely to God's work, it is almost certain that he does not mean that henceforth he will be a champion of justice in human relations, that he will see the facts brought out and right done; that he will do his share to untangle that snarl of ancient precedents called the common law and make the word "legal" synonymous with the word "just"; no, he means that he is going to become a preacher. The religious ideal of the people is not an ideal embracing their whole life. The church has so long restricted religious effort to saving one's own soul and the souls of others, that only the time and effort given to that [77] are supposed to be a service of God, and only those who give their whole time to that kind of work are understood to have devoted their lives completely to God's service. It is only when a man understands that this earth with all it contains is to become the habitation of God; that all the homely services and relations of human life, if rightly done, are a loving service of the brethren and hence of Christ; and that any improvement in the method and spirit of human relations is the perfection of God's will; only then can the whole life of the common man become a sacrifice and his plain daily toil a love-offering to God. The saving of souls has hallowed the work of the preacher. The saving of the world will hallow the life of the farmer who toils for humanity's daily bread; of the engineer who bridges chasms and holds back the seething river from the cottages of his brothers; of the teacher who unfolds [78] the germs of talent created by God and by Him destined to be unfolded; of the mason and carpenter and glazier and plumber, who build safe and dry and sunny houses in which little children will not be strangled to death by poison germs; of preachers who unfold the principles of justice and mercy; of lawyers who apply the former and of doctors who apply the latter; and of legislators who find ways for incorporating both. Doubtless all these have been hallowed before. God has looked upon many a workman's work and many a housewife's ceaseless round of duties and seen in that the real sacrifice of their lives, even though they themselves may have looked for it in other things. Doubtless too there have always been noble souls in all stations of life that have well understood this truth of the possible sanctity of the whole life of man. But I affirm that it is not the common thing among [79] religious people. An understanding of it would be a gospel to many a man who desires to serve God, and thinks now that he can do so only by the scraps of his life. It would enlist the services of those who have no gift of introspection, of preaching, or of dealing with souls. If Christian people would begin to do their daily work in such a way as best to serve their brethren and therewith their King; if they refused to enter into occupations in which they saw no benefit to men and hence no benefit the

Kingdom of God; then we should all find our common life uplifted by a great thought, the industry of the world affected by a new spirit, and some lines of business would either cease or be transformed; for there are some occupations of which it would be hard to say how they serve the good of men. Of them perhaps it would be true that they could be sainted only by their death.

We reiterate it: the religious [80] ideal of the average Christian embraces only a small portion of his life; the larger portion of it is touched by the religious purpose only insofar as he aims not to let it get in conflict with his Christianity. His business life is Christian in what he refrains from doing, and not in what he does do. The ideal of the Kingdom of God on earth is an ideal capable of embracing every useful human activity and of making it sublime. It can give unity to human life and abolish that frequent and fearful discrepancy between religious profession and business action which is the withering disease of modern Christianity.

This all-embracing aim is able also to enlist the abilities and interest of all men. There is a diversity of gifts. Not all have the gift of prophesying or teaching. Some have the gift of superintendence and management; some of mechanical dexterity, of making something out of nothing. Such men and women may have the love of God and man in their hearts, but how shall it find an outlet? The only way [81] now appointed for them is with a feeble, stammering tongue to speak of inward experiences and to address themselves to inward needs. The known sincerity of such men makes their expressions effective, and yet that is not what they can do best. Get them to cut garments in a sewing school or nail up boards at a picnic and see with what ability and alacrity they do that. The church cannot furnish them many opportunities for these gifts as it now works; but if all life became an effort to realize the Kingdom of God, then we should see a blazing forth of these faculties. The religious life, now pent up and forced to find an outlet through one narrow channel, would flow out freely on all sides and carry its blessings.

We surmise that it is the untrue division of the Christian ideal which has brought about the unequal representation of the sexes in the churches. The proportion at present is usually three women to two men; in European countries it is less than that. And if men followed their own inclinations without the attractive constraint of those whom they love, there would probably [82] be fewer men yet. Why is this? Surely not because one half of the human race is created better than the other. We do not expect to see the same preponderance of women in heaven. Men are more prone to the palpable sins of the flesh, but the subtler sins of the lust of the eye and the pride of life are perhaps even more destructive of the divine life.

It is not that men are naturally more wicked, less sensitive to moral impulses and less capable of sacrifice, than women. The fault is that no religious ideal is offered them capable of enlisting to the full the masculine faculties. Woman has her in life and man has his. They may overlap, but they are not the same. And their gifts correspond to the office they are to fill. Woman is endowed with a delicate sensibility, a faculty of divining emotions and of tenderly touching them and altering them which only the poets among men can equal. Her whole calling in life teaches her to deal with the inward life and to nurture its frailest efforts into strength. A [83] religion of the perfection of the personal life is her religion. It concerns her brother also, but it does not satisfy him. The man's life is turned out upon the world. That is his domain. Whether he will or not, it captivates his interest. Why are political meetings crowded with men while the churches are empty of them? Why are countless men working with sacrifice of money, time and strength, in the labor and social movements, who have only a shrug of the shoulder for the church? Is it because they are worldly and the church spiritual? Let who will believe that that is the sole cause. It is because in spite of the rottenness of politics and the many evil concomitants of the labor movement, they feel that here is an effort to carry righteousness into the life of mankind along the lines in which their interest and ability lies. Let a preacher in the course of his sermon make a reference to or take an illustration from politics or the social [84] question, and he will see the eyes of the men brighten, their necks crane forward and an interested look come over their faces. Is that a proof of their carnal mind? How is it that so many of the strongest and most virile ministers "cannot let politics alone"? We see in all this a groping of man for his share in the work of God, a reaching out for the neglected half of the Christian ideal. What they ignorantly worship, the church should declare unto them, in order that the vast amount of truly religious work which is now branded as secular and regarded as almost illegitimate, may stand forth as truly a service of God and may enlist the love and enthusiasm of God-driven men.

The two aims of the Christian revolution, the perfection of the individual and the perfection of society, blend and pass into each other; so do the offices and faculties of man and woman. Yet the directions of the one aim corresponds to the bent of woman's genius, the other to the inclination of man's [85] ability. The fact that religious work as it now stands is not enlisting the same proportion of men as of women, and that many of the noblest men find nothing to attract them in the church, furnishes another presumption that we have left out one term of the Christian synthesis and ventilated the rounded perfection of Christ's revolutionary aim.

And, finally, the combination of the two aims is necessary for the attainment of either. That the perfection of human society cannot be attained without changed lives to attain it, is plain enough. But it is equally true that the life of the individual cannot be perfected except by seeking the perfection of society. One of the fundamental teachings of Jesus is that by seeking our life we lose it, and by losing it we gain it. Avarice that gets no enjoyment out of its wealth; social selfishness that blights love and friendship and so destroys the pleasures it seeks; the life of pleasure that becomes blasé; the life of intellectual [86] self-culture which turns on itself in doubt, gaining keenness and losing firmness, rich in perceptions and bankrupt in convictions; these are demonstrations of Christ's law of life on lower planes of life. Wherever human life turns in upon itself and seeks its satisfaction and perfection in itself and not outside itself, it is distorted and foiled. And what holds of every other form of life, holds of the religious life also. He that seeketh his own religious life, shall lose it. Who is the most likely to be acknowledged before the judgment seat of Christ, he that has sought to save his own soul by penances, contemplations, exercises, by striving against faults and seeking after virtues; or he that forgets his states and feelings in the active work for the all-around welfare of his fellows? Where shall we seek the Christ? In the hermit's solitude or in the busy towns of Galilee?

"Activity" has become the motto of modern religious life. But when the newly awakened heart asks: "what shall I do?" it finds but few avenues for going forth into the world with blessing. Speaking in [87] prayer-meeting, visiting hospitals, teaching a Sunday School class, praying with inquirers, joining mission bands, above all giving money and attending church, these are the activities which we declare religious. And it is most lovable to see how moments of rest are utilized and strength is poured out in these efforts which are called dear to the Master. But again we assert, these lines of work are not fitted to the gifts of all, and still less are they fitted to the time and resources of all. Many of the activities recommended by modern church life are aristocratic activities. The average working man and his wife have no time to attend many meetings, and to spend afternoons in hospitals and among the poor. They can give only the scraps of their time to such work and then it means a sacrifice of rest and recuperation. And the working people, remember that, are the people. They constitute human society, and not the people who have leisure. If therefore we desire to teach the bulk of mankind how to attain [88] the divine personal life, we must be able to show them how they can spend themselves for others in that which occupies all but a fraction of their lives, their daily work. If they can consciously spend themselves in that for love of God and men, then they have the exercise of their own spiritual life which will give them spiritual health and vigor. They will strengthen the eternal life in them by working for the Kingdom of God outside of them.

Practically there are numberless plain men and women who in the round of daily work are growing up into self-forgetful Christian characters. Many of them think they serve God in their meetings only, but their lives are more correct than their religious theorizing. They are spending themselves in their entire lives, and their characters show the effects. They, and not those who have time for all societies and meetings and religious self-culture, are the elect and beloved of God. What we desire is that they should do their daily work intelligently and consciously as a part in the maintenance and upbuilding of God's Kingdom on earth, that so the full force of the religious principle may be brought to bear on it, and that they may have the full conscious enjoyment of the religious life which they really possess.

[89]

CHAPTER III.

THE REVOLUTIONARY POWER

It is worth much to perceive that things are not as they should be and to long for their betterment. It is worth more to have a clear and great ideal of how things ought to be. But unless there is a power to overcome the inertia of conservatism, to overthrow the angry resistance of selfishness, and to fashion the better ways of life, the ideal will remain a dream, a solace to the solitary thinker, a transient home-sickness to him that hears it, and no more. It is pathetic to see how many longings and efforts have wasted themselves in the history of mankind, like the blossoms of the orange-tree in the hot-house, that drop and leave no fruit. Noble souls have been pregnant with ideals, and there was no power to bring forth. Spirits have brooded over the chaos, but no creative word was spoken.

The Christian revolution is distinguished not only by the splendor and comprehensiveness of its ideal, but also by the power inhering in it and pushing towards realization. It was that which struck the observant eye of Paul, himself a restless mover among men. The Jews had an ideal in their law; they also had zeal; and yet [90] they had no power to attain. On the other hand it was the power joyously to achieve what Judaism painfully strove for, to which he pointed as the characteristic of the Christian life. It was the fleet-limbed strength, the hurling, earth-girding force in it, of which he boasted and which he opposed without shame to all the pride of the antique world.

What are the forces which originated and sustain the Christian revolution?

There were three forces through which the Old Testament prophets expected the renewal of the world and the perfection of the theocracy: the Messiah as the perfect theocratic king; the general outpouring of the spirit of God; and the purified and glorified nation as the seat of God's manifestation. There are three forces in Christianity in which these three expectations have found their fulfillment: Christ, the Spirit, the church. And these three are the revolutionary forces which are to realize the revolutionary program discussed in the preceding chapter.

I. Christ was the initiatory power of the Kingdom of God. With his coming the Kingdom began. All who had preceded him, had their faces turned to the future, and spoke of that which was to come. Even John did only a preparatory work; he was leveling the road for the entrance of the King; his baptism was but a cleansing with water to prepare for the baptism of spirit and fire; he himself claimed to be only a **[91]** Voice, a solemn figure pointing towards the greater One that was to come.

On the other hand Jesus turned the future into the present tense. The Kingdom of God was here. While men were questioning about its coming, it was in the midst of them. His demonstrations of power were the tokens of its presence. When he began, the Kingdom of God was a hope; he created the actual fact, till he could call his disciples blessed for seeing and hearing what the prophets had desired in vain.

And as he initiated the movement, so he sustains it. He is still the compulsory power, the fashioning force.

It cannot be our task here to discuss the nature of Christ, or to attempt to exhaust the eternal significance of his work. We have simply to state the historical fact that Jesus Christ is the prime force in the Christian revolution, and to make clear to ourselves the ways by which his force was exerted and is still exerted to change human society.

1.) And first we mention his teaching as the expression of his view of the world. His teaching taken by itself would tend toward a reversal of values and **[92]** a reconstruction of society.

The Prince of this world is also the father of lies. His power of the air is marvelously used in creating optical delusions. The great seems small and the small great; the serene face of goodness seems distorted into a grin and the narrowest pride and selfishness is rounded out to the fullness of virtue, when seen in these curved mirrors of his. It was so in the times of Jesus, and one of his most pressing duties was to clear the air of delusions and bid this lying devil be gone. He had to restore the spiritual eyesight of his people and teach them to see all things in their true proportions, as God sees them. Men had persuaded themselves that God was a step-father, weakly fond of one nation and making Aschenbrödels of all the other nations for its sake. They were convinced that God was exceedingly pleased with having a large number of animals slaughtered and burned for him, and with having great performances of white-robed people with marches and counter-marches, with singing and trumpet-blaring. They imagined that he liked to have them recite long prayers at particular hours of the day, and to have them wear little leather boxes strapped on their arm and forehead while doing so. Consequently those persons [93] who were most exact in performing these things; who gave a tenth of their income to religion even down to the mint and cumin that grew in a corner of their backyard; who recited their prayers faithfully even if they happened to be standing on a street-corner when the hour arrived; were considered the most holy people and the special darlings of God, while those who were too hard-worked to get all these little niceties by heart were lumped as a desperate and accursed lot. As for irreligious or profligate people, the chief duty of man was to keep away from them and let them go to destruction as fast as they could.

We know what a battle Jesus fought against these lies and how he labored to set up the true standard of goodness. He chilled their Jewish conceit by stories of Samaritan generosity. He walked rough-shod over their elaborate piety of fastings and washings. Against the reverence of sacrifices he was always quoting the prophetic motto: "Mercy, not sacrifice." He passed by the learned theologians as incapable of receiving the knowledge of God and gathered the common [94] people about him as capable of understanding the deep things of God. He told the pious people that the harlots and sinners were nearer the Kingdom of God than they. He knocked the mumbo-jumbo idol of Pharisaism from its pedestal and let all men see that there was nothing in it but wind, cobwebs and dirt.

It is almost amusing for us today to watch the pillars of Jewish society from this distance and see how they took the knocking down of their houses of cards. At first they were piously horrified. "Why," they gasped, "why, he doesn't wash his hands before he eats! He misuses the blessed Sabbath for healing people! He eats and drinks as much as he wants to! He, – yes, he actually does, – he sits down at the same table with publicans and sinners, and lets harlots touch him! And he wants to be a Rabbi? A holy man? He is a glutton, a wine-bibber, a friend of sinners, a Samaritan, a demoniac! He is possessed by Beelzebub, the biggest devil of them all!" After a while their tone changed. They had surveyed him from the secure height of their established religious infallibility. They had discussed the question whether he was to stand or fall. Now they perceived that it was a question [95] of their own standing or falling. The people heard him gladly. They were drinking in his words. His words carried a strange authority with them. He said a thing, and everybody said: "Of course, that's plain; there is nothing to be said against that." The people were swinging away from their old religious authorities. If this went on, they would be left high and dry as useless teachers and bad men. Society must be saved; the Law was attacked; religion itself was at stake; incidentally their own standing was in danger. We know the outcome.

Now this revolutionary influence of Christ's teaching is still felt. Society is much the same from age to age. We have our sham substitutes for godliness. We have our little lawyer's precedents and penny rules as to which actions are allowable for religious people and which are not. We have our brutal and lawless classes, and we have our respectable saviours of society. The gnat is still strained and the camel swallowed. Mint, anise and cummin are still tithed, and justice, mercy and faithfulness forgotten. And so we **[96]** need Christ's teachings. If any man will train his judgement by laying it parallel to the judgement of Jesus, he will soon find himself hewing close to the mark. He will find his judgements diverging considerably from the standard judgements of contemporary society. In time he will find that he is himself a revolutionist.

We cannot overestimate the effect which the teachings of Jesus have had in the course of centuries in training men to see clearly and judge fearlessly. It is true that many of the most radical teachings of Christ are tacitly left on one side by the average religionist. Over others the scribes have spun that same mystifying web of tradition, explanations and limitations, by which in Christ's time they had made the law of God of no effect. And yet there are his sayings. They have to be preached from. They have to be explained to open-eyed children and young people. Something of their sharp edge is felt through all the silken wrappings. And occasionally some man falls to unwrapping them. He finds they were made to be **[97]** used, and he uses them. He proclaims: "Christ meant what he said." He finds wise men maundering over some Gordian knot, some insoluble problem of humanity. A flash of Christ's word, an antithesis, a parable applied, and the knot falls, cut asunder. Then the wise men arise and cry: "Stop him; he is a crazy fanatic; a crank; crucify him." And so the revolutionary force of Christ's teaching goes on.

That is the wonderful thing about the teachings of Jesus, that they do not grow old. Rabbi Hillel said wise things before him, but we can easily spare the flower of Jerusalem's learning for the words of the Galilean peasant. Philo of Alexandria was good, profound, eloquent, but his writings are a weariness to all except the student of history. Socrates has had the pens of Xenophon and Plato to record him and explain him, and his intellectual midwifery is always interesting and stimulating; but lives are not changed by Socrates to-day; brave men do not fight the battles against the nether powers with words of Socrates as their weapons. This young and uncultured man of Nazareth has given the final and satisfactory expression to many of [98] the darkest truths of human life. We have not passed beyond his words, either in form or substance. Lassalle has been called the Messiah of socialism. He was a man of profound learning, of flashing and supple mind. He gave a powerful impetus to the social movement. His memory is reverenced; his speeches are still widely read. But the demands formulated by him and in which he saw all hope, have even now, a few decades after his death, become antiquated. They were carried for a while in the party platforms for his sake; now they have been dropped. His party has passed beyond him. The Messiah of socialism has been exhausted. Christ has not been exhausted. His party, the church, is charged with slowness and uselessness. But it is not because she has outstripped Christ, and still insists on cumbering herself with his worn-out teachings; but because she lags so far behind him, and has cut the tendons of his teachings and lamed them by tradition and false interpretation. A church based absolutely on the teachings of Jesus would be the most revolutionary society on earth, and its platform would be further ahead of existing [99] conditions than any party platform formulated in this age of platforms.

2.) But the chief power of Christ does not lie in his teachings. His words were only a partial expression of himself; he is more than they. It is the personality of Jesus Christ in which the secret of his power lies. We have declined the task of discussing here the nature of Christ; but in surveying the velocity of the current originated by him, we cannot help trying to get some approximate estimate of the power that entered human history in the person of Jesus.

He is himself the best witness concerning himself. Going back to the oldest and safest records of his sayings, we find high utterances concerning himself. He calls himself the desire of prophets and kings; the culmination of Old Testament history; greater than Jonah; greater than Solomon; more than the temple; the Lord of David; the Lord of the Sabbath. He claims the right to forgive sins; he promises to confess before the Father those who confess him; he that receives him, receives Him that sent him; blasphemy against him is a sin so serious, that he especially asserts that it can be forgiven. All things have been delivered to him of the Father; he will be the [100] judge of all the nations of the earth. He calls himself the Son of Man, a name that he fashioned for himself; it asserts his humanity, and yet implies that he is Man in a unique sense. He calls himself the Son of God in a manner and in a sense different from those whom he taught to call God their Father. He was conscious of a unique intimacy with God, knowing Him and known of Him in a way which could not be asserted of others (Mt. 11, 27). All this shows that he was conscious of a relation both to God and to humanity in which he stood solitary; of a personality which transcended that of all other historical persons in value; and of a power to fulfill the entire past, to initiate a new era, and to give the ultimate realization to the aspirations of humanity.

The same impression of an immeasurably great personality grows on us if we study the records of his life simply as candid students of history, and watch the impression he made on his contemporaries. Here was a man who without the easy pedestal of birth, rank, wealth or learning, yet attracted all eyes. The people hung upon him, wondering, doubting, guessing; willing to believe him, if he proclaimed himself the Messiah; insisting, even against the potent authority of the hierarchy, that he must be a prophet, Elijah, Jeremiah, or someone of the greatest. Here was a man of the people who could meet the learned and exceedingly able lawyers and theologians of his day with **[101]** their own weapons and disarm them with easy superiority, till they took their refuge, first in slander, then in violence. And, what seems to us one of the strongest historical proofs of the greatness of Jesus: here was a man who walked in simplicity, in poverty, homeless, weary sometimes and hungry, not withdrawing from men in austere loneliness, but mingling with them in the disenchanting smallness of daily life; and yet those who knew him best, exalted him most. At a time when his popularity was waning; when he was wandering as a fugitive in Northern Galilee; when the immense intellectual and moral weight of the teachers and leaders of the people, so calculated to shake the judgment of the simple, was thrown dead against him; at a time when all the popular glory of the first days of his ministry was veiled by adversity and lack of success, his disciples leaped beyond the average impression of the people, repudiated the judgement of the hierarchy, broke with all the Jewish standards of Messianic greatness, and asserted as the result of their maturing conviction that he was the Messiah, the Son of the living God. How great was this personality, which in spite of the paralyzing pressure of outward disappointment, could call forth such a confession? **[102]** It would be easy to leap at once to the theological dogmas of the later church and assert the very highest things concerning the person of

Christ. But we prefer the slower method of historical study to build up in our minds some approximate conception of the greatness of Jesus. We know how Paul conceived him. To him Christ was the second Adam; the center of a new humanity; the source of a current of life greater than the current of death which had swept in through the first Adam; he was the Lord, through whom are all things; the head of the church and its life-giving spirit; the coming judge, the restorer even of the travailing creation. Now it is true that Paul confessedly takes no interest in narrating the facts of Christ's life and quoting his sayings. He refuses to know Christ merely after the flesh. His Christ was the risen, glorified, spiritual Christ, present in the church with palpable power. Yet he built up his conceptions on historical facts. From the few instances in which the need of others compelled him to step down and demonstrate the stability of his foundations, we see that he knew the facts of Christ's life, and that his knowledge was the result of extensive, scrutinizing, even doubting inquiry. He was a reasoner by nature, and he had been convinced in spite **[103]** of doubt and denial. Therefore we can conclude from the loftiness of the speculative structure erected by him that he fully trusted the strength of its historical foundation. Again we ask, what must this personality of Jesus have been, if very shortly after his plain life, when his memory was still spotted with the fresh blood of an accursed criminal execution, Paul could put his foot on that cross which to so many Jews was the insuperable stumbling-block, and proclaim Jesus as the glorified Lord of the world, for whose exaltation the highest Messianic theology and the wealth of Alexandrian philosophy scarcely furnished him adequate expressions?

The same argument holds in qualified form concerning the conception of Jesus expressed in the Apocalypse, one of the earliest writings of the Christian church, and in the Fourth Gospel, one of the latest. It was because the glory of the man Jesus in grace and truth was so great, that the spiritual eye discerned in him the eternal Word made flesh. The portrayal of the Christ of the Fourth Gospel is distinct from the words, the gait, the look of the Jesus of the other three gospels. **[104]** And yet for all these centuries the church, though always feeling the diversity, has not felt any necessary incongruity between the one figure and the other. The Galilean Jesus of Matthew, Mark and Luke, is able to bear the exceeding weight of glory of the incarnate Word and Life. So great was he.

The larger perspective of later ages has not reversed the verdict of his first followers. Not only that countless sincere hearts have found in him the way, the truth, the life, their see, and have confessed the name of Jesus to be above every name known to them. Even those who have refused their consent to the doctrines of the church concerning him, have testified frankly to the immeasurable greatness of his personality. From his pantheistic standpoint Spinoza said as much as he could, when he called Christ "the temple of God, because God has given the greatest manifestation of himself in Christ." Goethe says: "Let culture progress, let natural science expand and deepen, let the human intellect grow as it will; it will never get beyond the elevation and ethical culture of Christianity as it shines in the gospels." Strauss, the great negative critic, whose attacks on the old guarantees of faith have been so terrible because there was so much powerful historical work **[105]** in them, has repeatedly conceded the possibility of proving, that it will be forever impossible to pass beyond Christ in religion, and hence in the highest department of life; that at all events he stands in the first rank among those who have educated humanity to higher ideals; that all religious life finds its full development in him, and that all our extension and elaboration, making the best use of what he has given, can only furnish grains of sand to the eternal structure, for which Jesus laid the mighty corner-stone.

We hear many bitter words against the church in these days; but seldom do we hear a word against Christ. The church is hissed; Christ is cheered. And the accusers of the church pay an involuntary tribute to Christ when they condemn the church by comparing it with its founder. Judged by comparison with any other organization the church stands high enough; judged by Jesus as the standard, its deficiency is painfully evident.

Now this great personality, Jesus Christ, has entered humanity as a force. He threw himself with all his strength into the history of our race. And we assert that he is now a revolutionary force, changing individuals and revolutionizing nations. We assert **[106]** that the personality of Christ has in a few nations overcome the inertia and retrogression everywhere else visible, and has started them upon that series of revolutionary eras by which they are hewing their way toward the perfect society. What we have said concerning the power of his personality has shown us that there was force enough in him to do what we say. It remains to make clear to ourselves how his personality exerts this force.

We have spoken of the force of his teachings. But the difference between moral and religious teaching in the abstract and the same teaching personified and realized is vital. Jesus embodied his teaching, and Christianity is built up, not so much on the doctrine, as on the person of its founder.

In the first place teaching merely in words is never intelligible beyond a certain circle. It requires some intellectual ability and training to grasp the profounder truths of life when put in words. Religions not founded on persons have usually been esoteric religions; they have been the property of a limited circle of intellects, while the mass of the people caught only the drippings of truth that leaked out in simple precepts of morality, or found embodiment in ritual, which spoke [107] in action. There was perhaps never a community so saturated with religious thought as the Jewish people; yet the Rabbis called the common people accursed "because they knew not the law." If Jesus was to establish a religion of the common people, a religion of which fishermen could be the teachers and which could in its perfection become the possession of the meanest slave on a Roman latifundium, then a doctrine in words would not do. A doctrine in a man would; for there is that in us all which understands a human nature. It is the most incomprehensible and the most comprehensible thing in the world to us. Watch a child looking at a stranger with the wide, searching eye and bestowing its confidence or dislike as the result of its scrutiny. If truth can find expression in human nature, then it has found expression in the most perspicacious, the most universal and the most elastic language. It is the language common to the rich and the lowly. It is the language that holds good though the boundaries of many nations be traversed. It is the language which does not become fossilized with the lapse of time. The words of the Nicene Creed, its distinctions of person and [108] substance, though recited so often in many churches, are meaningless babble to ninety-nine percent of those who hear it. Christ is just as intelligible to a church sexton to-day as he was to the porter that swept out the hall in Nicea after the Council adjourned. "The Word made flesh" is the necessary condition of a truly universal religion, for no other expression of truth can serve for all classes, all nations, all times, and all grades of spiritual development. In Jesus we find all these requirements, and therefore his personality has that power over humanity which a luminous Shechina of God, dwelling in the midst of us, must have.

In the next place the embodiment of truth lends it a compulsory power which the clearest statement in words cannot give it. The attempt has frequently been made, and with some success, to parallel the sayings of Jesus by similar sayings of the Rabbis, of the Shastras, and of Greek and Roman philosophers. Why should they not have said similar things? It would be no guarantee of the correctness of Christ's thoughts, if no one had ever sought the solution of life's problems in the [109] same direction. But if such collections of similarities are to prove that there was no difference between Christ and other wise men, they skip lightly across the immense chasm that yawns between dreams and realities. What noble words Seneca spoke and what a mean man he was. Those Stoic dreams of the brave, wise man were partly rhetorical coruscations, partly longings. They were moral intoxications, followed often by weariness, despair and suicide. Cicero sadly confesses the non-existence of the ideal of wisdom and virtue that he was portraying. (Tusc. 2,22: *in quo perfecta sapientia, quem adhuc nos quidem vidimus neminem, sed philosophorum sententiis, qualis futurus sit, si modo aliquando fuerit, exponitur.*) An ideal of goodness which is known never to have existed and to be unattainable, is not only without power; it is enervating. It substitutes the shrug of skepticism for the enthusiasm of faith. It benumbs self-forgetfulness even in the honest and makes them seek satisfaction in the appearances of virtue, which at least bring the admiration of others, rather than in virtue itself. [110] On the other hand the fact that truth and goodness are realized, immediately lays them upon all consciences with compulsory power. They are possible, are they? Well, then they are necessary. Preachers can speak all they please about the beauty of humility, of surrendering privileges and becoming brothers to the lowly. Men yield a ready assent, and live as they lived before. But let some man voluntarily strip off his purple and fine linen and work as a Connecticut factory operative or as a Russian moujik, and the world is moved. Consciences are stricken; minds become restless; longings are hardened into purpose; in a greater or less degree imitation follows.

It is thus that Jesus has lent to the moral conceptions of humanity a force which the clearest perception of them and the most lucid statement never did lend them and never could have lent them. He has furnished us with the demonstration of a life completely filled with God and absolutely mastered by goodness. Henceforth none of us can be satisfied with anything less. And as a matter of fact there is no impulse which even approaches the force which Jesus [111] Christ exerts upon those who lay themselves open to his influence, in perpetually raising their ideal and driving them toward it.

But we have pointed out that the thoughts of Jesus are revolutionary thoughts, and his activity was a revolutionary activity. His judgements did not coincide with the judgements current in his day; in many cases they directly contravened them. He did not admire what others admired. He scorned their models of virtue, and found goodness where they felt only contempt. His whole life incarnated those principles which contradict the ruling principles of existing human society. Hence wherever his personality gains influence over a human soul, the result will be, that that soul will go forth to live a revolutionary life. And the abiding power of the personality of Jesus is seen in the fact that although elements of society really hostile to Christ have so often and so generally obtained control of the church, and turned Christianity into a conservative and reactionary force, yet somehow his true character is forever bursting forth and impelling new men to [112] revolutionary efforts.

Furthermore, the personality of Jesus is so powerful a force by the sanity and harmony of its qualities. Any student of history knows that there is no impulse comparing in power with that of a living religion. The trouble is, that religion has so often spent its force by tearing its possessor loose from human society, setting him to lacerate his back with lashes, laming his joints by standing on a pillar, wasting his time on reciting prayers, or grimly locking him up on the Sabbath to examine his inward states and to torture his children with devotions that they have no taste for. It is wonderful. The energy and persistence developed is worthy of admiration. But it is force wasted. It is pounding the sea, which closes again on the blow. If all the force spent in the deserts of the East and the monasteries of the West had been exerted upon the world, instead of spending itself upon tearing men loose from their friends, stifling their love and choking down their longings, the world might by this time be a very different world.

But again, when religion has been brought to bear on practical life, it has often bruised itself to [113] death by the wild onset of fanaticism. The Jews rising under false Messiahs; the Anabaptists erecting a spiritual Kingdom at Münster; Quakers running naked through London with pans of brimstone on their heads, calling for repentance; the dervishes of the Mahdi storming against a fire that no European discipline would face; – is there nothing admirable in these to the thoughtful man? And yet how often have men discarded all religious enthusiasm, because the fire-cracker enthusiasm of these hotheads has sputtered itself out, leaving nothing but smoke, and perhaps a conflagration.

Now compare with these two extremes the equipoise of the life of Jesus. Here was quiet patience with heroic bravery; the most daring innovation with the most loving conservatism. It is he who has demonstrated the possibility of resting in God without leaving the world, and of living in the world without forgetting God; of obeying the spirit without asceticism, and of eating and drinking without serving the flesh. He was both the Son of God and the Son of Man, and showed that he did not cease to be the one by **[114]** becoming the other. He alone has fully married the real and the ideal, the life here and the life beyond, the inward perfection and its steady reconstruction of the outward imperfection. No spirit soared so high, and none was more sensible and sane.

And just this combination is the most difficult thing to teach by verbal instruction. Tell a man to have neither pride toward God nor servile fear of Him, and how shall he do it? Tell him that mere external performances are nothing in the sight of God, and that mere ecstatic raptures of the spirit are equally nothing, and see whether he will hit on something that does avail. The efforts of theology to find a reconciliation between the holiness of God and His love in the abstract are very perplexing. But let these apparent contradictions be actually united in a person, whose life is yet not contradictory, but consistent and lovely, and we draw a sigh of relief; we draw near that person; we come under his influence, and we feel the same harmonious wholeness of life developing in us.

Such men as John the Baptist knock more rudely at the door of **[115]** the world and demand admission for heaven. But Jesus brought heaven into the world and commended it to the love of men, and so, even though they killed him, the Kingdom of heaven is here and has gained its habitation through the influence of his personality. But where heaven is, sin leaves, and if sin leaves, this world is revolutionized. It will be only a question of time when the new force shall have penetrated everything.

The Kingdom of God presupposes a reconstruction of the life of this world, till in spirit and form it shall be the doing of the will of God. Jesus bore the Kingship of God within him. He saw (all) things as God views them, and his actions were done in entire obedience to the will of his Father. Hence the words in which he expressed his views of the world contradicted the lying views of society, and his actions likewise disobeyed the rules of propriety and right set up by society. In his words and in his actions we have the manifestations of his personality. His personality **[116]** therefore was in opposition to the existing life of humanity. But this opposition did not remain confined to his person. By that inalienable influence which every human being for good or evil exerts upon all others that come in contact with it, his thought and action would attract others. That influence increases in geometrical ratio with the greatness of the personality exerting it. The personality of Jesus was immeasurably great, and even without any exertion on his part, he would have drawn men out of their grooves into his. But Jesus deliberately exerted all his power to that end. His teaching came over men with all the inherent force of truth against which there is no appeal except denial. The teaching was made directly intelligible by being incarnated in his life. It thereby also gained the compulsory power which truth in action always has, and at the same time his life commended his radical [117] teaching by showing the healthful balance which was possible along with all its forward push.

Thus Jesus won those to him who loved the light. They opened their hearts to his influences and put themselves under his guidance. His power became the supreme power in their lives.

The same influence still continues from the historical Christ across all these centuries. Men still absorb his words and reconstruct their lives more or less to accord with them. His personality also acts upon all who put themselves in contact with it. There are many who have vowed loyalty to the Man of Galilee, and are satisfied if they can in any way execute the desires of him they call Master. They love him with a unique love. And upon all who have courage to pass by the false Christ which men who have the spirit of this world have set up to deceive us; upon all who push on to behold the sad, earnest face of the Son of Man, comes the spirit of battle. If the Master fought, so must we. If his battle was against the great ones of the earth on behalf of the people, we know who [118] is our enemy too. If he found the bitterest enemy of his Father's will in religious bigotry and Pharisaism, we know where we shall find it to-day. He shows us the direction and lends us the impulse. The cross of the MacGregors had to be carried on. So must the cross of the Christ. And if fear and loneliness come upon us, we gain renewal of strength from him who also wrestled with fear and darkness and then went forth in calmness and strength.

The center of the Messianic hope was the Messiah, the perfect King of his people. Jesus did not fulfill all the conceptions of the Jewish nation concerning the Messiah. He wielded no rod of iron; he piled up no heaps of the slain; he did not robe himself in magnificence like Solomon. His nation saw no regal power in him. Pilate, the Roman, thought he knew the aspects of royalty, and when he saw that pale and forsaken figure before him, he asked in scornful surprise: "Thou –art thou a king?"

"Thou sayest it; I am a king," was the answer. And thousands of quivering lips have since echoed it: "Thou sayest it, O Pilate; he is a [119] king." Royal not by gorgeous trappings bought with the sweat of his people; imperial not by the glint of bayonets; but the King of Men, glorious by the sweetness and strength of his life; powerful by the attraction of love and gratitude; and by the compulsion of truth and right. The Jews expected the Messiah as an Oriental autocrat. But despotisms are passing away. The greatness won by force is gaining less and less of admiration. The discernment of humanity is growing clearer. Men love heroism, self-sacrifice, love. Jesus has himself been the foremost force in bringing about this change, and in turn he reaps the reward of his work. The less men acknowledge the sovereignty of brute force and the more they yield their willing loyalty to the spiritual power of character, the more will Jesus become King of Humanity.

II. The second force by which the Old Testament prophets expected the perfection of the theocracy was the Spirit of God. That Spirit which had been the exclusive privilege of a few chosen men, of kings and prophets and priests, would be poured out on all, on old and young, on the great and the lowly (Joel 2, 28-29), and thus that knowledge of God's will **[120]** which had hitherto been imparted by the few to the many, would become the common property of all (Jer. 31, 31-34; Is. 54, 13). This inward knowledge of God, this writing of the law on the hearts by the Spirit of God, would make it possible to abrogate the old covenant of outward law and compulsion, and to institute the new covenant of loving obedience. Where thus the Spirit was poured out upon the people, it would be like water upon the thirsty, and like floods upon the dry ground; there would be a glad life like the sprouting of young grass, like the luxuriance of the willow withes along the water-courses (Is. 44, 3-4).

At the beginning of the Messianic era this prophecy was renewed by John. He depreciated himself in comparison with the greater one that was to come, and his own baptism in comparison with that which was to be administered by the Messiah. He said the two would compare as water with fire. His ministry was the ministry of repentance; his baptism was the baptism of repentance. He had power to call men to cut loose from the old and to wash off the former life. He had no power to inaugurate the new era and to **[121]** implant the principle of a new life. That remained for the Messiah and the baptism in spirit.

Jesus adopted the very words of John and renewed the promise (Acts 1, 4-8). It would be a misconstruction of his words and the subsequent facts, to regard this gift of the Spirit either as the natural reason of man, or as that enlightening influence which God exerts upon all men, or as elevation of character, or as mere enthusiasm. It was not natural reason; at least Paul perceived a very profound difference between the clear-sightedness and intellectual ability which distinguished the leaders of existing society, and the insight resulting from the possession of the Spirit (I Cor. 2, 6-16). It was not the general enlightening influence of God; the Fourth Gospel evidently distinguishes between the Logos which is the light of men and illuminates every man; and the Paraclete that was to complete the work of Christ. It was not synonymous with elevation of character; the apostles had been undergoing a process of spiritual education under Christ in faith, love, obedience and knowledge, yet Christ bids them wait for something additional. It **[122]** was not a boiling up of enthusiasm over the fire of opposition; it lasted too long and was apparently too objective a reality in the church to admit of that explanation. It was a gift, an impartation from God, not a product from within. The church in Jerusalem (Acts 2), the converts at Samaria (Acts 8, 14), the household of Cornelius (Acts 10, 44), the men at Ephesus (Acts 19, 1) had at one time not had the Spirit, and then they had received it. The power of that Spirit was a solid fact in the experience of the churches (I Thess. 1, 5). In writing to the Galatians Paul assumed their recollection of the coming of the Holy Spirit as a matter of course, and simply questions whether they at that time received it by the performance of Jewish rites or by the preaching of Christ's glad tidings (Gal. 3, 1). It was so universal in the church that Paul denied the title of Christian to all that did not have it and did not feel its guiding activity (Rom. 8, 9, 14). It was so palpable a possession that he calls it the earnest, the tangible pledge, the first part payment of the redemption for which the early church was so anxiously waiting in suffering. **[123]** If the epistles of Paul are taken simply as historical evidence concerning the life and condition of the early churches, they demonstrate the existence of a new spiritual force in the world, which Paul found only in connection with the gospel of Christ, and which he regarded as neither the product of environment, nor as the evolution of personal character, but as an abiding contact between the spirit of man and the Spirit of the living God.

Now, this new force is a revolutionary force. It must be, because it is of God, and must unceasingly protest against the saying and doing of lies, against impurity and meanness, against injustice and oppression; it must work toward truth, right and love.

And examining its historical effect we find that it is indeed a revolutionary force.

1.) First of all it frees man from that slavery which comes closest home to all of us, the enslavement of our ethical and spiritual nature under the cravings of our animal **[124]** nature. We all feel that the moral demands within us are the higher and ought to rule; and we all know that in most men they are overpowered by the brutal instincts and do not rule. Every man feels at least an occasional pang of sorrow at this fact. And the more earnest writhe under the consciousness of their impotence and cry out for some power to deliver them from the body of this death in life. Paul asserts that such a power exists. He asserts that what man cannot do even under the stimulus of a high moral law, is accomplished by the indwelling of the Spirit of God (Rom. 7, 15-8, 11). There is an enfranchising power in it. A man who is born from above (John 3, 3-6), and in whom the Spirit of God dwells (Rom. 8, 9), no longer has the same purposes and desires that he had before (Rom. 8, 5). Not that the old desires have been annihilated, but the center of gravity in the man is shifted from the brutal to the spiritual, and the desire to eat and to drink what he pleases is held in check by the love and tenderness for others who may be injured **[125]** thereby (Rom. 14, 14). The chief good becomes not to fill his stomach at any cost, but to be conscious of a right life, to be at peace with himself and his brothers, and to have the glad and quickening contact with the Holy Spirit. That fellowship and oneness with God is a prophylactic against any debasement of body and soul (I Cor. 6, 15-20). As long as the Spirit is kept supreme, the fruits of a man's life will not be a rank growth of lasciviousness and angry jealousy, but a harvest of peace, kindness, gentleness and self-control (Gal. 5, 16-24). In place of the excitement of revelling he has the healthy stimulus of a glad and thankful frame of mind, filled with services of helpfulness (Eph. 5, 18-21).

In short, that first and worst servitude, the slavery of man to his own baser desires, which compel him to do what he hates, and degrade him in his own sight if not in the opinion of others, – that slavery can be broken by the revolutionary power of the renewing and indwelling Spirit of God. Through that a man can become a freeman, lifting up his head before God and men. It makes him sane, sound, strong, a well-grained stone in the living temple of humanity. **[126]** 2.) In the second place the Spirit is a revolutionary force by emancipating men from the thraldom of superstition. Religious superstition has doubtless been one of the most paralyzing, benumbing forces in the world. It makes the African shiver at a black stump. It drives hundreds of thousands of people annually to the shores of Holy Ganges and to the grave of the Prophet, wasting them with the fatigues of travel and making them bearers of disease for themselves and others. Even in enlightened Europe there is Rome with its relics and Lourdes with its water, and as we write, the city authorities of Treves [Trier] are building three railway stations, laying double streetcar tracks and granting hundreds of saloon licences in view of the multitudes that are expected to visit the supposed garment of Christ which is to be exposed to the sight of the faithful.

One way of combatting superstition is by ridicule, exposure and denial. It examines the bones of the 10,000 virgins at Cologne and declares that in the first place there are not enough bones there to supply 10,000 virgins with their necessary anatomy, [127] and in the second place many of those that are there, never belonged to female skeletons. It watches the liquefaction of the blood of St. Januarius, and discovers that the miracle times itself by the church clock and not by solar time. The effect of this method of reasoning is twofold. Some, especially women, shut their eyes very tight and insist that they take all the more satisfaction in believing it, because science calls it absurd. Others, especially men, say: "We have been fooled, have we? Well then the whole thing is rot. Away with priests, away with God, away with moral obligations! Henceforth we believe what we see, and do what we dare." If they succeed, they produce atrophy of their higher nature; they lose all reverence; their moral fibre gradually grows flabby; they become what they desire to be, intellectual animals. If the suppressed part of their nature asserts itself in spite of them, their superstition merely changes its form; they are frightened by black cats and falling salt-cellars and the number thirteen, and attach themselves as blindly to [128] their favorite form of scepticism and their party, as their wives follow the priests and their church. One devil has gone out, but another has come in, and it is a mooted question in demonology, which of the two is the worse. The Latin nations of Europe will afford pathological cases enough to anyone who desires to investigate the question.

True Christianity applies a different method. It recognizes in superstition the helpless groping of a legitimate but underdeveloped instinct. It sees the caged bird flutter when the time comes for the southward flight, and it does not cut off the fluttering wings, but it opens the cage, lets the air and sunshine stream into the room, and says: "Now fly!"

Does the Samaritan woman reverence places, balancing the sanctity of Mount Gerizim against the holiness of Jerusalem? The answer is not that there is no use in worshipping God at all, but that he who approaches the Father in spirit and truth can draw nigh to Him anywhere and find Him. Have men been accustomed to enter temples with awe because God is there, and to bow before alters with [129] reverence because of the Real Presence in the host? Their true emancipation is not in thinking that God is nowhere near, not even in temples, but in experiencing the contact and presence of the Eternal One in their own souls. Then they will know that the Shechina is in no temple so palpable and near, as in the temple of a God-conquered body (I Cor. 6, 19), and in a community of spiritual men (I Cor. 3, 16; Eph. 2, 22). If they seek God, they will not travel hither or thither to get near Him, but will withdraw into the silent solitude of their own hearts and there God will meet them. He that knows God within him, is free from the superstition of holy places.

And from the superstition of ritual and sacred actions. Judaism was full of that; sacrifices, circumcision, ceremonial washings, the Tephillin on arm and forehead in prayer, the performance of the Paschal ritual, the reciting of the Shema, the punctilious observance of the Sabbath—all these were actions in themselves holy. God was pleased if **[130]** they were performed and displeased if they were not. This also was a bondage from which it was hard indeed to free men. And here again the possession of the Spirit is the enfranchising power. Paul compares the ritualists in their slavish piety and the children of the Spirit in their free service to the son of Hagar the handmaid and the child of Sara the free woman (Gal. 4, 21-5, 1). The Spirit was everywhere working out a free and truthful life that was not chained to set words and fixed actions, but sought its own natural expression. It is the undying merit of Paul that he cut the Jewish fetters by which the young church was bound, protested against the bondage of antiquated forms (Gal. 5, 1), refused the "weak and beggarly rudiments" (Gal. 4, 9), and insisted on liberty for the Spirit of God to do its transforming work (II Cor. 3, 6-18). But a mere refusal of the old forms would have availed nothing unless there were a new and creative spirit. It is not: "where the old forms are abolished, there is liberty"; but "where the Spirit of the Lord is, there is liberty." Unless that Spirit is present, there will always be forms to which men cling. Men have made a form of Christianity **[131]** itself. The Jews strapped on the Tephillin for prayer; Christians dip their finger in water and make the sign of the cross. The Jews substituted another word whenever the dread name of Yahweh occurred in the reading of the Scriptures; Christians bow their backs whenever the name of Christ occurs in the liturgy. The Jews thought circumcision a saving performance; Christians sprinkle a child with water and mutter a formula and expect that to alter God's feelings toward that child. How Paul would cry out against these modern Galatians who have indeed forsaken the old Jewish yoke that galled his shoulder, but have constructed a like fabric out of Christian observances, still trusting in saving performances and formulas, turning his own passionate appeals for freedom into a new law of Moses which they may read with a veil over their face! Are we saved by faith or by manipulations? Does the Spirit create its forms, or the forms conjure up the Spirit?

Set rites and creeds and forms are the grave clothes of a dead faith. The living Spirit alone is strong and daring enough to strip them off and stand forth in the strength of life. Where the [132] veneration for sacred forms increases, it is an almost certain sign that the Spirit is departing and that hence a substitute has to be found. The form of godliness is most exalted where the power of godliness is vanishing. On the other hand where the living Spirit grows dominant, forms become of slight account. They are used or not, as occasion teaches, but there is no compulsory holiness in them. The holiness is in the Spirit which uses the forms, and beside that wonderful presence all dead things seem as naught.

3.) In the third place the Spirit is revolutionary force, because where it comes, it breaks the power of priestcraft. This also is one of the evil forces that has kept humanity in bondage. The medicine-man of North America, the rainmaker of Africa, the augur and haruspex of ancient Rome, the priestly orders of Egypt, the scribes of Judea that laid heavy burdens upon the people, these all have wielded a power over men more tyrannical than the violence of kings and more blighting to the free development of human society. So almost universally has religion been bound up with the domination of priests, [133] that some honest students of history have identified the two and cast them overboard together. We feel under no compulsion to do so. Enemies of popular liberty have quoted the sad words of Madame Roland when she was led to the guillotine: "O Liberty, what crimes are committed in thy name," and have reasoned that liberty is evil because evil things are done in its name. We hold that just because liberty is one of the sublimest possessions of man, therefore will some commit atrocities to gain it, and others will use it to cloak their own selfishness. The same thing is true of religion. It is because religion is one of the potent forces of human life, that it has been used by designing men to fasten their power over their fellowmen. What noble aspiration is there which has not been thus misused? Sexual love, patriotism, the faculty of self-sacrifice – they are all used to bit and bridle the people.

Now the power of priests lies in this, that they claim for themselves some exclusive knowledge of the will of God and some exclusive right of approach to him. The Sudanese rain-maker alone knows the proper incantations to break the drought. The priest of Poleramma is the one [134] that knows just how to beat the tom-tom and offer the sacrifice in the way that will please the terrible Goddess of Disease and cause her to depart from the Hindu's favorite child. The Judean scribe had the knowledge of the Law, in the doing of which lay salvation, and therefore he had to be held in reverence.

Men want to approach God, to know His will and be assured of His favor. They do not know how, and feel unfit for it. They will submit to the direction of those who profess to know, and who claim by some title of caste or initiation to be qualified for approaching God.

How shall men be emancipated from this bondage of ignorance? Here also we deny that the liberation can be a merely negative one. The human heart demands truth; it demands God. Demolish the power of one sort of priesthood and yet leave the people as they are, and they will run after some other sort. It will be a change of manner, not of things. The only true emancipation is for a man to have the truth and the voice of God within him by the Spirit of God. The prophets hoped for that: "This is the new covenant that I will make with the house of Israel; **[135]** I will put my laws into their mind, and on their heart also will I write them. And they shall not teach every man his fellow-citizen, and every man his brother, saying: 'Know the Lord!' for all shall know me, from the least to the greatest of them" (Jer. 31, 33-34). Christ promised the fulfillment of this in the sending of the Paraclete, the Spirit of Truth, who would dwell in his disciples, teach them all things, remind them of what they had heard, make clear to them what they had seen but not understood, and guide them into the truths too great for them as yet (John 14, 17, 25; 16, 12-14). This spirit did come. It proved to be a Spirit of "wisdom and revelation in the knowledge of God," an "enlightening of the eyes of the heart." As Jesus foretold, it made of his unlettered followers "prophets and wise men and scribes" (Mt. 23, 34), stewards over a treasure of knowledge from which they could bring out new and old. Paul claimed for those who had the Spirit, a great and general knowledge of moral and spiritual truth (I Cor. 2), an open-eyed vision of **[136]** God, which far transcended what the painful scrutiny of the Rabbis could discern in their sacred writings (II Cor. 3). John distinctly declares that the Christians are of age; he himself has no desire to treat them as if they were still in tutelage, but simply offers his thoughts and counsels for their aid: "Ye have an anointing from the Holy One, and ye know all things. I have not written unto you because ye know not the truth, but because ye know it." "These things have I written unto you concerning them that would lead you astray.

And as for you, the anointing which ye received of him abideth in you, and ye need not that any one teach you" (I John 2, 20-21, 26-27). This is not the language of hierarchy, but of a mutually helpful fraternal society. The Epistle to the Hebrews is the record of a struggle for freedom, for a universal priesthood, for the right to do without priests and to approach God directly.

It is no argument against what we have said, that Christianity soon developed a finely graded hierarchy, evolved its "means of grace" which only an ordained clergy could administer, substituted the absolution of the priest for the free approach to God, and made the hierarchy the sole stewards of the truth and possessor of the Spirit. It simply proves what we assert, that no change of forms [137] can emancipate, but only the possession of the Spirit. He that has its witness in his heart needs no churchly sacraments to assure him that he is a child of God. He needs neither "the Holy Church" nor a "historic episcopate" to mediate between him and the God who is so near to him. He needs no infallible church, no flawless system of theology, and no arbiter of the faith in the editorial chair of a denominational newspaper, to tell him what he will have to believe, if he wishes to please God. There is a Comforter and Admonisher within him that opens his eyes and gives him a lively relish for the truth in the Bible or wherever he may find it in the thoughts of the great congregation of the faithful in all ages. "The truth makes free," says Christ: free from Pharisaic infallibility too; free from fear of the Jerusalem hierarchy. The "spirit of truth" is the emancipating power. He that truly possesses it can smile at excommunications, laugh at interdicts, shrug his shoulders [138] at the devil's cry of heresy, for, like Stephen who was full of the Holy Ghost, he sees his Lord present while the Sanhedrin gnash their teeth at him. He is free from priestcraft. The Spirit has made him free.

4.) The Spirit is a revolutionary power because it is the constructive power of a new society. Mere protests against existing conditions are not enough to evolve better conditions. It may be worth much to knock down the walls of an old and useless building; but those who can do that are not always able also to make the nobler edifice rise from the debris. There are tremendous destructive forces now at work in all the civilized nations, trampling on superstitions, protesting against unjust laws, bending like Samson against the pillars that support modern society. We cherish the confidence that in the long range of history these forces also will be seen to have been God's ministers. Superstitions ought to be killed; unjust laws ought to be abolished; existing society is rotten and ought to be buried. But the question which we anxiously put to ourselves again and again is this: Have these forces [139] the power to do anything more than destroy? Have they creative power?

In the arraignments of existing religion and politics and social order we always notice that the protests are much stronger than the positive propositions for something better. It is nearly all criticism, very little synthesis. Naturally a man grumbles at the bad food, before he calls for something that he would like better; and yet when he proposes to us to reject our entire bill of fare and our whole system of cooking, we must insist that he prove his ability to concoct something better, before we allow him to throw our dinner out of the window.

We ask not for a detailed plan of the new society. Such a demand is unreasonable. But we do ask to see those qualities of mind and heart which can cement men together into a better social structure. Peacefulness, self-control, love of right, and mutual forbearance are some of the virtues, the diffusion of which makes a happy social life possible, but they are not virtues that grow in any superabundance among [140] men. The number of people who feel the cravings of other people's stomachs as keenly as their own, are few. The men who will not oust a rival in love if they can do it, are also few. Selfishness is the primary force of human life, and selfishness is only to a very limited extent a unitive force. It unites men under the pressure of need. Even wolves unite to hunt when they are famished, but they snarl and bite at each other when they have run down their prey. Every higher form of society demands a surrender of selfishness under the impulse of larger thoughts and ideals. The lower form cannot be safely abandoned until that higher principle is present in the people, which is to underlie and fashion the better form of society.

Now we fear that which the destructive power of the modern iconoclasts is evidently very great, their constructive power, I fear, will be feeble. The average liberal in religion can destroy a nation's reverence for the Bible, but can he give the people a book in its place which will better educate the young, comfort the weary, and nerve the strong man to renewed fortitude? We confess that the system [141] of ethics colored with current philosophy, which is usually offered us in place of the old faiths, looks very slender to us. It may serve as a staff on ground smoothed out by the labor of ages, but I fear it would snap like a reed in the hour of a man's passion, or when a nation descends into the valley of the shadow of death, as nations sometimes must.

The same thing is true of the political and social revolutionists. They are destroying; can they upbuild? Will the men who are so wonderfully holding together now during their fight, hold together when the victory is won and peacefully and gladly cooperate in building up the details of the new structure? History does not make us very sanguine. The French Revolution is a noble chapter in history. Its aims were admirable. Many of the laws passed were ideally just. But they did not stick. It was like modeling a statue of soft butter. Men passed resolutions like angels and hated one another like demons. And this glorious movement [142] of freedom ended in feverish spasms. The gospel according to Jean Jacques Rousseau brought no millennium. "The Rights of Man" was a good cry to knock down with; but to build up we need a people that will respond to the cry of "the Duties of Man," and that is not a cry to which the average man lends a ready ear. We fear too, that the anger, distrust and hate which some social reformers are systematically infusing into the people, does not make the people better fitted for the future work of upbuilding. It is an excellent method of evoking cheers from a meeting, of gaining a temporary advantage from an employer, and of hastening the overthrow of society; but what material will the men thus trained be for the positive work afterwards? The armed men that sprang from the dragon's teeth sown by Jason, slew one another. Make the beast that lurks in man sullen and snarling, and one day it will turn and rend you.

Now we assert, what will doubtless draw a mocking smile from some, that Christianity is a constructive power that has in it the creative principle of a new society. We need not tell [143] those who have read the preceding pages, that we do not call everything Christianity which calls itself so. We mean neither the Christianity of princes nor of well-fed priests; neither that of the benevolent bourgeois who gives alms to keep the people contented and respectful, nor that of the tradesman who tries to make his ledger balance well both for this life and the life to come. We mean the Christianity of Jesus, which under the power of his Spirit has existed through the centuries, in various forms, always more or less despised, but always vital and energetic. That Christianity, we say, has in it the constructive power, because it has in it the Spirit of God.

The Christianity of the early church did knock down the wall of partition separating Jews from Gentiles. It did undermine the old principle of coherence which makes the Jews to this day a separate people. But the common possession of the Spirit was the bond of a new unity, by which Jews and Greeks grew into one body (I Cor. 12, 13). And only those who know the strength of the prejudices **[144]** that kept them apart, can estimate the strength of the force that drew them together, however imperfectly, in the Christian churches. Christianity at that time proved able to abolish the old forms of national coherence, without however leaving the individual isolated, because it united Jew and Greek and barbarian into a new society. The small patriotisms by which men have hitherto been united are also giving way today to the larger patriotism of humanity. This is well if there is a new principle of unity strong enough to bind together so large a mass. The only such principle that we can see is the idea of the brotherhood of humanity, which was first asserted by Christianity as an actuality, and for which Christianity is still the most powerful feeder, as soon as the brotherhood gets beyond phrases and selfishness. Christian missions, with all their shortcomings, are after all the only force which drives men from their own kinsmen into strange nations in order to carry the seed of a nobler life to them. Traders and emigrants may carry civilization incidentally, but they go for their own sake. Even the unselfish explorer and man of science **[145]** goes out in order to carry at least knowledge back with them. It is the Spirit of Christ alone which breaks down national barriers in order to lift up the low members of humanity to the same level with the rest of the family.

Again, the Spirit of God has proved itself the power to establish a form of society, not only more comprehensive in its scope, but higher in its nature. The church in Jerusalem was a social body that "walked in the fear of the Lord and in the admonition of the Holy Spirit" (Acts 9, 31). And of this body we read that "they were together, and had all things in common; they sold their possessions and goods, and divided them to all, according as any man had need. And day by day, continuing steadfastly with one accord in the temple, and breaking bread at home, they did take their food with gladness and singleness of heart, praising God, and having favor with all the people." We do not discuss here the question whether this life was meant to be permanent and universal in the churches, nor whether this was **[146]** a rational and scientific polity or not. But this is plain, that under the first powerful impulse of the Spirit men united in a new society, in which the divisive force of selfishness was broken, where love and generosity were the rule, and men lived a glad, thankful and single-hearted life. Suppose the experiment did fail. Most first experiments fail. But if the Spirit is present, it will impel to ever new efforts to incorporate it. That Spirit has remained, though by no means co-extensive with so-called Christendom. There was love among the early Christians, love so earnest that heathen writers ridiculed it, imposters abused it, and dark suspicions were current that so unheard-of an affection must be based on a sinister community of crime. That Spirit of God has given, as M. de Laveleye says, the most powerful impulses toward liberty and an ideal society up to the present day.

Even its enemies must acknowledge that a true Christian morality and religion is a strong conservative and cohesive force. It gives stability to what it has once undertaken to support. England **[147]** has for centuries had more and purer Christianity in it than the other European nations. It has since the Reformation been the birth-place of all the progressive religious movements. And England has also been the nation which has kept up the steadiest march toward civil liberty. It has been the nation which gained reforms and kept them. It has been the nation that has planted colonies which have the faculty of making free institutions work, while heathen nations plant despotisms, and European nations with a more paganized Christianity have planted colonies, which are republics in name and often despotisms in fact.

Christianity has been the most fertile parent of advanced social experiments. We shall speak of them later. It has experimented with communism before science touched it. And it can be demonstrated that of all the communistic colonies the only ones that have maintained permanent inward peace and prosperity are those which were held together by religion. Of course the maintenance of a socialist colony **[148]** is a difficult task, but these experiments show that Christianity has a greater unitive and organizing force than secularism. The unity of the Spirit is the bond of peace. The fellowship of the Spirit was Paul's basis of appeal for mutual forbearance and service (Phil. 2, 1). Jealousy and strife were to him a demonstration of a lack of the Spirit (I Cor. 3, 1). The Spirit gives and stimulates the faculties of mutual service which serve for the organic upbuilding of a new society (I Cor. 12, 4). It seems to us that the diversity of organizations in religious life, the fertility of Christianity in creating new forms of life, is even to-day far greater than that of secular society.

Therefore in the face of all the appalling sloth of so-called Christians, we assert that the Spirit of Christ is a revolutionary power for constructing a more perfect society. It is subversive of national and class distinctions, and contains the principle of a race unity. It stimulates to endeavor after juster and more merciful forms of social life, and produces that responsiveness **[149]** to duty, that love and forbearance and peace, which are the necessary conditions of making more perfect social institutions stick and work. We hold it probable, that if sweeping changes are to come, the Christian people will be found to be the stable element in the new society, and that to them it will fall to give shape and permanence to those of the modern revolutionary ideas which shall stand the trial of fire.

5.) Once more the Spirit of God is a revolutionary force because it creates the temper, wisdom and power of the revolutionary propagandist.

Of this we have the authoritative example in Jesus himself. Before he entered on his active work, he was, as Peter expresses it, "anointed with the Holy Spirit and with power" (Acts 10, 38). Under the impulse of that Spirit he was led into the wilderness to settle the great questions of the work before him (Lk. 4, 1). In the power of that Spirit he began to preach "good tidings to the poor, release to the captives and liberty to the oppressed" (Lk. 4, 14, 18). Through the force of that Spirit he grappled with **[150]** the sinister malevolence of lost souls, spirit to spirit, and overcame it (Mt. 12, 28).

He promised to his disciples the same power for the propaganda before them (Acts 1, 8; John 14, 12), and the same God-given wisdom (Lk. 12, 11-12; 21, 12-15). History shows that they received both. We find these plain country-people speaking to the cultured inhabitants of the metropolis with great boldness, and with entire fearlessness facing and accusing the great council of their nation, which to their minds must have seemed more august than any tribunal on earth would seem to us. And this boldness is given as the very consequence of their possession of the Spirit of God (Acts 4, 31). They defied judicial injunctions (Acts 4, 19) by their own sense of right, and rejoiced in suffering for their cause (Acts 5, 41). Such a character as that choice man Stephen is an almost ideal revolutionary character (Acts 6-7), and he was a man "full of faith and of the Holy Spirit" (Acts 6, 5).

As for wisdom, we find that also with the men upon whose untried shoulders rested the burden of guiding a great international movement, with all the forms of a new society to find, **[151]** and the most difficult questions to settle. They claim to have been guided by the Holy Spirit singly and as a body, not only on general questions, but about single practical points (Acts 15, 28; 13, 2-4; 8, 29; I Cor. 7, 40).

It seems to us that to possess this Spirit is the most effective revolutionary equipment.

He that has it, is independent above anyone in the world. He has the great Companion ever with him, whose presence Jesus declared to be better than his own visible companionship. (Jo. 14, 17). He can at any time lean back and feel the Eternal Rock supporting him. He stands among his neighbors in state and church, sharing with them, serving them, but not mastered by them. He does not draw his notions of right from public opinion nor limit them by existing laws; he has a higher canon within him, by which he judges what he sees (I Cor. 2, 15) and where necessary strives to change it. The feeble aspirations of his fluttering human spirit are borne up on the eagle-wings [152] of that mightier Spirit (Rom. 8, 26). His conscience is quickened and steadied by reference to that inward guide (Rom. 9, 1). Who has undertaken the work of a true herald of righteousness and mercy without growing disheartened in time at the dead weight of selfishness to be removed? Who has not felt the leaden heaviness of polite scorn, trembled at the angry mutter of the multitude and "battled with a dreadful ache at heart," as he saw before him "that loneliest solitude, the silent desert of a great new thought"? The true revolutionist, the pilgrim of this world, the child of eternity, needs that abiding Presence, if he would have wisdom not to stumble at the critical movement, boldness not to flinch, strength to seize the opportunity, and a serene and hopeful faith that even a desert wind cannot scorch (Eph. 3, 14-21).

And finally we must call attention to the fact that the two forces, Christ and the Spirit, are not two distinct forces, different perhaps in character and demands and dividing our allegiance. Jesus speaks now of himself being with [153] and dwelling in the disciples, and now of the Comforter abiding in them (Mt. 28, 20; John 14, 18-19; 15, 5; 14, 16-17). In the seven epistles of Revelation it is always the "Son of God," he that "was dead and lived again," that speaks; and yet every epistle closes with the words: "He that hath an ear, let him hear what the Spirit saith." Paul speaks interchangeably of Christ living in him (Gal. 2, 20) and the Spirit dwelling in him (Rom. 8, 9), of Christ in us as the ground of our hope of glory, and of the Spirit as the earnest and the firstfruits of our inheritance (Eph. 1, 13; Rom. 8, 23). Luke speaks in one breath of the Holy Spirit forbidding Paul to preach in Asia, and the spirit of Jesus not suffering him to go into Bithynia (Acts 16, 6-7).

We have no desire to dogmatize about this. But this easy interchange of expression certainly shows that the idea of the glorified Christ and of the Holy Spirit were for all practical purposes about identical to the early Christians. And we appeal to the experience of those who have a living sense of being acted upon by the Spirit of God, whether they ever conceive of him as anything but the Christ [154] whose words they have heard and whose person they have loved as they have seen him in the Gospels? Do they not feel the personal nearness and guidance and love of their Friend and Master? If so, then we may unite the discussion of these two forces and regard it as the discussion of the twofold influence of the one force, the Logos of God, first by the perennial influence of his historical manifestation in humanity, and then by his abiding personal influence upon and in our own hearts. It is one electric current, here kindling the resisting medium of the carbon point into illuminating splendor, and here running with silent power through the coils of wire, turning dead bars of iron into irresistible magnets. **[155]** III. The third power by which the Old Testament prophets expected to see the glorious future realized was the purified and glorified nation as the seat of God's manifestation. This expectation finds its fulfillment in the church. The historic personality of Jesus; the all-pervading Spirit of God touching the spirits of men; and living men in whom these two other forces have wrought a change and found a dwelling-place; these are the revolutionary forces working in humanity toward the reign of God on earth.

Jesus sought to duplicate himself in his disciples. He singled out among the multitude of people with whom he came in contact, those who by repentance had put away the evil deeds which would otherwise have made them recoil from him (Jo. 3, 20), and who by faith in him had opened their souls to all impressions coming from him. By every holy bond he attached them to himself. He walked with them and talked with them. Patiently he planted his ideas in their minds; utilized every moment of sorrow, of wonder, of sin, of hearty admiration to bring them to look at things in his way. He made them his companions, called **[156]** them his friends (Jo. 15, 14); ranked their nearness to him above that of kinship (Mt. 12, 46-50). He wanted to be their shepherd whose voice they would know and respond to (Jo. 14, 4, 14). He wanted to be as meat and drink to their spiritual natures (Jo. 6, 35; Mt 26, 26-29). He wanted his life to be in them as the sap of the vine courses in the branches (Jo. 15).

In a great measure he succeeded. Their hearts were plastic to his touch. They loved him. They found the chief good of their life in him. His thoughts became their thoughts. His sympathies and antipathies were theirs. Christ was formed in them. Paul in surveying his life saw the Paul-life all merged in the Christ-life; it was no longer he that lived; it was Christ. Both during Christ's life on earth and after, it was true in greater or less degree as Paul says: "We all, with unveiled face reflecting as a mirror the glory of the Lord, are transformed into the same image from glory to glory." They lived over again the life of Christ.

And as they lived over again his life, so they could continue his work, every one according to the measure of Christ's **[157]** life in him. As he was the light of the world, so they could be lights shining in the darkness. As he was the saving power, so they could be salt preserving the world from putrefaction.

And as they repeated his life and his work, so they would re-experience his sorrows and sufferings. If the world had hated him, it would hate them in the measure that they were like him (Mt. 10, 24-25). Many of them drank the same cup that he drank and were baptized with his baptism. It was not Paul alone that has carried in his body the dying of the Lord Jesus, and made up what was left of the suffering of Christ for men.

Since then there has been a long, long series of Christ-like lives on earth, of men and women in whom Christ has taken form. History has recorded some of them; but history itself is but slowly being christianized; it is only gradually learning to apply Christ's standards of greatness. It has wrapped the saint's robe about many a cloven hoof. It has left many a saint's aureole hidden under the felon's cap. Many it has forgotten forever. And yet they belonged to the assembly of the first-born who are enrolled in heaven. **[158]** They fed the hungry, clothed the naked, and cooled the feverish brow with the touch of love. They resisted injustice and poured oil in the wounds of its victims. They sought for truth when men had to pass through torture chambers to find her. They resisted prejudice, flung their reputation aside to grapple with bigotry, and stepped down the marble stairs of privilege to make the cause of God's poor their own. What a history that would be, if any man could read it, the history of all the truly Christian lives on earth! What a diversity there would be; the daring and the tender; the nurse-maid of babes and the ruler of states; all the shades of speculative opinion; men in the church and men out of the church; there would be first who would be last, and last who would be first. But this would characterize them all, that they were revolutionists, whether they knew it or not; that they tried in some way to overturn the throne of Satan and endeavored to make this world a habitation for God. A Christ-like life without putting forth Christ-like words and deeds is a delusion. And a putting forth of Christ-like words and deeds without checking evil and extending God's reign is inconceivable. Every **[159]** such life furnished a fulcrum for God's lever; a conservative influence to preserve whatever of purity and justice had already been gained; a source from which rivers of living water moistened the earth round about and prepared a place for whatever seeds of truth a future hand might drop.

But the scattering of isolated revolutionary personalities through society by no means exhausts Christ's conception concerning the human agencies in his revolutionary work. Christ established the church, and this formation of a revolutionary community is essential to his work. **[160]** Jesus not only bound men to himself; he bound them to one another. He founded a community, created a corporate feeling which differentiated them from the mass of men, gave them laws of their own, and established the rudiments of an internal organization. He prayed for their unity. He expected them to continue in this society after his own departure.

They did continue so. The interlacing fibres held true through the shocks of disappointment and persecution. After his death they naturally came together. After the resurrection they sought to perfect again their mutilated organization, showing thereby the sense of their unity, and the consciousness of a united mission (Acts 1, 15-26). This organizing impulse continued. They instituted new offices when needed (Acts 6, 1-6) and settled pressing questions in common (Acts 11, 1-18; 15, 1-29).

The expressions used by the apostles show that they regard the church as the new theocratic society and as a coherent organism. Peter calls it the elect race, the holy nation, God's own people, a holy and royal priesthood, a flock, a brotherhood, a spiritual house built up of living stones. Paul speaks of it as of a temple of the Spirit, a habitation of God. With him the conception of the church as a body, an organism with **[161]** various functions and differentiated organs, and yet with a unity of life, is fundamental for all his thinking and decisive in the smallest practical questions.

Christianity is not therefore a new philosophy, which a man may entertain in isolation. Christ's purpose was the establishment and extension of the Kingdom of God, the regeneration of human society. To this end he established an organization which was to be at the same time a realization of the Kingdom within its own limits, and the instrument for its propagation. Within this society Christ reigns; here his laws prevail and his spirit is the governing force. And from this society in turn his assimilating and conquering forces go out to extend the territory of his dominion. If Christ's purpose had been merely the conversion of individuals, the formation of the church would have been useful but not essential. Because his purpose was the immediate establishment and extension of a Kingdom, a society was absolutely essential.

And what are the functions of this society? **[162]** 1.) The first function of every organism is to maintain and strengthen its own peculiar life; and the first duty of the church is to maintain in its entirety, in its various local branches, and in its individual members, that life and spirit through which and for which it exists.

It is constantly absorbing new individuals who have the principle of the new life in them, but whose thoughts and habits have not yet been penetrated by it. The church has to nurture and train them, and to call forth the ripe fullness of the Christian virtues. It performs for the new-born spirit the same which the family performs for the infant. It furnishes the warmth and shelter within which the young life can grow. Jesus spoke of his disciples as being like mother, brothers and sisters to him (Mt. 12, 46-50). He promises those who have forsaken their property, or been cast off by their family, that they shall find compensation for it even in this life. Where there is a true Christian community this promise is realized in it; and on the other hand many a young faith has been snapped by the first storm of ridicule and opposition, because it stood like a solitary **[163]** sapling.

The church is to protect the growing faith until it is emancipated. There is strength in numbers. Few men can bear to stand entirely alone; certainly the young should not prematurely be exposed to so heavy a trial. When all the world counsels selfish prudence and worldly wisdom, a man may know in his soul that Christ is right against the world, and yet in the hours of weariness and fear it is a wonderful help to have others beside you who are one with you. Christ himself felt the need of the church in Gethsemane.

While he had been with the disciples, he had protected and encouraged them. Is it not as a substitute for his personal presence that at the same moment with the announcement of his departure, he lays upon them the new commandment of brotherly love? (John 13, 33-34). The visible brotherhood stands in the place of the visible Christ. We can watch this educational attitude of the church in Paul's letters. There were many in the churches who had not yet emancipated themselves from the old reverence for special **[164]** forms, the observance of sacred days, and the habit of regarding some food as ceremonially impure. When these people tried to foist their baby-jackets on the lusty limbs of the young church, Paul resisted them almost fiercely. But when it was a habit of mind which they were not yet able to strip off, he shows the utmost consideration for them, and advises those who had attained a broader view, voluntarily to descend to the lower position, as an elder brother shortens his steps that the younger may keep pace with him (Rom. 14).

But while the church protects the weak and gains for them free play to develop, it is not an institution to keep the weak brethren weak. It nurtures, but it also stimulates.

It makes it possible for the individual to obtain an insight into truth which he would never reach unaided. We all draw our ideas from a great public treasury. In secular life we are "heirs of all the ages." In our language, our literature, our inventions, our current conceptions [165] of life, we have a capital to which we are heirs at birth, and with which we are free to operate. Thus every new individual receives as a gift "a pair of seven-mile boots; he travels in twenty years a distance that humanity has traversed in twenty thousand" (Schäffle, I, 397.) The same is true in religious truth. Peter alone rose high enough to declare Jesus to be the Messiah, but the declaration, once made, became the property of all. There is in the church a certain quantity of truth in solution, with which he that moves in it becomes saturated almost without knowing it. The quantity varies in different Christian circles. But even where there is poverty of thought it is safe to say that the church furnishes to the individual more than he could acquire by himself. The church does for the spiritual life of a young member what a cultured family circle does for the intellectual and aesthetic life of its young members. Therefore Jesus could say that the feeblest member of the new society stood higher than the greatest prophet of the old.

Again, the church creates for its members a higher ethical standard than they would occupy if unaided. The church cherishes a high moral ideal; not as high as it should be; not always higher than that of individuals outside the church; but [166] probably always higher than the ideal generally prevailing in the world about it. And it not only passes laws, but it has sanctions to enforce obedience to them. Every society cultivates certain virtues and succeeds in infusing these into its members. It is the power of society which makes these moral precepts operative. Bravery is the prime virtue cultivated by army life, and cowards are scarce among army officers; on the other hand chastity and temperance are not considered as peculiarly soldierly virtues, and hence they are not nearly so frequent. The Indians prize stolid endurance of pain, and their young braves attain it. The Jesuit Order and the Salvation Army require obedience, and obedience flourishes among them. In short the demands made upon us by the society in which we move and the good opinion we prize, are for most of us the strongest incentives to right conduct.

Now here is a society which in most cases comprises for its members the best persons of their sphere of life. This society makes certain demands on the moral lives of its members. Those who respond to the demand are rewarded by the approval and respect **[167]** of men and women whom they themselves approve and respect. Those who disobey feel themselves under a cloud of suspicion and disapproval, and, what is hardest of all to bear, of sorrowing love. The effect of this cannot be overestimated. It rises with the intimacy existing in the brotherhood and with the holiness and discerning justice of its members. In one of the communistic communities of America the custom at one time existed of having a periodical meeting in which the members were reproved by one another for faults shown. The practice was discontinued after a time; not because it failed of effect, but because it was too painfully effective. Christ's rule of church discipline is based on this same principle. A reproof of three persons is more powerful than by one; and a reproof by the community is more powerful still, and indeed the last resource (Mt. 18, 15-20). In his promise to be present where two or three are gathered in his name it is likewise implied that he is present in a community in a manner different from his presence with an individual. He simply emphasizes that this peculiar operation **[168]** begins even with the smallest community, with but two or three (Mt. 18, 20). In the same way he invests the community with the power to forgive or retain sins; and a community does possess that power in the measure in which it has the Holy Spirit (John 20, 22-23). A striking instance of the moral force of a judgment passed by such a community is preserved in the case of Ananias and Sapphira.

The possibilities of moral impulsion inhering in the community have perhaps never yet been tried to the utmost. It is a power that must be reckoned with in the forecasts for the future development of humanity. Men doubt if it will be possible to relax the restraints of force and the driving power of hunger. Probably not, unless some other force is substituted. But such a force does exist in the social appetite, the hunger for approval, the natural faculty for imitation and emulation. In a bad society that appetite works toward the bad; a young tough and a young "society" man are both impelled to evil by the desire to stand well with their set. But in a healthily constructed society that appetite might do wonders. Here also it is **[169]** true: "To him that hath, is given, and from him that hath not, is taken even that which he hath."

A true religious community, therefore, small enough for all to know everybody, homogeneous enough for the members to be intelligible to one another, and holy enough to represent God, exercises an immense influence upon the moral life of its members. It not only imparts an ideal to them; it lays that ideal with effective force upon their consciences. It makes virtue and self-sacrifice contagious. The zeal for martyrdom in the early church was due to the spirit of the community more than to the courage of the individuals. The church can create any virtue in its members that it undertakes to create. It has in America in a high degree made the demand for chastity and temperance effective. On the other hand the business morality of its members is extremely open to reproach, because the church has been sadly backward in setting up a true ideal of business honesty and in outlawing those who transgress it.

Thus the church maintains [170] and strengthens its individual life in the members of its body. It brings them into direct contact with a large quantity of truth and wisdom, which they absorb and then carry out into the world. It replenishes in them that warmth of faith in the invisible realities, which the chilling contact of the world steadily withdraws. It lays upon their conscience a code of morals higher than that of the average humanity about them, and enforces its performance. It thus makes possible that revolutionary influence which consecrated men exercise upon the world about them; and by keeping alive the revolutionary spirit in them, it in turn ensures the assimilation of the newly entering members, and thus its own enduring vitality. The church in maintaining its own life is the nursery of Christian revolutionists.

We are as conscious as anyone how far the church has practically fallen short of this ideal. Its shortcomings are great in the standard of truth and righteousness which it has in various ages laid upon its members. They are even greater in the back of true Christian com-[171] munities. In some European countries there is no such thing as a body of people who gather in the consciousness that they are one in life, in order to build up that life in themselves. Frequently the church resists bitterly the formation of such circles. Yet the organizing instinct of Christianity, like the ideal aspirations of humanity, has never been absolutely repressed by human tyranny. The danger to the churches in America lies perhaps in two directions: first, that the ethical standard of the church is kept so little above the standard of the world, that "joining the church" implies no cross to be taken up, no profit to be abandoned, but rather a social function to be performed; thus worldly people flood the church under churchly forms, and the church loses its integrity and vitality. Second, that the churches, especially in the cities, mainly for pecuniary and aesthetic reasons, are swelled to an abnormal size. Their members are unknown to one another. They can go and come, do right or wrong, and no one knows. They are like young men afloat in a big city with no eye upon [172] them. A church suffering with hypertrophy of that sort may present a glowing appearance, but it is a sick organism, unable to perform the functions of a true Christian community.

2.) The next function that the church, like every other organism, has to perform, is that of growth.

It seems as if it were a divinely implanted impulse in every man to make propaganda for the moral and religious truths that have taken hold of himself. The same Providence that has provided some seeds with wings and others with hooks which carry them abroad, has had this care for the propagation of the truth.

In addition to that the duty of making disciples is enjoined upon us by Christ himself. He sent the twelve into the white harvest field of Galilee (Mt. 9, 36-10, 1). He sent them out at the end to make disciples of all nations (Mt. 28, 19). We see this discipling impulse at work in Peter's and Stephen's preaching, in Philip's conversation with the chance passer-by, in the dismissal by the church at Antioch [173] of its choicest men, in Paul's laborious missionary journeys, and in the entire history of the centuries. Every man feels that duty upon him, who holds, or thinks he holds, any truth which others do not possess. Every really living religious organization tries to multiply its members.

The danger in all this is, that it will be proselytizing and not discipling. Jesus says of the propaganda of the Pharisees that they were compassing sea and land to make one proselyte, but that when he had become so, they made him twofold more a son of hell than they themselves were (Mt. 23, 15). There is a difference between imparting to a man what one is conscious of possessing which would be a blessing to him; and trying to draw him in to feed one's pride in the organization and to sustain one's own confidence by the increase in members. Proselytizing is a grave danger in our churches and denominations, and those who are always appealing to the love of the people for their church or their denomination, are directly inciting to it. Yet as a general [174] thing it is probably true that missionary zeal is an indication of life, and its absence an indication of decay. Heretical parties that make a vigorous propaganda usually treasure some vital truth amid all fantastic trappings, and thoughtful men would do well to stay their denunciation and lovingly inquire what truth of God is striving to get itself born there.

The church will always be fairly safe in its endeavors to increase its membership, if it keeps its moral demands well above those prevailing in the world about it. If union with the church means a renouncing of reputation and profit, a selfish man will stay out, and the Christian who has become ambitious or avaricious will go out or be put out. If baptism, which Christ has placed at the door of the church, means really a putting off of many pleasant and luscious things, and a possible joining to the sufferings and the dying of Jesus (Rom. 6), then he only will ask for that initiation who has staked his all on Jesus Christ, as Israel staked their all on Moses at the Red Sea (I Cor. 10, 2). Christ showed **[175]** no anxiety of not having enough followers, but a great deal of not having the right sort. He warned men not to be like a man who begins to build a tower and has to stop when it is half-way up; or like a king that begins a war with an insufficient army. Let them count the cost before they join themselves to him. Let them remember that it may mean separation from family, loss of property, loss of life (Lk. 14, 25-35). Would they follow the Son of man? Then they must take the risk of being more homeless than the foxes and the birds of the heaven (Mt. 8, 18-22). Would they have eternal life? Let them sell all they have and give it away; a soldier in the skirmish-line of battle cannot carry a Saratoga trunk on his back (Lk. 18, 18-30).

The church is a picked company of soldiers whose efficiency depends more on their quality than on their number. The Broad Church thinkers are entirely right in insisting that the church is to benefit not only a small circle of the elect, but all men and the entire life of humanity. But they are wrong in thinking that this can best be accomplished by admitting everybody into the church by baptism **[176]** at birth. Christ was wiser. The same error underlies the zeal of many evangelicals in multiplying their members. Because they have made of Christianity merely a system for saving individuals, they naturally try to multiply those individuals. But in point of fact they are in danger of repeating the error that has been committed ever since Constantine, of making the church co-extensive with the nation. It becomes almost a matter of course for the children of Christian parents to join the church when they reach a certain age. The churches are scooping in the world and they are in danger of being swamped. Like Gideon's army they are too many to rout the Midianites.

Christ commanded an unremitting propaganda. He himself has given the example of an unwearying proclamation of the truth. But he was very wary about receiving men into his community. He discouraged them rather than the reverse. And the loftiness of the duties that he imposed on them was a self-acting check. He was constantly applying the winnowing fan. Here as everywhere, the Master is wiser than his prudent followers. [177] 3.) We have spoken of the self-preservation and growth of the church. But no organism is destined by God to live unto itself. It has an office in God's world corresponding to its individuality and endowment. Least of all was the church formed merely for its own sake.

The Christian church is not like the community on a Cunard steamer, shut off from the world and viewing the passing craft through opera glasses. Jesus did not join the Essene communities, who tried in solitude to live a pure and loving life. He founded a society which was to lead in the thick of the world a life higher than that of the world. Such a society must influence the general life about it, even if it should make no effort in that direction. It could not assert and live up to a system of ethics different from and superior to that of other men without influencing the standard of right everywhere. It could not cherish a supreme spiritual idealism without stimulating the ideal aspirations which God has implanted in every human being. The pillar of fire could not dwell [178] in Israel and be invisible to others. The knowledge of God's love and righteousness could not burn within the church and yet no ray of it lighten the darkness without.

But the church is distinctly forbidden to hide its light under a bushel. It was purposely mixed into the world as a woman carefully kneads the leaven into the dough. Activity is made the duty of the church; it is a steward managing the master's property according to the master's purposes; a servant doing business with trust funds. Jesus expected the multitude of its fruits to work toward the knowledge and exaltation of God among men (Mt. 5, 16; Jo. 15, 8). Paul trusted in the church, in spite of the weakness and lowliness of its members, to overcome the pride of Greek philosophy and Roman power (I Cor. 1, 26-29). He expected the manifold wisdom of God to be made known even to principalities and powers through the church (Eph. 3, 10). These expressions cannot be pressed to mean merely an extension of membership. They refer to the struggle of the church as a spiritual power with the spiritual forces ruling in the world [179] as a whole, and its victory [for] them. As Neander says (*Laben Jesu*, p. 136): "The aim toward which history is moving is, that Christianity is to become the world-governing principle." There are only three possibilities. It can flee out of the world; it can become like the world; it can make the world like itself. The first is asceticism, disobedience and cowardice; the second is suicide; the third is ceaseless conflict till a final victory. Which tallies with Christ's purpose? All his frequent sayings about taking up the cross, forsaking property and family, incurring suffering and death, have no sense, unless the church is to impinge upon the world and suffer from its angry reaction.

And such has in fact been the history of the church, and most so when it had most life. The antagonism between the free spirit of Christ and the ceremonialism of the Jews was not fully realized by them till they saw it demonstrated in the life of the church, in the violation of Sabbath laws and the neglect of ceremonial washings **[180]** by the disciples (Mt. 15, 1-20; Mk. 2, 23-28). The influence of Paul's continued preaching at Ephesus made itself felt in the trades that catered to superstition (Acts 19). Christianity is a force even in those who neither believe in it nor love it. It has been said with entire justice by James Russell Lowell that the high morality maintained by those who have thrown off the dogmas of the church, is yet due to the inherited purity and the moral atmosphere which generations of Christianity have created for them. It is the fashion at present to abuse the church for its conservative and reactionary influence on political and social progress. If by the church is meant the various ecclesiastical machines with titled and salaried hierarchies, then the church deserves much of the abuse that it gets. If, however, Christianity is fairly taken as a spirit and life which has hovered like a tongue of fire over consecrated men, and swayed the nations like a wind from heaven, then it must in fairness be conceded that the influence of Christianity on the **[181]** race has been incalculable. Schäffle, speaking of Christianity in his sociology, says: "The religious life has been a force of the first magnitude in the history of the world. It is as perceptible to-day as ever before that history turns on the axis of religion." A. Lange, who will not be charged with undue favor to Christianity, says in his *Geschichte des Materialismus* (1st ed., p. 535): "In surveying history in its grand total, it seems to me hardly doubtful that we may ascribe not only our ethical, but even our intellectual progress in large part to the moral but continuous influence of the Christian ideas." He adds, not without truth, as we shall see: "but that these ideas can develop their full effect only by breaking the ecclesiastical and dogmatic forms."

We ask now: How is the church to influence the world and overcome it? We grant that the church can withdraw individuals from the world. Can it do more? If so, how? What relation to secular society does the church demand for itself?

We can conceive of four diverging opinions.

First, that church and state [182] are co-extensive and synonymous. This is the ideal aimed at in the union of church and state. Every child becomes by birth a member of the state, and almost at the same time a member of the church by baptism. The prince is head of the state and also summus episcopus and head of the church. But the practical difficulties of this conception are too great even for those who ought logically to be its supporters. It is too clamorous a fact that church and world are not circles with an equal radius and that they will not coincide. So the realization of this view is postponed to another world and in practice the second view is adopted (Papal States?).

The second view is that the organs of the church and the organs of the state are distinct, but that the church is higher than the state and dominates it. This is the Roman Catholic idea of the two arms, which caused the medieval struggles between the popes and the emperors. The Roman Catholic church holds that all power is entrusted to it as to the vice-regent of Christ; princes hold their power by gift of the Church. The Church is independent [183] of the State, but the State is dependent on the Church. The church passes its own canonical laws, to which alone its ministers are subject. But the secular laws are subject to its revision, and the legal tribunals of the state are also the executors of the behests of the church. For instance, the church examines all literary publications, and the State destroys the books condemned by the Congregation of the Index. The church tries heretics and hands them over to the secular arm for execution of its sentence. That is the Catholic ideal of the theocracy.

The Catholic Church is right in asserting that the moral and spiritual life is superior to secular life and ought to govern it. It is wrong in binding up the moral and spiritual forces with a single organization, and confounding the supremacy of the latter with the rule of the former. It makes the Kingdom of God synonymous with the Kingdom of the Church. They are not necessarily synonymous. They have often been directly contradictory. [184] Just as the Old Testament church withstood Christ, so not only the Catholic church, but all the old and established churches have withstood him (Bishops in Parliament). Power has made them conservative. They have lost the revolutionary impulse. They have substituted the craftiness of politicians for the righteous zeal of prophets. The management of their affairs are gradually entrusted not to the most Christlike of their members, but to the ambitious, wealthy, worldlywise and scheming among them. There are those who hold the age of a church and the unbroken continuity of its organization to be the first proof that it is really the church of Christ. The very reverse seems to us to be true. The older and more firmly established a church is, the less likely is it to be spiritual and progressive. Therefore to construct an ecclesiastical organization and entrust to that the supreme guidance of the entire machinery of secular society is not only paralyzing to secular government, but destructive to the reign of God in that nation. The best service that can be rendered to the church is to keep it out of power.

This theocratic ideal therefore, which confounds the reign of God with the supremacy of an ecclesiastical [185] machine, is false, and, indeed, contradictory to the teachings of Jesus. Church and State will each do its work best, if its machinery is entirely unconnected with the machinery of the other. This has made the idea of religious interference in politics so odious that ecclesiastics interfere not for the sake of infusing righteousness, but of getting power for their church. That is the sure mark of the ecclesiastic as against the Christian, that he cannot distinguish between the progress and power of Christianity and the progress and power of his church.

Our reply to this second view, therefore, is that not only the supremacy of the church organization over the secular organization, but any mixture or inter-relation of the two, is detrimental to the very work which the church is to do for secular life. It unchristianizes the church, and when the salt loses its savour, wherewith shall society be salted?

The third view of the relation of the church to secular society is that the church should be indifferent to affairs of state. Its business is [186] to save souls. It is possible to live a Christian life in any form of society, therefore the forms are indifferent. This world is to pass away; it would be a waste of time to do anything for it. We must simply keep our lamps trimmed for the coming of the Master. If the world gets any indirect benefits from the life of the church, very well; but we need not aim to impart these benefits. A man may vote and do his duty as a citizen, but he does so as a citizen and not as a Christian. Christian morals are for regenerate men; it is an illusion to think of inducing the state to adopt them.

This position, so frequent in America, is the historical outcome of the protest against Catholicism. The Catholic church made the salvation of the individual dependent on the church and its means of grace; it exalted the church and depreciated the individual. Calvinism repudiated the church, exalted the individual by placing him solitary over against his God, and bent its energies to the salvation of individuals by personal experiences. In justly emphasizing this side [187] of the truth, it lost sight of the importance of society, and of the bearing of Christianity on the social organism. In addition to this, the type of Christianity prevailing with us is derived from the dissenters of England, who for generations had to battle for the right of simply being let alone by the State in doing their work of soul saving. They saw in the Established Church an evil union of church and state, and their thoughts on the relation of church and state were mostly limited to a protest against the Establishment. But both the religious value and independence of the individual, and the divorce of church and state, are now with us recognized facts; and it is time for us to examine candidly whether we have not burnt down the house to kill the rats, when we abandoned the theocratic idea in protesting against a false conception of it.

We have shown at length in the preceding that the very idea of the Old Testament is the interest of God in the life of human society, and that this **[188]** interest was not abandoned but adopted by Christ. Here is secular society, created by God, affecting us all, a power for good or evil, capable of being influenced by moral ideas. Shall that be indifferent to us? It is not. It is not indifferent to the most ardent believer in the speedy coming of Christ. He looks well to the plumbing of his house, to the social purity of the nurse that cares for his children, to the decency of their playmates, to the moral tone of the college to which he sends his boy, to the safety of the neighborhood in which he builds his house. Is not all that part of secular society? Is he selfish enough to look to the safety of his own family in these regards, and not to the safety of the thousands of families more helpless than his, whose health and safety and happiness depend in vast degree on the good or evil actions of their town, their state, their nation? Common sense teaches us all to value highly the character of the society we ourselves live in. Christian sense ought to make us take the same interest in the character of the society in which others live. Shall it be indifferent to us whether **[189]** the community of which we are part and on which we have influence, legalizes oppression, encourages vice, and commits a perennial murder of the innocents? To have the power to stop evil and not to do it – what is that?

We are pointed of the non-interference of Christ in affairs of government, and to the indifference of the apostles to politics and to social questions. Three cases are especially pointed out in which Christ refused to interfere. The case of Caesar's tribute money (Mt. 22, 15-22); of the Jewish tax (Mt. 17, 24-27); and of the division of an inheritance (Lk. 12, 13-21). It is argued from these cases that Christ draws a sharp line through human life, dividing it into secular and religious affairs, and that he renounced all jurisdiction or interest in the former. This interpretation has been originated by people who did not believe in Christ's ethics and supposed that Jesus did not either. Suppose that a Roman or Jewish tax-collector would come to Jesus and demanded the tax; suppose it were an onerous and excessive tax; suppose that the collector had after the manner of Oriental **[190]** officials, added his own bakshish to the legal amount. What would Jesus do? "If any man would go to law with thee and take away thy coat, let have thy cloak also" (Mt. 5, 40). He would quietly pay the amount demanded, and then perhaps just as quietly tell the man that he was endangering his soul through covetousness. He would reserve his right of judging whether the demand was just or not, and of saying so too; but he would not violently resist evil. That he preserved his inward freedom of judgment is evident from his conversation with Peter on the payment of the half-shekel (Mt. 17, 24-27). He felt that he was a child in his Father's house and free to go and come; yet he paid what people demanded "lest he cause them to stumble." In the third case (Lk. 12, 13-40) he refused to interfere for two reasons. First, it was not his business to be a judge or divider. The laying down of large principles and the investigation of specific instances are distinct functions. A pastor in a New England village might be very much interested in the labor question, and yet wisely **[191]** refuse to decide whether a firm could and ought to grant a particular rise in wages demanded by their men. His second reason for refusing is also apparent from the context. "Take heed, and keep yourselves from all covetousness." The whole request, to his mind, proceeded from covetousness, the vice that animated the rich fool of whom he goes on to speak, and that caused all this fretting and worrying over the future, which frustrates the enjoyment of life and destroys man's trust in God. He took no interest in helping this man to squabble with his brother, and to get a lot of money which would ruin his soul afterwards. Christ's attitude toward wealth in general makes his attitude in this case entirely natural and logical. But was he indifferent to social inequality? Read the parable of Dives and Lazarus. Was it nothing to him when widows were wronged out of their houses and oppressed by unjust judges? Read the parable of the unjust judge and the rebuke to the Pharisees. Verily it is the old blindness of the scribes over again, when men assert that **[192]** he was indifferent to justice and mercy in daily life, who made such indifference the sufficient ground for condemnation on the day of judgment (Mt. 25, 31-46). The parable of the Good Samaritan is being re-enacted on a grand scale in our day. Entire classes of society are being stripped and beaten by robbers. Is it again the priest and

Levite who pass by, busy in matters of religion, and the heretic and alien who lends a hand? Or if they come upon the robbers in the very act of their guilt, shall they assure the robbers of their divine right to rob, and wait on one side till the victim is half dead, and then begin their charitable care for him?

We are told that the apostles attempted no interference in politics and no leveling of social classes. It is true. Paul told Philemon to treat his runaway slave Onesimus kindly; he did not tell him that slavery was wrong. What a stock-in-trade that was for the advocates of slavery forty years ago! But, Paul to the contrary notwithstanding, we have abolished slavery and hold it to be wrong. The same thing is **[193]** going to be done with the social questions now before us, and those who hide behind Paul's noninterference are again going to bring shame upon Christianity. Their guilt lies in making of Christianity a set of rules instead of a living spirit. The question is not what Paul did then, but what he would do now. He was in his day a radical, who made havoc of old laws and notions, and cleared the deck for a new society. Thanks to his gallant fight, modern society has in some points passed leagues beyond the society in which he moved, and now his radicalism becomes our conservatism. He that adheres most strictly to Paul's rules of conduct, will most fatally deny Paul's principles and spirit. His decisions on what was lawful and prudent to do are buoys which he anchored at the farthest points to which in his day the channel of the future had been explored. We shall use them best by keeping to the direction he marked out and passing beyond them, and not by padlocking our boat to his buoys. The early Christians **[194]** did not try to ameliorate poverty by legislation, did they? How could they? Did Nero ask them for advice about his laws? Did Roman procurators invite them to vote on a constitutional amendment forbidding the persecution of Christians? They were glad if they could keep clear of politics and continue their hand-to-hand work in peace. It is different with us. We are now the citizen kings of our country, and it will be as criminal for us to leave unjust laws on our statute books, as it would have been for a converted king in the first century any longer to oppress his subjects.

The idea that the followers of Christ can be indifferent to the conditions of society about them finds some show of defense in the letter of the Scriptures, but it is condemned by the spirit of Christ. Such indifference is sin. Its guilt increases with the spread of democracy which thrusts power upon us, and with power responsibility. It denies Christ's conception of religion, who taught us that there is no way of treating God right except by treating our fellow-men right, and that the only plane upon which Christianity can be exercised is the plane of social life. **[195 - Blank] [196 - Blank]** **[197]** It remains to find a fourth conception of the relation of the church to secular life which will avoid the evil of the others. Indifference is wrong. A union of organization is dangerous. We want a separation of the organizations, and an interpenetration of influences. The church must be independent of the state, neither oppressed by its commands nor bribed by its support. And it must as a body abstain from all attempts to control the machinery of government or to fill its offices. On the other hand it is free to influence the ethical conceptions of the people and to stimulate the people to righteous actions. And under our form of government the convictions of the people are the final source of legislation. All influence exerted upon the mind of the people will finally issue in concrete form.

The church has the prophetic office in humanity. Because it is in contact with God, its conscience quickened, its ethical discernment clarified, its moral courage and **[198]** energy strengthened, it is to be the teacher of society. It is to discern injustice where it is hidden to others by force of habit. It is to hear the sob of pain in the outcast classes whom others pass unheeded. It is to detect the sallow face of tyranny hiding behind the mask of patriotism and benevolence. Who is fit to do this if the church is not? Society rolls heavily on its way. What has always been so, seems divinely right to the mass, even if it is diabolically wrong. They must be made to see. Men feel their own pains acutely, but they are dull to the sorrows of others which they have never known. Men with the divining-rod of sympathy must pass through the nation and stop and say: "there is a deep well of tears here, hidden underground." Men must be made to feel. Men are slothful to self-sacrificing action. They see a wrong; they call it wrong; but they do not stop it. They must be made to act. They need leaders who will show the way, and if need be, break a way with the spears in their breast. **[199]** There was a time when the life of a nation depended on the goodness of a monarch and his subordinates. Then it was proper for influential men to exert moral influence on the king and expect great things from his personal justice and benevolence. But with the rise of democracy the people have become the sovereign. The personal character of our chief magistrate means far less to us than the personal character of an absolute king means to his subjects. The moral education of the people is the formation of the future. That task is the rightful province of the church. The permanence of free institutions and the health of a nation depend on the general diffusion of intelligence and morality. The church can diffuse them. If in the swirling eddies of modern life a heap of ignorance and filth is swept together, and the cumbersome machinery of government is slow to reach it, the church is mobile and can invade it with light and cleanness. It can kindle the flame of patriotism and devotion to the public good in the hearts of the young. [200] Nations are moved by currents of thought and feeling that sweep through them. Sometimes these thoughts are just and noble, and yet find but slight response. Often they are base, originated by demagogs and inciting to evil passions, and they find a ready response. The nation is like the resonant case of a musical instrument; one side vibrates and the whole resounds. It is of the utmost importance that the just emotions shall be passed on and bad emotions stopped. We could conceive of an enlightened, spiritual church, spread through all the nation, deaf to party cries, alive to the voice of right. A cry of angry passion is raised by a designing party leader; paid newspapers take it up; party followers declaim; newspapers in search of sensations respond; the people are roused; they think there must be something in so much noise; their pride is stroked with nettles; there will be an outbreak. But now these emotions find everywhere points of resistance. The most respected people everywhere treat the matter calmly and with sense. They act as bits of non-conducting medium on an electric current; like the soft [201] pedal of a piano on a sound. They frustrate an attempt on the welfare of the nation, and discourage similar attempts for the future. But suppose that a just and true thought is uttered, which ought to receive public attention. It conflicts with established interests; no large party advocates it; some newspapers are studiously silent; others distort the matter; the people are not awake to the importance of it. Now again that wide-branching nervous apparatus of righteousness responds. It sends thrill upon thrill through the body politic. The people wake up. Newspapers find it profitable to discuss the cause. Finally selfishness itself takes it up. The social organism, like the human body, has its nervous apparatus. The nerves which look to the gratification of the lower and selfish instincts are always alive. They work almost by reflex action. But it is of the highest value to have a nervous system which finds its centre in the conscience and will respond to the nobler sensations. This function can be exercised by the church.

But if it is to exercise this function, the church must be enlightened enough [202] not to be hood-winked by ecclesiasticism of any sort. And above all it must have a standard of public ethics superior to that prevailing in politics. It must be clear on the application of Christian principles to public affairs.

That clearness is lacking as yet. Men of refined moral sensibility in private life have a crude and rudimentary conscience for public life. This is an evil effect of the past. When the people had no power in the state, there was no need of instructing them how to use such power. Now the need has arisen. The people have public duties and they should have public ethics. Steam and electricity are drawing society together and compacting it. The functions of the state are bound to increase. The welfare of the individual is becoming increasingly dependent on social action and construction. Who is to teach the people what public righteousness is? Shall they be left to the newspapers, or to the tender mercies of the vote-hunting stump orator? A new need has arisen for Christian teaching and the church is very slow to respond. **[203]** On the whole Christian thinkers are discouraged from giving attention to social and political questions. There is a feeling that they are passing beyond their calling. Evangelistic and edifying preaching and writing is the only sort that finds real approval. But to our mind the very fact that the staid denominational papers and the wealthy men in the church discourage the handling of social questions is presumptive evidence that they ought to be handled and that that is the sore spot of our church life. Christianity has fairly penetrated the simpler relations of individual and family life with its ethical ideas. But the more complex relations of industrial and political affairs have not yet been so penetrated, and the church is so far from making a Christian public morality effective, that it is not even approximately clear in its own mind what a Christian public morality would be. Schäffle in his great work on "The Formation and Life of the Social Organism" says (I, 417):

> "A true public morality has not yet come into effect. If not only a private morality for private citizens, **[204]** but a public morality for public relations really prevailed to-day in the family of Christian nations, then entire classes of the people could not be abandoned to wretchedness and legally disinherited by the jobbing of the exchange, and whole nations could not be given over to military despotism. The chief source of social misery at present is not that our private ethics is not applicable to public affairs, but that a public morality for the more complex public affairs does not exist; morality has lagged behind the glorious progress of intellectual culture."

If morality lags, it is because the morality-making organism lags, and that organism is the church. Christian people will do well to give all cheer to those who have bravely put their hand to this tremendous task, and to ward off as enemies to the Kingdom of God those who would drug the body of Christ into stupor.

This we hold to be the duty of the church toward the collective life of humanity. By its keener sensibility it is to notice wrong and suffering where others do not see it and call attention thereto. By the guidance [205] of the Spirit it is to have a clearer perception of ideal justice than others and is to impart this to society at large. By its superior moral daring it is to sustain the unpopular causes until they have become popular. It is to resist the materialistic and pessimistic tendencies of literature and philosophy by its pure spiritualism, and stimulate the idealism and the devotion to duty latent in men. Lotze says: "Only the single living spirits are the centres of force in the course of history; all general ideas which are to be realized and to become a power, must first be condensed in their living individualities, and then by action and reaction among them spread out and obtain general recognition." It is exactly this prophetic office which the church is to fulfill. It multiplies the number of such centres of power and stimulates them by association. Therefore its effect is not to be measured by the number of its converts only. It is well known that judged by the converts Christian missions are not gaining on heathenism, but the reverse. But the Christian ideas of God, the Christian [206] ethics, the duty of mercy and self-devotion, are spreading faster than the converts. Christ commanded to disciples – not of all men, – but all nations, and it looks as if Japan, India and China were to be brought under the actual sway of Christ faster in the bulk than in minute particles.

4.) Finally it is a function of the church to lead society in action. We have discussed the prophetic office of the church in leading the moral <u>thought</u> of humanity. But it is not to stop with thought. Philosophy is content to teach and to disseminate ideas, and for that reason philosophy is always the property of the few. As long as an idea remains abstract it will leave the mass of men indifferent; they see nothing in it. "Action is the word of the people," says Mazzini. "It would be false," says Schäffle, "to expect the progress of ethics merely from the extension of the circle of <u>ideas</u>. Great aims of <u>action</u>, of practical association, are the means of causing popular feeling to give birth to higher ethical norms" (I, 605).

Plato dreamed of an ideal republic; Christ instituted it. The Christian church [207] immediately realized just those social principles which humanity has been in travail with for the last 150 years. If the church has backslidden often, it has repented often; and the ideal and impulse have never been totally lost.

The splendid parole of the French Revolution: "Liberty, equality, fraternity," contains the social principles of the church.

There is liberty in it. It knows no compulsion save that of love, and no command apart from the categorical imperative of duty.

There is equality in it. Again and again the apostles tried to carry the fashion of the rest of the world into their little society, and to have ranks and grades of honor. Jesus always rebuked it. "Ye know that [208] the rulers of the nations lord it over them, and their great ones exercise authority over them. Not so shall it be among you; but whosoever would become great among you shall be your minister; and whosoever would be first among you shall be your servant; even as the Son of man came not to be ministered unto, but to minister, and to give his life a ransom for many." The only title to greatness in the new society is service. The only way to honor is in stripping one's self of it. Is there any higher ideal than that? And yet the equality desired by Jesus is not the dead level equality of the doctrinaire. He recognizes the difference of endowment and the aristocracy of character. He founds the apostleship. He singles out Peter as the solid man whom he can trust for yeoman's service. Not all are qualified for leadership. Setting the born leaders at work is no violation of equality, but communism in the highest form of property: human ability.

There is fraternity in it. And on that score even its gainsayers must acknowledge the pre-eminence of the church. Fraternity was the weak point in the triad of the French Revolution. Men had [209] far more to say about liberty and equality than about fraternity. But see the young church. They were "one heart and soul"; "they had all things in common"; there was "not among them any that lacked." No suffering nor inequality was tolerated (Acts 6, 1-6). We see them gathered at night to pray for one of their number who was in prison (Acts 12, 12). We see them falling upon the neck of a parting brother, kissing him and weeping sore (Acts 20, 37). What a spirit of tenderness, of mutual forbearance, of anxiety for one another's welfare breathes from their letters, their greetings, the little incidental remarks! That is the social spirit. Right is the chisel that smooths the stones; love is the mortar that holds them together. The society of the future is to be an edifice of wider arches and bolder curves than the present. But that will throw a greater pressure on every stone. Will they stand the strain? Will they hold together? It may be that the builders of the future will yet come to the church to learn what cements it so well. Churches quarrel, it is true; so do denominations. But observation inclines us to believe that they are far more peaceful and compact than lodges, trade unions and political [210] associations.

Christ included those superb words in his idea of society. But he did not, like the revolutionary parties of to-day, wait with their realization for a distant future. He began straightway. He lived in a society that always extorted obedience by force. He asked for obedience, but only the obedience of freedom. He lived in a society organized throughout on the aristocratic plan and without even the idea of equality before the law. He abrogated rank, and made the towel with which a slave washes the feet of the master to be a badge of distinction and the symbol of citizenship in his Kingdom. He lived in a society cleft and rent like volcanic ground after centuries of earthquakes; fissures made by nationality, by creed, by rank, by pride of learning. He laid the hand of the Jew in the hand of the Samaritan and said: You are brothers; love each other. He said to the man of wealth and rank: Leave your wealth, step down from your privileges, that you may be a brother to us. Jesus anticipated the evolution of centuries, and by anticipating it, brought it about. [211] Sociology to-day has no image to represent a true society more perfect than that by which Paul expressed the nature of the Christian church: a body with many members. Paul formulated the theory; Christ created the fact.

The maintenance of a true Christian community is itself a prophetic action. It educates its members; it educates its beholders, just as the mere existence of the North American republic has influenced the political thought of the world.

But the idea of the church as Christ's body has another side to it. Paul uses the illustration mainly to teach the dependence of all the members on Christ, the head, and their interdependence on one other. But without in any way straining the simile, we may say too, that Christ's body is Christ's means of action. As a man's hands carry our the will of his mind and his tongue speaks his thoughts, and as the mind is powerless without the body, and hampered by a paralyzed body, so the spiritual Christ makes himself practically felt in human affairs through the church. [212] It furnishes him with lips to speak his thoughts, with feet to go his errands, with hands to lift up the sick and to check the blow of cruelty. Generally speaking, if the church is paralyzed and irresponsive to the will of the Head, or if it has fallen to reveling and made itself drunk with the wine of Mammon, then the will of Christ will remain unperformed. Who will say how often that has happened?

But when the church performs the office of a sound body, it will not only speak Christ's thoughts, but repeat his actions. He went about doing good, relieving suffering and drying tears. The church has done much in the same direction. Hospitals did not exist before the Christian era. There was some organized care for orphans in imperial Rome, but they were cared for, not so much because they were destitute, as because they were children of Roman citizens. Christian philanthropy has always carried the first torch into the dark sub-cellars of human society. **[213]** Christianity drove Howard into prison reform. Christianity moved to the institution of ragged school, of the Raube Haus, of the great institutions for the epileptic at Bielefeld. The work which makes life tolerable to the blind and the deaf-mute is still mainly in Christian hands. The Catholic Sisters of Mercy and the Protestant deaconesses have carried mercy into war itself. The Red Cross shows the animating impulse by its form. The educational work for the colored people, for the Indians, for heathen nations, is almost entirely in the hands of the church. It furnishes the workers, a[nd] it furnishes the bulk of support.

Revolutionary agitators often cry down this work of charity. Ther[e] is evil in it, especially if the causes producing wretchedness are left untouched, and only the effects are [to] be healed. And yet the church is truer in its instincts of humanity than those who would let misery pile up in order to use its stench as a means of agitation. The Christian charities keep alive in society the tenderness for suffering and the ind[igna]tion against the wrong that cau[ses] **[214]** it, and that indignation gives the moral dignity to social reform agitation, which would otherwise be a selfish clamoring for rights. The most effective protest against wrong is not raised by the man who paces up and down with folded arms and pours forth abuse, but by the man who pillows the victim's head on his breast and then says to him that struck him: "This is your work." When the Christian church, in caring for the suffering, begins to see who causes the suffering and boldly to say what it sees, its protest will borrow a double force from its self-sacrifice.

Apart from the actual suffering alleviated or prevented by the charitable work of the church, it serves a prophetic purpose. It serves to bring society generally to the same humane position. The charities begun by the church are taken up by the state. At first hospitals were maintained only by private charities; now it is part of the functions of a municipality to care for the sick. Institutions for the blind and deaf are established or subsidized by state or county appropriations. The care of the strong for the weak **[215]** of the community for its members, which was at first voluntary, becomes compulsory. It was religious; it has become civil. The ethical standard of society has been raised by Christian action as well as by Christian thought.

The historical Christ; the invisib[le] Spirit; the visible church; the[se] are the forces of God in human history. And they are revolutiona[ry] forces.

Christ initiated the revolution[n,] marked out its direction, warned against the dangers, organized his army, carried the revolutionary standard before them, and consecrated the cause with his blood.

Through his Spirit he is still invisibly but powerfully present with his army. His Spirit strikes the shackles of baseness and superstition from their limbs and puts them on their feet as freemen. It binds them together by remo[ving] **[216]** old prejudices, and infusing love and a common enthusiasm. And it works among them a constant renewal of energy and sacrifice to carry forward the struggle to the end.

Every man who has promised allegiance to Christ and has his Spirit within him, is a revolutionary element, carrying on a guerrilla warfare, if no more. But in spite of apparent disjointedness there is a secret unity among them. Recruits are sought, filled with the enthusiasm of the army, and instructed in the warfare. The army resists the present Prince of this World by word and deed, levies the authority of his laws, refuses to submit to his officers, levels his entrenchments, and builds others where the flag of the true King is kept flying, and whence the conquered territory is maintained and extended.

[217]

CHAPTER IV

THE NEW LAW

The religion of Jesus is above all things a practical religion. It is life within, but not a life that stays within. Its source is from above; its manifestation is on earth. ("Faith apart from works," says stern old James, "is dead" (James 2, 26). Claiming to know Christ, and yet not keeping his commandments, is a lie, says tender John (I John 2, 4). This whole central doctrine of the Kingdom of God on earth gives the lie to any Christiani[ty] so spiritual or otherworldy that it does not change the manner of life of all who accept it.)

Jesus founded a new and higher community on earth, and that implies ne[w] and higher laws. His community is revolutionary and in opposition to the existing state of things; to be in keep[ing] with this character, the new laws must also differ from the existing rules of life.

Quite in accord with this supposition we find that as soon as the tendencies of his teaching were clearly understood, Jesus was charged by the representatives of the old order with "destroying the law and the prophets." He emphatically denied th[e] **[218]** charge. He said that it was not his purpose to destroy, but to fulfill and establish. He illustrated his meaning in the case of several of the main moral laws (Mt. 5, 21-48). The old law forbade murder under penalty of the judgement. Very well; Jesus did not break down this law and permit murder. He was so far from it that he considered a man who only hated his brother as worthy of the judgement which the old law set upon murder, and the use of the commonest words of abuse, to his [mind] were worthy of cognizance by the sup[...] court of the nation and of punish[ment] in the Gehenna of fire. It was the same w[ith] other commandments. The old law fo[rbade] adultery. Jesus forbade it too and every lustful look in addition. Th[e] old law forbade false swearing. Je[sus] forbade all swearing, and of course w[hen] his disciples swore no oath at all [...] could not well wear a false [...]. It was not the purpose of Jesu[s] to break down the difference [be]tween right and wrong, good and evi[l] and to give his followers a reckless licence. About the circle of the law he described another, concentric with that and enclosing it. In that se[nse] he did not [d]estroy, but fulfil it. [219] Yet there was a sense in which Jesus was breaking down the law. If the form of the legislation was confused with its essence, and its interpretation with its spirit, then he found himself in decided conflict with it. It is very possible that at the early stage of his work when he preached the Sermon on the Mount he was not yet fully conscious how much the law as the scribes held it differed from the law as it appeared to him. It is the privilege of a young man who is still in retirement, that he can gather from the ideas confronting him in society those which find him, and the detached though[ts] which he expresses to older men may meet with their approval. But when he enters on public life, he must think and say, not what he loves to think of, but what is needful to be said. The people perhaps are intensely interested in questions to which[h] he has given no thought because they seemed to him idle or indifferent. He and others became conscious of the real divergence of thought between him and the people, and the interest of truth compels him to take the con[tro]versial attitude more than he [had] ever expected. Jesus also advan[ced] in wisdom. He met questions [one] [220] by one. The peculiarity of his knowledge was not that he knew all things at once, but that he knew each thing rightly when he met it. His tone toward the representatives of the old law became more controversial as he went on; it was because he perceived more and more clearly how far he and they were apart.

When he asserted his allegiance to the law, he was thinking of the law as he had it in his heart. When the Pharisees charged him with breaking down the law, they were thinking of the law as they had it in their minds. And those two laws were different laws, just as the Christianity of George Fox, the Quaker, and that of John Henry Newman were different Christianities.

He found himself at variance with them in the application of the law to single cases. They found a world of difference between swearing by the temple and by the gold of the temple, by the altar and by the gift on the altar (Mt. 23, 16-22). Catching water that fell from the sky on the Sabbath, and catching water that fell from a wall, made all the difference between righteousness and sin. With [221] that sort of casuistry he had no patience. If that was their law, he had to knock it down because it obstructed the ways of God. They were forever sitting up rules; he was forever getting at principles. And the man who has found a principle, moves on different lines than the man who follows a rule. The man with a rule gives five cents to every beggar that asks. The man with a principle may give nothing to one, and a whole day's time and five dollars to the next. To the man with a rule he seems a very irresponsible and incomprehensible creature. It is a paradox when James calls the perfect law a law of liberty (James 1, 25). Law and liberty seem contradictions. Yet that law of liberty is the law of the Christian commonwealth. Its full-grown citizens have freely accepted it and freely they follow it. They discern the real nature of every case, and follow that and not the outward appearance. So they cross and re-cross the usual lines of conduct, and seem to the staid planets of a wee solar system as eccentric as a comet; a[nd] **[222]** yet the comet is as consistent as they only in a wider orbit. Jesus was always puzzling the people. He preached purity and associated with the impure. He worked a miracle for a beggar and refused it to a king. He called men to come to him, and when they came he warned them off. He spoke with the utmost frankness and again refused to speak when it seemed most needed (Mt. 21, 23-27). Against that kind of men the cry of lawlessness will always be raised. And justly. They are a disturbing element. Their influence is revolutionary.

So that was the general attitude of Jesus to the law as he found it. In general he considered his influence to be conservative and not destructive. He established no new principles of morality. He accepted those which have their basis in the nature of man and have been expressed with greater or less clearness in all human societies. But he also regarded them as merely approximate, susceptible of extension in scope, of greater clearness in statement, and **[223]** of more wisdom in application. And by changing the degree of emphasis, by grouping them about a central principle, by lending them a new impulse, and by endowing men with the Spirit as their interpreter, he has in effect established a new system of ethics.

The central principle of his system is the law of love. In that hangs the whole law. He that loves a man will not rob him. He that truly loves a woman will not wrong her. Love gives the quick discernment for the sorrows and joys of the loved one, and the readiness to keep sorrow away and bring joy near even at cost to one's self.

Christ loved. All the parts of his life open to that key. Even his anger, his denunciations, his prophecies of woe were due to his love. Therefore his follower must love. A lack of love gives the lie to all professions of attachment to God (I John 4, 20-21). It vitiate[es] religious belief, knowledge, charity, martyrdom itself (I Cor. 13, 1-3). It turns the odor of sacrifice into a stench before God (Mt. 5, 23-[...]). **[224]** Love covers faults and wakes all excuses that can be made; therefore cruel words and harsh judgments are sin, for they proceed from a lack of love (James 3, 11).

Love not only refrains from doing wrong. It implies doing good. Love is the unifying impulse. Love is the self-imparting impulse. To have seen another hungry, thirsty, naked, or in distress, and not to have shared with him, convicts a man of lovelessness and ranges him on the left side in the day of judgement (Mt. 25, 31-46). The law of Christ is not only to put no unnecessary burden on your fellows, but to take some of their burden on yourself (Gal. 6, 2). The law of Christ knows no limit of love either in its breadth or in its depth. In breadth it floods over the demarcation of family, kinship, nationality, race. It wipes out the line between Jew and Samaritan, Greek and Barbarian, Saxon and Celt, orthodox and heretic. In depth it stops only where the fountain of life springs up. The laying down of life has both demonstrated the nature of love to us, and made the laying down of our own lives a duty (I John 3, 16). Negatively Christian love means abstinence from harm; positively it means the **[225a]** bestowal of good at cost to ourselves.

The kind of love on which Christ was compelled to dwell most, was love unrequited. It is natural to love where we are loved. Even publicans and Gentiles do that (Mt. 5, 43-48). The real test of the divine love begins when love finds no response, or the response of hatred. It is only when we are able to love our enemies, to do good to those who hate us, and to pray for those who despitefully use us, that we give proof of being sons of our Father in heaven. Christian love begins where natural love stops. Therefore Jesus has dwelt especially on that which lies beyond.

If we are wronged, Jesus commands us to forgive, whenever he who has wronged us desires our forgiveness, even though it be seven times in one day (Lk. 17, 4). Not to forgive is to put ourselves outside the pale of God's forgiveness (Mt. 6, 14-15), for our debt to God is to our neighbor's debt to us, as twelve million dollars is to thirty-five dollars (Mt. 18, 21-35). If the other has no sense of wrong, it is still not right for us to leave the matter as it is. The initiative **[225b]** of reconciliation lies with us (Mt. 5, 23-24) and we are not excused till we have tried all means to convince him of his wrong (Matt. 18, 15-17). The desire to forgive must always be present. Christ prayed the Father to forgive those who crucified him, although they asked for no forgiveness. He forgave Peter though we know of no request for forgiveness, but only of tears. Love survives wrong.

And love overcomes wrong. It is natural to resent wrong. The resentment of wrong in others is the utterance of the same moral nature in us which, as the voice of conscience, protests against wrong in ourselves. We are right in resenting evil; we ought to resent it and stop it. But the question is, how? The old way is that of retribution. It turns back the evil upon him who has committed it. If he has robbed his neighbor of an eye, that neighbor or someone else in his stead must rob him of an eye also. Thus the protest of society against wrong is expressed, and future outbreaks of evil are checked by the fear of suffering in one's self the pain which one inflicts. That is the old law: "an eye for an eye, and a tooth for a [226] tooth." Jesus does not condemn this law any more than he condemns the law not to kill, not to swear falsely, and to love your neighbor. Like these others it is a good law as far as it goes, but it is not effective enough to satisfy him. He was more desirous of checking evil than anyone else, and yet he forbade his disciples to resist evil by returning it in kind. Why? Because he found that evil can best be checked by not returning it.

Suppose a man strikes you on the right cheek. You strike him back. Very likely you strike him harder than he struck you. He gets angry. He has quite forgotten that he was the aggressor and feels only the tingling of his own cheek. It is three to one that he will strike once more, and that you will part in a blaze of anger, and like Sampson's foxes will carry the fire into all the neighborhood. You have not checked evil but sown it abroad. Or take the more favorable case; suppose that the matter rests after you have returned the first blow. Certainly there will be no love between you. [227] The aggressor, if he is very impartial, will think you are quits; and if he is only an ordinary man, he will think himself hard used and pass his anger on to somebody else, his wife perhaps, or his children. There is no repentance in the matter, no recognition of the wrongness of wrong. The man may become more careful of his fists, especially toward you who have proved the possession of an equal pair. Otherwise there is nothing altered. The chastised dog fears the whip, but remains a dog. And the man, having been subjected to the same argument for righteousness as the dog, learns the same lesson of prudence, and what else can he learn?

Now suppose Christ's way is adopted. The blow is given, but none is returned. The evil stops there. He that receives it, certainly does not pass it on. And as for him that gave it, he is almost sure to feel regret very soon after. He will feel small and mean, and long for a dark place in which to hide himself. Paul has compared the pain suffered by those who have thus had evil answered by kindness with the pain of burning coals tangled in the hair **[228]** and burning through the scalp (Rom. 12, 20). It is an excruciating image, and sounds as if Paul had gone through the experience. The return of the blow would have aroused pugnacity, wounded self-love, vanity, everything that blurs and confuses the moral judgement. The blow given and not returned stands in naked meanness, and compels even the man who gave it to take the part of the innocent sufferer. The evil has been checked. It has been confined within the narrowest compass, and its repetition has been rendered unlikely all around. Evil has been overcome by good.

A brief survey would show how prominent this law was in Christian teaching. Jesus states the principle, and explains it by three supposed cases; the command in every case is, quietly to submit to the wrong, and even to do more than is demanded (Mt. 5, 38-42.) When the disciples proposed after the fashion of Elijah to call down fire on a Samaritan village which had refused the simplest duty of hospitality, he rebuked them (Lk. 9, 51-56). An ancient gloss adds his words: "Ye know not what manner of spirit ye are of." Christ never used his power to harm. This became so well understood that men who were convinced of his miraculous power offered him affronts without fear. In Gethsemane he forbade his disciples from **[229]** resisting what surely was a great wrong, and before Pilate he declared that this nonresistance was delibera[te] and essential to the nature of his Kingdom (Mt. 26, 50-53; Jo. 18, 36). Paul repeatedly warns against rendering evil for evil (I Thess. 5, 15; Rom. 12, 17). He calls it a defect to have a lawsuit at all, and says the normal thing for a Christian would be to submit to wrong (I Cor. 6, 7). He begs his brethren not to let their minds be embittered by the persecutions they were suffering, but to bless their persecutors, to do good to their enemies, and to leave vengeance to God (Rom. 12, 12-21). And Peter speaks of the patient endurance of wrong as the chief way of following in the footsteps of him "who, when he was reviled, reviled not in again, and when he suffered, threatened not" (I Peter 2, 19-24; 3, 8-18). There are few Christian teachings so frequently and emphatically stated, and few so little obeyed or even comprehended.

Perhaps it is because this law is distinctively Christian. Only a Christian can make it work. The man who submits to wrong must be a brave man, so that it will be apparent [that] his submission is not due to cowa[rdice.] He must also be a man who ca[n] **[230]** discern [the] wrong [and point it out,] if necessary. Submission does not imply silence. When Jesus was struck in the high priest's court, he did not strike back, but he calmly pointed out the wron[g] (John 18, 22-23). In many cases no word at all will be necessary. The unconscious bearing of the man will show that he is neither too dull nor too cowardly to resist, but that in him the majesty of goodness has been insulted. Another thing needful is love for the offender. If the blow is taken with sullen bitterness or with proud scorn, it will have no softening and overcoming influence.

But given a man with the righteousness, courage and love of a true Christian, and submission is the most effective treatment of wrong. It stops it. Retribution does not. It is like that experiment in physics: a row of balls hang side by side; one is moved and swings against the next; that recoils and clashes against the first, and soon the whole row are battering against one another till finally the force is lost by friction. The law of the conservation of energy holds in the moral [231] [world too. But if a good man receives] the shock and lets the vibrations of pain run through his own heart alone, the evil has been caught and extinguished. It is the heroism of the soldier who clim[be]d on the roof and rolled on the fire-brand which endangered the city. In fact it is the idea of the cross of Christ. Evil always brings suffering, somewhere, to someone. The old method of retributive punishment is to turn it back on him who sent it out and let him feel the consequence. Christ's method is for the innocent to take its full force and lovingly to let the evil-doer go free. He trusted to suffering love in his own case; he expects us to trust in it too. His disciples will best prove their faith in the overcoming power of Christ's suffering, by testing the power of voluntary suffering for sin themselves. If they have more faith in the restrictive power of violence than in suffering love, they profess themselves followers of Moses rather than of the Christ. There may be cases where the application of force is necessary by a Christian man; perhaps with children, or with persons whose moral sense is too dull to be alive [232] to anything but physical pain, if there be any such. But when a man undertakes to visit punishment, he takes upon himself the office of God, to whom vengeance belongs. Let him look to it that he has the calm justice of God and the sorrowing love of God, and that there is no personal anger in him, for the wrath of man worketh not the righteousness of God, not even the wrath of exasperated parents.

The central commandment of the Christian law is love. It excludes all wrong-doing as a matter of course. It demands in addition the relieving of suffering and the bestowing of good to the utmost limit of our strength. The law is not abrogated by any conduct of others. If they sin and repent, we are to love and forgive. If they sin and repent not, we are to love and reprove. If they do wrong to us, we are to love and suffer, leaving the sin to God to requite if He will, but taking the sinner for us to soften and save if we can.

There are some applications of these principles which are not expressed in the New Testament, and which yet ought to be made. We should debase **[233]** Christianity into a mere set of rules, if we drew only the inferences which the New Testam[ent] drew. Our times demand new applica[tions] of the eternal truth, and we are free to make them.

1.) Jesus spoke a profound truth when he put the same penalty on hate that former times had put on murder. There is an organic connection between hate and murder. Hate is murder in solution. Murder is hate crystallized.

But the connection does not end with actual cases of murder of which the courts take cognizance.

God has so ordered it that life originates through love, and the two everywhere stand and fall together. Love is the oxygen that feeds the flame of life, and when there is no love life darkens and dies. This fact is most clearly discerned where life is feeblest and most dependent on love. Some years ago it was shown that in Paris of the children brought up by their parents only 18 % died in their first year; of those given out to board after the French fashion, 29 % died; and of the children committed to foundling **[234]** asylums 66 % died in the first year. (This latter figure has decreased of late years.) In the great foundling asylum in Moscow 367,788 children were received between 1763-1856, and of these 288,554 or 79 % died in infancy. It must be taken into consideration that the parents of such children often transmit the germs of disease to them. But even then it is plain that, other things being equal, the child that lives under the care of love has better chances of life than the child under the sanitary care of doctors and nurses. Illegitimate children, whose coming is often hailed with less joy than their going, show a terrible rate of mortality. Of 1,000 legitimate children born in Berlin, 1878, 103 died in the first quarter and 65 in the second; while of the same number of illegitimate 261 died in the first and 113 in the second quarter. In some cases there may be purpose in it; in most cases it is simply lack of love.

Love gives a hold on life. On the whole the cares of life rest more heavily on the married, yet, from the 25th year up, the death-rate of the unmarried is nearly double that of the married; the proportion of cases of insanity is similar. **[235]** An increase in Christianity in any country ought to show itself in a decrease of the death-rate, especially of the young and feeble.

If there is a heavy mortality of the latter, it may be due to other causes; but the Christianity of that country is under indictment.

2.) There were several cases of sudden death reported to Christ. A number of Galileans had been killed by Pilate. The tower of Siloam had fallen and crushed eighteen men. The people of Christ's day evidently had the same interest in bloodcurdling accidents that people general have to-day. These cases set them to thinking and questioning about the guilt of those so killed. Jesus denies that they had guilt about all others, and, in addition, his answer indicates that he took little interest in the matter and tried to turn the public attention to the moral condition of the people at large which was threatening a national catastrophe (Lk. 13, 1-5).

The interest in striking occurrences is an indication of an undeveloped moral judgement, which responds only to powerful irritants. The matters of greatest importance are not those which occur occasionally, but those **[236]** which are at work constantly. If an orphan asylum should burn down and kill 100 children, a cry of horror would go through the land. But year by year not one hundred, but thousands of children die a premature death in our great cities just for lack of air and sunshine; which, being interpreted, means just by reason of high rent and land speculation. It is not after the spirit of Christ to fix our eye only on the extreme and shocking cases of suffering or murder, and be blind to the ceaseless suffering and murder of whole classes of society. That we should do, but not leave this undone.

3.) True love does not wait for evil to be done before it sees it. Wise love will exert itself more in warding off evil than in curing it.

The Christian church has done most nobly in healing the wounds of humanity after they had been smitten. That was by precept and example taught in the **[237]** New Testament. But there, on the whole, the church has stopped. It has considered the pound of cure better than the ounce of prevention. It is not justified in this by the absence of preventive measures in the New Testament period. The church had no influence on legislation then. Its hands were more than full with cases of suffering demanding immediate relief. Besides, it considered the period till the reconstruction of humanity through the second coming of Christ so brief, that any efforts requiring time would have seemed foolish.

Affairs have changed. Christian men are a power in the world. They can prevent as well as cure. It must be plain to any candid observer that a very large share of the misery of men is not caused in the first place by the fault of the individuals. Temperance reformers began by working on individuals, but experience has driven them more and more to seek social remedies first. They found that drunkards [238] create saloons, but that saloons even more create drunkards. They have refused to go on merely curing the drunkard after he has been made. They see that the best way to cure them is to stop the making of them so far as society can. This is hard common sense, and Christian people may as well make up their minds to apply the same principle to other sources of evil and suffering.

For instance, the "fresh-air work" is annually growing in our cities, and it is a most Christian thing to color those pale cheeks with the flush of health. But why let the cheeks get pale? Why wait till the work of slow murder is half done? Is there nothing to prevent it? Of course there is. Land speculation is the chief cause of city crowding, as the saloon is the chief productive cause of drunkenness. Speculative land-prices rise by the sufferings of women and children. Why should Christian men wear out their strength in curing the effects of the evil and have no word about the evil itself?

Society dumps its moral offal of pauperism and crime upon the church [239] and says: "Here, take these and care for them." And the church works, and moans about the unceasing flood of evil and the hopelessness of the task. But what creates pauperism? Like all diseased tissues it is self-perpetuating to some extent. But what creates it in the first place and maintains the conditions for its growth? Surely it takes only a slight acquaintance with history and economics to discern some of the chief causes. What has pauperized Ireland? Its land system. What has ruined the sturdy Italian stock ever since the days of Tacitus, and turns it loose on our shores hardy and laborious, but stunted and degraded? The Italian land system. What is the fertile source of our own idle, vicious and criminal class? Vagrancy rises and falls with the price of grain. Industrial crises are marked by an increase in criminality. I have before me a table showing the criminal statistics of Massachusetts 1860-79. In every category of crime there is an upward wave from 1872-75. The total number of cases was as follows: 1870: 39,705; 1871: 39,873; 1872: 45,30[3]; [240] 1873: 46,137; 1874: 43,691; 1875; 40,411; 1876: 33,113; 1877: 31,694. The years 1872-75 were years of industrial pressure.

Suppose an Italian city, supplied with water by an aqueduct, suddenly finds it's supply failing. The people ascribe it to devil, to the visitation of God, or to the nature of things. They catch rain-water in tubs, dig ugly cisterns, go for miles to the river to bring water, and suffer terribly. The monks of the convent do all they can; they stint themselves of water, they care for the suffering, they moisten the parched lips of the babes with wine and make them drunk rather than let them go thirsty. There is an heretical, red-bearded Englishman visiting in the place. He tries to make the people understand that there must be something the matter with the aqueduct. They look at him coldly. He speaks to the monks. They answer: "We are too busy with caring for the suffering to have time for masonry. Besides, God has sent this suffering to give Christian charity a chance to show its healing power." The Englishman [241] shrugs his shoulders, hires men at his own expense, examines the aqueduct, locates the leak and presses forward to work till the break is stopped. Meanwhile the townspeople shake their head at the crazy Englishman; the monks mutter at the lovelessness of the Protestant, who scarcely stops on the way to give a fainting woman a drink from his flask, and cares more for stone and mortar than for his fellow-men. At last the work is done. The water flows again. The people say: "We have had hard times; now the times are better again." The monks admonish the people to praise God for his goodness. The Englishman dies of the effects of exposure in the sun. God alone knows whose love was warmest. But whose was wisest?

The apostolic church founded the order of deacons to avoid a social inequality and to make sure that all want was relieved. Our deacons still care for the poor after they have become poor. Would it not be entirely in keeping with the spirit of Christ, if some of the Nineteenth Century deacons should take it in hand to care for the poor before they have been made poor, by stopping [242] the causes that pauperize society? Why should the church of Christ drive a one-horse cart, while the church of Mammon runs an express-train with all modern improvements? The devil and his servants are entirely willing to have the church take away their used-up victims and care for them, if only they can go on using them up.

Two things combine to produce sin: the outward opportunity and the inward inclination. The church tries to decrease the inward inclination and it does well. But if at the same time the outward temptation is increased, the inward gain is equalized and lost. Christ recognizes the force of this outward factor when he bids us pray: "Lead us not into temptation," and when he says that the man who causes one of the most insignificant of his fellow-beings to sin, had better be sent to the bottom of the sea with a mill-stone round his neck. What an inarticulate moan is forever going up to God: "Lead us not into temptation!" Shop-girls who want to remain innocent; [243] women who struggle to keep up a clean and decent home; men who desire to do an honest day's work. There are all grades of weakness among them. Increase the pressure by one ounce and some of them go down. Increase the industrial pressure, and thefts increase, divorces increase, suicides increase, youthful prostitutes increase. Hear their cries as they go under, and the ruined homes, the blasted reputations, the broken hearts swirl by on the flood. Is there any help? Who does not by this time see that these "glutted markets," these "money stringencies," are due to the reckless covetousness of powerful men, who coin money out of the sufferings of others? Verily Christ will have to take the rings of Saturn as mill-stones for the necks of some men now living, if the Christ on the throne views their guilt as the Galilean Jesus did. "Lead us not into temptation!" Hear that cry, church of Jesus, thou body of Christ! This too is a work for thy hands. Wait not till they have fallen, till shame has died, self-respect vanished, the blood has been [244] tinted, the imagination poisoned, the spring of life befouled, and hope has fled. Then the awful word of Christ takes effect: "From him that hath not is taken even that which[h] he hath." Every loss prepares for the next. If rescue is still possible, it will be only so as through fire; rescued and rescuer alike will com[e] off with eye-brows singed.

4.) Christ takes the old morality for granted, and sets in where that stops. Civil society can ask nothing more than: "Be just to one another." Christ adds: "Love one another." Civil society cannot demand more than: "Give thy neighbor <u>his</u> own." Christ says: "Give him <u>thine</u> own."

But mark well: Christ's commandment of love presupposes the world's commandment of justice. Justice is the foundation on which love can build its temple. Unless the foundation is there, the walls will crack.

It is necessary to say this because so many try to be loving without being [245] just. Suppose a factory owner grinds down his men to starvation wages and pockets the increased profit. His wife and daughter are tenderhearted women. They find destitution, sickness and ignorance all over the village. They spend their time and strength in helping cases of need. The husband and father is a church member and a generous man. He lets them have all they need for charity. He builds a chapel and endows a reading room. And yet the whole thing is false. He tries to make injustice and love pull in one harness. It will not work. Probably he will complain that his men are an ungrateful lot, who never appreciate what his family does for them. The moral judgment of the men is more correct than his. They ought not to be thankful. He is giving them as a gift what belongs to them by right. Working-men are fond of saying: "We want justice, not charity." It is a good saying. Perhaps it would be better yet to say: "First justice, then charity." After justice [246] has been done, there will still be ample room for love, and then it will be love indeed, and not "charity."

This demand the lower classes have a right to make of all who possess wealth, ability, or education, and who call themselves Christians: "First give us what is ours by justice; then if you wish to do anything for us from love, we shall appreciate your love. But if you do not love us enough to be just to us, do not call it love."

5.) Stopping wrong by suffering it is certainly the method commanded by Christ. It is not to the credit of the church that only a few sects and individuals have accepted the commandment in earnest. Most Christians relegate this morality to the Millennium, on the ground that in existing society a man acting so would be stripped and beaten up. It is a question whether he would or not. There are those who have tried it and assert that they suffer fewer injuries than before, and that certainly they fret and fume less over those they do receive [247] and therefore have a serener and sweeter life of it. The man that beats about him most wildly will be stung most, – by bees and men. There are always compensations in obedience to Christ which we discover only when we trust ourselves to him. A man taking upon himself this commandment might think that he was about to lose his life, and find to his surprise that he had gained it.

But suppose he did suffer under it and was buffered about more. What is that to the Christian? It is not the part of love to inquire about its own sufferings, but about the good of the loved one. Is it because in spite of our praise of love we think of our own welfare first, that we refuse to let the blow rest on us, but insist on passing it back to him who gave it? There are probably many young Christians who ardently desire some way to serve Christ and to suffer for him. This is a short road to the cross and open to all. We can all suffer for the sins of our friends, and, by suffering without resentment, show both the sinfulness of the sin, and [248] the forgiving goodness of love. And this martyrdom has this advantage over other kinds that it brings no publicity and fame with it to poison the heart of the martyr with pride, but acts quietly like oil on the angry waters of the sea, of which but a very little will calm many breakers.

Now while we accept this as the perfect rule of Christian conduct, it is necessary to remember that there are many approximations to it. As we have seen, Christ does not reject the old law of retribution as wrong, but as imperfect and dangerous. He rejects it because it is likely to recoil on him that uses it (Mt. 26, 52); and because it belongs to those who love themselves more than the wrong-doer. Yet he that resents wrong done to himself is a better man than he who is too cowardly even to do it. And he that forcibly resists wrong done to others is far better than he who is indifferent to it. If a man cannot rise to the best and most effective way of treating wrong, then it will be better if he resists evil by force than to let it run its unhindered course. [249] It is necessary to remember this in our judgement of the actions of others. When we see the stern Ironsides of Cromwell going into battle with prayer and psalms; when we see the soldiers of Young Italy striking for the unity of their country, we can render all praise and honor to the patriotism, the love of right, the self-sacrifice, that utters itself in iron and blood. Their actions are immeasurably above those who crouched by their hearth and mumbled piety. The question is whether there is not a way more brave still and more effective.

Force has this evil about it, that it ranges the noblest virtues on the side of wrong and makes even wrong look noble. The bravery of the Parliament troops was met by the gallantry of the Cavaliers who rallied round poor King Charles. Charles the First and Louis the Sixteenth were neither great nor good. If men are to die for treason at all, these two probably deserved it more than nineteen twentieths of the men who have been executed for treason in England and France. But in executing them, the patriots furnished martyrs to [250] a bad cause. Half of Europe wept at the sorrow of the kings. A hair from those poor heads became a treasure, an heir-loom, a spur to bravery. Tenderness, pity, chivalry pleaded for what was bad. Each execution was followed by the restoration of monarchy. If the cause of freedom gained through the two revolutions, it was in spite of, and not because of, the violence used. The influence of the French Revolution in loosening the shackles of the European nations has been immeasurable. But how much greater would it have been, if the Reign of Terror had never stained the cause of liberty with blood? At first all Europe sympathized with it; the reversal of feeling set in with the increase of violence, and to-day the majority of men know only of the terrors and not of the glories of that uprising.

It cannot be denied that forcible resistance to wrong has done good. But the good is so mixed with evil, that often the [251] social body is more prostrated by the effects of the medicine than by the sickness. Slavery has been overcome in our country by force. It had to be overcome somehow, and all honor to those who poured out life, happiness, property, to overcome it. But who can survey the terrible cost of life to both sides, the resentful anger which is so slow to die out between North and South, and especially the present sad condition of those on whose behalf all the sacrifices were made, without wondering whether there was no other way.

There are painful struggles before the civilized nations now. There are vested wrongs that must be overthrown. If blood is spilt, it will be spilt as justly as any other that has flowed on earth. And yet the saddest day for the cause of the People will be the day when they begin to shed blood. While they suffer violence they have all but the small interested minority on their side. As soon as they use violence [252] they will have on their side only the reckless men and the justest men. All that lies between will see the blood on their hands and see nothing else, and the cause of God and the People will have to wait for another era before it can recover from that defeat in victory. It will be well for the workingmen of America and all who lead them to think this out well before the time of need comes, because their enemies understand it well already, and will not fail to provoke them to violence.

But for those who warn the people against force and insist on a moral revolution, it is needful to remember the responsibility they assume. Here are wrongs that God is calling on this generation to remove, if He ever called on any generation to do anything. There are hands outstretched to seize them and tear them, and feet ready to trample them into the dust. We Christians say: "Hold! use no violence; trust to the power of truth and righteousness; [253] agitate, persuade, protest, but do not strike." We have a right to say that only if our spiritual weapons are really more effective than powder and steel. And they will be more effective only if the blade of truth is ground sharp on the rough stone of suffering, and if they who wield it have cut loose from family and ambition and love of ease, and march against wrong like the black Brunswick hussars, who wore the skull and cross-bones on their helmet in token that they gave no quarter and asked for none. That was the spirit of Jesus. If we had men of that spirit, a force revolution would be unnecessary; and if we do not have them, it will be inevitable.

[254] In surveying the ethical applications which Jesus made of his cardinal doctrine concerning the relation of man to man, we find first that he protested against all exalting of man over man in rank. It is not love when a man gathers every little chip of wood under his feet to raise himself half an inch above his fellows and down at them with condescension.

He ridicules the small ambition which scrambles for a high seat at a dinner-party, loves to be surveyed in a front pew in the synagogue, and takes the deferential greetings in the market-place as a rooster swallows a choice slug, with closing of eyes and side-ward cocking of head (Mt. 23, 6-7; Lk. 14, 7-11). He advised them as a mere matter of prudence to leave it to others to exalt them instead of doing it for themselves.

The system of giving and taking titles seemed to him born of the same spirit of self-exaltation. He forbade his disciples either to assume titles or to use them in addressing others (Mt. 23, 8-12). **[255]** The form which pride took in so religious a community as Judea was especially repulsive to Jesus. He saw the religionists stopping short on the street-corners when the hours of prayer came, and going through their devotions in the sight of all; and he knew that the beholders were by no means out of the thoughts of those who seemed so absorbed in talking to God. He saw them make a studied display of their benevolence to the beggars. He saw them assume sombre looks and a disheveled appearance to announce to all the world that they were fasting. "Ah, Jochanan is fasting again; how pious that man is." Using the worship of the Father as stilts on which to mount above one's brethren was a vile prostitution of the holy to the mind of Jesus (Mt. 6, 1-18; 23, 5). In the parable of the Pharisee and Publican he has given the classical portrayal of this religious ambition, which fasts and gives tithes in order to have the satisfaction of thanking God that it is "not as the rest of men" (Lk. 18, 9-14). One main reason why he forbade judging one another, was that the judging **[256]** spirit is the spirit of pride. It warms the cockles of our heart to pat our brother on the back and say: "Brother, on the whole I approve of you; but –ahem!– you have a mote in your eye which hinders it from being as clear and bright as you perceive mine to be."

Therefore in legislating for the new community, Jesus forbade his subjects from exalting themselves above one another. It was difficult to wean his disciples from that desire. Their hope of the speedy erection of a temporal kingdom fostered any latent ambition. They quarreled repeatedly about their future grades of rank. Once the mother of two of them tried by a bit of feminine diplomacy to pre-empt the chief positions for her sons (Lk. 22, 24-27; Mt. 20, 20-28).

Jesus unflinchingly resisted that tendency. When they wanted to know who was greatest in the Kingdom, he told them that unless they turned and became like children, they would not get into the Kingdom, let alone be great in it (Mt. 18, 1-5). He often held up the child-like spirit as the **[257]** untainted spirit of true humanity. For children with all their frank little egotisms, are all democrats, till they have been spoiled by their elders. A little prince would make mud-pies with a street-arab, if he was let alone, and consider himself in the best of company. As he condemned pride and ambition, so Jesus praised the qualities of meekness, purity, mercy, simplicity and peacefulness, as belonging especially to the Kingdom (Mt. 5, 3-9). He asked men to learn of him to be meek and lowly of heart, that so they might shake off the heavy yoke of ambition and resentment, and find rest for their souls (Mt. 11, 28-30). John tells how, on the last evening of his intercourse with the disciples, he performed the office of a menial, washing their feet and drying them, in order by this object lesson to impress it on their minds, that the greatness to be sought by them consisted not in exacting service from others, but in serving them (Jo. 13, 1-17). It is a sad example of the way men have distorted the teachings of Jesus, that by some the foot-washing, which was meant as a typical case of a universal [258] duty, has been turned into a sacrament, and is perform as such even in latitudes, where cow-hide boots, instead of dusty sandals, have to be taken off to permit it. If we mistake not both the pope and the Czar, annually wash the feet of a fixed number of beggars to demonstrate to the Lord Christ that they are the humble and self-forgetful servants of their fellow-men.

In this respect the ethics of Jesus is distinctly opposed to that prevailing in the world. For in all the world men lord it and rule it, and allow themselves to be called Benefactors, Highnesses, Gracious Majesties, and what not (Mt. 20, 25; Lk. 22, 25). Jesus says: "Be not like them. There are some who will stand higher than others in the sight of God, and in the sight of men too. But they are not those who try to stand higher, but those who abandon all thought of how they will stand, and simply love and serve." That law has once for all been fixed by the example of the Son of man, who, if any, had a right to honor, but who [259] sought pre-eminence only in being everybody's helper and giving up his life as a ransom to free the lives of others (Mt. 20, 28).

We notice in the writings of the early church that this quality of Jesus and this precept had especially impressed the apostles. Paul exhorts his friends at Philippi to do "nothing through self-seeking or vainglory, but in lowliness of mind to count each the other better than himself;" and thus to "have the same mind in them which was in Christ Jesus," who surrendered every privilege and stepped down, step by step, till he reached the depth of poverty, ignominy and suffering (Phil. 2, 3-8). So to James it seems painfully incongruous to introduce any difference in rank into the Christian church. The "faith of our Lord Jesus Christ" and the "respect of persons" have nothing in common. To honor a rich man more than a poor man is a violation of the royal law of love (James 2, 1-9). He warns the men against the covetous, jealous spirit, which snares for honors as a dog for bones (James 4, 1-10). And with the same purpose in mind Peter and Paul both beg the women not to load themselves with ornament, or to take pride **[260]** in the material and cut of their dress. In a society where women are uneducated and do not mingle on equal terms with the men, their social ambition goes mainly toward the quantity of their jewelry and the elaborateness of their dress. Perhaps it never quite leaves that; and we have all observed that a bit of gold or a few yards of shimmering stuff can serve its wearer as a satisfactory vantage-ground, and may disturb the fraternal equilibrium of an entire social circle. For a man to endeavor to outstrip others by his wealth, honor or ability, and for a woman to take pains to outshine others by her beauty and social position, is the same ambition in different spheres, and its effect is equally disastrous in either case, and equally destructive to Christ's society and the Kingdom of God.

We find, then, that Jesus bids us stand side by side as brethren of equal rank. Any attempt of an individual to raise himself above the rest by titles, social distinctions, or displays of religious superi- **[261]** [ori]ty, he condemns as evil. He desires that we shall forget to consider what men think of us and how we stand, compared with others, and shall give ourselves entirely to serving others and lifting them up. And he who does that most fully, not with a Uriah Heep, conscious, self-congratulating humility, but with unconscious sincerity, shall be the greatest in the Kingdom.

There is profound wisdom in the radical position taken by Jesus against pride and all its works.

Religious pride is self-sufficiency and independence of God, and that is isolation and death. At the root of Paul's speculative protests against salvation by works lay a very practical experience. He knew from experience that the close attention to religious performances, this keeping of a cash account with the Almighty and crediting one's self with so and so many good deeds, begot a pride which was spiritual death, and made religious men be bad men. Therefore he insisted on including all under condemnation, that all might be dependent on the **[262]** grace of God, "lest any man should boast." Paul was right.

> "Man's weakness is his glory, for the strength
> Which raises him to heaven and near God's self,
> Came spite of it. God's strength His glory is,

For thence came with our weakness sympathy
Which brought God down to earth, a man like us" (Browning's Paracelsus).

Paul's protest was leveled against a religious aristocracy. He aimed to bring all men down on one plane before God, and to unite them in one great brotherhood of sin and redemption. Even for the work done by him and others he refused praise. They were but husbandmen, planting or watering; but it is not the husbandman who gives the seed the faculty and the means of growth, but God. "What hast thou, that thou hast not received?" he asks, and "If thou didst receive it, why dost thou glory, as if thou hadst not received it." Modern science entirely confirms the major premise of Paul's syllogism, and from the ethical conclusion there is no escape.

And social science confirms the correctness of Christ's protest against the stratification of society in ranks and **[263]** classes. What is the general tendency toward democracy and the gradual abolition of hereditary privileges but history's assent to the revolutionary dogmas of Christ?

The existence of higher classes is a damage to themselves and to the body of a nation. They are exposed to special temptations and there is no force to exact from them obedience to the corresponding obligations. Those who should speak to them sternly, plead gently. They are up in a rarefied atmosphere whither the voice of truth sounds but faintly. It is painful to see how much more sedulous the church has always been in preaching the duty of the people to the princes than in pointing out the duty of the great toward the people. The upper classes appear to get the very best quality of preaching, but they are in fact suffering with a self-imposed famine of the word of God; that is, of what would be the word of God to them. They would not tolerate it, if they did hear it. There is an inward obstacle in the heart of those who are fed with honor against the plain truth of Christ. "How can ye believe, who receive glory one of another?" says Jesus (John 5, 44). **[264]** He seems to have had little hope of the upper classes. Those who did feel drawn to him, had the usual timidity of the privileged classes and feared to side with him, "for they loved the glory that is of men more than the glory that is of God" (Jo. 12, 42-43).

No part of humanity can stand it to be in any degree severed from the great body. The prisoners in Russian prisons suffer under their isolation, and the Czar and his nobility suffer under it in another way. There is a moral obliquity about it which distorts the entire life, and even cripples the intellectual faculties. The nobility of Europe has had the most extraordinary opportunities for producing at least intellectual work of value. They have had heredity, wealth, associations, familiarity with art, travel, everything in their favor. But considering these odds, what have they done in poetry, in art, in natural science, in the severer departments of philosophical research? In the list of soldiers and statesmen the names of ancient families occur more frequently; but then, these careers were almost closed to all but the nobility. And in how many cases [265] did the titled general gain the royal praise, when the real work had been performed by men unknown to history. It is interesting, also, to notice that both in the English and the French revolution, when a chance was given for the military talent of the common people, generals arose who stand head and shoulders above the average of those produced by an aristocratically graded military service. Free contact on terms of equality with the great body of humanity is the necessary condition of moral health, and hence indirectly of intellectual greatness.

Dividing off humanity into horizontal layers imposed one above the other is really equivalent to the formation of separate humanities. It is the devil's denial of God's doctrine that all man are of one blood and brothers. As Mrs. Browning says, there are more infidels to Adam than professed infidels to God. It is vain to comfort ourselves that Christianity can bridge the chasms. Christianity bridges them best by closing them. While they exist it can signal across them, run baskets across them on pulley-lines, and show its good will, but that sort of engineering [266] has its natural limits. Christian sympathy, it is true, works downward; but natural sympathy works sideways, in horizontal lines. Our real intelligence and love goes to those who are akin to us in manner of life, in education and views.

A businessman has a neighbor whom he has met in a friendly way off and on for twenty years. He also has a book-keeper, who has been with him for twenty years, with whom he has been in contact for hours every day, and whose probity he sincerely respects. The neighbor and the book-keeper both die in one week, and our friend learns that in each case the family has been left in want. How will his sympathy go out in either case? He may do more for the book-keeper's widow, but will it be with the same feeling with which he offers his assistance to the widow of his friend? Will it not be pity in the one case and true sympathy in the other?

The differences of rank are real differences. Surely modern literature is sufficient evidence for that. Where in ancient Greek literature the will of the gods or Fate is the obstacle against which human freedom clashes; [267] in modern literature it is the established difference in rank against which love or ambition beats its wings. And if sexual love, the most powerful passion of life, finds it hard to bring two persons together who are separated by rank, then Christian love will find it hard too. For the Christian love of the upper classes cannot well manifest itself in anything but a mild benevolence; "love" is diluted into "charity."

A class inevitably substitutes a class code for Christ's morality. What is proper becomes of more importance than what is right. Kingsley has a neat touch in his "Yeast." The game-keeper's ballad with the lament of the preacher's widow is read to the squire.

> "A labourer in Christian England,
> Where they cant of a Saviour's name,
> And yet waste men's lives like the vermin's
> For a few more brace of game.
> There's blood on your new foreign shrubs, squire;
> There's blood on your pointer's feet,
> There's blood on the game you sell, squire,
> And there's blood on the game you eat."
> "You villain," interposed the squire, "when did I ever sell a head of game?"

Killing men is inhuman; selling game is ungentlemanly. The squire resents the latter charge.

The life of a privileged class is an unsound life. It is less open to radical moral truths. It is subject to class [268] prejudice rather than to justice. It struggles against very great obstacles in endeavoring to obey Christ's law of love. It is like a camel going through the eye of a needle.

It is not for us to say that men in the upper classes cannot be Christians. It may be possible to support life in a glass vessel from which the air is partly pumped out. It may be possible to balance one's self along the straight and narrow way with a tremendous burden on one shoulder and an empty bag on the other. But it is unnatural and un-christian. And it must be remembered that it is to some extent voluntary. It is possible to step down and become a man. That is what Christ advised a wealthy young aristocrat to do. He did not do it.

We have spoken of the effect of class isolation on the isolated class. But the condition of any part of the social body must affect the whole. It is only truth to say that whatever good the upper classes generate, e.g., culture, refined taste, etc., has to be carried downward by force and purpose, as a balloon of gas has [269] to be dragged down; but that the corruption trickles down of itself. The licentiousness of an idle class has to be fed by the working class. Their luxury and display generates the love of luxury in those who can afford it less. This love of pleasure, this wasting of substance on dress and ornament, this living beyond their means, which is justly deplored in working people at present, has been aroused by the luxurious living of the rich. You may preach simplicity and contentment all you please. As long as there are those who live in idleness and waste, you are telling men to resist or reverse the law of gravitation. God has planted the love of the beautiful and the desire of imitation into the heart of man. It is the faculty by which he progresses. In a true society the aesthetic faculty is incentive to a nobler life, and we praise those who give up some of their daily bread if necessary, in order to enjoy the higher life of art and literature. In a false and classified society this same love of the beautiful and this same readiness to sacrifice [270] the lower needs to the higher, becomes a cause of destruction. *Corruptio optimi pessima.* The daughter of the workingman has a taste for natty bonnets, and a woman's touch for soft and clinging stuffs. She too could lean back in an open carriage or enjoy a box at the opera. If she copies her "favored sister" so far as she can with cotton velvets and Bowery theaters, has her favored sister the right to lift up the first stone? How many young girls in our cities suffer always the tortures of Tantalus? They hunger for beauty and refinement, and beauty and refinement are dangled up and down, up and down, within an inch of their famishing lips, in the stores, on the streets, in the novels they read, even in the churches they go to. And then the tempter shows them a shortcut to it all. Verily it is a marvel and cause to praise God, that the bulk of our people are as pure and true and solid as they are in the face of such influences of corruption as are represented in the "higher classes" of city society. We fear that if Jesus should walk on Fourteenth Street in [271] the afternoon and watch the women then, and walk there again in the evening and see the other women so like them in dress and gait and even perfume, only everything a little louder, he would place the mill-stone of this awful responsibility around many a neck covered with lace – or nothing. The stumbling blocks over which girls and men stumble at night, have been strewn there during the day.

It is idle to seek a remedy in begging wealthy women to dress more plainly. When will moralists cease to plaster cracked walls with untempered mortar? How long in this age of science will they try to do away with effects and leave the causes at work? Why try to conceal the appearances of inequality and leave the inequality in existence?

As long as there are upper classes, there will be men and women so near them that they may hope by effort to rise into them. And this hope will not generate noble qualities in them. It will drive the women to display, to petty scheming, to the wasting of their own lives and the lives of their children in [272] the soul-pulverizing machine call "society." It will drive the men to race and tear in their business, to skim close to the precipice of dishonesty, to turn the screw tighter on their employees, – all to furnish their wives and daughters with the necessary stepping stones to mount into these upper classes. Young men of ability and aspirations have to forsake the pride of rectitude and the strength of unselfish daring. They must curry favor, win influence; anyway, every way they must rise. Rank, wherever it exists, is a devourer of youthful promise. Rank is the worst court of divorce; it divorces true love, and pronounces its benediction over that most insidiously destructive form of prostitution, marriage for position or money.

It behooves Christian people to recognize that Christ is against inequality, and that he denounces the effort to create inequality as hostile to the nature of the Kingdom of God on earth. Therefore they should welcome and foster every effort to abolish the causes of inequality [273] and thus to remove the over-powerful temptations from the members of the upper classes, and give them a fair chance to become good men and women. Nor should a follower of Christ wait till the slow change of society rectifies these evils. The command to depart from unrighteousness and to join the society of Christ lies upon him for immediate obedience. If he is on the house-top, let him come down and tread the solid earth. If he is on the earth, let him not try to get astraddle of a roof-beam. Christian young men in business should refuse to join in the chase for wealth, for wealth will infallibly carry them into the dangerous classes. Young men in intellectual pursuit should refuse to join in the chase for titles, offices and distinctions, for if they strive to win the proud distinction of being called Rabbi, they will have to fight shy of the Galilean heretic. Daudet's *L'Immortel* is a striking commentary on Christ's condemnation of titles. It shows how even so respected an institution as the French Academy exercises a baleful influence of temptation, awakens [274] small ambition, fosters the meanest jealousies, strait laces courageous utterance, and freezes love and friendship. Like all caricatures the book exaggerates; but like all good caricatures it is an approximate portrait. The duty of resisting this ambition lies especially on the clergy. If they fix their eye on a title, or on a bishop's chair, the locks of their strength are cut. They will not fight Jehovah's battles, but grind the corn of the Philistines. "He that hates not titles, newspaper puffs, and his own promotion, cannot be my disciple."

The obligation to break the force of ambition lies especially on the women. We think it is fair to assert, that the larger part of the scrambling of men for place and money is done under the conscious or unconscious impulse of the women they love. The better a man is, the more will he prostitute himself to give his wife the social station which she desires. It would be a stern and rare type of virtue in a man to be practically a brother of the poor, if his wife desired to be a sister to the rich and [275] he could satisfy her desire by a slight lowering of his moral aspirations. It will be a great day for humanity when Christian young women refuse to bestow their love on young men who are so hostile to the Kingdom of God as to desire to "rise in life," instead of desiring to raise life.

Perhaps it may be necessary to add as the closing word on this subject, that equality does not mean uniformity. Whenever a proposal is made for a juster construction of society, the cry is immediately raised: "You want to have a dead level of uniformity. God created inequality; you cannot abolish it by act of Congress." We ought to be beyond such objections, in America at least. The experience of the American republic ought to have demonstrated that an equality of political rights for all citizens does not mean an equality of political wisdom and power, but that in a nation in which Abraham Lincoln could cast but one ballot, he could sway millions of hearts and command their wealth and heart's blood. It is probably true that there will always be inequality of ability. The number of born leaders is always [276] limited. Society will always group itself about its leaders, and the process of finding these leaders and putting them into the position in which their ability will have full play, is one of the most serious tasks of humanity. The old method has been to select the oldest sons of certain men; a method which has the advantage of stability and of very little else. An isolated class is least fit for true leadership, because it is out of contact with the people, has least comprehension for their true need and least inclination to serve them. Men of the people are the true leaders of the people. But as long as there is a pseudo-aristocracy to dazzle the vulgar eye and deflect the popular judgement, it will be much harder for the true aristocracy of intellect and character to gain the positions belonging to them of divine right.

It is not those who ask for equality that desire a dead level; it is those who desire to perpetuate hereditary inequality that practically keep the mass of the people, with all its latent powers, down on the dead level of a scramble for bread. [277] The family demonstrates the coexistence of equal rights with unequal powers. From the father down to the baby there is a long gradation of ability, but there is a single grade of dignity, and no right to exploit the weak. What father would tolerate it, if the older children, because they are stronger and know more, should set up the claim of doing least, eating the best, and occupying the parlor alone while the others crowd into a cubby-hole? And if we, being evil, desire to see equality among our children, how much more shall our Heavenly Father desire equality among us? [278] Christ's law of love is violated as soon as we love others less than ourselves. One way in which this greater love for self is manifested and satisfied is by seeking special honor for ourselves; of that we have just spoken. Another way is by acquiring property at the expense of others, or keeping it for ourselves when others need it more. On this section of the law Christ's commands are especially full and emphatic.

Jesus of course recognizes that we have need of property. As we have life, so we need food to preserve it and clothing to shelter it, and our Father in Heaven who has given us life, desires that we shall have all that is needful, and has made most ample provision for us (Mt. 6, 25-34). So we are to do our work, cheerfully garner its produce, and eat of our Father's bounty with thankfulness of heart. It is foolish to worry and fret about the morrow, saying: "What shall we eat? What shall we drink? Wherewithal shall we be clothed?" All our fretting will accomplish little. The wisest way is to bear the burden of every day as it comes, and let the morrow be anxious for itself. [279] If God finds food for the birds of the heaven, that sow not, reap not, and have no barns into which to gather their surplus, how much more is our life assured, who are of more account than they, in that we can sow, reap, and gather into barns? And if God clothes the lilies with beauty, though they toil and spin not, why should we fret about our clothing, to whom he has given cleft hands to take the material of all creation and fit it to our wants? (Lk. 12, 22-31).

Above all we are to remember that our material needs are only the foundation for the higher and real life. If like Martha of Bethany, we are so absorbed in setting a good table that we let the choicest spiritual food pass by untasted, we are not choosing the good part. A body cannot well have two centres of gravity; and a life cannot well be devoted to the anxious care for material things and have much time and strength left for thought and for converse with the unseen. We cannot serve God and [280] Mammon.

If another is in need and we have what he needs, of course we should give it to him. We should consider his needs and not our profit. We should not be carefully calculating the help we give our brother, and wondering whether we shall get it all back. Any man will lend to another on good security; he need not be a Christian for that (Lk. 6, 30-34).

This seems to be Christ's ideal: every man working cheerfully, eating contentedly the fruit of his labor, making the life of the body the foundation for the spiritual life, and sharing with his brother who happens to be in need. The same conception was in John's mind, when he advised men to live simply and honestly, and to share with the needy, as the best preparation for the new society of the Messianic era (Lk. 3, 10-14). For a short time the church at Jerusalem realized this ideal, where they shared according to their needs and took their food with gladness and singleness of heart (Acts 2, 44-47; 4, 32-35). Such a form of society would indeed be one in which gladness would [281] spring up like a fountain to sweeten the air. Love would be easy and mutual service a pleasure.

Now Jesus saw men living far differently. He saw them fretting and worrying for the mere food and drink. He saw them saving and stinting themselves to lay up treasures for the future, and when they had succeeded, leaning back with a sigh of satisfaction: "'There, my soul, it is done now; thou hast much goods laid up for many years; take thine ease, eat, drink, be merry." He saw that this care and this love for wealth was in many choking down higher thoughts, as the luxuriant thorns of Palestine outstrip the slow-growing grain (Mt. 13, 7, 22). He saw that when a man was once entangled in the meshes of wealth there was next to no hope that he would break loose and become a member of the Kingdom and a lover of the truer life (Mt. 19, 23-26). He saw that in this mad scramble to secure themselves, men could so far forget the love they owe their fellowmen, that one man could be carousing [282] in purple and fine linen, while another lay at his gate day by day in rags and hunger (Lk. 16, 19-21).

Of course this is foolish and wicked. But what shall we do? Shall we say: A man must be *too* absorbed in money-getting; he must not become *too* rich; he must not forget the poor entirely? In other words shall we acknowledge the necessity and rightfulness of the scramble, but try to dull the roughest edge and check the worst brutality of it?

Jesus was far more radical. His demands cannot be designated by any milder word than revolutionary. He forbids the hoarding up of unused property entirely (Mt. 6, 19-20). He ridicules a typical case of selfish thrift, calls the man a fool, and shows how God snuffed out the light of his life when it was just beginning to sputter in the richest fat (Lk. 12, 13-21). He tells the story of a man who made clever provision for the future by giving away right and left what happened to be in his power now; and he advises the possessors of the mammon of un- **[283]** righteousness to do the same, because at the coming of the Messianic Kingdom its use will collapse, and their only chance then will be that they have made friends among the children of the Kingdom, who will mercifully receive them into their tabernacles (Lk. 16, 1-13). When some of the Pharisees "who were lovers of money" turned up their noses at this story, (as the Greek has it, Lk. 16, 14), he told them another of a rich man who failed to use his wealth thus, and one day found himself in the torments of Hades (Lk. 16, 19-31). A rich man who seemed really willing to him, he advised to get rid of his wealth as a preliminary, but found to his sorrow that in this case also the love of property was too much for the man (Mt. 19, 16-22). One case is recorded in which a man of position and wealth, touched by the brotherly freedom of Christ's presence, determined to give away one half of his property outright, and with the other half to make good all moral claims against him by paying them fourfold. This was indeed a camel going through the needle's eye and coming out on the other side without its humps. The words **[284]** with which Jesus received this announcement evince the liveliest satisfaction (Lk. 19, 1-10).

In short Christ forbids the citizens of his Kingdom from pile up wealth, and where it is already piling up, he commands them to disperse it. It takes little imagination to picture the changes which obedience to his command would produce in society.

Of course the representatives of things as they are, take no delight in these teachings. They would very willingly exchange them for more teaching on the nature of God or on love in general. The treatment of Christ's teachings on property is one of the most interesting chapters in the history of morals. The critics get at it by criticism. They doubt the genuineness of the parables of the Rich Fool, and of Dives and Lazarus. Luke who reports most of these sayings seems to them tainted by Ebionite ideas and so far untrustworthy. Others who regard Jesus merely as a teacher like others, – like themselves, for instance, – frankly contradict him. He was "a good soul, but a limited intellect," and knew **[285]** nothing about political economy. The greater part of the church of course is more reverent. It carefully leaves the shell of his teachings intact and scrapes out the contents by a proper exegesis of this sort: "It is true that Jesus called the rich farmer a fool, but that was because the man did not remember the shortness of life. It is true that Jesus sent Dives to Hades, but that was not because he was rich, but because he did not look after Lazarus; moreover the chief point of interest in that parable is not its bearing on wealth, but its revelations concerning the future life. It is true that Jesus bade the young ruler give away his property, but that was because in this special case his heart loved wealth more than God; if he had said, 'Yes, Lord, I will,' he might have kept it with safety, for then his heart would have been free. As for the parable of the unjust steward – well, that is a very difficult passage, on which we are reluctant to venture an opinion. The communism of the church at Jerusalem was peculiar to it alone, and God [286] seems to have expressed his disapproval of it, for a few years later the church at Jerusalem was poor, which was probably the result of that communism. The command to give to him that asks and to lend without expectation of return must be interpreted by sanctified common sense, which tells us that indiscriminate charity is a great evil. On the whole the teaching of Jesus must be considered in its general balance, especially with an eye on that notable text: "The poor ye have always with you." Moreover Abraham and Solomon were rich, the apostles had boats, and Paul bids the rich not be highminded, but says nothing about giving away all their property. Whereby we see that Christ expected rich and poor to dwell together that in their interchange of love Christianity might be exercised. The rich must keep within the civil law, not acquire too much, give away at least a tenth of their income, and not set their heart on their wealth."

As a consequence of this dulling off of Christ's teaching we have a state of things in the church of Christ which is doing more to make Christianity [287] a by-word and a hissing among the civilized nations than all the higher criticism in the world. The salt has lost its savour, and men are trampling it under foot, as Jesus promised they should. The writings the Old Testament prophets show that in their day drunkenness existed and lewdness was rampant; but the sin which they denounce over and over and over again is neither intemperance nor unchastity, but the covetousness of the powerful which results in the oppression of the weak. With Christ the same proportion holds. There is no other ethical topic to which the Gospels devote so much space as to questions of property. Even Paul calls the love of money the root of all evils (I Tim. 6, 5-10). On the other hand in the modern church a man must deal very carefully with questions of property. He may speak as plainly as he pleases against intemperance, but let him weigh his words well if he deals with injustice. Is it not by the wincing of the patient that the physician detects the seat of disease? The New Testament puts lasciviousness and covetousness on an equal footing of guilt. Does the church do the same? We have [288] heard of many exclusions from church fellowship for causes of impurity. But though the writer has made continued inquiry, he has so far heard of but three cases of exclusion for covetousness. They occurred in small and poor churches, and in two cases out of the three the proof of the covetousness was that the persons concerned contributed nothing to the church, though well capable of doing so. There are thousands of inquiries to be dealt with every year by Christian ministers and some of them are rich. Suppose we grant that the demand made of the young ruler was exceptional and not a general rule. Still his case must recur now and then. Has anyone ever heard of a Christian minister repeating Christ's demand? The writer knows of one case where an able bodied man, living "on his income," was refused admission to a little church till he should earn his living, because the Bible said: "He that will not work neither shall he eat." The man acknowledged that the [289] point was well taken, and, at the time when we heard of the matter, was looking for work.

We assert that the church is, on the whole, more backward on this department of the ethics of Jesus than on any other. And yet it is exactly on this territory that the world is fighting its battle in this generation. The social question is confessedly the question of our age, and the social question deals primarily with property. If therefore we undertake to set forth the bearing of Christ's teaching more fully, we do so for the sake of the Kingdom, and not because we expect to reap any harvest of love or gain through it.

It seems to us, then, that the teaching of Jesus on property is an entirely plain doctrine, coherent in itself and well backed by reason, so that there is no excuse for those who make it nebulous. When Jesus says that there is something in wealth which makes the entrance into the Kingdom next to impossible for its possessor, he must mean that the possession of wealth is very closely bound up [290] with injustice and selfishness, which are the contradiction of the justice and love of the Kingdom. Let us examine why they are so closely bound up.

1.) In the first place it is not possible to get great wealth except by offending against justice.

If we run over in our mind the large fortunes of our own country, we find that they are nearly all traceable to the following sources: city real estate, mineral lands, banking, monopoly of means of traffic, speculation in stock or produce, and patents. It can, I think, be demonstrated that there is an element of injustice and lovelessness in every one of these, and that it is this element of injustice and lovelessness which gives these lines of business their productive faculty. Without going into economic discussion or attempting to support our assertions by reasoning, we can indicate where the wrong seems to lie.

In the real estate of cities, growing as our American cities mostly do, **[291]** there is an increase in the value of the ground which is not traceable to the labor or expense of the owner, but which is due to the existence and industry of the entire community. It should therefore in justice return to the community to serve in defraying the expenses of the communal life. Instead of that it goes to the private owners, and it is this and not personal exertion which has built up the estates of the Astors, Goelets, Rhinelanders, of Snug Harbor, Trinity Church, Grace Church, Collegiate Dutch Reformed Church, etc. It is the effort to appropriate this public product which causes speculation in city real estate, keeps city lots vacant, and causes the crowding of our cities. The price of the vacant land rises chiefly because the people are so crowded and suffer so, that they are willing to pay more to escape. Land values rise by the sweat of men and the suffering of women and children. Is it not injustice and lovelessness to accept wealth at that price? If Christ came to New York would he approve of wealth drawn from city real estate? **[292]** A second source of wealth is the possession of land giving access to mineral wealth, e.g., to deposits of coal, silver, iron, oil, etc. Men need these minerals for their work or their comfort. Those who work these deposits and prepare the material for use are justly entitled to a return for their labor and expense. But it is well known that the price charged for these products in many cases includes not only a return for labor and expense, but a payment for the substance itself. This is just only if the substance, the iron or coal, really belonged to the so-called owners. It does not. They did not make it or cause it to be buried there. It is part of the means of life which God has prepared for all his children. Individuals hold it only by right of appropriation. Suppose a mother were obliged to leave her children for a day. She leaves the pantry well stocked. But the oldest boy in her absence makes a claim of owning the goodies, and **[293]** the hungry little ones are obliged to surrender their playthings if they want any. That boy will be spanked when his mother comes home. He might perhaps have demanded a reward if the eatables were stored on the top shelf which only he could reach. But to ask pay for the food itself was injustice. And it was also lovelessness, for he got the playthings only because his brothers and sisters suffered. The cost of Anthracite coal in New York is said to be about twice the cost of production and transportation. That extra fifty percent creates the wealth of the mine owners, and in that fifty percent lies their injustice, and their lovelessness; for men pay so much, because cold hurts, rheumatism tortures, and pneumonia kills.

A third source of wealth is banking, the commercial management of money. In this also there is a legitimate service to be rewarded and an unjust privilege which is the chief source of profit. The subject is too intricate to be briefly stated. The people of the United States are [294] rapidly coming to see that the medium of exchange, the commercial life-blood of the nation, has been manipulated in the interest of the banking business; legislation conferring unjust privileges has been served, artificial stringencies created, and times of national distress, like the Civil War, have been dexterously used to enrich those who had money and still further to deplete those who had none.

A fourth source of wealth is the ownership of the means of traffic, railroads, street-cars, telegraphy, telephone, etc. All these are undertakings which cannot come into being unless public properties are granted for their use and public rights exercised on their behalf, and it is this public element in them which lifts their profit above that of ordinary business. There would be no injustice in the private working of railroads, if a profit were made only on that which the private [295] persons really contribute to their working, but in that case the fortune of the Vanderbilts and Goulds would never have been made. The injustice consists in making private profit out of the monopoly feature, which is a contribution of the public. The lovelessness consists in making dearer than need be the cost of transporting the means of life, and of making difficult or impossible the visiting of friends or lovers, the change in climate for the sick, and all the intercourse of men in which the chief enjoyment of life consists.

A fifth source of wealth is speculation in stock or produce. Here also there is a legitimate foundation and an unjust superstructure. Brokerage is a necessary function of a complex commercial system. But by plain brokerage men do not grow rich. The fortunes made on change are not the pay for work done, though we confess that the howling done in the New York Stock Exchange or the Chicago Wheat Pit deserves a larger pay than most other physical labor. A railroad [296] president once said to the writer: "These men who go up and down town on the L roads between five and eight, they really do something; they add value to what they work on. But we who go down town at ten create nothing; we only try to take things away from one another." It was good-humored self-ridicule and exaggeration, but it was also truth. The fortunes changing hands in the Produce Exchange must finally come from somewhere. The men who make them stand as middle-men between the farmers who raise the grain and the people who eat it. Whatever is lost in the transit between the farmer's hand and the laborer's mouth, must be a loss to either of these or both. It will be difficult for the speculators to prove that their service in meditating between producers and consumers is worth the profit extracted by them out of the business. And if they artificially enhance the price of that by which the people live and without which they suffer, where is their justice and love? [297] The last source of large fortunes mentioned is the possession of patents. An inventor of anything useful to men ought to be rewarded. He ought in many cases to be rewarded more highly than many poor inventors are, who are compelled to part with their rights under pressure of need and see them exploited by others. There are only some patents which are, as it were, the padlocks which individuals have succeeded in fastening on the doors giving access to new forces or materials of nature; these can be made the source of immense profit, and this profit is due not so much to the invention as to the natural force which lies back of it and which man stands in need of. In that case our parable of the boy and the pantry is again to the point. It is hardly true to say that without the holder of the patent that force would not have become available. In the case of almost all great inventions a number of men reached the idea almost simultaneously; and as the patent litigations show, it is often due only to the wildest haste that one man succeeds in putting in his claim before the other. Mankind needs that force of nature and [298] mankind will get it, if not through one man, then through another. And it is questionable justice that the man who has struck the last blow of the pick at which the water gushed out, shall have the right to wave thirsting humanity back and for a long term retail the water at his own price. It is the greatness of the possible unearned gain which dazzles so many honest men, sets them to leave their trade, go to inventing, and finally lose their family happiness and perhaps their minds over it. The lovelessness of those who exploit the monopoly in their inventions is even more apparent than the injustice. For instance the company controlling the Westinghouse brake charges a heavy price for every car supplied with their brake. As a consequence the freight-trains of most railroads are still provided only with the old hand-brake, the operating of which entails a steady annual loss of life by accidents, and another steady loss of health by exposure. Of course the railway companies might introduce the brake in spite of its cost, but the cost certainly is deterrent. If the patent is finally introduced, it will be because the [299] loss of life and consequent expense compels to it. So here again the wealth is made by the suffering of others.

To these sources most of the large American fortunes are traceable, and if businessmen are at present gaining wealth fast, it will usually be found that one or more of the aforementioned sources is tapped by them. But if our reasoning is only in a measure correct, it would be impossible to gain large fortunes in these ways without constantly setting justice and love aside.

And even in the common business life of to-day it is hard to see how a man may acquire wealth fast under ordinary circumstances, and yet have a tender regard for justice and love. The golden rule of competitive industry is to buy in the cheapest market and sell in the dearest; that is, to give your neighbor as little as you can and to get as much from him as you can. That may be justice, but is it love? Would not love require that you should give the product of your work as cheaply as you can afford, and pay your brother for his work as much as you can afford? We are not so sanguine that [300] we hope to see the law of the market reversed. Nor can a man at present entirely avoid acting according to it even in buying a loaf of bread. But is it not true that he who would gain wealth in a business life governed by that law, must appropriate that law and act heartily according to it? And if he does, he will surely take advantage of the needs of his neighbor. He will watch for opportunities to buy when his neighbor is pressed for money, and has to sell cheaply. He will try to sell that which men are most in need of, in order to get the highest price from it. It is all coining money out of your fellows' distress.

A party of travelers came to the camp of an Arab sheik, astray, footsore, and quite out of food. They asked for bread, for dates, for milk, for anything to eat. The sheik ordered his servants to bring out a tempting array of food, but when the strangers were about to fall to, he asked them first to pay him twenty pieces of gold. The indignant travelers exclaimed against such extortion, for the food was not worth a single piece. The [301] Arab smiled benignly and said: "Allah, whose name be blessed, brought a stranger here a year ago who slept in my tent. Going, he left a foreign book which with the aid of an interpreter I have read. It is entitled Political Economy. From this book I have learned that the price of a thing is not what it cost me to produce it, but what I can get you to pay for it. I learned also that it is a law of heaven that every man buys in the cheapest market and sells in the dearest. You are my dearest market. I have not a complete monopoly of food in this desert, for there is another camp five miles from here. But you are weary, the night is falling, and you cannot expect me to show you the way. The price is high, but the food is worth more to you. You are free to buy or not to buy. The food is mine to sell or not to sell. This is a free contract." The travelers paid twenty pieces of gold and swore. The sheik blessed Allah for revealing to him the wisdom of the foreigners.

We have taken an extreme case [302] to display the principle in its crudest form. But is it not true that he who pushes this principle to its farthest feasible limit, avails himself of the needs of others, and that only he who pushes it with cleverness and determination can acquire wealth in modern business life?

Indeed, the entire wages system is a system of taking advantage of our fellow-men. An employer pays his men not according to what they produce, but according to what he can get them to work for. And he can get them to work for less than the net proceeds of their labor, because they are in need of food and shelter, and for some reason can find no chance to employ their labor in such a way as to get the whole proceeds. That is taking advantage of their necessity (for his own advantage), and that is not love.

It would be easy to extend this discussion indefinitely to show that it is hard for any man to engage in business to-day [303] without being in constant temptation to close his heart to generosity and manly squareness; and that it is hard indeed for a man greatly to "prosper" in business without succumbing to the temptation.

We do not mean to deny that men who have gained wealth, are tender husbands and fathers, and generous friends. Some of the most terrible men on the Street are known for their delightful family life. We do not mean to assert either, that they are always conscious of doing wrong when they employ the means of money-making which all the world about them is employing. The guilt of social wrong lies on the entire society which permits it to exist. There is not a thinking man in America who is not to some extent responsible for every exploitation of human weakness under our business system. And yet we cannot, as some do, put the whole blame on the system. Within certain limits the individual is free to obey the [304] system or not to obey it. And it would he hard to persuade us that, for instance, the directors of the New York Elevated Roads, when they united their lines and watered their joint stock to escape paying over part of their profit over to the public according to law, were not conscious of doing wrong.

In short it is hard for a rich man, who has gained his riches himself, to enter the Kingdom, because money-getting is not well compatible with the justice and love of the Kingdom of Jesus. It is still true, as in Paul's day, that "they who desire to be rich fall into a temptation and a snare and many foolish and hurtful lusts, such as drown men in destruction and perdition" (I Tim. 6, 6-10). And yet men think themselves happy if they have a chance of falling into that temptation and think their lives well spent if they can see their children firmly caught in that snare. **[305]** 2.) As a man cannot wall gain wealth without sacrificing the Christian virtues, so he cannot well possess wealth without damage to his own soul.

The common church doctrine is that it does not matter how much a man has, but how he uses what he has. People are fond of quoting Christ's explanation as reported by Mark (10, 23-24), "how hard it is for them that trust in riches to enter into the Kingdom of God." But that is exactly the meaning of Christ, that they who have riches are so certain to put their faith and their heart into them. Christ expressed a profound fact when, in connection with his commandment not to hoard wealth, he said: "for where thy treasure is, there will thy heart be also." It is a magnetic force, the sinister attraction of the Hort of the Nibelungen, to which even they are victims who think they are masters of it. Mr. Charles Dudley Warner in his "Little journey in the World," a novel of delightful delicacy and self-control, has told **[306]** the story of the gradual crumbling of a noble character under the influence of wealth and society. Our fiction is full of such, and our real life fuller yet.

We frequently hear protests against the habit of denouncing the rich as a class and lauding the poor as a class. It is asserted that both have equal temptations and equal chances of being bad. I deny it. If the chances are equal, why does Christ make them unequal? Why does he say that it is hard for a rich man to enter the Kingdom, and not that it is hard for any man? Why does he pronounce blessings upon the poor, upon those that hunger now and weep now, and woes upon those who are rich, and upon those who are full now and laugh now? (Lk. 6, 20-26). It is tried to explain this passage spiritually, of spiritual humility and weeping for sin, and of religious self-satisfaction and carelessness. But that does violence to the text taken by itself. Matthew gives the beatitudes a more spiritual turn (Mt. 5, 3-9); but unless we would reject either account as unfaithful, we must suppose that [307] the same class was poor, hungry and crushed in temporal affairs, and lowly, meek and mourning in religious needs. If we picture to ourselves the Galilean peasants flocking about Christ we can easily understand the union of bodily and spiritual needs. There were many like the palsied man, who needed to hear the word of bodily and spiritual help. Those throngs who followed Christ into the desert places, were so hungry for righteousness that they listened to him all day, and so inured to physical want that they had made no provision for a lunch-basket on leaving home, as a better-fed people is sure to do. In the psalms and prophets the "poor man" is also the weak and God-fearing man, who puts his trust in Jehovah in the face of the oppression of the mighty. Matthew and Luke have each given one side of the Old Testament *Aniyim*, when the one reports Jesus calling "the poor" blessed, and the other "the poor in spirit." And those who to-day side with the poor as a class against the rich as a class are quite in harmony with Biblical conceptions. [308] The brightest virtues and the truest lives are with the common people, to-day as in Galilee; not with the pauper class, nor with the upper class, but with the great body of the people who earn their living in the sweat of their brow. They do not get a dollar without doing an ample dollar's worth of work for it, whatever others may do. They suffer wrong far oftener than they do it. Men call them discontented. They are not. They are not as impatient, as restless, as lustful for change, as *blasè* to the simple pleasures of life, as those who have all the appliances for happiness. Their patience is a marvel. It is no wonder that poets and artists who have once come to know them, love them and pour the richest colors of their sunsets about the peasants' prayer and work. Christ loved them too.

The poor are brave; the rich are timid. The common people fought the Civil War, while the rich made money out of it. The wealthy classes of England [309] sided with the slave-holders; the poor cotton-spinners of England, when once they understood the bearings of the war, sided with the North and starved. The year 1848 was the revolutionary year of the European peoples. The general distrust of the future found its accurate barometer in the savings banks. They showed a general decrease in the number of accounts and a tendency of the people to keep their cash in hand or to hide it in old boots. But this timidity was greater in the larger accounts. In the savings banks of Saxony the accounts under 20 Thaler actually increased from 1847-48 by 4.4%. Those between 20-50 Thaler decreased 1.1%; 50-100 Th.

decreased 3.6%; 100-200 Th. decreased 7.9%; over 200 Th. decreased 11.3%. That is to say, the poorest people, to whom their few thaler meant most, were yet the most hopeful and stable element. The timidity and anxiety increased in rapid ratio with the wealth of the depositors. This timidity of wealth makes it a reactionary element in every reform. **[310]** The greatest generosity is not found with the rich. Their gifts are heralded and praised. They have all the incentives of ambition and public admiration to spur them to liberality. And yet it is not the rich who cast in much, who get the praise of the just man sitting over against the treasury. It is the poor widow who gets his praise. It is rare that any rich man gives as much, proportionately, as many laboring man gives habitually. Probably any pastor of a working class congregation has seen gifts which, according to Christ's method of bookkeeping, would count for more than anything he has read about in the papers. Even if the rich man and the poor man give in the same proportion, their gifts are not equal. If a workingman earning $15 a week gives a tenth, he has $13.50 left to support himself and his family. If a rich man earning $150 a week gives a tenth, he has $135 left to support a family which is probably smaller. The amounts needed for the absolute necessities of life **[311]** is about the same for every man's stomach. Cut that out of the $13.50, and there is not much left; cut it out of the $135, and there is a great deal left which can go for the unnecessary. The man who gives $15 out of $150 is like a man on a cold day wrapped in warm clothing, fur-coat, fur-cap, fur mittens, and a light muffler about his throat. He meets a freezing child, takes off the muffler, gives it to the child, turns up his fur collar and goes on about as comfortable as before. The man giving $1.50 out of $15 is like a man wearing a single thin over-coat and giving that to the child, while he goes on beating himself with his arms to keep warm. How much would the wife of a rich man have to put down as a charity subscription in order to equal the sacrifice of a woman who bends over the wash-tub all week, and who after finishing her day's stint, goes over to a sick neighbor to do up her week's washing? And such unpretentious deeds of love and heroism are being done all the time, and without making a fuss about it. **[312]** The possession of wealth is the insidious destroyer of character. The children of the rich are exposed to sore temptations. It would be easy to find middle class families who can trace their family back for generations of solid, clean, capable men of business or the professions, and the stock is still as good as new. Rich families deteriorate. A New York paper recently reported in column on column the marriage of the heir of one of the wealthiest families of the city.

He is the third of his line. The paper gave a very good cut of the founder of the family's wealth; a broad, strong German face, with firm chin and vaulted forehead. It also gave a cut of the grandson. Perhaps it was an unkind cut, but the falling off was sad. Rich men's boys easily go astray. Rich men's daughters are often married for their money, and the children of a money marriage are not like the children of a love marriage.

But more insidious is the **[313]** deterioration of the finer faculties of the soul, of truthfulness, simplicity, generosity, daring. Wealth blights these. The social forms of high society are full of untruth. Life is artificial. The simple verities of life become nebulous, themes for conversation, flints out of which to strike the sparks of wit. The perceptions are keen, but knowledge and obedience are divorced. Such society is the hot-bed of skepticism. It is sterile of high thinking and of courageous action. Young men of promise who marry rich wives, seldom do anything great. A rich man cannot well fight the cause of the people, which is the cause of God. London society is the undoing of popular reformers. Send a man to Parliament, let him be invited in a few social circles, let him get money enough to keep a horse of his own, and his politics change. Poor people need their children for their support in old age, but they send them out as foreign missionaries. Rich people have enough to support themselves and to make life easy for their children on the foreign field. We hear occasionally of a wealthy man's daughter who **[314]** desires to go, but she does not go. Her parents cannot spare her.

Was the case of the young ruler, who turned away sorrowfully, an isolated case? Did Christ mean anything less than he said, when he called it hard for a rich man to enter the Kingdom? Is it not a solemn truth that a man's life consisteth not in the abundance of the things that he possesseth? Then why do Christian men desire to possess much? Why do they spur their children on to gain much? And why do Christian ministers not warn those who are about to slay their higher life on the altar of Mammon, as they would warn them if they saw them drifting into intemperance or licentiousness?

3.) In the getting and in the having of riches there is danger to their possessor; therefore Christ warns against getting them, and commands the surrender of them. But in addition to that, the owner of wealth is not qualified for citizenship in the Kingdom, because its citizens must build up, and not destroy, the perfect human society. Now the rich, as a **[315]** class, do not make a true life easy for the rest of mankind, but hard.

It has come to be a proverb, that the tramp is the corollary of the millionaire. Where Dives is, Lazarus must be too, if not at his gate, then on Blackwell's Island or in the East Side Tenement. If some have more than they earn, others must have less than they earn.

But neither wealth nor extreme poverty is conducive to the best life. Each is full of temptations; the subtle and gilded temptations for the rich, the sordid and brutal for the poor. But the guilt for both classes of temptation lies on the rich. No one compels the rich to be rich; the poor, on the contrary, though individually they may often be at fault, are not poor because they love to be so, but because they are compelled to be so.

The condition in which men are most secure against temptation and the most useful constituents of society, is when they work steadily for their daily bread, without the immediate pressure of want or the haunting fear of it, with a comfortable **[316]** home and leisure enough to read a good book, to see their friends, and to take an interest in public affairs. That used to be the condition of life in America. A nation consisting of such men is a great nation. The English yeomen were the material for England's greatness and freedom. With the growth of a wealthy class, this middle class is cut into, at once from the top and the bottom. There are districts of Germany divided into farms; there are others divided into great estates and worked by laborers. Where will the most solid men be raised? Where will public safety and decency be most insecure? The farm laborer is the complement of the landed proprietor; the city proletarian is the complement of the money king.

The very poor, whose lives are squalid and insecure, are the first victims to temptation. Every added pressure carries some of them out from honesty into crime, as every icy wave loosens a feeble grasp in the spars of the shipwrecked **[317]** vessel. M. Parent-Duchatelet examined carefully into the history of 5183 prostitutes in Paris. He found that 2398 had been put on the downward path by some first sin of frailty. 2696 had gone into it because they were generally poor and wretched, or without relatives and helpless; 37 to feed old parents, 29 to maintain younger brothers and sisters, 23 because they found no other way of supporting their own children. Of 3084 whom the same careful investigator examined as to their occupation, he found that only three had a little property, a fixed income of from 200-1000 Francs. It is the "fingers thin" that "push from them faintly want and sin." When want becomes too strong, the sin is pushed away no longer. In England the number of youthful prostitutes rises above the average in years of scarcity, and falls below it in years of plenty. It would remain to be seen how the percentage would decrease if all the girls had a fair chance of a good living and a happy marriage. We repeat what we have already said: the outward temptation and the **[318]** inward desire combine to produce sin. Therefore Christ bids us pray our Father not to lead us into temptation. The church as the body of Christ is to serve in answering this prayer. It is to lessen temptation and not to increase it. But the existence of wealth increases temptation. It first takes from the poor and renders them needy. Then it comes and tempts them with wealth in accumulated splendor, and plunges them in sin. It is those who make rent artificially dear, that make homes hard to form. It is those who make coal artificially dear that drive the lonely young man or girl into the bright and warm palaces of sin. There are two destructive and dangerous classes. The one is at the top, the other is at the bottom. But it is the strong, who have elbowed their way to the top who will be held responsible for themselves and for the weak ones whom their climbing feet have pressed down into the mud. And after they have pressed them down, they turn around and ask: "Why are you so dirty? Why do you delight in groveling in the mire?" **[319]** Wealth dissocializes society. All that we have said on that score about rank holds of wealth, because wealth to-day confers rank. The wealthy man is not the brother of the poor man, whatever moral somersaults he may perform to make himself believe so. It would take a great soul indeed for him not to patronize his poor neighbor. And it will take a greater soul yet in the poor man to accept the advances of his rich neighbor as the friendship of an equal. Wealthy men who really try to meet the poor on their own terms, are constantly foiled by the suspicion and sensitiveness of the poor. It is the price which they have to pay for their wealth. They gain dollars and lose brothers.

Christianity desires to bind humanity together. Differences in wealth cut it asunder. Christianity desires to remove the stumbling-blocks from the path of the weak. Wealth strews them broad-cast. Shall the enemy who sows the tares be hired to help in the husbandry of the Kingdom of God? Does it seem so strange that Christ demands of high officers in the army of Mammon, that they **[320]** shall resign their position and strip off their insignia, before they enlist as soldiers in the army of God?

4.) And finally wealth is incompatible with the Kingdom, not only because it harms its possessor and stumbles others, but because if it does enter the Kingdom, it corrupts Christianity itself. And if the devil can unsalt the salt and sterilize the leaven, he will pat himself for a good day's work.

The admission of wealth into the church has delayed the acceptance of Christ's law. We may as well be frank. We Christians <u>are</u> anxious for the morrow. We do not give to him that asks, nor lend to anyone that requires a loan. We do not give our cloak to him that takes our coat. We insist everywhere on strict obedience to the plain commands of Christ, and yet we do not even pretend to obey these precepts. Why not? In most cases probably because we want the things ourselves, and do not propose to give them away. But some **[321]** have actually tried this "promiscuous charity" and have found that it worked harm. What shall we say then? Was Christ less wise than we? Or did he solemnly enjoin duties which he did not expect anybody to live up to till the Millennium?

Hardly. The difficulty lies here: that rich men try to make ethics work which were meant for men who live the simple and natural life enjoined by Jesus. If a man has a great pile of wealth, more than other people about him, of course they all lust for it and try to get some share of it, and if it were known that he would give to anyone that asks, they would quickly relieve him of his surplus. Indeed, it sometimes seems to us, that the assurance with which people ask of those who possess, and the resentment which they feel when refused, is due to the deeply implanted instinct of human brotherhood. That instinct makes us risk our lives to rescue a drowning beggar. Why should it not make the beggar feel that if his brother has bread, he has a right to part of it? Here also corruption of the noblest instinct is the worst. **[322]** But if a man who lives day by day on the produce of his toil, is asked for help by a man in want, there is nothing much to arouse the man's cupidity. He can only be made free to a seat at the table, or to an extra coat. Or if he wants to borrow, he will find no tremendous sums to be drawn. He may borrow a tool, or some seed-corn. But whatever he gets, there will always be the sense: "my brother is stripping himself for my sake; he will eat less; he will have no extra coat." And this sacrifice in the giver does act as a check on the receiver, except in the case of very abandoned characters. Instead of encouraging shiftlessness, it would reprove it.

There are many good, plain people who by natural instinct obey this law of Christ. Their task is made difficult for them by the false conditions created by the wealthy, and by the pauper habits awakened and fostered by the existing inequalities. Many a farmer in times past would never have let a wayfarer pass from his door hungry or without shelter. But since **[323]** the distress has become frequent in the manufacturing centers, and men out of work first had to take to the road, and then by idleness and vicious companionship have learned to love it, the farmer has had to be more careful of the tramp. The just suffer for the unjust. The disease germs bred in a filthy neighborhood float over into the cleanly home. The plain man in the country is hindered from obeying Christ's law by the effect of wealth-gathering in the cities.

In the same way Christ's law of trust has been made difficult by wealth. He bids us live like the ravens and lilies. But how can a man live so, when it is almost a certainty that he will be laid off two months out of the twelve? When improvements in his trade are projected which will make half the men useless? When twenty men answer an advertisement for a single man? Even the lily would droop and lose its smile, if flag-stones were laid about it on every side, catching the rain, and heavy foliage were trained above it, intercepting the [324] sunshine. Suppose a few ancient ravens should set up a claim of owning the fields, and exact every third worm or grain as rent for the privilege of scratching in their fields, would not a look of care come over the new raven's face too. Christ bids us seek the Kingdom of God and God's righteousness, and all "these things" would be added to us. It is very true; in the measure in which God's will and God's justice orders human society, in that measure will the needs of our life be satisfied without fretful worry. And those who for private profit keep the Kingdom at a distance make it hard to live a life of trust. The rich cannot well live it. He that has a number of Government bonds between him and starvation may think he trusts God, but in fact he trusts God plus the bonds. And for the poor the life of trust is also made hard. Who will talk of trust to a farmer whose back is bent and whose hands can hardly straighten out, and who yet is running behind every year, thanks to scarce money and a plentiful tariff? [325] Who will talk of trust to a small store-keeper whose trade is being absorbed by the big bazaars, and who cannot keep up a whole store on profits with which they only keep up only a single counter? If a man loves wife and children, his very love will throw him into feverish anxiety and make him disobey Christ.

So we lay it upon the disobedience to Christ's primary law against riches, that all the minor laws of charitable help and of trust are made impossible to the rich and difficult to the poor. Every step toward the social equalization of wealth will bring Christ's ethics within the bounds of the possible. If the unrighteous sources of wealth will be cut off, there will be no such inequality of possession as there is now. There cannot be. Men are by nature unequal, but they are not unequal enough to justify anything like the present inequality of [326] wealth. And when the weakness and inertia of generations of poverty shall have been eliminated by plentiful food and intellectual stimulus (and America has proved that it can be done in two generations), then the inequality will be still more reduced, and we shall have that soundest and most delightful society, the society of intellectual and social equals.

Then, with the assured basis of life which nature conquered by man will give, with no haunting fear of starvation, a life of trust in God and of flourishing in the sunshine of his love, will be possible to more than the most heroic souls. "Ah, but Christ says: The poor ye have always with you." Yes, Christ was right as usual. At least eighteen centuries have corroborated his words. Perhaps he foresaw that there would be always people who would seize on a text like that and run it like a hand-spike into the wheels of social progress, and thus keep the poor in society. But there will always be the poor. There will always [327] be slaves to passion who will waste their substance. There will always be the sick who need a friendly hand. There will always be the aged and the very young, who will need protection and love. There will always be the widowed, who have buried their beloved; and the lonely ones, who have never possessed their beloved. Truly there will always be the poor, and opportunity enough for suffering to do its chastening work, and for love to do its healing work. And if all the other poor should fail, there would still perhaps be one so feeble that he could not distinguish a declarative sentence from an imperative, and would insist on changing: "The poor ye have always with you," into "Strive to have the poor always with you."

In a community governed by righteousness there would still be opportunity for love. And only there could love do its unhampered work. The fault in our modern charity is that love is made to do the work of justice, and that is an upside-down arrangement which makes even the simple precepts of Jesus [328] appear unwise and impracticable. Such masses of poverty as our great cities possess have not been created by private fault or misfortune, but by social injustice, and therefore of course private charity cannot cope with it, but social justice must put a stop to its production. Charity is best administered by personal friends and neighbors. They know best when the other is in need, and what he needs, and when they help the suffering one out, it has no pauperizing effect. There is still a vast amount of this mutual help among the working classes. When the number of sufferers becomes so great, or their friends are so destitute, that a great charitable machinery is necessary, it is in itself a proof that there is something wrong in society. And then the best love will be that which, while relieving the greatest distress, labors away to remove the social injustice. Charity can never be more than supplementary to justice. All honor to the workers in the charitable societies; but they know best the weary hopelessness of their task. They [329] know how often they do evil by doing good, and how charity itself becomes destructive. The idea of charitable machinery! That means loving machinery, and how can machinery love, even when loving women are part of it? Truly has Lowell said:

> "Not what we give, but what we share,
> For the gift without the giver is bare."

Modern charity divorces the gift and the giver. The giver does not know the receiver and the receiver does not know the giver. No wonder Christianity of that sort becomes an evil.

And, as we have said, this prostitution of religion itself is brought about by the alliance of Christianity and wealth. Religion should do away with riches. Instead of that it allows wealth to manufacture poverty, and then accepts the alms of wealth to undo in a lame fashion the evil that has been wrought. But instead of undoing it, it adds new evils. And so the evils roll into a snarl that men despair to see unwound. Nor will it be, except by a Christianity that does not fear to be radical and revolutionary. Public justice; and then private charity; that is the only true order. [330] We have tried to show that the co-existence of wealth and poverty makes the morality of Jesus difficult of comprehension and still more difficult of obedience. And it is also true that it corrupts the spirituality of the Christian religion.

Is it not a significant fact that wherever modern civilization with its contrasts of rich and poor is greatest, there materialism and unbelief is greatest also? What great city is there in civilized nations, that is not godless? The proportion of church attendance is everywhere smallest in the great cities. Why is this? It would be foolish to assign it to only one cause, but we are surely not wrong in attributing part of it to the existence of wealth and poverty.

The wealthy class which contaminates the morality of the working classes, also saps their religious faith. The wealthy classes of England and America are still religious after the velvet-bound-prayer-book fashion. Religion is part of respectability. But on the Continent where the rich have emancipated themselves, they are the bearers of a [331] practical materialism which justifies itself by a cynical skepticism. How has France come to be irreligious?

Her irreligion is not of recent growth. It began in the dissolute aristocracy of the last century, which settled God with an epigram. From there lust and unbelief, uniting in a deadlier poison, trickled down into the lower classes. Robespierre objected to atheism because it was aristocratic. The same thing has been true in Germany. A Socialist in the Reichstag charged the bourgeoisie with having made unbelief fashionable, and of being the originator of the pessimistic materialism of the common people. And now the wealthy classes in Europe, having made religion contemptible to the people by their ridicule of it, make Christianity hateful by enlisting the church on their behalf. They have found that the wind they have sown, has raised them a harvest of whirlwind. They tremble at the red terror and beckon to the priest to exorcise it. And the priest founds charitable institutions with the rich man's money, and preaches to the **[332]** masses that "the rich and the poor must dwell together," and that we must "give honor to whom honor is due."

Another cause for the religious indifference of the great cities, is the grinding hardness of the life of the poor. To live away from the mountains, the meadows, the sea, and from all the handiwork of God; to be cooped up in a story street with nothing but brick and iron; to live all the day among whirling wheels making a few mechanical motions; to drag a weary body home only to find a querulous wife, a sloppy supper, a dingy bed; if these are not enough to take the ideal thoughts and aspirations, to which religion appeals, out of a man's heart, what is? What is there of God in the dreary labyrinth of the East End of London, or in the drearier rectangles of the East Side of New York? What language would God speak to a Job living in a tenement? How would he make known his majesty to one who has never seen the Pleiades through the city smoke, who sees the treasures of **[333]** the snow only in the slush, and inspects leviathan and behemoth behind the bars at Central Park? How' can we complain because the Socialists' ideal is an idealized factory and a glorified tenement house? That is what we have shut the working people up to. How can we complain that they believe in materialism and hold the whole world to be a great machine with merciless cogs, a world of matter, in which brute pleasure is the aim and brute force and selfishness the means? That is the sort of world they live in. The marvel is that any trace of the ideal remains in them. This unbelief and religious indifference of the masses is another count in the indictment against our unjust and loveless civilizations, and since Christ and humanity cannot call the whole corporation to account just yet, the warrants are out against its directors and agents, the protagonists, the embodiment, tools and profiters of the evil. Let not the wealthy classes protest indignantly against the judgement everywhere beginning. It is God's judgement through humanity. [334] But the most effectual damage done to Christianity lies in this, that wealth and power gain control of the church and use it as a tool. Constantine was the far-seeing man to begin it and in the most varied forms it has continued to this day. The process is very natural. The clergy are educated. They find more affinity among the wealthy than among the poor and ignorant. Their natural drawing is away from the poor. It is only a powerful spiritual impulse and conviction which can keep them down with the people. The same fact appears with labor leaders, and all other leaders of the people. Then when the interests of the poor clash with those of the rich, they incline to side with those who possess so much more enlightenment and refinement, everything that passes for a higher life with all except the most spiritual eyes. Then there is the fact that with the help of the wealthy and powerful so much good can be done. Have influence with a king, and you can get immunity from taxation for the church lands. [335] Have influence with a rich man and you can build a hospital. Is it not the duty of the servants of God to cultivate the wealthy, persuade them to consecrate their talents to the service of the Lord, and then teach the people gratitude to their benefactors? Would it not be wrong to offend them by hasty words?

Some of the best impulses have made good men subservient to the wealthy and have silenced their tongue against wrong. The wiser among the wealthy know the power of ideas, and of a clergy rising as tribunes of the people. They are trained and dexterous in using influence, social favor, and patronage to tie the young reformer with silken bands.

It cannot be denied that the church as a whole, while it contains good democratic material, is largely under aristocratic management. That will not be denied concerning the Roman Catholic Church with its monarchical constitution, nor concerning the established churches of Protestant countries. The minister is allowed considerable freedom of movement, but there are limits, as [336] he knows after he has passed them, and as his wife knows before he passes them. Our American churches are the continuation largely of dissenting movements in Europe, which sprang up among the people, and therefore contain a more popular religion and a more republican form of government. But even in the freest denominations wealth is making its power felt. The forms of worship are becoming refined. The aesthetic element is becoming more prominent. There are wealthy congregations and poor congregations. And the wealthy churches make their power felt in the denomination, for from them come the sinews of war. Religion needs money, a great deal of it, and therefore those who have money are important persons to the Kingdom of God. They are elected into the boards of Home and Foreign and City Mission Societies, Education Societies, Church Edifice Societies, every sort of societies. The men of whom Jesus said that they shall with difficulty get into the Kingdom have checkmated him. They have got **[337]** in and they run things. The minds that have discovered the ways of making money out of the poor, sit in the board and devise ways of carrying good tidings to them. The hearts that have proved their proficiency in worldly wisdom, now meditate the deep things of the Spirit. Above all they deliberate on "how to reach the masses." Ah the confession that lies in that threadbare phrase! So we have to reach them? There is a gulf fixed between us? We are not the masses, not of them, not in them; we are above somewhere, discussing how to reach them. The cork is trying to dive into the water. There was a time when the Christians were the masses, fishermen, tent-weavers, low-browed slaves, garlic-eating Jews, a sinister mass to fill the mind of the philosopher with disgust and the mind of the statesman with vague alarm. That is all changed now. The cross is on our highest domes. We wear it as an ornament in gold and jewels. Christianity now is great, recognized as a power. The princes of the world lay their trophies **[338]** at its feet.

And there are the people down yonder. We ought to reach them. We ought to persuade them that "at the foot of the cross alone the social question can be solved." Instead of that they run after agitators and demagogues.

It was the first Sunday in May. I rode through London on the top of a bus. It was very quiet. Well dressed people were going into the churches. Well dressed people were going into the chapels. Fine quarters and dingy quarters; but where were the vulgar herd? Ah here they come; a mob rolling through the street, ragged boys, jeering girls; a little string of blue and red in the middle; a big drum, a few plain, sober, bright-eyed faces. God bless them; they are still of the people. We approach Hyde Park. What a crowd! Thousands, tens of thousands, hundreds of thousands. They are talking, making love, lying on the grass, eating oranges. These are the people. There is no end to the march; brawny union black-smiths, haggard non-union **[339]** sweated tailors. Yonder are the platforms, a dozen of them, every one with a band of speakers. There is John Burns; that yonder is Tom Mann. John Burns is the man who for weeks got up every morning at four, harangued the starving dockers, infused courage into them, persuaded them not to use violence, and then went off to his shop to earn his living. Tom

Mann is the fellow who heard that in a certain trade chemicals were used dangerous to health. He got himself employed and worked till his hands were raw and bleeding, that he might help the men by knowing the business. There is a cart with an Episcopalian minister side by side with a Jewess, the daughter of Karl Marx.

I met a friend, a cultured American gentleman. I thought of the churches in Belgravia and these crowds, and I asked: "Where would Christ be, if he were in London?" "He would be here, for he had compassion on the multitude." "Would he speak from the tail of a cart, as he spoke from the tail of a boat?" "Probably."

A few days later I came into Westminster Abbey when they were **[340]** consecrating three bishops. Over the heads of the congregation I caught a glimpse of a solemn procession in the nave, garments, robes, gilt crucifixes. I returned an hour later; they were still consecrating the bishops. I went off for lunch and came back; the bishops were still on the make. Now, how can we more readily imagine Jesus? In an archbishop's robe bowing, kneeling, marching, wheeling, and all that to get a man fit to be a successor of the apostles and to draw a salary? Or on the tail of a cart talking to the multitude on the social question? Which would seem to him more important for the Kingdom of God on earth?

The interests of the leaders of the various churches and the interests of Jesus do <u>not</u> go in the same direction. The public sentiment of the churches as expressed in the most influential religious papers (with a few notable exceptions) sympathizes with the movements of the common people only when they are directed by the wealthy, and not when they are indigenous in the **[341]** masses. We have noticed that religious papers scarcely ever announce the success of a strike, but seldom fail to announce the collapse of one. And yet, more strikes succeed than fail. It shows where the editorial sympathy lies in the weary struggle of the people.

> "Have ye builded your thrones and altars then
> On the bodies and souls of living men?
> And think ye that building shall endure
> Which shelters the rich and crushes the poor?"

We have given much space to this discussion, not because we love it, but because it is sorely needed. The secular and religious press extol the rich and their works and represent them as prime movers of social progress and pillars of godliness. Christ's teaching flatly contradicts that. And since his teaching on this point has been so generally suppressed, we have set forth fully the reasonableness of his opposition to the gathering of wealth. We restate once more his positive teaching.

He desires that every man shall work and live on the proceeds. He forbids us to insure ourselves against [342] the future by the hoarding of wealth, because we are sure to fasten our heart to our treasure. He bids us not worry about the future, but to seek the establishment of the Kingdom of God on earth, and then a life of simple trust will be easy. He commands us to share with one another as any man needs it, and this mutual help of the community affords the stability and the insurance against cases of sickness or distress. Any attempt to gather wealth for one's self he condemns. He gives no limit of what is permissible, because in a fraternal community the entire community would rise in comfort, and it would then be lawful for a man to have what would be unlawful if he had it for himself alone. Wealth is relative. He is rich who has more than others. The efforts for prosperity should tend to raise the whole plane of life and not to raise one above the plane. If any man is rich, he should divest himself of his wealth and turn it to public uses.

It will not do for Christians to wait for society as a whole to reach a better life. They must anticipate [343] the progress of society by private action, and by anticipating it, speed it on. Except your righteousness exceeds the righteousness of political economy, ye can in no wise enter the Kingdom.

Such anticipation will of course make it impossible for a man pluck the best fruits of the existing conditions. It will to some extent keep him poor and despised. In how far he has to fall in with present conditions in order to sustain his own life and the life of his family, he must let the Spirit teach him. There is no law for him except the law of the Spirit. If he saves up the seed-corn for next year's harvest; if he lays by something to educate his children; if he lays by something for his wife's old age, who will condemn him, until we have a society Christian enough to relieve the individual of self-insurance. If a man has consecrated his ability to the advancement of the Kingdom, and he feels that it would be equivalent to the destruction of his life to live as low as the lowest, let him take what comfort he needs for his best work. A famished town has often given double rations to the [344] soldiers on the ramparts. A boat-load of ship-wrecked sailors would do well to allow a double portion of crackers to the mate who alone knows navigation. And the worker for the Kingdom will find that the poor are very ready to allow him better comfort than they have, if they see that he is fighting their battles. It is all his, provided he is Christ's. And if a man finds that he would injure his brother by giving him what he asks, let him refuse it. A father or elder brother may refuse something to a lad whom he dearly loves. But let such a man look to it that his refusal is due to the love he bears his brother and not to the love he bears himself. The new law of Jesus is no law set in ordinances. It prescribes no dead rules. It is a compass pointing ever to the perfection of justice and love. He that carries it is free to turn out of his way for trees and rocks. A man may perhaps obey Christ's law best at times by disobeying it. The Spirit is the freest taskmaster. He that has it, can go and come at pleasure, and yet he is absolutely bound, a bond servant of Jesus Christ. [345] While we are to anticipate the development of society by private action, we have not exhausted our responsibility thereby. We know what kind of society Christ desires, and we can further every movement of corporate society in that direction. The abolition of every unjust privilege of wealth-gathering will tend toward the social equality desired by Jesus. It will make a natural life easier for the poor, and remove the temptation from the rich. And in addition every social action tending to fraternal co-operation and unity of interest among men will be an incorporation of Christ's thoughts in the institutions of mankind. Negatively, the abolition of injustice; positively, fraternal association among equals; these are to be simultaneously the social words of the future. [346] We have spoken of Christ's law of love as it finds expression in an equal regard for my brother's life and my own life, his honor and my honor, his prosperity and mine. There is one other department of our reciprocal duties, more confined in scope, but of the greatest importance: the relation of one half of humanity to the other half, of sex to sex.

It goes without saying that Jesus hated impurity and forbade it. He accepted as a matter of course the ancient law against adultery. But he did not, like the Decalogue, stop with acts of impurity, but brought the conscience of his followers to bear on the thoughts, which precede and generate the acts. Impure actions are not an absolute standard of guilt. There are those who have never done the wrong, but who have always loved it. And there are those who by their evil surroundings have been led to do the wrong before they loved it. Men judge what they see; God looks at the heart; and for the followers of Christ it is necessary to adopt God's standard so far as it is possible for man. [347] Now, while Jesus advocated and represented a higher standard of purity than his times, he was freer in his intercourse with women than the customs of his times sanctioned. He freely opened a conversation with a woman whom he chanced to meet alone at a well. The disciples who represented public opinion, on their return "marvelled that he was speaking with a woman." Moreover Jesus knew, what they did not know, that conversation with this particular woman was not conducive to a good reputation in that neighborhood. Again, in the case of the woman who was "a sinner," he quietly submitted to her approach and touch. There was not the least attempt in the entire scene to keep her at a distance. And in his conversation with his host he made no effort to establish his own prophethood, which had been challenged, but championed the woman by making the noble spring of her action clear (Lk. 7, 36-50).

If this was his bearing in extreme cases, it may be supposed that he would maintain the same frank bearing toward women in general. He was a frequent guest in the home at Bethany. Several women seem to **[348]** have been part of the little traveling company. It would have been safer for him to keep at a greater distance from them. The records of the early church have preserved no slanders against him on this score. But it is hardly possible that the world in his case forgot its readiest resource to blacken a purity that condemns it. It would have been easy for him to assume the reserve which a Rabbi's position almost demanded. That he did not do so, is itself a declaration. The barriers erected between men and women are confessions of weakness; an increase of purity makes greater freedom possible. And greater freedom in turn produces purity of mind.

On the whole there is a surprising scarcity of utterances on this matter in his teachings. When he did speak of it, it was in reply to questions. He did not voluntarily return to it, as he does to the subject of ambition or wealth.

The questions on which his opinion was called out by others, covered the debatable ground where conscience is most ready to find excuses for itself and **[349]** to fortify itself by law and custom. For what causes may a man divorce his wife? May he marry again? May she marry again?

The first principle laid down by Jesus is, that marriage ideally does not admit of dissolution. There is that implanted in man and woman at creation, which makes a union between them unlike any other human relation, surpassing even the relation between parents and children in closeness. It makes the two one, a complete Man. For man to meddle with this union and tear it asunder to gratify a fit of anger, a new lust, or a desire of profit, is an interference with the laws of God and an undoing of his doings (Mt. 19, 1-6).

The only thing that can justify the dissolving of the relation on the part of one, is if the other has cut the bond which first united them and which constitutes the peculiarity of marriage. Interference with marriage sows the seed of every trouble. It sends the woman out into life disgraced, torn out of her natural family relation, without means of income, and thus peculiarly liable to temptation, and herself a cause [350] of temptation (Mt. 5, 32). It implicates the man and the family that receives her. The damage done by dissolving the family life is in exact proportion to the fundamental social importance of the family, and to its blessings when good. The number of divorces is found to bear a very close correspondence to the number of illegitimate births, showing that there is a unity of cause. It has been found too that even to-day, when a woman is not nearly so helpless outside of the family relation as in Christ's time, divorced women furnish far more than their proportion of criminality. Statistics also corroborate Christ's suspicion of second marriages. In Holland and Saxony the number of divorced women marrying again is twice as great as the proportionate number of widows marrying again, although in general the widows would be considered more eligible than they. There is therefore very often a second marriage in the background.

When the Pharisees objected to Christ's position on the indissoluble nature of marriage, that Moses had [351] made regulations about divorce, he replied that Moses had done so "for your hardness of heart, but from the beginning it hath not been so" (Mt. 19, 8). In other words, Moses came as near the ideal law as the condition of his countrymen would permit. Jesus does not appear to censure such approximate legislation; he merely insists that they shall keep the divine ideal before them, and not be content to drop down on a standard or morality set up for past times and evil men. They are not to turn the permission of Moses into a command.

And then he spoke of a higher standard yet, of a voluntary renunciation of marriage for the sake of the Kingdom of God (Mt. 19, 11-12). He that has put his whole life into that is not troubled, as the disciples were, to see marriage stripped of its convenience. But Jesus knew that a life of such devotion is not given to many, and he imposes the duty on no one (Mt. 19, 11).

There is one other point on which he expressed himself emphatically. Among the notions of the future life entertained by the Jews was that [352] of the continuance of the sexual relations. The descriptions of the Rabbis were often gross and sometimes beastly. The Sadducees used this to ridicule the whole idea of a future life. They imagined the tangle in which family affairs would be after the resurrection, if all the relations of this life were to be resumed. Jesus took the position of neither Pharisees nor Sadducees. He asserted the future life, but denied that the marrying and giving in marriage would continue there (Mt. 22, 23-33).

This is probably the sum of the distinct teachings of Jesus on the relation of men and women. The beautiful passage of Christ and the woman in the temple we are unable to accept as authentic. There are several inferences to be drawn from them, however, upon which we shall touch below.

The teaching of Paul is very full and its influence on the church has been great. It will be useful to sum it up.

His warnings against impurity are frequent. It was the besetting sin of the Greeks, and all who lived among them were exposed to the contagion. It was constantly invading the church, just as it does in heathen **[353]** nations still. The council at Jerusalem considered it necessary to except it expressly from the general liberty given to the Gentile Christians (Acts 15, 29), and Paul emphatically refused to place it among the actions neither good nor bad in themselves, such as the keeping of days and the eating of certain food (I Cor. 6, 12-20). He asserted that it is impossible to hold an act of impurity at arm's length; it involves the whole being and infallibly debases it.

Concerning marriage he expressed his opinion very fully, though he claimed no categorical authority for his advice, but only that consideration which is due to the thoughts of a man who "has received mercy of the Lord to be trustworthy" (I Cor. 7). He denies that there is any wrong in marriage, and protests against the beginnings of asceticism which were manifesting themselves in the church (Col. 2, 20-23; I Tim. 4, 1-5). He holds that for some it is the only safety, and that they ought to marry. Yet for those who have power over themselves he thinks it best that they remain as they are. The time is short till the coming of the Lord. **[354]** Just as he advises the Jew to remain a Jew, and the Gentile to remain a Gentile; the freedman to remain so and the slave to be content as a slave; so he advises the married not to shake off the tie nor the unmarried to enter it. If a man does marry, he will have the distress of seeing his wife and children involved in the coming persecutions. Alone they have only himself to care for. And finally, if a man or woman is married, it is natural and inevitable that part of their interest and work is given to their family, and thus some of the strenuousness of their efforts for the Kingdom will be lost. Paul himself, therefore, remained unmarried. He claimed the right to be married like other apostles, but freely renounced it, just as he made no use of his right to receive a salary. He refused to get as much out of life as he could, lest in using the world to the full, he should get to serving it.

We proceed now to draw several inferences from these teachings, and hope that we shall do no violence to them. [355] 1.) The first evident inference is, that Jesus worked in the direction of the permanence of marriage, and not the reverse. It is safe to say that he would not sympathize with those who hope for benefits from its easy dissolution. Everything that would tend to make it a union of life and for life would meet with his encouragement; everything which would tend to make it the legalized method of self-gratification, to be dissolved when the passion has lost its fire, would meet with his resistance. No man can dissolve such a relation without secret damage to his own best life, and without involving others in sorrow. It would require good [356] cause indeed to perform a psycho-surgical operation of so serious a character.

But as Jesus would resist a pressure against the bond of marriage from within, so he would resist all unnecessary pressure from without. There are such pressures in which no single person, but the whole society furnishes the weight. The statistics of morality show that divorces increase in years of scarcity and industrial anxiety. It seems that the worry and anxiety for the future, the snappy temper of a hungry stomach and of feet weary with searching for work, chafe through many a bond that would otherwise endure. Here also God distributes the responsibility justly. But would it not well befit those who profess themselves anxious for the sanctity of marriage to hold aloof from it anything that would endanger it? Another fact of importance is that the proportion of divorces is smallest for the wage-workers, and greater for the educated and wealthy classes. This fact is no contradiction of the preceding statement, that financial [357] distress increases divorces. For want is a relative term. Want means for every man less than he has been accustomed to have. A businessman would consider himself in great want if he came down to the earnings that seem prosperity to the daylaborer. No, this fact indicates that increasing intelligence and education do not solve moral questions, but make them more acute. It shows that unless morality keeps progress with education, education contains a menace to society. In France the liberal professions contain about 2.4 % of the population, but between 1843-67 they brought in 23.29 % of all the petitions for divorce. This fact supports our assertion that the life of the upper classes is overwrought and unhealthy. A family in which husband and wife both have their stint of daily work to do, in which the pleasures are simple instead of highly spiced, and no ennui begs the devil to make the house his home, is fairly safe against the main causes of divorce.

2.) The second inference from Christ's teaching is, that he was standing **[358]** up for the women. The Pharisees were asking for what cause a man might divorce his wife. Nobody thought of asking when a woman might divorce her husband. Women were not doing it. In that condition of society marriage was the only vocation, the only road to social respect, the only harbor of safety for a woman. She had everything to gain by its stability. She had everything to fear from a law which put her at the mercy of her husband's moods. That this was the actual bearing of Christ's declaration concerning the permanence of marriage, is evident from the rueful exclamation of the disciples: "If the case of the man is so with his wife, it is not expedient to marry" (Mt. 19, 10).

It is well to bear this in mind, for the decision of Jesus is most often being turned against the women to-day. They are bidden to submit to cruelties and all injuries, as long as the husband does not sin against the one point named. By the change of social con- **[359]** ditions obedience to the letter of Christ's teaching may offend against its purpose.

3.) The entire question of marriage and divorce is better taken hold of before the marriage than after it. The best way to diminish divorces is to diminish the number of marriages that will end in divorces.

The pairing off of young people always has been and always will be full of uncertainty and possibilities of heart-ache and disappointment. But it is safe to say that it will go on most smoothly where the following conditions are fulfilled: a community without great differences of rank and wealth, so that the choice will be independent of money considerations; a community with a neighborly social life, so that young people can freely meet and take time to develop their predilections; an education and independent position for the girls, which will make them partners joining the firm with an equal stock of working capacity, and not suppliants waiting **[360]** for somebody to support them. Our highly developed city life furnishes none of these requisites. The community is stratified, and everybody tries to crawl from one story of the house into the next higher. Young men marry capital for their business. For young women their marriage is the one business chance of their life time, and they must be on the alert accordingly. These considerations are not so decisive in America as yet, as they are in "the better classes" in Europe, but we shall inevitably get there, if American social conditions go on developing in their present direction. And when once love-marriages become rare, farewell to the promise of the American stock.

The second condition of a neighborly social circle is almost nonexistent in a modern great city, at least for the mass of its inhabitants. Tenement house life is the death of family sociability. Young men do not meet their [361] future wives in the sacred atmosphere of the home. They "get mashed on them" on the street, in the Elevated, or in the public ball-room. They fall suddenly in love, and after marriage they fall just as suddenly out of it. They do their love-making under the electric lights of Tomkins Square and whisper their vows in the shrieks of the merry-go-round at Coney Island. Our great cities are sand-heaps, piles of human atoms. They lack the elementary structures of a social organism, within which the family can build itself up. This also is upon the heads of those who are robbing the people of homes by their avarice.

And finally it is notorious that women are not on an equal footing with men in view of marriage. It is a crying pity to see how girls are forced out of their natural modesty by their false position. Everything is involved for them in being well married. They have to study to be attractive. They have to use means of attraction which operate more speedily, but which for that very [362] reason give a less permanent basis to love. They are compelled to take a man whom they respect little and love less, because their mother whispers that there may not be another chance. On the other hand among the young men the bachelor life is becoming more frequent. As single men they can have a standard of living which the support of a family would immediately cut down. They can have the enjoyment of women's society without its burdens. The increase of unmarried men is always a sign of a rotting civilization. Here again the remedy lies deep. Only a healthy society, in which life is simple and a living certain, makes the formation of families safe and desirable for the men, and makes woman for her own sake a treasure to be sought after, a helpmate and not a burden, a giver of comfort and not a despoiler of it.

There is perhaps nothing that so concerns the lover of his country and of humanity, as the safety [363] of the family life. Corrupt the spring of life and the whole stream is poisoned. Preaching will do something to maintain good morals. But the best way to keep them good is to keep them natural. Unnatural conditions are bound to breed evil. Army life is an unnatural life, and consequently the standing armies of Europe furnish the greatest percentage of sexual extravagance and disease, as well as of crime and suicide.

Everything that hinders the ready formation of marriages is a cause of social corruption. In Bavaria the percentage of illegitimate births was formerly 22 %. It sank to 18 %, and again to 12.79 % when legal obstacles to marriage and to the freedom of business life were removed. Industrial pressure acts as forcibly as law to diminish marriages. The maximum number of marriages coincides with the minimum price of grain. Once more we assert that those who artificially disturb and depress the industrial prosperity of the people, bear the guilt of checking marriage, and of driving the sexual [364] impulse to seek illicit means of gratification. Women yield to temptation, and in turn become tempters. And so the evil perpetuates itself.

Let those who obey Christ and desire purity and a healthy family life, begin their work where it will tell best. Let them help to do away with the bitter need of the poor and the rotting superfluity of the rich, which combine to produce prostitution. Let them help to do away with the tenement house by reforming the land system. Let them press forward the education and financial independence of women. Let them in every way help to abolish the chances of dishonest gain, which have poisoned the social body with the malarial fever of covetousness. The love of money is the supplanter of family love. **[365]** The ethical relations which we have so far discussed, are the relations of individual to individual. It is true, we have everywhere been compelled to take the wider outlook and notice the bearing of individual relations to the whole of human society. As a great writer on ethics has said: "There is no longer any private morality." Humanity is drawing together by a thousand forces. And as vibrations travel fastest through the densest bodies, so the moral movements of the social atom communicate themselves most quickly in the most social society. It is one of the pressing duties of religious men to insist on this fact of solidarity and press its ethical importance home to the conscience of every man.

But in addition to this ever-present social background of private morality, every man is placed over against organized society, the state. The state renders us service and exacts duties from us. What attitude does the **[366]** Christian take to its demands?

Three cases can arise. The state may demand of us duties which serve our interests and commend themselves to our conscience. In that case our duty is, plainly, to render all assistance required, and more.

In the second case the state may demand of us what conflicts with our interests without conflicting with our conscience; for instance, in the levying of burdensome taxes, the vexatious interference with the freedom of personal movement etc. In such cases the general law of non-resistance to evil holds as anywhere else. So Jesus submitted to the soldiers sent to arrest him. So he paid the temple tax, though his half-smiling colloquy with Peter shows that he did not much relish it (Mt. 17, 24-27). And so also he advised the Jews to pay the Roman tax. What if they did give Caesar his own? That did not hinder them from giving God the spiritual service that He demanded. Of course in a modern popular government, with the greater rights, we have also the duty to strive for a change **[367]** in laws which we consider oppressive and undesirable. But that does not interfere with personal submission to them. A man may courteously pay the custom's duty on a book which he is importing to furnish him the material wherewith he may overthrow that very duty.

The third case presents by far the greatest difficulties. The state may demand of us something which conflicts with our conscience. It may at the same time damage our interests, or possibly benefit them, but it compels us to do wrong. Shall we obey the authority of the state, or the authority of our conscience?

Theologians have in times past given answers to this question which bound the individual conscience under the divine right of the king who could do no wrong. Rebellion was regarded as always wrong. And the stay for this doctrine which has given a long license to wicked men and hindered the enfranchisement of the people, was taken from the Scriptures. Does not Paul say: "Let every soul be in subjection to the higher powers; for there is no power but of God, and the powers that be are ordained of God. Therefore he that resisteth the power, withstandeth **[368]** the ordinance of God"? (Rom. 13, 1-7). So it was argued, that whatever government exists, is of God, and to resist it is rebellion against God. But they refused to see the reason which Paul assigns for his advice: "For rulers are not a terror to the good work, but to the evil....He is a minister of God, an avenger for wrath to him that doeth evil. Wherefore ye must needs be in subjection, not only because of the wrath, but also for conscience sake." Obedience therefore is due because civil government stands up for good against evil, and thus demands the free approval of our moral judgement. But suppose there is a government which persistently terrorizes the good and favors the evil? Suppose that it approves itself, not by isolated errors, but by its settled policy, a minister of Satan, an avenger for wrath to him that doeth good? Then what? Paul's command falls to the ground with the reason given for it. It may be objected that Paul wrote this injunction of obedience while evil men wore the imperial purple. It is true; yet the injustice of Roman rule has often been exaggerated. It was burden- [369] some; it was cruel when its own supremacy was endangered. So is the rule of England in India, but like the English rule the Roman government was the justest, on the whole, that the world had seen. Even the much abused Pilate stood firmer in the defense of innocence than many an American police justice would do, if all the Irish politicians of his district demanded the committal of an obnoxious Italian. To him it was a question between his own political existence and the life of a strange fanatic with a touch of sublimity. He was only not absolutely just.

A passage in the first epistle of Peter (2, 13-17) throws light on the purpose of Paul's command. Peter bids his friends be subject to anything that the king or his deputies command, because they are set to punish evil and reward good. "For so is the will of God, that by well-doing ye should put to silence the ignorance of foolish men; as free, and not using your freedom for a cloke of wickedness, but as bondservants of God." These young Christians had been drinking of the new wine of freedom, and they were getting unsteady on their feet. [370] Paul was always warning against the abuse of freedom in private morality. The same danger threatened in public life. The Christians, conscious of having in them a higher norm of life, were inclined rudely to walk across established customs and civil laws, and thus to create the impression that they were refractory and impertinent disturbers of society. The same danger is noticeable on foreign mission fields. The converts are inclined to hold their heads very high and make themselves obnoxious. It is the danger of every transition period. It is the same vexatious and amusing swagger that we all know in lads outgrowing their boyhood. Now, in the early days of Christianity this was a serious matter. Christianity was a new phenomenon and was being observed with a critical and unfriendly eye. Men would judge it by its worst. These immature members who used their new freedom as a pretty covering for what was after all self-indulgence, were endangering the whole movement. Both Paul and Peter told them that one of the chief uses of freedom is not to use it, and that existing institutions had a solid foundation of justice and usefulness [371] underneath them, and were not to be lightly set aside.

But this free and manly submission to existing institutions, though known to be imperfect, is a very different thing from a slavish obedience which surrenders the personal conscience to the keeping of government. There was nothing servile about John the Baptist before Herod. There was not the budging of one inch in Jesus before the high-priest: "if I have spoken evil, bear witness of the evil; but if well, why smitest thou me?" (John 18, 23). He met the foxy curiosity of Herod with impenetrable silence, and the polite incredulity of Pilate with a self-possessed dignity that is admirable. Certainly there was nothing cringing in the bearing of Stephen before the Sanhedrin (Acts 7, 51-60). Nor in that of Paul: "God shall smite thee, thou whited wall; and sittest thou to judge me according to the law, and commandest me to be smitten contrary to the law?" (Acts 23, 1-5). We love him as much for this passionate outburst of insulted innocence, as for the courteous self-control that followed. But the plainest declaration of the Christian position was made by Peter before the Sanhedrin. He boldly charged **[372]** them with injustice in their official capacity, and refused obedience to their commands in so far as they ran contrary to the will of God (Acts 4, 10, 19). "We must obey God rather than men" (Acts 5, 29). And, what is the crucial point, he claimed the right to interpret the will of God for himself, and to set his interpretation over against the interpretation of the highest authority that he knew of. It was the Declaration of Independence of the individual conscience, which received its ultimate expression by Luther at the Diet of Worms.

If the state demands that a citizen shall believe, say or do, what he, after due deliberation and consultation with others, considers wrong, he may and must refuse obedience. Abolitionists were right in disobeying the fugitive slave law. The Quakers were right in refusing to take oaths. The Mennonites were right in refusing to serve as soldiers. When the wrong consists in any single demand, passive resistance to that one demand coupled with open protest against it, will usually be effective, though it always entails suffering on some. After much chicanery the Mennonites have wrested exemption of military service even from the Russian government. An interesting **[373]** case is told of a chaplain in the Civil War. It was against his conscience to kill anybody, but he was no coward. In battle he was forward in every charge, whooping and shouting, but carrying his rifle idle in his hands.

The matter is more complicated when the national wrong cannot be so directly reached, but is bound up in the general life of the State. In civilized politics the peaceful redress of injustice is now so open, that it would be wrong for anyone to take more stringent measures until he has done all that is possible along the prescribed course of redress. But there are cases where a passive refusal to be implicated in a wrong might become necessary. For instance, if England should begin another opium war, would it not be right for

Christian citizens to refuse the payment of taxes, part of which would be used for the maintenance of iniquity?

We speak only of passive resistance, because we hold that to be in the end the quickest, the most effective, and the cleanest method. Jesus rejected armed resistance even against the most crying wrong (John 18, 36.) But those who do not share that conviction against the use of force, can with difficulty **[374]** show why armed resistance against a wrong done by civil government is not permissible. If one nation may fight another nation to resist the searching of ships on the high seas; if a colony may fight the mother country to resist an oppressive tax; why may not part of a nation resist another part inflicting a wrong upon them? It may justly be demanded that those aggrieved shall seek redress peacefully. But what if peaceful redress is denied? What if, as in Russia, the public voice is stifled, even the humblest petition draws down cruel punishment on the petitioners, and the aspirations of patriotism and popular devotion which would be the pride of other countries, are treated as crimes? What if in the struggle of an oppressed class for its rights, the oppressors should pack juries, procure special legislation, mislead public opinion by corrupting the press, slander the champions of the poor, and in every way defeat the legitimate efforts for justice? What if experience should gradually lead the oppressed to despair of making headway **[375]** by the peaceful presentation of their rights, and should teach them that there are some men with whom a little fright goes farther than much argument? What if some state should one day appear not to be the organized people at all, but an organized class rebelling against the unorganized people? Then those who believe in the use of force against rebellion would find the same guns used, only pointed in the opposite direction, and they could raise no just protest against it.

This is the attitude of the Christian toward government: devoted assistance when government seeks the right; submission to troublesome burdens if they fall on him and do not compel a participation in wrong; passive resistance and public protest against compulsory participation in wrong-doing. And the judgement in every case lies with the individual conscience, which, however, is bound before God to have sought all light and wisdom obtainable, before it sets itself against public action. **[the text on page 376 is crossed out] [377]** The moral life of man is active in three directions: in his relations to his fellow-men; in the conscious maintenance of his own personality; in his fellowship with God. We have attempted in the preceding sections to set forth Christ's law concerning the relations between man and man. We pass now to the moral actions which turn back on the man's own life. Of course, in point of fact the two divisions run into each other. A man's bearing toward his neighbor determines his own life, and a man's personal integrity affects his neighbor.

The first duty of man to himself is to maintain his consistency, his unity of life, his truth. Hypocrisy, double-mindedness, is one of the few sins to which Jesus gave no quarter. A man may be bad and a slave to his passions, but as long as there is an acting connection between his outward moral bearing and his inward moral life, so long moral power can be exerted upon him to help him. But when you talk truth to a man and he answers [378] you piously, and yet his heart is far from what he says, what can you do for such a man? He is like a patent churn with a broken shaft; you turn the crank, the cogs rattle, but the wheel stands still.

The simplest form of truthfulness is to speak the truth, to let your yea mean yea and not nay.

Men find that inconvenient. Lying is very easy. So they lie. But that again is inconvenient, for there are occasions when truth is really necessary, for instance in making a contract or in bearing witness in court. Then the universal distrust of one another is felt to recoil on every one concerned. So they have invented a method of securing truth and fidelity in these special cases. They compel the person bearing witness or giving a promise to call on some higher being, or something sacred to him, to visit punishment on him in case of an untruth, and they trust to the man's superstitious fear to keep him from untruth in that case. This is called swearing, and false swearing has ever been considered [379] very wicked, while false talking is of little importance.

Christ levels this artificial distinction. He ridicules the invoking of heaven or earth, which are the throne and footstool of God and have nothing to do with the wee unite of a man who stands there swearing. Swearing is based on superstition and its special influence falls both for him who believes that God hears nothing and for him who believes that God is present at his lightest word as well as at his solemn oath.

But the worst feature about swearing is its untruthfulness. It proceeds from a consciousness of untruthfulness which needs a special asseveration. The really truthful man says "yes" and is done with it. It does not occur to him that anything more is necessary to secure belief. The untruthful man suspects distrust, and seeks to prevent it by confirming his words by oaths. While the Decalogue demanded veracity only in witnessing in court, Jesus demands truth everywhere. While the old [380] law forbade false swearing, Jesus forbade all swearing, and expected his followers to be so genuine in their truthfulness, that their yea would mean yea to all men. If they should yield to the custom of swearing, there was danger that in their minds also the distinction between solemn utterances for which truth is necessary, and common occasions at which untruth is permissible, would be built up again.

It does not appear that the Christian world has made much progress in the obedience to this command of Jesus. It has outlawed profane swearing, and perhaps diminished the kind of swearing that Peter dropped into in the court of the highpriest. But the solemn swearing is still in vogue, and it is often maintained that Jesus made no reference to that. But that also is condemned by its fruits. The oath of Herod and the vow of Jephtha are typical cases, how men are entrapped by an oath to do what they know to be wrong (Mt. 14, 1-12). The oath of loyalty to a sovereign has often in history constrained the consciences of good men to act against the welfare of their country. In his vow of celibacy the young Catholic priest makes a [381] solemn promise, which at the moment of his consecration he may be perfectly minded to keep, but which in after years may become a two-edged sword keeping two lives asunder that ought before God to unite. So the vows of secret societies are either superfluous mummeries, or if they mean anything they ought not to be sworn. No man has the right to give his conscience into the keeping of another man, or of a soulless corporation. He has not even the right to sell his own future, by promising forever to abide by rules of conduct which future years may show him to be inadequate or wrong. It may be objected that matters would not be changed if men regarded their plain yes as good as an oath. Theoretically not; practically they would be changed. Somehow the senseless literalism of the oath does not attach to the plain promise even of the most honest man. He feels bound to the spirit of the promise, but not to its mere form, which may be rendered hostile to the spirit by the change of events.

In short, Christ's suspicion of oaths is well founded. The Christian should need no oath to secure belief in his assertions, and should use no oath to bind himself for a future which he does not know. The inward consistency of his life, the steadfastness of his principles, will be a sufficient guarantee for those who have to trust him. [382] And if Christians can use their influence to abolish oaths in civil life, they will probably do no damage. The way the oath is administered in our law-courts and by our public notaries awakens neither reverence nor superstition. The main reason why men lie less under oath is because they are liable to prosecution. If that is retained there will be little decrease in judicial truthfulness. And there will be this gain. At present the word of the most dissolute and of the most honest man in a township are supposed to be of equal value if they are under oath. Yet they are not. A clever rascal may take care to keep within the letter of the law and yet distort the whole case. Why not let the honest man's testimony have the additional weight to which his honesty entitles it, by letting every man's yea and nay stand on its own strength?

In the next place Jesus taught that a man's words judge him. "By thy words thou shalt be justified, and by thy words thou shalt be condemned." For "out of the abundance of the heart the mouth speaketh." Generally speaking, a man's words are the barometer of his soul. Therefore Jesus treated it so seriously [383] when the Pharisees insinuated that the Spirit which was overcoming the demoniacs was a Satanic spirit. It is the last stage of a soul's decay when it cannot distinguish between white and black, between God's Spirit and the Devil. About everything else a man may be in doubt, even about the Son of Man, and a word against him can be forgiven. But the Spirit comes with immediate conviction to the heart of every man; and when a man by his words shows that he has lost his sense of the Spirit, those words pass an irretrievable judgement upon him (Mt. 12, 22-37).

But words do more than express an inward state. They clinch a conviction. This also Jesus recognized. When their minds were ripe for it, he gave the disciples an opportunity to express themselves in regard to him. And when Peter, speaking the mind of all, asserted that he was the Messiah, the son of the living God, Jesus hailed this expression as an epoch in his work, and began from that time to open up a new reach of thoughts to them (Mt. 16, 13-21). Such an expression of thought is like a stone put under the wagon-wheel in driving up a hill; it secures the distance that has been gained and gives the horse breath for the next pull. The Declaration of Independence was made with an effort. It was the wave-crest of patriotic daring. Only a part of the young nation rose so high. But when the declaration [384] was once put forth, it stayed, and drew the next step after it. Therefore Paul couples the believing of the heart and the confession of the mouth together, like the driving of the nail and the clinching of it (Rom. 10, 10). And therefore Christ has instituted baptism as the emphatic public expression of that faith and that committal to obedience which has taken place in the silence of the heart. The two things belong together. The outward expression without the inward reality is vain; the inward reality without the outward expression is incomplete and in danger of dying still-born.

But Jesus was not the man that judged words by a superficial judgement. He puts the greatest value on words, and then again he disparages words. It was only in so far as to his discerning spirit they really indicated the state of the heart, that he cared for them at all. If they were contradicted by the acts of the speaker the words were bubbles of wind. Acts are a more conclusive criterion than words, because they come more slowly and cost more. Therefore not all that say "Lord! Lord!" shall enter the Kingdom but those who do the will of the Father (Mt. 7, 15-27). Words are blossoms; actions are fruit. Not the son who says "I go, sir," is dear to the father, but the son that does go. If Christ has to choose between words without action **[385]** and actions without words, he prefers the latter (Mt. 21, 28-32).

It is the peculiar danger of religious men and religious communities, that their words are so likely to be different from their actions. In a community like that of the Jews, like England under the Puritans, or like any church to-day, there is a standard of religious thought and utterance which is adopted without effort, and most successfully reproduced by those who have the glibbest tongue. This religious vernacular of the community is modeled on the utterances of really spiritual men, used perhaps in moments of profound emotion. Thus the utterances of the pulpit or the prayer-meeting soar high, but the actions dangle down below somewhere. Again it often happens that a man has in his youth possessed a living faith, but that under the cares of life and the deceitful of riches it has oozed away. The high-water mark is still visible. The man remembers what a life with God is. He retains the expressions which his inward life formed for itself in the Springtide of his spirit. So the grasping, covetous old man speaks with the accents of love and damns the religion he praises. Therefore Paul warns against prophesying beyond the proportion of our faith (Rom. 12, 6). This religious lying is an awful danger. It is detestable to Christ. It is the **[386]** fawning kiss with which Judas shows his intimacy with the Christ whom only a little before he sold for thirty pieces of silver. It is the lie of Ananias, who gave a fraction of his possession and hoped thereby to get the credit of a complete consecration. We know how this leaven of hypocrisy had penetrated the Jewish church at the time of Jesus. The first epistle of John shows that it was at work on the early church also to destroy its whole-heartedness. "He that saith, I know him, and keepeth not his commandments, is a liar, and the truth is not in him" (2, 4). "He that saith he is in the light and hateth his brother, is in the darkness even until now" (2, 9). "Whoso hath the world's goods, and beholdeth his brother in need, and shutteth up his compassion from him, how doth the love of God abide in him? My little children, let us not love in word, neither with the tongue, but in deed and truth" (3, 17-18). How the modern church stands condemned before such words! In Lowell's "Parable" Christ revisits the earth to see how men believe on him. The chief priests and elders receive him and show him that in church and palace and judgement hall his image high over all. But Christ walks sadly through all the splendor. He **[387]** leads forth "an artisan, a stunted, low-br[owed] haggard man, and a poor girl whose f[...] thin pushed from her faintly want and sin." And as the priests and rulers draw back their robes, Jesus points to the two and said: "These are the images ye have made of me." Walk through Fifth Avenue and Madison Avenue, and admire the double rows of lofty spires rising amid sumptuous mansions. Then walk to the East or to the West, as you please, and see the double rows of lofty tenements, ornamented with iron fire-escapes. Add the minus quantity to the plus quantity, and see whether the sum is plus or minus. The net value of a city's or nation's Christianity is represented by its lowest class, not by its highest. And the existence of a sumptuous Christianity in the midst of a destitute population is prima facie evidence of untruth.

The only hope for the church is if it can be pushed forward to accept Christ's standard of practical life, and to put itself into antagonism against gilded wrong. Then it will get into trouble, and the hypocrites will decamp.

Christ abhors double-mindedness. He refuses even the universal loan of truth to those who are not straightforward and genuine (Mt. 21, 25-27). He measures the value of an action by its spontaneity. It was the heartfelt **[388]** sincerity of the multitude's jubilations at the entrance into Jerusalem, which made their Hosannas so delightful to him. "Master, rebuke thy disciples," said the Pharisees, who loved shouting only when it was done by salaried Levites from the approved "Pharisaic Hymn and Tune Book." But Christ answered: "I tell you that, if these shall hold their peace, the stones will cry out." There are occasions that call for noise, and then the most disordered shouts are melodious in Christ's ear. But the sweetest music in his honor is like a rattle of tin-pans, if it is gotten up to order.

It was the spontaneity of Mary's gift which touched him at Bethany. The disciples were calculating about precisely the best way to invest the cost of the ointment in charity. Jesus sided with feminine feeling against masculine hard-headedness. With their prudence they were letting his heart starve for a little love in those days of bitter need. She divined it, and lavished the costly stuff on him in a flood of sweetness.

On the other hand it was the lack of spontaneity which struck a chill into him in the religious devotions that he watched about him. [389] Men gave alms and watched out of the corners of their eye for public approval. They fasted and advertised the piety of their stomachs by the sadness of their countenances. They prayed and meanwhile calculated their increasing reputation. Yes, by the terrible irony of sin through which the deceiver at last becomes self-deceived, they got so that they thought they could impose on the Almighty himself, and make Him mistake the multitude of their words for fervor (Mt. 6, 1-18). As an old lady once said to the writer: "I never feel really blessed in my public prayers, till the tears come." So she watched the swelling of her lachrymal glands as she prayed to God.

To sum up: Jesus demands wholeness of life, a correspondence of our words to our actions, and of both to our inward life. The value of words and acts depends entirely on their ingenuousness and spontaneity. Religious actions lose their value by side-thoughts and calculations of profit. Chronic separation between the heart and its manifestations induces spiritual paralysis and death. [390] The second duty of man to himself is to keep his higher life supreme. For though a man "delight in the law of God after the inward man," yet he "sees a different law in his members, warring against the law of his mind, and bringing him into captivity under the law of sin which is in his members." That there is this conflict of desires we all know by experience. It is the problem of every religion and philosophy. And everyone who has not darkened the lamp of his soul by lust or by speculation, knows it as an absolute verity, that the voice of the spirit is the voice which he should obey, when it contradicts the clamor of his body.

Christianity teaches: first, that this inward conflict exists; second, that it is the common and natural thing to obey the flesh; third, that this obedience produces inward corruption and ends in death; fourth, that by faith in Christ man comes in contact with the life of God and receives power to overcome the domination of sin and to obey the spirit; fifth, that the culmination of this progressive victory is eternal life. [391] But this victory requires constant effort and watchfulness. He that stands, always has to take heed lest he fall. The attraction of the world operates on our lower nature as incessantly as the force of gravitation. Our hearts are always in danger of being "overcharged with surfeiting and drunkenness and cares of this life" (Lk. 21, 34). Therefore we must "watch and pray, that we enter not into temptation," for though the spirit be willing, the flesh is weak (Mt. 26, 41). There is a limit to every man's strength of resistance. And there is a vulnerable place in every man's life, though as with Siegfried it be only the size of a linden-leaf. Every man knows where it is. Therefore let him take heed lest he expose it to the enemy whose spear hovers ready. His weakness is probably bound up with his strongest affections. But though it be dear to him as the apple of his eye or as his trusty right hand, let him cut through; it will ruin his soul (Mt. 18, 8-9). It may be a book, a habit, a companion, an ambition; it is very likely to be wealth. The best thing is amputation, performed even a little above the diseased spot to make sure. That **[392]** was Paul's mind for himself (I Cor. 9). He saw others venturing very close to the boundary line of the permissible, and he saw some throw up their hands as they went over the precipice. He refused to go as far as he dared to go. He preferred voluntarily to surrender some of his just privileges. He had a right to the sweet comforts of married life as well as other apostles. But he knew that the mated bird seeks a nest; the restless missionary would begin to shorten his flights; he would begin to tremble at mobs and dungeons; and the work which God had laid upon his soul would remain incomplete. He shook his head and remained alone. He had a right to support at the hands of these whom he served. If the herdsman everywhere has a right to eat of the milk of the flock which he tends, surely one carrying the highest treasures of truth and knowledge may claim the means of life from those whom he blesses. But Paul refused support. He preferred to stitch tent-canvass for a living and preach for nothing. He was bound not to let the noble race of his **[393]** life slow down into a leisurely amble for his daily bread. If an athlete could freely refuse the delicacies of life to keep his muscles firm and to gain a wreath of pine-twigs, surely Paul could abstain from some things to win the unfading wreath of honor which God bestows on a righteous and heroic life.

The abstinence which Christ demands is not weak and colorless. Christian virtue is not absence of faults. Jesus had no love for the negative characters; for the man with one talent who does not waste it, but just wraps it in a napkin and does nothing with it; for the virgins who wake up at the critical moment to find out that they have no oil and are useless in the procession; for the fig-tree that does not do the one thing for which it was planted; for the respectable people who lived in the midst of the poor, the hungry, the naked, but only did nothing for them. Decide yourself, says Christ; be either for or against me; if you are not for me, I count you on the other side. The man that is simply not bad is like an empty house free to the first batch of demons that passes by. [394] Wherever Jesus found energy, daring, insistence, he praised it. What an eye he had for the heroism in John's character. John was none of your reeds wobbling in the wind; none of your pretty courtiers in soft raiment; he was a man; he was a granite pillar and not a plaster-cast. Herod could break him but never bend him. There, said Jesus, that is the character of the Kingdom; the men of violence, who storm in by force, are the ones to take it (Mt. 11, 7-12). Three men came to him who wanted to follow him. Yes, said he, you may come; but you must come right away; and you will risk it that you will be more homeless than the jackal and the swallow. If you are of the sort that puts its hand to the plow, but keeps its head turned back with a longing look at the cool fence-corner and the lunch-basket, you had better stay away (Lk. 9, 57-62). The kind of faith that Jesus praises, is not the faith that sits down in an upholstered elevator and tries to believe that it believes that the elevator is sufficiently [395] strong to carry it up. Christ's ideal of faith is the faith that mounts on the roof and tears up the shingles, if it cannot get in by the door; the faith that climbs into a sycamore tree to see Christ, forgetful of respectability; the faith that without a word leaves nets and boats and follows the call of the nobler future; the faith that leaves the publican's counting-house without stopping to balance accounts and collect outstanding debts; the faith that beats a rattattoo on a friend's door at midnight, wears out a judge who cares for neither God nor men, and turns a brusque word of refusal into a still more pleading appeal.

While it is necessary for men to abstain, Jesus does not put the emphasis on abstinence, but on energy. He does not pray for his followers that they be taken out of a tempting world, but that, living in the world, they overcome it. There are two ways of preserving purity. One way is to keep out of sight and hearing of all that may [396] sully. The other way is to face evil and grapple with it. A lad, delicately nurtured in a pure family circle, may have the purity of innocence. A preacher, living amid vice and foulness, may have the purity of holiness. And that is the Christian purity.

Christ has put himself in contrast with John the Baptist: "John came neither eating nor drinking, and they say, He hath a devil; the Son of man came eating and drinking, and they say, Behold, a gluttonous man, and a wine-bibber, a friend of publicans and sinners!" They were one in their energy. But John's energy carried him out of the world into the desert; Christ's energy carried him out of the desert into the world. And yet he remained pure. Thrust the nozzle of a garden-hose into a street-puddle and turn the water on; will the mud of the puddle enter the hose?

It is well known that the Christian church has not always taken this view of Christ's teaching. It has taken John the Baptist as its model more frequently than Christ. The piety of centuries was ascetic. The hermit, the celibate, was considered more holy **[397]** than the married man of business. Flight from the world was the only sure way of salvation. Even to this day the predominant feature of Christianity in the mind of the people is the abstinence from certain pleasures.

It can fairly be maintained that asceticism had an influence for good. It was a passionate protest against the contagious sensuality of pagan life. And there is an abiding reason in it, as we saw in Paul's case. It is better voluntarily to abstain from some things that are permissible, than to push liberty to the very edge.

But the great fault of the ascetic tendency is that it substituted the salvation of one's soul for the Christian aim of establishing the Kingdom of God. By that silent substitution the words of Christ took on a different meaning. Jesus spoke of abstinence from marriage "for the Kingdom of heaven's sake" (Mt. 19, 12). Paul practiced it. It is simply the renouncing of family happiness in order to concentrate one's whole life on the establishment of God's will on earth. In that sense it is only doing with the **[398]** sublimest and all-inclusive patriotism what many a young volunteer has done who left his bride unwed to fight his country's battles. But a narrower Christianity turned Christ's unselfishness into a selfish love of one's own soul, to the salvation of which our own tenderest impulses and perhaps the happiness of others has to be sacrificed.

Jesus in a measure loosened the bonds of his family, and substituted the community of his disciples for it. They were brother and sister and mother to him. It is that loosening of natural bonds and that growing strength of spiritual kinship which every man has felt who has ever consecrated himself to a great cause and joined a noble movement. It is the lot of every revolutionist to turn from the tears of parents or to draw from the clasp of loving hands. And as long as the revolutionary character of Christ's purpose is recognized, there is nothing strange in his demand that every man who comes to him must hate his own father and wife **[399]** and children and brethren, yea and his own life. But when that revolutionary purpose is forgotten the command becomes harsh, brutal, inhuman. To give up one love for the sake of a larger love is right and natural. Every man does it who leaves his parents to cleave to his wife. Every man does it who, like Hector of Troy, leaves Andromache and his child to fall for his fatherland. But to give up the love of others from love of ourselves and our salvation is not an expansion of life, but a contraction. A man leaving his family to enter a monastery and spend his time telling beads and singing vigils, has no business to take Christ's words into his mouth.

If Christianity is a revolutionary movement for the emancipation of humanity, the Christian doctrine of self-sacrifice is reasonable and noble. Horatius who held the bridge; Winkelried who broke a way for liberty; the Spartan heroes of Thermopylae anointing their hair for the last battle as for a feast; indeed every noble deed that has kindled the imagination of our **[400]** boyhood down to that of the last locomotive engineer who drove his engine crashing through the debris on the track to cut a way for the train, they all contain the element of self-sacrifice for others. Christ gave the ultimate expression to it and made it a universal law. It is the carrying into action the principle of loving our brothers.

But the whole principle is immediately vitiated if the sacrifice is made for ourselves. If a man cuts down his food to ten boiled peas a day to feed others, it may be unwise, but it is grand. But when a man might have more, but confines himself to ten peas, that he may torture his flesh and win merit with heaven, we wonder at it, but we do not admire it. It is true that devotion for others will bring reward; "he that loses his life for my sake, shall find it"; but if he loses his life in order to find it and not in order to help others, then the other half of Christ's word is applicable: "he that seeketh his life shall lose it."

Asceticism, then, contains a solid **[401]** basis of sense. When in any given case the natural desires of life conflict either with the rights and well-being of others, or with our own nobler nature, there is nothing for it but resistance. So far most will agree. And, furthermore, when in surveying our life as a whole, we perceive that our dangers lie along certain lines and that even a moderate indulgence may endanger our self-control or chill our spiritual ardor, it is wise to restrict ourselves voluntarily. So far goes the asceticism of the New Testament. It does not go far enough to take a man out of human society nor to annihilate the natural impulses with which God endowed him. Christ has once for all demonstrated the possible holiness of common human life. Christianity would lift man up, not by making him less man, but by making him truly man. For, as Pascal says, "man is neither angel nor beast; and the trouble is that he who would make an angel of him, makes him a beast."

Wherever Christianity appears to demand a stricter asceticism, it is not [402] asceticism at all, but concentrated devotion for the good of humanity. He who gives himself to the Kingdom of God will be scourged like a monk; but unlike a monk it will not be himself that swings the scourge in the lonely cell, but others will swing it over him in public life.

The cause of false asceticism everywhere we seek in the substitution of personal salvation for the establishment of the Kingdom of God in the teaching of the church. That has twisted the words of Christ out of their natural meaning. That has diverted the energy of religious men from public affairs and concentrated it on themselves. That has produced a false type of godliness. Not till the doctrine of the Kingdom of God shall have entered once more into the consciousness of the church, and Christianity shall become a revolutionary movement, will Christian morality lose its unworldly pallor, and become once more the sublimest type of civic virtue. Then no Christian revolutionist [403] need be anxious about inflicting pain upon himself. Others will do it for him. [404] We have spoken of the law of Christ as it regulates our actions toward our fellow-men and toward ourselves. It remains to speak of the actions in which our relation to God is expressed,—if there are any such.

In Jewish society there were a multitude of actions, performed not because they were a help to man, but because they were supposed to be pleasing to God. Men fasted; not for the good of their digestion, but to please God. Men washed their hands; not to get the dirt off, but to undo any defilement which might have been contracted in the sight of God by touching somebody who had touched a dead body. Men painfully abstained from work on the Sabbath; not to have a good rest from their work, but to please God. In short there were a thousand and one actions, which might or might not bring some advantage to men, but which were not performed for the sake of men, but for the sake of God. Aside from good effects on men, the actions themselves were supposed to please God by the very fact of their performance. [405] The most cursory reader of Christ's life must have noticed that these ceremonial laws were the main cause of contention between him and the representatives of the orthodox religion, and that Christ differed from them not in the strictness of his observance, but in its looseness. A more careful reading shows only one ceremonial law, the observance of which he enjoined, and that was the law commanding a leper who believed himself healed, to be examined by the priest and to make an offering of purification. There was a sanitary basis to this law. The priest was the public officer who had to guard the community against the rash readmission of the quarantined lepers. Jesus knew that the men whom he healed, were sound, but he desired that they subject themselves to the regular civil procedure with all that pertained to it (Mk. 1, 40-45; Lk. 17, 11-14). **[406]** There is one other instance in which it may seem, as if Jesus displayed zeal for ceremonial law. On his last visit to the temple, he drove out those who were selling the objects needed for sacrifice, saying: "It is written: My house shall be called a house of prayer; but ye make it a den of robbers." But a closer examination shows that here also his interest was for humanity and against ceremonialism. Those who were marketing the sacrificial animals and changing the secular money of the pilgrims for the temple shekel which alone was permitted for offerings, were serving the interests of ceremonial worship, but their Oriental chatter, their Jewish greed of barter, robbed the place of its sanctity, sullied the thoughts of reverence with the heat of covetousness, in short, turned the place into a robbers' den. Immediately afterward the blind and lame crowded to Jesus to be healed, and the children, taking up the cry of the morning's procession, shouted their silvery hosannas about the temple court. That Jesus permitted; but now the ceremonialists were **[407]** indignant. That was their difference of attitude. To their mind the covetous clatter of trade was no defilement, as long as ceremonial objects were being bought and sold; but a crowd of dirty beggars limping or leaping about, and a rabble of children shouting Hosannas to their enemy were an intolerable profanation. Jesus exactly reversed it. Ceremonialism was not sacred to him; the needs and joys of humanity were (Mt. 21, 12-16).

Against some of the ceremonial rules of Jewish society Jesus offended by neglect.

He failed to fast like the Pharisees. The disciples caught his indifference and also ate as they pleased. The Pharisees objected (Mk. 2, 18-22). Jesus replied: "Why should they fast? They are happy now, and not sorrowful. They are like the friends of the bridegroom, and no one fasts at a wedding. The time of sorrow will come for them, and when it is natural to fast, then let them fast." Jesus also fasted while he was struggling through his temptations in the wilderness. There are times of trial in which fasting is natural, and then it is also legitimate. But Jesus went farther. **[408]** He implied that fasting was part of an antiquated formalism which would not harmonize with his new life. To put his disciples with their new ideas to observing the old fast days would be like putting fermenting wine into old wine-skins, or like patching a piece of harsh, undressed cloth on a garment falling to pieces with age. Better keep it off; there will only be a worse cracking and tearing.

Another neglect noticed by the Pharisees in the disciples, was their failure to perform the ceremonial washings before they took food (Mt, 15, 1-2, 10-20). When they took Jesus to task for this, he flatly denied that there was any sense in their purifications, on the ground that what touches a man or what he eats, has no influence whatever on the purity of his heart or on his standing before God. That is determined entirely by his inward life and by the thoughts and words and deeds proceeding from him. This was a clean-cut contradiction of the very basis of ceremonialism. No wonder the Pharisees were offended (v. 12).

There were other ceremonial laws against which he offended, not by **[409]** neglect, but by actual violation of them. One of them was the understanding that every pious man, and especially a rabbi pretending to holiness, should keep at a distance from all suspected and unclean persons. Jesus shocked this prejudice thoroughly. He made a point of seeking the society of publicans and sinners, and of getting into conversation with Samaritans. In this also he justified himself by the prophetic motto: "Mercy, not sacrifice," showing that he discerned in the protest of the Pharisees the old clashing of ceremonial piety with mercy and love.

But the most frequent conflict was about the Sabbath law. The Jewish regard for the Sabbath was extremely strict. The Gospels narrate six instances in which Jesus broke the law openly and with determination (Mt. 12, 1-8; 12, 9-14; Lk. 13, 10-17; 14, 1-6; John 5, 1-18; 9, 1-41). Most of them were cases of healing. The ceremonialism of the religious leaders had to such an extent hardened their hearts to the simplest feelings of humanity, that they were chagrined to see a human being relieved of suffering. It is amusing to notice the argument which Jesus usually employed to bring their cruelty home to **[410]** them. He appealed to their selfishness: "Who of you shall have an ass or an ox fall into a well, and will not straightway draw him up on a Sabbath day?" Nobody, of course. But you see, the ox or ass belonged to them, and the suffering man or woman did not, and that makes all the difference in the world.

There was one case, however, in which the violation consisted not in the relief of the sufferings of another, but in the satisfaction of a simple need of nature by the disciples. They were hungry on the Sabbath, and walking through fields of grain they plucked off some ears, rubbed out the corn and ate it. According to the Pharisaic code this was work, and the Pharisees spoke out their horror. Jesus found a precedent which would avail with their lawyer-souls. He reminded them that David and his men had once when hungry eaten the sacred shew-bread, which the priests alone were allowed to eat. Hunger therefore had the right of way over ceremonial restrictions. The plain needs of humanity are the solid first facts of life, the corner posts, beams and girders of the social structure; [411] everything else, even their ceremonial law and their Sabbath, was a supplement and a completing of these, and if it contradicted them, it and not they would have to go. "The sabbath was made for man, and not man for the Sabbath," and therefore the Son of Man, as the representative of humanity and the interpreter of its needs, is "lord even of the Sabbath," and can reduce its observance back to those limits within which it will be a blessing and not a curse to men. So even the Sabbath is stripped of its ceremonial sanctity and its observance based on its usefulness to man (Mk. 2, 23-28).

The hostility of Jesus to ceremonialism grew as he advanced in his work. When he declared his allegiance to the law in the Sermon on the Mount, it does not appear that he was thinking of its ceremonial features at all, for the laws mentioned by him to illustrate his meaning are moral laws. The distinction between moral and ceremonial laws did not exist with the Jews. To them law was law. Jesus did not define the distinction, but he made it practically. When he was compelled [412] by the attacks of the Pharisees to declare his attitude on the ceremonial laws, he declared them partly useless, as fasting and washing; partly put on a wrong and inhuman basis, as the Sabbath law; partly imperfect stages in the development of religion, as the hallowing of special places (John 4, 19-24). But the more he came in conflict with the Jewish religionists, the more did he perceive that ceremonialism was not merely an imperfection of religion, but very apt to be the most stubborn obstacle to a true religion. Those who were most concerned about the traditions of the elders, were most inclined to set at nought the primary commandments of God. Under the pretext of religion they neglected the simplest duties of life (Mt. 15, 1-9). Those who were most minute in tithing mint, anise and cumin, were for that very reason likely to pay little attention to justice, mercy and faith (Mt. 23, 23-24). It is just the temper of the ceremonialist to strain out the gnat and swallow the camel. Those who are full of uncleanness within are [413] most likely to ornament and whitewash the exterior by outward performances indicating religious zeal (Mt. 23, 25-28).

So Jesus has in his parables repeatedly taken the ceremonialist as the type of all that is unlovely and antagonistic to the spirit of the Kingdom. He paints for us the pompous Pharisee, strutting in the very presence of his God because he fasted twice a week and gave the tithes promptly; the surly elder brother, grumbling at the return of the prodigal; the priest and Levite slipping by the man groaning on the Jericho road. Has Jesus anywhere said a good word for ceremonies? He mentioned no ceremonial command in summing up the law for the young ruler. He certainly has woven for the Pharisee "the Nessus-garment of ridicule" which he wears to this day and which has made his name and character common property in every literature. He has warned most emphatically against imagining that ceremonial performances can supplant justice and love, or that any sacrifice will be acceptable before God while he who brings it is not at peace with his fellowmen (Mt. 5, 23-24). [414] We conclude, then, that Jesus recognized no actions as being in themselves holy and for their own sake constituting a service of God. He of course he recognized prayer as the natural expression of loving fellowship with the Father. But even prayer is robbed of its idea of merit. Let a man talk to God naturally as his needs require, but let him not think that God cares for the prayer itself, for the length of it, or the beauty of it, or the set form of it (Mt. 6, 5-15). As for the rest, the acts with which you would serve God, do to man. Receive the most humdrum creature for Christ's sake and you receive Christ; and receiving Christ, you receive God. What need of performing ceremonies to please God, when you can always please him by serving your neighbor? Christ has not, as the Catholic Church teaches, one vicar on earth, but a billion. If you desire to lay a sacrifice at the throne of the King, his plenipotentiary stands ready, commissioned to receive it. Who? The man next [415] to you (Mt. 25, 40-45).

Of the existing acts of a ceremonial nature Jesus left none in existence as ceremonies. He instituted, however, two acts which are in a sense ceremonial, baptism and the Lord's supper. Each is the expression of an inward relation to the unseen Christ. The one is the bath of consecration, the other the meal of fellowship. The one gives conscious and public expression to the free act of the individual, by which he renounces his old life and stakes his all, for life and death, on Jesus Christ. The other is the common meal by which the Christian brotherhood remembers the free and loving death of its Master, and re-affirms its spiritual fellowship with him, its dependence on him, and its loyalty to him. The one marks the inception, the other the continuation of the freely chosen discipleship.

In instituting these outward expressions for spiritual facts, Jesus recognized that necessary trait of human nature, which demands a body for the spirit, an incarnation for the [416] unseen, a "local habitation and a name" for the intangible life of the soul. And the acts, which are created by the inward life, in turn strengthen the inward life. The Marseillaise was the embodied spirit of the French Revolution, but the singing of it in turn propagated and confirmed that spirit. The "stars and stripes" are the symbol of American patriotism, but the sight of the flag in turn kindles and fans the flame of patriotism. So baptism and communion are the result of existing spiritual discipleship; but when thus used, they not only express but establish that discipleship. And when, as they ought, these acts coincide in time with their spiritual equivalents, the two are fused into one, like soul and body, and those who speak of the entire procedure may describe it by either of its constituent parts or by both jointly. That is the New Testament usage.

But it is a very different thing when the outward act is performed with the expectation of thereby creating the spiritual fact; when baptism is [417] performed on an involuntary and unconscious individual, not to declare faith and loyalty and a new life, but to create them; when communion is performed, not as the expression of a fellowship with Christ strong enough to demand an expression, but as a rite, which by its mere performance conveys some mysterious blessing. Then the body is expected to create its soul and life. That is the same reversal of nature and good sense which Jesus opposed in the Jewish notions of purification: it is not the bodily act which purifies or defiles the soul, but the reverse. As men have turned the democratic simplicity of Christ's commonwealth into an ecclesiastical aristocracy, so they have turned his spiritual worship into a system of rites and performances. It is apostasy. This is indeed heresy, not against the letter of a dogma, but against the very spirit of Christianity. The veneration of rites is either due to religious childhood which has not yet attained to the emancipation of the spirit, or to religious senility, which seeks [418] to disguise its impotence by dye and rouge.

Ceremonialism was the first intestine enemy of Christianity. For the enemies who maligned Paul at Corinth and destroyed his work in Galatia, were ceremonialists, who insisted on binding up the limbs of a live faith in the grave-clothes of a dead religion. The Jerusalem council, under the leadership of Peter, built a dam to ward off this destruction from the non-Jewish Christians. The dead works against which Paul protested as powerless to save, were not works of justice or love, but ritual performances, circumcision, keeping of feasts and Sabbaths, the eating of some food and the ceremonial rejection of other food. Such actions might at one time have been commanded, he says; but they were only weak and beggarly rudiments; they were the shadow of a man, falling before him, like him in outline, but not his substance. Since Christ had come, the performance of such things was not **[419]** an advance but a retrogression. It might be necessary for some in a transition period to retain the old forms; Paul himself did so; but they must be inwardly superior to them, freely subjecting themselves to them as to an onerous duty for the sake of those who were still so weak that they could not discern between the Spirit and forms. The heroic battle of Luther against dead works and for faith, was also a battle against ceremonialism. The dead works that Luther had in mind, were masses, processions, crosses, holy water, relics, and all the paraphernalia of outward performances in the Catholic church of his day.

Ceremonialism is the symptom of spiritual decay. A dying faith utters itself in dead works. The Spirit is life; it can utter its life by anything. And then, infallibly, those who have no life and yet desire the appearance of life, seize on those expressions of a living Spirit and turn them into ceremonies.

Therefore the church must be [420] forever on the watch against them. Here also eternal vigilance is the price of liberty.

Christ permits us to utter our filial relation to God in words; only he demands that these words shall be true and shall really utter something. He has also given us two acts, by which we can more impressively utter the two central facts of our Christian life; and here too the first demand is, that they shall be true and utter what they are meant to utter. All other service of God is to find its vent in the service of man. He that serves man for God's sake, serves God. And he that does not serve man, does not serve God, though he have a callous on each knee by much praying; though he wear out the cushions of his church pew; though he read his Bible every day and allow no fire in his house on the Sabbath; though he pray in public like an angel and exhort like an archangel; it is in the ear of God like the banging of a restaurant gong, and like a boy's toy drum. **[page 421 is blank] [422]** There remains one more question concerning the law of Christ, a question not concerning his teaching on any single duty, but concerning his teaching on the nature of duty, on responsibility and reward.

The fact of our responsibility is self-evident. We know we are responsible, and that is about as much as can be said concerning it. We are responsible for what we are within the limits of our freedom. And we are responsible for our influence or lack of influence on the world according to the law of solidarity. None of us lives to himself. God has kindled no light of any sort in us to have it concealed under a bushel. The mere existence of the light proves that it was meant to shine and bless. The cause and nature of our responsibility are repeatedly represented by Jesus under the likeness of a trust. We are responsible for what we have, because we did not give it to ourselves. It is a fund entrusted to our management. A trustee differs from a servant in the freedom of his management. He is not under the daily and minute orders of a master. He knows the purpose of his trust; he knows the spirit of him who entrusted it; within those limits he is free to deal. But he is just as responsible as, or even more responsible than, a servant. He will have to give an **[423]** account of his management some day. And while all allowances are made, if he can show that he has acted in good faith according to the purpose of the trust, no allowance whatever is made, if it appears that he has appropriated the trust funds to private uses. The parables of the talents and pounds do not bear on money alone. There was probably no great amount of wealth to be managed by those to whom Jesus told the parable of the pounds on the way from Jericho to Jerusalem. It refers to intellectual ability and attainments, hereditary strength of will, knowledge of truth, beauty of person, physical strength, social position, in short everything which constitutes a working capital in human society. Of course it applies to money also. If any man claims the right to have more property than his fellows, he can justify his claim only by regarding it as a trust. But in that case he will have to demonstrate that he can use it for them better than they could use it for themselves. He places himself voluntarily under the law of trusts, and that law is all the more inexorable because it gives such latitude. Can anyone assert that the wealthy classes on the whole **[424]** have not yielded to the temptation of trusteeship, the temptation to embezzle trust funds? What business corporation would tolerate such a board of trustees as the people of the United States possess in their wealthy men? The grievance is all the greater because the stockholders of the defrauded corporation are the poor, the widows, the orphans. What shall the master of a steward do, who instead of serving the household, begins to act as its master and tyrant, to "beat the menservants and the maidservants and to eat and drink, and to be drunken"? (Lk. 12, 41-46). Every trustee against whom there is well-grounded suspicion by the lavishness of his own outlay and the meagreness of his expenditures for the trust purposes, that he is appropriating the funds, may be summoned to give an account. God has reserved the grand jury and the Supreme Court of the world to himself, whither he may summon evil-doers against whom no plaintiff rises, and to which those who are unjustly judged on earth may still appeal. But he has [425] instituted a minor court on earth in which humanity sits as jury. Before that court the wealthy classes of the civilized nations are now being called to give an account of their trusts. Humanity is only doing its duty before God in calling them to account.

The degree of our responsibility, according to Christ's teachings, is exactly graded according to our knowledge, opportunity and ability. The degree of knowledge in the slothful servant measures the number of stripes which he deserves (Lk. 12, 47). The opportunities enjoyed by Capernaum, the Galilean cities, and the men who listened to Jesus, made their unbelief and disobedience more culpable than the sins of the proverbially wicked, of Tyre and Sidon, of the accursed Sodom, of Nineveh whose wickedness rose up before God, and the generation destroyed by the flood (Mt. 11, 20-24; 12, 41-42). Ability measures obligation: "to whomsoever much is given, of him shall much be required" (Lk. 12, 48). The Jews, Paul says, shall be judged according to the high law which they possess, and the Gentiles by whatever knowledge they have (Rom. 2, 12-15). [426] And as reproof and punishment fall heaviest on those who have done least in proportion to their great abilities, so praise and reward is meted out most richly to those who with small opportunities have done most. The widow's two mites, in Christ's sight, are more than the large gifts of the rich, because they are a sacrifice, a surrender of part of herself (Mk. 12, 41-44). It is effort and sacrifice which tells before God; it is the leaving of houses and brethren and lands for Christ's sake, that shall "receive a hundredfold and inherit eternal life" (Mt. 19, 29). The parable of the talents and the parable of the pounds are alike in their general idea; but there is this difference: in the former two servants start with unequal capital, and present gains which, though unequal in amount, in each case are 100 percent of the capital, and they receive exactly the same commendation; in the latter parable the servants begin with equal capital, but present unequal gains, and their reward is unequal and exactly in proportion to the percentage of their gains (Mt. 25, 14-30; Lk. 19, 11-27). [427] This is a principle of obligation which the world has only to a small extent approximated. In family life that standard prevails sometimes; some parents have loving insight enough to praise their children according to their efforts, and not according to the result of their efforts. But the world at large does not reckon that way. It regards the quantity and quality of the finished product and not the effort that lies behind it. It employs women or children to do the work which men did, and for their greater efforts pays them less. It worships success and not sacrifice. Christ's principle of measuring desert would be revolutionary, if applied. It would level some reputations and exalt others. It may be that some day even the reward paid for work will be measured in some degree by Christ's standard. It is certainly achievable that admiration be more justly distributed in the future. Every man can help to that. He can refuse to admire a public benefaction given from a man's superfluity, and can search out cases in which a sacrifice has been made and hold **[428]** them up to admiration. Every such effort will correct the public standard of judgement. The church itself is derelict. The writer has seen bulky gifts hailed with acclamation by religious assemblies. He has heard pastors in ministers' meetings narrate with grief the death of Mr. Dives, who had left $100,000 for a memorial church bearing his name, while ten millions went to his weeping relatives. He has seldom, if ever, heard any public mention at the death of a poor woman, whose back had grown bent and her joints rheumatic over the wash-tub, and who had yet been cheerful, helpful, bringing up her family honestly, perhaps rising early on Sunday morning to teach a class, and ever with a dollar to spare for the Johnstown flood, the famine in China, or some neighbor poorer than herself. And yet there are many such. Christian men should deliberately refuse to measure gifts and efforts by their size, but make the degree of sacrifice, so far as it can be ascertained, the measure of their admiration. **[429]** Christianity clearly holds out a reward to goodness and warns wrong of the punishment in store. There is a "righteous judgment of God; who will render to every man according to his works; to them that by patience in well-doing seek for glory and honor and incorruption, eternal life; but unto them that are self-seeking, and obey not the truth, but obey unrighteousness, shall be wrath and indignation, tribulation and anguish, upon every soul of man that worketh evil" (Rom. 2, 5-9). It is inevitable. It must be so. As surely as cause follows effect, so surely must a bad life be followed by different results than a good life. This certainty is constantly added in the Christian teachings as an additional incentive to righteousness. Christ warns us to forgive, that we may be forgiven, and not to judge, lest we be judged (Mt. 6, 14-15; 7, 1-2). In exhorting to plain trust in God he dwells on the uselessness and inquietude of anxiety (Mt. 6, 25-34). Paul assures his friends that their labor is not in vain in the Lord, and he quickens his own **[430]** weary steps by the thought of the crown of righteousness which the righteous Judge will give to his faithful servant. The

Apocalypse is always holding out the reward "to him that overcometh," and John speaks of the richer life awaiting those who are even now children of God, and admonishes them to purify themselves in view of this hope.

But while Christianity plainly and often speaks of the certainty of reward, it forbids us to do the right for the sake of reward. It holds it up as an encouragement, but not as a cause for right action. It asserts the utility of righteousness, but it repudiates the utilitarian basis of morality. It insists that it is blessed to give, but does not command us to give that we may be blessed.

Jesus condemns the alms-giving which is done with an eye to a reputation of benevolence (Mt. 6, 2-4). He bids us purposely to single out those actions for which we can expect no return; to invite to dinner those by whom we do not expect to be asked for breakfast (Lk. 14, 12-14); to do kindnesses to those from whom we expect no **[431]** kindness in return (Lk. 6, 31-35). The utilitarian morality is the morality of natural selfishness, which even bad men know well how to handle; only the morality which does good for its own sake, independently of considerations of usefulness, allies us to God, who does even so. The "golden rule" contains a rough and ready method of finding out what is right; it does not contain the motive of doing right. We are to do to others <u>as</u> we would have them do to us, and not in order that they may do the same to us.

> Our heart demands the belief that
> "It's wiser being good than bad;
> It's safer being meek than fierce;
> It's fitter being sane than mad."

The moral universe would crash about us, if it were not so. Even the most heroic soul needs that conviction for itself. There may be moments in which the good man, standing in the flood of adversity and seeing no star of hope to herald relief or vindication, can yet be calm and hold to the right because it is right and not because it is good. But soon the heart will protest, and demand **[432]** like Job, at least to believe that its "avenger liveth and shall stand forth in later days." It may by faith defer the vindication to future ages or another world, but somewhere God must prove himself just.

But this hope is the divine food of the persecuted prophet at the river Kerith, and not the sauce of Ahab's feast. To taste the power of the coming era belongs by right to those who have left the full enjoyment of the present era. It is misused when it is offered as a bait to induce a grudging hand to let slip some present enjoyment.

Jesus had no love for the dickering spirit. He spoke of treasures laid up in heaven, but whenever anyone tried to calculate his savings or asked for the vouchers, he was reproved. When Jesus had asked the young ruler to leave all things and he had refused, Peter, with the naive selfishness of an Oriental, reminded the Master that the disciples had left all and had followed him; "what then shall we have?" Jesus promised [433] full reward, to them and to all who have left anything for his sake. But he immediately went on to narrate a story of a man who hired laborers to work in his vineyard, and when evening came, paid every man justly, but some more generously than seemed right to others. So some began to haggle, and to demand his generosity as their right, and were rebuked (Mt. 19, 27-20, 16). The point of the story is turned against the mercantile spirit of the disciples. He condemns the arrogance which thinks it has not only done all that could be demanded, but has even put the Almighty under obligations. He bids us do our duty cheerfully, and after we have done it all, still regard it as merely our duty (Lk. 17, 7-10).

The fact of reward and punishment has been misused in the church. The calculating spirit has been catered to. The Catholic church sets a price on its prayers and processions. The reciting of one sort of prayer cuts down purgatory by two hundred days and of another by three hundred. This cannot fail to have the effect of fixing the minds of the people on that. [434] They do good, but the edge is taken off from their goodness by the calculation of how much reward it is going to bring them. The natural bias of man is toward selfishness anyway, and there is no need of giving it artificial incentives. Protestantism meant to cut off the mercantile method of piety by denying all merit whatever to human actions and making every man absolutely dependent on divine grace and mercy. It has, I think, succeeded in eliminating the idea of earning reward from the single acts of goodness, but it has so persistently held up the hope of heaven and the fear of hell as the reasons why men should do right, that these have after all become the dominant incentives of the mass of church members in Protestant countries. The single acts of religion and morality are not supposed to earn anything, but everything is humped together and reward expected. It is a longer headed selfishness than that which seeks immediate gratification, but it is selfishness still. The [435] farmer who deposits [the] proceeds of his market sales in the bank on Saturday instead of investing it in a store suit or mixed drinks, is a prudent man; by and by he will use his savings to buy another meadow lot.

On Sunday he abstains from carrying in his hay, misses a whole working day, walks three miles in the broiling sun to the meeting-house, where he succeeds in keeping awake part of the time. He is looking for "the welfare of his soul," his "eternal well-being." He is the same prudent man in the one case as in the other; it is in each case his "well-being" that he is thinking of; only one investment is to realize in this world, and the other in the next.

We do not condemn this. It is natural. We doubt if such considerations can ever be entirely eliminated. They are present even in the love of parents to their children, of husband and wife. That self-control which can renounce immediate gratification for the sake of some larger and higher profit in the future, is the necessary condition of all noble pursuits and of an established society. We do not even [436] say that the alternative of reward or punishment, of heaven or hell should not be held out to men to arouse them to righteousness. In the parable of the unjust steward Jesus appealed to the rich by their faculty of forecasting the future. It was perhaps the only nerve of their stunted conscience which could be made to respond to the galvanic current of truth. But it seems to us that the habitual and exclusive use of this incentive, in much of the popular preaching even of our day, carries with it a serious danger. It hardens men in their selfishness, instead of rousing them out of it. It changes the range of it and not the quantity of it.

Our natural impulse is to sacrifice others to ourselves. The danger of much of our current Christianity is that we learn to sacrifice ourselves to ourselves. True Christianity educates us toward sacrificing ourselves to others, to humanity, to God. That can be learned only if there is an aim constantly before us calling for self-forgetful service and enlisting all our strength. In fixing our mind [437] on that we shall forget to fix it on ourselves. The church must begin once more to preach the Kingdom of God as the central and all-embracing doctrine. That will draw us out of ourselves. And in forgetting ourselves and not seeking our lives because we seek the Kingdom, we shall find our lives. By ceasing to strive for individual perfection, we shall attain a truer and more harmonious perfection. If necessary, let the call be to those who are too engrossed in their gain to care for the Kingdom: "Save yourselves." But to those who do care, let the word be: "The Kingdom of God." And if, in the long and often seemingly hopeless battle against vested wrong and willful ignorance, the heart of the revolutionary soldier of God grows weary, if he looks back at profits spurned and honors untested, then he can justly look forward to the rest that is reserved for the people of God, and hear by faith the words of his Master: "Well done, good and faithful servant, enter thou into the joy of thy Lord." **[page not numbered]** The Kingdom of God is based, not on material, but on spiritual forces. Its advance columns are the invisible hosts of new hopes, new aspirations, new repentances, new convictions. The primary work of the Christian propaganda consists in the propagation of Christ's ideas.

We must "preach the Gospel." But preaching means to be a herald, and the Gospel means Glad Tidings. To carry glad good news as a herald is not to drone over threadbare ideas dressed up in worn-out illustrations. Such a gospel is no news at all, and such preaching is no heralding.

We are told that we must preach "the old Gospel." If men mean by that the everlasting verities of human life, of its slavery under sin and its possible redemption by Jesus Christ, then we like "the old gospel" well. But if they mean – as in fact they mostly do, – that we must express those eternal verities in the terminology of past ages, and limit their application to those circumstances of life, to which men in the past were by their historical condition compelled to limit them, then we object. We refuse to imprison the living Spirit **[page not numbered]** even in its own words. We have no desire to play the part of the Judean religionists over again, who loved the past revelation of God so well, that they would accept no present revelation of his.

The Spirit of God, the great Teacher, is no pedant, that knows nothing beyond the once invented formulas and rules. The God who has adapted plant and animal life to the exigencies of climate and soil in such marvelous diversity, will surely have as closely fitting a religious garment for the multiform spiritual life of humanity. Let every bird sing its own note. Let every man utter the word that God has spoken in his heart. And let every generation formulate in its own vernacular the eternal truths of Jesus. Only then will it be a Gospel to preacher and hearer, and not a study in dead languages.

And as the Spirit must be free to choose its manner of expression, so it must be free to turn the point of its weapon where it will in the shifting battle of history. For the issues change. If the Reformation laid the stress of its preaching on dead works and a living faith, it may be that our age must spurn the dead faith **[page not numbered]** and demand live works. **[page not numbered]**

CHAPTER 5.

THE REVOLUTIONARY PROPAGANDA

We have discussed the aim which Christianity has set for itself. We have reviewed the forces and laws at its disposal. It remains for us to examine the laws and methods of its progress, the history of its advance in the past, and the present condition of the Christian revolutionary movement.

But at the outset we are met by an objection: "You propose to examine the methods of the revolutionary progress. Is there any progress at all? Is Christianity a victorious force? Can the aspirations of humanity for purity, righteousness, freedom and peace, produce anything more than the feverish tossings of a prisoner in chains, the oscillating equilibrium of a pair of scales, the rush of the surf up the beach which yet ever retreats with a moan? Will God conquer?"

The heart of faith can give no answer save the answer of Columbus. The Ocean waste seems limitless; the promised land is long in appearing; but we refuse to turn back. Every prophet soul has believed in the ultimate [page not numbered] victory of God and right. Isaiah saw the mountain of Jehovah exalted in the last day above every mountain. The seer of the Apocalypse saw one riding forth on whose garment was written: "King of kings, and Lord of lords," and he heard a voice as the voice of rushing waters, saying: "Hallelujah, for the Lord God Omnipotent reigneth." Paul believed that the time would come for every knee to bow in the name of Jesus and for every tongue to confess him Lord. And Jesus? He had a better right to despair of the world than the easy pessimist of to-day. He did his utmost and the world crushed him. Did Jesus believe in the triumph of righteousness? We hear a cry from the darkness: *Eli sabachthani*. We see him sigh: "When the Son of man cometh, shall he find faith on the earth"? And yet he believed. In the face of death he asserted the triumph of right in his own person: "From henceforth shall the Son of man be seated at the right hand of the power of God" (Lk. 22, 69). Even that sigh of doubt was but the fringe of his energetic promise that God will surely avenge his elect who cry to him day and night against their oppressors (Lk. 18, 1-8). [page not numbered] To do the right against all considerations of utility is the categorical imperative of duty. To believe in the triumph of right against all appearances of defeat is the categorical imperative of faith. To deny the former is moral suicide. To surrender the latter is religious suicide.

In so far as Christianity is identical with righteousness and with the cause of God, its ultimate victory is certain. But by asserting that, we do not assert that it is victorious at all times and all along the line.

Public thought in America is so far from doubting the value of life and the triumph of right, that it is in a perpetual chuckle of satisfaction at "the progress of the world." Hoary wrongs are crumbling; the nations are marching toward popular liberty; steamboats are getting faster, kings rarer, creeds more liberal; what more would you have? **[page not numbered]** Give humanity free play and we shall have the millennium here on schedule time.

This hopefulness is probably due partly to our youthfulness, and partly to the idea of evolution which has saturated our thought. We conceive of the world rolling slowly out into the light of day; therefore every step must be day-ward, every change must be an improvement, every new idea must approximate more nearly to the truth than the one it supplants, every tendency must be just. That is the way in which evolution has taken hold of the popular mind.

But this view is not accurate. Evolution—granting it proved,—teaches the possibility of change for the better, not the certainty of it. Environment may modify backward as well as forward. Degeneration is as much a scientific fact as development. The forces of death and destruction press hard on the forces of life. The assumption that, on the whole, evolution is moving forward and upward, rests partly on sight, but even more on faith. [page not numbered] The matter becomes even more doubtful when the idea of evolution is applied to human history. The nations of the earth have not moved forward with unfaltering march. Concerning some the proof is wanting that they have ever been lower than they are now. Of others proof is abundant that they have been higher than they are now, and, having come down, they apparently propose to stay down. In Egypt, in Central America, in Asia Minor, in Greece, the monuments of a higher civilization look down on a degenerate state. In India and China there is stagnation, if not degeneration. In fact it looks as if every nation had its period of childhood and its teens, and then, when growth is most rapid and life most luscious, it is stung by some hidden disease and sapped of its virility. It declines, and henceforth is old. Some have collapsed quickly. Others have stood erect for centuries, and perhaps, like Italy, have risen to a second period of glory. There **[page not**

numbered] are only a few of the nations, whose track through the last two thousand years seems headed toward the Kingdom of God. It is a wavering, lagging line, yet it goes forward. And they seem to have the faculty also of planting new and vigorous societies, and of putting a thrill of life into their paralytic sister nations.

In short, while we hold fast our faith in the destiny of humanity and in the capacity of every nation to grow up into an ever higher stature and, for aught we know, into an endless bloom of manhood, yet history solemnly tells us that there are lost nations as well as lost individuals. "Many are called, but few are chosen." The Bible itself tells of a nation, elect of God, which failed in the hour of its visitation, and its vineyard has been taken "away from it (Canaanites)."

History does not encourage [page not numbered] the rollicking optimism, which trust humanity, and especially in the United States, to come down every time feet foremost, like a cat. Nations also have to strive with fear and trembling to be saved. For humanity also the gate is narrow and the way to life is straight.

It is a goodly doctrine, that of human progress. It is very sweet to man. It is delightful to know that after a few more hampering traditions and worn-out institutions are knocked away, humanity will ride down into the perfect life like a ship from her dock into the sea. The presupposition of this doctrine is, that man is by nature good and tends upward, if only he is not dragged down by outward forces. The writer is frank to confess that he once felt all the attractions of this view of life. But he has been obliged to yield it up and to say now with Browning:

> "The candid incline to surmise of late
> That the Christian faith may be false, I find.
> I still, to suppose it true, for my part,
> See reasons and reasons; this, to begin: [page not numbered]
> 'Tis the faith that launched point-blank her dart
> At the head of a lie, – taught Original Sin,
> The Corruption of Man's Heart."

It is not true that man tends by nature upward. It is the downward way that is easy; the upward way is steep and toilsome. It requires no effort for us to yield to temptation; the effort comes when we try to resist. The number of those who overcome even the natural intellectual inertia is small. Educational institutions do not sustain themselves; with few exceptions they would collapse if the benefactions of individuals or the taxing power of the community were withdrawn from their support. We have to pass laws to get children into school and to keep them out of the saloon. In Europe the theatres giving the classic plays have to be subsidized; those rendering adapted French plays need no subsidy. (Newspapers)

That none of us individually drifts into purity, justice and unselfishness, we all know. And humanity as a whole would likewise, if let alone, by no means roll into the Millennium, but by a broad and easy track into a hell on earth, **[page not numbered]** into rottenness, beastliness and self-destruction. What association of men or what human institution does not sag downward? What political party does not grow corrupt? What church does not tend toward formalism and worldliness? What charitable society is not in danger of becoming uncharitable? What educational system or institution does not stiffen into pedantry to the stifling of intellect? What body of law needs no effort to exhume justice buried under its legal decisions like Nero's guests under his shower of roses?

And not only is the natural tendency downward by mere moral inertia. We have to reckon also with the fact that there is such a thing as conscious, determined, malicious love of evil. The natural thing is to do evil, because it looks sweet before it is done; then to do it again, because it has acquired power, and thus to continue the downward course. But all this while the man knows it to be wrong; he wishes that he did not **[page not numbered]** do it; he is pained to see the young and innocent acquiring the same habit. But it seems to be possible for the human spirit to give itself to evil and to love it, to take delight in ensnaring the innocent, to corrupt their minds systematically, to interfere consciously with the efforts to better society, and not to only to turn sideward with a hiss at the approach of purity, but to strike a poisoned fang into its heel. If those who have consciously abandoned the principle of selfishness and handed themselves over to love, are children of God, then such are children of the devil. They bear the mark of the beast on brow and hand, on intellect and action.

Now, such men and women have power. There are periods of history which, like a forest tract with charred trunks, show the passing of one of these human firebrands. And what these Catilinarian spirits have been in the larger territory of history, their smaller kindred, smiling behind the saloon bar, button-holing in local politics, promenading on the city streets, telling anecdotes on the kegs of a village grocery, or laying snares in drawing-rooms, are to the social circle within which they move. **[page not numbered]** If a determined good man has power, so has a determined bad man. He can even with the same exertion of force accomplish more, because he appeals to the lower instincts of lust, hate, pride, and needs only to draw out the pegs to set the log rolling. These forces have to be reckoned with. They add momentum to the natural downward drift of humanity. Therefore our wrestling is not merely with the natural weakness of flesh and blood, but "against the principalities, against the powers, against the world-rulers of this darkness, against the spiritual hosts of wickedness."

Let us have no illusions. The world will not evolve into a Kingdom of God by natural processes. It is uphill work. It is a battle. Every inch will have to be fought for.

But neither let us have any cowardice; especially no croaking sloth hiding under a religious garb. We *must* conquer. We may use the old crusaders' cry with a purer right than they: "*Deo le volt.*" God wills it! [page not numbered] And what, then, shall lift humanity up, if the force that raises it, is not naturally inherent in it? Water cannot rise higher than its source. An effect cannot contain more than its causes. One epoch of history cannot be greater and nobler than the one out of which it has grown, unless an additional force has entered into its composition. Whence does that force come in human history?

The same question has been raised concerning the asserted upward evolution of the organic world below man. If the higher forms of life have developed from the lowest, what has pushed them up? Those who believe in God, have not hesitated to reply: God. He is immanent in the world, forever active and working. It is his force and his guidance which moulds his existing works into higher forms.

We take exactly that position concerning the life of humanity. God is in it. "The Father worketh hitherto." His will is set toward the Kingdom of God on earth. His Spirit works upon the spirits of men and of nations. Within limits known to Him, and for reasons known by Him, He suffers their disobedience and resistance. But He wearies not. His force is still put forth. And **[page not numbered]** the medium through which it is most exerted, are those human spirits who have freely surrendered themselves to the will and service of righteousness. There God gets a purchase on humanity. There he can grip it. Such spirits he fills with the ideas and impulses which their time needs in order to take the next step forward, and through these channels the forces of God flow out into humanity. These are the prophetic souls. In them and in their work lies the hope of humanity's progress. The upward forces communicated through them have to overcome the downward inclination of flesh and blood, as life in the physical world overcomes the force of gravity.

The hope of the world therefore lies in religion. Politics cannot lift man; at its best it removes hindrances to his uplifting or refrains from laying stumbling-blocks in his way; at its worst it defeats the aims of justice and lends tools to the leagued interests of oppression. Its power in either direction is immense. But it never creates moral forces; it simply yields to them.

Even education does not **[page not numbered]** lift man. It enhances his power either for good or evil. It refines his good or evil enjoyments. But it does not make him good. France is the living demonstration of that to our day. They dress better and converse better at Paris than the rest of us do; they write a more brilliant style, coin cleverer epigrams, and see plays more intelligently. But in spite of that, France supplies the world with lasciviousness and with virulent unbelief.

No, as Mazzini said: "You seek to perform a work of regeneration, and you hope to accomplish it by banishing every religious idea from your work! Politics merely accepts man as he is. The religious idea alone has power to transform. It is the very breath of Humanity; its life, soul, conscience and manifestation. Humanity exists only in the consciousness of its origin and the presentiment of its destiny; and only reveals itself by concentrating its powers upon some one of the intermediate points between these two. Now this is precisely the function of the religious idea. That idea constitutes a faith in an origin common [page not numbered] to us all; sets before us, as a principle; a common future; unites all the active faculties on one sole center, whence they are continuously evolved and developed in the direction of that future, and guides the latent forces of the human mind towards it." (p. 36.)

But when we speak of religion, we do not include everything that claims that name, nor exclude everything that disclaims that name.

Source: "Christianity Revolutionary" Manuscript, Walter Rauschenbusch Family Collection, RG 1003, American Baptist Historical Society, Atlanta, Georgia. Transcribed by E. Colford.

An Overarching Theme
The Kingdom

Editorial Introduction

The Kingdom of God was theologically and ethically central to Walter Rauschenbusch's thinking. His interpretation moved beyond the contemporary premillennial "kingdom is coming" to a present manifestation of the reign of God. In many ways, Rauschenbusch's "kingdom" was an American kingdom, defined by contemporary American political and social ideals. Yet, Rauschenbusch did not jettison completely the notion of the complete fulfillment "in another epoch."

THE KINGDOM OF GOD

BY WALTER RAUSCHENBUSCH

"History still turns on the axis of religion," says Shäffle, in his great work on sociology. Those who study the life of a great city, and especially those who desire to awaken it to righteousness, cannot afford to overlook the ideas current in its thought-life, and should hail with satisfaction any effort to make religious impulses come down with a heavier and more direct impact on municipal life.

An organization has recently been formed by Christian believers, called "the Brotherhood of the Kingdom." Its members believe that the idea of a kingdom of God on earth was the central thought of Jesus, and ought ever to be the great aim of the church. They are convinced that this aim has largely dropped out of sight, or has been misunderstood, and that much of the social ineffectiveness of church life is due to this misunderstanding. Therefore, they have organized "in order to re-establish this idea in the thought of the church, and to assist in its practical realization in the world."

The idea of the "Kingdom of God" has gone through many changes in the history of Christianity. At present we can distinguish five different senses in which the term is used.

The common people generally understand by the "Kingdom of God", or the "Kingdom of Heaven", the blessed life after death—heaven. It is a condition to which they expect to come to them. Perhaps the most vivid proof for the prevalence of this conception of the "Kingdom" is the fact that the description of the New Jerusalem, in the Book of Revelation, is popularly supposed to describe heaven, while the author meant to describe the perfect city to the established on earth at the return of Christ.

Men of a mystical mind have usually seized on the idea of "the Kingdom of God" to designate that inner life of the Spirit which, to their minds, constitutes the highest gift of Christianity. Men of that turn of mind frequently slight the questions of dogma and of ecclesiastical organizations, which absorb others, and they need some term not stamped with a technical sense by church usage. Their favorite passage is "The Kingdom of God is within you".

Men of ecclesiastical temper use the term synonymously with the "Church". The Church sums up the total of divine forces in the world to their minds, and so they can make it co-terminus with the church.

Men with whom the second coming of Christ is a living hope, have restricted the term to the reign of Christ to be established after His return.

Men who are interested in movements that extend beyond the existing work of the church, and are pushing out under religious impulses into new fields of Christian activity, have seized on this term as one large enough to include everything else *plus* the work to which they are giving themselves. So at the beginning of foreign missionary activity its pioneers loved to speak of "the enterprise for the extension of the Redeemer's Kingdom." And at present those who labor for a righteous social order, under religious impulses always raise the standard of "the kingdom of God."

Which of these ideas is right? We reply they err by defect. The Kingdom of God is larger than anything contained in any one of these ideas. It stands for the sum of all divine and righteous forces on earth. It embraces all pure aspirations God-ward, and all true hopes for the perfection of life. It is a synthesis combining all the conceptions mentioned above, and if we could combine them in such a synthesis, it would prove to be like some chemical compounds, more powerful than the sum of all its parts.

In the common conception of the Kingdom as heaven, we must recognize the truth that we have here no abiding city. Life at its best is transitory and unsatisfactory. The perfection of our personality is not attained on earth. Even if humanity lives on and marches toward the golden city of the Ideal, the weary toiler to whom its progress is due drops by the wayside, and his feet never enter the city of his longings. An ideal which is to satisfy all the desires of the human heart and is to embrace perfect man as well as the perfect Man, must include a heaven beyond death.

In the mystical conception of the Kingdom as the inward fellowship with God, we must recognize the justice of human yearning for the living God. A righteous and happy intercourse with our fellow-men, in a true human society, will not satisfy the heart completely. Deeper then the hunger and thirst for God Himself. It would be a mistake on the part of those who labor for a perfect humanity to rule out the efforts of religion to bring men into personal intercourse with the living God.

We must recognize the importance of a living Church within the Kingdom. It must not dwindle. It is the channel through which ethical impulses pour into humanity from God. Yet the Church and the Kingdom are not identical. We are the Church as we worship together; we are the Kingdom as we live justly and lovingly with one another.

We must recognize the justice of the millennial hopes. They stand for the force of Cataclysms in human history; for the direct interference of God in the life of nations; and for the ultimate victory of right and love in the conflict of the ages.

But finally, we must insist that the Kingdom is not only in heaven, but is to come on earth; that while it begins in the depths of the heart, it is not to stay there; that the Church does not embrace all the forces of the Kingdom and is but a means for the advancement of the Kingdom; that while the perfection of the Kingdom may be reserved for a future epoch, the Kingdom is here and at work. The Kingdom means individual men and women, who freely do the will of God because they love it; who have fellowship with God, and therefore live rightly with their fellow-men. And without a goodly number of such men and women no plan for a higher social order will have stability enough to work. But the Kingdom also means a growing perfection in the collective life of humanity, in our laws, in the customs of society, in the institutions for education, and for the administration of mercy; in our public opinion, our literary and artistic ideals, in the pervasiveness of the sense of duty, and in our readiness to give our life as a ransom for others.

With most social reformers it is the former aspect which needs emphasis; with most religious people, it is the latter.

Source: Brotherhood of the Kingdom Leaflets, Number 4. (Reprinted from the *City Vigilant*, May 1894). Copy from Scrapbook, Walter Rauschenbusch Collections, American Baptist Historical Society, Atlanta, Georgia. Transcribed by W. Brackney.

A Gifted Writer

Editorial Introduction

From his days as a secondary school student Rauschenbusch read widely in literature and imitated what he read. This gift continued in German as well as he studied at the Gymnasium. Having read the English writers like Richard Heath, Charles Kingsley and F. W. Robertson, he frequently tried his hand in stories and editorials. His target was his pastoral situation in Hell's Kitchen in New York City. This selection demonstrates his concern for his neighbors in the tenements, exploited by runaway capitalists and businesses with little concern for the sick, old, or children. His use of dialogue and metaphor are remarkable.

“BENEATH THE GLITTER”

“Why, yes, it is a pleasant evening. Out to see life in New York City, eh? Well, Saturday night is a good time to see it on this avenue. Lots of people. Hold on there! That fellow nearly took my hat off. Rather interrupts conversation to squeeze through and dodge around.

“Fine sight, you think? Yes, the stores are bright, people well-dressed mostly; they all look busy and happy, as they push by. Got to do their shopping for Sunday, you know, and their love-making for all the week. “The world is not so bad a world as some would like to make it.’ That’s your verdict, is it, from what you see” You’ll go and pooh-pooh this talk about want and degradation and the iron law, and all that. Well, go ahead, you’ll only be one of a crowd who know the family because they’ve looked at the front door, and say the elephant is a tree, because they stumbled against his leg Getting made, am I? Oh no, only a bit wild. You’d do the same if you had eyes to see.

“There, do you see that big clothing house on the corner there? Brilliantly lighted; show windows gorgeous; all hum and happiness. But somewhere in that big house there’s a little bullet-headed tailor doubled up over the coat he is to alter, and as surely as I know that my hand is pressing your arm, I know too that he is choking down the sobs and trying to keep the water out of hus eyes. Why? Because his little girl is going to die tonight and he can’t be there. Consumption, pulmonary. Been wasting away for months, can’t sleep except her head is on his breast. And then he can’t sleep when her panting is in his ears. He has just been draining his life to sustain hers, and yet Minnie is all the world to him. She’s the only drop of sweetness in his cup; all the rest is gall. Hard work; nothing to look forward to’ wife grown bitter and snarling; and tonight the girl dies. How do I know? Just been there. Her forehead is getting clammy and her whole body rocks with the effort to get breath. She’s whispering, ‘Tell my papa to come,’ but he’ll not be there before one o’clock tonight. Saturday night, you know; very busy; sorry, but can’t spare him. O yes, you can say that: ought to go home, permission or none; but that means throwing up a job that he has been hanging to by his finger nails. It will be six months before he gets another. And so he has to sew away and let his little girl die three blocks off. When he gets home he can sob over her corpse; what more does he want? Exceptional case, you think. Not a bit of it. It's the drop on the crest of the wave, but there are a million other drops underneath it, all hurled along, or that one drop wouldn't be so high.

"Do you see that old woman with the basket just turned into the street? Yes, the little one with the shawl over her head. Well, that is one of the meekest souls in this city. She and her husband live in two little rooms in a rear house. They pay about the lowest rent I have found in this neighborhood, $6 a month. He earns from $1.50 to $3.00 per week, so you can figure how much they live on. Lazy? No, sir! They have just toiled and toiled all their lives. She has kept house and borne children and washed and scrubbed and saved. Why aren't they better off, you ask? That's what I want you to tell mer. Here are these two old people standing at the close of a life of work and frugality, and watching old age and helplessness creeping down on them. And what have they got to face it with? A bit of bare furniture; one son who drank and has drifted out of their sight; another son a barber, who just scrapes together enough to feed and clothe his family while they live and to pay off their funeral expenses after they die; a few graves across the river; a hope in heaven, and $70 in the savings bank. Ah, you say, that's something. Yes, it is something, more than I've got; but no soul knows how they stinted to get that much, and what an anchor of hope that little sum is for the coming years. And they gave me a dollar 'for the heathen' the other day. Case for charity you say. Yes, daub your walls with mortar to fill up the cracks; but what makes the wall split up so, anyway?

"Do you see that girl in front of…got to go, eh? Bored you, didn't I? Yes, guess I am something of a crank on these things. Wish you'd trot around with me for a week; you wouldn't think so highly of things as they are. Good night, my boy."

Source: *Christian Inquirer,* New York (1887). First published in the daily press. Also reprinted in Dores R. Sharpe, *Walter Rauschenbusch* (New York: Macmillan, 1942), 81-82.

Professor of Church History

Editorial Introduction

Rauschenbusch had a first-rate education for a clergy of his era, especially given his studies in Germany. The earned Ph.D. degree was just coming into vogue among a few institutions in the United States as he began his pastoral career. He was certainly qualified to teach in basic theological disciplines and this was realized in his appointment to the German Department at Rochester Seminary in 1887. In 1902, however, at the invitation of his president, Augustus H. Strong, Rauschenbusch embarked upon a new academic discipline, church history. He realized the inadequacy in academic terms of his preparation and he worked doubly hard to research and prepare lectures. In spite of his hearing problems and weak voice, he was a popular teacher and managed to read widely in the literature and publish important articles, especially on the Anabaptist reformers. His greatest assets in the field were his capacity in the German language and his embracement of the German historicist school that overwhelmingly defined his academic orientation. The following essay presents a well-argued appreciation for historical studies, notably for ministry.

"The Value and Use of History"

Walter Rauschenbusch

It is still necessary to persuade ministers that history is important to them. Before the Reformation few priests had ever read the New Testament through and they had no sense of obligation in that direction. Today ministers do not have to be told that they must study the Bible, but they are, on the whole, as indifferent about history as Catholic priests used to be about Bible study. In fact, with the average Protestant minister the Bible itself has cut under the study of other historical books by monopolizing his interest for one supreme collection of literature.

Our American intellectual life is far less saturated with historical knowledge than European life. Perhaps the fact that we have so few historical relics in our country that lead our thoughts backward may be one cause for this. Everything is new, even in the old parts of our country, and the new parts are decidedly raw. We rarely here feel the thrill of historical veneration which we feel in England or Italy. I dare say that the assertion of Graham Brooks is true that "no people was ever born so gayly and so confidently indifferent to history and experience as the people of the United States."

In characterizing the American spirit, Kipling says that our eyes are "swift for the instant need of things. "That practicalness of mind is our strength and our weakness. For the rough and ready needs, it is swift of action, but the finer and more spiritual things are often thrust aside by the "practical instinct." A speaker is voted "punk" if he deals with anything six months old. There is no market for historical knowledge. I rarely have any call for historical addresses, and when I am requested to speak on a historical subject, it is usually to serve some denominational glorification. Consequently, when we Americans make generalizations, being ignorant of history, we fall back on general principles that we get out of our own heads. "practical men" are often the giddiest theorizers of all. An eminent college professor told me recently that the Scotch students who have been brought over here by the Young Men's Christian Association for summer conferences feel that American students are ahead of them in the capacity to organize, but that otherwise they have little to learn from us. On the other hand the world of scholarship has long sat at the feet of Germany, for German thinking gets its orientation always from a profound insight into history.

We might excuse our common people if they have no time for history. But we might expect a knowledge of history in college-trained men. Yet I think most seminary professors will agree with me that we do not often get men from college who have a well-developed historical point of view and method. We have to make elaborate efforts in our seminaries to give it to them. Professor Stevens felt that the historical insight of college graduates had seriously declined in recent years through the weakening of the classical studies in the colleges. The classics were historical source material. Their study demanded historical side reading, and in some students the reading of ancient literature created an intimate sense of the life of the past and so gave them an instinct for history.

The Cultural Influence of Historical Studies

The influence of the teaching ministry depends on the largeness and maturity of the minister's personality. Look back over the men whop moulded your life in the pulpit or lecture room, and see if this is true. Such men fertilize and expand the mind. They have the capacity of suggestiveness. An evangelist may be narrow and yet get results by force and intensity. A great teacher must have breadth and generosity. A friend asked me recently, "Why do all the evangelists hold the old views of the Bible?" I replied, "Why do all the great teachers hold the new views of the Bible?" The evangelists can bank on the capital accumulated for them by the teachers of past generations, but the teachers of to-day are laying up the fund of new convictions on which the evangelists of tomorrow will draw.

History is not the only cultural influence. Natural science gives clearness of mind, analytical powers, moderation of judgment. The study of poetry and literature gives refinement and sensitiveness. But history above all gives us roundedness and maturity and richness. Goethe says:

"Wer in der Weltsgeschicte lebt,
We r in die Zeiten schaut und strebt,
Nur der ist wert zu sprechen and zu dichten."

That is, only a man saturated with history has a right to be heard. We can readily distinguish a man who has traveled and mingled with the large affairs of life from an honest and earnest farmer's boy. History is the nearest substitute for large experiences. It supplies the wisdom of age in youth.

Historical knowledge is not the remembrance of a string of dates and facts any more than a man's travels are the number of miles he has railroaded. Wisdom comes by being part of things, by having the life of men and nations run through the mind and having assimilated it, so that one can say, "I am a part of all I have known." A wise man enjoys folks. Lincoln did: and so did Jesus. We should have an appetite for human qualities just like a dog loves scents. The stage driver, the old farmer, the pert young girl, the old Quaker lady, are all wonderfully interesting and human. The provincial mind scorns what is different; it settles a man by calling him a "Dago," a "Dutchman," or a Unitarian. In the same way, we should enjoy the history of other nations and tomes just because they are different from our own and give us a new flavor of humanity which widens our experience.

Ministers especially need this breadth of interest and this keen love of humanity. Our professionalism may dry up our intellect. A teacher who merely drills for examinations, a lawyer who read law merely to win cases, and a minister who merely "runs a church" are all mere mechanics in their profession. Their skill is indispensable to them, but will they have the largest results in making richer, sweeter, broader men and crating the wider sympathies that we need? There is not much wisdom or vision in the typical hustler. I would rather embrace a buzz-saw than take him to my heart.

History and Preaching Material

Many ministers appreciate historical reading chiefly as a source for fresh anecdotes and illustrations. The trouble is that most of the historical facts of that kind are not so. There is hardly a single homiletic anecdote from history that will bear scrutiny. Constantine's vision of the cross, the Emperor Julian's surrender to Christ in death, Luther's inkwell, his chained Bible and his climbing of the sola sancta at Rome, along with Newton's apple, are all short-weight goods.

A far wider appeal to history is possible, but it is difficult to use it with the ordinary audience. On a large scale there is a vast number of historical situations which offer splendid material for inductive moral reason. But the trouble is that our people rarely know the facts to which we should want to refer. Ewe should have to make a laborious exposition first before we could draw our conclusion, and it takes unusual skill to condense such information. At an Alumni dinner in New York I recently pointed out to an eminent

Presbyterian minister that the effort of our federal government to tame the trusts and compel them to submit to the law of public welfare is precisely analogous to the conflict of the kings with the great feudal nobles in the Middle Ages. My friend admitted my point, but thought that people would think it idiotic if it were set forth. The ignorance of our audience frustrates the really effective use of history. We would profit by a general rise in culture among our people.

Nevertheless, I advocate the use of historical narrative in religious teaching. Why not tell the Bible stories as of nobody had ever heard them? Many of our people never have, in fact. When we sing "Tell Me the Old, Old Story," we really mean "Tell me the old, old doctrine." We rarely narrate the story of redemption. In children's services especially, direct story telling from the Bible would be highly valuable. Some time ago the editor of a great magazine, who is himself as realistic novelist, asked me to write Bible stories for his magazine. He is not at all a religious man, but he had read a volume of Bible stories in his boyhood and had a profound respect for their qualities as stories. The Bible stories may be told aloud because they were first made by telling them aloud. Many of them originated through long oral repetition. They had a social authorship. That gives them their compactness and their wonderful epic qualities. and occasionally turn myself into a troubadour of the gospel. If I were a pastor once more, I should develop my romancing and dramatic abilities and occasionally turn myself into a troubadour of the gospel.

The Contribution of History to the Minister's Comprehension of the Bible

The interpretation of the Bible is a recognized task of the minister. The emphasis on the Bible is partly due to Protestant tradition. Protestantism was forced to emphasize the authority of the Bible in order to smash the authority of the Roman Catholic Church and its scholastic theology. On the other hand, the emphasis on the Bible is also due to the unique and external value of the Bible for religious inspiration and instruction. Personally, I have always loved exegetical sermons, and my complaint is that so few of them are preached.

But the Bible is history. When we insist on the supremacy of the Bib le, we insist that history is superior to dogmatics. The dominance of history in modern thought began with the early Protestant insistence on the grammatical and historical interpretation of the Bible. To interpret the Bible well, we need historical knowledge, historical method, and historical spirit. Otherwise, we shall merely put our own ideas into the Bible and fetch them out again and then claim divine authority for our own pet ideas.

The question, how much religious outlook and insight a given section of the Bible will furnish us, depends partly on our previous historical knowledge. For instance, unless we know something of Greek rhetoric and allegorizing and disputativeness, we shall not understand Paul's fear of it. The author of Acts is profoundly interested in the conflict of the apostles with sorcerers and magic. Aside from a few weird ladies, who act as clairvoyants and mediums on our back streets, we see very little of sorcery nowadays, and unless we know something of it from history, we shall slight these stories which, to the readers of Luke, were among the strongest proofs of the redemptive power of Christianity.

Historical knowledge fertilizes our detailed exegesis. Grammatical exegesis is merely a hod-carrier and mortar mixer. Unless it leads up to biblical theology and the historical understanding of the Bible, it may divert our minds from more useful things.

Every biblical book originated in a definite historical environment. Within that environment it was full of meaning and power. As soon as it is taken out of that environment, it is inevitably distorted and changed, even with the most reverent care. Every living thing is beautiful and absolutely fit in its own place. For instance, a lobster down among the rocks on seaweeds is a wonderfully capable and well-made creature. The same lobster on ice in as meat market seems an absurd and curious beast. The Apocalypse was a martyr book, written in an atmosphere of pressure and fear. When it is read today in a congregation rustling with silks and sleek with wealth, it is like the poor lobster on ice. Galatians and Romans were written to set Christianity free from Jewish ceremonialism and sacramentalism. Paul's theology was elaborated for that purpose, and when it is taken out of that historical surrounding, we are unjust to it. The doctrine of election developed by Paul was never meant to formulate the eternal relations of God to the human soul, but to explain the terrible question why Israel had not yet begun to come over the Christ in a body. All these books lose something of their true proportion and lifelikeness when they are detached from their historical background.

It is profoundly interesting to know from later history the effect of certain biblical passages. For instance, the allusions to Mary in the New Testament resulted in the tremendous spiritual edifice of the worship of Mary in the Greek and Roman Church. The lovely stories of the infancy of Jesus have furnished support for the elaborate speculative Christology of later centuries. The saying of Jesus to Peter became the foundation stone for the amazing institution of the papacy. The usual Protestant interpreter slips away over that passage. To the historical student it is one of the most important in the New Testament. Such passages, then, are like the boyhood picture of some great man in which we can trace the soft lineaments of the stern face which later moulded history.

The Bible is always in danger of slipping away from realty into unreality. Because it is marked off from all other historical material by the doctrine of revelation and inspiration, it is turned into divine doctrine and law and exempted from the processes to which ewe subject all other books. Just as conservatives today are fighting against historical criticism, their forefathers fought against the revision of the received Greek text on the basis of older manuscripts. Many plain people in America even objected to the Revised Version because it seemed to tamper with the inspired word of King James' Version. The treatment of the Bible seems like profound reverence, but in the long run it harms the Bible. It takes it out of the realm of reality and thrusts it into the realm of fairy tale and legend where all things are radiant with strange and hidden lights. Minds that love illusions may love that kind of Bible. Minds that love reality instinctively turn from it, and it is no true service to the Bible to alienate that class of minds.

The historical interpretation of the Bible will save it from seeming unreal. Most of the popular skepticism disappears when the Bible is connected with all other religious history. Most of the doubts are directed against nonhistorical interpretations.

Our Larger Christian Heritage

The individual is always small and transitory. His life is too short to learn much through his own experience. We get most of our knowledge and wisdom by inheriting the accumulations of knowledge supplied to us by society. The question then is whether we draw on a social life that is rich and modern, or one that is poor and backward. A boy who grows up in one of our rural sections and gets his religion from some small and reactionary sect is a disinherited soul. We must tap the largest and richest currents of spiritual tradition. The sectarian spirit, which says, "I am of the party of Paul," or "I am of the party of Apollos," narrows our capacity for growth, because it shuts us up to a single monotonous influence. Calling a denomination Catholic does not save it from that narrowing exclusiveness. The Roman Catholic

Church and the High Church Episcopalians are among the most sectarian of all religious people. Among the classroom sayings of President E. G. Robinson was this: "When any church says that it alone is the true church and there is no other, take your hat."

Historical study is a truly catholic influence. It shows that every religious body has much to blush for init own history and much to admire in others. Each church is but a partial reflection of the truth. But the Church of Jesus Christ in its totality has a sublime authority. Its fundamental truths are the most valuable things humanity possess.

The study of history will take us beyond our contact with our own denomination and put us in touch with the wider tendencies and movements of all Christendom.

I have to warn you that while all churches will assent to the propositions in general, no denomination likes that spirit in particular. Every church wants to be something special, unique, and holy. It loves the history that feeds ots pride and resents the history which teaches it humility, Almost every denomination has some kind of sacred history draped about itself which it will not readily allow its professors of history to handle roughly. When the historian Macaulay was a lttle boy, he already had his phenomenal memory and vocabulary. One day he had laid out the backyard into fields and lots by little fences of sticks and stones. While he was away the hired girl swept it all aside. When he came back and saw his work undone, he stamped his foot and shouted: "Cursed be Sally! For it is written, 'Cursed is he that removeth his neighbor's landmarks'!" This expresses quite fairly the average feeling toward historians who meddle with denominational landmarks.

History and the Scientific Understanding of Life

Some of us have worked in a biological laboratory. We know the difference between watching life itself moving, changing, and developing under our eyes, and seeing all this on stationary pictures and charts. Embryology prolongs the lines of observation backward; paleontology runs it still farther back. The observation of real life has created the scientific attitude and the modern world. It has not only taught greater accuracy and truthfulness, but changed life from a static into a dynamic thing. This has been one of the greatest psychological changes in modern times.

Now, history is the biological laboratory of humanity. We can cross rabbits or sweet peas and in a few years we have many generations on which we can base our deductions In human life we cannot follow the final effects, say of alcoholism, venereal diseases, or religious unbelief, until several generations have completed their life, and that takes more than a century. The biological study of social institutions and ideas takes far longer still. For instance, no one could judge adequately of the historical effects of Protestantism when it was merely a hundred years old. Many of its effects are still maturing to-day in the rise and decline of nations. Therefore all sciences dealing with human life have adopted historical methods, for instance political economy. This is the special mark of the modern intellect as compared with Roman, Saracen, or mediaeval culture, and accounts for the immense results achieved by applied modern science. The monster should not spin a silken cocoon of doctrine and ecclesiastical illusion around himself but should have a full share in this modern scientific understanding of life.

The Moral and Spiritual Effects of Historical Study.

Historical study trains the critical faculty. In the ancient world, the writing of history was noncritical and artistic; its aim was to please. In many cases we can trace how the famous historians embellished their sources to make the story pretty. The capacity to be accurate in stating the truth is a late and rare development of the human mind. Modern scientific and historical methods have greatly increased this capacity. What we call criticism is trying to separate truth from falsehood, and those who denounce criticism ask us to accept the assertions of a past generation without testing them. It is a spiritual tragedy that the church in the past has so often condemned this chef agent of veracity. In the Leibnitz Museum at Hanover, in Germany, I found a bill printed in imitation of a Continental two dollar bill, asking all "to commemorate the centennial year of your country by obtaining a convertible life policy in the United States Life Insurance Company." I applied critical methods and asked the director of the museum to eliminate this fake from the collection of coins. Unless we train our people to critical sincerity, we leave them open to all kinds of seduction, ready to accept the fake books of the Mormon Church, the fake oath of the Knights of Columbus, etc. A minister or teacher who has drugged his own critical faculties and persuades others to do the same is an untrustworthy and dangerous leader.

The study of history, however, should train us to couple the critical instinct with modesty and reverence. The self-sufficient, know-it-all attitude of young students of criticism has created proper distrust. True knowledge of history makes us realize that the world is more complicated than we used to think in our youth, and that our two-penny intellect is really not big enough to run it nor even to understand it. Anyone trained through history knows that he can at most approximate the truth and will never have to reach it perfectly. It is like complete satisfaction; if we say we have it, that shows we haven't got it. But if the study of history makes us modest, truthful, open-minded and childlike, it is a real sanctifying influence.

It does more. It creates awe and reverence, like the view of the starry firmament. Indeed, it is so vast that it overpowers. Bishop Stubbs said: "He who devotes himself to the study of history may be a wiser, he will be a sadder man." The same, however, is true of the knowledge of life itself. As the wise man in the Bible said: "With increase of knowledge, there is increase of sorrow." The great artist Duerer, who was himself a profound intellect, has pictured Melancholy seated and pondering, with astronomical and mathematics apparatus and all the instruments of knowledge about her. We can only dimly feel in history the working of a righteous law and a holy purpose. Sometimes we see beneath all events a Supreme Mind and Reason, but it is always elusive, and in the main we have to walk by faith. Long occupation with history at best will not leave us with rosy optimism, but with calm serenity and humble faith.

History and Social Conceptions

In recent years we have been getting some glimpses of a social conception of the gospel of Christ. If we approach the social service problem only from the practical point of view, it will not affect our thinking deeply. We need an intellectual basis for our social interest, and we can get it only through historical study. Our theology, psychology and philosophy concentrate their interest on the mind of the individual. History, on the other hand, is interested in the permanent and organized life of great groups of men, and cares for individuals only when they are the exponents or creators of organized, collective life. Only in history do we learn to think in social categories and to see the continuity of social forces and movements. So history gives us a feeling for the life of the community and a realization of its immense power in shaping the life of all its members. On this intellectual basis we can do our practical social work.

The Influence of Historical Study on Practical Action

All study should result in wisdom and validate itself in action. History should help us discern what movements in present life are likely to be fruitful and which are foredoomed to failure. For instance, it ought to help us choose between democracy and monarchy, between a society founded on equality of opportunity and one founded on special privilege. Humanity had had a long experience with agricultural land; in some countries the land has been in the hands of those who actually worked it; in others it has been owned by great proprietors who farmed the farmers. This experience with the agricultural means of production seems to me decisive in judging the present tendency in our country to concentrate the industrial means of production in the hands of a small and powerful class. Must we make the same mistake over again, or can we learn from history? I should think historical study would make a man practically immune toward Sabbatarianism or Adventism. They belong to the past. History can teach us to discern the great and small, the sterile and fruitful.

This is a very serious matter for ministerial leadership. Men trust us, and we can seal their minds against things they ought to know, or we can open their minds to powerful truths. For instance, if a minister indoctrinates his people with the premillennial scheme, which idealizes early Christianity, and describes all modern life as decay and "signs of the times," he therewith sterilizes the intellect of his congregation. I believe that the historical conception and theory taught by premillennialism is one of the most powerful obstacles to all social effort, especially in our denomination. If generally accepted, it would keep the church standing in dress parade and leave the fight for justice and fraternity to irreligious men.

Historical Studies and Prophetic Power

Our ideal is a teaching ministry. But the rabbis of the Jews were a teaching ministry too. So were the mediaeval scholastic doctors. They were teachers; but were they prophets of God? The prophetic mind must have moral will, forward movement, the power of moral indignation and hope. The scribe sees God in the past and also in the far future; the prophet sees him right now, and in the immediate future. The scribe sees his will as written law; the prophet feels it as a living force and as fire in his bones.

The prophetic mind always has a wide social outlook and political consciousness. No ancient or modern prophet has been without that. On the other hand, religious individualism has very little vision. The expounding of past predictions is sometimes called prophetical study. But it is no more prophetic than playing with building blocks is architecture.

Now we need history for a real prophetic outlook. The finest sections of the historical books of the Old Testament were written by men of the prophetic mind, those portions which appeal least to the religious mind of our day were written by men of priestly mind. The prophets always appealed to history.

A minister can have prophetic qualities if he lives the right life for it. He must live a life which is morally above that of the world about him, and keep his soul open to the divine voice. He must have hatred for collective wrong and stand for righteousness, even when wrong seems more prosperous. The world and the church are in constant need of renovation. We need the prophetic succession even more than we need the apostolic succession. But unless the prophet is fortified with historical wisdom, he is likely to be a fanatic. Of Lord Acton it has been said: "To Acton history was the master of political wisdom, not a pursuit but a passion, not a mere instrument but a holy calling, not *Clio* as much as *Rhadamanthus*, the avenger of innocent blood."

So rich and manifold are the uses of history. The chief fountains of wisdom are honest work, loving intercourse with men, and prayer. But for the wider wisdom needed for large leadership, there is nothing like the study of history.

Killikelly: *Curious Questions in History*, 3 Volumes. Desmond: *Mooted Questions of History*. Hertslet: *Treppenwitz der Weltgeschicte*.

Source: Address Delivered at the Special Session of Rochester-Colgate Theological Seminaries, May 1914. Reprinted from *The Record* 9 (Nov. 1914). Transcribed by W. Brackney.

Denominational Identity

Editorial Introduction

Walter Rauschenbusch was a life-long Baptist. He attributed this identity to his upbringing, particularly his father. He was educated at two Baptist-related institutions: the University of Rochester and both the English and German departments of Rochester Theological Seminary. His church affiliation was with the German Baptist Conference, originally a domestic mission project of the American Baptist Home Mission Society. He was baptized at the Andrews Street Baptist Church in Rochester. As a part-time minister, he was a student pastor in a German Conference church in Louisville, Kentucky. His first full-time pastorate, Second German Baptist in New York City, was affiliated with the German Conference and also the Southern New York Baptist Association, as well as receiving funding from the New York Baptist City Mission Society. He was ordained by the Second German Baptist Church in New York. In Rochester, he returned to his home congregation, the Andrews Street Church. As a theological educator, Rauschenbusch taught at Rochester Theological Seminary, an official institution of the American Baptist Board of Education and the Northern Baptist Convention when it was formed in 1907. A significant amount of Rauschenbusch's essays were published in Baptist journals. From 1892-97 he was secretary of the Baptist Congress, a national gathering of Baptist pastors and educators.

In Rauschenbusch's interpretation of Baptist identity, he connected with the Anabaptist tradition and the Free Church movement in Germany. He especially valued the individual and social aspects of Baptist life, the requisite religious experience and non-creedal aspects, and the nature of democratically-governed congregations. He was much taken with the missionary spirit of the Baptists and considered offering himself as an appointee of the American Baptist Missionary Union.

Why I am a Baptist

BY PROFESSOR WALTER RAUSCHENBUSCH

PRELUDE

Why am I a Baptist? Well, at the outset, because my father was one.

He was a Lutheran minister in Germany; he came to America, got into contact with the Baptists, found in their teachings the truths that he had been groping for and, under great loss of position and trouble of soul, became a Baptist. If he had remained a Lutheran minister in Germany, I should probably not be a Baptist minister in America. There is no use in denying that our family relations and the training of our childhood exert a very strong influence on all of us and determine our religious affiliations for us. In countries that have an "Established Church" it is considered a horrible and impious thing for anyone to leave the religion of his fathers, and even in our country, which is the paradise of religious liberty and individualism, only a minority of persons are so strongly swayed by individual convictions that they can break the soft and twining bonds of family love and family tradition. Most men are Catholics or Protestants or Jews, because their parents were Catholics or Protestants or Jews, and that's all there is of it. If the angels tonight should steal a hundred Baptist babies and replace them by Episcopalian babies, it is fair to assume that the babies which might have grown up to champion episcopacy and the apostolic succession and the Prayer Book, would learn to smile the smile of conscious superiority at those very things. There are some of us who have become Baptists from simple conviction, and have had to leave the denomination of their parents to follow where truth led them. But the majority of us were born in Baptist families, and I am one of that majority.

But that expresses only half of the truth. We are Americans because we were born so. But it is our duty and our right clearly and increasingly to understand what our country stands for and to adopt as our personal principles those ideals of democracy and equality on which our national life is founded. We are Americans by birth, but we must become Baptists by conviction. And no man is a true Baptist until his inherited tendency has been transformed into conscious purpose. In a big freight yard you can watch a locomotive distributing a freight train over the various sidings. It will bunt a car along and let it roll along by itself. The car moves, but it moves by the power of inertia. It has no living energy in it. By and by it will slow up and stop. No Baptist boy or girl ought to grow up to resemble that car. They must develop their own Baptist convictions and run under their own steam. They have inherited a great legacy of truth; let them learn what is already theirs; let them hold by the surer title of personal acquisition what is theirs by hereditary right.

I began by being a Baptist because my father was, but to-day I am a Baptist, because, with my convictions, I could not well be anything else. I now stand on my own feet and am ready to give an account of the faith I hold. It is a good thing to raise the question: "Why are you a Baptist?" I wish all our church members had to answer it clearly and fully. It is possible to be a Baptist on small grounds or on large grounds. Some man will say: "I am a Baptist because the Greek word baptizo means immerse. That is quite true, but that is a pretty small peg to hang your religious convictions on. A near-sighted child was taken to the Zoo and stood in front of the lion's cage. The lion's tail was hanging down through the bars. "But I thought the lion was different," said the child, "it looks like a yellow rope." So there are Baptists who have hitherto discovered only the tail-end of our Baptist ideals and convictions, and it is no wonder that they turn out as narrow as the tail they devoutly believe in. It is possible to play "Nearer, my God, to Thee" with one finger on a little reed-organ of four octaves. But it is very different music when the same melody is played with all the richness of full harmony. Little beliefs make little men. Many Baptists are cut on a small pattern because their convictions are so small.

The minds of men are widening today. There are large thoughts pouring and flooding all about us. And men who have grasped great ideas in one part of their life feel impatient with petty ideas in any other part of their life, especially in their religion. Only a large faith, built on generous, gigantic lines will win the thoughtful men and women of the future. I do believe that we Baptists have a magnificent body of truth - free, vital, honest, spiritual, and wholly in line with the noblest tendencies of our age. But we must realize its largeness and present it in all its out-of-door greatness and freshness, and not show people a few dried plants and stuffed animals as exponents of the Promised Land to which God has led us and to which we invite them.

In the next issue of the MONTHLY I shall try to set forth some of the convictions that have become dear to me personally. I cannot guarantee that my ideas will measure up to the full Baptist stature. Indeed, the likelihood is all the other way. No one man is likely to see the whole, nor even to say the whole of what he sees. If I fall short, this is a free country, and anybody is at liberty to hoist the Baptist colors on a taller pole than mine.

Why I am a Baptist-My First Reason

SECOND PAPER IN THE SERIES-BY PROFESSOR RAUSCHENBUSCH

Religion has taken a great variety of forms in the various Christian bodies. Take a solemn mass in a Roman Catholic cathedral, with the dim religious light, the swelling music, the candles, the trooping of the priests and acolytes, the wafting of the incense, the tinkle of the bell, the prostration of the people as the wafer is miraculously transformed into the very body of the Lord. Take on the other hand a little experience meeting in a country church where one simple soul after the other arises to tell in rude words of its dealings with God. How far apart they are! And yet it is only fair to believe that all Christian bodies aim at the same thing: to bring the human soul into saving contact with God through Christ and to secure for it the knowledge and power of a holy life. Let us rejoice that we are all one in that fundamental aim.

But on the other hand it is only true to assert that some religious bodies seek to attain that aim by means that hinder the soul from finding God more than they help it. Judaism, too, sought God with its elaborate temple worship, its bloody sacrifices, its detailed forms. But Christ taught us to approach God by a simpler and more spiritual way. The all-important question of just where to worship and how to worship was relegated to the background as obsolete and outgrown for those who had learned to worship God in spirit and in truth. All religious bodies carry with them a good many clinging remnants of their childhood stage, beliefs and customs that were superstitious in their origin and never belonged to genuine Christianity. And some religious bodies have squarely refused ever to strip these things off; they cherish remnants of heathenism as their most precious and fundamental possessions. Thus it becomes a matter of importance for an intelligent Christian to inquire where he can find Christianity in its least adulterated form. Where is the fundamental aim of bringing the human soul into saving fellowship with God attained most clearly? Where is worship most spiritual? Where is attention least diverted from what is essential in the religious and ethical life?

I have repeatedly attended confirmation services in the Lutheran Church and was deeply interested in them. The children there are examined as to their knowledge of the catechism and of passages of Scripture. They recite them from memory. I wish Baptist children knew as much of the Bible and the hymns of the church by heart. I regard the systematic instruction given for months previous to confirmation as one of the finest features of the Lutheran Church and wish we could copy it. It offers an unrivalled opportunity for a devout pastor. But when the mental exercise of memoriter recitation is made the test for admission to the Church and its sacrament, personal experience is supplanted by something totally different and inferior. I know from personal contact with the people how many get the impression that such instruction makes a person a Christian.

Now consider how great a thing it is for a church body to assert that a man may and must come into direct personal relations with God, and to adapt all its church life to create such direct and spiritual experiences in men. I have met people in other churches who not only have no such experience themselves, but they doubt if anybody can have it. It seems presumption to them for a man to assert that he knows he has received pardon from God and is living in conscious fellowship with him. Yet what is all the apparatus of church life good for, if it does not help men to that experience?

The Christian faith as Baptists hold it, sets spiritual experience boldly to the front as the one great thing in religion. It aims at experimental religion. We are an evangelistic body. We summon all men to conscious repentance from sin, to conscious prayer for forgiveness. We ask a man: "Have you put your faith in Christ? Have you submitted your will to His will? Have you received the inward assurance that your sins are forgiven and that you are at peace with God? Have you made experience of God"? If anyone desires to enter our churches we ask for 'evidence of such experience and we ask for nothing else. We do not ask him to recite a creed or catechism. The more simple and heartfelt the testimony is, the better we like it. If it is glib and wordy, we distrust it. Experience is our sole requisite for receiving baptism; it is fundamental 'in our church life.

We apply the same test as our ministry. The first thing we ask a candidate is about his conversion and Christian experience. The next thing we ask him is if he is conscious of being personally called to the work of the ministry; that also probes for experience with God. Finally we ask him for his views of doctrine, but there, too, we discourage any mere recitation of what is orthodox, and are best pleased if all his intellectual beliefs are plainly born of inward conviction and experience.

Thus our church membership and our ministry are both based on religious experience. So is the ordinary course of our church life. Take our churches right through and nothing so draws and wins them in preaching as the note of personal experience of God; nothing so touches and melts them in the social meetings as the heart-note of experience. When we insist so strongly on true baptism, it is not an insistence on external forms, but a protest against any external form that has no experience back of it. Baptism of believers is an outward act plus an inward experience. Infant baptism, we believe, is an outward act minus any inward experience, and we will have none of it.

In this direct insistence on conscious personal experience a true Baptist Church is about as clear-cut and untrammeled as any religious body can well be. The Roman Catholic Church, for instance, also seeks to put a man in contact with the grace of God, but the grace of God is received through the sacraments. In the regenerating water of baptism, in the mysterious wafer of the communion, in the absolution pronounced by the priest in the sacrament of penance, they say a man meets God. But does he? Or does he only meet the Church? Has the Church not interposed a lot of man-made ceremonies between the soul and God, so that thousands who punctiliously go through all this ritual never experience God in fact, and are kept from doing so by the very things in which they are taught that they meet him?

Some churches make much of ritual and sacrament, in the belief that this furnishes access to God. Others make much of a formulated creed, in the belief that correct intellectual comprehension is the fundamental thing in the Christian life. Baptists have simplified ritual until we have only two obligatory ritual actions left, baptism and the Lord's Supper, and we insist on experience as the essential ingredient in these too. We believe in clear convictions of truth, but we have no formulated creed to which anybody, minister or layman, is required to assent. Intellectual statements of belief are useful if they are the outgrowth of personal experience; if not, they are likely to be a harmful substitute for experience.

The great mass of men take their religion at second hand. Some strong religious soul in the past has had a real experience with God. He tells others about it; they believe it and then take their belief in his experience as a substitute for having any such experience themselves.

The religion of the past is deposited in the Bible, the creeds, the rites and beliefs of the Church, and men devoutly rehearse all that and assent to it, and think that is religion. It is no more religion than moon-light is sunlight. The thoughts and experiences of others are invaluable to us because they enrich and broaden our own, but in religion nothing will take the place of personal experience. In the study of the natural sciences the modern method is to put the student into direct contact with nature. The dissection of a single animal will give more realizing knowledge of biology than the best text-books in which a student reads what others have observed. Baptists believe in advanced methods in religion. They confront the soul with God.

Experimental religion is necessarily free and voluntary. Men can compel attendance at the mass. They can compel subscription to a creed. They cannot compel an inner experience. It has to be free and spontaneous. And nothing has any value in the sight of God that is not the free outflow of the man's life. What would we care for the compulsory love of a wife or child? What does God care for compulsory faith and adoration? When we insist on experience, and not on ritual or creed, we place religion where it is necessarily free, and then, if it is freely given, it has value in God's sight.

Experimental religion is more likely to have an outcome in moral life than any other kind. In the lower forms of heathen religion ritual is nearly all there is of religion; morality is only an incidental outcome. Every real rise in the evolution of religion makes it less ritual and more ethical. In the higher forms of religion there is always danger of gliding back into the lower stages, and of emphasizing ritual at the expense of morality. When we insist on repentance from sin and submission to the will of God, that is a religious experience directly leading to a higher moral life. Such religion lends the most powerful reinforcement to ethical duty and is of high service to the common life of humanity.

We can see how profoundly important such a direct experience of God is from the fact that in times of doubt it is often the only thing that remains unshaken. Many a man has felt his intellectual beliefs crumbling away, and yet his faith in God has weathered the storm like a granite cliff. When arguments went to pieces, he could still say: "But I know that God made a new man of me; the experience I had in years gone by is just as certain to me as that I am alive." And on that basis he was able to build up a wider faith. A church that helps men to personal experience of religion therefore helps them to the most essential and abiding thing in the moral and spiritual life.

I like to think also that a church body which demands religious experience and that alone is deeply democratic. It takes a trained mind to understand the fine distinctions of the creeds. It takes a good deal of historical information merely to understand the ritual and symbols of some of the old churches. If anybody knows just what each garment means which a Catholic priest wears before the altar, and how this garb originated and what changes it has passed through, he knows enough history to write a book. On the other hand, experience of God is open to the simplest mind, just as love is. A little child can love before it can think. A poor German or Italian mother can not follow the new learning which her children get in this country, but she can outclass anybody in loving them. The intellect is aristocratic; human love and religious faith are both democratic.

We Baptists insist on personal experience as the only essential thing in religion, we are hewing our way back to original Christianity. The gorgeous ritual that drapes the limbs of the ancient churches was wrought out piece by piece in later generations, and modern historical scholarship is constantly making it clearer that the shimmering silk of which those garments are made and the golden threads with which they are embroidered, were taken from the heathenism of the ancient world. The insistence on correct thinking, on exact orthodoxy of definition, was likewise a product of Greek intellectualism after Christianity had amalgamated with the Greek civilization of the heathen world. These things were not part of Christianity as the apostles knew it. Much less were they part of the Christianity of Jesus himself. Original Christianity was exceedingly simple; it was just a new life with God and a new life with men. Faith in Christ was a spiritual experience. Those who believed in him, felt a new spirit, the Holy Spirit, living in their hearts, inspiring their prayers and testimonies, melting away their selfishness, emboldening them to heroism. Paul called that new life "faith." That word with him does not merely mean an intellectual belief. It is a kind of algebraic symbol, expressing the inner religious experience and life in Christ.

I am a Baptist, then, because in our church life we have a minimum of emphasis on ritual and creed, and a maximum of emphasis on spiritual experience, and the more I study the history of religion, the more I see how great and fruitful such a position is.

When I claim such a purely spiritual religion for Baptists, I am well aware that not all Baptists possess it. Many do not even realize that that is the essence of our Baptist faith. We have some who insist on immersion in a purely legal and ritualistic spirit. We have others who would be only too glad if we had an iron-clad Baptist creed with a thousand points that they might insist on it. I know, too, that "experience" with very many is a very shallow emotion, copied often from others, and passing away again without changing life and conduct at all, unless it be to add religious conceit to all other faults. This is the smallness and pettiness that is inseparable from human life. But our Baptist faith, like our American political constitution, is founded on great principles, and even if some misuse it, or misunderstand it, or are inwardly traitors to it, its greatness lifts others up to it. Baptists uphold Baptist principles; and Baptist principles in turn lift up Baptists."

Why I am a Baptist - My Second Reason

THIRD PAPER IN THE SERIES-
BY PROFESSOR RAUSCHENBUSCH

In the last issue of the Monthly I set forth how important and valuable it seems to me that Baptists in all their church life emphasize the necessity of personal experience with God and thus confront the soul with Him to work out its spiritual salvation. As Moses or Elijah or John the Baptist met God alone amid the lonely crags of the desert, so we want every man to go into that inner solitude of his own soul where no man can follow him, to hear the still small voice of the Eternal and to settle the past and the future with the great Father of his spirit.

But religion is not a purely individual matter. Nothing in human life is. We are social beings, and all elements of our life come to their full development only through social interchange and co-operation. A man working alone is an inefficient producer; by division of labor and co-operation the productive efficiency of all is multiplied. A person educating himself is at a great disadvantage compared with a student who has teachers and fellow-students to stimulate him. Our pleasures, our affections, our moral aspirations are all lifted to higher power and scope by sharing them with others. An isolated individual is to that extent a crippled man. We never realize all our powers and enthusiasms until we shout with others in a public meeting, or keep step with others to the drum-beat, and see the flag, which is the symbol of our common life, leading us forward.

It stands to reason that religion, too, demands social expression, and will come to its full strength and richness only when it is shared with others. And so in fact we find it. There is a sweetness in private prayer, but there is an additional thrill when we join in a heartfelt hymn and are swept on the wave-crest of a common emotion. Most of us have come to the great religious decision in life only under the influence of social emotion. With most of us the flame of religious longing and determination would flicker lower and lower in the course of the years, if it were not fanned afresh by contact with the experiences and, the religious will-power of others. When Jesus said that where two or three are gathered in his name, he is in the midst of them, he expressed the profound truth V that his presence is fully realized only in a Christian society; it may be a very small group, but it needs at least one other human heart next to ours to be fully sensible of the Christ.

The Christian church gets its justification from these fundamental facts of human nature. It is not an end in itself. It is always a means to an end. It is to create and foster the religious life in the individual; it is to build up the Kingdom of God in all humanity.

Christians have had no end of controversy about the proper organization of the church. The Roman Catholic Church holds that there is no true church apart from the bishops and the Roman pope. Pope Boniface VIII in 1302 solemnly asserted: "The one and unique church has one body, and one head, namely Christ, and the vicar of Christ, Peter, and the successor of Peter. Further we declare, assert and define that for every human being it is absolutely essential for salvation that he be subject to the Roman Pontiff." Pope Pius IX in 1854 reiterated that "it is part of faith that outside of the apostolic Roman church no one can be saved". The Episcopal church holds that all ministerial authority is derived through the ordination coming down through the historic episcopate, and that Presbyterian and Baptist ministers, while they may be very good men and blessed of God in saving souls, are not ministers of the Christian church in the proper sense. Thus the one church makes salvation and the other makes ministerial authority depend on connection with the right church organization. There are Baptists, too, who are ready to assert that none but a Baptist church is a true church at all.

To my mind the essential matter is not that a church body is very ancient, or that it has a continuous history, but that it embodies the Christian spirit in he method of its organization, and by its very constitution offers the largest possible opportunity to its members to live a truly Christian life together. The fundamental question is not even whether a certain church order is biblical, but whether it is Christian. The Bible merely helps us to see if it is Christian.

Now I think our Baptist church organization, though it is faulty in many ways and though it creaks and groans as it works along, just as all other human organizations do, is built on very noble Christian lines and therefore it is dear to me.

It tries to create an organization of really Christian people. It admits to membership only those who deliberately apply for it and who can assert that they have met Christ and love him and want to follow him. It scrutinizes their statements to save them from self-deception and votes to receive them only if it feels confident that there is a real beginning of conscious spiritual life. It also eliminates from its membership those who are manifestly not living Christian life. It may make many mistakes in receiving too quickly and in excluding too slowly, but at least it tries to keep its membership clean and homogeneous. Churches may become so worldly that it is hard to see any line dividing them from the world, but still the principle is embedded in the very constitution of our church life, and that always offers a ready possibility of reformation. On the other hand with other churches their very constitution works the other way. Individual pastors in such churches may strive to create a really Christian fellowship, but their churches neutralize these efforts by admitting everybody through the gate of infant baptism.

Our churches are Christian democracies. The people are sovereign in them. All power wielded by its ministers and officers is conferred by the church. It makes ample room for those who have God- given powers for leadership, but it holds them down to the service of the people by making them responsible to the church for their actions. That democracy of the Baptist churches is something to be proud of. One of the noblest elements in the life of our Teutonic ancestors was that their village communities governed themselves in the town meeting. That has been called the mark of the Aryan race. It was the germ of all popular liberties. A Baptist church meeting is exactly that sort of self-governing assembly of the people. It is more democratic than delegated government by a presbytery. It also corresponds more completely to primitive Christianity. The farther we get back to apostolic Christianity the completer is the democracy we encounter. The Roman Catholic Church is a benevolent despotism. All power flows from the pope downward. That type of church organization originated under the despotism of imperial Rome and has perpetuated the political ideas and customs of that epoch. Government by bishops also has strong affinities for a monarchy. As James I said: "No bishop, no king". He saw in the bishops the best props against Puritan democracy. Our congregational government originated in a great wave of popular democracy in England, and has embodied and perpetuated the democratic ideals of the Puritan Revolution. I am proud to think that our church life is in harmony with that great ideal of government of the people, by the people and for the people, which mankind is slowly toiling to realize.

Our Baptist churches recognize no priestly class. Our ministers are not essentially different from the laity. According to Catholic and high church views a priest receives an indelible character in ordination which enables him to do things which no other man can do. We take no such view of our ministry and I thank God we do not. The havoc which priestly assumption of power has wrought in the history of the church is incalculable. The priest is an inheritance from heathenism. He is needed only if there are magical sacraments to be offered or administered. Jesus was not a priest, nor the creator of priests. Other churches have only a vague line of demarcation between the church and the world, but a very sharp line of demarcation between the ministry and the laity. We reverse that. We have a sharp line of demarcation between church and world, but only a vague line between ministry and laity. Which is most Christian?

We have no hierarchy within our ministry. We have no rector above the vicar, no bishop above the rector, no archbishop above the bishop, no pope above them all. Jesus bids us call no man father or master, but all of us are to be brethren, and, the only greatness is to be by preeminent service Matthew 23:1-12). That settles all hierarchies for me. Some have greater natural gifts than others, and that inequality should be frank1y recognized. Some have a holier 'character and deeper spiritual insight, and they should have honor and leadership accordingly. But fraternity in the ministry.

Our churches have home-rule. Each church is sovereign in its own affairs. In that respect we follow the same principle on which our country is built up. One cause why our cities are so badly governed is because they lack home-rule and are run by distant State legislatures. Every man knows best where the shoe pinches him, and every community on the whole is best acquainted with its own affairs. The self-government of our churches does not hinder them from joining with others in fraternal cooperation, in associations and State conventions, in city mission societies and national missionary organizations. I do think, however, that our Baptist churches have lagged in this voluntary cooperation, and have too generally allowed each church to struggle along as best it could. In Rochester, for instance, we have no adequate organic expression of our unity.

Our Baptist churches decline all alliances with the State. They accept no dictation from the State in their spiritual affairs. They ask no favors from the State, except that they accept such exemption from taxation as the State grants to all institutions which labor for the common good and not for private profit. Baptists insisted on separation between church and State at a time when the principle was novel and revolutionary. Some Baptists seen to think that this separation is based on the idea that the spiritual life has nothing to do with the secular life. I utterly deny that assertion and think it a calamitous heresy. Our Baptist forefathers insisted on that separation because they saw that it wrought mischief when unspiritual men, actuated by political or covetous motives, tried to interfere with the centers of religious and moral life. To let the churches alone meant to let the religious and moral life of the nation work out its own problems unhampered and unthwarted by baser considerations and forces. But in turn it was also found that the political life of the nation is freed from a warping and disturbing influence when ecclesiastical questions are removed form politics. Other churches have had to be wrenched loose forcibly from their hold on public income and political power. Baptists have the far nobler and prouder position of declining these things voluntarily and of being pioneers in that principle toward which the civilized nations are slowly drifting.

My second reason for being a Baptist is, then, that Baptist churches in their very constitution approximate Christian principles of organization and give a fair chance to any Christian community to form a Christian social life. They seek to organize communities of really Christian people. They trust the people with self-government and form Christian democracies. They have mo priestly or clerical class set apart from the people. They have no graded hierarchy in the ministry. Their local churches combine home-rule with fraternal cooperation. And they are on principle free from any entangling alliance with non-religious forces.

I know well that Baptist churches have not lived up to these magnificent principles. Churches, like individuals, are in perpetual danger of backsliding. There are churches that admit almost anybody and exclude scarcely anybody. There are Baptist churches in which a small junta of men rule and democracy has become a mere name. There are Baptist ministers who are priestlier in spirit and temper than the present pope. But it is a great thing for a nation to have adopted a constitution guaranteeing freedom, even if that nation is ridden by bosses and sold out to those who pay; it is a great thing for a young man to have committed himself definitely to a life of unselfish service, even if he is often led away by selfish impulses; and it is a great thing for a body of churches to have embodied such advanced Christian principles in their very constitution, even if individually or collectively they drop below them.

WHY I AM A BAPTIST - MY THIRD REASON

FOURTH PAPER IN THE SERIES-
BY PROFESSOR RAUSCHENBUSCH

The first reason which I gave for embracing my Baptist inheritance with heartiness and intelligence was that personal religious experience is cultivated among Baptists. The second was that our church organization is approximately Christian in its essence. My third reason deals with the conception of worship.

I can best make this clear by going back a little into the history of religion. In the rude and primitive forms of religion, worship is mainly an attempt to "get on the right side" of the gods. Men are afraid of the terrible powers of nature, of thunder, disease, blight, flood and drought, and they try to placate and conciliate the supernatural beings who show their displeasure by sending these terrors on helpless mortals. So they offer sacrifices and piteous prayers, just as they would bring gifts and wail before the angry human despots with whose ferocity and whims they were well acquainted. Men want good harvests, health, offspring, revenge and protection, and they tell the gods of their wants and bring them presents to win their help and favor. To ward off evil and to secure favors is the main object of worship in these lower stages of religion.

But each god has his peculiar tastes and disposition which must be consulted. One god likes rice and flowers; another wants the smell of burning mutton or beef another insists on human blood. They have their sacred places where they have appeared and where they can best be approached. They have their sacred names and formulas by which they can be summoned. And they have their priests, who are experts on all these matters, and are allowed to draw near the god and offer sacrifices on behalf of the ignorant and unclean folk-for a consideration. These forms of worship are handed down from generation to generation, and are carefully preserved in the memory of the experts, for their effectiveness depends on the very wording of a prayer or on a prostration to right or left. In heathen Rome the priests muttered ancient prayers which they no longer understood. Religion is marvelously conservative about the forms of worship. All old religions are full of petrified usages.

In a higher state of religious development men want Personal contact with the deity. They have a sense of impurity and defilement. They are told that by being bathed with water or anointed with oil, or touched with hot blood-all, of course, with the proper magic formula,- they will be supernaturally cleansed and made holy and freed from the power of the evil forces. Men now have a deep sense of the frail and perishable nature of mortal life; they long for immortality and the assurance of it. They are told that if they pass through certain mysterious rites, they will come under the protection of the gods who rule the hereafter amid will be saved from death; or something of the divine life will enter into them and survive death. Thus in this higher stage of religion men seek expiation of guilt, freedom from impurity, victory over death, direct and concrete contact with the deity. In this stage, too, the forms of worship are supposed to be of the utmost importance. If they are not performed exactly, they lose their power.

To anyone who knows the dense pall of superstition that has hung over mankind, it is a wonderful relief to pass from this smoke of incense and burnt-offering to the outdoor air and sunlight in which Jesus walked with his Father. The crew of supernatural despots who want sacrifices and who love to see men cringe and implore has vanished away, and the Best Being in the universe bows down with fatherly love. Holy places, holy times, holy formulas, holy experts are all left behind, and the only thing God asks for is love for himself and love for our fellowmen. The old cowering fear of the slave is gone, and instead we see the free love and obedience of the son and child of God. Jesus did not pray because he had to or because he wanted to get something from God, but because he loved to pray and speak to his Father. To become a disciple of Jesus means to learn to think of God and live with Him as Jesus did, and to let all life he transformed by that new knowledge and faith.

Paul understood Jesus. His contest against the Law was a mighty effort to cut away the old forums of religion that cramped amid gagged the spirit of religion, and to set Christians free to look at Christ before them and to listen to the Spirit within them. Read Romans 8 or Galatians from that point of view.

But the old religious habits of mind were very strong in men. It took hard work to emancipate the Jewish Christians from their old Jewish forms of religion, and the people who had lived in heathenism very soon created a new system of ceremonialism, which had a Christian face but a pagan spirit. Christianity had only two religious acts in which form counted for anything, baptism and the Lord's Supper; one was a bath, the other a meal. These two simple acts of daily life were used to express great spiritual thoughts. But men with pagan habits of mind seized on these and saw in them just what they were looking for. Baptism was to them a mystic cleansing which washed away guilt and defilement, a magic bath from which a man rose regenerate as a new man with the past all cleaned away. When they heard the words "This is my body, this is my blood," they felt that in some mysterious way Christ was really present in the bread and wine, and when they swallowed the elements, his divine life entered into them and gave them the assurance and power of immortality. These superstitious ideas became ever more powerful and concrete as time passed; they were adopted by theologians and defended as part of the essence of Christianity. Gradually it was believed that Christ was not merely present in the sacrament; the bread and wine were actually changed into his body and blood and chewed with the teeth, and this new body of Christ, which was created under the magic formula of the priest, was offered anew to God in the sacrifice of the mass. A new priesthood early grew up, equipped with mysterious powers to consecrate the sacraments and to forgive sins. Additional sacraments were developed. Christianity once more had its holy places, holy times, holy formulas, its sacrifice and incense, its set prayers and all the apparatus of worship, just like the heathen religions, only more so. Through it all still breathed the spirit of Jesus with pitying and saving power, but the saving power was largely in spite of what was called Christian worship, and not by means of it. And this established religion was exceedingly conservative and anxious to keep things just as they had been, and refused to let the spirit of Jesus educate it up to better things. Just as the ancient heathen priest in Rome muttered formulas in a dead language, so the Christian priest in Rome chants his formulas in Latin, which was a living language when Christianity began and is now a dead language. The Greek Church, too, uses a ritual language which has become unintelligible to the people. This is merely a trifling indication of the petrifying conservatism in religion.

The Reformation was a rising of the religious and democratic and national spirit against this dead inheritance of the past. Among other things the Reformation simplified worship and swept out a great mass of superstitious ceremonial. In some countries the break from Catholic forms of worship was far more thorough than in others. The Calvinistic churches in Switzerland, France, Holland, Scotland and parts of Germany were very thorough; the Lutheran churches in Germany and Scandinavia not quite so thorough; and the Church of England least of all. The Baptists, and all those bodies with whom we are historically connected, marched in the vanguard of Protestantism. That is one reason why I am a Baptist, because by being a Baptist I am a radical Protestant. I can help to cleanse Christianity of the mass of heathen influence which leaked in during the early centuries and was afterward so religiously preserved and cherished. I can help to bring humanity to that simple, ethical, spiritual worship which Jesus taught and which has been so sadly overlaid by the gilded and jeweled worship of a paganized church.

Baptists are, in fact, more Protestant than the great Reformers on some points. The Reformers all retained infant baptism. But infant baptism was part and parcel of that very paganizing tendency which I have tried to describe. It grew out of a double root: the belief that original sin damns even infants to hell; and the belief that baptism regenerates. If baptism saves and if children need salvation, of course human love wanted the children to be baptized in order to save them from the risk of hell. There was wide-spread doubt about infant baptism at the beginning of the Reformation, but to reject it would have meant churches of baptized believers and would have unchurched the great mass of men. The Reformers recoiled from so sweeping a change, largely for political reasons, and infant baptism was maintained, defended and extolled. It was an alien element in Protestantism, and has been most subtly influential in opening the door to other alien elements in worship, organization and doctrine. It is now slowly dying out. Modern Protestant Christians no longer believe that unbaptized infants go to hell through their original sin, nor do they believe that baptism regenerates. And if a baby does not need baptism and if baptism does not do it any good, why should the baby be baptized? Other sentimental reasons are now used to prop the custom, but the number of infant baptisms is constantly decreasing.

People are sensibly concluding to give their children a chance to be baptized when it will mean something to them. Of course, Baptists have largely helped to bring this result about. They made a cleaner sweep of the old pagan leaven at the outset, and the slow development of the purified Christian spirit in modern Protestantism is swinging their way.

The real worship, the only thing that God really cares for, is a Christlike life. To live all the time in the consciousness of the love and nearness of God, to merge all our desires and purposes in His will, to walk humbly before Him and justly and lovingly with all men, this is the real Christian worship. Without that no prayer, no song, no "divine service" on Sunday is more than discordant noise in the ears of God. That is what Paul meant when he tells us to offer our bodies, our own selves, as a living sacrifice, and says that will be our "reasonable service," that is, our rational form of worship. He was well acquainted with many irrational forms of worship. When James says that a pure and undefiled "religion" consists in helping the helpless and keeping ourselves unspotted from the world, the word "religion" means liturgy or ceremonial. A loving and pure life is the true liturgy of Christian worship.

The life of Jesus was as full of religion as a nightingale is full of song or a rose full of fragrance, but the bent of his life was away from the inherited forms of worship, and he can scarcely be said to have taught new forms. He taught a prayer when his disciples asked for it, but that prayer was not meant to teach utter simplicity. In our common worship we shall come closest to the spirit of true Christianity if every act is full of joy in God and his fellowship, love for one another, hatred for all evil, and an honest desire to live a right life in the sight of Christ. Our worship should eliminate as far as possible all selfish greed, all superstition, and all untrue and unworthy ideas about God. It should clear our conception of the right life by instruction our moral nature; it should give our will strong, steady, lasting impulses toward righteous action; and it should breed and foster habits of reverence and the faculty of adoration.

For all this the way is cleared in our Baptist religious life. It is made easy for us to be simple, truthful, spiritual. We are not led into temptation to slop back into superstition by the survival of pagan forms in our ritual. If our service has a fixed liturgy with responsive features and artistic adornment, that is not necessarily a departure from Baptist fundamentals. "When two do the same thing, it is not the same thing." Just how much spirituality and essential religion there is in a given Baptist church service, is another question.

That depends entirely on the men and women who engage in it. It may be utterly barren and dead. But even then there is an advantage in our simplicity of form, for the deadling will not be hidden and masked by the borrowed life of mere ceremonial. An unspiritual priest may sing the mass more beautifully than the sweetest saint, but a Baptist minister or church can not be dead ling without having men know it and then there is a fair chance for repentance.

Why Am I a Baptist - My Fourth Reason

CONCLUDING PAPER IN THE SERIES BY PROFESSOR RAUSCHENBUSCH

Religion appeals to the whole of man and finds expression in the various sides of his nature. There is an intellectual element in all religion, and that grows stronger as we follow the development of religion from the rude and barbarous peoples to the civilized nations. We can not help reflecting on this world about us and this soul within us. How did the world originate? Was it made by a good or a bad power, with a wise purpose or through folly? If a good being made it, why is there so much suffering and evil in it? How did sin and death come into the world? How can man be saved form sin and its penalty? What comes after death? What is the future of the world and of the human soul? These are questions with which natural science and philosophy deal, but they are also religious questions and a religious man craves an answer, and seeks in some way to build up a satisfactory and harmonious edifice of thought in which his intellect can dwell content.

But the answer which contents a man at one stage of his life is outgrown at the next stage. If he is a growing man, his belief must keep on growing and adjust itself to his expanding information. The same thing is true of mankind at large. If an African chief believes that the world ends on the other side of the mountains and that his god makes a new sun every day and extinguishes it in the evening that is a satisfactory scheme of the universe for him, but not for a boy of ten in our schools. If Christians in the Middle Ages believed that our earth was the universe, and that the stars were set in various crystal globes which revolved around the earth, that was a religious and scientific conception of the universe which satisfied men in that day, but we live in a vaster world now, and a man would commit intellectual suicide if he tried to "stand pat" on that explanation of God's universe. To the moral feelings of a past age it seemed quite right and fair that God should condemn men for a sin which Adam committed and that all heathen were hopelessly lost. Our moral judgment has been made more tender and true by the more searching tuition of the spirit of Christianity, and we repudiate such ideas about God's dealings with mankind. It is of the utmost importance that the individual and the race shall retain the capacity for growth in religious thought. It is fatal to make the religious thought of one age binding for a higher age. It condemns a grown man not to put away childish things, but still to think and talk like a child.

Yet that is what religion has very commonly done. After Christianity had become the State religion of the Roman Empire under Constantine the Great, it was a matter of great concern to the emperors that the Church should remain united and not be broken up by bitter doctrinal fights. So, if some doctrinal question was giving trouble, they summoned a great council of bishops and had them decide by a mere majority vote on the profoundest questions. Moreover these councils were usually packed and engineered by wire-pulling exactly like modern political conventions, and the result was usually reached by compromises or intimidation. Yet when the result was reached, it became the binding law of orthodoxy, and men believed that the Holy Ghost, who had promised to lead the Church into all truth, had guided the decisions. Such a general council could not err, and its decisions were binding on all Christian thinkers. Such infallible decisions increased as the centuries went on, and each was riveted around the intellect of the Church like an iron hoop around a barrel. Hoops are good around barrels, but I should not advise putting nice, tightly fitting hoops around the body of a growing child. It is hard to overstate the damage that was done to the intellectual and moral and religious growing power of humanity by this incubus of dead authority. For instance, the doctrine of transubstantiation, that is, the belief that the bread and wine of the Lord's Supper are actually changed into the flesh and blood of Christ, was the product of the Dark Ages. When education and science were at their lowest stage, when the civilization of the ancient world lay buried tinder the raw barbarism of the Teutonic tribes, when superstition sprouted like toad- stools in the dark, this belief was evolved which laughs at common sense and reason. But the Catholic Church solemnly adopted it, and now American Catholic scholars of the twentieth century have to believe it. And they do. But they can not without crippling their intellect in other ways.

While the Reformation was in progress, the Reformed bodies also produced creeds in plenty. They grew at first out of political necessities. For instance, in 1530 the Lutheran party in Germany was in great danger of being persecuted and suppressed by the Emperor. At the Diet of Augsburg they presented a Confession, a summary of their belief, to show that they agreed with the Catholics on all vital points and were not so bad as they had been made out to be. This Augsburg Confession was drafted by Melancthon, who was by nature a timid soul and at that time desperately frightened, and he kept all the braver assertions of the Reformation carefully out of sight. It is easy to sympathize with this conciliatory attitude in that dangerous situation. But this Confession afterward was adopted as one of the creeds of the Lutheran Church and still has to be accepted and subscribed as a binding statement of Gospel truth. It is very hard, almost "impossible," to get rid of a creed again after it is once adopted. Our Presbyterian brethren have long been restless under the straight Calvinism of their Westminster Confession, and it has cost them a long struggle to secure some modification of it. The great church historian Harnack, knowing how tenaciously creeds cling to a church, was lost in admiration when our American Presbyterians first began to make the effort.

Now we Baptists have no authoritative creed. Our ministers and professors are not required solemnly to declare that they adopt some obsolete statement as their belief and will always teach that. We have a couple of summaries, called the New Hampshire and the Philadelphia Confession, which are often adopted by newly organized churches, but no one is compelled to use them. So far as I remember I never read either of them until I had been several years a Baptist minister, and when I did read them, I was not interested in them. This freedom from creeds has left Baptists free to grow without jars amid struggles. We used to be strict Calvinists, just like our Presbyterian brethren, and we, too, have insensibly grown away from rigid Calvinism, but we have had no creed to tinker and no conflict about it. Like Topsy, we just "growed."

Yet Baptists have been remarkably free from doctrinal vagaries. They have not moved zigzag, but in a fairly straight line. There was enough conservative instinct to balance their thinking without carrying a big stick of timber on their shoulders to balance them.

Baptists have always insisted that they recognize the Bible alone as their sufficient authority for faith and practice. There are, indeed, many Baptists who have tried to use the Bible just as other denominations use their creeds. They have turned the Bible into one huge creed, and practically that meant: "You must believe everything which we think the Bible means and says." They have tried to impose on us their little interpretation of the great Book as the creed to which all good Baptists must cleave.

But fortunately the Bible is totally different from a creed. A creed contains sharply defined and abstract theology; the Bible contains a record of concrete and glowing religious life. A creed addresses itself to the intellect; the Bible appeals to the whole soul and edifies it. A creed tells you what you must believe; the Bible tells you what holy men have believed. A creed is religious philosophy, the Bible is religious history. A creed gives the truth as it looked to one set of clever men at one particular stage of human history; the Bible gives the truth as it looked to a great number of God-filled men running through many hundreds of years. The strength of a creed is in its uniformity and its tight fit; the beauty of the Bible is in its marvelous variety and richness. A creed imposes a law and binds thought; the Bible imparts a spirit and awakens thought.

Any collection of historical documents, growing right out of human life, would be more useful and instructive to after-times than the cleverest piece of abstract thinking done by a single man or group of men. The epoch-making treatises of the past grow obsolete with fearful rapidity; human nature with its love and hate and fear and hope and sin and passion is always the same, and what was true in the days of Rameses II under the shadow of the pyramids, is true in the days of Roosevelt I under the shadow of the skyscrapers. Hence creeds are dead and the Bible is alive. And such a life in it! A unique and gifted nation, with a lofty conception of God and a thrilling faith in him, preserves the thoughts of its most daring thinkers, its prophets and revolutionists, its poets and religious historians, and the whole collection throbs with the living breath of God-if only we have a mind to respond. And then comes the Highest One of all, the Son of God and the King of Humanity, and his life and thought are preserved in artless books, and the powerful impulse which he gives to human souls records itself in a series of letters and tracts, and these are added to the Old Bible of the Jewish people as the New Bible of the Christian people.

These books are the deposit of the purest and freshest form of Christianity. It is the mountain-brook before it has grown muddy in the plain by the inflow of other waters. The New Testament has been the conscience in the heart of the Church, always warning and recalling it from its sinful wanderings. It is still calling us up higher to-day, beyond traditional Christianity to the religion of Christ. In the New Testament lies the power of perpetual reformation for the Church. Baptists, in tying to the New Testament, have hitched their chariot to a star, and they will have to keep moving.

It seems to me a great thing that Baptists are not chained by creeds, but have taken the Bible as their authority. The full significance of that principle has never yet appeared among us. We have paralyzed the Bible by turning it into a law-book and a collection of proof-texts. We have often refused to take it in its own plain meaning and to comprehend the larger sweep of history in it. We have fussed about trifles in it and have missed the greatest things. We have reduced it all to a single level, as if Esther was equal to Isaiah, and the Old Testament to the New, and Zephaniah or Jude to our Lord Jesus Christ. But my faith is that the old veil of Moses will yet be taken away from the Bible and its full light will break forth.

This is the last reason which I shall give for being a Baptist. Baptists have not bound the religious intellect by the adoption of a creed, and they have undertaken to learn the Bible can tell them and to guide their life thereby. This is to me a satisfactory adjustment between the two great principles of Freedom and Authority; between the initiative of the individual and the authority of the church; between faithfulness to the past and obedience to the call of the future. I do not mean that Baptists have been faultless in their application of these principles; they have sinned and bungled more often than not. But the principle is right and has a saving power of guidance in it.

POSTLUDE

Herewith ends this little series. The articles written off-hand and amid the pressures of work, and their faults crave a kindly judgment. My hope was that a few people might actually take time to read them and be helped to a clearer understanding of their own faith and the nature of our denomination would get some new light by approaching the familiar subject by fresh ways.

Sometimes while writing these articles I felt in doubt whether I was doing good or harm. I should do harm if I gave Baptists the impression that "we are the people and there are no others." We are not a perfect denomination. We are capable of being just as narrow and small as anybody. There are fine qualities in which other denominations surpass us. I do not want to foster Baptist self-conceit, because thereby I should grieve the spirit of Christ. I do not want to make Baptists shut themselves up in their clam-shells and be indifferent to the ocean outside of them. I am a Baptist, but I am more than a Baptist. All things are mine; whether Francis of Assisi, or Luther, or Knox, or Wesley; all are mine because I am Christ's. The old Adam is a strict denominationalist; the new Adam is just a Christian.

Source: *The Baptist Commonwealth.* 5 December 1912, pp. 8-9; 12 December pp. 6-7; 19 December, p. 6.

Select Walter Rauschenbusch Correspondence

LIFE-LONG FRIENDSHIPS AND INSIGHTS

Walter Rauschenbusch enjoyed lifelong friendships from his days as a student at Rochester Free Academy. He corresponded with Edward Hanna (1860-1944), who took orders in the Roman Catholic Church, and became Archbishop of San Francisco, and Munson Ford, who became a local businessman. The correspondence with Munson Ford illustrates details of Walter's early student ministry in Kentucky, plus his school life at Gütersloh Gymnasium, as well as the ongoing nature of a close personal friendship. The Ford correspondence transcribed below is the oldest extant documentation for Walter's early life.

A.

Walter Rauschenbusch to Munson Ford 12 November 1882

Mr Munson Ford, sen

My dear fellow,-

So you want a description of my whole vacation-trip, do you? Well I'm very much afraid you will not get it, poor fellow! I tell you what, I have had to write a description of that several times to different people & as the German phrase is, it hangs out of my throat. Not the memory of it, that is a constant source of enjoyment, but the description of it. So you must wait till I come back & get it from me personally. Perhaps I shall go to Switzerland & Italy before I return, then I shall be still really aglow. I expect to pass my final exam in February or March, the written part will be done in January probably, that is the more important, the oral is done just before dismission in presence of a high and mighty government official, who takes the examination into his own hands when he sees it don't go. And there is such a thing as getting left, doesn't occur very seldom either. I ought to be grinding like a wind-mill but I haven't settled down to it yet. You must know Munson, that I have changed very much since I came hither, grown quite lazy in fact & I haven't been able to rally enough to go to work in earnest even with the exam confronting me like the jaws of lion (pretty simile isn't it).

Well after the final ordeal, which by the way is considered comparatively the hardest of all the examinations through which German students have to pass & those are many & hard, after that, I say, I hope to stay a few months in Europe yet to travel-for I haven't seen anything of the world yet & to pursue some studies for which I might never here after have time. I desire very much a close aquaintance with Greek literature, especially Plato and Sophocles, with whom I am very much in love, & with German literature. The latter is very fascinating study for me & I should like to devote more time to it than I have as yet been able to do in America I shall not have the material at hand for it. Then I want to go to Italy see Hanna & return to home sweet home in June or July, perhaps I shall be in time for the [Delta] Upsilon farewell supper & for commencement, to see you in your glory. How will that be, old fellow?...

B.

Walter Rauschenbusch to Munson Ford, 31 December 1884

My Dear Munson,-

Your letter of July 15 and your postal of Nov. 15 are both before me; so is the new year;--I write. In fact I don't know any earthly reason why I did not write long ago. I thought of you often, I had time enough, I like you as well as I ever did 7if you were here at this moment I should enjoy a talk with you immensely. So the only reason that did not write to you at any single time.

I see in your letters you wish to know more about my first pastorate in Louisville. Well that seems very far in the past now; but it forms a very pleasant remembrance indeed. It was only a very small flock but a very neglected one. Sins of pastor and sins of member had created distrust & contempt among outsiders. Internal dissensions had banished the spirit of brotherly love. Everybody was sorely discouraged & very many were very hungry which was the best thing about the church. I began with the determination to raise the spiritual standard of every Christian among them as far as he or she would let me. I worked a great deal from house to house poohooed & frowned on their backbiting stories, reconciled those who hated each other & tried everywhere to awaken in their hearts the love of Christ as the only sure cure for their love of self & sin. Then I preached as well as I could & had the satisfaction to see the congregation almost double in 3 months. I organized the young people, gave Bible readings & got $20 a month; when I left the place I was as thin as a ghost, but I rejoiced in a number of conversions, I saw the numbers again united by their common affection for their common Master, I saw them deeply affected when I said farewell to them at the little social they gave me, & I was satisfied. I don't write this with a boastful spirit, Munson; I am proud of my diligence & application, for of that any man may be proud & I got a better opinion of myself in that respect than I had before. But as for the success and the blessing, I am not proud of that. Again and again I said to myself this Summer "How foolish I sh'd be, were I to attribute this to myself! This is beyond my vainest imaginings about my own powers; there is One behind me, I am but the instrument in his hand."

You can imagine that three months of such work have an influence on one's ideas & ideals. It is now no longer my fond hope to be a learned theologian and write big books; I want to be a pastor, powerful with men, preaching to them Christ as the man in whom their affections & energies can find the satisfaction for which mankind is groaning. And if ever I do become anything but a pastor, you may believe either that there was a very unmistakeable call to duty in that direction.

My studies here are progressing quietly. I don't mean to fail in my standing, yet I no longer regard them as an end in themselves, if I ever did. I look more for the great thoughts that shake mankind, than for certainty in regard to a disputed date in Acts or an obscure root of a Hebrew verb.

From Ed Hanna I had a letter dated Aug. 17; but it was so full of a compendium of Roman Catholic systematic theology, that it fairly squelched me for a time& I have not had the cheek to answer him with my low gossip. He has received all the orders, has the "*character indelibis*" as priest, is bound to eternal virginity etc. Should you ever write to him you would have to address him now with Rev. He will finish there about the time that I do here. I called on Miss Page in the beginning of this term & found a young gentleman by the name of Hawthorne visiting her; the other day I called again& low he was still there. In other respects she seems to be well.

Last night I went over to see Miss Davis & had a very good time with her. There is an air of purity and childlikeness about her which is very charming compared with the self-possession of the average American girl; her oddity only makes it the more piquante, so that I find her in spite of her oblique stare and undesirable homeliness a much more pleasing companion than Miss Page with all her natural & acquired "smartness." Don't imagine however, because I have mentioned several calls to young ladies, that I have any habits tending in that line. I enjoy them when I do make them, but on the whole, I find myself better without.

Now I have talked a great deal about myself: Do thou likewise, that is to say, talk about yourself for that is what I want to know most; how are you getting along in business? How does your place look? How are your parents? Have you got as handsome a pair of burn-sides & such a charming mustache as I have? Well write soon, old fellow & we'll start the carts into a trotting match. My mother sends kind regards. My father is in Cleveland. Remember me to your father and mother.

Yours W. Rauschenbusch

Source: Rauschenbusch Family Collections (RG 103), American Baptist Historical Society, Atlanta, Georgia.

A Potential Foreign Missionary?

By the later decades of the 19th century Rochester Theological Seminary became a leading resource of potential candidates for American Baptist missionary service. Beginning in 1865, the Rauschenbusch Family rendered distinguished service in India through the labors of John E. Clough (1836-1910) and his wife, Emma (1859-1940; Walter's older sister). Upon the recommendation of John Clough, E. F. Merriam, secretary to the American Baptist Missionary Union, was disposed to contact Rauschenbusch regarding discussions in the Board about his possible appointment to India. R. R. Williams of Buffalo, New York, was a member of the American Baptist Missionary Union Board. The correspondence below illustrates the process that ended in no further discussion of missionary service for Walter.

A.

E. F. Merriam to Walter Rauschenbusch 16 August 1886
American Baptist Missionary Union
Tremont Temple
Boston, Mass.

Rev. Walter Rauschenbusch.

My dear Brother: Your esteemed favor of the 13th instant came this morning, and it gives me great pleasure to know that you are prepared to consider the work at Ramapatam. It would be desirable for you to go out before the 1st of December, in order to have as much of the cool season in India as possible to take the burden of the Seminary from Dr. Clough, who is weighed down by his own work at Ongole which few men could carry alone. Yet it is far more important to secure the right man for this important post; and in order to do this we ought to wait until we are sure of our way; and we would be willing to await the convenience of the right man. It would better to wait a year than to make a mistake in this very important matter.

Dr. Williams' father-in-law is Mr. Henry Wills of Buffalo, N.Y. and I presume they will go there immediately on reaching this country. I will write to Dr. Williams to arrange an interview with you as soon as possible. I suppose they will arrive before Sept. 1. Any further information I can give you I shall be glad to afford and if after investigation you think you will go to India, please let me know and I will arrange for you to meet the Executive Committee. Please write me freely in regard to this matter. I shall be glad to help you all I can.

Your brother in Christ, E. F. Merriam, Secys. Asst.

B.

E. F. Merriam to Walter Rauschenbusch 29 Sept 1886

Rev. Walter Rauschenbusch
141 West 45th St., New York, NY

My Dear Brother

The subject of your appointment to the Presidency of the Telugu Theological Seminary at Ramapatam was again considered by the Executive Committee at their meeting on Monday. The most flattering testimonials to your abilities and attainments have been received. Yet some of those who wrote most highly of your personal qualities felt, as I intimated in my last letter, that it would be better for you to have a few years' experience before assuming the duties of such a responsible and important position as that under consideration. The committee therefore decided that it is not expedient at present to appoint you to the Presidency of the Ramapatam Seminary, but I hope the missionary work may yet have the benefit of your service. Praying that the Lord may greatly bless you in all your labors.

Yours sincerely, E. F. Merriam, Secys Asst.

Source: Rauschenbusch Family Collection, American Baptist Historical Society, Atlanta Georgia.

A Gifted Hymnist

Though much hampered by profound deafness, Rauschenbusch maintained a lifelong love for music. In his pastoral years, he authored several hymns or anthems, mostly in German, and co-published with Ira D. Sankey, Evangeliums Lieder, 1 and 2 *(1897). He was a contributor to* Gesangbuch der Deutschen Baptisten-Gemeinden *(1916), the official hymnbook of the German Baptists. The selection below, likely composed in the later 1880s, he considered an 'anthem.' The original was signed by Walter. The tune he selected ("Whitehead") also accompanied the popular contemporary hymn, "Faith of Our Fathers."*

"O God, We Thank Thee" (Tune: Whitehead)

O God, we thank Thee for this universe, our home; for its vastness and its riches and for the manifoldness of its life!

We praise Thee for the arching sky and the blessed winds for the driving clouds and the constellations on high!

We praise Thee for the salt sea and the running water, for the everlasting hills, for the trees, and the grass under our feet!

Grant, we pray Thee, a heart wide open to joy and beauty, that we shall not pass heedless and unseeing, when e'en the thornbush by the way-side is aflame with the glory of God!

Through Jesus Christ our Lord, Amen.

WALTER RAUSCHENBUSCH

Source: Folder 1023, Rauschenbusch Papers, North American Baptist Heritage Commission Archives, Sioux Falls Seminary, Sioux Falls, South Dakota. Courtesy Philip E. Thompson.

Professional and Personal Social Concerns

Walter Rauschenbusch was continually reviewing and assessing world affairs and emerging concerns in his own home town, Rochester, New York. In **Selection A** below, he wrote to his beloved wife, Pauline, concerning a possible outbreak of diphtheria in the city. It was a deadly disease in this period in American cities, mostly due to inadequate sanitary conditions, and affecting children. His family was not affected, but he assumed a personal responsibility for finding ways to alleviate the spread of the disease. In **Selection B** below, he joined with the faculty of Rochester Theological Seminary, prominent clergy, and civic leaders of Rochester in addressing Russian Czar Nicholas II's plan for disarmament. The Rochester community of pastors/leaders supported the initiative that led ultimately to the first Hague Convention (1899) which brought about an international consensus on disarmament, the laws of war, and war crimes.

A.

January 8th, 1902.

Dear Pauline,-

I am in quite an anxious frame of mind. This evening at five I met Mrs. Guth and Dr. Adams coming down the stairs, and I inquired if anyone were sick, and learned that young Liebig has a bad case of sore throat, which might turn out to be diphtheria. I told Dr. Adams of our trouble, in order to help him in the diagnosis, and he was evidently glad of the hint to keep a look-out in that direction. To-morrow will probably show if any rash developes (sic).

I have not been in direct contact with him, his class does not meet me till to-morrow. But if scarlet fever breaks out in the building, it will be a bad business for me. It may come from a totally different source, but I shall get the blame, and one can't tell how far it may have done and how many will get it.

And I confess that I feel we have not taken full precautions of late. Dr. Adams at once inquired about my clothes. I said it had been disinfected, but personally I fear it was in a perfunctory fashion. And we have grown careless of late. I was painfully surprised the first time I came to the door and found Miss D at table with you. We have no guarantee that she will not carry it to the two little ones still. And even if they are immune, it infects the house, and we shall not be inwardly free when we have merely disinfected the two sick-rooms by and by. My fear about Liebig may prove groundless, but the case has brought things home to me more. I think we better pull up sharp a while again and be more conscientious toward others. We don't want to inflict the danger on them under which we have suffered.

With love,
Walther

Source: Box F-5, No. 75, Rauschenbusch Correspondence, (Walter, Pauline), North American Baptist Heritage Commission Archives, Sioux Falls Seminary, Sioux Falls, South Dakota. Transcribed by Philip E. Thompson.

B.

Dear Sir and Brother:-

On August 29 the rescript of the Czar was published setting forth the steady and draining growth of military armament and calling on the Powers to consult how this waste of treasure and life could be checked. This proclamation has since been supplemented by several definite proposals: to keep military stores and budgets stationary for a fixed period; to consult about future reduction of armaments; to restrict the use of high explosives; to exclude any of still higher power; to forbid the throwing of high explosives from baloons, the construction of rams and the use of submarine torpedoes; to neutralize vessels engaged in saving those wrecked in naval battles; and to accept the principle of mediation and arbitration as far as possible.

These proposals have been received favorably by the Governments, somewhat cynically by many reviewers, and with a growing interest by the people as they begin to comprehend the sincerity of the Czar and the potential relief and peace in his bold deed. Efforts are being made, especially in England, to give public sentiment of the aggressively Christian nations a chance to utter itself. Is it not time for America to do the same? The experiences of the past year and the present war-like temper of people make it all the mote imperative for those who proclaim the thoughts and spirit of Jesus to further any movement that makes for the peace of nations.

The undersigned, drawn together by this desire, have resolved to ask you and all the ministers of our city to devote one sermon, if possible, on the 19th of February to a discussion of great historical opportunity and of the cause of international peace in general. An effort will also be made to have the matter presented in the public schools, the labor unions and other organizations.

Will you kindly notify our secretary whether our request commends itself to your judgment? If you think well of it, please have the enclosed resolution or one similar to it voted upon at your meeting and return the blank to the secretary. The information thus collected will be forwarded to the President of the United States and the Czar of Russia.

F. L. Anderson,	W. C. Gannett,	W. Rauschenbusch,
C. L. Barbour,	Max Landsberg,	H. H. Stebbins,
W.T. Brown,	F. D. Leete,	J. W. A. Stewart,
R. R. Converse,	N. Millard,	A. H. Strong,
W. D. Doty,	J. H. Pattison,	W. R. Taylor.

Source: "Circular Letter, 1899", Rauschenbusch Papers, North American Baptist Heritage Commission Archives, Sioux Falls Seminary, Sioux Falls, South Dakota. Courtesy of Philip E. Thompson.

THE SCHOLAR ON READING AND HIS LIBRARY

Walter Rauschenbusch collected a fine scholar's library rich in English and German titles. At his death, his library was distributed among students and pastors in the German Baptist community in Rochester. In the short essay below he gave his opinion about literacy and the pleasures of owning books.

WHY PEOPLE SHOULD OWN AND READ BOOKS

Our nation does not buy solid books. Even the figures for the best sellers for books that are supposed to be epoch-making in their line, are curiously small when one thinks of this enormous nation of potential book-buyers.

We are rich enough to buy books. Probably we are not civilized enough. In education great masses of our people have passed from the public school to the high school in recent years. Some day, let us hope, the masses will graduate from the periodical to the book.

I have a large professional library at my disposal, from which I can borrow freely. But a book doubles or trebles its value for me when I can mark it up, and that I can do only with my own books.

When I have marked or double-marked a sentence or paragraph, I have passed a verdict on it. I have made up my mind on it, and in making up my mind I have molded my mind. When I put down a question mark on the margin, I have exercised my critical faculty and the issue raised between the author and me has become a little clearer to me. Marking up a book comes close to having a personal discussion with the writer.

Then again, when I take up a marked book later, I can recall the argument easily by the passages marked. The trail is blazed. And now I can pass judgment on my own judgments. The doubt which I expressed in the question mark is gone now, or it has stiffened into denial. I can pat myself on the back for my youthful discernment.

But all this is possible only with a book I own.

Walter Rauschenbusch

Source: *Philadelphia North American* 26 April 1913

A GENEROUS MENTOR IN MINISTRY

Walter Rauschenbusch wanted to be a writer. He thought of his theological and ethical works as invitations to his readers to become active in social transformation. He saw his students and those recently appointed in pastoral ministry as a first-line of army workers in his cause. In **Selection A** below, in 1907 he advocated ministry as an intellectually broadening profession, thus illustrating his growing liberal lines of thought and a magisterial idea of Christian ministry. In **Selection B** below, in 1912 another anonymous donor made it possible for Rauschenbusch to give complimentary copies of his second great book, *Christianizing the Social Order*, to recent theology graduates across the country. A professor himself, his first disciples were his students.

A.

Dear Sir:-

Through the generosity of a friend I am enabled to present this copy of "Christianity and the Social Crisis" to you as a gift on your entrance into the Christian ministry. It is his hope that it will be a leaven in your life and work.

The ministry is the greatest and most glorious of all professions. Yet actually it has often narrowed the men who have entered it. It is of the highest importance that you lay hold of your life's task---whether at home or abroad---in the spirit of a missionary, as an apostle of a mighty Gospel that is to revolutionize both men and institutions, and to turn the anarchy and sinfulness of our present life into a kingdom of peace and love.

It is the hope of the giver and the writer that this book will help you to see and to face the larger tasks of Christianity, and we send you Good Cheer as you join the ranks of the greatest army that ever was.

Yours for the Kingdom of God,

Walter Rauschenbusch

Source: Walter Rauschenbusch Scrapbook, 1911-1912, p. 49. Rauschenbusch Family Collection, RG 1003, American Baptist Historical Society, Atlanta, Georgia.

B.

March 1st, 1913

Dear Sir:-

A limited number of the members of your Class have been selected on the basis of scholarship to receive a copy of "Christianizing the Social Order" as a gift. I beg to congratulate you on being of that number and trust that the achievements of school life will be a guarantee of high achievement in the severer tests of life.

The friend who presents this book to you believes in its message and wants to see the able young minds of the ministry awakened to the questions discussed in it. He hopes that you will read it soon and thoroughly, and will discuss it with your fellow-students, so that when you pass out into the work of Christian ministry, you will have a somewhat matured understanding of these fundamental moral problems of our age, and can help to mobilize the Christian Church for the work of christianizing the social order.

I join you in gratitude to the generous giver, and remain,

Yours for the Kingdom of God,

Walter Rauschenbusch

Source: Folder 985, Rauschenbusch Collection, North American Baptist Heritage Commission Archives, Sioux Falls, South Dakota. Courtesy of Philip E. Thompson.

Responses to Last Published Work

Responses from friends, fellow scholars far and wide, came to Rauschenbusch upon the publication of his major works. Below are two examples from theologically informed readers to his last book, A Theology for the Social Gospel *(1918). In* **Selection A** *below, Vida D. Scudder (1861-1954), a professor at Wellesley College and a social activist, was critical of Rauschenbusch's attacks upon Roman Catholicism. In* **Selection B** *below, Gerald Birney Smith (1863-1929), a leading liberal theologian at the University of Chicago, was dubious of Rauschenbusch's idea of the Christological origins of the Kingdom of God.*

A.

Wellesley, Mass.
March 27, 1918

My dear Dr. Rauschenbusch:-

How late I am in acknowledging the copy of your book, with that delightful inscription. I love to be called Brother and Comrade, in spite of the sex discrimination involved. Of course you know that my great desire is to get your feeling and interpretation over into the Anglican Communion. For this very reason I have stressed, you may think unduly, our points of difference with you in the Review which you will see some day. I wanted to forestall the difficulties which our Church people will feel. But for all the positive side of your book, I am deeply grateful.

Not for a moment should I think of denying to you the title of Mystic. It is a question of the value placed on one type of mysticism, that which is quite unrelated to our fellow-men. I do profoundly honor and value this special type, believing it to be the root from which the fair flower of human love may spring. You, I think, are unduly afraid of it.

I am glad indeed that your book is finding its own, and the people who repudiate it may be the very ones to be most affected by it in the long run.

Fraternally yours,

Vida D. Scudder

Source: Vida Scudder to Walter Rauschenbusch, 27 March 1918, Rauschenbusch Family Collection, RG 1003, Box 35, Correspondence Files, 1917-1918, American Baptist Historical Society, Atlanta, Georgia.

B.

April 30, 1918

My dear professor Rauschenbusch:-

The main theological event of the year in Chicago has been the reading and discussion of your book. I intended to write to you sooner about it; but to tell the truth, I did not get time to it all through until recently. My students have been most enthusiastic over it. In one of my classes, I asked for reviews of it; and student after student wrote in such a way that I could see that in many cases the reading of that book will constitute a spiritual birthday. If this is some reward to you for the writing of it, you ought to have it for all that it is worth.

I envy your social vision, and your happy way of expressing yourself. These strenuous days of thinking make us see how completely the religious, to say nothing of the material welfare of men is at the mercy of social ideals. A day of crisis for the church is here. If we have not a vigorous social gospel, Christian institutions will become second rate survivals. And you have given the cause this tremendous boost, just when it is most needed. God bless you.

If I wanted to, I could raise one or two theological questions. I will mention just one. According to your exposition, Jesus was the initiator of the Kingdom; but I had the feeling that you had left Jesus socially unrelated to a certain extent. What would be the effect on your theology, if instead of the somewhat Ritschlian position of masking Jesus the de novo initiator, you should interpret Christianity as the outgrowth of a complex social situation, in which Hellenic as well as Judaic forces were positively present. Jesus' message would be relative to his own age, rather than a socially unexplained superhuman norm for all ages. It is the spirit and the religious power of his ideals rather than their exact content which become significant for us, in that case. Did Jesus really "initiate" the Kingdom? Did its beginnings not reach far back of him? Is there anything in his message which he does not share with the prophets of Israel and with the modern social prophets? Can we have a "social gospel", in which Jesus is valued in individualistic terms, by being set off as an "initiator" rather than interpreted as a "sharer."

But I did not mean to enter into a theological argument. Nor do I want you to feel that you must answer my questions. They are so petty in comparison with the brace, inspiring message of the book, that I am almost ashamed to entertain them at all. The main thing is to get the content of our modern social faith persuasively expressed, rather than to be precise over technical theological method. And here you are the teacher to whom we all gladly go to school.

I am distressed to learn of your poor health. I hope a period of rest will set you up again. We need your prophetic voice sadly in the days that are before us.

Sincerely and gratefully yours,
Gerald Birney Smith

Source: Gerald Birney Smith to Walter Rauschenbusch, 30 April 1918, Rauschenbusch Family Collection, RG 1003, box 35, Correspondence Files, 1917-18 American Baptist Historical Society, Atlanta, Georgia.

The Faith of a Prophet

Toward the end of his life in 1918, Walter reflected on his pilgrimage in faith. In this "Affirmation," he exhibits his theological priorities, his overarching emphasis upon the Kingdom of God, and his optimistic views of life in general. Cast in the shape of an evangelical confession, it bears witness to his evangelical and liberal perspectives. Alongside his last book, A Theology for the Social Gospel, *it may be considered a theological testament.*

AN AFFIRMATION OF FAITH

I affirm my faith in the reality of the spiritual world, in the sacred voice of duty, in the compelling power of truth and holiness, in prayer, in the life eternal, in him who is the life of my life and the reality behind all things invisible. I rejoice to believe in God.

I affirm my faith in the kingdom of God and my hope in its final triumph. I determine by faith to live day by day within the higher order, and divine peace of my fatherland, and carry its spirit and laws into all my dealings in the world that is now.

I make an act of love toward all fellow men. I accept them as they are, with all their sins and failures, and declare my solidarity with them, if they have wronged or grieved me, I place my mind within the all-comprehending and all-loving mind of God, and here and now forgive, I desire to minister God's love to men and offer no hindrance to the free flow of his love through me.

I affirm my faith in life. I call life good and not evil. I accept the limitations of my own life and believe it is possible for me to live a beautiful and Christ-like life within the conditions set for me. Through the power of Christ which descend on me, I know that I can be more than conqueror.

WALTER RAUSCHENBUSCH

Source: Folder 1022, Rauschenbusch Papers, North American Baptist Heritage Commission Archives, Sioux Falls Seminary, Sioux Falls, South Dakota. Courtesy Philip E. Thompson.

A Rauschenbusch Bibliography

Bibliographies

Bibliography of Materials by and about Walter Rauschenbusch in the American Baptist Historical Society Library. Rochester, NY: American Baptist Historical Society, 1967.

Brezina, Christoph. See below "Von der Erweckungsbewegung zum "Social Gospel": Walter Rauschenbusch Herkunft, Umfeld und Entwicklung bis 1891" Ph.D. Dissertation, Philipps-Marburg Universität, 1993.

Selected Bibliography-Project MUSE.

Muse.jhu.edu/books/9780813162898/9780813162898-13 pdf.

Stackhouse, Max. *Bibliography of Walter Rauschenbusch.* Cambridge, MA: Harvard University, 1964.

Vanderberge, Mary E. "Walter Rauschenbusch and the Social Gospel: A Select Bibliography." Rochester: 1970.

Primary Documents

Brackney, William H. *Baptist Life and Thought, 1600-1980.* Valley Forge, PA: Judson Press, 1983; 1998.

Ferm, Robert L. *Issues in American Protestantism: A Documentary History from the Puritans to the Present.* Garden City, NJ: Anchor Books, 1969.

Handy, Robert T., editor. *The Social Gospel in America 1870-1920: Gladden, Ely, Rauschenbusch.* New York: Oxford University Press, 1966.

Hudson, Winthrop S., editor. Walter Rauschenbusch: Selected Writings. New York: Paulist Press, 1984.

Landis, Benson Y., compiler. *A Rauschenbusch Reader: The Kingdom of God and the Social Gospel.* New York: Harper and Brothers, 1957.

Mays, Benjamin E., editor. *A Gospel for the Social Awakening: Selections from the Writings of Walter Rauschenbusch.* New York: Association Press, 1950.

Moehlman, Conrad H. *A Rauschenbusch Sourcebook with Commentary.* Los Angeles, 1953. (Microfilm).

Proceedings of the Baptist Congress, 1885-1912.

Rauschenbusch, Ernst, and Frederich Voigts, Walter Hermann. *Latomiablumen: Dichtergrüse fur die Schwestern aller Freimaurer.* Frankfurt an Main: Grobel, 1885.

Rauschenbusch, Walter. "August Rauschenbusch." *Baptist Home Mission Monthly* 20/9 (September 1898): 323-324.

______. "About Politics" *For the Right*, I (March 1890): 2

______. "Aim of Social Christianity." *The Gazette* (Delaware, Ohio), 1911.

______. "American Christianity and the National Life" *The Standard,* 52 (1915): 1303-05.

______. "Auch ein amerik amicher Professor, Nachruf von Alfred Hess." *Christlichte Welt,* 33 (1919): 9.

______. "Augustus Hopkins Strong: An Appreciation." *Rochester Baptist Monthly* (November 1906).

______. "Augustus Rauschenbusch: An Address by His Son, Walter." *Rochester Democrat and Chronicle,* 27 October 1900.
______. "Autocracy and War: Germany's Evil Heritage." *Rochester Democrat and*
______. *Chronicle,* 1 July 1918.
______. "A Word for the Little Churches." *The Examiner,* 10 March 1892.
______. "The Baptist Contribution" *Freedom and the Churches*, edited by Charles W. Wendte. Boston, MA: American Unitarian Association, 1913, 1-10.
______. "Baptist Work in Germany." *National Baptist,* 31 July 1884.
______. "Baptists and Social Progress." *Minutes of the Pittsburgh Baptist Association*, 75-87.
______. "Be Fair to Germany: A Plea for Open-mindedness." *The Congregationalist,* September, 1914.
______. "The Belated Races and the Social Problems An Address Before the American Missionary Association." *Methodist Quarterly Review,* 63/2 April 1914: 252-257.
______. "Beneath the Glitter." *The Inquirer,* 1887.
______. "Between Eras: From Capitalism to Democracy: Albion W. Small." *The*
______. *American Journal of Sociology,* 19/6 (1914): 853-854.
______. "Breaking Bread." *The Independent,* 48 (March 1896).
______. "The Brotherhood of the Kingdom." *National Baptist*, 26 October 1893, p. 683.
______. "Can a Christian Be a Socialist?" *The Philadelphia Press,* (27 February 1893).
______. *Cement of Society.* Boston: MA: The Pilgrim Press, 1912.
______. "Centralization of Baptist Polity" *Thirteenth Annual Session of the Baptist Congress.* New York: Baptist Congress Publishing Co., 1896), 57-60.
______. "The Charm of Jesus" (with Gustav Zart). New York: T. Y. Crowell, 1899.
______. *Cherkvata I Obshtestveniiat Prievrat.* Samokov, Bulgaria: Pechatnitsa pri Amerikanskitie, n.d.
______. "The Church and Money Power" *Proceedings of the Baptist Congress* 1893. (Paper read Dec. 5, 1893).
______. "Christ the Emancipator." WR Files, ABHS.
______. "Christ the Source of All Our Good." *The Treasury,* 18 (February 1901): 757-58.
______. "Christi Person und Werk in Der Predeiger D. Hermann Gebhardt." *The American Journal of Theology,* 3/2 (1899): 430-431.
______. "Christian Socialism" *A Dictionary of Religion and Ethics*, edited by
______, Shailer Mathews and G. B. Smith. New York: The MacMillan Co., 1921, 90-91.
______. "Christian Socialism and the Brotherhood of the Kingdom: An Interview with Walter Rauschenbusch." *The New York Press,* 3 June 1894.
______. "Christian Union as an Historical Problem." Clipping in CRDS Library.
______. "Christianity a Democratic Religion." 2/3 *City Club Bulletin* December 1890.
______. *Christianity and the Cooperatives.* Chicago, IL: Cooperative League of the U.S.A., 1957.
______. "Christianity and Social Problems." *The American Journal of Theology,* 15/1 (1911): 146-148.
______. *Christianity and the Social Crisis.* London: MacMillan, 1907; 1913.

______. "Christianity and the Social Crisis" In *Callings: Twenty Centuries of Christian Wisdom on Vocation*, edited by William C. Placher, 377-84. Grand Rapids, MI: William B. Eerdmans Publishing Co., 2005.
______. *Christianity and the Social Crisis in the 21st Century: The Classic That Woke Up the Church.* Edited by Tony Campolo and Paul Rauschenbusch. New York, NY: HarperOne, 2007.
______. *Christianity and the Social Sciences.* New York and London: Macmillan, 1908.
______. *Christianizing the Social Order.* New York, NY: The MacMillan Company, 1912; 1926. 2010 (Baylor University Press)
______. "Christlicher Socialismus einst und jetzt." *Christliche Welt,* 23 (1909) 538-42
______. "Christmas Message." *Life and Labor,* 2/12 Dec. 1912, no 24.
______. "The Church and Its Attitude to The Labor Movement" *Iron Molders Journal,* October, 1898.
______. "Church and Money." *The National Baptist,* 23 March 1893.
______. "The Church and Money Power" *Eleventh Annual Session of the Baptist Congress.* New York: Baptist Congress Publishing Co., 1894, 10-17.
______. "Church and Social Questions." Council of Women for Home Mission Conservation of National Ideals, pp. 99-122.
______. "Church and Socialists: An American View." *Evening Gazette* Aberdeen Scotland, 3 May 1911.
______. "The Church and Social Questions." *Conservation of National Ideals* New York: Fleming H. Revell Co., 1911, 99-122.
______. "The Church's Duty." *Rochester Herald* 4 September 1899.
______. "The City." *Rochester Daily Advocate,* 23 April 1904.
______. "The Comenius Society." *Examiner* 70/5 (4 February 1892): 2.
______. "The Coming of the Lord." *Report of the Amity Missionary Conference, Fifth Annual Conference Report* (1895), 3.
______. "Comments on Strikes for the Eight Hour Day." *City Club Bulletin* 1/9 June 1890: 2.
______. "Conceptions of Missions." *The Watchman,* 24 November 1892.
______. "Conservation of the Social Service Message" in *Men and Religion Forward Movement*, Vol. 2: 121-125.
______. "A Conquering Idea." *The Examiner,* 21 July 1892. Clipping, CRDS.
______. "The Conservation of the Social Service Message" *Messages of the Men and*
______. *Religion Movement.* New York: Association Press, 1912 II: 121-25.
______. "Contribution of Jesus to the Social Movement." *The Springfield* (Mass.) *Union* 29 January 1910.
______. "Contributions Socialism Has Made to the Social Feeling of Which We
______. Are All Conscious." *Rochester Democrat and Chronicle* 13 December 1909.
______. "The Culture of Spiritual Life." *Rochester Baptist Monthly* November 1897. Clipping CRDS.
______. "The Czar's Peace Proposal." *The Pittsburgh Post,* 6 March 1899. Clipping, CRDS.
______. *Dare We Be Christians?* Boston, MA: The Pilgrim Press, 1914.
______. *Das Leben Jesu: Ein systematischen Studiengang.* Cleveland, OH: Bickel, 1895.

______. "The Deacons of the New Testament." *Homiletic Review,* 38 (December 1899): 539-43.
______. "Degrees." *The National Baptist,* 31 August 1893.
______. "Der Einzelkelch in Amerika" *Monatschrift fur Gottesdienst und kirchliche kunst* Nr. 10 October 1904.
______. *Deutsche Trinksitten in amerikanischer Beleuchtung: Rede.* Hamburg: Deutschlands Grossloge IIdes I.O.G.T., 1912.
______. "Devotion to Truth." *Colloquium,* November, 1899, Clipping, CRDS.
______. "Die Bible oder die ganze Heilige Schrift des Alten und Nuen Testaments." New York: Amerikanische Bibel-Gesellschaft, 1870.
______. "Die Bruder Alfonso und Juan de Valdes. Zwei Lebensbilderr aus Geschicte der Reformation in Spanien und Italien. *The American Journal of Theology,* 7/1 (1903): 162-163.
______. Die Evangelisation mit Besonderer Rücksicht auf die Heilgungsbeweggung." *The American Journal of Theology,* 3/4 (1899): 861.
______. "Die Geschicte der Idee des Reiches Gottes." Eine Rede [gehalten beim Schulanfang der deutschen Abteilung des theologischen Seminars in Rochester, NY, am 12 September 1902].
______. *Die Politische Verfassung unseres Landes: Ein Handbuch zum Unterrichte fur die deutsche-amerikanische Jugend.* Cleveland, OH: Bickel, 1902.
______. "Discipling vs. Proselytizing" *Report of the Amity Conference Third Annual Conference Report,* 1893, 32.
______. "Dr. Fox on the Causes of Poverty." *Christian Inquirer,* 5 April 1894.
______. "Dr. Willmarth and the Kingdom of God." *National Baptist,* 14 December 1893.
______. "Does the New Testament Provide a Definite and Permanent Church Polity?" *Twenty-Second Annual Session of the Baptist Congress.* New York: Baptist Congress Publishing Company, 1904, 108-15.
______. "Dogmatic and Practical Socialism." *Rochester Herald,* 14 March 1901.
______. "Drop a Nickel in the Slot." *For the Right* I January 1890, 3.
______. "The Economic Base of Democracy." *Ford Hall Talks,* 7 February 1915.
______. "The Education of a Jesuit." *The Standard,* 20 June 1893.
______. "Der Einzelkelch in Amerika: Brief an Professor Spitta." *Monatsschrift fur Gottesdienst und kirchliche Kunst* 9 (October 1904): 303-06.
______. "Emotionalism in Religion" *Eleventh Annual Session of the Baptist Congress.* New York: Baptist Congress Publishing Co., 1894, 33-34.
______. "England and Germany." *The Watchman,* 16 November 1899. Clipping, CRDS.
______. "Ethical Versus Forensic Conceptions of Salvation." *Eleventh Annual*
______. *Session of the Baptist Congress.* New York: Baptist Congress Publishing Company, 1894, 76-78.
______. "Die Evangelisation mit Besonderer Rucksicht auf die Heilgungsbewegung." *The American Journal of Theology,* 3/4 (1899): 861.
______. "An Executive Genius, Joseph." *The Sunday School Times,* 12 October 1901.
______. "For the Right Does Not Endorse the Citizen's Movement." *For the Right,* 1 July 1890, 1.
______. "The Freedom of Spiritual Religion." *Brotherhood Leaflets.* Philadelphia, PA: American Baptist Publication Society, 1910.

______. "The Fruition of the Spirit." *Report of the Amity Missionary Conference, Second Annual Report*, 1892, 9.
______. "Funeral Tribute to Harrison E. Webster." *Union University*. New York: Lewis Publishing Co., 1907, 1: 378-83.
______. "Further Discussion." *National Baptist,* 28 December 1895.
______. "Die Gemeind und der Staat." *Wort und Werk,* November 1892.
______. *Die Geschicte der Idee des Reiches Gottes*. Eine rede von Walter Rauschenbusch. Rochester, NY: 1902.
______. "Die Heilsordnung." *The American Journal of Theology* 3/2 (1899): 430.
______. "Die Parusie Christi." *The American Journal of Theology* 3/3 (1899): 602-603.
______. *Die Religiosen Grundlagen der Sozialen Botschaft*. Erlenbach-Zurich: Rotapfel Verlag, 1922.
______. *Der tod in dichtung philosophie undkunst*. GDR?: Steinkopff Darmstadt, 2012.
______. "Discipling versus Proselytizing." n.p., n.d., ABHS files.
______. "Does Rochester Want Competing Gas Companies?" *The Rochester Economic Club*, Feb 27, 1902*
______. "Dr. Fox on the Causes of Poverty" *Christian Inquirer,* 5 April 1894.
______. "The Education of a Jesuit." *The Standard,* 29 June 1893.
______. "England and Germany." *The Watchman,* 16 November 1899.
______. *Evangeliums Lieder* (with Ira Sankey). New York: The Bigelow and Main Co., 1897.
______. *For God and the People: Prayers of the Social Awakening*. Boston, MA: Pilgrim Press, 1910.
______. *For the Right*. 1889-1890 (periodical).
______. "For the Right Does Not Endorse the Citizen's Movement" *City Club Bulletin* 1/10 (July 1890): 1.
______. "Forces At Work in the Social Movement" *The Association Seminar* Intl YMCA College, Feb. 8, 1913.
______. *Fur Gott und das volk*. Gottingen: Vandenhoek and Ruprecht, 1928.
______. *The Freedom of Spiritual Religion*. Philadelphia, PA: American Baptist Publication Society, 1910.
______. "Das Fussachen." *Der Sendbote* (20 January 1887).
______. "George C. Coleman." *American Magazine* 72 (June 1911): 183-85.
______. "Good Men and Good Government" *The City Club Bulletin* 1/11 August 1890 2.
______. *A Gospel for the Social Awakening*. Edited by Benjamin E. Mays. New York: Association Press, 1950.
______. "Ideals of Social Reformers." *American Journal of Sociology* 2.2 (1896): 202-219.
______. "Enoch Pond Lectures on Applied Christianity at Bangor Theological Seminary, January 1915." WR Files, ABHS.
______. *Evangeliums Lieder, 1 and 2 mit Deutschen Kernlieden ausgewalt und herausgebeben von Walter Rauschenbusch und Ira D. Sankey*. Chicago, IL: Bigelow and Main, 1897.
______. "Gambling." *The Club Bulletin* 2/2 (November 1890): 3.
______. *Gesangbuch der Deutschen Baptisten-Gemeinden*. Cleveland, OH: Verlag des publikations-vereins oer Deustchen Baptisten 1916.

______. "The Genesis of 'Christianity and the Social Crisis.'" *Rochester Theological Seminary Bulletin* (November 1918): 51-52.
______. "George C. Coleman." *American Magazine* 72 (June 1911): 183-85.
______. "Die Geschicte der Idee des Reiches Gottes." Reprint of address at the opening of school year of the German Department of Rochester Theological Seminary, September 12, 1902. Scrapbook, CRDS.
______. "Good Men and Good Government." *For the Right* 1 (August 1902): 2.
______. "The Gospel for the Men of Today." *The Congregationalist and Christian World,* September, 1911.
______. "Handdelsgewinn und nationale Ehre" *Christlichte Welt* (12 August 1915, 644-47.
______. "Harrison Edwin Webster, LLD '68." *Union University Quarterly,* August, 1906: 121-124.
______. "Heil, Suffield." *Songs of Suffield.* New York: Bigelow and Main Co., 1892.
______. "High Rent and Low Morals." *National Baptist,* March 1889.
______. "How Rich Have I a Right to Be?" *The Altruistic Review,* August 1894.
______. "The Ideals of Social Reformers." Report of the Brotherhood of the Kingdom, Third Annual Conference Report" (1895) and *American Journal of Sociology* (2 September 1896): 202-19.
______. "The Imperative Demand." *Christian Socialist.* 11 (15 March 1914): 5.
______. "The Imprecatory Psalms." *The Inquirer,* 1892.
______. "Impressions of the Northfield Meeting." *The Inquirer,* 1887.
______. "The Influence of Historical Studies on Theology." *The American Journal of Theology.* 2/1 (January, 1907): 111-12.
______. "The Influence of Mazzini." *Colloquium,* November 1899, Clipping, CRDS.
______. "The Interpretation of the Life of Church and State." in *Proceedings of the Baptist Congress* 1889. (Read at Toronto, 13 November 1889).
______. "Introduction to the Study of Church History" *Rochester Theological Seminary Bulletin* (Spring, 1906).
______. "Is the Baby Worth a Dollar? *The Ladies Home Journal* 27 (October 1910): 19.
______. "Is the Woman's Movement Going to Save Society? *Ford Hall Talks,* 2/28 (26 April 1914).
______. "It Shall Be (The Kingdom of God is Coming)." *City Club Bulletin* 2/6 March 1891," 5.
______. "Jesus and the Social Problems of Our Age." Galley proofs, WR Files, ABHS.
______. "Jesus as an Organizer of Men." *The Biblical World* 11.2 (February 1898): 102-111.
______. *Jubilee: A Study Resource for the Bicentennial.* Nashville, TN: Upper Room, 1976.
______. "Justice and Brotherhood" *The Path of Labor.* New York: Council of Women for Foreign Missions, 1918, 165-87.
______. *Kann ein Christ auch ein Socialist sein? Vortrag von Walter Rauschenbusch, Gehalten im Deutschen Christlichten verein junger manner von Philadelpia.* Philadelphia, PA: Druck von H.R. Grassman, 1894.
______. "Karl von Hase, ein Deutscher Professor." *The American Journal of Theology,* 5/4 (1901): 799-801.

______. "Keep Them Separate." *Church and State*, 2/4 January 1891: 3.
______. "The Kingdom and the Church." *Report of the Brotherhood of the Kingdom, Second Annual Conference Report* (1894): 37.
______. "The Kingdom of Evil." In *Creation and Humanity: The Sources of Christian Theology*, edited by Ian A. McFarland, 262-67. Louisville, KY: Westminster John Knox Press, 2009.
______. "The Kingdom of God." *The Kingdom*, 1/1 (August 1907).
______. "Der Kirche Kraft." *The Morning Journal, German Edition*. New York: 2 December 1895.
______. "Kirche und Soziale Bewegung in Nord Amerika" *Christliche Welt* 22 (1908): 346-349; 367-370; 395-99; 410-414.
______. "Labor Day Address." *The Standard*, 64 (1918): 184-85.
______. *Das leben Jesu. Ein systematischer stuiengang fur jugendvereine und bibelklassen.* Cleveland, OH: K.P. Bickel, 1895.
______. "The Lessons of Economic History" *Proceedings of the Baptist Congress*, 1898. (Read at Buffalo, 16 November 1898).
______. *Le Plat de Lentilles, quelques chapitres de Christianizing the Social Order*. Trans. S. Godet. Paris: Fischbacher, n.d.
______. "A Letter: On the War." *The Standard*, 65 (1918): 1409-10.
______. "Letter Dated July 20, 1907, Marburg in Germany, to the Brotherhood of the Kingdom." *The Kingdom*, 1/2 (September 1907).
______. *Leben und Werken von August Rauschenbusch, Professor am theologishen Seminar zu Rochester in Nordamerika angefangen von ihn selbst, vollendet und herausgegeben von seinem Sohn Walter Rauschenbusch.* Cassel: Kommissionsverlag von J.G. Oncken, Nachfolger (Gmbh). 1901.
______. "Lent Has Real Value for All of Us, Especially the Rich, Lest They Forget!" Published in 8 city papers, March 1914.
______. "The Life of Dollinger." *American Journal of Theology*, (Fall, 1903): 734-743.
______. "Limits of Immigration." *Seventh Annual Session of the Baptist Congress.* New York: Baptist Congress Publishing Co., 1888, 86-87.
______. "The Literary Work of George Dana Boardman." *The Examiner*, 14 May 1904.
______. *The Little Gate to God.* New York: The Federal Council of Churches, 1918.
______. "Living by the Rule of Loving One's Neighbor." *For the Right*, 1 (February 1980): 2.
______. "The Loneliness of Noah." *Sunday School Times*, 6 July 1901.
______. "The Lure of the Pastorate." *Rochester Theological Seminary Bulletin* (May, 1914): 8.
______. "Lutherische Dogmatik." *The American Journal of Theology*, 5/3 (1901): 611-615.
______. "Luthers Auffassung der Gottheit Christi." *The American Journal of Theology*, 6/3 (1899): 859-860; 630-631.
______. "Luthers Theologie in ihrer Geschictlichen Entwiclung und ihren Inneren Zusaammenhang." *The American Journal of Theology*, 6/3 (1902): 592-593.
______. "The Making of an Executive Genius." *Sunday School Times*, 43/41 Oct. 12, 1901.
______. "The Man Who Wrote the Acts." *Sunday School Times* 28 December 1901.
______. "Members One of Another." *The Christian Endeavor World*, 21 December 1911.

______. “Modern Judaizers.” *The Sabbath Outlook*, June 1892.
______. “Movement Against Alcoholism in America.” *International Congress of Free Christianity and Religious Progress.* Berlin, 5-10 August 1910, 588-599.
______. *The New Evangelism*. New York: *The Independent*, 1904.
______. “Notes on Church History.” 1905. WR Files, ABHS.
______. “The Obligations of the Childless.” WR Files, ABHS.
______. “Old Folks in the Twentieth Century.” *The Ministry,* July 1914*
______. “On Monopolies.” *Proceedings of the Baptist Congress*, 1889. Read at Toronto, 12 November 1889.
______. “Mr. Haldeman’s Millenarianism.” *The Examiner,* (18 June 1903).
______. *Osons-nous etre Chretiens? Traduit de l’Anglais par Robert Farelly.* Paris: Libraire Fischbacher.
______. “Our Guests.” Rochester, NY 1897-1903. WR Family Guestbook, WR Files, ABHS.
______. “Our Mixed Civilization.” *The Examiner,* 25 August 1892.
______. “Most Radical of Revolutionaries.” *Rochester Democrat and Chronicle* (March 1, 1899).
______. *The Movement Against Alcoholism in America: An Address Delivered at the World Congress of Free Christianity and Religious Progress, Berlin, August 7, 1910.* Pamphlet in CRDS Library.
______. “Municipal Ownership.” Rochester Post-Express (21 June 1901).
______. “Natural and Artificial Monopolies.” *Eighth Annual Session of the Baptist Congress.* New York: Baptist Congress Publishing Co., 1890, 55-61.
______. The New Apostolate.” *Report of the Amity Missionary Conference, Sixth Annual Conference Report.* (1896).
______. “The New Evangelism.” *The Independent* (12 May 1904): 1055-59.
______. *The New Evangelism.* New York: Rufus Weeks, 1905.
______. “Non-Partisan Political Ideas.” *Rochester Democrat and Chronicle* (29 October 1908).
______. “The Old Religious Faith and the New Social Gospel Enthusiasm. *Ford Hall Talks* (28 May 1916).
______. “Opening Gun for the Czar” *Rochester Democrat and Chronicle,* 21 February 1899.
______. “Our Attitude Toward Millennarianism” *The Examiner,* 24 September 1896 Clipping, CRDS.
______. “Our Mixed Civilization *The Examiner,* 15 August 1892 Clipping, CRDS.
______. *The Path of Labor.* New York: Council of Women for Home Missions, 1918.
______. “Pensees de Walter Rauschenbusch.” *Le christianisme social,* 35 (October 1922): 832.
______. *Perpetuating the Memory of Walter Rauschenbusch.* Rochester, NY: Colgate Rochester Divinity School, 1928
______. “Political Liberty and Social Equality.” *The City Club Bulletin,* 1/12 Sept 1890: 2
______. *Die Politische verfassung unseres lands (Civil Government of the United States) Ein handbuch zum unterriche fur die Deutsch-Amerikanische Jugend.* Cleveland, OH: Verlag von P. Bitter, Manager. 1902.

______. *Pour Dieu et pour le people, prieres du reveil social.* Trans. A.P Bovet. Paris: Fiscbacher, 1914.
______. *Pourquoi je suis baptiste.* Traduit par G. Brabent, Pasteur. Paris: Mazarine, n.d.
______. "Practical Application of Christianity to Social Conditions." *The Transcript* (30 November 1908).
______. "Practical Cures for Social Wrongs Under Individualism." *The Treasury,* 17 (April, 1900): 930-34.
______. "Practical Measures of Socialism." *The Treasury,* January 1901.
______. "A Prayer for the Church." *Watchman Examiner,* 24 April 1919.
______. "A Prayer in time of War." *The Independent,* 80/12 (5 October 1914).
______. *Prayers.* Translated by Motoi Kurihara. Kyoto, Japan: 1932.
______. *Prayers of the Social Awakening.* Boston, MA: The Pilgrim Press, 1910.
______. "The Present and the Future." *Post-Express.* 25 November 1898.
______. "Priere contre l'impurete." Le christianisme social, 34 (February/March 1921): 251.
______. "Priere pour les femmes qui travaillent." Le christianisme social, 43 (February-March 1930): 270.
______. "Priere pour les vrais amants." Le christianisme 34 (February-March,1921): 212.
______. "Private Profit and the Nation's Honor: A Protest and A Plea." *The Standard* 62/47 (31 July 1915): 1486-1487.
______. "Private Profit and the Nation's Honor." *Christlichte Welt,* 29 (1915): 195ff.
______. "The Problem of the Black Man." *The American Missionary, New Series,* 5 (March 1914): 732-33.
______. "Professor Vedder's New Book on Socialism." *The Standard,* 59 (1912): 1276.
______. "Prophetic Character of the Anabaptist Movement." *Rochester Democrat and Chronicle,* 15 September 1903.
______. "Private Profit and the Nation's Honor: A Protest and a Plea." *The Standard,* 62 (1915): 1486-1487.
______. "Proposed Cures for Social Wrongs." *The Treasury,* 17 (February 1900): 768-71.
______. "Proposed Cures for Social Wrongs Under Individualism" *The Treasury,* April 1900.
______. "The Pulpit in Relation to Political and Social Reform" in *Proceedings of the Baptist Congress,* 1892. (Read at Philadelphia, 19 May 1892.)
______. "Railroads and the Press." (Title?) 2/6 March 1891: 4.
______. *A Rauschenbusch Reader: The Kingdom of God and the Social Gospel.* Edited by Benson Y. Landis. New York, NY: Harper and Brothers, 1957.
______. "Recent Literature in Church History" *The American Journal of Theology* (March, 1906): 338-343.
______. "The Re-Evaluation of Values." WR Files, ABHS.
______. "Regenerate Church Membership." *Rochester Baptist Monthly,* March 1903.
______. "The Rejection of Jesus." *The Inquirer,* 1889.
______. "Relation of Church and State." *Eighth Annual Session of the Baptist Congress.* New York: Baptist Congress Publishing Co., 1889, 138-40.
______. "Relation of the Ministry to Social Questions." *The Dawn,* 21 November 1892.

______. "Relation of the State to Semi-Public Corporations and their Employees." *Thirteenth Annual Session of the Baptist Congress.* New York: Baptist Congress Publishing Co., 1896, 132-33.

______. "The Relation of Theology and Religion." *Twenty-Second Annual Session of the Baptist Congress.* New York: Baptist Congress Publishing Co., 1905, 89-92.

______. "Religion the Life of God in the Soul of Man." *The Baptist Magazine* (London) May 1909. (Paper Read at New York State Conference of Religion, 20 November 1900.)

______. "The Religion of the Passion Play." *The Independent* 69 (29 September 1910): 689-693.

______. "The Religious Quality of Social Work." *The Christian Commonwealth, Supplement.* London: 31 July 1912.

______. *Report of a Committee to Consider Our Present Condition as a Denomination and to Make Suggestions for Its Improvement.* New York: 1895.

______. "Report of a Talk to Sunday School" *Rochester Democrat and Chronicle,* 25 (January 1913).

______. "Report of a Y.M.C.A. Committee to Investigate Social Conditions of Men and Boys in Rochester. *Rochester Union and Advertiser,* May 30, 1904.

______. *Report on the Industrial Situation at Muscatine, Iowa.* New York: Federal Council of Churches of Christ in America, 1912.

______. "Revelation: An Exposition." *The Biblical World,* 10/2 (August 1897): 94-103.

______. Review of *Das Abendmahl im Urchristendum*, by J. Hoffman, *American Journal of Theology* 10 (April 1906): 342-44.

______. Review of *Der Index der Verbotenen Bucher, Ein Beitrag zur Kirchen---und Literaturgeschicte*, von Dr. Fr. Heinrich Reusch, Bonn, 1883 und 1885." *The Baptist Quarterly Review* (October 1886): 564-567.

______. Review of *Die Anschauung der Reformatoren vomgeistlichen Amte*, by W. Thomas, *American Journal of Theology*, 6 (July 1902): 631.

______. "Review of Die Brüder Alfonso und Juan de Valdes, by William Schlatter, *American Journal of Theology*, 7 (January 1903): 162-63.

______. "Review of *Christi Person und Werk in der Predigt*, by D.H. Gebhardt, *American Journal of Theology* 3 (April, 1899): 430-431.

______. "Review of *The Church's Task Under the Roman Empire*, by Charles Bigg, *American Journal of Theology*, 10 (April 1906): 337-39.

______. Review of *Ephemeriden des Isch-Schachefeth,* by L. Rymarski, *American Journal of Theology*, 2 (October 1898); 959.

______. Review of *Erkennen und Schauen Gottes*, by L. Weiss, *American Journal of Theology* 3 (October 1899): 859-60.

______. Review of *Die Evangelisation mit besonderer Rücksicht auf die Heiligungs bewegung,* by T. Hardeland, *American Journal of Theology*, 3 (October 1899): 861.

______. Review of *Genugsamkeit und Vielseitigkeit des Neutetstamentlichen Kanons,* by C. F. Nosgen, *American Journal of Theology*, 2 (July, 1898): 719.

______. Review of *Das Heil der Welt,* by J. Pierning, *American Journal of Theology*, 2 (October 1898): 955.

______. Review of *Die Heilsordnung*, by Emil Wacker, *American Journal of Theology*, 3 (April 1899): 430.

______. Review of *Ignaz von Döllinger*, by J. Friedrich, *American Journal of Theology*, 7 (October 1903): 733-43.
______. Review of *Karl von Hase*, by R. Burkner, *American Journal of Theology*, 5 (October 1901): 799-801.
______. Review of *Luther's Auffassung der Gottheit Christi*, by C. von Kugelgen, *American Journal of Theology* 6 (July 1902): 630-31.
______. Review of *Lutherische Dogmatik. American Journal of Theology* 5 (July 1901): 611-15.
______. Review of *Luther's Theologie*, 2 vols. 2nd ed., by J. Kostlin, *American Journal of Theology*, 6 July 1902): 592-93.
______. Review of *Die Materialisierung Religiöser Vorstellungen*, by Ernst Bittlinger *American Journal of Theology* 10 (April 1906): 340-42.
______. Review of *Das menschlich Anziehende in der Erscheinung Jesu Christi*, by G. Zart, American Journal of Theology, 3 (January 1899): 221.
______. Review of *Die Parusie Christi*, by H. Dieckmann, *American Journal of Theology*, 3 (July 1899): 602-03.
______. Review of *Religions et Sociéties*, by T. Reinach, et.al., *American Journal of Theology*, 10 (April 1906): 339-40.
______. Review of *Das Sakrament des Heiligen Abendmahls*, by J. Gemmel, *American Journal of Theology* 2 (July 1898): 719.
______. Review of *St. Pauli Brief an die Galater*, by W. F. Besser, *American Journal of Theology*, 3 (October 1899): 848.
______. Review of *St. Pauli Brief an die Römer*, by W. F. Besser, *American Journal of Theology*, 3 (January 1899): 211.
______. Review of *Skizzen aus dem Leben der alten Kirche*, by T. Zahn, *American Journal of Theology*, 3 (July 1899): 603-04.
______. Review of *Über die Aussprüche Jesu an Petrus*, by W. Beyschlag, *American Journal of Theology*, 2 (July 12898): 719.
______. Review of *Wesen und Wirkung der Taufgnade*, by H. Cremer, *American Journal of Theology*, 3 (October 1899): 859.
______. "Revolutionary Ancestry of Baptist and Congregational Churches." *The Springfield (Mass.) Republican*, 1 December 1908.
______. "Revolutionary Religion." *Rochester Democrat and Chronicle*, 1 March 1909.
______. *The Righteousness of the Kingdom*. Edited by Max L. Stackhouse. Nashville, TN: Abingdon Press, 1968.
______. "Rights of the Child in The Community." *Religious Education*, 10/3 (1915): 219-225.
______. *Samfundets Kristianisering*. Trans. Eugene Hanssen. Kristiania Steenske Bogtrkkeri og Forlag, 1914-15-16.
______. "The Saving Efficacy of Money." *The Inquirer*, 1887.
______. "The Second Commandment: Love to Man." *The Inquirer*, 1889.
______. *Selected Writings*. Edited by Winthrop S. Hudson. New York, NY: Paulist Press, 1984.
______. "The Servant Girl Question." WR Files, ABHS.
______. "The Service of the Church to Society." *The Treasury*, 17 September 1899, 393-97.

______. "Services Which the Church Can Render to Society." *The Canadian Baptist* 10 November 1910.
______. "Should Deal with the Living Present." *San Francisco Star,* 9 July 1943.
______. "Sinful Mercy." *The Sunday School Times,* 31 August 3 1901.
______. "The Single Tax." *For the Right*, 1 February 1890, 3.
______. "Skizzen aus dem Leben der Alten Kirche." *The American Journal of Theology* 3/3 (1899): 603-604.
______. *The Social Awakening in the Churches of America.* International Congress of Free Christianity and Religious Progress. Berlin: 5 August 1910.
______. "Social Background, Spirit, and Message of the Bible." *Rochester Theological Seminary Bulletin, The Record,* 69 (November 1918): 54-63.
______. "The Social Call to the Lutheran Churches of America." *The Lutheran Observer* 28 January 1910.
______. "Social Ideas in the New Testament." *The Treasury,* 17 (June 1899): 155-59
______. "Social Ideas in the Old Testament." *The Treasury,* 16 (March 1899): 871-76.
______. "The Social Ideas of Paul." *Report of the Brotherhood of the Kingdom Sixth Annual Conference*, 1898.
______. *Social Kristendom.* København: Nyt nordisk Forlag, 1931.
______. "The Social Mission of Baptists." *The Christian Socialist* 4/21 (1 November 1907).
______. "The Social Movement and the Higher Life in Our Country." *Rochester Democrat and Chronicle,* 16 November 1899.
______. *The Social Principles of Jesus.* New York, NY: Association Press, 1916; 1919; 1921; 1939.
______. "The Social Program of the Church." *The South Mobilizing for Social Service.*
______. Nashville, TN: Southern Sociological Congress, 1913, 504-11.
______. "Social Solutions in the Light of Christian Ethics." *The American Journal of Theology* 15/1 (1911): 146-148.
______. *Social Suggestions for Program-Makers.* Philadelphia, PA: American Baptist Publication Society, 1912.
______. "The Social Value of Women." WR Papers, ABHS.
______. "Socialism." *Rochester Herald,* 11 November 1908.
______. "Socialism Is Coming." *The Call,* 28 January 1909.
______. "Socialism is of Two Kinds: The Preached and the Dogmatic Contrasted" Rochester Democrat and Chronicle 25 February 1901.
______. Sociální Zásady Ježíšovy. Praha: Y.M.C.A., 1926.
______. "Some Moral Aspects of the 'Woman Movement'". *The Biblical World* 42.4 (October 1913): 195-199.
______. "Some Results of the Conference on Social Problems." *The North American Student,* June, 1914.
______. "Some Words About Socialism in America." *For the Right* (1 April 1890): 3.
______. "Speaking in Tongues: What Was It?" *The Watchman,* 30 September 1897.
______."The Spiritual Criticism of the Bible." *The Examiner,* 9 November 1905.
______. "St. Pauli Brief an die Galater in Bibelstunden fur die Gemeinde Ausgelegt." *The American Journal of Theology* 3/4 (1899): 848.

______. "St. Pauli Brief an die Romer, in Bibelstunden fur die Gemeinde Ausgelegt." *The American Journal of Theology* 3/1 (1899): 221.

______. "The Stake of the Church in the Social Movement." *American Journal of Sociology* 3/1 (July 1897): 18-30.

______. "State-Help versus Self-Help, or Paternalism in Government" *Sixteenth Annual Session of the Baptist Congress.* New York: Baptist Congress Publishing Co., 1898, 107-16.

______. *Suggestions for Organization of Local Chapters of the Brotherhood of the Kingdom.* New York: n.d.

______. "Sunday School Lesson on Sampson." *The Inquirer,* 1888.

______. "The Superior Social Efficiency of Modern Christianity." *Homiletic Review,* May 1906: 337-341.

______. "Thanksgiving Meditation." *The Watchman,* 23 November 1905.

______. "That Boston Fad." *The Inquirer,* 1889.

______. *A Theology for the Social Gospel.* New York, NY: The Macmillan Company, 1917.

______. *A Theology for the Social Gospel* (Chinese Mandarin). Shanghai: Christian Literature Society, 1923.

______. "Le XIII chapitree aux Corinthiens applique aux affaires en style modern." Le *christianisme social* 36 (November 1923): 869-71

______. "Thoughts on Prayer. *Rochester Baptist Monthly,* January 1901.

______. "Toward the German Churches in the West" (With L. Kaiser), 1898.

______. "Tradition as a Formative Influence in Baptist Doctrine and Church Life." *Twelfth Annual Session of the Baptist Congress.* New York: Baptist Congress Publishing Co., 1895, 36-38.

______. "The Trend Toward Collectivism." *The City Club Bulletin* 5/10 19 April 1912" 123-130.

______. "A Trip to the Pacific *Rochester Theological Seminary Bulletin* 66 (May 1915): 50.

______. "The True Foundation." *Monroe County Mail,* Monroe, NY: 11 August 1904.

______. *The True American Church, Great Christian Groups that Belong Together.* New York: 1914.

______. *To the Deacons of Our Churches.* New York: n.d.

______. "The Unspoken Thoughts of Jesus." *Modern Sermons.* 8, (1909), pp. 23-32.

______. *Unto Me.* Boston, MA: The Pilgrim Press, 1912.

______. "A Valedictory Message. A Letter of Walter Rauschenbusch." *The Standard* 65/48 (3 August 1918): 1409-1410.

______. "The Value and Use of History." *Foundations* 12/3 (July-September 1969): 263-272.

______. *Vår mastares liv: En systematisk undervisningskurs för undomforeningar och bibelklasser.* Stockholm: B. M:s bokf, 1925.

______. "La vision du nouveau christianisme." *Le christianisme social,* 33 (January 1920): 3.

______. "Walter Rauschenbusch: His Personal Testimony." *Watchman-Examiner,* 6 (1918): 985.

______. "Walter Rauschenbusch (1861-1918): Champion of the Social Gospel." In *Theology in America: The Major Protestant Voices from Puritanism to Neo-Orthodoxy,* edited by Sydney E. Ahlstrom. Indianapolis, IN: Hackett Publishing Company, Inc., 2003. Pp. 531-586.

______. "Walter Rauschenbusch's letzter Gruss." *Christlichte Welt,* 33 (1919): 576.

______. *Wanted: A New Type of Layman. Brotherhood Leaflets* and *The National Baptist*, 8 March 1894.

______. "War and Hate: A Reply." *The Standard.* 64 (1916): 296-297.

______. "War and the Loss of Love." *The Standard* 63 (26 August 1916): 5.

______. "Watering Stock" Unpublished. WR Files, ABHS.

______. "The Welsh Revival and Primitive Christianity." *The Examiner,* 15 June 1905.

______. "Wesen und Wirkung der Taufgnade." *The American Journal of Theology* 3/4 (1899): 859-860.

______. "Letter of Walter Rauschenbusch on the War." *The Standard* 65 (1918): 1409-1410.

______. "What Help Does Modern Christianity Give Us on Modern Social Problems?" *The Examiner,* 3 November 1904.

______. "What Is a Christian Nation?" *Proceedings of the Religious Education Association.* Rochester, NY, 5-7 February 1907.

______. "What Stephen Did for the Christian Church?" *Sunday School Times.* 8 February 1902.

______. "What's the Matter with Rochester?" *Rochester Democrat and Chronicle,* 4 April 1904. (Speech delivered before the Labor Lyceum in Council Chambers).

______. "Where Does It All Come From?" *For the Right,* 1 (November 1889): 3.

______. "Where Dr. Rauschenbusch Stands." *Maritime Baptist,* 3 July 1918.

______. "Who Shall Educate: Church or State? *Seventh Annual Session of the Baptist Congress.* New York: Baptist Congress Publishing Co., 1889, 28-31.

______. "Why Has Christianity Never Undertaken the Task of Social Reconstruction? *Report of the Brotherhood of the Kingdom*, Twelfth Annual Conference, 1906, 28-29.

______. "Why I am a Baptist." *Baptist Commonwealth.* 5 December 1912, pp. 8-9; 12 December, pp. 6-7; 19 December, p. 6.

______. *Why Playgrounds Should Be Municipal.* New York: Playground and Recreation Association of America, 1916.

______. "Why Should People Own and Read Books?" *Philadelphia North American* 26 April 1913.

______. "Wie die Bedingungen fur eine sociale Wirksamkeit des Christentums mit der Zeit sich verändert haben." *Christlichte Welt* 23 (27 May 1909): 511-516.

______. "Will the Church Disappear?" *Ford Hall Folks,* n.d.

______. "Woman's Work in the Church." Report of the Amity Missionary Conference, Fourth Annual Conference Report (1894): 1.

______. "A Word for the Little Churches." *The Examiner,* 19 March 1892.

______. *Yhteiskuntaelaman uudistus Kristinuskon hengessa.* Trans. K. Eeil Roine 1917-1918

______. "Yielding Our Rights." *Sunday School Times,* 20 1901.

______. "You Did It Unto Me." *Proceedings of the National Council of Charities and Correction.* Fort Wayne, IN: Fort Wayne Printing Co., pp. 12-17

______. "Zehn goldene Regin fur junge Christen." *Der Sendbote,* 16 February 1887.

______. *The Zurich Anabaptists and Thomas Münzer.* American Journal of Theology 9 (January 1905): 91-106.

Stuber, Stanley I. *The Christian Reader: Inspirational and Devotional Classics.* New York: Association Press, 1952.

Biographies; Biographical Sketches

Aiken, John R. "Walter Rauschenbusch and Education for Reform." *Church History* 36/4 (1967): 456-469.

Altschuler, Glenn C. "Walter Rauschenbusch: Theology, the Church, and the Social Gospel." *Foundations* 22 (1979): 140-151.

Argow, W. S. "The Centennial of Walter Rauschenbusch." *Baptist Herald* 28 (Sept. 1961): 14-15.

Barnes, Sherman B. "Walter Rauschenbusch as Historian." *Foundations* 12 (July- September 1969): 254-62.

Bartlett, Gene E. "Rauschenbusch: A Portrait in Perspective." *Missions* (October 1961): 23-26.

Batten, Samuel Zane. "Walter Rauschenbusch." *The Social Service Bulletin* (Methodist Episcopal Federation for Social Service) Sept. 1918: 2.

Beach, Waldo and H. Richard Niebuhr. "Walter Rauschenbusch." In *Christian Ethics; Sources of the Living Tradition.* New York, NY: Ronald Press Co., 1955. Pp. 444-474.

Beckley, Harlan. *Passion for Justice: Retrieving the Legacies of Walter Rauschenbusch, John A. Ryan, and Reinhold Niebuhr.* Louisville, KY: Westminster John Knox Press, 1992.

Bowden, Henry Warner. "Walter Rauschenbusch and American Church History." *Foundations* 9 (1966): 234-50.

Brachlow, Stephen. "Walter Rauschenbusch" in *Baptist Theologians*, edited by Timothy George and David Dockery. Nashville, TN: Broadman Press, 1990.

Brackney, William H. "Rauschenbusch, Walter" in *Historical Dictionary of the Baptists, Second Edition.* Lanham, MD: Scarecrow Press, 2009, p. 470.

Brackney, William H. "Walter Rauschenbusch: Then and Now" *Baptist Quarterly* 48/1 (January 2017): 23-46.

Cauthen, W. Kenneth. "The Social Gospel: Walter Rauschenbusch" in *The Impact of American Religious Liberalism.* New York: Harper and Row, 1962.

Cross, F. L. "Rauschenbusch, Walter." *Oxford Dictionary of American Biography.*

Dahlberg, Edwin and John Skoglund. *Reminicences of Walter Rauschenbush.* n.p., 1973.

Daniel, C. A. "Walter Rauschenbusch as I Knew Him." *Michigan Christian Advocate* 24 November and 1 December 1938.

Davis, R. Dennis. "The Impact of Evolutionary Thought on Walter Rauschenbusch" *Foundations* 21/3 (1978): 254-271.

Dickinson, Richard. "The Church's Responsibility for Society: Rauschenbusch and Niebuhr: Brothers Under the Skin?" *Religion in Life* 27 (1957-58): 163-71.

Dittberner, Job L. *Walter Rauschenbusch: The Progress of Religion: A Study in Pre- War Religious Optimism.* n.p., 1968.

Doerries, Reinhard R. "Walter Rauschenbusch." *Die Neueste Zeit* 10/1 (Spring, 1985): 174-184.

Duff, E. "Rauschenbusch, Walter" in *New Catholic Encyclopedia.* New York: McGraw Hill, 1967, Vol. XII, p. 94.

Duinen, Corrie. *Walter Rauschenbusch: Moralist or Prophet?.* The Netherlands, n.p., 1992.

Ede, Alfred J. "The Social Theories of Walter Rauschenbusch and Vatican II in Dialogue" *Foundations* 18/3 (1975); 198-208.

"Edwin Dahlberg in Conversation: Memories of Walter Rauschenbusch" Transcribed by John E. Skoglund. *Foundations* 18/3 (1975): 309-317.

Evans, Christopher H. *The Kingdom is Always but Coming: A Life of Walter Rauschenbusch.* Grand Rapids, MI: William B. Eerdmans Publishing Co., 2004.

Fosdick, Harry Emerson. "An Interpretation of the Life and Work of Walter Rauschenbusch," in *A Rauschenbusch Reader: The Kingdom of God and the Social Gospel,* compiled by Benson Y. Landis. New York: Harper and Brothers, 1957.

George, Timothy, and David Dockery. *Baptist Theologians.* Nashville, TN: Broadman Press, 1990.

Handy, Robert T. "Walter Rauschenbusch" in *Ten Makers of Modern Protestant Thought.* New York: Association Press, 1958.

Handy, Robert T. "Walter Rauschenbusch in Historical Perspective." *Baptist Quarterly* 20 (July 1964): 313-21.

Higgins, Paul L. *Preachers of Power: Henry Ward Beecher, Phillips Brooks, and Walter Rauschenbusch.* New York: Vantage Press, 1950.

Hopkins, C. Howard. "Walter Rauschenbusch and the Brotherhood of the Kingdom." Church History 7/2 (1938).

Hudson, Winthrop S. "A Lonely Prophet: The Continuity of the Great Tradition" *The Great Tradition of the American Churches.* New York: Harper and Row, 1953.

Hudson, Winthrop S. "Rauschenbusch—Evangelical Prophet" *The Christian Century.* 24 June 1953, pp. 740-42.

Hudson, Winthrop S. "Walter Rauschenbusch and the New Evangelism." *Religion in Life.* 30 (1961): 412-30.

Hunt, George Laird. *Ten Makers of Modern Protestant Thought: Schweitzer, Rauschenbusch, Temple, Kierkegaard, Barth, Brunner, Niebuhr, Tillich, Bultmann, Buber.* New York: Association Press, 1958.

Hutchinson, William R. *American Protestant Thought: The Liberal Era.* New York: Harper and Row, 1968. Chapter 10.

Hutchinson, William R. *The Modernist Impulse in American Protestantism.* Cambridge, MA: Harvard University Press, 1976, Chapter 5.

Jaehn, Klaus Juergen. *Rauschenbusch, the Formative Years.* Valley Forge, PA: Judson Press, 1976.

Johnson, Carl E. "The Present and the New Past: Some Timely Reflections on the Rauschenbusch Legacy." *Perspectives in Religious Studies* 14 (Summer 1987): 135-36.

Johnson, Karl E. *Walter Rauschenbusch as Historian.* n.p., 1977.

Kittler, Glenn D. *Profiles in Faith.* New York: Coward-McCann, 1962.

Langford, S. Fraser. "The Gospel of Augustus H. Strong and Walter Rauschenbusch" *The Chronicle* 14/1 (1951): 3-18.

Lippy, Charles H. "Rauschenbusch, Walter." *Oxford Dictionary of American Biography.*

Livingstone, E.A. "Rauschenbusch, Walter (1861-1918)." Oxford University Press, n.d.

Lundin, Roger and Mark Noll. *Voices from the Heart: Four Centuries of American Piety.* Grand Rapids, MI: Eerdmans, 1987.

Lundsten, B.A. "The Legacy of Walter Rauschenbusch: A Life Informed by Mission." *International Bulletin of Mission Research* 28/2 (2004): 75-79.

McBirnie, William Stuart. *Walter Rauschenbusch: Apostle of the Social Gospel.* Glendale, CA: VOA, 196-?.

McGiffert, Arthur C. "Walter Rauschenbusch: Twenty Years After." *Christendom* 3 (Winter 1938): 96-109.

McGuire, William and Leslie Wheeler, "Walter Rauschenbusch." Encyclopedia Article, n.d.

McKelvey, Blake. *Walter Rauschenbusch's Rochester.* Rochester, NY: Rochester Public Library, 1952.

Marney, Carlyle. "The Significance of Walter Rauschenbusch for Today." *Foundations* 2/1 (January, 1959): 13-26.

Meyer, F. W. C. "Walter Rauschenbusch." *Bulletin of the German Department of the Rochester Theological Seminary, Jubilaumsgabe.* (July 1927): 47-50.

Meyer, F. W. C. "Walter Rauschenbusch: Preacher, Professor, and Prophet" *The Standard,* 3 February 1911.

Minus, Paul. *Walter Rauschenbusch: American Reformer.* New York, NY: The MacMillan Company, 1988.

Moehlmann, Conrad Henry. "The Life and Writings of Walter Rauschenbusch." *Colgate-Rochester Divinity School Bulletin* (October 1928): 32-37.

Moehlmann, Conrad Henry. *Walter Rauschenbusch and His Interpreters.* Chester, PA: Crozer Theological Seminary, 1945.

Moellering, R. L. "Rauschenbusch in Retrospect." *Concordia Theological Monthly* 27 (1956): 613-633.

Moore, James R. "Walter Rauschenbusch and the Religious Education of Youth." Religious Education 68 (1973): 435-453.

Muelder, Walter G. "Walter Rauschenbusch and the Contemporary Scene." *The City Church* (March-April 1957): 10-12.

Muller, Reinhart. *Walter Rauschenbusch: Ein Beitrag zur Begehnung des deutschen und amerikanischen Protestismus.* Leiden: E. J. Brill, 1957.

New World Encyclopedia. "Walter Rauschenbusch." *www.new worldencyclopedia.org/index.php?title=Walter Rauschenbusch*

Niebuhr, Reinhold. "Walter Rauschenbusch in Historical Perspective." *Religion in Life* 27 (Autumn 1958): 527-36.

Nixon, Justin Wroe. "The Realism of Rauschenbusch." *The City Church*, (November-December 1956): 5-7.

Nixon, Justin Wroe. "The Social Philosophy of Walter Rauschenbusch." *Colgate- Rochester Divinity School Bulletin* I (1928): 103-09.

Nixon, Justin Wroe. "Walter Rauschenbusch: After Forty Years." *Christendom* 12 (1947): 476-485.

Nixon, Justin Wroe. "Walter Rauschenbusch: Ten Years After." *The Christian Century* 8 (November 1928): 1359-61.

Nixon, Justin Wroe. "Walter Rauschenbusch: The Man and His Work." *Colgate-Rochester Divinity School Bulletin* 30 (1958): 21-32.

Noble, David W. *The Paradox of Progressive Thought.* Minneapolis, MN: University of Minnesota Press, 1958. Chapter 10 deals with Rauschenbusch.

Ottati, Douglas F. "Forward" to *Christianity and the Social Crisis in The Library of Theological Ethics.* Louisville, KY: Westminster John Knox Press, 1991.

Oxford Dictionary of American Biography, "Rauschenbusch, Walter." Vol. 18. (1999).

Oxnam, G. Bromley. *Personalities in Social Reform.* New York: Abingdon Cokesbury Press, 1950.

Pelikan, Jaroslav. *The World Treasury of Modern Religious Thought.* Boston, MA: Little, Brown, 1990.

"Professor Rauschenbusch as "a German"" *The Journal and Messenger* (7 February 1918): 7.

Ramsay, William M. *Four Modern Prophets: Walter Rauschenbusch, Martin Luther King, Jr., Gustavo Gutierrez, Rosemary Radford Reuther.* Atlanta, GA: John Knox Press, 1986.

Raoshen, Bushi. *Rao Shen Bu Shi She Hui Fu Yin Ji.* Xiang gang: Ji du jiao fu qiao chu ban she yin xing, min 45.

Rauschenbusch, August; Walter Rauschenbush; Donald Harold Madvig. *Life and Ministry of August Rauschenbusch: Professor at the Theological Seminary in Rochester, NY in North America.* Sioux Falls, SD: North American Baptist Heritage Commission, 2008.

Rauschenbusch, Paul Brandeis. *Christianity and the Social Crisis in the 21st Century: The Classic That Woke Up the Church.* New York: Harpercollins, 2007.

Sharpe, Dores R. *Walter Rauschenbusch.* New York, NY: The Macmillan Company, 1942.

Sharpe, Dores Robinson. *Walter Rauschenbusch, A Great, Good Man.* n.p, 1939.

Sharpe, Dores R. "Walter Rauschenbusch As I Knew Him." *The City Church* (May-June 1956): 12-14.

Shriver, Donald W. "Introduction" to *A Theology for the Social Gospel, Library of Theological Ethics.* Louisville, KY: Westminster John Knox Press, 1997.

Singer, Anna. *Walter Rauschenbusch and his Contribution to Social Christianity.* Boston, MA: Gorham Press, 1926.

Skoglund, John E. "Edwin Dahlberg in Conversation: Memories of Walter Rauschenbusch." *Foundations* 18 (1975): 209-218.

Smucker, Donovan E. "Walter Rauschenbusch and Anabaptist Historiography" in *The Recovery of the Anabaptist Vision*, edited by Guy F. Hershberger. Scottdale, PA: Herald Press, 1957.

Smucker, Donovan E. "Walter Rauschenbusch: Anabaptist, Pietist and Social Prophet." *Mennonite Life* 36/2 (June 1981): 21-3.

Stackhouse, Max L. "Introduction" to *The Righteousness of the Kingdom* by Walter Rauschenbusch. Nashville, TN: Abingdon Press, 1968.

Starr, Edward C. "Walter Rauschenbusch, 1861-1918." Unpublished manuscript, American Baptist Historical Society.

Stormer, John A. *None Dare Call It Treason.* Florissant, MO: Liberty Bell Press, 1964. Chapter 7 deals with Rauschenbusch.

Strayer, Paul Moore. "Walter Rauschenbusch: An Apostle of the Kingdom." *Homiletical Review* (February 1919): 91-94.

Sturgess, William Krieger. *Walter Rauschenbusch: An Introduction to His Times, Life, and Thought*. Lexington, KY: Lexington Theological Seminary, n.d.

Tillman, William M. *Baptist Prophets: Their Lives and Contributions.* Brentwood, TN: Baptist History and Heritage Society, 2006.

Toulouse, Mark G. "Walter Rauschenbusch." Encyclopedia Article.

Tuck, William Powell. *Modern Shapers of Baptist Thought in America.* Richmond, VA: Center for Baptist Heritage and Studies, 2012.

Tull, James E. *Shapers of Baptist Thought.* Valley Forge, PA: Judson Press, 1972.

Vulgamore, Melvin L. "The Social Gospel Old and New: Walter Rauschenbusch and Harvey Cox." *Religion in Life* 36 (Winter, 1967): 516-33.

"Walter Rauschenbusch" *The National Cyclopedia of American Biography*. New York: James T. White & Co., 1926, XIX, 193.

Woyke, Frank H. *Heritage and Ministry of the North American Baptist Conference*. Oakbrook Terrace, IL: North American Baptist Conference, 1979.

Zenos, Andrew C. "Recent Literature in Church History." *The American Journal of Theology* 10/2 (1906): 334-362.

Zhensong, Zhao. *Raoshenbushi she hui fu yin ji*. Xianggang: Jidu jiao wen yi chu ban she, 1989.

Selected Book Reviews

"Christianity and the Social Order." *The Watchman* 2/8/08, p. 7.

Haldeman, I. M. *Rauschenbusch's "Christianity and the Social Crisis."* New York: Charles C. Cook, n.d.

Henderson, Charles R. "Book Review: Christianity and the Social Crisis." *The American Journal of Theology* 12/1 (1908): 172-174.

J. B. T. "A Theology for the Social Gospel." *The Sewanee Review* 26/4 (1918): 503.

Moellering, R.L. "Rauschenbusch in Retrospect" *Concordia Theological Monthly* 27 (August, 1956): 613-33.

Morse, R. Osgood. "Christianizing the Social Order." *Maritime Baptist* 22 October 1913.

Muelder, Walter G. "Walter Rauschenbusch and the Contemporary Scene" *The City Church* 8 (March-April 1957): 10-12.

Nearing, Scott. "Book Review: Christianizing the Social Order." *Annals of the American Academy of Political and Social Science* 48 (1913): 286.

Robertson, D. B. "Book Review: The Righteousness of the Kingdom." *Journal for the Scientific Study of Religion* 8/2 (1969): 337-338.

Smith, Gerald Birney. "Book Review: A Theology for the Social Gospel." *The American Journal of Theology* 22/4 (1918): 583-588.

Smith, Samuel G. "Book Review: The Church and the Changing Order." *The Biblical World* 31/3 (1908): 229-233.

"The Social Principles of Jesus." *The Biblical World* 49/4 (1917): 250-251.

Strain, Charles R. "Toward a Generic Analysis of a Classic of the Social Gospel: An Essay-Review of Walter Rauschenbusch." *Journal of the American Academy of Religion* 46/4 (1978): 525-543.

Dissertations and Theses (Unpublished)

Allen, Jimmy R. "Comparative Study of the Concept of the Kingdom of God in the Writings of Walter Rauschenbusch and Reinhold Niebuhr." Th.D. Dissertation, Southwestern Baptist Theological Seminary, 1958.

Andersen, Karl S. "Christian Witness in Contemporary Society in the Light of the Thought of Walter Rauschenbusch and Reinhold Niebuhr." B. D. Thesis, Andover Newton Theological School, 1962.

Anderson, David T. "Christian Discipleship and Social Solidarity: A Study of Walter Rauschenbusch and Richard T. Ely." Ph.D. Dissertation, Union Theological Seminary in Va., 1991.

Anderson, James R. "The Role of Walter Rauschenbusch in Christian Ethics." B. A. Thesis, Interdenominational Theological Center, 1964.

Bacon, Edward A. "Recalling Walter Rauschenbusch: Conversations on the Pastor's Role in Social Ministry." D.Min. Thesis, Andover Newton Theological School, 2013.

Ball, James Bernard. "Theologies of Social Transformation: A Study of Walter Rauschenbusch and Gustavo Gutierrez." Ph.D. Dissertation, University of Notre Dame, 2003.

Barchewitz, Wolf-Dieter. "Der Social Gospel Walter Rauschenbuschs als theologisches und hermeneutisches Problem." S.T.M. Thesis, Hartford Theological Seminary, 1951.

Barker, Frederick T. "The Doctrine of Sin in the Thought of Walter Rauschenbusch." Ph.D. Dissertation, Drew University, 1978.

Barnes, C. Gary. "An Analysis of Walter Rauschenbusch's Theology for the Social Gospel." Th.M. Thesis, Dallas Theological Seminary, 1983.

Barnette, Henlee H. "The Ethical Thought of Walter Rauschenbusch: A Critical Interpretation". Ph.D. Dissertation, Southern Baptist Theological Seminary, 1948.

Barrs, William Kenneth. "A Critical Survey of the Social Philosophy of Walter Rauschenbusch." Ph.D. Dissertation, Duke University, 1942.

Battenhouse, Paul F. "Theology in the Social Gospel, 1918-1946." Ph.D. Dissertation, Yale University, 1950.

Bayer, Susan. "Unconventional Evangelicals: The Bible-based Social Activism of Walter Rauschenbusch and Jim Wallis." M.A. Thesis, Georgetown University, 2006.

Beckford, James A. *New Religious Movements and Rapid Social Change*. London: Sage Publications, 1986.

Bertalot, Renzo. "The Roman Catholic Modernism and the Social Gospel: A Study of Their Common Premises in the Writings of Ernesto Buonaiuti and Walter Rauschenbusch." S. T. M. Thesis, McGill University, 1959.

Bishop, Richard S. "Walter Rauschenbusch and Social Christianity." B.A. Thesis, Cornell College, 1950.

Bockman, Peter W. "The Theology of Walter Rauschenbusch in Its Significance for Political Ethics." S.T.M. Thesis, Union Theological Seminary, 1961.

Bodein, Vernon P. "The Relation of the Social Gospel of Walter Rauschenbusch to Religious Education." Ph.D., Yale University, 1936.

Bond, Richard Ellison. "A Critical Analysis of the Concept of Justice in Paul Tillich, Heinrich Rommen, and Walter Rauschenbusch." Ph.D. Dissertation, Yale University, 1972.

Boudreau, Michael S. "The Emergence of the Social Gospel in Nova Scotia: The Presbyterian, Methodist and Baptist Churches with the Working Class 1880- 1914." M.A. Thesis, Queens University, 1991.

Bowman, Staci. "Walter Rauschenbusch: His Life, Theology, and Advancement of the Kingdom." M. A. Thesis, Lexington Theological Seminary, 2006.

Bresina, Christoph. "Von der Erweckungsbewegung zum "Social Gospel": Walter Rauschenbusch Herkunft, Umfeld und Entwicklung bis 1891" Ph.D. Dissertation, Philipps Marburg University, 1993.

Brummer, H. David. "The Doctrine of Sin in the Theology of Walter Rauschenbusch." B. D. Thesis, Concordia Theological Seminary (Ill), 1964.

Brunson, Drexel Timothy. "The Quest for Social Justice: A Study of Walter Rauschenbusch and His Influence on Reinhold Niebuhr and Martin Luther King Jr." Ph.D. Dissertation, Florida State University, 1980.

Burckhardt, Abel E. "Walter Rauschenbusch as a Representative of American Humanism." S.T.M. Thesis, Union Theological Seminary in New York, 1925.

Canipe, Christopher L. "A Captive Church in the Land of the Free: E.Y. Mullis, Walter Rauschenbusch, George Truett, and the Rise of Baptist Democracy. 1900-1925." Ph.D. Dissertation, Baylor University, 2004.

Carter, Purvis M. "The Astigmatism of the Social Gospel, 1877-1901." M.A. Thesis, Howard University, 1950.

Chapman, Leslie W. "Walter Rauschenbusch as a Prophet of the New Social Order." B. D. Thesis, Andover Theological Seminary, 1935.

Clark, K. Don. "A Study of the Social Dimensions of Christian Education in the Major Writings of Walter Rauschenbusch." M. R. E. Thesis, Emmanuel School of Religion, 1970.

Clemens, Eugene Philip. "The Social Gospel Background of the Federal Council of Churches." Ph.D. Dissertation, University of Pennsylvania, 1970.

Dale, Verhey Allen. "The Use of Scripture in Moral Discourse: A Case Study of Walter Rauschenbusch." Ph.D. Dissertation, Yale University, 1975.

David, William E. "A Comparative Study of the Social Ethics of Walter Rauschenbusch and Reinhold Niebuhr. Ph.D. Dissertation, Vanderbilt University, 1958.

Dupertuis, Jean. "Christianisme social" d'après Rauschenbusch." D.Th. Theol dissertation, University of Geneva, 1911.

Durfee, Harold A. "the Theologies of the American Social Gospel: A Study of the Theological and Philosophical Presuppositions of the American Social Gospel." Ph.D. Dissertation, Columbia University, 1951.

Eder, Benedict C. "A Study of Walter Rauschenbusch and His Influence on Church Leaders of Today." M.Div. Thesis, Concordia Theological Seminary, (Indiana), 1985.

Edwards, Joseph James. "The Theology of Walter Rauschenbusch." B. D. Thesis, Northern Baptist Theological Seminary, 1950.

Edwards, Wendy Deichman. "Josiah Strong: Social Reformer and Advocate of a Global Kingdom." Ph.D. Dissertation, Drew University, 1992.

Evans, Christopher H. "A Theology for the Middle Class: Social Gospel Liberalism and the Ministry of Ernest Fremont Tittle." Ph.D. Dissertation, Northwestern University, 1993.

Felski, Lorry W. "Science and the Radical Social Gospel in Western Canada." M. A. Thesis, University of Calgary, 1975.

Feltmate, Darrell. "The Help Should Be Greatest Where the Need Is Most: The Social Gospel Platform of the United Baptist Convention of the Maritime Provinces 1921." M.Div. Thesis, Acadia University, 1993.

French, Henry Frank. "The Concept of Church in the Theology of Walter Rauschenbusch." Ph.D. Dissertation, Drew University, 1986.

Fricke, Ernest Erwin. "Socialism and Christianity in Walter Rauschenbusch." Ph.D. Dissertation, University of Basel, 1965.

Garber, Rebecca P. "The Social Gospel and Its View of Women and the Woman's Movement." M.A. Thesis, Trinity Evangelical Divinity School (Deerfield, IL), 1978.

Gault, Michael. "The Basis of the Social Gospel: An Examination of Walter Rauschenbusch's Biblical Hermeneutic." Independent Studies Project, Hanover College, 2001.

Geiger, Rodney E. "Walter Rauschenbusch: The Social Gospel and Orthodoxy." Th.M. Thesis, Dallas Theological Seminary, 1973.

Gilbert, Neal. "Walter Rauschenbusch and the Social Dimension of His Christian Faith." M.A. Thesis, California State University, Dominguez Hills, 2007.

Hampshire, George W. "Northern Baptists and the Social Gospel." Th.M. Thesis, Eastern Baptist Theological Seminary, 1956.

Harris, Randy. "Current Thought in Churches of Christ about Social Concern in Light of Walter Rauschenbusch and Reinhold Niebuhr." M. A. Thesis, Harding Graduate School of Religion, 1983.

Harry, David R. "Two Kingdoms: Walter Rauschenbusch's Concept of the Kingdom of God Contrasted with the Theology of Revivalism in Early Twentieth Century America." Ph.D. Dissertation, Southwestern Baptist Theological Seminary, 1993.

Heinemann, Robert Leo. "The Social Gospel of Black Evangelicals, 1968-1975: A Study of a Rhetorical Attempt to Alter Three Race-Related Images." Ph.D. Dissertation, Ohio State University, 1975.

Heselgrave, D. Dennis. "The Relationship Between A.H. Strong and Walter Rauschenbusch at Colgate Rochester Divinity School." M.A. Thesis, Trinity Evangelical Divinity School, 1970.

Hoffmann, Warren John. The Homiletical Theory of Karl August Rauschenbusch and Walter Rauschenbusch: Implications for Contemporary Proclamation." Ph.D., Southern Baptist Theological Seminary, 1996.

Horne, Cleveland R., Jr. "Christian Economic Ethics: A Study of Contemporary Thought in the Light of the Works of Walter Rauschenbusch." Ph.D. Dissertation, Southwestern Baptist Theological Seminary, 1955.

Horton, Natalie R. "The Life, Work, and Influence of Walter Rauschenbusch" Th.M. Thesis, Central Baptist Theological Seminary, 1951.

Howard, Irving E. "The Nature and Origin of the Political Thought of Walter Rauschenbusch." M. A. Thesis, Clark University, 1953.

Htwe, Maung M. "A Prophetic Religion Curriculum for the Pwo Karen Theological Seminary in Burma (Myanmar)." D.Min. Thesis, Andover Newton Theological School, 2007.

Hudson, Frederic M. "The Reign of the New Humanity: A Study of the Background, History, and Influence of the Brotherhood of the Kingdom" Ph.D. Dissertation, Columbia University, 1968.

Huff, Ronald Paul. "Social Christian Clergymen and Feminism During the Progressive Era." Ph.D. Dissertation, Union Theological Seminary, 1978.

Jackson, David. "Walter Rauschenbusch from the Social Gospel to Neo-Orthodoxy." Independent Study Paper, Hanover College, n.d.

Jaehn, Klaus Jurgen. "Walter Rauschenbusch: Scholar-Preacher-Social Reformer, 1886-1891" M.Div thesis, American Baptist Seminary of the West-Berkeley, 1972.

Janson-Fugere, Roswitha. "Walter Rauschenbusch and the Kingdom of God: A Study of the Biblical Basis for the Structure of His Ethical Thought." M.A. Thesis, University of St. Michael's College, 1970.

Johnson, Carl Elbert. "Walter Rauschenbusch as Historian." Ph.D. Dissertation, Duke University, 1976.

Jolley, Steven W. "The Legacy of Walter Rauschenbusch in Twentieth Century Protestant Christian Ethics: An Essay in Theological Ethics." Ph.D. Dissertation, Fuller Theological Seminary, 2002.

Jones, Kirk B. "Kindred Visions: A Comparative Analysis of the Social Role of the Church in the Thought of Walter Rauschenbusch and Martin Luther King, Jr." Ph.D. Dissertation, Drew University, 1996.

Kerstan, Reinhold J. "Historical Factors in the Formation of the Ethnically Oriented North American Baptist General Conference." Ph.D Dissertation, Northwestern University, 1971.

King, William McGuire. "The Emergence of Social Gospel Radicalism in American Methodism." Ph.D. Dissertation, Harvard University, 1977.

Kiser, A. Melissa. "Walter Rauschenbusch: For God and the People." B.A. Thesis, Princeton University, 1975.

Landes, Scott D. "The Nature of Humanity and Sin in the Thought of Clarence Jordan and Martin Luther King, Jr. in Light of Walter Rauschenbusch's *A Theology of the Social Gospel*." Honors Thesis, Carson-Newman College, 1994.

Langevin, Eugene A. "A New Interpretation of the Social Theory of Walter Rauschenbusch." B.A. Thesis, Harvard University.

Lassen, Kara Marie. "Walter Rauschenbusch and the Social Gospel Reconsidered." B.A. Thesis, Butler University, 1996.

LeMasters, Philip. "A Critical Analysis of Walter Rauschenbusch and Gustavo Gutierrez' Respective Uses of the Kingdom of God as a Normative Symbol for Theological Ethics (Liberation Theology)." M.A. Thesis, Rice University, 1987.

Liever, Oscar W. "The Idea of the Kingdom of God as Reflected in the American Social Gospel, 1865-1917." Ph.D. Dissertation, Duke University, 1941.

Lindner, Eileen W. "The Redemptive Politics of Henry George: Legacy to the Social Gospel." Ph.D. Dissertation, Union Theological Seminary, 1985.

Lindsay, Natille P. "A Study of the Writings of Walter Rauschenbusch as Reflected in His Books on the Social Gospel." M. A. Thesis, Ouachita Baptist University, 1966.

Locke, Harvey James. "A History and Critical Interpretation of the Social Gospel of Northern Baptists in the United States." Ph.D. Dissertation, University of Chicago, 1930.

Magill, Sherry Patricia. "The Political Thought of Walter Rauschenbusch: Toward a Religious Theory of the Positive State." Ph.D. Dissertation, Syracuse University, 1984.

Maley, Leo C. "Walter Rauschenbusch's Socialism: Reconstructing an Argument with Implications for Contemporary Social Ethics." M.T.S. Thesis, Wesley Theological Seminary, 1992.

Massey, John David. "Solidarity in Sin: An Analysis of the Corporate Conceptions of Sin in the Theologies of Augustus Hopkins Strong and Walter Rauschenbusch." Ph.D. Dissertation, Southwestern Baptist Theological Seminary, 2000.

McClintock, David Alan. "Walter Rauschenbusch: The Kingdom of God and the American Experience. Ph.D. Dissertation, Case Western Reserve University, 1975.

McInerny, William F. "Scripture and Christian Ethics: An Evaluative Analysis of the Uses of Scripture in the Works of Walter Rauschenbusch." Ph.D. Dissertation, Marquette University, 1983.

*McNab, John. "Towards a Theology of Social Concern: A Comparative Study of the Elements for Social Concern in the Writings of Frederick D. Maurice and Walter Rauschenbusch." Ph.D. Dissertation, McGill University, 1972.

Meriwether, David P. "An Exercise in Ethical Method: An Analysis of the Ethics of Walter Rauschenbusch with Reference to His Views on Economic Morality." Ph.D. Dissertation, Duke University, 1986.

Mernitz, Susan C. "The Disintegration of Faith: The Social Gospel and Modern American Culture." Ph.D. Dissertation, University of Missouri-Columbia, 1986.

Meyer, Georg Gustav. "Theological Foundations for Social Action in the 19th and Early 20th Century: A Comparison Between Robert Baden-Powell, Mathew Arnold and Walter Rauschenbusch." M. Th. Thesis, University of Natal, Pietmaritzburg, 1995.

Mewborn, Michael P. "A Comparative Analysis of the Preaching of Walter Rauschenbusch, Charles Sheldon, and George W. Truett, as Related to Social Ministry." Ph.D. Dissertation, Mid-America Baptist Theological Seminary, 2014.

Morley, James William. "The Kingdom Come: An Analysis of the Thought of Walter Rauschenbusch." Ph.D. Dissertation, Harvard University, 1942.

Morton, Hilton O. "The Implications for Christian Education of the Social Teachings of Walter Rauschenbusch." B.D. Thesis, Duke University, 1938.

Mosher, Sheila P. "The Social Gospel in British Columbia: Social Reform as a Dimension of Religion, 1900-1920." M.A. Thesis, University of Victoria, 1974.

Nason, Gary Curtis. "New York State Baptists and the Social Gospel, 1900-1917." M.A. Thesis, University of Western Ontario, 1977.

Naumann Kurt. "Die Theologie des social gospel in Amerika: dargestellt an Walter Rauschenbusch; Versuch einer kritischen Würdigung." Ph.D. Dissertation, University of Tübingen, 1939.

Nelson, William D. "The Kingdom of God and Walter Rauschenbusch: A Synthesis of Personal Salvation and Social Transformation." D.Min. Thesis, Wesley Theological Seminary, 1989.

Niebuhr, Reinhold. "The Validity and Certainty of Religious Knowledge" B. D. Thesis, Yale University, 1914.

Norment, Owen L. "A Study of the Social Ethics of Walter Rauschenbusch and Reinhold Niebuhr." Th.M. Thesis, Union Theological Seminary in Va., 1959.

Ogden, Joslyn E. "Walter Rauschenbusch and Reinhold Niebuhr: Advocates of Christian Social Action." B. A. Thesis, Davidson College, 2000.

Ohlmann, Eric H. "The American Baptist Mission to German-Americans: A Case Study of Attempted Assimilation." Th.D. Dissertation, Graduate Theological Union, 1973.

Phillips, David D. "The Relation of the Social Gospel to the Kingdom of God Concept in American Neo-Liberalism." Th.M. Thesis, Dallas Theological Seminary, 1966.

Pittendrigh, Scott M. "The Religious Perspective of T.C. Douglas's Social Gospel Theology and Pragmatism." M. A. Thesis, University of Regina, 1997.

Price, Timothy Shaun. "An Evaluation of the Theology of the Kingdom of God as Demonstrated in Carl F. H. Henry's *The Uneasy Conscience of Modern Fundamentalism* Compared to the Views of Albert Schweitzer, C. H. Dodd, and Walter Rauschenbusch." M.A. Thesis, Southeastern Baptist Theological Seminary, 2007.

Prochaska, Joseph G. "The Theology of the Social Gospel: An Analysis of Rauschenbusch's System and Continued Influence." Th.M. Thesis, Western Conservative Baptist Seminary, 1975.

Rand, Francesca. "Theodore Dreiser and the Social Gospel: A Thesis in English." M.A. Thesis, State University College at Buffalo, 1996.

Rapske, Arnold. "The Kingdom of God as Interpreted by Baptists in America Since 1900." Th.M. Thesis, Northern Baptist Theological Seminary, 1956.

Robbins, Anna M. "Common Sense in Uncommon Degrees: Methodological Diversity in Twentieth Century Christian Social Ethics." Ph.D. Dissertation, University of Wales, Aberystwyth, 2001.

Rogers, Anna Kathryn. "The Social Gospel and the Doctrine of Progress." Ph.D. Dissertation, University of Chicago, 1937.

Rossol, Heinz D. "Walter Rauschenbusch as Preacher: The Development of His Social Thought as Expressed in His Sermons from 1886 to 1897." Ph.D. Dissertation, Marquette University, 1997.

Rowand, E. C. "The Contribution of Walter Rauschenbusch to the Christian Social Gospel." Th.M. Thesis, Pittsburgh-Xenia Theological Seminary, 1951.

Ryley, Thomas W. "The Social Gospel Movement During the Period of American Reform, 1880-1910." Ph.D. Dissertation, New York University, 1965.

Satta, Ronald F. "Rauschenbusch and Rochester: How He Applied His Own Social Gospel at Home." M.A. Thesis, State University of New York, College at Brockport, 1999.

Saxton, Colin B. "Life in the Kingdom of God: The Theology and Praxis of Walter Rauschenbusch." M.A.R, Thesis, Eastern Mennonite Seminary, 1991.

Schirmer, Carolyn Best. "Theological Method in Walter Rauschenbusch: An Analysis and Critique of His Use of the Bible." M.A. Thesis, The American University, 1968.

Schattenmann, Johannes. "A Critique of the American Social Gospel from the Standpoint of German Theology and Philosophy, with Special Reference to Walter Rauschenbusch and Harry F. Ward." Ph.D. Dissertation, 1928.

Scopino, Aldorigo J. "The Social Gospel in Connecticut: Protestants, Catholics, Jews, and Social Reform, 1993-1929." Ph.D. Dissertation, University of Connecticut, 1993.

Shelley, John. "Realism and Utopianism: Elements in the Construction of a Political Theology." Ph.D. Dissertation, Vanderbilt University, 1977.

Simpson, Thomas W. "Rorty and Rauschenbusch on Religion and Reform." M.T.S. Thesis, Emory University, 1999.

Singer, Anna M. "Walter Rauschenbusch and His Contributions to Social Christianity as Shown in His Writings." M. A. Thesis, University of Southern California, 1921.

Smucker, Donovan E. "The Origins of Walter Rauschenbusch's Social Ethics." Ph.D. Dissertation, University of Chicago, 1957.

Sonderregger, Hugo. "Die Idee des Reiches Gottes im Social Gospel nach Walter Rauschenbusch." S.T.M. Thesis, Union Theological Seminary (NY), 1937.

Stackhouse, Max L. "Eschatology and Ethical Method: A Structural Analysis of Contemporary Christian Social Ethics in America, with Primary Reference to Walter Rauschenbusch and Reinhold Niebuhr." Ph.D. Dissertation, Harvard University, 1964.

Super, Joseph Francis. "On Earth as It is in Heaven: The Social Gospel as a "Theology of Liberation." M.A. Thesis, Liberty University, 2009.

Tannassee, Geoffrey Y. "The Approach of Walter Rauschenbusch to the Social Gospel." B.D. Thesis, Waterloo Lutheran Seminary, 1966.

Terracini, Paul. "John Stoward Moyes and the Social Gospel: A Study in Christian Social Engagement." Ph.D. Dissertation, University of Sydney (AU), 2012.

Thornbury, Gregory A. "The Legacy of Natural Theology in the Northern Baptist Theological Tradition, 1827-1918." Ph.D. Dissertation, Southern Baptist Theological Seminary, 2001.

Trench, William Crowell. "The Social Gospel and the City: Implications for Theological Reconstruction in the Work of Washington Gladden, Josiah Strong, and Walter Rauschenbusch." Ph.D. Dissertation, Boston University, 1986.

True, David B. "Faithful Politics: The Tradition of Martin Luther King, Jr., Reinhold Niebuhr, and Walter Rauschenbusch." Ph.D. Dissertation, Union Theological Seminary (Va.) and Presbyterian School of Christian Education, 2005.

Tuck, William Powell. "The Concept of Soteriology in the Theology of Walter Rauschenbusch." Th.M. Thesis, Southeatern Baptist Theological Seminary, 1961.

Verhey, Allen Dale. "The Use of Scripture in Moral Discourse: A Case Study of Walter Rauschenbusch." Ph.D. Dissertation, Yale University, 1975.

Vickrey, Garrett. "From Stranger to Family: Hospitality and the Kingdom of God as Influenced by the Ethics of Walter Rauschenbusch and T. B. Maston." M.Div. Thesis, Wake Forest University, 2007.

Weatherly, Owen Milton. "A Comparative Study of the Social Ethics of Walter Rauschenbusch and Reinhold Niebuhr." Ph.D. Dissertation, University of Chicago Divinity School, 1950.

Weisser, Christa G. "The Life and Work of Walter Rauschenbusch and the Narrative Ethics of James Wm. McClendon, Jr." D.Min. Thesis, Sioux Falls Seminary, 2009.

Wessel, James H. "A Study of Walter Rauschenbusch and the Social Gospel." B. D. Thesis, Concordia Theological Seminary (Ill), 1965.

Williams, Claude J. "Walter Rauschenbusch: A Prophet of Social Righteousness." Th.D. Dissertation, Southern Baptist Theological Seminary, 1952.

Wilson, Lloyd T. "Restoring Communities and Restoring Hearts: Poverty, Relief and Urban Restoration Models for Concerned Christians." M.T.S. Thesis, Christian Theological Seminary, 2010.

Social Gospel (General); Social Christianity Backgrounds

Allen, Richard. *The Social Passion: Religion and Social Reform in Canada 1914-28.* Toronto, ON: University of Toronto Press, 1971.

American Institute of Social Service. *The Gospel of the Kingdom.* New York: American Institute of Social Service.

Baker, Ray Stannard. "The Spiritual Unrest." *American Magazine* (Dec. 1909): 176.

Baker, Ray Stannard. *The Spiritual Unrest.* New York: 1910, pp. 260-285.

Barbour, Robin. *The Kingdom of God and Human Society.* Edinburgh: T & T Clark, 1993.

Barnes, Sandra. "Black Megachurches: Social Gospel Usage and Community Empowerment." *Journal of African American Studies* 15/2 (2011): 177-198.

Baum, Gregory. *Religion and Alienation: A Theological Reading of Sociology.* New York: Paulist Press, 1975.

Bebbington, David W. "Baptists and the Social Gospel" in *Baptists Through the Centuries: A History of a Global People.* Waco, TX: Baylor University Press, 2010, pp. 121-138.

Bennett, John C. "The Social Gospel Today" in *The Social Gospel: Religion and Reform in Changing America,* edited by Ronald C. White, Jr. and C. Howard Hopkins. Philadelphia, PA: Temple University Press, 1976.

Bennett, John C. "The Social Interpretation of Christianity." In *The Church Through Half a Century: Essays in Honor of William Adams Brown,* edited by Samuel Cavert and Henry Van Dusen. New York: Scribner's, 1936.

Bennett, John C. *Social Salvation: A Religious Approach to the Problems of Social Change.* New York: Scribner's 1935.

Bernstein, Eduard. *Evolutionary Socialism.* New York: Schocken Books, 1899; repr. 1961.

Bernstein, Richard. *The Restructuring of Social and Political Theory.* New York: Harcourt Brace Jovanovich, 1976.

Boorstin, Daniel. *An American Primer.* Chicago, IL: University of Chicago Press, 1966.

Brackney, William H. "Legacy: The Social Gospel" in *Baptists in North America: An Historical Perspective.* Oxford: Blackwell Publishing, 2006, pp. 101-103.

Brown, Charles Reynolds. *The Social Message of the Christian Pulpit.* New York: 1906.

Carter, Paul A. *The Decline and Revival of the Social Gospel; Social and Political Liberalism in American Protestant Churches, 1920-1940.* Hamden, CT: Archon Books, 1971.

Cendron, Ivy. *Un'analisi escatologica della realtà: Il Movimento Social Gospel.* Bologna: Società Editrice Il Mulino, 2014.

Cobb, Stephen G. *Reverend William Carwardine and the Pullman Strike of 1894: The Christian Gospel and Social Justice*. Lewiston, NY: Edward Mellen Press, 1992.

Cort, John C. *Christian Socialism: An Informal History*. Maryknoll, NY: Orbis Books, 1988.

Curtis, Susan. *A Consuming Faith: The Social Gospel and Modern American Culture.* Baltimore, MD: Johns Hopkins University Press, 1991.

Dayton, Donald. *Discovering an Evangelical Heritage.* New York: Harper and Row, 1976.

Dorn, Jacob H. *Socialism and Christianity in Early Twentieth Century America.* Westport, CT: Greenwood Press, 1998.

Dorn, Jacob H. *Washington Gladden: Prophet of the Social Gospel.* Columbus, OH: Ohio University Press, 1967.

Dorrien, Gary. *The Democratic Socialist Vision.* Totowa, NJ: Rowman and Littlefield, 1986.

Dorrien, Gary. "In the Spirit of Abolitionism: Recovering the Black Social Gospel." *Tikkun* 31/1 (2016).

Dorrien, Gary J. *Reconstructing the Common Good: Theology and the Social Order.* Maryknoll, NY: Orbis Books, 1990.

Dorrien, Gary. "The Social Gospel: Washington Gladden, Josiah Strong, Walter Rauschenbusch, and Harry F. Ward." In *Social Ethics in the Making: Interpreting an American Tradition,* 60-145. Malden, MA: Blackwell Publishing Ltd., 2011.

Dorrien, Gary. "Social Gospels: Justification, Social Salvation, and Modern Theology." In *The Gospel of Justification in Christ: Where Does the Church Stand Today?,* edited by Wayne C. Stumme. Grand Rapids, MI: William B. Eerdmans Publishing Co., 2006, pp. 85-103.

Dorrien, Gary. *Soul in Society: The Making and Renewal of Social Christianity.* Minneapolis, MN: Fortress Press, 1995.

Dougherty, Mary Agnes. "The Social Gospel According to Phoebe: Methodist Deaconnesses in the Metropolis, 1885-1918" in Hilah F. Thomas and Rosemary Skinner Keller, eds. *Women in New Worlds: Historical Perspectives on the Wesleyan Tradition* Nashville, TN: Abingdon, 1981: 200-216.

Dupertuis, Jean. "*Christianisme Social" d'après Rauschenbusch.* Saint-Blaise: Foyer Solidariste, 1911.

Eighmy, John Lee. *Churches in Cultural Captivity: A History of the Social Attitudes of Southern Baptists.* Knoxville, TN: University of Tennessee Press, 1972.

Ely, Richard T. *Social Aspects of Christianity 7 Other Essays.* New York: Thomas Y. Crowell Publishing & Co., 1889.

Evans, Christopher H. *Perspectives on the Social Gospel: Papers from the Inaugural Social Gospel Conference at Colgate-Rochester Divinity School.* Lewiston, NY: Edwin Mellen Press, 1999.

Evans, Christopher H. *The Social Gospel Today.* Louisville, KY: John Knox Press, 2001.

Fishbuurn, Janet F. *The Social Gospel as Missionary Ideology.* Cambridge: Currents in World Christianity Project, 1998.

Fogel, Robert W. *The Fourth Great Awakening and the Future of Egalitarianism.* Chicago, IL: University of Chicago Press, 2000.

Fraser, Alexander. *The Social Gospel and the Bible: A Business Man Turns to His Bible to Learn the Truth Concerning the Social Gospel.* Pittsburgh, PA: A. Fraser, 1939.

Frederick, Peter J. *Knights of the Golden Rule: The Intellectual as Christian Social Reformer in the 1890s.* Lexington, KY: The University Press of Kentucky, 1976.

Frederick, Peter J. "What is the Social Gospel?" Temple University. www.temple.edu/tempress/cvhapter/100_ch 1. Pdf

Garriguet, Leon. *The Social Value of the Gospel.* London: Catholic Truth Society, 1911.

Gerson, Michael. "A New Social Gospel: Many Evangelicals are Chafing at the Narrowness of the Religious Right: A New Faith-based Agenda." *Newsweek* 148/18 (13 November 2006): 40.

Gonce, R. A. "The Social Gospel, Ely, and Commons's Initial Stage of Thought." *Journal of Economic Issues* 30/3 *Journal of Economic Issues.* (September 1996): 641-655.

Gorrell, Donald K. *The Age of Social Responsibility: The Social Gospel in the Progressive Era, 1900-1920.* Macon, GA: Mercer University Press, 1988.

Graham, William C. *Half-finished Heaven: The Social Gospel in American Literature.* Lanham, MD: University Press of America. 1995.

Handy, Robert T. *A Christian America: Protestant Hopes and Historical Realities, Second Edition.* New York: Oxford University Press, 1984, 135-147.

Hardman, Keith. *Issues in American Christianity: Primary Sources with Introductions.* Grand Rapids, MI: Baker Books, 1993.

Harnack, Adolf. *What is Christianity?* New York: Putnam, 1901.

Harper, Keith. *The Quality of Mercy: Southern Baptists and Social Christianity, 1890- 1920.* Tuscaloosa, AB: University of Alabama Press, 1996.

Heard, Gerald. *The Kingdom Without God: Road's End for the Social Gospel: Essays.* Los Angeles, CA: Foundation for Social Research, 1956.

Hilgard, Ernest R. "From the Social Gospel to the Psychology of Social Issues: A Reminiscence." *Journal of Social Issues* 42/1 (1986): 107-110.

Hinson-Hasty, Elizabeth. "The Future of the Social Gospel." *Theology Today* 66/1 (2009): 60-73.

Hofstadler, Richard. *The Progressive Movement, 1900-1915.* New York: Simon and Schuster, 1963; 1983.

Hopkins, Charles Howard. *The Rise of the Social Gospel in American Protestantism, 1865-1915.* New Haven, CT: Yale University Press, 1940.

Hutchinson, William R. "The Americanness of the Social Gospel: An Inquiry in Comparative History" *Church History* 44/3 (Sept. 1975): 367-381.

Jacobs, Pierre. "The Social Gospel Revisited: Consequences for the Church: Original Research." *Harding School of Theology Theological Studies* 71/3 (2015): 1-8.

Jenkins, Thomas E. "The Social Gospel and Its Critics: Walter Rauschenbusch, Reinhold Niebuhr, and J. Gresham Machen." In *The Character of God: Recovering the Lost Literary Power of American Protestantism.* Oxford, UK: Oxford University Press, 1997, 160-179.

Johnson, F. Ernest. *The Social Gospel Re-Examined.* New York: Harper and Brothers, 1940. (CRDS Rauschenbusch Lectures 1939)

Kanaley, Donald Edward. *A Study of the Relationship of Economics to the Doctrines of Modern Protestant Theology.* Np, 1955.

King, Martin Luther, Jr. *Advocate of the Social Gospel: September, 1948-March, 1963.* Berkeley, CA: University of California Press, 2007.

Laidler, Harry. *A History of Socialist Thought.* New York: Crowell, 1933.

Lasch, Christopher. "Religious Contributions to Social Movements: Walter Rauschenbusch, the Social Gospel, and Its Critics." *Journal of Religious Ethics* 18 (Spring 1990): 7-25.

Leonard, Bill J. "Baptists and the Social Gospel" in *Baptist Ways: A History*. Valley Forge, PA: Judson Press, 2003, pp. 217-219.

Lindley, Susan. "Neglected Voices and Praxis in the Social Gospel" *Journal of Religious Ethics* 18/2 (Spring, 1990): 91-98.

Lugan, Alphonse. *Social Principles of the Gospel*. New York: Macmillan Co., 1928.

Luker, Ralph. *The Social Gospel in Black and White American Racial Reform 1885- 1912*. Chapel Hill: University of North Carolina Press, 1991.

Macintosh, Douglas Clyde. *Social Religion*. New York: Charles Scribner's Sons, 1939.

Marty, Martin E. *Protestantism and Social Christianity*. Munich; New York: K. G. Saur, 1992.

Marzotto, Tessa. *L'ideale Social di Gesù: La Vera Filosofia del Vangelo*. Rome: Castelvecchi, 2014.

Mathews, Shailer. *Jesus on Social Institutions*. Philadelphia, PA: Fortress Press, 1971.

Mathews, Shailer. *The Social Gospel*. Philadelphia, PA: Griffith and Rowland Press, 1910.

McBirnie, William S. *The Social Gospel: A Perversion of the Christian Gospel*. Glendale, CA: Community Churches of America, 196-?.

McDowell, John Patrick. *The Social Gospel in the South: The Woman's Home Missionary Movement in the Methodist Episcopal Church, South 1886-1939*. Baton Rouge, LA: Louisiana State University Press, 1982.

McDurmond, Joel. God Versus Socialism: A Biblical Critique of the New Social Gospel. Powder Springs, GA: American Vision, 2009.

McLoughlin, David. "Catholic Social Teaching and the Gospel." *New Blackfriars* 93 (2012): 163-174.

May, Henry F. *The Protestant Churches and Industrial America*. New York: Harper & Row, 1949.

Metcalf, John. *John Metcalf's Testimony Against the Social Gospel*. Penn, Buckinghamshire: John Metcalf, 1995.

Miller, L. "Updating the Social Gospel for the 21st Century." *Religious Studies and Theology* 22/2 (2003): 33-39.

Morris, Calvin. "Reverdy Ransom, the Social Gospel and Race." *Journal of Religious Thought* 41/3 Spring/summer 1984).

Nicklason, Fred J. "Henry George: Social Gospeller." *American Quarterly* 22 (1970: 649-674.

Niebuhr, H. Richard. "The Attack upon the Social Gospel" in *The Social Gospel: Religion and Reform in Changing America*, ed. Ronald C. White, Jr. and C. Howard Hopkins Philadelphia, PA: Temple University Press, 1976.

Noble, David W. *The Paradox of Progressive Thought*. Minneapolis, MN: University of Minnesota Press, 1958.

Patterson, James Alan. "Christ, the Kingdom, and the Great Commission: The Impact of the Social Gospel on American Protestant Foreign Missions, 1890-1920." Evangelical Theological Society Papers, 1991.

Phillips, Paul T. *A Kingdom on Earth: Anglo-American Social Christianity, 1880-1940.* University Park, PA: Pennsylvania State University Press, 1996.

Piott, Steven L. *American Reformers, 1870-1920: Progressives in Word and Deed.* Lanham, MD: Rowman and Littlefield Publishers, 2006.

Pope, Robert. *Seeking God's Kingdom: The Nonconformist Social Gospel in Wales, 1906-1939.* Cardiff: University of Wales Press, 1999.

"Richard T. Ely: Lay Spokesman for the Social Gospel." *Journal of American History* 53/1 (June 1966): 61-74.

Rodgers, Ronald R. *The Social Gospel and the News.* Columbia, SC: Association for Education in Journalism and Mass Communication, 2011.

Rossinow, Doug. "The Radicalization of the Social Gospel: Harry F. Ward and the Search for a New Social Order, 1898-1936." *Religion and American Culture* 15/1 (January 2005): 63-106.

Sandeen, Ernest R. *The Bible and Social Reform.* Philadelphia, PA: Fortress Press, 1982.

Schneemelcher, Wilhelm and Gottfried Traub. *Religion und Sozialismus: Sieben Vorträge gehalten beim 5 Weltkongress für Fries Christentum und Religiösen Fortschritt, Berlin 1910.* Berlin: Schöenberg, 1910.

Small, Albion W. "Christianity and Socialism." *The American Journal of Theology* 17/2 (1917): 317-320.

Smith, Erin A. "What Would Jesus Do? The Social Gospel and the Literary Marketplace. *Book History* 10 (January 2007): 193-221.

Smith, Gary Scott. *The Search for Social Salvation: Social Christianity and America, 1880-1925.* Lanham, MD: Lexington Books, 2000.

Smith, Timothy L. *Revivalism and Social Reform in Mid-Nineteenth Century America.* Nashville, TN: Abingdon Press, 1957.

Social Suggestions for Program-Makers. Philadelphia, PA: American Baptist Publication Society, 1925.

Southern Baptist Historical Society. *Baptists and the Social Gospel.* Brentwood, TN: Southern Baptist Historical Society, 2000.

Strugnell, E. H. *Christ and Human Relationships: Five Studies Based on Rauschenbusch's Social Principles of Jesus.* Melbourne: Australasian Student Christian Movement, 1919.

Sugden, Chris. *Social Gospel or No Gospel?* Bramcote, UK: Grove Books, 1975.

Suttle, Tim. *An Evangelical Social Gospel? Finding God's Story in the Midst of Extremes.* Eugene, OR: Cascade Books, 2011.

Sweet, Leonard I. *Me and We: God's New Social Gospel.* Nashville, TN: Abingdon Press, 2014.

Thomas, Jacob. *From Lausanne to Manila: Evangelical Social Thought: Models of Mission and the Social Relevance of the Gospel.* Delhi: Indian Society for Promoting Christian Knowledge, 2003.

Tipple, John Ord. *The Capitalist Revolution: A History of American Social Thought, 1890-1919.* New York: Pegasus Books, 1970.

Troeltsch, Ernst. *The Social Teaching of the Christian Churches. 2 vols.* New York: Macmillan, 1931.

Tulga, Chester E. *The Case Against the Social Gospel: A Study in the Social Theology of the Prophets.* Chicago, IL: Conservative Baptist Fellowship, 1949.

Vollmer, Philip. *What Is the Social Gospel?* Philadelphia, PA: Commission on Social Service and Rural Work of the Reformed Church in the U.S., 1922.
Waldmeir, John C. *Poetry, Prose, and Art in the American Social Gospel Movement, 1880-1910.* Lewiston, NY: Edward Mellen Press, 2002.
White, Ronald C. *Liberty and Justice for All: Racial Reform and the Social Gospel 1875-1925.* San Francisco: Harper and Row, 1990.
"William Jennings Bryan and the Social Gospel." *The Journal of American History* 53/1 (June 1966): 41-60.
Williams, Preston N. *The Social Gospel and Race Relations: A Case Study of a Social Movement in Toward a Discipline of Social Ethics: Essays in Honor of Walter George Muelder.* Ed. Paul Deats. Boston, MA: Boston University Press, 1972.
Williams, Thomas Rhondda. *The Social Gospel.* Bradford: 1902.
Yeager, D. M. "Focus on the Social Gospel: An Introduction." *The Journal of Religious Ethics* 18/1 (April 1990): 3-6.
Zurlo, Gina. "The Social Gospel, Ecumenical Movement, and Christian Sociology: The Institute of Social and Religious Research." *The American Sociologist* 46/2 (2015): 177-193.

Social Christianity: English Backgrounds

Bebbington, David. *Evangelicalism in Modern Britain: A History from the 1730s to the 1980s.* Grand Rapids, MI: Baker Book House, 1989.
Blackwood, James R. *The Soul of Frederick W. Robertson: The Brighton Preacher.* New York: Harper and Brothers, 1947.
Briggs, John H. Y. *The English Baptists of the 19th Century.* Didcot: Baptist Historical Society, 1994.
Brook, Stopford A., editor. *Life and Letters of Frederick W. Robertson, M.A.* Boston, MA: Fields, Osgood & Co., 1870.
Brose, Olive J. *Frederick Denison Maurice: Rebellious Conformist.* Athens, OH: Ohio University Press, 1971.
Chadwick, Owen. *The Victorian Church, 2 Parts.* London: Adam and Charles Black, 1953.
Erskine, Thomas. *The Unconditional Freeness of the Gospel in Three Essays.* Edinburgh: Waugh and Innes, 1831.
Heath, Richard. *Anabaptism: From Its Rise at Zwickau to Its Fall at Munster, 1521- 1536.* London: Alexander Shepherd, 1895.
Higham, Florence. *Frederick Denison Maurice.* London: SCM Press, 1947.
Jones, Peter dA. *The Christian Socialist Revival 1877-1914: Religion, Class and Social Conscience in Late-Victorian England.* Princeton, NJ: Princeton University Press, 1968.
Kingsley, Charles. *Parson Lot, Cheap Clothes and Nasty.* London: W. Pickering, 1850.
Kingsley, Charles. *Water Babies: A Fairy Tale for a Land Baby.* London: Macmillan 1885.
Marchant, Sir James. *Dr. John Clifford, CH: Life and Letters and Reminiscences.* London: Cassell and Co., 1924.
Masterman, J. M. *Ludlow, Builder of Christian Socialism.* Cambridge: Cambridge University Press, 1963.
Maurice, Frederick. *The Kingdom of Christ.* London: Darton and Clark, 1838.

Maurice, F.D. *Theological Essays*. London: Macmillan, 1853.

Maurice, J.F. *The Life of Frederick Denison Maurice.* London: Charles Scribner's Sons, 1884.

McClain, Frank Mauldin. *Maurice: Man and Moralist*. London: S.P.C.K., 1972.

Norman, Edward. *Church and Society in England 1770-1970*. Oxford: Oxford University Press, 1976.

Pease, Margaret, and Heath, Carl. *Richard Heath, 1831-1912*. Letchworth, UK: Garden City Press, 1913.

Phillips, Paul T. *A Kingdom on Earth: Anglo-American Social Christianity, 1880- 1940.* University Park, PA: Pennsylvania State University Press, 1996.

Stubbs, Charles William. *Charles Kingsley and the Christian Socialist Movement*. London: Blackie & Son, 1899.

Thompson, David. "John Clifford's Social Gospel." *Baptist Quarterly* 31/5 (January, 1986): 199-217.

Vidler, Alec R. *The Theology of F. D. Maurice.* London: SCM Press, 1948.

Young, David. F. D. *Maurice and Unitarianism*. Oxford: Oxford University Press, 1992.

The Social Gospel and Walter Rauschenbusch

Aiken, John R. *Walter Rauschenbusch and Labor Reform: A Social Gospeller's Approach.* New York: n.p., n.d.

Allen, Robert A. "Walter Rauschenbusch and the Protestant Response to the Social Crisis, 1886-1898." Paper, ABHS files.

Altschuler, Glenn C. "Walter Rauschenbusch: Theology, the Church, and the Social Gospel." *Foundations* 22 (April-June 1979): 140-51.

Baker, R. S. "The Spiritual Unrest, A Vision of the New Christianity, conversation with Professor Walter Rauschenbusch." *American Magazine,* December 1909.

Bawer, Bruce. "Rauschenbusch's Kingdom" in *Stealing Jesus: How Fundamentalism Betrays Christianity*. New York, NY: Broadway Books, 1998, 91-108.

Beckley, Harlan. *Passion for Justice: Retrieving the Legacies of Walter Rauschenbusch, John A. Ryan, and Reinhold Niebuhr.* Louisville, KY: Westminster John Knox Press, 1992.

Bennett, John C. "The Social Gospel:" in "Theology for Preaching," Conference on Interpreting the Faith, 7 July 1977 at Union Theological Seminary in Virginia, sound recording.

Binkley, Olin T. "The Social Gospel of Walter Rauschenbusch and Its Relation to Religious Education." *Review and Expositor* 42/1 (1945): 87.

Blake, C. N. "New Century, Same Crisis: Walter Rauschenbusch & the Social Gospel." *Commonweal* 134/18 (26 October 2007): 19-22.

Blake, Casey Nelson. "Private Life and Public Commitment: From Walter Rauschenbusch to Richard Rorty." In *A Pragmatist's Progress?: Richard Rorty and American Intellectual History*, edited by John Pettigrew, pp. 85-102. Lanham, MD: Rowman and Littlefield Publishers, Inc., 2000.

Bodein, Vernon Parker. "The Development of the Social Thought of Walter Rauschenbusch." *Religion in Life* 6 (Summer 1937): 420-431.

Bodein, Vernon Parker. *The Social Gospel of Walter Rauschenbusch and its Relation to Religious Education.* New York: Yale University Press, 1944.

Canipe, Lee. "Walter Rauschenbusch and the Democratic Kingdom of God." In *A Baptist Democracy: Separating God from Caesar in the Land of the Free*, 52-87. Macon, GA: Mercer University Press, 2011.

Cassedy, Steven. "Walter Rauschenbusch, the Social Gospel Movement, and How Julius Wellhausen Unwittingly Helped Create American Progressivism in the Twentieth Century" in *Sacred History, Sacred Literature: Essays on Ancient Israel, the Bible and Religion in Honor of R. E. Friedmann on His Sixtieth Birthday*, edited by Shawna Dolansky. Winiona Lake, IN: Eisenbrauns, 2008.

Clark, Kenneth W. "Walter Rauschenbusch." *Duke Divinity School Bulletin* 23/1 (February 1958): 1-11.

Curtis, Susan. "American Protestantism at a Crossroads." In *Critical Issues in American Religious History: A Reader*, edited by Robert R. Mathisen. Waco, TX: Baylor University Press, 2001.

Curtis, Susan. "Walter Rauschenbusch: 'Bound Up By a Thousand Ties'." In *A Consuming Faith: The Social Gospel and Modern American Culture.* Columbia, MO: University of Missouri Press, 2001, 101-13.

Daly, Lois K. "Passion for Justice: Retrieving the Legacies of Walter Rauschenbusch, John A. Ryan, and Reinhold Niebuhr." *The Journal of Religion* 74/4 (1994): 582-583.

Davis, Dennis. "The Impact of Evolutionary Thought on Walter Rauschenbusch." *Foundations* 21 (July-September 1978): 254-71.

Dietrich, Suzanne de. *L'Evangile Social de Jesus.* n.p, nd.

Dorrien, Gary J. "Society as the Subject of Redemption: Washington Gladden, Walter Rauschenbusch, and the Social Gospel." In *Economy, Difference, Empire: Social Ethics for Social Justice.* New York, NY: Columbia University Press (e-book), 2010.

Dorrien, Gary. *Soul in Society: The Making and Renewal of Social Christianity.* Minneapolis, MN: Augsburg Fortress, 1995.

Dyrness, William A. "Forays into an American Gospel: Walter Rauschenbusch and Robert Schuller." In *How Does America Hear the Gospel?*, 106-131. Grand Rapids, MI: William B. Eerdmans Publishing Co., 1989.

Dyrness, William A. *How Does America Hear the Gospel?* Grand Rapids, MI: Eerdmans, 1989.

Evans, Christopher H. "Gender and the Kingdom of God: The Family Values of Walter Rauschenbusch." In *The Social Gospel Today*, edited by Christopher H. Evans. Louisville, KY: Westminster John Knox Press, 2001, pp. 53-66.

Fishburne, Janet Forsythe. *The Fatherhood of God and the Victorian Family: The Social Gospel in America.* Philadelphia, PA: Fortress Press, 1981.

Fishburn, Janet Forsythe. "Walter Rauschenbusch and 'The Woman Movement': A Gender Analysis." In *Gender and the Social Gospel,* edited by Wendy J. Deichmann Edwards and Carolyn De Swarte Gifford, 71-86. Chicago, IL: University of Illinois Press, 2003.

Gladden, Washington, and Richard T. Ely, and Walter Rauschenbusch. *The Social Gospel in America.* New York: Oxford University Press, 1966.

Gorrell, Donald K. *Walter Rauschenbusch and the Social Awakening of the Church.* Boston, MA: Intercollegiate Case Clearing House, 1974.

Haldeman, I. M. *Professor Rauschenbusch's "Christianity and the Social Crisis."* New York: Charles C. Cook, 19--?.

Handy, Robert T. *The Social Gospel in America 1870-1920: Gladden, Ely, Rauschenbusch.* Oxford, UK: Oxford University Press, 1966.

Handy, Robert T. "Practical and Prophetical Aspects of the Social Gospel, Charles R. Henderson and Walter Rauschenbusch." *The Chronicle* 18/3 (July-Oct 1955): .

Herron, George D. *Social Meanings of Religious Experiences.* New York: Johnson Reprint Corp., 1896; 1969.

Hopkins, C. Howard. "Walter Rauschenbusch and the Brotherhood of the Kingdom." *Church History* 7/2 (June 1938): 138-156.

Hudson, Winthrop S. "Walter Rauschenbusch and the New Evangelism." *Religion in Life* 29 (Summer 1961): 412-30.

Jonge, Haijo de. *Walter Rauschenbusch en de Werkelijikheid van het Godsrijk: een Onderzonoek naar de Beteknis en Doorwerking van zijn "Social Gospel."* Gorinchem: Narratio, 2002.

Kearley, Bruce. *Walter Rauschenbusch and Oliver Jackson: A Comparative Study in the Social Gospel Tradition.* n.p, 2011.

Kroeker, Peter Travis. "The Cooperative Commonwealth and the Kingdom of God: The Social Gospel Quest for a Public Morality." In *Christian Ethics and Political Economy in North America: A Critical Analysis.* Montreal, QC: McGill-Queen's University Press, 1995, 19-44.

Langford, S. Fraser. "The Gospel of Augustus H. Strong and Walter Rauschenbusch." *The Chronicle* 14/1 (January 1951): 3-18.

Lasch, Christopher. "Religious Contributions to Social Movements: Walter Rauschenbusch, the Social Gospel, and Its Critics." *The Journal of Religious Ethics* 18/1 (1990): 7-25.

"Lascopara di un proeta Americano." *Bilychnis.* Vol. 12 (1918).

LeMasters, Philip. "Discipleship and Political Action." In *Discipleship Between Creation and Redemption: Toward a Believers' Church Social Ethic,* pp. 1-18. Lanham, MD: University Press of America, Inc., 1997.

Lotz, Philip H. *Founders of Christian Movements.* New York: Association Press, 1941.

Massanari, Ronald Lee. "The Sacred Workshop of God: Reflections of the Historical Perspective of Walter Rauschenbusch." *Religion in Life* 40 (Summer 1971): 257-66.

McLintock, David A. "Walter Rauschenbusch: The Kingdom of God and the American Experience."

Moore, James R. "Walter Rauschenbusch and the Religious Education of Youth." *Religious Education* 68 (July-August 1973): 435-53.

Mueller, Reinhart. *Walter Rauschenbusch: Ein Beitrag zur Begegnung des deutschen und des amerikanischen Protestantismus.* Leiden, Netherlands: E. J. Brill, 1957.

Nelson, Janet R. "Walter Rauschenbusch and the Social Gospel: A Hopeful Theology for the Twenty-First Century Economy." *Cross-Currents* 59/4 (2009): 442-456.

Nicbuhr, Reinhold. "Rochester Holds Lecture Week" (Reinhold Niebuhr's WR Lectureship) *The Christian Century* (18 April 1934): 535.

Noble, David W. "Walter Rauschenbusch: Prophet." In *The Paradox of Progressive Thought.* St. Paul, MN: North Central Publishing Company, 1958, pp. 228-45.

Patterson, W. Morgan. "Walter Rauschenbusch: Baptist Exemplar of Social Concern" *Baptist History and Heritage* 7/2 (April 1972): 139-136; 7/3 (July 1972): 130-136.

Phillips, Paul T. *Kingdom on Earth: Anglo-American Social Christianity, 1880-1940.* University Park, PA: The Pennsylvania State University Press, 1996.

Piott, Steven L. "Walter Rauschenbusch and the Social Gospel." In *American Reformers 1870-1920: Progressives in Word and Deed.* Lanham, MD: Rowman and Littlefield Publishers, Inc., 2006, pp. 75-90.

Ramsay, William M. *Four Modern Prophets: Walter Rauschenbusch, Martin Luther King Jr., Gustavo Gutierrez, Rosemary Radford Reuther.* Atlanta, GA: John Knox Press, 1986.

Schneider, Michael. *The Christian Socialism of Walter Rauschenbusch*. n.p., 1961.

Shaw, R. W. "The Searchlight and Dr. Rauschenbusch." *The Baptist* Vol. 3. (1922).

Sheldon, Preston King. "Rauschenbusch: Prophet of Christian Socialism." *American Journal of Economics and Sociology* 3/1 (1943): 133-135.

Sleeper, Charles F. *A Study in the Theology of Christian Social Action: An Examination of the Works of Walter Rauschenbusch and Reinhold Niebuhr, and of the Approaches to the Problem Which They Represent.* Waterville, ME: Colby College, 1954.

Smucker, Donovan E. "Multiple Motifs in the Thought of Rauschenbusch: A Study in the Origins of the Social Gospel. *Encounter* 18 (Winter 1958): 14-20.

Smucker, Donovan. "Rauschenbusch's View of the Church as a Dynamic Voluntary Association." In *Voluntary Associations: A Study of Groups in Free Societies*, edited by D. B. Robertson. Richmond, VA: John Knox Press, 1966, pp. 159-170.

Spencer, John Michael. "Hymns of the Social Awakening: Walter Rauschenbusch and Social Gospel Hymnody." *Hymn* 40 (April 1989): 18-24.

Stackhouse, Max L. "The Formation of a Prophet: Reflections on the Early Sermons of Walter Rauschenbusch." *Andover-Newton Quarterly* 9 (January 1969): 137-59.

Steinkraus, Warren E. "Walter Rauschenbusch and Socially Conscious Religion in America." *Religion and Philosophy in the United States of America* 2 (1987): 713- 14.

Strain, Charles R. "Walter Rauschenbusch: A Resource for Public Theology." *Union Seminary Quarterly Review* 34 (Fall 1978): 23-34.

Torbet, Robert G. *History of the Baptists.* Valley Forge, PA: Judson Press, 1950, 1963, pp. 158; 425.

Trench, William Crowell. *The Social Gospel and the City: Implications for Theological Reconstruction in the Work of Washington Gladden, Josiah Strong and Walter Rauschenbusch.* Ann Arbor, MI: University Microfilms, 1986.

Tuck, William Powell. *A Revolutionary Gospel: Salvation in the Theology of Walter Rauschenbusch.* Macon, GA: Smyth & Helwys, 2015.

Tull, James E. "Walter Rauschenbusch: Prophet of Social Christianity." In *Shapers of Baptist Thought.* Valley Forge, PA: Judson Press, 1972, pp 183-208.

Vinz, Warren L. "Bifurcated Nationalism." In *Pulpit Politics: Face of American Protestant Nationalism in the Twentieth Century,* 19-42. Albany, NY: State University of New York Press, 1997.

Vulgamore, Melvin L. "The Social Gospel Old and New: Walter Rauschenbusch and Harvey Cox." *Religion in Life* 36 (1967): 516-33.

Ward, A. Dudley. "The Modern Amos." *Christian Action* (December 1968): 25-32.

Workman, Wilbur E. *Social Protests of American Protestants in the Late Nineteenth Century, with Special Emphasis on Washington Gladden, Edward Bellamy, Josiah Strong, and Walter Rauschenbusch*. Goshen College: 1950.

Rauschenbusch's Ethics

Atherton, John. *Christian Social Ethics: A Reader*. Cleveland, OH: Pilgrim Press, 1994.

Beach, Waldo and H. Richard Niebuhr. *Christian Ethics: Sources of the Living Tradition*. New York: Ronald Press Co., 1955.

Bodein, Vernon Parker. *The Development of the Social Thought of Walter Rauschenbusch*. Nashville, TN: Abingdon Press, 1937.

Boulton, Wayne G., and Thomas Kennedy; Alan Verhey. *From Christ to the World: Introductory Readings in Christian Ethics*. Grand Rapids, MI: Eerdmans, 1994.

Burrow, Rufus. *God and Human Dignity: The Personalism, Theology, and Ethics of Martin Luther King, Jr.* Notre Dame, IN: University of Notre Dame Press, 2006.

Dorrien, Gary J. *Economy, Difference, Empire: Social Ethics for Social Justice*. New York: Columbia University Press, 2010.

Dorrien, Gary. *Social Ethics in the Making: Interpreting an American Tradition*. Malden, MA: Wiley-Blackwell Publishing, 2009.

Fox, Richard Wightman. *Reinhold Niebuhr: A Biography, with a New Introduction and Afterword*. Ithaca, NY: Cornell University Press, 1985; 1996.

Haight, Roger. "Recent Catholic Social and Ethical Teaching in Light of the Social Gospel." *The Journal of Religious Ethics* 18/1 (April 1990): 103-128.

Handy, Robert T. "Rauschenbusch, Walter" in John MacQuarrie, editor, *A Dictionary of Christian Ethics*. London: SCM Press, 1967. 288-289.

Huebner, Harry John. *An Introduction to Christian Ethics, History Movements, People*. Waco, TX: Baylor University Press, 2012.

LaFollette, Hugh. *The International Encyclopedia of Ethics*. Malden, MA: Wiley- Blackwell, 2013.

Lewis, Paul. "Walter Rauschenbusch (1861-1918): Pioneer of Baptist Social Ethics." In *Twentieth-Century Shapers of Baptist Social Ethics*, edited by Larry L. McSwain and Wm. Loyd Allen. Macon, GA: Mercer University Press, 2008, pp. 3-22.

Lindsey, Susan H. "Neglected Voices and Praxis in the Social Gospel." *The Journal of Religious Ethics* 18/1 (April 1990): 75-102.

Maurice, F. D. *Reconstructing Christian Ethics: Selected Writings*. Edited by Ellen K. Wondra. Louisville, KY: Westminster John Knox Press, 1995.

McSwain, Larry L, and William Loyd Allen. *Twentieth Century Shapers of Baptist Social Ethics*. Macon, GA: Mercer University Press, 2008, pp. 3-22.

Mueller, William A. "Rauschenbusch, Walter" in *Baker's Dictionary of Christian Ethics*, edited by Carl F. H. Henry. Grand Rapids, MI: Baker Books, 1973.

Niebuhr, Reinhold. *An Interpretation of Christian Ethics*. New York: Harper and Row, 1935.

Niebuhr, Reinhold. *Faith and Politics: A Commentary on Religious, Social, and Political Thought in a Technological Age*. New York: G. Braziller, 1968.

Ramsay, Paul. *Basic Christian Ethics*. New York: Charles Scribner's, 1950.

Robbins, Anna. *Methods in the Madness: Diversity in Twentieth Century Christian Social Ethics*. Carlisle: Paternoster Publishing, 2004.

Robins, Henry B. *The Contribution of Walter Rauschenbusch to World Peace.* Rochester, NY: Colgate Rochester Divinity School, 1940.

Smith, Kenneth L and Ira G. Zepp. *Search for the Beloved Community: The Thinking of Martin Luther King, Jr.* Valley Forge, PA: Judson Press, 1974.

Smucker, Donovan E. "The Ethics of Rauschenbusch." In *On Being the Church: Essays in Honor of John W. Snyder,* edited by Peter Erb. Waterloo, ON: Conrad Grebel Press, 1992.

Smucker, Donovan, and Robert T. Handy. "The Origins of Walter Rauschenbusch's Social Ethics." *Church History* 65/2 (1996): 249.

Smucker, Donovan E. *The Origins of Walter Rauschenbusch's Social Ethics.* Montreal, QC: McGill-Queen's University Press, 1994.

Stassen, Glen H, and David P. Gushee. *Kingdom Ethics: Following Jesus in Contemporary Context.* Downers Grove, IL: InterVarsity Press, 2003.

Sundquist, S. E. "The Kingdom of God and the Theological Ethics of Walter Rauschenbusch. *American Baptist Quarterly* 22/1 (2003): 77-98.

Yoder, John Howard. *The Priestly Kingdom: Social Ethics as Gospel.* Notre Dame, IN: University of Notre Dame Press, 1984.

Theology and Rauschenbusch

Ahlstrom, Sydney E. *Theology in America: The Major Protestant Voices from Puritanism to Neo-Orthodoxy.* Indianapolis, IN: Bobbs-Merrill Co., 1967.

Aiken, John R. "Walter Rauschenbusch and Education for Reform." *Church History.* 36 (1967): 456-69.

Andjelic, Milenko. *Christlicher Glaube als Prophetische Religion: Walter Rauschenbusch und Reinhold Niebuhr.* Frankfurt am Main: Peter Lang, 1968.

Bowman, Matthew. "Sin, Spirituality, and Primitivism: The Theologies of the American Social Gospel, 1885-1917." *Religion and American Culture* 17/1 (Jan 2007): 95-126.

Braaten, Carl E. and Robert W. Jensen. *A Map of Twentieth Century Theology: Readings from Karl Barth to Radical Pluralism.* Minneapolis, MN: Fortress Press, 1995.

Brackney, William H. *A Genetic History of Baptist Thought.* Macon, GA: Mercer University Press, 2004, pp. 335-337.

Bryant, S. E. "The Optimistic Ecclesiology of Walter Rauschenbusch." *American Baptist Quarterly.* 27/2 (2008): 117-35.

Cauthen, W. Kenneth. *The Impact of American Religious Liberalism.* New York: Harper and Row, 1962.

Dexter, Lewis A. "Administration of the Social Gospel." *The Public Opinion Quarterly* 2/2 (April 1938): 294-299.

Dorn, Jacob H. "The Social Gospel and Socialism: A Comparison of the Thought of Francis Greenwood Peabody, Washington Gladden, and Walter Rauschenbusch." *Church History.* 62 (March 1993): 82-100.

Dorrien, Gary. *Economy, Difference, Empire Social Ethics for Social Justice.* New York: Columbia University Press, 2010.

Dorrien, Gary J. *The Making of American Liberal Theology: Idealism, Realism, and Modernity, 1900-1950.* Princeton, NJ: Princeton University Press. 2007.

Dorrien, Gary J. *Reconstructing the Common Good: Theology and the Social Order.* Maryknoll, NY: Orbis Books, 1990.

Dorrien, Gary. "Thy Kingdom Come: Walter Rauschenbusch, Vida Scudder, and the Social(ist) Gospel." In *The Making of American Liberal Theology: Idealism, Realism, & Modernity 1900-1950,* pp. 73-150. Louisville, KY: Westminster John Knox Press, 2003.

Duke, David Nelson. "Theology Converses with the Biographical Narrative of Walter Rauschenbusch." *Perspectives in Religious Studies.* 18 (Summer 1991): 143-58.

Ede, Alfred J. "The Social Theologies of Walter Rauschenbusch and Vatican II in Dialogue." *Foundations.* 18/3 (July-September 1975): 198-208.

Edwards, R. A. R. "Jane Addams, Walter Rauschenbusch, and Dorothy Day: A Comparative Study of Settlement Theology." In *Gender and the Social Gospel,* edited by Wendy J. Deichmann Edwards and Carolyn De Swarte Gifford, pp. 150- 66. Chicago, IL: University of Illinois Press, 2003.

Everett, Daniel J. Interpreting Salvation, Personal Versus Social: A Late Nineteenth Century Case Study—Walter Rauschenbusch and A.B. Simpson. Evangelical Theological Society, 1991.

Fennell, Robert. "Renewing the Social Gospel through the Doctrine of Passability." *Toronto Journal of Theology* (2008): 125.

Fishburn, Janet F. *The Fatherhood of God and the Victorian Family.* 1981.

Fishburn, Janet Forsythe. *The Social Gospel as Missionary Theology.* Cambridge: Currents in World Christianity Project, 1998.

French, Henry F. *Theodicy in the Work of Walter Rauschenbusch.* (Japanese) National Diet Library, 1986: 15-34.

Gardner, Robert G. *Walter Rauschenbusch: Christocentric Prophet of the Kingdom.* n.p., 197-?.

Hambrick-Stowe, Charles E. "For God and the People: The Spirituality of Rauschenbusch—and Dubois—A Century Later." *Spiritus: A Journal of Christian Spirituality.* 1/2 (2001): 217-231.

Harris, Mathew L. *Rauschenbusch's Regurgitations: Rob Bell's Promotion of a Realized Eschatology and His Alignment with Walter Rauschenbusch and the Social Gospel Movement.* Lynchburg: Liberty University, 2010.

Hartzler, Lynn P. *Walter Rauschenbusch's Concept of the Kingdom of God: A Definition and Study of Some Implications.* n.p., 1954.

Hutchinson, William R. *American Protestant Thought: The Liberal Era.* New York: Harper and Row, 1968.

Hudson, Winthrop S. "Walter Rauschenbusch and the New Evangelism." *Religion in Life* 30 (Summer, 1961): 412-30.

Kerr, Hugh T. *Readings in Christian Thought.* Nashville, TN: Abingdon Press, 1966.

Knudten, Richard D. *The Systematic Thought of Washington Gladden.* New York: Humanities Press, 1968.

Lindsey, William D. *Shailer Mathews's Lives of Jesus: The Search for a Theological Foundation for the Social Gospel.* Albany, NY: State University of New York Press, 1997.

Lindsey, William D. "The Social Gospel and Feminism." *American Journal of Theology and Philosophy* 13/3 (Sept. 1992): 195-210.

McFarland, Ian A. *Creation and Humanity: The Sources of Christian Theology.* Louisville, KY: Westminster John Knox, 2009.

McGrath, Alister. *The Blackwell Encyclopedia of Modern Christian Thought.* Cambridge, MA: Blackwell Publishing, 1995.

Moore, James R. "Walter Rauschenbusch and the Religious Education of Youth." *Religious Education* 68/4 (1973): 435-453.

Nash, Robert N. "Walter Rauschenbusch, the Pope, and the New Evangelism." *Perspectives in Religious Studies* 42/2 (2015): 159-74.

Nelson, Janet R. "Walter Rauschenbusch and the Social Gospel: A Hopeful Theology for the Twenty-First Century Economy." *CrossCurrents.* 59/4 (December 2009): 442-456.

Niebuhr, H. Richard. *The Kingdom of God in America.* New York: Harper and Brothers, 1937.

Peerman, Dean G., and Martin E. Marty. *A Handbook of Christian Theologians.* Cleveland, OH: World Publishing Co., 1965.

Peitz, Darlene Ann. *Solidarity as Hermeneutic: A Revisionist Reading of the Theology of Walter Rauschenbusch.* New York: Peter Lang Publishers, Inc., 1992.

Reed, Ralph. *Active Faith: How Christians are Changing the Soul of American Politics.* New York: Free Press, 1996.

Rynbrandt, Linda. "Caroline Bennett Crane and the History of Sociology: Salvation, Sanitation, and the Social Gospel." *The American Sociologist* 29/1 (1998): 71-82.

Singer, Isidore. *A Religion of Truth, Justice, and Peace: A Challenge to Church and Synagogue to Lead in The Realization of the Social and Peace Gospel of the Hebrew Prophets.* New York: The Amos Society, 1924.

Smith, H. Shelton. *Changing Conceptions of Original Sin.* New York: Charles Scribner's Sons, 1955. Chapter 9 deals with Rauschenbusch.

Smucker, Donovan E. "Multiple Motifs in the Thought of Rauschenbusch." *Encounter* 19 (Winter, 1958): 14-20.

Stackhouse, Max L. "The Formation of a Prophet: Reflections on the Early Sermons of Walter Rauschenbusch." *Andover Newton Quarterly* 9 (1969): 137-159.

Strain, Charles R. "Walter Rauschenbusch: A Resource for Public Theology." *Union Seminary Quarterly Review* 43 (1978): 23-24.

Toulouse, Mark G. and Duke, James. *Sources of Christian Thought in America.* Nashville, TN: Abingdon Press, 1999.

Verhey, Allen D. *The Use of Scripture in Moral Discourse: A Case Study of Walter Rauschenbusch.* Ann Arbor, MI: University Microfilms, 1976.

Welch, Claude. *Protestant Thought in the Nineteenth Century. 2 vols.* New Haven, CT: Yale University Press, 1972; repr. 1985.

Wilson, John E. *Introduction to Modern Theology: Trajectories in the German Tradition.* Louisville, KY: Westminster John Knox Press, 2007.

Canadian Sources: Social Gospel; Walter Rauschenbusch

Allen, Richard. "The Social Gospel and the Reform Tradition in Canada: 1890-1928." *The Canadian Historical Review* 49 (December 1968): 387-88.

Allen, Richard. *The Social Gospel in Canada: Papers of the Interdisciplinary Conference on the Social Gospel in Canada, March 21-24, 1973 at the University of Regina.* Ottawa, ON: National Museums of Canada, 1975.

Allen, Richard. *The View from Murney Tower: Salem Bland, the Late Victorian Controversies, and the Search for a New Christianity.* Toronto, ON: University of Toronto Press, 2008.

Antonides, Harry. *Stones for Bread: The Social Gospel and Its Contemporary Legacy.* Jordan Station, ON: Paideia Press, 1985.

Blaikie, Bill. *The Social Gospel & Globalization.* n.p., 1996. *The Canadian Baptist.* 1900-1920.

Cook, Ramsay. *The Regenerators: Social Criticism in Late Victorian English Canada.* Toronto, ON: University of Toronto Press, 1985.

Crysdale, R. C. Stewart. *The Industrial Struggle and Protestant Ethics in Canada.* Toronto, ON: Ryerson Press, 1961.

Elgee, William H. *The Social Teachings of the Canadian Churches: Protestant; The Early Period, Before 1850.* Toronto, ON: Ryerson Press, 1964.

Finkel, Alvin. *The Social Credit Phenomenon in Alberta.* Toronto, ON: University of Toronto Press, 1989.

Forbes, Ernest R. "Prohibition and the Social Gospel in Nova Scotia." *Acadiensis* 1 (Autumn 1971):

Fraser, Brian J. *The Social Uplifters Presbyterian Progressives and the Social Gospel in Canada, 1875-1915.* Waterloo, ON: Wilfred Laurier University Press, 1988.

Grant, John Webster. *The Church in the Canadian Era.* Burlington, ON: Welch, 1988.

Helmes-Hayes, Rick. "Building the New Jerusalem in Canada's Green and Pleasant Land: The Social Gospel and the Roots of English-Language Academic Sociology in Canada, 1881-1921." *Canadian Journal of Sociology* 31/1 (2016): 1-52.

Ives, Andrew. "Christians on the Left: The Importance of the Social Gospel in the Canadian Social Democratic Tradition." *Revue/LISA* 9/1 (April 2011): 188-204.

Lam, Vincent. *Tommy Douglas.* Toronto, ON: Penguin Canada, 2012.

Levy, George E. The Baptists of the Maritime Provinces. Saint John, NB: Barnes-Hopkins, 1946.

Longley, Robert S. *Acadia University 1838-1938.* Wolfville, NS: Acadia University, 1939.

MacLean, M. C. "Social Service: An Announcement and a Platform." *The Canadian Baptist* 59 (April 10, 1913): 4.

The Maritime Baptist, 1880-1920.

Marshall, David B. *Secularizing the Faith: Canadian Protestant Clergy and the Crisis of Belief, 1850-1940.* Toronto, ON: University of Toronto Press, 1992.

The Messenger and Visitor. 1920-1940.

Minutes of the Board of Social Service of the Maritime United Baptist Convention, 1921-1948.

Moir, John S. "The Canadian Baptist and the Social Gospel Movement, 1879-1914." In *Baptists in Canada: Search for Identity Amidst Diversity,* edited by Jarold K. Zeman. Burlington, ON: G. R. Welch, 1980.

Rawlyk, George A. "The Champions of the Oppressed? Canadian Baptists and Social, Political, and Economic Realities." *McMaster Journal of Theology* 1 (1990):

Rawlyk, George A. *Champions of the Truth: Fundamentalism, Modernism, and Maritime Baptists.* Montreal, QC: McGill Queens University Press, 1990.

Saunders, S.A. The Economic Welfare of the Maritime Provinces. Wolfville, NS: Acadia University, 1932.

Sharpe, D. R. "Why Should We Make the Forward Movement an Unqualified Success?" *Maritime Baptist* 20 January 1920, 3.

Sholdice, Mark. "Brotherhood Extended to All Practical Affairs: The Social Gospel as the Religion of the Agrarian Revolt in Ontario." *Journal of Religion and Popular Culture* 25/3 (2013): 358-371.

Walsh, H. H. *The Christian Church in Canada.* Toronto, ON: The Ryerson Press, 1956, 326-341.

Wilson, W. D. and H.R. Boyer, "Temperance and Moral Reform: Report of the Committee." *United Baptist Convention of the Maritime Provinces Year Book.* Saint John, NB: United Baptist Convention of the Maritime Provinces, 1917.

Zeman, Jarold K. *Baptists in Canada: Search for Identity Amidst Diversity.* Burlington, ON: G. R. Welch, 1980, pp. 47-159.

Archives (Includes Personal Papers, Records, Memorabilia)

Rauschenbusch Materials at Ambrose Swasey Library, Colgate Rochester/ Crozer Divinity Schools

General Note: Colgate Rochester Divinity School (formerly Rochester Theological Seminary) was the original location of institutional records and the beginnings of a Rauschenbusch Collection dating from the 1920s. Later, Rauschenbusch's student secretary, Dores R. Sharpe, added his collection of Rauschenbusch materials. When the Samuel Colgate Baptist Historical Library of the American Baptist Historical Society was moved from Rochester to Atlanta, Georgia, only a small amount of Rauschenbusch material remained in the School's archives, plus the institutional records relating to the Rauschenbusch era.

Record Group I. Rochester Theological Seminary Faculty Meetings

Minutes: Vol. I 1850?-1912? [Not Available]

Minutes: Vol. II: 1912 – 1920

Minutes: Vol. III: 1920-1928

Record Group II. Rochester Theological Seminary Board of Trustees and Executive Committee

Board of Trustees Minutes, Vol. I May 7, 1889 through July 12, 1928 Executive Committee Minutes, Vol. 1: June 3, 1867 through May 11, 1883 Minutes, Vol. 2: May 23, 1883 through May 7, 1904 Minutes, Vol. 3: June 6, 1904 through May 17, 1921

Record Group III. Walter Rauschenbusch Scrapbooks

Walter Rauschenbusch Scrapbook 1912

Walter Rauschenbusch Scrapbook 1914

Walter Rauschenbusch Scrapbook 1915

Walter Rauschenbusch Scrapbook 1916

Walter Rauschenbusch Scrapbook 1917

Record Group IV General Files

Series [Box] 1

Walter Rauschenbusch: Prayers
Series [Box] 2
Walter Rauschenbusch: Framed Photos, Rochester Theological Seminary
Series [Box] 3
Perpetuating the Memory, etc. Series [Box] 4
Memorial Record
"Why I Am a Baptist"
Series [BOX] 5
"Theology for the Social Gospel"
Series [BOX] 6
Journal Articles about Walter Rauschenbusch
Series [Box] 7
Undated Miscellaneous

Rauschenbusch Material at Sioux Falls Seminary, Sioux Falls, South Dakota
General Note: Sioux Falls Seminary, formerly North American Baptist Seminary, was established as the German Department of Rochester Theological Seminary in Rochester, New York. Walter Rauschenbusch was a graduate of the German program and a faculty member in the Dept. from 1897 to 1902. The material listed here was identified by Jackie Howell and presented to this bibliography kindness of Dr. Philip Thompson.

Rauschenbusch Series 1
Rauschenbusch – Walter materials – primarily correspondence
223* Walter Rauschenbusch – Phillippus von Mazedonian
224* Walter Rauschenbusch – *Neque honestam neque utilem fuisse Catonis de Carthagine delonde senteatiem*
837 Walter Rauschenbusch – letter to FWC Meyer Dec 30, 1892
785* Walter Rauschenbusch – Essay on tasso (German)
933* Walter Rauschenbusch – Essay – Ermahnt Pendar mit Reicht
1842 Walter Rauschenbusch – Clausuraufsatz – Weshalb bewundern Dilattanten, weshalb kunstrichter die lookoongruppe
934 Walter Rauschenbusch – 1842
49 Walter Rauschenbusch – letter to Mrs. Doring Dec 17, 1889
845 Walter Rauschenbusch – letter to aunt February 2, 1894
846 Walter Rauschenbusch – letter
848 Walter Rauschenbusch – letter to Maria July 13, 1886
849 Walter Rauschenbusch – letter to aunt July 14, 1886

Rauschenbusch Series 2 – Letters to F.C.W. Meyer 1884-1893
847 August 16, 1884
850 June 22, 1886
852 July 15, 1886
851 August 12, 1886
853 September 23, 1886
822 May 5, 1887
823 May 31, 1887

824 June 25, 1887
825 July 21, 1887
826 July 25, 1887
828 August 9, 1887
827 August 17, 1887
829 August 27, 1888
830 Sept 1, 1888
831 October 7, 1890
832 January 10, 1890
834 October 10, 1892
835 October 13, 1892
836 December 22, 1892
838 November 1, 1893 (receipt)
843 January 24, 1893
841 October 17, 1893
840 October 27, 1893
839 November 3, 1893
842 January 12, 1893
844 -- 1893
854 October 30, 1886
855 November 5, 1886
856 November 29, 1886
833 October 7, 1890 (to church at New Haven)
111 November 3, 1890
837 December 30, 1892
857 January 31, 1899
858 January 22, 1899
859 December 23, 1899
860 February 1, 1900
862 February 20, 1900
861 September 11, 1900
953 February 13, ____
954 nd

Rauschenbusch Series 3

Edward Hanna letters to Walter Rauschenbusch 1881-1887 (Hanna was a classmate)

950 Aug 9, 1879
951 Nov 30, 1879
947 Feb 21, 1880
948 Aug 12, 1880
949 Nov 7, 1880
938 Jan 6, 1881
939 Mar 1, 1881 (handwritten, 4 pages)
940 Apr 10, 1881 (handwritten, 4 pages)
941 July 31, 1881
952 Summary of Hanna's letters to Walter Rauschenbusch
(prepared by Joyce Ringering – typed, 1 page)

955 Feb 14, 1882
956 July 28, 1882
957 Oct 10, 1882
958 Nov 23, 1882
959 Mar 12, 1883
960 Apr 19, 1883
961 May 27, 1883
960 Oct 21, 1883
963 Jan 25, 1884
964 Aug 17, 1884
965 Apr 26, 1885
966 Nov 4, 1885
967 Jan 10, 1887 (handwritten, 4 pages)
968 Apr 9, 1887 (handwritten, 3 pages)
969 Sept 30, 1887 (handwritten, 3 pages)

Rauschenbusch Series 4

Rauschenbusch, Walter – letters to Aunt Lina (Pastor Karl) Doring 1873-1892 letters in German

(* Typed copy and typed English translation done in 1960's-1970's)

132 October 6, 1873
910 July 22, 1882
911 June 9, 1883
92 March 21, 1884
131 Postcard – nd
127 March 21, 1886
52 *December 14, 1886
64 April 12, 1887
91 March 11, 1889
59 August 18, 1887
48 *July 4, 1889
125 December 5, 1889
49 *December 17, 1889
128 July 22, 1891
54 *March 3, 1892
74 August 20, 1892
53 *December 20, 1893

Rauschenbusch Series 5

Rauschenbusch, Walter – letter to Maria Doring 1873-1892 letters in German (Lina's daughter)

(*Typed copy and typed English translation done in 1960's-1970's)

56 *November 14, 1880
55 *January 14, 1887
57 *December 12, 1888

Rauschenbusch, Walter – letters to aunt 1883-1894 letters in German
(if all to same aunt – would be Aunt Lina as Aunt Maria died in 1888)

120 Mar 24, 1883

146 Nov 6, 1884
849 July 14, 1886
858 Oct 14, 1891
932 Oct 22, 1893
953 Dec 20, 1893
845 Feb 2, 1894

Rauschenbusch Series 6

Letters & postcards to Max Leuschner 1902-1906

977 October 13, 1902
1085 June 20, 1904
1084 July 4, 1904
1049 July 1, 1905
1087 December 28, 1905
1086 January 12, 1906
981 August 19, 1906

Rauschenbusch Series 7

Letters to Pauline Rauschenbusch (wife) 1901-1903 (Handwritten in English)

85 May 26, 1901
67 May 27, 1901
65 May 28, 1901
86 May 29, 1901
87 May 30, 1901
84 May 31, 1901
78 June 1, 1901
68 June 3, 1901
89 June 4, 1901
77 June 6, 1901
93 November 25, 1901
90 January 2, 1902
75 January 8, 1902
76 November 19, 1902
71 November 20, 1902
66 June 13, 1903
79 June 15, 1903
72 June 17, 1903
62 July 21, 1903

Pauline Rauschenbusch – letters received [typed and translated] 164 *September 16, 1908 from Elisabeth

165 *January 31, 1909 from Elisabeth
166 *

Rauschenbusch Series 8

Gribel, Minna – letters to Walter Rauschenbusch 1892-1900

95 August 28, 1892
96 July 29, 1893
99 November 22, 1896

97 January 1, 1897
101 June 24, 1897
98 July 12, 1897
100 November 16, 1897
140 February 13, 1898
102 October 7, 1898
141 December 9, 1898
139 February 23, 1899
103 June 15, 1899
142 June 9, 1899
238 July 9, 1899
104 September 2, 1899
143 December 8, 1899
107 postcard – nd
106 letter – nd
105 February 13, 1900

Rauschenbusch Series 9

Doering, Maria – letters to Walter Rauschenbusch
909 May 27, 1891
??? any more
56 Nov 14, 1880

Rauschenbusch Series 10

271 nd WR: What shall we do with the Germans? (10 pages)
330 1912 WR: Deutche Trinksitten in Amerikanischer Beleuchtung
[German drinking habits in America] 333
WR: What shall we do with the Germans? *Examiner* Jan 10,
786 1892 WR: Sermon: "The Resurrection" April 4, 1892
787 1885 WR: Sermon: Col 1:21-22 [preached in Louisville] 788 1904
WR: Sermon: "The Sower" May 13, 1904
792 1885 S WR: Sermon: Botschafter am Christi Staff [Ambassadors
for Christ] preached in Louisville
978 WR: The little gate of God [poem – 9 copies] 979
WR: Photographs of Walter Rauschenbusch
794 WR: Miscellaneous notes on the Social Gospel
930 WR: Essay: John Milton als Staatsmann [John Milton as a statesman] 784
WR: Wie verhalten sich die Griechischen Haupttugenden zu den Christlichen?
[How do the Greek cardinal virtues relate to the Christian?] 257
WR: Geniessen ist Schön, Entsagen ist schön [enjoyment, self-denial] 220
WR: Wurde Karl der Growwe von Alkuin König David genannt
221 WR: Die Poesie u. Gesang haben gawaltigen Einfluss Auf das Gemut
[The poetry and song have tremendous influence on the mind] 223
WR: Phillippus von Mozedonian
224 WR: Neque honestam Neque utilem fuisse Caton is de Corthagine
delmde sententiem
160 WR: Sieben Unterhaltungen mit Jungen Christen

Seven conversations with young Christians [leaflet printed in New York] 785
WR: Essay on Tasso (in German)
988 WR: Fellowship of Baptists 1942 Annual Meetings program

Rauschenbusch Series 11

933 WR: Essay: Ermahnt Pindar mit Recht
1842 WR: Clausuraufsatz – Weshalb bewunderin Dilattanten,
Weshalb Kunstrichter die Laokoon gruppe
934 WR: (no title)
846 WR: letter
175 Walter and Pauline wedding announcement
176 Rauschenbusch, Caroline – legal paper (indenture) for
Walter Rauschenbusch – April 14, 1897
[Gives Walter responsibility for her property in the US] 163
Remembrances of Walter Rauschenbusch – New York ministry
864 Bericht des Committees ueber die 10. Jahresfeier von Br.
Walther Rauschenbusch's Predigtamt [Report of the Committee
about the 10th anniversary of Bro Walther Rauschenbusch's ministry] 869 Biographical data on Walter Rauschenbusch (notes on scratch paper from publication Society)
883 1907 Postcard to Walter Rauschenbusch – (Author's Clipping Bureau)
937 WR: Autobiography of Patsy Rauschenbusch (a dog)
980 Colgate-Rochester Divinity School Foundation – lectureship
perpetuating the memory of Walter Rauschenbusch
982 WR: A prayer for our country and people
983 Book Reviews by Sharpe on writings of Walter Rauschenbusch;
Also a 5 page biography
985 WR: form letter when giving his book [used to recognize scholarship] 987
WR: Against War (1 page statement)
WR: Fellowship News May 1942

Rauschenbusch Series 12

992 1942 Halle Brothers Company – invitation to reception for
Sharpe's biography of WR, Apr 16, 1942
996 1942 Book Jacket from Sharpe's book of WR Biography
1014 WR: Prayer for Teachers
1020 Leuschner, Martin: "The Influence of Professsor
Walter Rauschenbusch on Ethical Thinking" Dec 13, 1927
1021 1914 Dr. Josiah Strong – Quote concerning Walter Rauschenbusch
– January 30, 1914
1023 Rauschenbusch, Walter – "Oh God, We thank Thee" (Anthem)
1029 Reviews of books by Walter Rauschenbusch
1030 Rauschenbusch, Walter – Aus dem Leben Jesu [From the Life of Jesus]
–a series of lectures April-June 1896 – text & 3 points – German
1034 Rauschenbusch, Walter Die Stille Pforte [The quiet gate] 1041
Rauschenbusch club program April 1924
1059 Quotes from Walter Rauschenbusch writings *The Epworth Herald*, p. 498,
August 17, 1935

1061 Donovan E. Smucker. Rauschenbusch after 50 years. *Christian Century* April 17, 1957
1062 Herbert E. Langendorf. A Man ahead of his time. *Together* July 1963
1065 Missions – November 1957 – Editorial and news article concerning Walter Rauschenbusch
1047 WR: "Too much churchliness and denominational Disunion"
1048 WR: Defense of "an alle, die es angeht" [to all whom it may concern] Published in *Der Sendbote* April 14, 1897
1050 WR: "Das Leben Gottes in der Menschenseele" ["Life of God in the human soul"] *Der Sendbote* Jan. 15, 1902
1051 WR Poem – 1987
1053 WR: 1861-1918 A Tribute
1057 WR: The True American Church 1914 – leaflet
1069 Gene E. Bartlett – Rauschenbusch, Portrait in Perspective *Mission* October 1961

Rauschenbusch Series 13

1070 Nixon, Justin Wroe: Walter Rauschenbusch: Man and His Work – lecture presented on Rauschenbusch Day, September 11, 1957
1071 Whitesell, Faris D.: Who was Walter Rauschenbusch? *Watchman Examiner* Oct 3, 1957
1073 WR: The Postern Gate (poem) 1918
1976 Carl Schneider, "Frieda Rauschenbusch Fetzer," article published in *Der Wahrheitszuge* 1934
1092 Photos of August and Caroline Rauschenbusch
1116 WR: Letter to class of 1902 – May 12, 1904
1054 Winifred Rauschenbusch Rorty. Letter to Martin Leuschner Oct 30, 1961 concerning Walter Rauschenbusch, Rochester Bulletin 286-7 Mar 1934
902 Birthday Greetings to Walter Rauschenbusch Oct 2, 1911
900 WR: Avers US frowns on Germans Newspaper clipping Sept 5, 1915
1015 Wording of a tablet in 2nd German Baptist Church, New York, honoring Walter Rauschenbusch
1063 Robins, Henry Burke. The contributions of Walter Rauschenbusch to world peace pp. 149-154
1066 The Social Gospeler – Article in *Time*, Nov 18, 1957
1043 Leuschner, Martin. "Walter Rauschenbusch and our Day" (handwritten, 24 pages) read x3 1934-35
1058 Meyer, F.W.C. "Rauschenbusch Aflame for God" *Baptist Herald,* Oct 1, 1936, pp. 304-305
1068 Ensley, F. Gerald. Walter Rauschenbusch: Prophet of the Social Gospel. *Together.* July 1963, p. 30
1067 Walter Rauschenbusch. Crusaders of History
1052 Dahlberg, Edwin T. "Walter Rauschenbusch, Prophet of the Social Christianity" (12-page leaflet published by Colgate Rochester Divinity School, ND—after 1942
1072 Payne, Ernest A. The prophet of the social gospel. *Baptist Times,* Dec 19, 1957, p 6

1022 Rauschenbusch, Walter. An affirmation of faith (typewritten, 1 page)

Rauschenbusch Series 14

1060 Hudson, Winthrop S. "Rauschenbusch – Evangelical Prophet." *The Christian Century* June 24, 1953, p 740-742 (legal size pages)

820 Daniel, C.A. Some Reminiscences of my friend, Walter Rauschenbusch (handwritten, 28 pages)

88 Newman, Albert Henry. Letter to Walter Rauschenbusch. Mar 28, 1905 (handwritten 2 pages)

959 Hanna, Edward J. Letter to Walter Rauschenbusch. Mar 17, 1883 (handwritten 2 pages)

807 Faunce, W.H. Letter to Rauschenbusch. Jan 29, 1909 (typed with handwritten note 2 pages)

795 Rauschenbusch, Pauline – Christmas Letter Dec 20, 1944 (typed, 1 page)

793 Walter Rauschenbusch – John 13:33-35 Sermons preached at Louisville, Kentucky, May 24-Aug 9, 1885 First sermon (typed – in German, 9 pg)

1024 The social triumph of the ancient church – Shirley Jackson Case. Walter Rauschenbusch and his contribution to Social Christianity & Rochester Lectureship Foundation (handwritten, 2 pages)

83 Schmidt, Nathaniel. Letter to Walter Rauschenbusch. Nov 3, 1903 (handwritten, 4 pages)

82 Williams, Leighton. Letter to Walter Rauschenbusch. Sept 16, 1905 (tyed, 2 pages)

Concerning Walter Rauschenbusch. *Rochester Bulletin* pp286-287, Mar 1934

Brachlow, Stephen. Walter Rauschenbusch biography (typed 31 pages). Delivered at Convocation, NABS, 1986

Rauschenbusch Material in American Baptist Historical Society (ABHS)

General Note: The Samuel Colgate Baptist Historical Library of the American Baptist Historical Society is the repository of the largest collection of Rauschenbuschiana in existence. It includes the massive Rauschenbusch Family collections (including his children and some grand-children), a subset, the Dores R. Sharpe Walter Rauschenbusch Collection, and related personal papers collections, and institutional records. ABHS also has extensive magazine, newspaper, and journal files from the era of Rauschenbusch. The Collections were relocated from Rochester, New York, to Atlanta, Georgia, where they are housed on the Cecil B. Day Atlanta Campus of Mercer University.

The Rauschenbusch Family Collection (RG 1003)

Chronological Span: 1836 – 1979, bulk 1890-1920

Physical Contents: 66.8 linear feet

Background of the Collection
Rauschenbusch family materials have been coming to the American Baptist Historical Society since 1969, when Carl Raushenbush shared genealogical charts and photographs that his sister Lisa had been storing. Walter Rauschenbusch's student, one-time secretary, and friend Dores Robinson Sharpe preserved many of WR's papers when the family opposed making them accessible to the public. He acquired even more when he gained Pauline's support in preserving her husband Walter's papers. In 1980, Sharpe's donation of his Dores R. Sharpe Collection of Walter Rauschenbusch Papers, amassed over decades, formed the backbone of the ABHS Rauschenbusch Family collection. In 1981 and 1982, Stephen Raushenbush sent a large collection of materials, and Richard Rorty donated materials on Winifred Raushenbush Rorty.

As for other Rauschenbusch family members, some highlights include daughter Winifred's writings on immigration and race relations. Walter's son, Stephen's papers include writings on the Vietnam Peace Proposal, the Biscay Offensive in 1942 and consultant work for the National Parks Association, articles on peace written jointly with his wife Joan, and even a story by their son, Burns. A second son, Paul, is represented by works on unemployment compensation co-authored with his wife Elizabeth. The collection also includes third son Carl's writings on labor. There are a few items by daughter Lisa on theatre and literature. The extended family (Döring, Rorty, Schaefer, and Clough related families) are also represented in papers and photographs in the collection, including sister Emma Rauschenbusch Clough's published dissertation on Mary Wollstonecraft, and books on Baptist mission work in India.

The comprehensive ABHS inventory, begun by Susan Eltscher in 1985, and substantially updated in 2018 by Jill Sweetapple, and frequently refined, is available through the ABHS online catalog: https://libraries.mercer.edu/archivesspace. The box listing and abbreviated content descriptions, were compiled by William H. Brackney from the comprehensive ABHS inventory.

Box #	Content Description
Box 1	Lectures: Church History; Manuscript chapters; D. R. Sharpe organization of WR material
Box 2	Lectures and Notes: Church History: Early Church; doctrines; special topics
Box 3	Lectures, book chapters, clippings: Topics: Medieval, Reformation; Anabaptists; Separatists
Box 4	Lectures, Addresses: American Church history: denominations
Box 5	Course Materials: American Christianity; Reformation in Germany; Lutheranism
Box 6	Course Materials: Baptism; Cult of Mary
Box 7	Course Materials: Democratic religion; Satan; alcoholism; missions
Box 8	Resources and Writings: 1909-1913
Box 9	Resources and Writings: historical topics; WR child class-book; German essays; "On the Synagogue"
Box 10	Notes and Addresses: the Parables; physiology; ordination; zoology; life of Paul

Box 11 Lecture Notes and Addresses: the ministry; care of the poor; education; the woman's movement
Box 12 Lecture Notes: Socialism; Baptists; Alcoholism; social awakening; personal religion
Box 13 Addresses and Lectures Notes: German religion; industrial education; Jesus and social questions
Box 14 Lectures: Baptists; Lord's Prayer; Women; Awakenings; Gale Lectures; Social Service
Box 15 Writings, Lectures, Correspondence: 1890s: Czar and Peace; social redemption
Box 16 Correspondence: 1886-1908
Box 17 Correspondence: 1910-1912
Box 18 Correspondence: 1912-1913
Box 19 Correspondence: 1913-1914
Box 20 Correspondence: 1915-1916
Box 21 Correspondence: 1908-1919 (John D. Rockefeller)
Box 22 Correspondence: 1908-1944
Box 23 Correspondence: 1898-1917
Box 24 Correspondence: 1909-1937; Artifacts pertaining to Pauline Rother
Box 25 Artifacts; Clippings, Biographical material; Hist. of Second Baptist Church, NYC
Box 26 Correspondence; notecards; clippings, 1896-1918; WR prayers, poems
Box 27 Correspondence: 1911-1918
Box 28 Clippings; poetry; pamphlets
Box 29 Lectures: Taylor Lectures; reviews of books; Mss. of "A Theology of the Social Gospel"
Box 30 Correspondence: 1890s-1917; hymns; Earl Lectures
Box 31 Correspondence; financial records; Rochester Seminary; Rochester public schools
Box 32 Correspondence: Family: Pauline, children
Box 33 Correspondence: 1908-1946: family; poetry collection; photographs
Box 34 Correspondence; Notebooks: 1912-1927
Box 35 Correspondence: 1940s; Clippings; family legal documents; misc. photographs
Box 36 Correspondence: Pauline, her family; greeting cards; mss: "Dare We Be Christians?"
Box 37 Photographs; Rockefeller Correspondence
Box 38 Correspondence: Pauline, Caroline: 1879-1920
Box 39 Correspondence: Pauline, family: 1892-1930; receipts
Box 40 Correspondence: Pauline, family: 1920s
Box 41 Correspondence: Pauline, family
Box 42 Correspondence: Pauline, Walter, family: 1907-1940
Box 43 Correspondence; clippings; notes; D.R. Sharpe-related
Box 44 D. R. Sharpe resources and materials
Box 45 Correspondence; clippings: Pauline, family: Pauline; about WR
Box 46 Correspondence: Pauline, children: 1910-1943
Box 47 Correspondence: Pauline, children, Caroline Schaeffer

Box 48 Correspondence: Walter to Pauline: 1890s
Box 49 Biographical details; correspondence: Pauline, children clippings: 1940s
Box 50 Correspondence: Walter (from hospital, 1918)
Box 51 Correspondence: WR Last will; photos; school notes: 1880s
Box 52 Pauline material: lecture notes; mss. "New Evangelism"; "Social Questions in Bible"
Box 53 Correspondence; family: 1918: death of WR
Box 54 Correspondence: 1902-1918; reviews; reports; notes
Box 55 Correspondence: 1889-1917
Box 56 Correspondence: 1913-1937; clippings
Box 57 Clippings: 1914-1919; Correspondence: 1897-1902
Box 58 Correspondence: 1897-1900: H. L. Morehouse; Rochester Seminary German Dept.; programs
Box 59 Addresses; correspondence; Lecture Notes: 1886-1917
Box 60 WR Diary 1888-1891; manuscripts; articles in German
Box 61 Lecture notes in German; correspondence: 1880s; photographs; outline for "Christianity Revolutionary"
Box 62 Lecture Notes (in German); reading notes; address on "Life of Dollinger"
Box 63 Lecture notes: "Jesus: Organizer of Men"; correspondence: Pauline: family
Box 64 Correspondence: 1901-1927
Box 65 Correspondence: Pauline, children
Box 66 WR Diary 1908; correspondence: WR to family
Box 67 Correspondence: WR, Pauline: 1892-1942
Box 68 Correspondence: WR, Pauline: 1904-1918; clippings
Box 69 Photos; Correspondence: Pauline, children, 1918-1946
Box 70 Correspondence: Pauline, family: 1926-1947; clippings
Box 71 Correspondence: 1908-1938: Pauline, WR, children
Box 72 Correspondence: 1909-1945: Pauline
Box 73 Correspondence: 1904-1945: Pauline
Box 74 Photographs: miscellaneous
Box 75 Correspondence: 1893-1944: Pauline
Box 76 Correspondence: 1917-1946: Pauline, children
Box 77 Correspondence: 1919-1945: Pauline, children
Box 78 Correspondence: 1911-1943: Pauline, children
Box 79 Correspondence: 1904-1957: Pauline, children
Box 80 Correspondence: 1910-1943: WR; Pauline, children
Box 81 Correspondence: 1914-1940: Pauline, children, Caroline Schaeffer
Box 82 Correspondence: 1882-1939: Pauline, children
Box 83 Correspondence: 1910-1944: Pauline, children
Box 84 Correspondence: 1918-1945: Pauline, children
Box 85 Correspondence: 1919-1942: Pauline, family
Box 86 Correspondence: 1914-1939: Pauline, children
Box 87 Correspondence: 1873-1946: Pauline, WR, family
Box 88 Correspondence: Pauline, children; Stephen Rauschenbusch Papers
Box 89 Correspondence: 1908-1936: Pauline, family, Stephen

Box 90 Correspondence: Stephen Rauschenbusch works, papers; Caroline Rother correspondence
Box 91 Correspondence: 1893-1946; Pauline, family
Box 92 Correspondence: 1894-1936: Pauline, children
Box 93 Correspondence: 1919-1944: Pauline, children
Box 94 Correspondence: 1904-1945; articles, clippings: 1874-1918; genealogical information; photo
Box 95 Photos; obituaries; memorabilia: Pauline's engagement; Rauschenbusch Fellowship of Baptists
Box 96 Lecture Notes: G. C. Fetter: 1912-1913; WR Journal: 1895; correspondence: Winifred and WR
Box 97 Correspondence, writings, clippings, notes: Winifred Rauschenbusch
Box 98: Correspondence: 1907-1918: Pauline, Walter, family, D. R. Sharpe
Box 99 Correspondence: Correspondence, clippings, articles: 1899-1917
Box 100 Stephen Rauschenbusch: Writings, Correspondence, Papers, Clippings: 1939-1979
Box 101 Stephen Rauschenbusch: Correspondence, Papers, Speeches: 1933-1970
Box 102 Winifred Rauschenbusch Papers: Writings, Pamphlets, Manuscripts, Notebooks: 1926-1963
Box 103 Winifred Rauschenbusch Papers: Photos, Manuscripts, Correspondence; Rorty Family Papers: 1928-1953
Box 104 Winfred Rauschenbusch: Manuscripts; Esther Rauschenbusch; Lisa Rauschenbusch Correspondence: 1927-1972
Box 105 Winifred Rauschenbusch Papers: Writings, Correspondence: 1940-1972
Box 106 Winifred Rauschenbusch Papers: Correspondence, Manuscripts; James Rorty: 1917-1967
Box 107 Winifred Rauschenbusch Papers: Writings, Family Info, Clippings, Correspondence: 1932-1978
Box 108 Winifred Rauschenbusch Papers: Correspondence: 1919-1978: James Rorty
Box 109 Winifred Rauschenbusch Papers: Biography of Robert Park; Photos; transcript
Box 110 Lisa Rauschenbusch Papers: Photos; Transcript; Play; Notebooks: 1962-1965; Correspondence; Clippings
Box 111 Lisa Rauschenbusch Papers: Notes, Clippings; Manuscripts; Correspondence: 1908-1949
Box 112 Lisa Rauschenbusch Papers: Correspondence, Manuscripts; Notes; Legal Documents: 1940-1962
Box 113 Lisa Rauschenbusch Papers: Thesis; Correspondence: 1946-1961
Box 114 Winifred Rauschenbusch Papers: Correspondence: 1908-1979; Lisa Correspondence: 1935-1944; Diaries; Photo Album
Box 115 Lisa Rauschenbusch Papers: Diaries: 1971-1973; Correspondence: 1955-1964
Box 116 Lisa Rauschenbusch Papers: Correspondence: 1955-1964; Diaries 1957
Box 117 Winifred Rauschenbusch Papers: Clippings; Correspondence: 1943-1967; Clippings
Box 118 Winifred Rauschenbusch Papers: Photos, Clippings; Correspondence: 1934-1977; Manuscript

Box 119 Lisa Rauschenbusch Papers: Correspondence: 1957-1977; Notes on "King Lear" Play
Box 120 General Family Correspondence: Winifred; Walter; family; Lisa; Pauline: 1912-1973
Box 121 General Family Correspondence: Pauline; Caroline Schaeffer
Box 122 General Correspondence: Clippings; Manuscript; Artifacts; Correspondence: Josephine Joan Rasuchenbusch: 1942–1977
Box 123 Photographs of Rauschenbusch Family
Box 124 General Correspondence: Pauline; Walter; Stephen: 1881-1957
Box 125 Photographs of Rauschenbusch Family
Box 126 Walter Rauschenbusch: Sermon Notebooks
Box 127 Walter Rauschenbusch Sermon Notebooks
Box 128 Walter Rauschenbusch Sermon Notebooks
Box 129 Rauschenbusch Photographs; August Rauschenbusch Material; Rauschenbusch Family; Walter Rauschenbusch, Bibliography and Diary
Box 130 General Correspondence: Walter; Lisa Datebook; Photos; Autograph Album; WR Gardening Notes
Box 131 Walter Rauschenbusch: Lecture Notes; Typescript: "A Theology of the Social Gospel"
Box 132 Walter Rauschenbusch: Lecture Notes; Correspondence: 1914-1917; Mss: "Life of Jesus"
Box 133 Walter Rauschenbusch: Lecture Notes; Correspondence: 1893-1897: Nathaniel Schmidt; Wax Cylinders; Amity tracts
Box 134 Index Card File
Box 135 Index Card File
Box 137 Index Card File
Box 138 Index Card File
Box 139 Index Card File
Box 140 Artifacts
Box 141 Artifacts: Wax Cylinders (WR voice)
Box 142 Artifacts: Wax Cylinders (WR voice)
Box 143 Newspaper Clippings 1907-1909
Box 144 German Sunday School Lessons; Clippings from the Baptist Congress, *Examiner*
Box 145 Articles by WR
Box 146 German Articles
Box 147 Correspondence; Postcards: 1884-1908
Box 148 Newspaper and Magazine Clippings: 1888-1889
Box 149 Hilmar Rauschenbusch: German articles; family honors
Box 150 Walter Rauschenbusch Articles
Box 151 Miscellaneous: Obituaries and Clippings: 1890-1891
Box 152 Walter Rauschenbusch: Articles; Manuscripts: 1897-1902
Box 153 Walter Rauschenbusch: Articles; Sermons on various topics: 1901-1910
Box 154 Brotherhood of the Kingdom: Conferences; various articles: 1886-1890
Box 155 Miscellaneous: "Effectiveness of Religion": 1903-1907

Box 156 Miscellaneous: Newspaper clippings: 1911-1912; Walter and Pauline Wedding Announcement
Box 157 Miscellaneous: Newspaper Clippings about strikes, unions, German affairs
Box 158 Miscellaneous: Newspaper Clippings re: Dr. Pierson: 1903-1904
Box 159 Miscellaneous: Newspaper Clippings: 1910
Box 160 Walter Rauschenbusch Scrapbook: 1912-1914
Box 161 Artifacts: August Rauschenbusch memorabilia; plaster reliefs of Walter; printing plates
Box 162 Artifacts: Family Bibles
Box 163 Artifacts: Ernst Augustus; Walter; Pauline Rother
Box 164 Artifacts: Walter graduation: Rochester Free Academy; Rauschenbusch Family Genealogy charts to 17th century; photos of Rauschenbusch home in Rochester
Box 165 Artifacts: photographs
Box 166 Walter Rauschenbusch, "Christianity Revolutionary" used by Max Stackhouse; Remarks on mss. by Nathaniel Schmidt
Box 167 Artifacts: Photographs: August Rauschenbusch; property photographs
Box 168 Scrapbook and journal, summer vacations: 1911-1915
Box 169 Vacation journals: 1911-1915
Box 170 Family Member Contents: initials "J.R." [James Rorty?] 1958 Diary; photograph album; Postcard
Oversized Box Walter Rauschenbusch D.D. degree, University of Rochester: 1902; Elizabeth, Rauschenbusch diploma, East (Rochester) High School: 1921

Additional Collections and Print Matter related to Walter Rauschenbusch in ABHS:

RG 1016 Papers of George Dana Boardman, Jr.
Contemporary of Rauschenbusch in the Baptist Congress
RG 1021 Papers of John E. Clough
Brother-in-law to Rauschenbusch who implemented social gospel principles in India
RG 1026 Papers of Edwin Dahlberg
Student secretary of Rauschenbusch, social activist, and national ecumenical leader
RG 1044 Papers of Winthrop S. Hudson
Colgate Rochester church historian and biographer of Rauschenbusch
RG 1062 Papers of Judson Wroe Nixon
Rochester Seminary faculty colleague and faculty successor to Rauschenbusch
RG 1084 Papers of Leighton Williams
Close confidante of Rauschenbusch and co-founder of the Brotherhood of the Kingdom; son of William R. Williams
RG 1120 Papers of Johann Gerhard Oncken
Major leader of Baptists in Germany and founder of Hamburg Seminary
RG 1125 Papers of John Davison Rockefeller
Donor and friend to A.H. Strong and Rauschenbusch Family
RG 1141 Papers of William R. Williams
Pastor of Amity Baptist Church, New York
RG 1159 Augustus Hopkins Strong

President of Rochester Theological Seminary and mentor of Rauschenbusch

RG 1246 Dores R. Sharpe
Student secretary of Rauschenbusch and promoter of Social Gospel in US and Canada

RG 1363 Conrad H. Moehlman
Student of Rauschenbusch, professor at Rochester Seminary, and Rauschenbusch biographer

RG 1369 Nathaniel Schmidt
Close confidante of Rauschenbusch and co-founder of Brotherhood of the Kingdom; professor of biblical studies at Colgate Theological Seminary

RG 1393 Robert T. Handy
American religious historian, biographer of Rauschenbusch and Social Gospel advocate; Professor and Dean at Union Theological Seminary, New York

Relevant print matter that pertains to Rauschenbusch: *For the Right* (newspaper Rauschenbusch fostered and contributed to); *The Watchman*; *The Examiner*; *The Standard*; *Proceedings of the Baptist Congress*; *The American Baptist* (and all inclusive titles); Ford Hall Forum; Federal Council of the Churches of Christ in U.S.; Baptist Association minutes for southern New York, Monroe County/Rochester; the German Baptist Conference; the records and publications of the Brotherhood of the Kingdom (*For the Kingdom*); and publications of the Hamburg Seminary.

Rauschenbusch Material in Theologischen Seminars, Elstal, Germany

General Note: The Theological Seminary in Hamburg, Germany, established by J. G. Oncken in 1880, has been a center of Baptist life in Europe. It accumulated an extensive library and growing amount of historical material while in Hamburg. During World War II the seminary was damaged and many materials lost. With its move to Elstal near Berlin, the Seminary library has become again the principal resource center for Baptists in Germany and beyond, including especially the Oncken Archiv. Walter Rauschenbusch had numerous correspondents on the faculty and copies of his works and works about him are housed at Elstal.

1. August Rauschenbusch: Unpublished Works (umfasst vier Kartons, unverzeichnet) 4 boxes enthält vor allem: (includes especially):

-Zeugnisse (grade reports)

-Konvolut Kindheit und Gymnasialzeit (material on childhood and time in school)

-Briefe an und über A. Rauschenbusch während seiner Gymnasialzeit in Elberfeld von seinem Vater und seiner Mutter 1831- (letter to and about A.R. during his school years in Elberfeld by his father and mother from 1831 ff.)

-Briefe aus der Zeit der Krankheit und dem Anfang der Bonner Zeit 1836-1840 (letter from the time of his illness and the beginnings of his time in Bonn 1836-1840)

-Briefe seiner Eltern an A. Rauschenbusch 1837-1840 (letters by his parents 1837-1840)

-Schriftwechsel zwischen A. Rauschenbusch und der Langenberger Gesellschaft 1845-1854 (Kopien) (copies of exchange of letters between A.R. and the Langenberg Society 1845-1854)

-Entwürfe von Reden, Predigten in Altena und anderswo, Briefe und Fragmente seiner Tätigkeit 1840 (drafts of speeches, sermons in Altena and elsewhere, letters and fragments of his actitivities, 1840 -)
-Unterlagen von Enthaltsamkeitsvereine (brochures of temperance societies)
-Unterlagen aus seiner Altenaer Zeit 1841-1845 (material from his time in Altena 1841-1845)
-Briefwechsel Drucksachen betr. (exchange of letters and brochures)
-Briefwechsel 1828-1867 (exchange of letters 1828-1867)
-Predigten 1840-1842 (sermons 1840-42)
-hs. Notizen, Zeitungsausschnitte, Broschüren (handwrittten notices, newspaper clippings, brochures).

August Rauschenbusch: Published Works

August Rauschenbush, Leben und Wirken von August Rauschenbusch
______. Handbüchlein der Homiletik für freikirchliche Prediger und für Stadtmissionare
______. Die Wallfahrt nach Zionsthal
______. Auserlesene biblische Historien aus dem alten und neuen Testamente nachHübner
______. Die Nacht des Westens
______. Die Pilgerväter oder Geschichte der christlichen Aussiedler von Neu=England
______. Die Pilgerväter oder Geschichte der christlichen Aussiedler von Neu=England
______. Die Entstehung der Kindertaufe im dritten Jahrhundert n.Chr. Und die Wiedereinführung der biblischen Taufe im sechenten Jahhundert n. Chr.
______. Biblische Frauenbilder zur Erbauung und Belehrung christlicher Frauen und Jungfrauen
______. Der Ursprung des Sonntags
______. Sollen wir Samstag oder Sonntag feiern?
______. Sind Menschen und Affe Stammverwandt
______. Der Ursprung des Sonntags
______. Wo hat Kain sein Weib hergenommen
______. Statuten des christlichen Enthaltsamkeits-Verein
______. Anweisungen für Auswanderer nach Nordamerika
______. Beschreibung einer Seereise von Bremen nach Rem-Dorf
______. Sollen wir Samstag oder Sonntag feiern?
______. Ist der Sonntag heidnischen, päpstlichen oder christlichen Ursprungs
______. Ist der Sonntag heidnischen, päpstlichen oder christlichen Ursprungs
______. Der Ursprung des Sonntags
______. Die Entstehung der Kindertaufe im dritten Jahrhundert n. Chr. Und die Wiedereinführung der biblischen Taufe im sechenten Jahhundert n. Chr.
______. Lebensgeschichte von Roger Williams, erstem Baptistenprediger in Nord-Amerika und Gründer des Staates Rhode-Island

Materials Relating to Hamburg Seminary (yet to be classified)

-Faculty Minutes
-Trustee Minutes

-Publications by Faculty
-Annual Catalogues, calendars
-Historical materials, photos relating to the Seminary

Zeitschriften (Newspapers/Periodicals)

Der Sendbote (1920-)
Missionsblatt der Evangelisch-Taufgesinnten (1844-1878)
Der Wahrheitszeuge (1879-1941)

Rauschenbusch-Related Correspondence at Rockefeller Archive Center, Sleepy Hollow (Pocantico Hills), New York.

General Note: In the early 1890s Rauschenbusch met John D. Rockefeller through the friendship of President Augustus Hopkins Strong. Mr. Rockefeller was generous to the Seminary, providing scholarship, building, and general funds. Rockefeller and his wife, Laura Spelman, became close friends with the Rauschenbuschs, particularly reinforced by the Rauschenbusch's visits to New York City. Mr. Rockefeller was fond of Pauline Rauschenbusch. The Rockefeller Archives contain useful correspondence between the two families.

In the "Dimes" Catalog, the following entries are listed in The John D. Rockefeller papers, Letterbooks, Series L (FA431), "Outgoing Correspondence":

Rauschenbusch, Walter
Vol. 220; page 261
Rauschenbusch, Mrs
Vol. 068; page 449a
Rauschenbusch, P.E. Mrs.
Vol. 043; page 428
Rauschenbusch, Pauline E.
Vol. 249; page 655
Rauschenbusch, W.
Vol. 026; page 80
Vol. 031; page 82, 140
Vol. 034; page 71
Vol. 035; page 188
Vol. 063; page 204
Vol. 077; page 426
Vol. 090; page 263, 365
Vol. 091; page 62
Vol. 094; page 180

Vol. 242; page 434
Vol. 248; page 112
Rauschenbusch, Walter M[rs] Vol. 075; page 136
Vol. 212; page 66
Vol. 215 page 144
Vol. 218; page 470
Vol. 234; page 336
Vol. 236; page 157
Vol. 237; page 52
Vol. 239; page 69
Vol. 246; page 68
Vol. 247; page 70
Vol. 300; page 35

INDEX TO VOLUMES I-III